Historical Dictionary
of the
French Revolution,
1789-1799

Historical Dictionaries of French History

This five-volume series covers French history from the Revolution through the Third Republic. It provides comprehensive coverage of each era, including not only political and military history but also social, economic, and art history.

Historical Dictionary of the French Revolution, 1789-1799
Samuel F. Scott and Barry Rothaus, editors

Historical Dictionary of Napoleonic France, 1799-1815
Owen Connelly, editor

Historical Dictionary of France from the 1815 Restoration to the Second Empire
Edgar Leon Newman, editor

Historical Dictionary of the French Second Empire, 1852-1870
William E. Echard, editor

Historical Dictionary of the Third French Republic, 1870-1940
Patrick H. Hutton, editor-in-chief

Historical Dictionary of the French Revolution, 1789-1799

Edited by
SAMUEL F. SCOTT
and
BARRY ROTHAUS

Greenwood Press
Westport, Connecticut

Library of Congress Cataloging in Publication Data

Main entry under title:

Historical dictionary of the French Revolution,
  1789-1799.

  Bibliography: p.
  Includes index.
  1. France—History—Revolution, 1789-1799—
Dictionaries. I. Scott, Samuel F. II. Rothaus, Barry.
DC147.H57   1985   944.04′03′21   83-16625
ISBN 0-313-21141-8 (lib. bdg.)
ISBN 0-313-24804-4 (lib. bdg. :v.1)
ISBN 0-313-24805-2 (lib. bdg. :v.2)

Library of Congress Catalog Card Number: 83-16625
ISBN 0-313-21141-8
ISBN 0-313-24804-4 (v.1)
ISBN 0-313-24805-2 (v.2)

First published in 1985

Greenwood Press
A division of Congressional Information Service, Inc.
88 Post Road West
Westport, Connecticut 06881

Printed in the United States of America

10 9 8 7 6 5 4 3 2 1

Contents

Contributors

L. J. Abray, Scarborough College, University of Toronto, West Hill, Ontario, Canada

Thomas M. Adams, Transylvania University, Lexington, Kentucky

Effie Ambler, Wayne State University, Detroit, Michigan

Leon Apt, Iowa State University, Ames, Iowa

Eric Arnold, Jr., University of Denver, Denver, Colorado

Charles Bailey, State University of New York, College of Arts and Science at Geneseo, Geneseo, New York

Keith Baker, University of Chicago, Chicago, Illinois

H. Arnold Barton, Southern Illinois University at Carbondale, Carbondale, Illinois

Vincent W. Beach, University of Colorado, Boulder, Colorado

Georgia Robison Beale, Madison, Wisconsin

Paul H. Beik, Swarthmore College, Swarthmore, Pennsylvania

Lenard Berlanstein, University of Virginia, Charlottesville, Virginia

J.-P. Bertaud, Sorbonne, Paris, France

Richard Bienvenu, University of Missouri, Columbia, Missouri

Marc Bouloiseau, Nice, France

Ronald J. Caldwell, Jacksonville State University, Jacksonville, Alabama

Raymond L. Carol, St. John's University, Jamaica, New York

Jack Censer, George Mason University, Fairfax, Virginia

Nupur Chaudhuri, Kansas State University, Manhattan, Kansas

Clive Church, Eliot College, University of Kent, Canterbury, United Kingdom

Susan Conner, Tift College, Forsyth, Georgia

Marvin R. Cox, University of Connecticut, Storrs, Connecticut

Robert R. Crout, University of Virginia, Charlottesville, Virginia

V. M. Daline, Institute of History, Moscow, U.S.S.R.

Philip Dawson, Brooklyn College (CUNY), Brooklyn, New York

Theodore A. DiPadova, Russell Sage College, Troy, New York

William Doyle, University of York, Heslington, York, United Kingdom

Melvin Edelstein, The William Paterson College of New Jersey, Wayne, New Jersey

Elizabeth Eisenstein, University of Michigan, Ann Arbor, Michigan

David M. Epstein, University of Tulsa, Tulsa, Oklahoma

Howard V. Evans, Central Michigan University, Mount Pleasant, Michigan

Robert Forster, The Johns Hopkins University, Baltimore, Maryland

James Friguglietti, Eastern Montana College, Billings, Montana

John G. Gallaher, Southern Illinois University at Edwardsville, Edwardsville, Illinois

Clarke Garrett, Dickinson College, Carlisle, Pennsylvania

Charles A. Gliozzo, Michigan State University, East Lansing, Michigan

Jacques Godechot, Université de Toulouse-Le Mirail, Toulouse, France

Ralph W. Greenlaw, North Carolina State University at Raleigh, Raleigh, North Carolina

William D. Griffin, St. John's University, Jamaica, New York

Vivian Gruder, Queens College (CUNY), Queens, New York

James R. Harkins, Wilfrid Laurier University, Waterloo, Ontario, Canada

Robert D. Harris, University of Idaho, Moscow, Idaho

Jonathan E. Helmreich, Allegheny College, Meadville, Pennsylvania

Arthur Hertzberg, Columbia University, New York, New York

Patrice Higonnet, Harvard University, Cambridge, Massachusetts

Robert B. Holtman, Louisiana State University, Baton Rouge, Louisiana

Gerlof D. Homan, Illinois State University, Normal, Illinois

James N. Hood, Tulane University, New Orleans, Louisiana

Donald D. Horward, The Florida State University, Tallahassee, Florida

Lynn A. Hunt, University of California–Berkeley, Berkeley, California

Maurice G. Hutt, University of Sussex, Brighton, United Kingdom

Frank A. Kafker, University of Cincinnati, Cincinnati, Ohio

Thomas E. Kaiser, University of Arkansas at Little Rock, Little Rock, Arkansas

Gary Kates, Trinity University, San Antonio, Texas

Michael Kennedy, Winthrop College, Rock Hill, South Carolina

Ernest J. Knapton, Chatham, Massachusetts

James M. Laux, University of Cincinnati, Cincinnati, Ohio

Robert Legrand, Abbeville, France

Charles A. Le Guin, Portland State University, Portland, Oregon

James A. Leith, Queen's University, Kingston, Ontario, Canada

Colin Lucas, Balliol College, Oxford, United Kingdom

Jay Luvaas, Army War College, Carlisle, Pennsylvania

John Lynn, University of Illinois, Urbana-Champaign, Illinois

Martyn Lyons, The University of New South Wales, Kensington, New South Wales, Australia

Scott Lytle, University of Washington, Seattle, Washington

John P. McLaughlin, The University of Western Ontario, London, Ontario, Canada

Gordon H. McNeil, University of Arkansas, Fayetteville, Arkansas
Walter Markov, Karl-Marx-Universität, Leipzig, German Democratic Republic
Claude Mazauric, Université de Provence, Aix-en-Provence, France
Jeffrey Merrick, Barnard College, New York, New York
Andrew C. Minor, University of Missouri, Columbia, Missouri
Kate Norberg, University of California–San Diego, La Jolla, California
Alison Patrick, University of Melbourne, Parkville, Victoria, Australia
Jeremy Popkin, University of Kentucky, Lexington, Kentucky
Mary Ann Quinn, The Papers of the Marquis de Lafayette, Cornell University, Ithaca, New York
Clay Ramsay, Palo Alto, California
R. Barrie Rose, The University of Tasmania, Hobart, Tasmania, Australia
Steven T. Ross, Naval War College, Newport, Rhode Island
Barry Rothaus, University of Northern Colorado, Greeley, Colorado
Gail S. Rowe, University of Northern Colorado, Greeley, Colorado
Ambrose Saricks, University of Kansas, Lawrence, Kansas
Samuel F. Scott, Wayne State University, Detroit, Michigan
Monika Senkowska-Gluck, Warsaw, Poland
Joseph I. Shulim, Forest Hills, New York
Michael D. Sibalis, University of New Brunswick, Fredericktown, New Brunswick, Canada
Morris Slavin, Youngstown State University, Youngstown, Ohio
Melvin Small, Wayne State University, Detroit, Michigan
John Spears, Baltimore, Maryland
Martin S. Staum, The University of Calgary, Calgary, Alberta, Canada
Bailey Stone, University of Houston, Houston, Texas
Daniel Stone, The University of Winnipeg, Winnipeg, Manitoba, Canada
George V. Taylor, The University of North Carolina, Chapel Hill, North Carolina
Louis Trenard, Université de Lille, Lille, France
Robert Vignery, The University of Arizona, Tucson, Arizona
Michel Vovelle, Université de Provence (centre d'Aix), France
Henry S. Vyverberg, Southern Illinois University at Carbondale, Carbondale, Illinois

Preface

This dictionary had its inception following a series of discussions between the present coeditors. We had taught undergraduate and graduate courses in the French Revolution for over thirty years collectively, one of us at Wayne State University, the other at Wayne and at the University of Northern Colorado, and each of us had spent research time in France at various archives. As friends, we shared our teaching and research methodologies, and our professional concerns. At one point or another in every conversation we had, talk invariably turned to the lack of a single, easily obtainable, and cohesive work that would present students of the French Revolution with the basic facts and interpretations surrounding persons and events connected with that cataclysmic upheaval. Such information, we believed, would be of enormous value to students, who ordinarily would not have sufficient knowledge of the sources to know where to look for accurate data. A sophisticated work of this sort would also be of significance to mature scholars of the Revolution. Familiar as they are with the sources, they often lack the time to examine them even when the material is available in their college or university library.

We observed additionally that although comprehensive historical dictionaries exist in English for virtually every other area of world history, no equivalent historical dictionary in English—or recent work in French—existed for historians of the French Revolution—this despite the fact that much significant research and writing on the Revolution is conducted by English-speaking historians and that interest in the Revolution remains uniformly high in English-speaking universities on both sides of the Atlantic.

During early spring 1978, we met in Detroit to begin the actual planning of a historical dictionary of the French Revolution to overcome these scholarly gaps. From the beginning of our discussions, we agreed that the scope of the Revolutionary decade, the enormous impact it has had on the modern world, the sweeping reforms it engendered, and the many interpretations of its causation and progress during the decade before Napoleon was so vast and complex that if the work were to succeed, we would have to seek the aid of other specialists in specific areas of the Revolution. Consequently 165 personal letters were sent worldwide to scholars of the Revolution requesting their participation in this project. We were astonished at the number of positive responses and extremely gratified that our proposal for an English-language historical dictionary had elicited such enthusiasm from academicians. In the end we secured the agreement of over ninety historians of the French Revolution from Australia, Canada, East Germany, France, Poland, the Soviet Union, and all geographic areas of the United States to contribute articles on their specialties. This gathering together of such a galaxy of scholars for a dictionary of the French Revolution was indicative to us of the professional need for this work.

After examining innumerable reference works, texts, and monographs treating the Revolution, we selected for inclusion in the proposed dictionary some 525 separate entries germane to the history of the French Revolution. In our selection process, and the ultimate assignment of entries to our contributors, we assumed that each specialist would probably desire maximum space to develop the topics within his or her area of expertise. But as editors we also recognized that it was impossible to grant this license, for it would make the dictionary unmanageable in terms of length. While we wished to present as broad a spectrum as possible in this collaborative effort, the length of articles had to correspond with the importance of the entry in the context of the Revolutionary decade. In short, it was our view that Maximilien Robespierre merited more space than his brother, Augustin.

The choices we have made for scholarly examination may not meet with universal approbation. We believe, however, that no important element of the Revolution has been omitted. We have strived throughout this work to establish the proper balance among Revolutionary personalities, events, and constitutional developments so that every significant and representative figure and event has been examined and interpreted. Each article, moreover, has appended to it a bibliography ranging from one to seven titles. Thus, should additional research or inquiry on a specific topic be contemplated, the student or scholar would have available the most reliable sources. We have also added to every entry a list of cross-references of related entries in the dictionary so that as well rounded an analysis as possible of the subject may be presented.

In editing these interpretive essays, we refrained deliberately from imposing our own judgment on the writings of our colleagues, although we repeatedly checked factual accuracy. Every effort was made to hold to the language submitted by the authors. When necessary, however, articles were reduced in length, and sentences and paragraphs were restructured to fit the stylistic format we had adopted. In no case did we make substantive changes in the text of an entry without the permission of the author concerned. Translations from the French were done by the coeditors. We were aided significantly in translations from the German and Russian by Professors Morris Slavin and Walter Markov, each a contributor to this work, and Steven Schuyler, currently on the staff of Harvard University.

Bibliographical information was provided by the contributors to supplement each of their entries. Because this project extended over five years from inception to conclusion, with contributions being received by the coeditors throughout this period, in the summer of 1983 all authors were given the opportunity to update their bibliographies. The vast output of literature on the French Revolution during the 1978-83 period led to significant additions to almost half the entries, as well as to several textual changes occasioned by new interpretations, information, and statistical data being made available. We believe that the currency and the authoritativeness of the dictionary's bibliographies reflect our intention to make it a complete reference work. It is our hope that readers will be as pleased as we are with the care with which each specialist has selected the most relevant sources to sustain his or her work.

We acknowledge with deep appreciation the work of the ninety-six scholars whose contributions made possible *A Historical Dictionary of the French Revolution*. We are confident that their efforts will stand the test of time and that all students of the French Revolution will be grateful for this invaluable resource. We also thank Tricia Kessel, Ginny Corbin, Donna Monacelli, and Jane Hobbs for their unsung but not unappreciated typing efforts. We would be remiss, too, if we failed to recognize the support engendered for this project from Greenwood Press, which plans to publish similar historical dictionaries for nineteenth and twentieth century France. Our special thanks go to Cynthia Harris, a gentle but persuasive and persistent reference editor.

We cannot conclude these remarks without offering a paean of praise for our families whose time we stole and whose lives were made occasionally unbearable by our desire to be perfectionists. Gratefully, we thank Denise, Margie, Eric, Elizabeth, Leslie, Robert, and Timothy.

S. F. S.
B. R.

Abbreviations of Journals in References

Am. Hist. Rev.	American Historical Review
Am. J. of Psychoanalys.	American Journal of Psychoanalysis
Am. Sociol. Rev.	American Sociological Review
A.N.	Archives Nationales
Anj. hist.	Anjou historique
Ann. de Bourg.	Annales de Bourgogne
Ann. de Bret.	Annales de Bretagne
Ann. de l'Est	Annales de l'Est
Ann. de Norm.	Annales de Normandie
Ann. du pr. de Ligne	Annales du prince de Ligne
Ann.: Econ., soc., civ.	Annales: Economies, sociétés, civilisations
Ann. hist. de la Révo. française	Annales historiques de la Révolution française
Ann. Report of the Am. Hist. Assoc. 1904	Annual Report of the American Historical Association for the Year 1904
Ann. révo.	Annales révolutionnaires
A.P.	Archives parlementaires de 1787 à 1860, première série (1787–1799), ed. J. Mavidal and E. Laurent
Ass. bret.	Association bretonne
B.N.	Bibliothèque nationale
Bord. et les îles brit.	Bordeaux et les îles britanniques du XIIIe au XXe siècle
Bull. de la Comm. hist. de la Mayenne	Bulletin de la Commission historique et archéologique de la Mayenne
Bull. de la Soc. des Antiq. de Norm.	Bulletin de la Société des Antiquités de Normandie
Bull. de la Soc. hist. de l'Orne	Bulletin de la Société historique et archéologique de l'Orne
Bull. de la Soc. roy. de Vieux Liège	Bulletin de la Société royale de Vieux Liège

Bull. d'hist. écon. et soc. de la Révo.	Bulletin d'histoire économique et sociale de la Révolution française
Bull. of the Inst. of Hist. Res.	Bulletin of the Institute of Historical Research
Bull. of the J. Rylands Lib.	Bulletin of the John Rylands Library
Cah. d'Hist.	Cahiers d'Histoire
Cah. ht.-marnais	Les Cahiers haut-marnais
Can. Slav. Papers	Canadian Slavonic Papers
Ch. Hist.	Church History
Comp. Stud. in Soc. and Hist.	Comparative Studies in Society and History
Econ. Hist. Rev.	Economic History Review
Econ. Rev.	Economic Review
Eighteenth Cent. Life	Eighteenth Century Life
Eighteenth Cent. Stud.	Eighteenth Century Studies
Eng. Hist. Rev.	English Historical Review
Europa	Europa: A Journal of Interdisciplinary Studies
Eur. Stud. Rev.	European Studies Review
Fr. Hist. Stud.	French Historical Studies
Hist. bladen	Historische bladen
Hist. J.	Historical Journal
Hist. Papers, Can.	Historical Papers, Canadian Historical Association
Hist. Reflec.	Historical Reflections
Hist. Stud.	Historical Studies (Melbourne)
Jahr. für Gesch. Ost.	Jahrbucher für Geschichte Osteuropas
J. des Débats	Journal des Débats
J. of Mod. Hist.	Journal of Modern History
J. of the Hist. of Ideas	Journal of the History of Ideas
Mél. de. sci. relig.	Mélanges de science religieuse
Mém. de l'Acad. Natl. de Metz	Mémoires de l'Académie Nationale de Metz
Mém. de la Soc. d'Hist. de Bret.	Mémoires de la Société d'Histoire et d'Archéologie de Bretagne
Mém. de la Soc. éduenne	Mémoires de la Société éduenne
Mém. de l'Inst. hist. de Prov.	Mémoires de l'Institut historique de Provence
Mém. de la Soc. Archéol. de Tour.	Mémoires de la Société Archéologique de Touraine
Mod. Lang. Notes	Modern Language Notes
Nice hist.	Nice historique
Paris et Ile-de-Fr.	Paris et Ile-de-France
Past and P.	Past and Present
Pol. Sci. Q.	Political Science Quarterly
Pol. Theo.	Political Theory
Pro. of the Cons. on Revo. Eur.	Proceedings of the Consortium on Revolutionary Europe, 1750–1850

Pro. of the Roy. Mus. Assoc.	Proceedings of the Royal Musical Association
Pro. of the WSFH	Proceedings of the Western Society for French History
Pub. Opin. Q.	Public Opinion Quarterly
P.V. des A.	Procès-verbal des Anciens
P.V. des C.C.	Procès-verbal des Cinq-Cents
Rech. sov.	Recherches sovietiques
Red Riv. Val. Hist. J. of W. Hist.	Red River Valley Historical Journal of World History
Réim. de l'Ancien Moniteur	Réimpression de l'Ancien Moniteur ... depuis la réunion des Etats généraux jusqu'au Consultat, mai 1789–novembre 1799, avec des notes explicatives
Rev. de l'Anj.	La Revue de l'Anjou
Rev. de la Révo.	Revue de la Révolution
Rev. des Deux-Mondes	Revue des Deux-Mondes
Rev. des Et. hist.	Revue des Etudes historiques
Rev. des Et. Mais.	Revue des Etudes Maistriennes
Rev. des ques. hist.	Revue des questions historiques
Rev. d'hist. dipl.	Revue d'histoire diplomatique
Rev. d'hist écon. et soc.	Revue d'histoire économique et social
Rev. d'hist. litt. de la France	Revue d'histoire litteraire de la France
Rev. d'hist mod. et cont.	Revue d'histoire moderne et contemporaine
Rev. du d-h. siècle	Revue du dix-huitième siècle
Rev. hist.	Revue historique
Rev. hist. de Bord. et de la Gir.	Revue historique de Bordeaux et de la Gironde
Rev. hist. de la Révo.	Revue historique de la Révolution française
Rev. hist. de dr. franç. et etr.	Revue historique de droit français et étranger
Révo. française	La Révolution française
Stud. in Burke	Studies in Burke and His Time
Stud. in Eighteenth Cent. Cult.	Studies in Eighteenth Century Culture
Stud. on Voltaire and Eighteenth Cent.	Studies on Voltaire and the Eighteenth Century
Trans. of the Amer. Phil. Soc.	Transactions of the American Philosophical Society
USF Lang. Q.	USF Language Quarterly
Vie Judic.	La Vie Judiciaire
Wm. and Mary Q.	William and Mary Quarterly

L

LACEPEDE, BERNARD-GERMAIN-ETIENNE DE LA VILLE, COMTE DE (1756-1825), naturalist. See SCIENCE.

LACOMBE, CLAIRE (1765-?), actress and leader of the Société des citoyennes républicaines révolutionnaires. Born in Pamiers (Ariège), Lacombe was the daughter of B. Lacombe and J.-M. Gauche. Her childhood cannot be traced, but by the early years of the Revolution, she had become an actress, playing in Lyon in 1790-91, then in Marseille and Toulon. She came to Paris in the spring of 1792. There is no direct evidence about her political sympathies prior to her arrival in Paris, but friends lobbying later for her release from prison claimed that her Revolutionary and republican sentiments had harmed her career in the south.

Once in Paris she quickly entered public life. On 25 July 1792 she delivered to the Legislative Assembly a patriotic address in which she attacked the marquis de Lafayette and noted that as a childless, single woman, she could do what mothers could not: attack the nation's enemies directly rather than by raising virtuous children. On 10 August 1792, she used her theatrical and oratorical talents to stir up the men participating in the attack on the Tuileries. For this she earned a civic crown and the praise of the *fédérés*.

Her next known appearance was before the Jacobins on 3 April 1793. By mid-August 1793 she had emerged as the new leader of the Société des citoyennes républicaines révolutionnaires, a women's club founded the previous May by P. Léon. In its early days, this society had supported the Montagnards against the Brissotins and had condemned J. Roux and the *enragés*. Lacombe's emergence as leader was apparently the result of a power struggle within the society. It signaled a major realignment, as the Citoyennes now turned against the Jacobin leadership and supported the *enragés*. The shift did not go unopposed within the society, and the Jacobins were able to collect statements from dissident *citoyennes* who accused Lacombe of sympathy for the Lyon rebels, of immorality, and of treasonous attacks on members of the Committee of Public Safety, particularly M. Robespierre. On 26 August 1793, Lacombe went to the Convention to castigate its members for their lukewarm attitude toward counterrevolutionaries and to demand that the Constitution of 1793 be put into effect. She continued this campaign through September. On 16 September 1793, members of the Jacobin club accused her of lobbying for the release of aristocrats (the ex-mayor of Toulouse and his nephew) and of counterrevolutionary attacks on the emergency Republic. Lacombe, who was present, was not permitted to speak. The Jacobins ordered the Citoyennes to purge their leadership and demanded the arrest of those purged. Lacombe spent the night in custody but was released when the Halle au Blé section could find nothing compromising in her papers. She promptly published a report on the incident, attacking F. Chabot, who had criticized her sympathy for T. Leclerc, an *enragé* journalist. |She then proceeded to involve the Citoyennes in a battle with the women of les Halles over the wearing of the Revolutionary cockade and the Phrygian bonnet and over the policing of the maximum on prices. Violence flared several times before the market women succeeded in trouncing Lacombe and her followers on 28 October 1793.

These disturbances gave the Convention its excuse to close the society and to ban all women from public life on 30 October 1793. Two weeks later Lacombe was to play Liberty in a festival of reason, but for her, political liberty was at an end, although she may have spent the next months working behind the scenes with the Hébertists. By March 1794 she was arranging her return to the provincial theater, but on 31 March she was arrested and held without trial until 18 August 1795. Early in 1796 she resumed her acting career in Nantes. In 1797-98 she again played in Paris. Nothing is known of her later life.

L. J. Abray, "Feminism in the French Revolution," *Am. Hist. Rev.* 80 (1975); D. G. Levy, H. B. Applewhite, and M. D. Johnson, eds., *Women in Revolutionary Paris, 1789-1795* (Urbana, 1979); R. B. Rose, *The Enragés: Socialists of the French Revolution?* (Sydney, 1965).

L. J. Abray

Related entries: CHABOT; *ENRAGES*; GIRONDINS; LECLERC; LEON; MONTAGNARDS; ROUX.

LAFAYETTE, MARIE-PAUL-JOSEPH-ROCH-GILBERT MOTIER, MARQUIS DE (1757-1832), general, deputy to the Assembly of Notables, the Estates General, and the Constituent Assembly, commander of the Paris National Guard. During the American War of Independence, Lafayette served with great distinction in the Continental Army. Following his return to France in 1782, he was promoted to the rank of *maréchal de camp* and awarded the Cross of Saint-Louis. During the following years, he became greatly involved in reform movements in France and the United States. During his 1784 tour of the United States, he urged a stronger central government, a national militia force, free trade, and the eventual abolition of slavery. In France he sought greater freedom of religion and a reduction of governmental regulation of trade. As a member of the Assembly of Notables in 1787, he protested the abuse of royal properties.

During the spring of 1788, he returned to military service as commander of an infantry brigade, but his career suffered as a result of his public support for the Breton nobility's protest against the Plenary Court. On 5 March 1789 the nobility of the *sénéschaussée* of Riom selected him as a deputy to the Estates General. Although he refused to leave that assembly because of his instructions from his constituency, he became active in the National Assembly on its dissolution. Three days after taking the oath on 8 July, he proposed a declaration of rights. On 13 July he was named vice-president of the Assembly, and on the day after the fall of the Bastille he led a deputation of sixty members to Paris. There the municipality proclaimed him commander of the Paris militia, which—with the assistance of a committee from the arrondissements—he soon transformed into the Paris National Guard.

It is claimed that he was responsible for proposing on 17 July the merging of the Paris colors—red and blue—with the royal white to form the national cockade. Lafayette's essential interest in establishing the National Guard was to secure the reforms of the Constituent Assembly in a peaceful atmosphere. When J.-F. Foulon and L.-B.-F. Bertier de Sauvigny were assassinated, he offered his resignation on 23 July but was prevailed on to withdraw it. During the march on Versailles of 5-6 October 1789, Lafayette and his troops followed the crowd, and, when they broke into the palace, his personal intervention calmed the situation. On 4 February 1790 he refused the command of all National Guard units throughout the realm. On 12 May 1790, Lafayette and others founded the Society of 1789, which later became known as the Feuillants.

In a show of national unity for the principles of the Revolution of 1789 and its oath of allegiance "to the nation, the law, and the king," a national *fédération* of representatives from National Guard units around the country was held in Paris on the first anniversary of the fall of the Bastille. Lafayette presided over the ceremony, with the king and queen present, and C.-M. Talleyrand celebrating Mass.

During the next year, Lafayette's efforts to maintain order and security until the constitution was completed forced him to take actions that increased his unpopularity on the Left and Right. In late August he lent his support to F.-C.-A. marquis de Bouillé's repression of the military mutiny at Nancy. On 28 February he supported the disarming of a group of men who had taken a position in the Tuileries claiming to defend the royal family. When the king attempted to go to Saint-Cloud during Holy Week (April 1791), the National Guard units impeded his departure, believing he was attempting to escape. Lafayette offered his resignation at their disobedience, believing that every citizen had a right to the free exercise of religion. After the royal flight to Varennes, the Jacobins accused Lafayette of collusion. Finally, on 17 July a group gathered in the Champ de Mars at the altar of the Fédération to sign a petition demanding that the Assembly replace the king by constitutional means. The Assembly urged that Lafayette disperse the mob out of fear for their well-being. When the group resisted, they were fired on by the National Guard.

On 18 September Lafayette at the head of the National Guard assisted in the proclaiming of the completion of the constitution. With that, the Constituent Assembly dissolved on 30 September and Lafayette's purpose fulfilled, he resigned on 8 October. In his honor the Paris National Guard offered him a golden sword, and the Paris municipality ordered that a bust of Washington be presented to him. The general then retired to his château in the Auvergne. In the days that followed, he rejected an offer to become an administrator of the department of Haute-Loire, as well as one to be *chef de légion* of the fourth division of the army of Paris.

As a result of increasing war tensions from the *émigrés* and the elector of Trier, L. Narbonne, the minister of war, announced on 14 December 1791 the creation of three armies, with Lafayette to command that of the center. Lafayette could not refuse to come to the defense of the constitution. He went to Paris to accept command and then left for Metz to organize his forces. The campaign of 1792 began in May. Yet events in Paris seemed to be a greater threat to the national security to Lafayette. Following the invasion of the Tuileries on 20 June, the general hurried to the Legislative Assembly to criticize that violence. His appearance on 28 June caused much discontent from the Left, and his prompt departure on 30 June did not stop the complaints. The events of 10 August further outraged Lafayette, who believed them a violation of the constitution. He opposed them and publicly addressed his troops on the matter on 13 August. The following day he had the municipal officials of Sedan arrest the commissioners of the Assembly who had been sent to advise the troops of the change in government. On 17 August the Executive Council ordered his removal from command, and two days later the National Assembly declared him in rebellion. That same day, Lafayette and twenty-two members of his general staff crossed the border at Mouzon. They were arrested by Prussian sentinels at Rochefort.

Lafayette was taken prisoner and transferred to a number of locations in the days that followed: Namur on 25 August, Luxembourg (3 September), Coblentz (15 September), Wesel (18 September), Magdeburg (31 December), and Neisse (16 January 1793). In May he was transferred from Prussian custody to the Austrians, who imprisoned him at Olmutz. There he remained in squalid conditions until a special provision of the Treaty of Campoformio secured his release, which occurred on 19 September 1797. Lafayette took up residence first in Holstein, then Holland. On hearing of the coup of Brumaire, he hurried to Paris under an assumed name. In May 1800 his name was stricken from the list of *émigrés*. From his estate at Le Grange-Blesneau in Seine-et-Marne, he rejected offers of a seat in the Senate and the ambassadorship to the United States. On 15 March 1802 he requested his retirement from the army.

E. Charavay, *Le Général La Fayette 1757-1834* (Paris, 1898); L. Gottschalk and M. Maddox, *Lafayette in the French Revolution*, 2 vols. (Chicago, 1969-74); S. J. Idzerda and R. R. Crout, eds., *Lafayette in the Age of the American Revolution, 1776-1790*, 5 vols. (Ithaca, 1977-); Lafayette, *Mémoires, correspondances et manuscrits du général La Fayette*, 6 vols. (Paris, 1837-38); C. de Tourtier-Bonazzi, *Lafayette: Documents conservés en France* (Paris, 1976).

R. R. Crout

Related entries: ASSEMBLY OF NOTABLES; BERTIER DE SAUVIGNY; BOUILLE; CHAMP DE MARS "MASSACRE"; ESTATES GENERAL; FEUILLANTS; JACOBINS; MUTINY OF NANCY; OCTOBER DAYS; 10 AUGUST 1792.

LA FORCE. See PRISONS.

LAHARPE, FREDERIC-CESAR DE (1754-1838), Swiss patriot. See HELVETIC REPUBLIC.

LAKANAL, JOSEPH (1762-1845), educator, legislator, academician. The family name was Lacanal, but early in the Revolution he adopted the spelling Lakanal to set himself apart from brothers who remained royalist. At age eleven Joseph entered the collège d'Esquille at Toulouse and at eighteen was beginning to teach. Continuing his own studies at the University of Angers, "Josephus Lacanal" was recognized as *maître-ès-arts* by that faculty on payment of the required fee of 21 *livres* in September 1786. Through the mid-1780s he was, first, professor of rhetoric at Bourges and then professor of philosophy at Moulins, where he was living when the Revolution began.

Although ordained, Lakanal was little inclined toward the active priesthood. He did serve one year (1791-92) as episcopal vicar to his patron, the abbé B. Font, constitutional bishop of Ariège; then, at age thirty, he was elected to the Convention by the department of the Ariège. In January 1793 he voted for the death of Louis XVI. The same month he was named a member of the Committee of Public Instruction, with which he worked throughout the Convention and into the Directory, often acting as *rapporteur* to the legislature. From 1795 until 1797, when he was dropped by lot, he represented the department of the Finistère in the Council of Five Hundred. In these crucial five years, he left Paris several times as representative on mission to supervise local administrations; the most important of these missions, to the Dordogne, lasted from October 1793 until August 1794. In the summer of 1799, even though no longer sitting in the legislature, he was appointed by the Directory to organize the four new departments on the left bank of the Rhine.

In the span of 1789-99, however, Lakanal is to be distinguished most by his focus on reshaping France's cultural institutions to fit and promote the republican regime. He labored prodigiously as sponsor, guide, and driving force in the transitions: from académies to Institut, from Jardin du Roi to Muséum national d'histoire naturelle, from the whole gamut of private schools and universities toward a state-run system of education.

After Brumaire, Lakanal remained in Paris as professor at the Ecole Centrale of St. Antoine; in 1804 he went to the Lycée Bonaparte as financial manager. In 1809, under the Empire, he was named superintendent of weights and measures for the departments of the Eure, Oise, Seine-Inférieure, and Somme. At the Institut, where he had been a member of the Classe des sciences morales et politiques from 1795 until it was abolished in 1803, he was transferred to the Classe d'histoire et de littérature ancienne.

For twenty-one years after the return of the Bourbons (1816-37) Lakanal lived in the United States: in Kentucky, in Louisiana, where he was briefly president of the College of New Orleans (1822-23), and in Alabama. Heartened by the Revolution of 1830 and deeply touched by his reinstatement in 1834 at the Institut (he had been dropped in its 1816 revision), Lakanal returned to France and took his place, vacated by the death of Garat, in the Académie des sciences morales et politiques, itself resurrected only since 1832.

The final years were marked by an especially close friendship with D. d'Angers, whose Lakanal bust (1840) now stands in the Institut.

J. C. Dawson, *Lakanal the Regicide* (New York, 1970); H. Jouin, "Lakanal et David d'Angers," *Rev. de l'Anj.* 88 (1902); H. Labroue, *La mission du conventionnel Lakanal dans la Dordogne en l'An II* (Paris [1912]).

G. R. Beale

Related entries: COUP OF 18 BRUMAIRE; EDUCATION; GARAT JEUNE; SCIENCE.

LALLY-TOLLENDAL, TROPHIME-GERARD, MARQUIS DE (1751-1830), Anglophile, deputy to the Estates General and National Assembly. When Lally-Tollendal was only fifteen, his father (Thomas-Arthur) was executed for alleged misconduct as commander of the French forces at Pondichéry during the Seven Years War. That did not prevent the young marquis from entering military service a few years later, though he resigned his captain's commission in 1785. In 1789, when he was elected as a deputy to the Estates General by the nobility of Paris, he was still actively petitioning the Parlement of Paris to clear his father's name. Lally's filial devotion and his passionate, even melodramatic, style at first attracted a number of admirers inside and outside the first Revolutionary assembly. So, too, did his decision to join the deputies of the Third Estate, along with forty-six other aristocrats, on 25 June in defiance of the king's orders. His election to the first Committee on the Constitution was proof of the high esteem he enjoyed in the early months of the Revolution. However, his subsequent reluctance to accept vote by head because it was not sanctioned by the *cahiers* made him look inconsistent at best; his emotional rhetoric gradually lost its appeal; and his close association with the moderate royalists known as *anglomanes* or *monarchiens* tarnished his reputation with both the more radical Revolutionaries and the ultraroyalists.

The deterioration of Lally's popular image began as early as 23 July 1789. On that date, remembering the politically inspired execution of his father, he denounced the murder by a Parisian crowd of the hated royal intendant L.-B.-F.

Bertier de Sauvigny. It was in response to his impassioned speech that A. Barnave uttered the famed words, ''Was that blood, then, so pure that it was such a great crime to spill it?'' In the months that followed, Lally continued to call for the suppression of lawlessness and supported the increasingly unpopular policies of the *anglomanes*. As early as 11 July, he had opposed as a practical matter the publication of a declaration of rights, while proclaiming support for the idea in principle. In August and September he declared himself in favor of a two-house legislature, an absolute royal veto, and a reconsideration of legislation ending aristocratic privileges.

Lally fled to Switzerland after the king and Assembly were forced to move to Paris in October 1789. After opposing the Revolution from exile for more than two years, he returned to Paris in 1792 to collaborate with P.-V. Malouet and A.-M. Montmorin in a desperate attempt to prevent total collapse of the monarchy. Arrested as a royalist shortly after the suspension of the monarchy on 10 August, he was released the day before the September Massacres and made good his escape to England. During his second exile, he published defenses of Louis XVI and the *émigrés*. He returned again to France after the Napoleonic coup in 1799 but took up residence in Bordeaux, shunning politics until the royalist restoration in 1815. Louis XVIII in that year appointed him to the Chamber of Peers and later called him to the royal ministry. He was elected to the French Academy in 1816. In 1830, a short time before the fall of Charles X, he died of apoplexy.

Lally-Tollendal did not match his fellow *anglomane* J.-J. Mounier in intellect, the comte de Virieu in boldness of spirit, P.-V. Malouet in practical good sense, or S. Clermont-Tonnerre in oratorical skill. But he played his Revolutionary role with the integrity, honesty, and courage that was typical of the *monarchiens*.

C. du Bus, *Stanislas de Clermont-Tonnerre et l'échec de la Révolution monarchique, 1757-1792* (Paris, 1931); J. Egret, *La Révolution des Notables; Mounier et les monarchiens, 1789* (Paris, 1950); L. de Lanzac de Laborie, *Jean-Joseph Mounier; sa vie politique et ses écrits* (Paris, 1887).

R. Vignery

Related entries: ANGLOMANES; BARNAVE; BERTIER DE SAUVIGNY; CLERMONT-TONNERRE; COUP OF 18 BRUMAIRE; MALOUET; *MONARCHIENS*; MONTMORIN; MOUNIER; SEPTEMBER 1792 MASSACRES; 10 AUGUST 1792.

LA MARCK, AUGUSTE-MARIE-RAYMOND, PRINCE D'ARENBERG, COMTE DE (1753-1833), deputy to National Constituent Assembly. La Marck, born in Brussels on 30 August 1753 into one of the oldest aristocratic families in Europe, was the fourth child of Charles-Léopold, duc d'Arenberg and Louise-Marguérite d'Engelbert. In 1773, he inherited the title of comte de La Marck and a German regiment in the service of France from his maternal grandfather, L. d'Engelbert, who had no direct male heirs. His French military career flourished during the *ancien régime*. La Marck became a brigadier, served in the important post of inspector general of the infantry, and played an important role in the formulation of infantry ordinances, which remained in effect for several decades.

Electoral regulations permitted the nobility in 1789 to elect La Marck, who was not a French citizen, as a deputy to the Estates General from the *bailliage* of Le Quesnoy where he held a fief. A constitutional monarchist and strong partisan of order and royal authority, La Marck became progressively alienated from the Revolution during the period of the National Assembly. He later admitted that he had made a major error in supporting the uprising of 1789-90 in Belgium against Joseph II.

La Marck had very close ties with the monarchy and with H.-G. R. Mirabeau. Stating that providence had erred in having Louis XVI as a king during a revolution, La Marck believed that the monarch's fatal flaws were apathy and the lack of resolution in the making and implementation of policies. By contrast, La Marck praised the queen's courage and determination, though not her sense of political judgment. La Marck became Mirabeau's closest friend and, although often distressed by the latter's demagoguery, felt that Mirabeau was sincerely devoted to saving the monarchs from the political dangers threatening them.

La Marck's major role during the Revolution was to serve as the main intermediary in arranging for Mirabeau to become a secret agent of the court and for the transmission of information between them. In this capacity, he played a central part in Mirabeau's conspiracy to restore the power of the monarchy through the escape of the king to the eastern frontier where he would abolish the National Assembly and create a new national legislature. La Marck recruited some of the conspirators, including the marquis de Bouillé, commander of the northeastern frontier. However, the cabal, the success of which La Marck had grave doubts about due to the apathy of the court, collapsed with the death of Mirabeau in April 1791.

Mirabeau's demise led to La Marck's main contribution to the historiography of the French Revolution. In fulfillment of a promise to a dying Mirabeau who wanted his conduct vindicated by posterity, La Marck arranged for the publication of the latter's correspondence with him, as well as other relevant documents. This collection, which includes a brief biography of La Marck, constitutes a valuable primary source on the early stages of the Revolution.

In October 1791, La Marck left France for Brussels in order to aid the comte de Mercy-Argenteau, former Austrian ambassador to France, in the latter's efforts to save the French monarchy and to restore order in Belgium. He became Mercy-Argenteau's private secretary and remained in that post until the latter's death in August 1794. The Austrian government then placed him on active duty at the rank of general-major and sent him on some minor diplomatic missions. In 1796, due to ill health, La Marck retired and lived in Vienna, where life was difficult for him because he had lost most of his wealth and properties with the French conquest of Belgium. After the fall from power of Napoleon, who had tried unsuccessfully to recruit him, La Marck returned to Belgium, where he lived quietly until his death on 26 September 1833.

A. de Bacourt, ed., *Correspondance entre le comte de Mirabeau et le comte de la Marck pendant les années 1789, 1790, et 1791*, 2 vols. (Brussels, 1851); Oliver J. G. Welch, *Mirabeau: A Study of a Democratic Monarchist* (London, 1951).

D. M. Epstein

Related entries: BOUILLE; MERCY-ARGENTEAU; MIRABEAU.

LAMARCK, JEAN-BAPTISTE-PIERRE-ANTOINE DE MONET, CHEVALIER DE (1744-1829), one of the most important naturalists of his time, who developed his own, controversial theory of evolution. Lamarck was born on 1 August 1744 at Bazantin in Picardy to a family of limited means. Destined for the church, he studied at the collège and subsequently the seminary of Amiens. In 1761 he enlisted in the army of marshal de Broglie in Hanover and was promoted to captain for his courage and determination. Poor health forced him to quit the service. He then studied medicine and botany at Paris. Deeply interested in systems of classification, he collected plants at the Jardin du Roi. A disciple of A.-L. Jussieu, he published *Flore française* (3 vols. in 1778, reedited with Candolle in 5 vols. in 1805). This work, for which L.-J.-M. Daubenton had drafted the "preliminary discourse," enjoyed a brisk success and opened election to the Academy of Sciences in 1779 to Lamarck. The great naturalist G. Buffon obtained for him a commission to travel in Europe as botanist of the king during 1781-82.

Lamarck collaborated in C.-J. Panckoucke's enterprise, the *Encyclopédie méthodique* (1783-1808). He immersed himself in herbal collections and followed the system of C. Linnaeus. In 1788 he was named conservator of the herbal collection and lecturer in the *Cabinet du Roi*. The Legislative Assembly suppressed learned societies, but the Convention reconstituted the Jardin du Roi under the name of the Museum of Natural History (10 June 1793) and confirmed the positions of twelve renowned scholars, the youngest of whom were G. Cuvier and Lamarck. The latter obtained the chair of zoology for the class of invertebrates. By his opening address, by his works, and by his lectures to the Philomathic Society of Paris, he showed himself a successor to Buffon, going beyond the technical aspect of the life sciences to philosophy and metaphysics. Admitted to the Institute in 1796, he published a *Bulletin des sciences*, which endorsed evolutionary conceptions of knowledge.

Under the Directory, he became interested in the evolution of the earth and the seas and in meteorology, but his principal work consisted of his hypotheses on the evolution of species, which was presented in *Recherches sur l'organisation des corps vivants, particulièrement sur leur origine, sur la cause de leur développement, des progrès de leur décomposition et celle qui amène la mort* (1802) and, above all, his *Philosophie zoologique* (2 vols., 1809). He did not accept the existence of species that were permanent and unchanging in their characteristics but insisted on the evolution of species through adaptation to changes in their environment. "Lamarckism" found a resolute opponent in Cuvier.

Besides the works cited, Lamarck published *Recherches sur les causes des principaux faits physiques* (2 vols., 1794), *Réfutation de la théorie pneumatique et de la nouvelle doctrine des chimistes modernes* (1796), *Mémoires de physique et d'histoire naturelle* (1797), *Systeme des animaux sans vertebres* (1801), *Hydrogéologie* (1802), *Annuaire météorologique* (1800-11), and *Extrait du cours de zoologie du Muséum d'histoire naturelle* (1812) which was expanded to seven volumes of *Histoire naturelle des animaux sans vertebres* (1815-22).

Having become blind at the end of his life, Lamarck was assisted by his daughter in the publication of *Mémoire sur les fossiles des environs de Paris* (1823) and *Système analytique des connaissances positives de l'homme* (1830), published after his death on 19 December 1829.

M. Bartélemy-Madaule, *Lamarck ou le mythe du précurseur* (Paris 1980); R. W. Burckhardt, *The Spirit of System: Lamarck and Evolutionary Biology* (London, 1977); L. Burlingame, "The Importance of Lamarck's Chemistry for His Theories of Nature and Evolution of Transformism," *13ᵉ Congrès Intern. Sc. Hist. Moscou* 3 (1970); H. Daudin, *Cuvier et Lamarck (1720-1830)* (Paris, 1926) and *De Linné à Lamarck (1740-1790)* (Paris, 1926); E. Perrier, *Lamarck* (Paris, 1925).

L. Trenard

Related entry: SCIENCE.

LAMETH, ALEXANDRE-THEODORE-VICTOR, COMTE DE (1760-1829), deputy to the Estates General and the Constituent Assembly. During the American War of Independence, Lameth served in J.-B.-D. Rochambeau's army. After returning to France he was promoted to colonel of the Chasseurs of Hainaut. In the Estates General, he served from the nobility of Péronne but soon left to join the National Assembly, where he joined his brother on the Left. On the night of 4 August 1789, he urged the abolition of the privileges of nobility. That same month he proposed that church properties serve as security for the creditors of the nation.

On 3 November Lameth proposed a decree forbidding the parlements from assembling and also dissolving the authority of the *chambres de vacations*. In the session of 15 May 1790, he joined with his brother to promote the right of the Assembly and not of the king to declare war. It was he on 13 June 1790, prior to the Fête de la Fédération, who urged the dismantling of the war trophies in the place des Victoires in esteem for the citizens of Franche-Comté and Alsace. In a speech on 2 August, he sustained the principle of freedom of the press.

Some of Lameth's most effective work in the Assembly was in its committees, especially those on the constitution, colonies, finances, and the military. On the last he made a significant report calling for reforms. On 20 November, Lameth became president of the Assembly. In February 1791 he joined the administration of the department of Paris. Following Louis XVI's acceptance of the constitution,

Lameth was one of the first to urge the continuation of the Assembly as a legislature.

When war was declared against Austria, Lameth joined the Army of the North as *maréchal de camp*. On 15 August 1792, the Legislative Assembly brought charges against him, but he fled with the marquis de Lafayette to the enemy lines where he was held and imprisoned with Lafayette. As a result of bad prison conditions, Lameth's health seriously deteriorated, and he was later released. While on his way to Bath, England, for the waters, he was intercepted by British authorities and expelled. He then proceeded to Hamburg where he joined his brother, Charles. Lameth returned to France in 1796 attempting to reestablish his citizenship, but after the coup of 18 Fructidor, he was forced to flee again, this time to Lausanne. As a result of pressure from the Directory, Swiss authorities expelled him, and he returned to Hamburg. On 28 April 1800, his name was removed from the *émigré* list, and he was allowed to return to France, where he became a prefect under Napoleon in the departments of the Basses-Alpes (1802), the Rhin-et-Moselle (1805), the Roer (1806), and the Po (1809).

A. de Lameth, *Examen d'un écrit intitulé Discours et réplique du comte de Mirabeau ... à qui la nation doit-elle déléguer le droit de la paix et de la guerre* (Paris, 1790) and *Rapport général sur la situation actuelle des frontières* ([Paris], [1791]); C. A. McClelland, ''The Lameths and Lafayette: The Politics of Moderation in the French Revolution, 1789-1791'' (Ph. D. dissertation, University of California, 1942); E. Welvert, ed., *Notes et souvenirs de Théodore de Lameth, faisant suite à ses Mémoires* (Paris, 1914).

R. R. Crout

Related entries: COUP OF 18 FRUCTIDOR YEAR V; 4 AUGUST 1789; LAFAYETTE; LAMETH, C.; LAMETH, T.

LAMETH, CHARLES-MALO-FRANCOIS, COMTE DE (1757-1832), deputy to the Estates General and the Constituent Assembly. Lameth served in J.-B.-D. Rochambeau's army during the American War of Independence and was there promoted to the rank of *aide-maréchal général des logis*. He was severely wounded in both legs at the siege of Yorktown. In 1788 Lameth became colonel of the Royal Cuirassiers. As a delegate of the nobility of Artois to the Estates General, he was one of the first of the nobility to join the National Assembly, where he was often found on the Left. He was an early proponent of the freedoms of press and religion. He opposed the motion of H.-G. R. Mirabeau to have the prince de Condé declared a traitor, and on 11 December he urged that only the king and dauphin be given legal privileges. After the flight of Louis on 20 June 1791, Lameth called for the renewal by legislative act of the oath of allegiance, and he urged the arrest of the marquis de Bouillé and other officers accused of aristocratic loyalties. On 5 July 1791 he was elected president of the Assembly. He used that influence to support the constitutional monarchy. At the beginning of the military campaign of 1792, Lameth took command of a brigade in the Army of the North. Following the events of 10 August 1792, he was discharged.

Shortly after he was arrested and taken to Rouen, where he was held for a month. After being freed, then denounced again, Lameth escaped to Hamburg, where he set up business as a merchant. He attempted to return to France in 1797 to regain his citizenship, but after the Fructidor coup he fled to Basel. Under pressure from the Directory, he was expelled and returned to Hamburg. On 21 April 1800, his name was stricken from the list of *émigrés*, and he returned to France. There he rejoined the army and was given an active command at Hanau in 1809.

C. A. McClelland, "The Lameths and Lafayette: The Politics of Moderation in the French Revolution, 1789-1791" (Ph.D. dissertation, University of California, Berkeley, 1942); E. Welvert, ed., *Notes et souvenirs de Théodore de Lameth, faisant suite à ses Mémoires* (Paris, 1914).

R. R. Crout

Related entries: BOUILLE; CONDE; *EMIGRES*; LAMETH, A.; LAMETH, T.; MIRABEAU; 10 AUGUST 1792; VARENNES.

LAMETH, THEODORE, COMTE DE (1756-1854), deputy to the Legislative Assembly. Lameth entered the navy at the age of fifteen. As an *enseigne de vaisseau*, he distinguished himself in campaigns under the comte d'Orvilliers and the comte de Guichen. He was wounded at the Battle of Grenada. Following his return to France, he was named *colonel en second* and later colonel of a cavalry regiment, the Royal-Etranger. In 1790 he was elected president for the department of Jura, and the following year he represented that department in the Legislative Assembly, where he was seated on the Right.

Lameth was one of the few deputies who voted against C.-E. Pastoret's motion for war on the Holy Roman Empire, and he also denounced the massacres of 10 August 1792. Shortly after, he went into seclusion on his brother Charles' estate in Osny. Learning that an order for his arrest had been issued by the committee of surveillance of Lons-le-Saunier on 3 November 1793, Lameth fled to Switzerland, where he resided at Nyon. In 1796 he returned to the Jura but was forced to flee again at the time of the Fructidor coup. This time he stayed in Lausanne. On 8 October 1798, the Directory placed him on the list of *émigrés*. Under the amnesty of Brumaire, he was restored to his full rights on 29 May 1800, and he returned to France.

B.N., Nouv. acquis. fr., 1387-1389, *Papiers du général Théodore de Lameth*; T. Lameth, *Mémoires*, ed. E. Welvert, 2 vols. (Paris, 1913); E. Welvert, ed., *Notes et souvenirs de Théodore de Lameth, faisant suite à ses Mémoires* (Paris, 1914).

R. R. Crout

Related entries: COMMITTEES OF SURVEILLANCE; LAMETH, A.; LAMETH, C.; 10 AUGUST 1792.

LAMOIGNON DE BASVILLE, CHRETIEN-FRANCOIS II DE (1735-89), judge and reformist keeper of the seals. This prominent minister of Louis XVI belonged to one of the most illustrious families of the high judiciary in Old

Regime France. Son and great-grandson of prominent Parisian *parlementaires*, great-nephew of chancellor Lamoignon de Blancmesnil, and nephew of the famed judge and Minister Lamoignon de Malesherbes, Chrétien-François II de Lamoignon quite naturally followed a legal career and harbored long-standing ministerial ambitions. Received as a junior magistrate in the fourth Chambre des Enquêtes of the Parlement of Paris in September 1755, Lamoignon became a president in the court's senior chamber in May 1758 and served in that capacity until his elevation to the post of keeper of the seals under Louis XVI in 1787.

Lamoignon's tenure in the parlement, like that of his colleagues, was interrupted during the 1771-74 interval marking R.-N. Maupeou's reformist chancellorship and the *parlementaires'* disgrace. Lamoignon's impatience with the *métier* of parlementary justice, and his willingness to have a hand in ameliorating that justice, were widely rumored and reliably reported by several of his confidants in the years following the reinstatement of the old judiciary in 1774. Consequently, he was mistrusted by most of the conservative elders of the parlement's senior chamber but favored by certain reform-minded and rebellious junior magistrates of the subordinate chambers of enquêtes and requêtes. Early in 1783 Lamoignon, a few like-minded senior jurists, and a coterie of zealous young judges from the lower chambers attempted to persuade their associates to define the major abuses in parlementary justice and to request that the crown eliminate those abuses. The resultant controversy of 1783-84 ended with the parlement's conservative leaders outmaneuvering Lamoignon's party; nonetheless, the affair promoted Lamoignon's reputation in enlightened circles at Paris and Versailles and foreshadowed his reforming judicial ministry of 1787-88.

That ministry was made possible early in 1787 by the impasse between Finance Minister C. A. de Calonne and the first Assembly of Notables. Calonne fell from office in April 1787; so, too, did Keeper of the Seals A.-T. Hue de Miromesnil, whose stewardship of justice since the disgrace of Chancellor Maupeou in 1774 had attracted notoriety for its frustration of judicial reform. Lamoignon received the seals on 13 April. Over the next seventeen months, utilizing the advice and talents of some of the foremost justices and lawyers of the realm, Lamoignon initiated significant reforms. In particular, the famous legislation of May 1788 broke the back of parlementary resistance to government policies by vesting a plenary court with the parlements' traditional power of registering (and remonstrating against) royal laws. The legislation of May 1788 also destroyed the parlements' monopoly of sovereign justice by portioning out that justice between the parlements and new law courts called *grands bailliages*. The May edicts ameliorated justice in other ways as well. They abolished the dread *question préalable* (the torture still used at times to compel convicted criminals to reveal accomplices) and in general mitigated the rigor of French criminal law. While not abolishing venality of office, Lamoignon's legislation set higher standards of competence for the personnel of the tribunals, requiring most notably that parlementary judges gain prior service in the lower courts. Furthermore, Lamoignon's reforms reduced the powers of seigneurial justice, abolished many useless fiscal and administrative courts, reorganized the process of judicial appeal in the interest of litigants, and in general strove to render French justice swifter, cheaper, and more equitable.

Although the keeper of the seals elicited much support from enlightened individuals within the upper ranks of society, he ultimately fell victim to royal weakness, government insolvency, bruised special interests, and the general constitutional uproar attending the 1787-88 pre-Revolution. Lamoignon's resignation on 14 September 1788 signified frustration of his hopes for judicial reform and signaled his final retirement from public affairs, but it could not dim his stature as one of the last great ministers of the *ancien régime*. Although Lamoignon's death on his estate of Basville during 1789 meant that he would not witness the Revolutionary and Napoleonic eras, his abortive reforms of 1787-88 anticipated the permanent transformation of French justice under the auspices of the new age.

J. Egret, *The French Prerevolution 1787-1788*, trans. W. Camp (Chicago, 1977); M. Marion, *Le garde des sceaux Lamoignon et la réforme judiciaire de 1788* (Paris, 1905); B. Stone, "The Old Regime in Decay: Judicial Reform and the Senior Parlementaires at Paris, 1783-84," *Stud. in Burke* 16 (1975).

B. Stone

Related entries: ASSEMBLY OF NOTABLES; CALONNE; JUSTICE; MALESHERBES.

LAPLACE, PIERRE-SIMON, MARQUIS DE (1749-1827), astronomer, mathematician, academician. Son of a cider manufacturer and a product of Benedictine and Jesuit schools, Laplace by 1789 had taught at the Ecole militaire, made important connections in the Parisian scientific community, and achieved membership in the Academy of Sciences. Reputedly favorable to the Revolution, he avoided an active political role and remained outside the public eye until after the Terror. In December 1794 he became assistant to J.-L. Lagrange (1736-1813) at the Ecole normale and in 1795 accepted appointments to the Bureau of Longitudes and the National Institute for Science and the Arts. Laplace continued to prosper under Napoleon I and the restored Bourbons. He was initiated into the French Academy, several foreign academies, and the Legion of Honor. He also acquired a title of nobility and served as minister of the interior, senator, and chancellor in the First Empire. His best-known publications, *La mécanique céleste* and *Théorie analytique des probabilités*, were brilliant syntheses of other scientists' findings. Although by choice he played no significant role in political events between 1789 and 1799, he exemplified the continuity of scientific advancement through the Revolutionary epoch.

J. Neyman and L. M. Le Cam, eds., *Bernoulli (1713), Bayes (1763), Laplace (1813): Anniversary Volume* (Berlin, Heidelberg, New York, 1965); E. Picard, 'Un double centenaire: Newton et Laplace, leur vie et leur oeuvre," in *Eloges et discours académiques* (Paris, 1931); G. A. Simon and K. Pearson, "Laplace, Notes on His Ancestry and Life," *Biometrika* 20 (1929).

R. Vignery

Related entries: LAMARCK, J.; SCIENCE.

LA REVELLIERE-LEPEAUX, LOUIS-MARIE (1753-1824), legislator, director, academician. Born of a propertied and professional family with roots in Anjou and Poitou, Louis-Marie was schooled from the age of thirteen in Anjou, first under the Sulpicians in Beaupréau and then in Angers at the collège de l'Oratoire from 1767 to 1772. His formal education was completed with three years at the University of Angers, where he was graduated *licencié-ès-lois* in 1775. There followed three years in Paris, where he was registered as an *avocat au parlement* and held a desk in a law office. There his older brother usually did his work while Louis-Marie explored the city and its resources in company with his former school comrade J.-B. Leclerc, with whom he was later to be elected to the Constituent Assembly.

Forsaking the practice of law in Paris, at age twenty-five he returned briefly to his home in Montaigu but stayed only until his parents decided he should establish himself at Angers. There he married J.-M.-M.-V. Boileau of Chandoiseau on 13 February 1781. After a year in Nantes, the young couple returned to Angers to manage their share of the Boileau inheritance.

Freed from the necessity of earning a living, Revellière-lépeaux abandoned law in favor of botany. (The name has been spelled in countless ways; the subject of this sketch himself settled on *L. M. Revellière-lépeaux*, with or without a hyphen, by the time he became director, and consistently signed in this fashion the rest of his life.) Along with Leclerc and another close friend, U. Pilastre, he helped found the local Société des botanophiles, of which he became president. In 1788, following the death of a professor of botany, Revellière-lépeaux was invited to give courses in that subject at the University of Angers. At last his profession seemed to be decided, but the next year was 1789. Standing as syndic of the commune of Faye and engaging in a brisk pamphleteering campaign, "Louis Marie de la Revellière de l'épeaux, Bourgeois" was the third of eight deputies elected by the third estate of Anjou. Pilastre and Leclerc were the first two of four alternates named. At the end of April, the three set out together for Versailles along with C.-F.-C. Volney, also a deputy.

Through the early months of the Constituent Assembly, "L. M. Delarevellière Delépeaux," as he then signed, stated graphically his tenets of equality with the second estate by persistently wearing colored costumes rather than the black officially prescribed for the Third Estate. He signed the Tennis Court Oath on the same page with H.-G. R. Mirabeau and M. Robespierre. Accustomed to associating with members of the Breton club, he helped found the Jacobin club but was one of the first to brand some of its members as factionist, and by July 1791 he had withdrawn. Undertaking his share of day-by-day committee work, in July 1789 he served as one of the thirty who considered how to go about making a constitution but was not a member of the Committee of Eight who actually drew it. His most important public speeches of the two years were directed against granting the veto to the king, allowing royal investiture of elected judges, and reelecting deputies to consecutive legislatures, though he approved delegates' sitting in alternate sessions. He supported the Civil Constitution of the Clergy but repudiated accepting the Catholic church as the sole state church.

During the constitutional monarchy, like many other former deputies, he served as administrator in his own department and in that capacity supported the new regime. Elected in 1792 to the newer and republican National Convention, he stood fearlessly in November to proclaim that this Convention in the name of the French nation would aid all peoples who wished to recover their liberty. His friends for the most part were Girondist, and he strongly mistrusted the Paris Commune, but he was not proscribed in May 1793 and continued expressing his opinions in the truncated Convention until August. Thereafter, hidden first by L.-A.-G. Bosc in the forest of Montmorency, then by M.-L.-N. Pincepré de Buire in Péronne, he survived to reenter the legislature in March 1795. There a much-applauded defense of secret treaties won him a place, first as secretary, then as president, of the body. From April 1795 he worked on the Committee of Eleven to prepare a republican constitution; the last two months of the session he spent on the still important Committee of Public Safety.

In six years Revellière-lépeaux rose from provincial deputy to become a co-head of state. On 1 November 1795 Revellière-lépeaux was elected, by a vote of 216 to 2 in the Council of Ancients, a member of the Executive Directory of France's first constitutional republic. He had stood at the head of the list submitted by the Council of Five Hundred, seventy votes higher than J.-F. Reubell, who was second on their list of fifty candidates. Only Revellière-lépeaux himself, and Pilastre at his insistence, had cast negative ballots.

Revellière-lépeaux' responsibilities were to take over a bloc of western departments for authorizing appointments and watching over other local business. He also promoted the reconstruction of cultural institutions: the Institut de France (where he was elected a member of the Classe des sciences morales et politiques), public celebrations and cults, schools, and patronage of science and the arts.

Using a vocabulary reminiscent of J.-J. Rousseau, Revellière-lépeaux as director propounded the inviolability of the general will, which he equated to the indivisibility of truth; his definition presumed a base of universality that left little room for divergence; parties to the right or left of his own positions were instantly suspect. He had also read C. de Montesquieu and seized on a version of that writer's concept of separation of powers. As a result, when in the spring and summer of 1797 L. Carnot proposed to break the impasse between councils and Directory by appointment of new ministers representative of legislative opinion, Revellière-lépeaux held with P. Barras and Reubell against an innovation that might have led to cabinet-parliamentary government, as it came to be practiced many years later. For a year and a half after Fructidor, Revellière-lépeaux stood firm against what he viewed as legislative pressure on executive power, when yearly elections returned legislators less amenable to leadership by the Executive Directory. He exhorted by proclamation and was willing to manipulate elections. Failing victory at the polls, he was willing to discredit elected deputies. The tide was running against his variation of Montesquieu but he survived until the last clearing out before Brumaire. On 30 Prairial Year VII, this once most popular director capitulated.

Afterward he lived a quarter of a century in seclusion, in and near Paris except for five years when he removed his family to La Roussellière, near Orléans. He went occasionally to look after interests in the west of France. Disassociating himself from any of the succeeding political regimes, he occupied himself exclusively with the education and establishment of his children and with the writing of his memoirs. He died at his apartment in the rue Condé, close by the Palais du Luxembourg, and was buried in Père-Lachaise.

A.N., series A F III, Cartons 314-637; H. Janeau, *Le Vendéen La Revellière-Lépeaux, Membre du Directoire, 1753-1824* (Poitiers, 1951); A. Meynier, *Un représentant de la bourgeoisie angevine, L.-M. La Revellière-Lépeaux, 1753-1795* (Paris, 1905); L.-M. La Revellière-Lépaux, *Mémoires*, 3 vols. (Paris, 1873); G. Robison, *Revellière-lépeaux: Citizen Director, 1753-1824* (New York, 1938; 1972).

G. R. Beale

Related entries: BOSC; CIVIL CONSTITUTION OF THE CLERGY; COMMITTEE OF PUBLIC SAFETY; COUP OF 18 FRUCTIDOR YEAR V; DIRECTORY; GENERAL WILL; ROUSSEAU; SELF-DENYING ORDINANCE.

LA ROCHEFOUCAULD-LIANCOURT, FRANCOIS-ALEXANDRE-FREDERIC, DUC DE

(1747-1827), reformer, philanthropist, and deputy to the National Assembly. Liancourt was born into one of the most ancient noble families in France, one in which both interest in the newest intellectual currents and concern for humanitarian reform were established traditions. In the 1770s, he was closely associated with the progressive circle of his aunt, the duchesse d'Enville, which included both the marquis de Condorcet and A.-R.-J. Turgot. At her salon he met all the leading figures of the Enlightenment and foreign celebrities as well. On a visit to England, Liancourt saw the improvements being launched there in farming and manufacturing and began his long and close association with A. Young, the English agronomist.

Following another family tradition, Liancourt had entered the army at fifteen. He served ably and rose quickly to the rank of major general. He also made the requisite visits to the court at Versailles, traveled widely, and personally supervised the management of his estates. He established a school for the orphaned sons of army officers, in which technical education was emphasized. He built mills for the making of textiles and tools, also providing a basic education for the children who worked in spinning mills.

In 1783 he succeeded his deceased father as master of the robes. He was thus in constant contact with Louis XVI, to whom he would be unswervingly loyal. Like many of the other great nobles, he found himself increasingly excluded from the favors of patronage and influence that were lavished on the queen's favorites, notably the unsavory Polignac clan. By 1787, he was among those great nobles calling for the reduction of the privileges of his own order, and in 1788 he was active in the Committee of Thirty, which was orchestrating a propaganda campaign for the creation of a constitutional monarchy. Elected by his order to the Estates General in 1789, he continued his efforts, declaring on 27 June that the nobility should give up its privileges because "We are citizens before we are nobles."

He continued to be the king's loyal friend and as master of the robes was an important link between the National Assembly and the court. Unfortunately, the Assembly's measures against such arrangements, aimed mainly at H.-G. R. Mirabeau, diminished his influence with the king. With Mirabeau, Condorcet, and the marquis de Lafayette, all colleagues from the old Committee of Thirty, he was active in the Société de 1789.

When the National Assembly ended, Liancourt sought and received appointment as commander of the army in Normandy. He tried to persuade the king to come to Rouen, where he would be under Liancourt's protection. It would have been entirely legal, despite post-Varennes restrictions on royal movement, but the queen persuaded Louis to refuse. On hearing of the events of 10 August 1792 and the imminent fall of the monarchy, Liancourt escaped to England, where he learned that his cousin, the duc de La Rochefoucauld, had been lynched by a mob and that he had inherited the title.

La Rochefoucauld-Liancourt spent seven years in exile, four of them in the United States, where he was impressed especially with the institutions for the care of criminals and the poor. He refused to have anything to do with the schemes of the counterrevolutionary *émigrés*. When Napoleon moved to political reconciliation by removing the proscriptions against those *émigrés* who had served in the National Assembly, La Rochefoucauld-Liancourt returned immediately to France where, despite the depletion of his fortune, he resumed the improvement of his estates. He served in the upper legislative chamber during both restorations and in the Chamber of Representatives during the intervening Hundred Days, but he found himself once again excluded from influence at court by the Polignacs and their ilk. He therefore threw himself into a range of philanthropic and humanitarian undertakings. He continued his interest in technical education, established welfare institutions of various kinds on American models, and was active in behalf of civil liberties and religious toleration until his death at the age of eighty in 1827.

H. Clergue, *Phases of France on the Eve of the Revolution* (London, 1922); F. Dreyfus, *La Rochefoucauld-Liancourt, 1747-1827* (Paris, 1903); D. Wick, "The Court Nobility and the French Revolution: the Example of the Society of Thirty," *Eighteenth-Cent. Stud.* 13 (1980).

C. Garrett

Related entries: COMMITTEE OF THIRTY; CONDORCET; LAFAYETTE; MIRABEAU; SOCIETY OF 1789; YOUNG.

LA ROCHEJAQUELIN, HENRI DU VERGIER, COMTE DE (1772-94), commander of the Grande Armée of the Vendée. La Rochejaquelin served with his cousin, the marquis de Lescure, in Louis XVI's Constitutional Guard, returning after 10 August 1792 to live near Bressuire in Haut-Poitou where, on the outbreak of insurrection in March 1793, he took a leading part in a skirmish that was the first of a series (Tiffauges, Beaupréau, Thouars, Parthenay and, on 25 May, Fontenay) that established his reputation for valor, honor, and simplicity of manner. Stories multiplied, entering into folklore: the Intrepid One leading, with his cousin, the charge across the bridge at Thouars (5 May), his galloping into Saumur alone (9 June) ahead of the Grande Armée on whose controlling council he sat and to the command of which he was appointed by that council when, with C.-M. Bonchamp dead and M.-L.-G. d'Elbée and L.-M. Lescure badly wounded at Cholet (17 October 1793), the army crossed the Loire.

Henri was a splendid leader of men, but despite the admiration he forced from the Republican general at Laval (23 October), probably not especially remarkable as a battle commander; and in the council his was not, especially after Granville (13-14 November) an unchallenged voice. He and A.-P. Talmont did, though, hold off the Republican attack at Dol (20-21 November) with skill as well as courage, but he was checked at Angers (3 December) and routed at Le Mans (12 December). Shortly afterward he, N. Stofflet, and a small band crossed the Loire and, learning of the army's dispersion at Savenay (23 December), headed into the *bocage*. Having met F.-A. Charette de la Contrie and agreeing they should operate separately, La Rochejaquelin soon demonstrated skill, the popular touch, and bravery in a series of raids and small-scale engagements, in the course of one of which he was shot (28 January). La Rochejaquelin's youth, impetuous character, and sacrifice were, like the piety and death of his cousin, the stuff of legend. This helped nourish a reputation that was boosted by the publication, during the Restoration, of the memoirs of Henri's brother's wife, the widow of Lescure; vastly successful, this "Gospel of La Vendée" exalted Henri, Lescure, and the Grande Armée at the expense, undoubtedly, of other royalist leaders and armies in western France.

C. L. Chassin, *Etudes documentaires sur la Vendée et la Chouannerie*, 11 vols. (Paris, 1892-1900); J. G. du Vergier de La Rochejaquelin, ed., *Mémoires de Mme. la marquise de la Rochejacquelin: édition originale* (Paris, 1889), on which see the comments by F.-A. Aulard in *Révo. française* 16 (1889) and by F. Uzureau in *Revue des facultés Catholiques de l'Ouest*, 15 (1905-06); M. Lidove, *Les Vendéens de '93* (Paris, 1971).

M. G. Hutt

Related entries: CHARETTE DE LA CONTRIE; *CHOUANNERIE*; VENDEE.

LASOURCE, MARC-DAVID ALBA (called LASOURCE) (1763-93), deputy (Tarn) in both the Legislative Assembly and the Convention. Lasource was born at Anglès, near Montpellier. He was baptized in "*le désert*," attended seminary at Lausanne and became a Protestant pastor in 1784. He was a pastor at Castres in 1791 when he was elected to the Legislative Assembly. An upright, learned man of courage and ardent convictions, he was one of the leading Brissotins in that body, associated closely with M. Isnard, the marquis de Condorcet, P.-V. Vergniaud, A. Gensonné, and M.-E. Guadet as well as with J.-P.Brissot. He supported Brissot on the colonial question, on which he urged the Assembly to oppose the planter lobby and protect white and mulatto alike. While deploring the massacre of the Glacière at Avignon, he urged the application of the earlier law of amnesty to Jourdan "coupe-tête" and others responsible for that massacre. He spoke out against the *émigrés*, the nonjuring priests, and the princes. One of the first to use the phrase, "the fatherland is in danger," he urged rearmament and joined Brissot in advocating war and in attacking royalist ministers, especially A.-M. comte de Montmorin. He also joined those who contended there was an Austrian Committee in the Tuileries seeking French defeat in the war against Austria. He had, in the meantime, come into conflict with M. Robespierre at the Jacobins (1 and 26 January, 1792) and also, more seriously, with J.-P. Marat, as he defended the marquis de Lafayette and other generals against Marat's attacks. He contended that Marat and the royalist journalist abbé Royau were agents of a common project to disorganize France (3 May).

On the dismissal of the Girondin ministers (13 June), he stood out in efforts to reunite the Revolutionaries against the crown. He attacked the report condemning the abortive insurrection of 20 June. He also attacked his former idol Lafayette (21 July); a month later he urged Lafayette's indictment. But when Robespierre urged the replacement of the Legislative by a National Convention, he retreated from insurrection, asking for the withdrawal of the *fédérés* from Paris (29 July), opposing the insurrection petition of the section Mauconseil, and taking part in the discussion of deputies of the Club Réunion who sought the indictment of Robespierre. On 10 August he joined Vergniaud in seeking only the suspension of the king. With Brissot and Gensonné he was elected to the Legislative's important Commission of Twenty-one.

Elected to the Convention, he was immediately chosen as one of its four secretaries, and he spoke out vigorously against the "despotism of Paris," which, he argued, ought to have only one eighty-third influence, like each of the other departments. He condemned, in particular, recent efforts, during the September Massacres, to bring about the deaths of leaders of the Legislative (25 September). He broke formally with the Jacobins. He urged the creation of a departmental guard for the Convention. In reply to C. Basire's favorable report on the state of Paris, he again spoke out against the despotism of Paris and against the September Massacres (6 November). A courageous opponent of the Mountain, he nonetheless pursued a moderate tack with respect to French occupation policies (24 October), and he voted with the Mountain with respect to the king's fate. Absent on mission at Nice with J.-M. Collot d'Herbois and J.-F.-M. Goupilleau when the vote was taken on the question of a popular referendum on the Convention's decision, he returned to Paris to vote for the death of the king and against the postponement of his punishment. In March (1793) he reported on the royalist La Rouerie affair, attempted to exempt the children of *émigrés* from legislation, and supported new legislation against foreigners, while opposing their blanket expulsion from France. But while still moderately Revolutionary, he continued to defend the Girondins against the Mountain. Following the March

Days, he took the lead in attacking G.-J. Danton, accusing him of being the accomplice of C. Dumouriez in an effort to restore the monarchy (1 April). He also attacked Marat as dangerous to liberty, while abstaining from voting for his indictment on the scruple that Marat had attacked him personally (13 April). In response to the section petition of 15 April, which sought the expulsion of twenty-two Girondins (including himself), Lasource replied by thanking the petitioners for now conspiring only against their honor rather than (as in the March Days) against their lives. He argued that Parisians were usurping sovereignty in claiming to speak for all of France. He pointed out that the departments could do the same, could ask for the expulsion of the deputies who represented Paris. "Would not this be feudalism, civil war, and the dissolution of the Republic?" (Aulard, p. 139). And he suggested as a remedy the review of all deputies by primary assemblies throughout France, a proposal rejected under the lead of the vacillating Vergniaud (16 April).

Lasource was one of the twenty-two Girondins whose arrest was sought on 2 June. He went into hiding and posted on the walls of Paris a placard accusing J.-R. Hébert, Marat, F. Chabot and others of counterrevolution, conspiracy, and tyranny by the insurrection (or coup d'état) of 2 June. Returning home on 22 July, he was placed under house arrest. Ill, he was placed in the Luxembourg with C.-A. Sillery whose arrest as an Orléanist he himself had sought three months before. He was one of the twenty-two Girondins to be indicted on 3 October, though J.-B.-A. Amar's report did not specifically mention him. He received little attention at the trial, during which Chabot recalled both his suggestion concerning the *fédérés* on the eve of 10 August and his opposition to Marat, and L. Maribon de Montaut spoke of his involvement in the Club Réunion. There was not much that could have been said, in fact, for he had supported the Revolution steadily and on many matters had voted with the Mountain. But he had been also the Girondins' bravest opponent of the Mountain and therefore was guillotined with them. According to the early historian C. F. Beaulieu, his fellow prisoner at the Conciergerie just before he died, he said of his Montagnard opponents: "I die when the people has lost its reason; you will die when it has recovered it" (Aulard, p. 141).

F.-A. Aulard, *Les orateurs de la Legislative et de la Convention*, vol. 2 (Paris, 1886); C. Rabaud, *Lasource* (Paris, 1890); M. J. Sydenham, *The Girondins* (London, 1961).

S. Lytle

Related entries: AUSTRIAN COMMITTEE; CENTRAL REVOLUTIONARY COMMITTEE; GIRONDINS; MONTMORIN.

LA TOUR DU PIN GOUVERNET, JEAN-FREDERIC (1727-94), general, deputy, minister of war. La Tour du Pin devoted his entire life to military service. He went on his first campaign at the age of fourteen in 1741; later in the War of the Austrian Succession, he fought under Marshal de Saxe. Soon after the close of that conflict, he attained the rank of colonel and led a regiment of *grenadiers de la France* during the Seven Years War. He later commanded line infantry regiments, including that of Piémont. By the time elections were held for the Estates General, he had risen to lieutenant general. Elected as a representative of the nobility, he soon won a reputation as a liberal noble and was one of the first to join the Third Estate in June. He was therefore an acceptable choice as the first minister of war to serve the monarchy and the now-victorious National Assembly. Louis XVI named him minister on 4 August 1789.

La Tour du Pin was a reformer in his own fashion, presiding over the first Revolutionary changes in French military institutions; however, he was also an *ancien régime* general, intolerant of the indiscipline and mutiny that plagued the army from 1789 to 1791. His reactions to the troubles of 1790 condemned his ministry. By repeatedly carrying his complaints to the National Assembly, he lost what credit he had once enjoyed. Most important, he headed the ministry at the time of the brutal repression of the Nancy mutiny in August 1790. General F.-C.-A. Bouillé did the dirty work, but when the National Assembly came to know the full story, La Tour du Pin was tarred with the same brush as Bouillé. The embattled minister held on for a time, but in late October the National Assembly decreed that he no longer enjoyed the confidence of the nation. The king, after first refusing his resignation, finally accepted it in November. La Tour du Pin then retired from politics and entered voluntary exile at Auteuil. There he was arrested in May 1793, released, and then arrested again in November. Called on to testify at the queen's trial, he damned himself by his show of respect for the doomed former monarch. In April 1794 he too went before the Revolutionary Tribunal and was himself condemned to death. His elder brother met a similar fate.

L. de Chilly, *Le premier ministre constitutionnel de la guerre, La Tour du Pin* (Paris, 1909).

J. A. Lynn

Related entries: BOUILLE; MUTINY OF NANCY.

LATOUR-MAUBOURG, MARIE-CHARLES-CESAR-FAY, COMTE DE

(1758-1831), deputy to the Estates General and the Constituent Assembly. Colonel of the Soissonnais Regiment at the time of the Revolution, Latour-Maubourg with the assistance of the marquis de Lafayette was elected a deputy from the nobility of Le Puy-en-Velay to the Estates General. He was one of the first of that order to join the Third Estate, and on 14 August renounced his hereditary titles in Languedoc. During the troubles in Avignon, he voted for its union with France. In 1791, Latour-Maubourg was one of the commissioners ordered to bring back the king following the flight to Varennes. As *maréchal de camp*, he accompanied Lafayette to the Army of the Center, and later he fled with him and shared his captivity. Freed in 1797, he went to Hamburg. After the Brumaire coup he returned to France and in 1801 was elected to the Corps législatif.

A.N., F[7] 4767; L. Mortimer-Ternaux, *Histoire de la Terreur* (Paris, 1863); C. de Tourtier-Bonazzi, *Lafayette: Documents conservés en France* (Paris, 1976).

R. R. Crout

Related entries: AVIGNON; LAFAYETTE; VARENNES.

LAUNEY, BERNARD-RENE-JORDAN, MARQUIS DE (1740-89), governor of the Bastille, who surrendered this fortress to Parisians on 14 July 1789 and was killed by a crowd later that day. Bernard de Launey (or de Launay, or even de Launai) was born at the Bastille in 1740. His father was the governor of the fortress, and he succeeded him in that capacity. He is primarily known for the role that he played 14 July 1789 and for his tragic death the evening of the same day.

As early as 7 July, Louis XVI had ordered Launey to put the Bastille in a state of defense in the light of the threat of popular disturbances in Paris when the dismissal of J. Necker, the minister, should become known. The garrison of eighty-two *invalides* (disabled veterans) had been reinforced by a detachment of thirty-two Swiss soldiers from the Salis-Samade Regiment. Ammunition had been gathered to supply the fifteen eight-inch cannons located on the towers, the three field cannons in battery in the courtyard, and the twelve rampart guns. The garden wall had been raised higher, the cannon embrasures enlarged, the drawbridge reinforced. Six cart loads of cobblestones and old scrap iron had been hauled up onto the walls on 9 and 10 July so that they could be hurled at possible attackers. On 12 July, 250 barrels containing 30,000 pounds of powder were transferred to the Bastille. Useless battlements and windows were boarded up with planks. However, the Bastille possessed only enough meat for one day and bread for two days.

Launey could have put up a resistance, but he was a weak and irresolute man, little disposed to fight, constantly afraid that his forces would be insufficient to resist a major attack. On 14 July at 10 A.M., demonstrators massed before the fortress, and a delegation of Parisian electors came to the Bastille. Launey received them very amiably and invited them to lunch. The delegation demanded that he remove from the towers the cannons trained on the capital, which he did immediately. But this gesture did not appease the demonstrators. A new delegation appeared before the Bastille around 1 P.M. to demand that Launey allow the Parisian militia, which had just been formed, to participate in guarding the fortress. Once again Launey was amiable but refused to surrender the fort to anyone, and he declared that he would defend it as long as he could but that he would not open fire if he were not attacked.

Firing began shortly after the departure of the second delegation. The demonstrators felt that they had been betrayed and began to assault the fortress. Today it is impossible to say if Launey ordered the shooting first or if the attackers took the initiative in firing. The committee of electors, hearing the noise of the fusillade, sent a third delegation to the Bastille around 2 P.M., but the battle was so intense that it could not enter. A fourth delegation also failed to accomplish its mission. It appears that this time Launey did nothing to halt the combat. Moreover, he would have been able to continue for a long time, without results, if some sixty French Guards had not arrived before the Bastille around 3:30 with four cannons that had been taken from the Invalides the same morning. The cannons were immediately set up in battery in front of the gate. It was clear that the Bastille was going to be invaded. With the garrison assembled, Launey then asked what action he should take. He proposed to blow the fortress up by lighting fire to the powder. But the majority of the *invalides*, who had already shown little enthusiasm for the struggle, declared that it was necessary to capitulate. The white flag was hoisted on the towers, the drawbridge lowered. The crowd rushed into the fortress. It was 5 P.M. The seven prisoners found in the Bastille were freed and Launey was arrested by one of the demonstrators named S. Maillard, the son of a bailiff, who would become famous during the September 1792 Massacres.

Maillard took away Launey's cane and sword and said that he wanted to take him to city hall. But everywhere there were cries of "Kill him!" During the trip Launey was insulted and injured. Finally, on arriving at city hall, he was torn away from his guards and an unemployed cook, named Desnot, stabbed him in the stomach with a bayonet. The governor fell into the gutter. He was finished off with swords and pistols. Desnot cut off his head, and the crowd promenaded it through Paris at the end of a pike, while making merry, during the night.

F. Funck-Brentano, *La Bastille, ses dernières années* (Paris, 1898) and *Légendes et archives de la Bastille* (Paris, 1898); J. Godechot, *The Taking of the Bastille, July 14th, 1789* (New York, 1970).

J. Godechot

Related entries: BASTILLE; BERTIER DE SAUVIGNY; MAILLARD; NECKER.

LAVAUGUYON, PAUL-FRANCOIS, DUC DE (1746-1828), diplomat, monarchist. His titled father was a tutor of the future Louis XVI. Lavauguyon's early career was largely in the military, although he also demonstrated a philosophical bent in publishing, being the author of a response to the abbé Mably's work on the nature of political society. Intertwined with advancement in the army were diplomatic missions; one, to Holland in 1776, had as its purpose the lessening of British influence in that country and was deemed a success for French foreign policy. Eight years later he was sent to Spain to consolidate relations between the two Bourbon monarchies. This mission was also a success; and the esteem of the Spanish king, Charles IV, for Lavauguyon was marked by the latter's being named knight of the Golden Fleece. He was recalled to France in July 1789 by Louis XVI to serve as his foreign minister in the short-lived Breteuil ministry (12–15 July). He was sent back to Spain as minister plenipotentiary to maintain royal ties in the face of a buildup of the British fleet.

In May 1790 a question was raised in the National Assembly relating to Lavauguyon's competence to remain in his post because of his hostility to the Revolution. He was replaced, but information, which had been slow in arriving, was received in Paris that, despite a Spanish freeze on export of funds, he had managed to obtain a substantial amount to ease the crisis in French finances. Lavauguyon had also obtained some relief from taxes for French businessmen in Spain, receiving from them, in gratitude, a sum of 83,000 French pounds for the national treasury.

He remained in Spain, representing the interests of Louis XVI, and after that monarch's death, he represented the interests of the French Bourbons. In 1795, he joined Louis XVIII in Verona and Blankenbourg, serving as one of his chief advisers. He became a member of the Clichyens and, as a constitutional monarchist, tried to heal the breach between that group and the absolute monarchists. Unsuccessful in his attempts and compromised by his son, the prince de Carency, who was informing the Paris government about *émigré* activities, he resigned in 1798 and did not reappear on the political scene until the Restoration.

J. Godechot, *The Counter-Revolution; Doctrine and Action, 1789-1804* (London, 1972).

R. L. Carol

Related entries: CHARLES IV; CLUB DE CLICHY; COUNTERREVOLUTION; *EMIGRES*; NOOTKA SOUND CONTROVERSY.

LAVOISIER, ANTOINE-LAURENT DE (1743-94), chemist, farmer general, and reforming administrator. Lavoisier was born in Paris 26 August 1743, the son of a prosperous councillor in the Parlement of Paris. He was educated at the collège Mazarin and received a law degree in 1764, but had already developed a keen interest in science. Both his intellectual development and his commitment to science were decisively influenced by the geologist E. Guéttard, who took the young Lavoisier on long field trips in 1763-64 and 1767.

In 1768 Lavoisier became an associate chemist of the Académie royale des sciences and rose rapidly in the scientific establishment, eventually serving as the Académie's director in 1785. His first truly significant scientific work began in 1772 when he conducted a series of experiments on combustion, which led to the destruction of the fallacious but universally accepted theory that matter contained a flammable substance or principle named phlogiston. Lavoisier's subsequent researches on the role of oxygen, on plant and animal respiration, as well as his contribution to a rational, uniform chemical nomenclature, together constituted a basic revolution in chemistry. By the time he published his *Traité de chimie* in 1789, he had earned the title of Founder of Modern Chemistry.

Lavoisier was the greatest of eighteenth-century French scientists, but he was also an exemplary *philosophe* in his indefatigable determination to harness scientific research to technological and social progress. The range of his interests and activities was also typical of the Enlightenment. In 1769 he purchased shares in the General Farm and was thereafter actively involved in the business of the syndicate, both as a wealthy financier and as one of its reforming administrators. After A.-R.-J. Turgot appointed him to the Régie des poudres (Commission on Gunpowder) in 1775, Lavoisier played a crucial role in the dramatic improvement in the quality and quantity of France's production of explosive chemicals. He continued to lead the commission until 1791.

In 1778 Lavoisier purchased the estate of Fréchines near Blois (Loir-et-Cher) and conducted experiments to demonstrate that scientific agricultural practices and sound management techniques were productive and profitable. His dedication to practical reform next manifested itself in his activities as a member of the Provincial Assembly of Orléans in 1787. He drew up most of the assembly's reports, and his written proposals illustrate the combination of lucid exposition, rational organization, and technical competence in finance, economics, and science that made him such an effective and sought-after administrator. He called for the abolition of the *taille*, proposed the establishment of a state-supported People's Savings Bank to provide a voluntary retirement fund for the poor, and addressed the problems of vagabondage, mendicity, and unemployment in his schemes for hospitals, workhouses, and prisons. His humanitarianism was more than abstract. In the winter of 1788-89 he lent at no interest considerable sums of money to the communes of Blois and Romorantin for stocking the grain markets and lowering the price of food.

Lavoisier was actively involved in the Revolution from its inception. A liberal aristocrat and physiocrat, he early supported progressive reforms. When the electoral assembly of the nobility of the *bailliage* of Blois convened, Lavoisier served as the secretary of the committee that drafted the nobility's *cahier*. The document was essentially reformist and liberal. It demanded a constitution, civil liberties, equality of taxation, a form of representation, and legal reform.

Lavoisier was chosen to be a substitute delegate to the Estates General. Although he did not participate in the events at Versailles, he approved of the transformation of the Estates General into the National Assembly and devoted himself increasingly to public service, even while continuing his scientific work and his financial activities. In 1790 he began to serve on the commission established to introduce a new system of weights and measures, and in the same year he became a member of the liberal Société de 1789. On Lavoisier's suggestion, the nationalized Royal Treasury was renamed the National Treasury, and in 1791 he was made one of its commissioners. In the same year he joined the Bureau of Consultation for the Arts and Crafts, a committee of scientists set up to encourage and reward technological innovation useful to the nation.

In June 1792 Louis XVI offered Lavoisier the post of minister of public revenue (*Contributions publiques*), but Lavoisier declined the offer because he felt that the Legislative Assembly had upset the proper balance of powers in the constitutional monarchy. Privately he expressed his disapproval of the leftward movement of the Revolution and especially regretted the necessity of arming the people. He nevertheless remained a steadfast supporter of the Revolution even after the overthrow of the monarchy. In 1793 he worked as a member of a commission appointed to draw up a plan for a national educational system that would emphasize technical education. His *Réflexion sur l'instruction publique* was printed for the National Convention, and Lavoisier himself wrote a projected decree to institute the reforms.

His services to the Republic were cut short by the decree passed in the Convention ordering the arrest of all former farmers general. Imprisoned at the end of November 1793, Lavoisier collected materials and wrote an able defense against the charges that the farmers general had been guilty of overcharging the government, late payments to the treasury, and adulterating tobacco with excessive and insalubrious amounts of water.

Despite his brochures refuting these accusations, the formal indictment of 5 May 1794 repeated the charges. The trial began and ended on 7 May. On 8 May 1794 Lavoisier was executed along with a number of other farmers general. The infamous remark attributed to his judge at the Revolutionary tribunal—"The Republic has no need of scientists"—is almost certainly apocryphal.

I. Duveen and H. S. Klickstein, *A Bibliography of the Works of Antoine Lavoisier, 1743-1794* (London, 1954) and *Supplement* (London, 1965); E. Grimaux, *Lavoisier, 1743-1794*, 3d ed. (Paris, 1899); H. Guerlac, "Lavoisier and His Biographers," *Isis* 44 (1954); A.-L. Lavoisier, *Oeuvres de Lavoisier*, 6 vols. (Paris, 1864-93; rep., New York, 1965); D. McKie, *Antoine Lavoisier, Scientist, Economist, Social Reformer* (New York and London, 1952).

R. Bienvenu

Related entries: BAILLIAGE; CAHIERS DE DOLEANCES; ENLIGHTENMENT; FARMERS-GENERAL; SCIENCE; SOCIETY OF 1789; *TAILLE.*

LAW, JOURDAN. See JOURDAN LAW.

LAW, TWO-THIRDS. See TWO-THIRDS LAW.

LAW OF 14 FRIMAIRE (4 December 1793), act of the National Convention centralizing the Revolutionary administration, often described as the provisional constitution of the Terror. It remained the charter of government until the decree of 7 Fructidor (24 August 1794), which had equivalent importance for the Thermidorian period.

The Law of 14 Frimaire ended the Terror's anarchic phase. From the beginning of 1793, new institutions had arisen to pursue a variety of Revolutionary goals, operating without clear guidelines from the Convention and with varying interpretations of their own authority. The regular municipal and departmental administrations, which were sometimes moderate, sedentary survivors of the regime of limited suffrage under the Constitution of 1791, were surrounded by surveillance committees, popular societies, Revolutionary tribunals, representatives on mission, and *armées révolutionnaires*.

Surveillance committees watched for signs of *incivisme* and employed the threat of arrest to enforce Revolutionary mores in their communities. Popular societies provided meeting places where militants pursued their political education by discussing national measures and acting on local questions (especially food supply). Revolutionary tribunals judged rebels, nonjuring priests, and people accused of counterrevolutionary activities or attitudes. Each of these bodies authorized its own commissioners to travel in its name and enforce its directives. The representative on mission, himself a commissioner of the Convention, animated all this activity; he was responsible to Paris for suppressing rebellion and uprooting reluctance in an assigned department. He organized committees and clubs where they did not yet exist and used them as sources of information for the purging of the regular administrations. He founded and staffed tribunals and often organized his own *armée révolutionnaire* to enforce his measures and those of the bodies he had created or purified.

It is probably a mistake to assign to this cluster of authorities the sole blame for the administrative chaos inherent in the internal and external situation of France during Year II. However, it is understandable that the Committee of Public Safety found it difficult to assert its central authority over the panoply of terrorist organs.

The Convention was struggling to limit the power of the Paris Commune, and much of the vigor of the law of 14 Frimaire is due to this. B. Barère was referring to the Commune when he asserted on 14 Frimaire that governmental measures would necessarily become counterrevolutionary when their execution was enforced by agencies other than the Convention. The articles of the law against combinations of subordinate bodies such as surveillance committees (section III, articles 16-17) were directed especially against the association of Paris sections.

In the provinces, however, the unlimited authority the Convention had given to representatives on mission was the major source of variance in the enforcement of its decrees. Desultory or self-glorifying dispatches from the representatives, arriving with a week or two's delay, could not provide the Committee of Public Safety an adequate check on the representatives' activities.

Finally, the extension of fixed prices for commodities had culminated on 29 September in the general maximum, which set official rates for all products and wages throughout France. The effort to coordinate and enforce a planned economy in wartime could only succeed through dynamic centralization.

The text of the Law of 14 Frimaire is divided into five sections. Section I deals with the printing, dispatching, and promulgation of laws. Section II creates a hierarchy for the execution of laws. Section III defines the competencies of various authorities in relation to one another. Section IV assigns the responsibility for reorganizing and purging local authorities to the Committee of Public Safety, acting through the representatives on mission. Section V establishes penalties at every administrative level for negligence or infraction.

Section I instituted an official *Bulletin des lois*, which was to print the text of new acts of the Convention within three days of enactment. Municipalities were required to promulgate the new law by reading it aloud in public within twenty-four hours of reception.

Section II begins by declaring the Convention to be the sole point of origin for all the activity of government. The law must be enforced literally and only the Convention may interpret it (article 11). The Committee of Public Safety was responsible for the conduct of all constituted authorities; the Committee of General Security for the civicism of individuals. The Executive Council—under the eye of the Committee of Public Safety—oversaw the execution of military, administrative, criminal, and civil law (article 4). The field of Revolutionary measures, both economic and political—the Terror and the general maximum—lay outside the Executive Council's competence. The Committee of Public Safety enforced Revolutionary measures through the districts—administrative regions midway between departments and municipalities. Municipalities and local surveillance committees were required to report to the district every ten days. (Paris was an exception; the committees of the capital were directly responsible to the Committee of General Security.) To give mobility to the districts' authority, the old *procureurs syndics* (public prosecutors) were transformed into national agents who traveled constantly through the districts enforcing the Revolutionary laws. The departments were demoted to a minor role—the care of tax collection and public works; they were bypassed as far as the Terror was concerned.

Section III defined the competencies of various authorities and confirmed the supremacy of the Committee of Public Safety. The committee was responsible for foreign diplomacy. It controlled representatives on mission, whose prerogatives were severely constrained. Representatives on mission had to correspond with the Committee of Public Safety every ten days. They could not delay or modify the committee's measures, remove generals without notifying the committee within twenty-four hours, or impose special taxes or raise local *armées révolutionnaires*. All the departmental *armées révolutionnaires* organized up to then by representatives on mission were abolished.

The Convention reserved the nomination of generals and admirals for itself by a procedure that traversed the Committee of Public Safety. Officials could no longer accumulate positions. The law expressly forbade an official to over-reach his powers geographically or otherwise, to communicate with other official bodies except by writing, or to seek to combine official bodies into regional federations.

Section IV ordered representatives on mission to complete the purge and reform of local administrations within six weeks' time.

Section V established a range of penalties for negligent or rebellious administrators. Deprivation of citizenship rights, confiscation of property, and (for some offenses) five years in irons were typical prescribed sentences. Counterfeiting of the *Bulletin des lois* was a capital crime.

The Law of 14 Frimaire also established a unified structure of command, founded on the practice of reporting at ten-day intervals. Municipalities and surveillance committees reported to districts; districts reported to the Committee of General Security. Departments, military and civilian tribunals, generals, and military agents reported to the Executive Council, which reported in turn to the Committee of Public Safety. Representatives on mission corresponded with the committee directly. The ten-day rhythm—derived from the Revolutionary calendar, then two months old—was uniform throughout the system and formed part of the Committee of Public Safety's vision of a coordinated Revolution.

The committee's letters accompanying the text of the Law of 14 Frimaire made constant analogies between the human body and the body politic. "Thus the action that commences in the heart of the Convention comes to its final point in you'' reads the letter that all surveillance committees received; "you are like the hands of the body politic, of which the Convention is the head and we [the Committee of Public Safety] are the eyes; it is through you that the national will, once having decided, strikes out.'' The Law of 14 Frimaire was conceived in these hierarchical terms, and the decadal rhythm in the flow of information was integral to the committee's organic analogy.

Classically, historians have described the Law of 14 Frimaire as ending the anarchic Terror, subduing its gamut of local agents, and preparing the way for a uniform Terror directed by the state. Recent research indicates that the most serious obstacles to a uniform Terror were not posed by the local popular forces and their committees and tribunals, who were largely in harmony with Montagnard policy, but by the representatives on mission whose measures often surpassed the pace of events in Paris. (J. Fouché's initiative in promoting dechristianization is a noteworthy example.) The Law of 14 Frimaire provided a statute for the control of representatives on mission, which proved crucial to the problem of controlling the course of the Revolution in the Year II.

The law also led to a general decrease in local and municipal elections. The cooperation between the representatives on mission and the Revolutionary clubs and committees, who together purged local administrations, led to increasing reliance on the clubs to indicate trustworthy provisional officials and to the suspension of local elections after 5 Brumaire.

In its creation of national agents, the Law of 14 Frimaire foreshadowed the Consulate. More dependent on Paris than the intendants and subdelegates of the Old Regime, the national agent was a functionary who, despite his local power, dared not risk an independent judgment. In him the first sketch of the future prefect can be discerned.

Finally, the Law of 14 Frimaire legitimized the power of the Committee of Public Safety. Nearly all of the reins of authority were now apparently in its hands, though the Committee of General Security remained the central agency of repression. However, the Law of 14 Frimaire must not be taken at face value. The Terror's administrative means never matched its ambitions. Centralization under eighteenth-century conditions bore little resemblance to its twentieth-century counterpart, and a decree's verbal harshness was also a measure of the difficulty of its enforcement. Perhaps it is best to say that the Law of 14 Frimaire was to the Convention's practice what the Constitution of 1793 was to its ideology: a charter of intent that made official a chosen direction.

The Committee of Public Safety's ensuing correspondence with representatives on mission shows that its attitude did not harden immediately; in many cases ten weeks went by before the most headstrong were brought to heel or removed from their posts. But the Law of 14 Frimaire had established the basis for such removal. It did serve to regulate the Terror—where desirable, when feasible.

A.P., vol. 80 (Paris, 1879-1913); C. Lucas, *The Structure of the Terror; the Example of Javogues and the Loire* (Oxford, 1973); P. Mautouchet, *Le gouvernement révolution-*

naire (Paris, 1912); M. Robespierre, *Oeuvres*, vol. 10, ed. M. Bouloiseau and A. Soboul (Paris, 1967); A. Soboul, "Problèmes de l'etat révolutionnaire," *Problèmes politiques de la Révolution française* (Paris, 1971).

C. Ramsay

Related entries: ARMEES REVOLUTIONNAIRES; COMMITTEE OF GENERAL SECURITY; COMMITTEE OF PUBLIC SAFETY; FOUCHE; LAW OF THE MAXIMUM; REPRESENTATIVES ON MISSION; SECTIONS.

LAW OF HOSTAGES (24 Messidor Year VII, 12 July 1799), decree passed after the *journée* of 30 Prairial Year VII (18 June 1799) intended to secure republican officials and their families, as well as those who had bought national property, from the increasing threat of right-wing violence. The decree was one of a series produced by the temporary victory of the newly elected, Jacobin-dominated legislature over the directors and was preceded by the new *levée en masse* and a forced loan on the wealthy, both passed on 9 Messidor (the loan in fact was not decreed in detail until 19 Thermidor, 6 August). The Law of Hostages could have been justified as an extension and a formalization of the hostage taking already used by General L. Hoche in dealing with insurrectionary communes in the west, but through its associations as well as its actual provisions, it recalled to its opponents—not necessarily all counterrevolutionary—the terrorism of the Year II.

The decree was to apply in any area officially proclaimed as subject to civil disturbance and could be applied where such a threat was thought to exist. In any such area, the relatives and connections by marriage of *émigrés* and suspect nobles, and the grandparents and parents of anyone known as a member of a counterrevolutionary gang, were to take collective and civil responsibility for any disturbance. Hostages, to be taken from such families, had to accept removal, under escort if necessary, to a designated center, where they were to stay at their own expense. Evasion of the removal order was to be treated as equivalent to emigration. For each attack on a Revolutionary official or ex-official, soldier, purchaser or owner of national property, or on the family of any other official, four hostages were to be deported and their property temporarily sequestered. No proof of complicity was required, and deportation could be avoided only if the hostage supplied evidence leading to the arrest and conviction of the guilty party. Heavy fines, payable for each offense and levied collectively on the families subject to the hostage order, were to be used partly to compensate the victim of the attack and/or his family and partly to reward informers. If the money available from fines was inadequate to pay compensation at the stipulated rates, the balance was to be made up by those liable to be fined.

A section of the decree dealing with brigands was both selective and repressive. Any artisan or poor peasant known to be in this category could secure an amnesty by establishing his social status and handing in a firearm in good order as a symbol of future good behavior, but if he did not accept the offer of amnesty, he would be classed as an *émigré* and shot on sight. Amnesty was specifically refused not only to leaders offending after an earlier amnesty but also categorically to *émigrés*, nonjuring priests, and anyone else at all, whatever his former status, who had ever held any form of privilege.

This legislation was reminiscent of the 1793 Law of Suspects but went further in that those affected by it were suspect because of other people's offenses of which they might not even be aware, much less be able to control. It allowed the administrative encroachment on what would normally have been the jurisdiction of judges, who were thought likely to be more lukewarm in dealing with brigands and their allies—perhaps in itself an echo of the Jacobin attitude to judges in 1792. In effect, it reflected the near anarchy that had developed in some provincial areas, especially the south and west, and contained an illuminating clause aimed at reducing the risk of kidnapping, which was apparently a real one for the families of well-known republicans. Those whom the decree was designed to protect were not necessarily violent radicals; in December 1799, C.-J.-E. Girard-Villars, an ex-*conventionnel* but also an antiregicide, died of the wounds he had received when *chouans* attacked his house near Chantonnay.

Although social distinctions were drawn, the logic of the decree was primarily political, reviving memories of *sans-culotte* extremism rather than dread of servile war in the classic sense. Among the offenses covered by it, the extortion of rent (by counterrevolutionary landowners?) was certainly one, but the others included arson and the destruction of crops, provisions that could have had the effect of amalgamating social with political protest and that clearly envisaged parts of the peasantry as a potentially counterrevolutionary force.

The fear that had evoked the decree also echoed 1793, being partly engendered by the prospect of both foreign invasion and civil war. Neither of these threats lasted very long. The invasion scare died by the autumn. A revolt centering on the department of the Haute-Garonne that broke out on 19 Thermidor (5 August) was serious but short-lived. As a result of this, a number of cantons were declared as disturbed, but it is not clear how far, if at all, the hostage decree was enforced. The suggestion that it helped to provoke the outbreak seems unnecessary as an explanation.

The neo-Jacobin resurgence that had made the decree possible was brief. By October, the directors had regained control, and in early November a commission was considering repeal. Napoleon abrogated it four days after his coup d'état on 22 Brumaire Year VIII (13 November 1799).

J. B. Duvergier, *Collection complète des lois* . . . , vol. 2 (Paris, 1825-28); J. Godechot, *Les institutions de la France sous la Révolution et l'Empire* (Paris, 1951); G. Lefebvre, *The Thermidorians and the Directory*, trans. R. Baldick (New York, 1964); M. Lyons, *France under the Directory* (Cambridge, 1975); J. H. Stewart, *A Documentary Survey of the French Revolution* (New York, 1951).

A. Patrick

Related entries: CHOUANNERIE; HOCHE; LAW OF SUSPECTS; TERROR, THE.

LAW OF SUSPECTS (17 September 1793), most important of the measures taken by the National Convention to provide a legal basis for the Terror. This act defined categories of people whom Republican authorities were enjoined to suspect of counterrevolutionary proclivities and to whom the extraordinary procedures of Revolutionary justice were to be applied: (1) those who by their behavior, personal relations, statements, or writings had shown themselves to be partisans of tyranny or federalism and enemies of liberty; (2) those who could not provide proof of their means of livelihood or of the fulfillment of their civic duties; (3) those who had been refused certificates of civicism; (4) public functionaries who had been suspended or removed from office; (5) those among former nobles and among husbands, wives, fathers, mothers, sons or daughters, brothers, and agents of *émigrés* who had not constantly demonstrated their attachment to the Revolution; and (6) those who had emigrated between 1 July 1789 and 8 April 1792, even if they had returned to France before or during the grace period specified in the measure enacted on the latter date.

Committees of surveillance in each of the communes of France were directed to draw up lists of such suspects within their jurisdictions, to issue warrants of arrest against them, and to seal their papers. Those thus marked for suspicion in whatever locality were then subject to trial by the Revolutionary Tribunal in Paris.

In the legal history of the Revolution, the Law of Suspects figures as the climactic legislation in the series of measures taken by the Convention—beginning with the creation of the Revolutionary Tribunal (10 March 1793) and culminating in the Law of 22 Prairial—that progressively weakened the legal procedures enacted by the Constituent Assembly for the protection of the individual. It supplemented the decrees of 10-12 March, which had initially and more narrowly defined categories of suspects (for example, all those who by their behavior, writings, and by the places they formerly occupied recalled usurped prerogatives), and the decree of 28 March 1793, which had stipulated that in all localities the names and qualifications of suspected counterrevolutionaries should be directly communicated to the Convention.

This legislation served as the basis for subsequent measures that intensified the Terror. This was specifically true of the questionnaire issued by the Committee of General Security in mid-Nivôse Year II (December 1793), the principal directives of which, calling for sterner measures against the agents of fanaticism, were presented as a commentary on the Law of Suspects, but the Law of 22 Prairial was also in an important sense an extension of the earlier act in that it reaffirmed its basic principle that those who might plausibly be suspected of subversion were to be suspected of subversion and in that its detailed provisions simply added more categories of suspects.

In the larger legal history of France, the Law of Suspects shares with other measures of Revolutionary justice the paradoxical distinction of reviving one of the principles of the Old Regime's *cours prévotales*, which earlier Revolutionaries had repudiated: special procedures for people without a regular station in society (*hommes sans aveu*). Inasmuch as the law extended the competence of the Revolutionary Tribunal, which was in turn directly responsible to the Committees of Public Safety and General Security, its passage marked a major stage in the consolidation of power by these latter bodies, and it served as their major legislative instrument when they implemented the policies associated with the Terror.

Considered in relation to the circumstances of its enactment, however, the Law of Suspects is significant as another in the series of acts—again beginning with the creation of the Revolutionary Tribunal—by means of which the Convention sought to institutionalize and in some degree moderate the punitive will of the Revolutionary crowds. Popular pressure for stringent measures against suspects, recurrent during the summer of 1793, had grown so strong by August that G.-J. Danton, on the twelfth of that month, asked for specific legislation to this effect—an initiative that led, on 31 August, to a proposal for a Law of Suspects, which was submitted to the Convention and rejected, ostensibly as too lenient.

The event precipitating the drafting and eventual passage of the definitive law was the *journée* of 5 September 1793, when crowds angered by the news of treason in Toulon and encouraged by the Commune and the Paris sections invaded the Convention and gave the appearance of reenacting scenes from the previous late May and early June, which had eventuated in the expulsion of the Girondins. The crowd's major demand was for the creation of revolutionary armies, to be accompanied by traveling Revolutionary tribunals, but it also expressed a need for elastically defined categories of suspects against whom this elaborate punitive apparatus could operate. The *conventionnels* who responded to these entreaties promised total satisfaction. J.-N. Billaud-Varenne suggested categories of suspects—insolent valets, businessmen, big *rentiers*, those who were litigious hagglers by essence, profession, or education—that in their specificity went beyond the *sans-culottes'* aspirations. In the aftermath of the incursion, however, action on the matter of suspects was deferred to the Committee on Legislation. The Law of Suspects resulted from the deliberations of this body between 6 and 17 September. The committee was chaired, and the law submitted, by P.-A. Merlin de Douai, one of the most eminent jurists of the Convention and the author of the measure rejected on 31 August. Enactment of the law did not end Parisian pressure for still sterner measures against suspects. On 10 October 1793 P.-G. Chaumette proposed to the Commune additional categories of suspects, which included those who, having done nothing against liberty, had done nothing for it either. Subsequently, in the Nivôse questionnaire, people suspected of excessive Revolutionary ardor became a category, and the Law of Suspects was used by the Committee of Public Safety against popular leaders whose pressure had done so much to bring it into existence. Post-Thermidorian *conventionnels* allowed the Law of Suspects to remain technically in force until October 1795, far longer than the Law of 22 Prairial, which was abrogated in the wake of M.

Robespierre's fall, and well after the suppression of the Revolutionary Tribunal on 31 May 1795.

P. Deshais du Portail, *La loi des suspects: son application à Nantes et dans la Loire-inférieure* (Rennes, 1938); L. Jacob, *Les suspects pendant la Révolution* (Paris, 1952); R. Roblet, *La justice criminelle en France sous la Terreur* (Paris, 1937); E. Séligman, *La justice en France pendant la Révolution* (Paris, 1913); H. A. Wallon, *Histoire du Tribunal révolutionnaire de Paris*, vol. 1 (Paris, 1880).

M. R. Cox

Related entries: BILLAUD-VARENNE; CHAUMETTE; COMMITTEE OF GENERAL SECURITY; GIRONDINS; LAW OF 22 PRAIRIAL; MERLIN DE DOUAI; REVOLUTIONARY TRIBUNAL.

LAW OF THE MAXIMUM (29 September 1793), legislation that established a partially controlled economy during the Year II. This was the second of three primary maximum decrees. The maximum of 4 May 1793 fixed prices on wheat and flour; the general maximum of 29 September 1793 fixed both prices and wages over a wide spectrum of primary commodities and production; the third, the maximum of 6 Ventôse Year II (24 February 1794) replaced the local prices of the second maximum with a schedule of national prices. On 4 Nivôse Year III (24 December 1794) the Thermidorians disestablished this system of price and wage controls. These were the basic laws of a complex of decrees and a torrent of administrative reporting that included not just fixed prices but administratively controlled distribution as well, all of it directed theoretically from Paris by the Commission of Subsistence and Provisions and backed by the authority of the Committee of Public Safety.

These controls were obviously a temporary retreat from the liberal economics of the bourgeoisie and were forced into place by the demands of the *sans-culotte* movement. For their part, the Montagnards acquiesced to this pressure in the spring of 1793, not because of any change in their own economic philosophy but to temporize with the popular pressures in Paris and to find administrative solutions to severe provisioning problems of the army and of Paris. The gap between the economic philosophies of this *sans-culotte* movement and the Montagnards can be seen in the exchange between J.-R. Hébert and M. Robespierre in mid-March 1794. The Hébertists, like the *Enragés* before them, promoted the *sans-culotte* commitment to an administratively controlled economy within a kind of egalitarian economic persuasion, coupled in the Year II to their demands for a war against the merchants. On the other hand, Robespierre, while defending the temporary economic controls of his government, insisted that commerce was not incompatible with liberty; indeed, it was essential to a permanent social structure; to destroy commerce was to destroy society. The maximums can be reasonably perceived from the social democratic perspective of the Year II as the necessary steps toward an egalitarian Revolutionary settlement and from the Montagnard strategy as necessary but temporary concessions to the imperious political and economic demands of 1793.

Those concessions began with the first maximum, passed on 4 May 1793. In face of the subsistence demands of both Paris and the army, as well as the popular pressures in Paris, the National Convention fixed the prices of grain and flour, gave the national and local governments the power to inventory, to requisition, and to monitor all grain sales, and limited all such commerce to public markets. Unfortunately, during the following summer months, the local officials who were to implement the law had little sympathy for it. If anything, the fear and disfavor it faced and the failure to implement it increased the problems that had inspired it. Grain commerce further contracted, the *assignat* continued its perilous decline, and popular demands in Paris grew louder. Such controls did have precedent in royalist administrative actions in the Old Regime, but implemented from above and understood by all to be temporary, they met little resistance then. In the summer of 1793, however, such controls had been forced from below and were of undecided duration, and they did meet massive resistance, both public and private. Rather than overcome this resistance, the moderates in the National Convention, assisted by an uncertain Montagnard leadership, sought alternatives to controls. By late August this temporization, frequently punctuated by further hollow control legislation, had failed, and the conditions it was to ameliorate continued to worsen. The *assignat* fell to an all-time low of 22 percent of face value, and the popular forces rallying behind the rhetoric of the *Enragés* reached a feverish pitch by the beginning of September. What was needed went beyond the simple existence of decrees. There was needed the machinery and the will to enforce these decrees against widespread resistance.

That will developed in the National Convention in the crisis of 4-5 September, while the machinery was constructed in the following months. The general maximum of 29 September displayed this will, the Terror; the Revolutionary government created this machinery. The second maximum was passed twenty-four days after it had been pledged to the crowd in the Convention. In fact, the fixed prices that were best executed, particularly in the provinces, were the maximums in cereal grains, which dated from the complete overhaul of the first maximum on 11 September. This decree along with the general maximum established the direction for an incredible administrative complex (in fact quite beyond the technical skills available). The economy did not become completely controlled, and large areas of economic activity escaped, but the crucial commerce in grain and flour throughout France, as well as the commerce in a number of primary commodities in Paris and the larger provincial capitals, did fall under rather rigid administrative control.

Resistance to these controls, whether public or private, was largely stifled through the legal powers of the Terror. Very few Frenchmen were actually executed for economic crimes, but the state, if unprepared to kill, was quite prepared to hurt. Arrests and confiscations ultimately brought most of France into line. By December the *assignat* had rebounded to 48 percent, and by and large the foodstuffs of France, in a very tight provisionary situation, were reasonably well distributed. But the success of the commercial controls, often referred to as the "economic terror," never really took on the nature of class war, as championed by the *sans-culottes*, nor was it ever perceived as anything but temporary by the National Convention. On 6 Ventôse Year II (24 February 1794), the centralizing and rationalizing logic of the Revolutionary government had completed a mammoth inventory of France, and the third maximum was passed. The late winter months of Year II found the Revolutionary government in an increasingly strong position, however, and when the voice of social democracy was quieted in late March with the purge of the Hébertists, the Montagnards were in a position to begin a disengagement from their economic controls. After the commissars on hoarding and the revolutionary armies had been disbanded, the government began to use its power to protect a freer commerce. Even before Thermidor, á seller's market began to emerge in which public officials were the largest buyers. By midsummer 1794, the government appeared much more prepared to enforce the maximum on salaries than on prices.

After Thermidor the weakening will behind the controls dissipated completely. Faster than the Thermidorians could dismantle the machinery of the Revolutionary government, private initiative restored a de facto freedom to the marketplace. The National Convention continued to pass laws to protect the supplies for the army and for large urban markets, particularly Paris, but prices continued to rise and the *assignat* to decline. From July until December 1794 the *assignat*'s face value fell from 34 to 20 percent. On 4 Nivôse Year III (24 December 1794) the National Convention removed all price controls and restored free trade inside France. Within twelve months, the *assignat* had fallen to less than 1 percent of face value, and a stagnant subsistence commerce had reduced the poor of France to the worst privations experienced in the Revolution.

J. Bertrand, *La taxation des prix sous la Révolution française* (Paris, 1949); P. Caron, *Le maximum général* (Paris, 1930); S. Harris, *The Assignats* (Cambridge, 1930); G. Lefebvre, *Etudes orléanaises*, vol. 2 (Paris, 1962); A. Mathiez, *La vie chère et le mouvement sociale sous la Terreur*, 2 vols. (Paris, 1927).

J. R. Harkins

Related entries: ASSIGNATS; *ENRAGES*; HEBERT; 9 THERMIDOR YEAR II; *SANS-CULOTTES*; TERROR, THE.

LAW OF 22 PRAIRIAL (10 June 1794), passed by the National Convention and intended to accelerate the procedures of the Revolutionary Tribunal of Paris and enlarge the numbers of those who could be brought before it for judgment. The Law of 22 Prairial specified that the Revolutionary Tribunal was intended to punish the enemies of the people and defined this category in such broad and vague terms that many sincere Revolutionaries believed themselves threatened by it. The law also divided the tribunal into four courts that were to function simultaneously, and it revised procedures so as to reduce seriously the possibility that any defendant would be found innocent. One of its provisions stipulated that the only applicable punishment for all offenses under the jurisdiction of the Revolutionary Tribunal would be death. The fear of many members of the

Convention that they or their relatives or friends would be arrested and tried under this law, even though they were innocent, furnished much of the motivation for the conspiracy by which the Robespierrists were arrested and later killed on 9 and 10 Thermidor (27-28 July 1794).

The Law of 22 Prairial defined the enemies of the people as those who committed the capital crimes made familiar in earlier legislation of the Terror, but it increased the number of capital crimes for which one might be recognized as an enemy of the people and attributed hostile motives to the expression of opinions that need not have arisen from counterrevolutionary intentions. Among those now defined as enemies of the people were the following:

> Those who have deceived the people or the representatives of the people, in order to lead them into undertakings contrary to the interests of liberty; Those who have sought to inspire discouragement, in order to favor the enterprises of the tyrants leagued against the Republic; Those who have disseminated false news in order to divide or disturb the people; Those who have sought to mislead opinion and to prevent the instruction of the people, to deprave morals and to corrupt the public conscience, to impair the energy and the purity of revolutionary and republican principles, or to impede the progress thereof, either by counter-revolutionary or insidious writings, or by any other machination; . . . Those who, charged with public office, take advantage of it in order to serve the enemies of the Revolution, to harass patriots, or to oppress the people; . . . .

In the clashes of judgment and opinion that characterized the committees, the Convention, the local administrations, and the Revolutionary clubs, it would be easy to find innocent acts that approximated those described and to attribute sinister motives to those who committed them.

With respect to procedure, the law weakened the right of the accused to challenge the evidence presented against him or to offer any on his own behalf. It provided defense counsel for calumniated patriots but not for conspirators. Especially formidable was article 13: "If either material or moral proofs exist, apart from the attested proof, there shall be no further hearing of witnesses, unless such formality appears necessary, either to discover accomplices or for other important considerations of public interest."

This law is said to have been prepared by G.-A. Couthon and M. Robespierre alone. B. Barère wrote in his *Mémoires* that no other members of the Committee of Public Safety knew of the law before Couthon presented it in the name of the committee, although since on that occasion Barère spoke in its support, it is possible that he had prior knowledge of it. Probably its authors did not anticipate the opposition it aroused. The problem as they saw it was that the prisons were crowded with suspects who had not been tried, and the traditional preoccupation of the courts with the validity of evidence and the rights of the accused would impede the kind of prompt justice the situation called for. Besides, they were accustomed to seeing justice in Revolutionary or extraordinary terms and saw no harm in changes that made the legal process more expeditious and (in a Revolutionary context) more reasonable.

As R. R. Palmer observes, the system they were proposing for the Revolution was similar to the one the Convention had approved on 10 May for the Commission of Orange, a Revolutionary court then operating in the southern Rhône valley. When Robespierre defended the Law of 22 Prairial, he emphasized that counterrevolutionary conspirators, assassins, and foreign agents were at large in France, and the Convention had to be defended against them; that the Revolutionary courts should not be handicapped under these conditions; and that since the law was intended exclusively for the punishment of enemies of the Revolution, only enemies of the Revolution would oppose it. D. O. Greer, however, has written that Robespierre and Couthon may have seen the Law of 22 Prairial as a complement to the decrees of Ventôse, which were intended not only to accelerate the judgment of the suspects but also, through the executions and the confiscations the executions entailed, to make additional wealth available for redistribution to poor patriots. If this is true (and Greer considers it only a hypothesis), the Law of 22 Prairial may have been intended to implement the Robespierrist policy of social revolution. That interpretation, however, remains to be confirmed.

Although there was considerable enthusiasm for this law in the Convention on 22 Prairial, there was also a serious and distrustful opposition. Having lost the vote of 22 Prairial on the law, the opponents obtained some relief the following day, when P.-A. Merlin de Douai carried a resolution to the effect that the Convention, in passing the law, had not intended to repeal the laws that barred bringing a representative of the people before the Revolutionary Tribunal unless the Convention had indicted him.

According to Barère, the Committee of Public Safety and the Committee of General Security met jointly in several evening sessions to consider how to repeal the Law of 22 Prairial. In one of those meetings, they called in Robespierre and L. Saint-Just and told them to repeal the law themselves on the following day, and the Committee of Public Safety made it clear that it would disavow the law. In reply, Robespierre and Saint-Just accused their colleagues of wishing to protect enemies of the people and to jeopardize the most sincere Revolutionaries. Robespierre and Saint-Just left, and Robespierre took no further part in the meetings of the Committee of Public Safety. According to Barère, this occasion produced a declaration of war between the Triumvirate (Robespierre, Saint-Just, and Couthon) and the two committees.

In operation the Law of 22 Prairial raised the activity of the Revolutionary Tribunal of Paris to the highest level in its twenty-three months of existence. During June and July 1794, the Tribunal sentenced 1,594 persons to death, about 58 percent of all the condemnations it ever pronounced. In the fourteen months before June 1794, it had condemned only 1,090 persons, about two-thirds as many as under the regime of Prairial. In the first ten days of June 1794, the average number of executions was seventeen per day; for the remainder of that month it was twenty-seven, and for July it was thirty. In August it fell to six for the entire month.

Apart from its effect on Revolutionary justice, the Law of 22 Prairial is significant in that it intensified the personal apprehensions and animosities that led to the conspiracy of 9 Thermidor, the deaths of the Robespierrists, and, ultimately, the dismantling of the Terror. It may be too strong to say, as did C. Brinton, that it destroyed Robespierre. Other events, including the proscription of the Hébertists and Dantonists, the astonishing popular adulation shown for Robespierre at the Festival of the Supreme Being, the creation of a special police bureau by the Committee of Public Safety, the victory of Fleurus that considerably reduced the urgency of the military threat, and the threats Robespierre made in the Convention on 8 Thermidor also counted in producing the motives for the conspiracy. But the Law of Prairial was as weighty as any of these.

J. L. Godfrey, *Revolutionary Justice: A Study of the Organization, Personnel, and Procedure of the Paris Tribunal, 1793-1795* (Chapel Hill, 1951); D. O. Greer, *The Incidence of the Terror during the French Revolution* (Cambridge, Mass., 1935); J. Hardman, ed., *French Revolution Documents*, vol. 2 (Oxford, 1973); P. Mautouchet, *Le gouvernement révolutionnaire* (Paris, 1912); R. R. Palmer, *Twelve Who Ruled: The Year of the Terror in the French Revolution* (Princeton, 1965); J. H. Stewart, *A Documentary Survey of the French Revolution* (New York, 1951).

                                                                              G. V. Taylor

Related entries: BARERE; COMMITTEE OF PUBLIC SAFETY; COUTHON; CULT OF THE SUPREME BEING; HEBERTISTS; 9 THERMIDOR YEAR II; REVOLUTIONARY TRIBUNAL; ROBESPIERRE, M.; SAINT-JUST; TERROR, THE; VENTOSE DECREES.

LE BAS, PHILIPPE-FRANCOIS-JOSEPH (1764-94), member of the National Convention and the Committee of General Security; a Robespierrist. Le Bas was born at Frevent, department of the Pas-de-Calais, where his father was a notary. After studying law at Paris, he was accepted in 1789 as an *avocat en parlement* and at the wish of his father began to practice law at Saint-Pol, near Arras. In 1791 he was elected administrator of the Pas-de-Calais, and in 1792 he was elected deputy of the Pas-de-Calais to the National Convention.

In the Convention, Le Bas chose to follow a role of self-effacement and resolute service to the Republic. Although he addressed the Convention on a few occasions, usually briefly and in the crisp and uncompromising style of a Montagnard, he seldom spoke in that body and purposely left the pursuit of notoriety to others. He is best remembered as a representative on mission to the armies and particularly as the collaborator and confidant of L. Saint-Just, who was engaged to his sister.

On 2 August 1792 Le Bas was sent on mission with A.-C. Duquesnoy to the Army of the North, which was then at Cassel, in Germany. On 22 October he and Saint-Just were sent to the Army of the Rhine in Alsace, and there they carried out a famous mission in which, by rigorous measures, they removed incompetent officers (some of whom were executed), restored discipline to the army, energized the Revolutionary authorities and the Jacobins, brought the local terrorists under control, and levied a forced loan on the rich. On 22 January 1794 they were sent on mission to the Army of the North. It was during that mission that they issued an order at Arras by which all nobles of four departments were to be placed under arrest. On 12 February they were recalled to Paris by the Committee of Public Safety, but they returned to the Army of the North on 29 April for a further month.

Because Le Bas was frequently absent from Paris, he rarely attended meetings of the Committee of General Security, to which he was appointed on 14 September 1793, but he was elected president of the Paris Jacobin club on 22 April 1794 and on 2 June was made one of the two administrators of the new School of Mars, which the Committee of Public Safety had established on the initiative of Saint-Just for the military training of boys of sixteen and seventeen. From the time Le Bas became an administrator of the school, he devoted himself entirely to it.

On 9 Thermidor Year II (27 July 1794), when the Convention decreed the arrest of M. Robespierre, Saint-Just, and G.-A. Couthon, Le Bas and the younger brother of Robespierre asked to be indicted along with them. For Le Bas, this was an act of loyalty to Saint-Just. Taken to one of the prisons, he was released by a jailor of the Commune and taken in triumph to the Hôtel de Ville, where the other arrested deputies, also released, gathered and conferred for several hours. When at about 2 A.M., groups loyal to the Convention entered the Hôtel de Ville, Le Bas killed himself with a pistol. He left behind a wife, the youngest daughter of M. Duplay (in whose house Robespierre rented a room) and her infant child. They along with Le Bas' father were imprisoned for conspiracy after his death.

A. Kuscinski, *Dictionnaire des conventionnels* (Paris, 1916); R. R. Palmer, *Twelve Who Ruled: The Year of the Terror in the French Revolution* (Princeton, 1971).

G. V. Taylor

Related entries: COMMITTEE OF GENERAL SECURITY; COMMITTEE OF PUBLIC SAFETY; REPRESENTATIVES ON MISSION; ROBESPIERRE, M.; SAINT-JUST.

LE BON, GUISLAIN-FRANCOIS-JOSEPH (1765-95), member of the National Convention and the Committee of General Security, deputy on mission. Le Bon is best remembered for his activities of 1793-94, when he was representative on mission to the departments of the Pas-de-Calais and the Nord, where he organized the agencies of Revolutionary government under the Law of 14 Frimaire (4 December 1793), and applied Revolutionary principles with energy and zeal. During the Thermidorian Reaction, he was imprisoned for several months, tried for terrorism, and guillotined at Amiens on 16 October 1795.

Le Bon was born at Arras on 25 September 1765. His family was not well-to-do. He was educated at the collège of the Oratorians of Arras and made his novitiate in that order in 1783 at Paris. He then began to teach philosophy at the collège of Beaune (Burgundy), where he showed more interest in the philosophic writings of the Enlightenment than in theology and the Scriptures. He was strongly influenced by the encyclopedists and by J.-J. Rousseau and could recite many passages from Rousseau's writings.

In 1789 Le Bon was ordained. As the Revolution developed, he at first applied himself only to teaching, but in 1790 he was a dedicated member of the Society of the Friends of the Constitution at Beaune and taught Revolutionary principles to his students, to whom he administered the civic oath. In June 1790 he broke with the Oratorians. He remained, however, a priest and during 1791-92 served as constitutional curate at Neuville-Vitasse, near Arras, and later as vicar of the church of Saint-Waast, in Arras. The summer crisis of 1792 affected him strongly. On 13 September he renounced the priesthood and the next day was elected mayor of Arras. He resigned that office on 5 December to accept election to the administrative council of the department of the Pas-de-Calais. On 1 July 1793, having previously been elected an alternate member of the National Convention, he joined that body in replacement of A.-G. Magniez, who had resigned.

On 29 October 1793 the Committee of Public Safety sent Le Bon to the Pas-de-Calais to suppress counterrevolutionary movements there, and from that time he was seldom in the Convention. His responsibility was soon extended to include the department of the Nord. Since the area under his jurisdiction was often threatened by invasion from the Austrian Netherlands, Le Bon saw the arrest and punishment of traitors and counterrevolutionaries as a crucial responsibility, as did the committee that had appointed him. Assuming that all nobles and nonjuring clergy were counterrevolutionaries and that it was urgent to collect the evidence that would convict them, he accelerated the arrest of suspects and the trial and punishment of all who could feasibly be indicted and saw to it that the revolutionary tribunals at Arras and Cambrai were not idle. Acquittals infuriated him. He reorganized the tribunal at Arras so as to reduce the likelihood that they would happen. In the Pas-de-Calais and the Nord, Revolutionary courts condemned 549 persons, accounting for 4.7 percent of the executions D. O. Greer tallied for France as a whole in reckoning the geographic incidence of the Terror.

Complaints against Le Bon's conduct of the Terror at Cambrai, Arras, and elsewhere flowed into the Convention, provoked by the massive arrest of suspects there and the volume of trials and executions, and by Le Bon's terroristic rhetoric, which seemed to threaten many whom he probably did not intend to punish. The deputy A.-B.-J. Guffroy, who represented Pas-de-Calais in the Convention and published a journal in Paris, conducted a vendetta against Le Bon that lasted until the latter's trial and execution in October 1795. But Le Bon was a member of the Committee of General Security. He also had the confidence of his fellow townsman, M. Robespierre, whose power in the Convention was very strong until June 1794, and he was always able to justify his conduct to Robespierre and other members of the Committee of Public Safety. On 21 Messidor (2 May

1794) B. Barère justified Le Bon's conduct to the Convention on the ground that the counterrevolutionary threat in Le Bon's departments was intense but acknowledged that Le Bon's measures were sometimes "a little severe." Le Bon's most recent biographer, L. Jacob, observes in his behalf that every execution in his departments was preceded by a trial, as was not the case, for example, at Nantes. But until it has been established that the counterrevolutionary threat in Le Bon's departments was as serious as he thought, it will remain impossible to decide whether his severity was fully justified.

In judging Le Bon, one must consider all his contributions to the beleaguered Republic of the Year II and not merely his record as a terrorist. He organized the Revolutionary government in his territory, maintained the authority of the Convention there, energized the Jacobin clubs, invigorated military recruitment, kept order in the rear of the army on the frontier, supplied and transported provisions to the army and the town, and worked to execute the Laws of Ventôse, which, if carried out, would have redistributed considerable wealth to the benefit of the elderly and the poor. One must also remember that Le Bon did not invent the Terror but implemented it as part of a national program, to which he was dedicated, of defending the nation and preserving the benefits of the Revolution. He was encouraged by the instructions he received from the Committee of Public Safety and by the rhetoric of those instructions, which was congenial to him. Like other Revolutionaries of the Year II, he was possessed of a Revolutionary state of mind that entailed what G. Lefebvre called a punitive will. Jacob says he was driven not by avarice or ambition but by the religion of the nation and the Revolution. During his many months of imprisonment after Thermidor, he saw men who during the Year II had shared his sentiments and goals falling into a Thermidorian mentality and becoming his accusers, but as a notorious terrorist condemned by public opinion before trial, he had nothing to gain from following their example and never disavowed the principles of a Robespierrist. At his death, he left a wife, whom he had married in November 1792, and a son who in 1845 published Le Bon's letters to his wife and in 1861 a biography of him.

D. O. Greer, *The Incidence of the Terror during the French Revolution* (Cambridge, Mass., 1935); L. Jacob, *Joseph Le Bon, 1765-1795: La Terreur à la frontière*, 2 vols. (Paris, 1933); E. Le Bon, *Joseph Le Bon dans sa vie privée et dans sa carrière politique* (Paris, 1861) and *Lettres de Joseph Le Bon à sa femme* (Châlons-sur-Saône, 1845); A. J. Paris, *La Terreur dans le Pas-de-Calais et le Nord* (Arras, 1864).

G. V. Taylor

Related entries: COMMITTEE OF GENERAL SECURITY; COMMITTEE OF PUBLIC SAFETY; ROBESPIERRE, M.; TERROR, THE; VENTOSE DECREES.

LEBRUN, PIERRE-HENRI-HELENE-MARIE (1753 or 1754-1793), journalist and foreign minister. Lebrun was born in Noyon of an obscure family, studied in Paris at the collège de Louis-le-Grand and at the Observatory, then became an ecclesiastic known as the abbé Tondu. He soon changed this career for that of a soldier and the name Lebrun but deserted after two years and worked as a printer.

A believer in popular sovereignty, the benefits of reason, and the theories of F. Quesnay and the baron de Montesquieu, he founded in 1785 at Liège the *Journal Général de l'Europe* (later edited from Herve). It was the first newspaper in the southern Netherlands to critique as well as to chronicle current events. Lebrun criticized the church, participated in the 1787 revolt against the prince-bishop of Liège, and praised Austrian reform authored by Joseph II.

His writings stimulated an invitation to Paris; in April 1792 Lebrun received a post in the foreign ministry under the C. Dumouriez cabinet. On 10 August 1792 he was appointed by the Legislative Assembly to the provisional executive council and named minister of foreign affairs. He negotiated with the Prussians for a possible armistice and assured the British that the Convention would not hold Belgium, while at the same time he opened the Scheldt to trade. Suspected by M. Robespierre of working with Dumouriez to save the king, he was attacked by the Mountain. Lebrun was arrested on 2 June 1793, during the proscription of the Girondists, and guillotined at the end of the year.

T. A. Dodge, *Napoleon*, 4 vols. (Boston, 1904); R. W. Phipps, *The Armies of the First French Republic and the Rise of the Marshals of Napoleon the First*, vol. 1 (London, 1926); H. Pirenne, *Histoire de Belgique*, 7 vols. (Brussels, 1909-32); S. Tassier, *Les démocrates belges de 1789. Etude sur le Vonckisme et la Révolution brabançonne* (Brussels, 1930).

J. E. Helmreich

Related entries: DUMOURIEZ; GIRONDINS; MONTESQUIEU; 10 AUGUST 1792.

LE CHAPELIER, ISAAC-RENE-GUY (1754-94), politician. Le Chapelier was born in Rennes on 12 June 1754 into a family that had produced illustrious lawyers since the early seventeenth century. His father, ennobled in 1769, was one of the most celebrated Breton jurists of his day and a spokesman for the cause of the Breton nobility against the crown. Le Chapelier himself won acclaim as a lawyer before entering politics on the eve of the Revolution as a leader in a campaign to have the *anoblis* (recently ennobled families) of Brittany recognized as members of the Second Estate in the elections for the Estates General. Rebuffed in this by the government in March 1789, Le Chapelier threw in his lot with the Third Estate, which elected him deputy for Rennes.

At Versailles he emerged as a radical who helped found the Breton Club and consistently opposed the privileged orders. His political skill and oratorical talent won him a major role in the National Assembly and great popularity in Paris. It was he who presided over the Assembly on 4 August 1789. Among many other initiatives, often taken as a member of the Constitutional Committee, he demanded the immediate nationalization of church lands in November 1789, attacked the estates and parlement of Brittany and Breton particularism in January

1790, called for the abolition of hereditary titles of nobility in June 1790, and proposed civic equality for Protestants in August 1790. The Right heartily detested him and lampooned him as "King Isaac" for his alleged ascendancy over his colleagues and the Paris mob.

Le Chapelier's predominant conviction was that France ought to be a united nation of equal citizens who, as he informed the king on 13 August 1789, would be responsible to the same laws, governed by the same principles, and filled with the same emotions. But he was never a democrat, despite his support of the radical cause in 1789. His popularity declined as he increasingly came into conflict with the Left. He opposed any measures against the *émigrés* and the nonjuring clergy as despotic and arbitrary. He was especially alarmed by the development of the democratic movement in 1791. He believed that while sovereignty resided in the nation as a whole, it could legally be expressed only within the National Assembly. On these grounds, he repeatedly denounced group petitions and popular political associations as unconstitutional.

The Law of 14-17 June 1791, commonly known as the Le Chapelier law, was a response to labor agitation, but it should be understood within the broad context of Le Chapelier's opposition to all forms of collective action by ordinary citizens. In the spring of 1791, Parisian workers staged a series of strikes for higher wages. In some trades, they formed associations to promote their economic interests and to negotiate with their employers. Le Chapelier, in the name of the Constitutional Committee, attacked these associations for their corporate spirit, comparing them to the guilds that the Assembly had abolished on 2 March 1791. Corporations no longer exist within France, he asserted. Nor, he continued, is there anything other than individual interest and the general interest. He insisted that wages were a matter to be settled by free discussion between employer and employee as individuals. The law he presented was intended to prevent all combinations (*coalitions*), whether by workers seeking to increase wages or by employers wanting to cut them. It banned all trade and professional associations formed by employers as well as employees, but most articles were directed specifically against workers. Workers as a group were forbidden to demand higher wages, to strike, or to harass those who might refuse to join a strike. The Le Chapelier law upheld, as a fundamental principle of post-Revolutionary society, an individualistic conception of labor relations. It was in this respect a logical consequence of the night of 4 August and the Declaration of the Rights of Man, which had together destroyed the corporate structure of the Old Regime. No one on the Left opposed it with the sole exception of J.-P. Marat, who did so for political and not social reasons. The Le Chapelier law remained in force until 1884. Moreover, articles 291 and 414-416 of the Penal code of 1810 restated and strengthened its main provisions. For over ninety years, the French state used this law to hinder the development of the labor movement yet almost never invoked it against employers' associations.

After the flight to Varennes, Le Chapelier's conservatism became even more pronounced. He left the Jacobin club for the Feuillants and as a constitutional monarchist urged a revision of the constitution to limit electoral rights. His political career ended with the National Assembly. He returned to Rennes, took up the practice of law once more, and involved himself in business. While in London in late 1792 (26 September-2 November) to negotiate the purchase of a shipment of rice, he was erroneously listed as an *émigré*. He managed to live undisturbed for the following eighteen months, possibly in hiding, but he had many political enemies, and he must have sensed imminent danger. In February 1794 he wrote a letter to the Committee of Public Safety. He admitted, in what he called his "profession of faith," that he had never wanted the Republic, but he declared himself now "its partisan and defender." He offered to go to England and, posing as a refugee, to spy for the committee.This extraordinary proposal could not save him. His arrest was ordered on 1 March 1794. The act of accusation charged that greed and ambition had led him to conspire with moderates and the foreign enemy to destroy the Revolution, but he was really put on trial for his political opinions. Le Chapelier was guillotined on 22 April 1794.

A.N., W 351, Le Chapelier's trial dossier; R. Kerviler, *Recherches et notices sur les députés de la Bretagne aux Etats-Généraux et à l'Assemblée Nationale Constituante de 1789*, 2 vols. (Nantes, 1885); E. Soreau, "La loi Le Chapelier," *Ann. hist. de la Révo. française* 8 (1931).

M. D. Sibalis

Related entries: DECLARATION OF THE RIGHTS OF MAN AND OF THE CITIZEN; FEUILLANTS; 4 AUGUST 1789.

LECLERC, JEAN-THEOPHILE-VICTOIRE (1771-?), *enragé* editor. Youngest of the *enragé* leaders, Théo Leclerc was born in La Cotte near Monbrison and was only twenty years old when he began his brief political career. Little is known of his early years except that Leclerc was the son of an engineer of bridges and roads. His youth also remains in obscurity until he enrolled in the National Guard of Clermont-Ferrand in 1789.

In 1790 Leclerc embarked for Martinique as a merchant clerk, but the island was in a state of insurrection, and Leclerc joined the patriot cause. Captured in March 1791, the youth was imprisoned for two months. He was then sent back to France where he enrolled in the First Batallion of Morbihan. Shortly after, he accepted a commission as spokesman for the Grenadiers de la Forêt.

Leclerc's commission sent him to Paris where in March 1792 he addressed the Jacobin club and the Legislative Assembly. His convincing oratory restored the honor of the soldiers. In another virulent address, Leclerc attacked the institution of the monarchy, reminding Louis XVI of the fate of Charles I of England and charging Marie Antoinette with discrediting her sex.

In February 1793, Leclerc went to Lyon to serve in the Army of the Alps, where he joined the radical Jacobins in their plans to annihilate the aristocrats. Less than three months later, he returned to Paris as *député extraordinaire* to the Jacobins, but he was soon released from his duties. Not only had he incurred the wrath of M. Robespierre, but the Parisian Jacobins agreed that he was damaging their cause by his "unabashed bloodthirstiness."

When the Girondins were overthrown, Leclerc saw himself as one of the moving forces, although evidence shows that he made only one brief appearance at a club meeting on 1 June. Leclerc soon returned to his philippics. He charged that the assumption that the Revolution was over was erroneous, and in demanding more stringent laws against suspects, he antagonized J.-R. Hébert. After a brief detention, in late June he returned to the rostrum of the Cordeliers club to support the *enragé* platform and to denounce the Dantonists. He was later purged from membership in the club.

After J.-P. Marat's assassination, Leclerc saw himself as Marat's successor, and he named his triweekly paper *L'ami du peuple par Leclerc* (20 July-15 September 1793). But Leclerc's position was more Lyonnais than orthodox Jacobin. His program, enunciated on 8 August and couched in strong language, promoted price ceilings, fierce army purges, and the formation of a Revolutionary army of loyal terrorists. It was punctuated with the continuing refrain that all speculators, monopolists, and rogues be sent *à la guillotine*!

Ironically, Leclerc was conscripted into the batallion of the Marat section in 1793, a decision he supported philosophically but attacked when he was the object of the draft. Stationed at La Fère, he continued to publish his paper, which eulogized the feminists of the *Républicaines révolutionnaires* and aimed barbs directly at the Jacobins who had been dubbed the "Capet of nine heads." Again he had overstepped his mark. A Jacobin committee was authorized to collect evidence against him, and on 16 September, the Jacobin club discussed his arrest. The warning was enough because *L'ami du peuple* ceased publication immediately.

Only a few other events figure in Leclerc's life. In November 1794, the former *enragé* married P. Léon who had founded the recently proscribed *Républicaines révolutionnaires*. They moved to the Vendée where they were both arrested in April 1794 for alleged activity in an Hébertist plot. After their release five months later, Leclerc collected his personal papers and returned to La Fère. After that time, no official notices mention Leclerc, and it can be assumed that he never returned to politics.

A.N. F[7] 4774[9]; A. Mathiez, *La vie chère et le mouvement social sous la Terreur* (Paris, 1927); R. B. Rose, *The Enragés: Socialists of the French Revolution?* (London, 1965); G. Walter, *La Révolution française vue par ses journaux* (Bourges, 1948).

                                                                        S. Conner

Related entries: CORDELIERS CLUB; *ENRAGES*; HEBERT; INDULGENTS; LEON.

LEFEBVRE, GEORGES (1874-1959), historian. Georges Lefebvre was born in Lille on 6 August 1874 into a family of small artisans and commercial clerks. He studied at the local *lycée*, thanks to a municipal scholarship, and later, again on a scholarship, at the Faculty of Letters of Lille where he was awarded his *licence* and *agrégation* in 1899. For a quarter of a century, he taught history and geography successively at the *lycées* of Cherbourg, Tourcoing, Lille, Saint-Omer, and Orléans and at the *lycées* Montaigne and Henri IV in Paris. After receiving his doctorate in 1924, he was appointed *maître de conférences* at the Universities of Clermont-Ferrand and Strasbourg and subsequently professor at the Sorbonne. In 1937, he succeeded P. Sagnac in the chair of the History of the French Revolution. Forced to retire in 1941, he was retained in charge of complementary courses. After the Liberation, he announced his retirement in 1945 and thereafter devoted himself entirely to directing the Institute of the History of the Revolution, which he had founded in 1939, and to his own research.

After the premature death of A. Mathiez in 1932, Lefebvre had been invited to take charge of the Society for Robespierrist Studies and of its review, the *Annales historiques de la Révolution française*. At the same time he assumed, in effect, the presidency of the *Commission économique et sociale de la Révolution française*, which J. Jaurès had created in 1904 and with which his name is still associated.

Both Lefebvre's audience and his work were considerable. He guided or inspired nearly all the work on the history of the French Revolution done throughout the world for half a century and produced a large number of reviews of works for specialized periodicals. His annual collations in the *Revue historique* were awaited with keen interest because his impartial judgment was so greatly appreciated.

A socialist and a Dreyfusard, a patriot enamored of liberty, faithful to his principles, devoted to his friends and those near to him, respectful of the dignity of others, he gave an example of a simple life, of a total disinterestedness, of professional conscience, and of daily effort to better know the land, the workers, and the economic and social structures of the past and more particularly of the period of the Revolution and Empire. At first he devoted his research to the study of the peasantry and its conditions. His doctoral thesis, *Les paysans du Nord*, is still definitive, as are his *Questions agraires au temps de la Terreur* (1932), his *Grande Peur de 1789* (1932), and his posthumous work *Etudes orléanaises* (2 vols., 1962).

A staunch partisan of scholarly research based on a methodical and objective analysis of the documents, nevertheless he did not sacrifice lively narration, which created a larger audience for his work. Nor did he disdain historical synthesis, where he could at the same time draw on his extensive reading and present his own conclusions. As a result, we have some genuine classics, which have been often reprinted and translated into all European languages; among these are *La Révolution française* in 1930 and subsequently *Napoléon* in 1935, both in the collection, "Peuples et civilisations." Other syntheses of his are less broad in scope but no less essential: *Les Thermidoriens* (1937), *Quatre-vingt-neuf* (1939), *Le Directoire* (1946), and *Etudes sur la Révolution française*, a collection of his principal articles.

A pioneer in many areas, he wanted to extend the scope of historical explanation to the maximum and to show the complex interaction of factors that retard and those that advance progress. Conceived as a discipline of the sensible world, history ought to collaborate with the natural sciences, biology, and medicine in order to establish the constants of human conduct. Toward the end of his life, Lefebvre accorded priority to the study of mental habits (*mentalités*), of existential needs, of the environment. His appeal was heard, and after his death in Paris on 28 August 1959, researchers oriented their work according to these perspectives and methods.

Ann. hist. de la Révo. française, special number 159, "Hommage à Georges Lefebvre," 32 (1960) and special number 237, "Georges Lefebvre, pour le vingtième anniversaire de sa mort," 51 (1979); B. Hyslop, "Georges Lefebvre, Historian," *Fr. Hist. Stud.* 1 (1960); R. R. Palmer, "Georges Lefebvre: The Peasants and the French Revolution," *J. of Mod. Hist.* 31 (1959).

M. Bouloiseau

Related entries: AULARD; GAXOTTE; JAURES; MATHIEZ.

LEGENDRE, ADRIEN-MARIE (1752-1833), scientist and academician. Born in Paris, 18 September 1752, Legendre was educated at the Collège Mazarin and taught mathematics at the Ecole Militaire from 1775 to 1780. He won the prize offered by the Berlin Academy in 1782 for a problem in ballistics and was admitted to the Academy of Sciences on 30 March 1783. His mathematical researches included important work on celestial mechanics, number theory, and the theory of elliptical functions. His publication (*Nouvelles méthodes pour la détermination des orbites des comètes* in 1805) of the method of least squares prompted a priority dispute with his more celebrated contemporary, C.-F. Gauss.

Little is known of Legendre's personal life or political activity during the Revolution. His most important public responsibilities were related to the introduction of the metric system. In 1787, he had participated in the geodetic measurements conducted jointly by the Paris and Greenwich observatories. One of the academicians charged in April 1791 to carry out the calculations to determine the standard meter, he withdrew from this task early in 1792. However, in 1794 he was head of a bureau of the Commission exécutive de l'instruction publique with responsibility for weights and measures, and in 1795-96 he served in the Agence temporaire des poids et mesures that supervised the introduction of the metric system. Elected to the Institut National in December 1795, he also continued his interest in the mathematics of the metric system as a member of the international Commission des Poids et Mesures. In 1813, he was appointed to the Bureau des Longitudes.

Legendre served as examiner in mathematics at the Ecole Polytechnique from 1799 to 1815. The *Eléments de géometrie* (1794), which he was commissioned to write for the Convention by its Committee on Public Instruction, remained the standard introduction to the subject, in France and abroad, for many decades. He died in Paris, 9 January 1833.

C. D. Hellman, "Legendre and the French Reform of Weights and Measures," *Osiris* 1 (1936); J. Itard, "Legendre," *Dictionary of Scientific Biography*, 16 vols. (New York, 1970-1980).

K. Baker

Related entry: SCIENCE.

LEGISLATIVE ASSEMBLY (1791-92), the legislature established under the Constitution of 1791 and officially entitled National Legislative Assembly; its first meeting was on 1 October 1791, its last on 20 September 1792. Designed to carry on routine, though important, functions in a context of stable political life, the Legislative Assembly never rose to the heroic level sometimes achieved by its predecessor, the Constituent Assembly. Its term was cut short as a result of the insurrection of 10 August 1792.

The Legislative Assembly had 745 seats. They were allocated among the 83 departments in proportion to three variables: number of active citizens (249 seats), total direct tax paid by the inhabitants (249 seats), and extent of the territory of each department (247 seats). The members were chosen in September 1791 by the electors. These, according to the constitution, amounted to 1 percent of the active citizens and therefore probably numbered about 42,000 men. In order to be eligible to be elected, one had to own land and pay a direct tax equivalent in value to a mark (244.5 grams) of silver. Such a sum would amount to about fifty days' wages for a skilled artisan; on the other hand, tens of thousands of men paid that much or more in direct taxes. The members of the Constituent Assembly were ineligible for election to the Legislative.

The social composition of the Legislative Assembly was very different from that of its predecessor. The clergy and the nobility had held, together, 49 percent of the seats in June 1789. Now they had no right to be represented as such; the ten bishops and eight *curés* who were elected were members of the constitutional church; a score of men who appear to have been nobles were elected; and the two groups together amounted to 5.5 percent of the Legislative Assembly. In 1789, of the Third Estate deputies, 21 percent held offices in the royal judiciary; in the Legislative Assembly, less than 6 percent had held such offices. Land-owners of middling to substantial wealth, among them many law graduates, the members of the Legislative Assembly in general had been active, even enter-prising, in the political life of the small towns where most of them lived.

The constitutional powers of the Assembly included several that have since become standard for any legislature: to propose and adopt statutes, establish and regulate taxes, authorize and supervise public expenditures, create and abolish official positions, control the coinage, determine the number of men and the rates of pay in the armed forces, declare war, and ratify treaties. Its control over its own sessions included the right to command the armed forces in whatever city in which it might meet (in fact, Paris). It had the power to impeach ministers and agents of the executive branch for malfeasance and the power to indict anyone for the attacking or conspiring against the security of the French state or the constitution.

The Legislative Assembly had no constitutional power to choose or dismiss ministers. Only the king had that authority. A member of the Assembly was constitutionally ineligible, while a member and for two years after, to be appointed minister or to receive any commission from the executive. The Assembly could not override a royal veto, which would stand until a third legislative session adopted the vetoed decree (at the earliest, May 1795). Nor could it propose any amendment of the constitution, for 1797 was the earliest date when the constitution itself would permit the amending process to begin.

The members elected in September 1791 saw their task as maintenance of both the monarchy and the constitution, which limited the monarch and which he had accepted reluctantly, as a temporary expedient. In the Legislative Assembly, two principal groups held somewhat differing views. The Jacobin minority wanted to force the king to cooperate with them, to repress priests who refused allegiance to the constitution, to penalize émigrés who hoped to overthrow the constitution, and to make war on other monarchs. A larger minority, the Feuillants, although having a divided leadership, believed in general that the way to defend the constitution was to rely on the monarch while seeking to advise him. Almost half of the legislators, prizing ther independence, had joined neither the Jacobins nor the Feuillants.

By the end of 1791, the pattern of relations between the majority of the Assembly and the king was clear: reciprocal suspicion and antagonism with regard to affairs in France, combined with willingness to join together to threaten and eventually to undertake war abroad. The agreement on a war policy was illusory; it covered ulterior motives that were totally contrasting. The king wanted Austrian and Prussian troops to defeat the French and restore his former authority. The leading orators in the Assembly wanted the king to help achieve military victory, which would strengthen the people's attachment to the constitution and render impossible any reversion to the Old Regime.

The course of the struggle between king and Assembly was marked by the principal decrees that the king vetoed and by the appointments and dismissals of ministers. He vetoed both the decree of 9 November 1791, which required gatherings of émigrés outside France to disperse within fifty-two days, and the decree of 29 November 1791, which imposed the civic oath requirement on nonincumbent clergymen as well as bishops and curés. He appointed as minister of war (7 December 1791) the comte L. de Narbonne, who was favored by some of the Assembly's leaders and who soon made it obvious that he was preparing for war.

In his effort to secure a dominant influence, Narbonne collided with the adviser whom the king himself preferred, A.-F. Bertrand de Molleville, naval minister. Each minister had adherents in the Assembly. Narbonne made Bertrand's position within the king's council untenable. Bertrand resigned. The king suddenly dismissed Narbonne. The Assembly fell into an uproar and proceeded to impeach the minister of foreign affairs, C.-A. Valdec de Lessart, who was removed from office pending trial. The king was prevailed on to appoint C. Dumouriez minister of foreign affairs (17 March 1792) and then to add to his council three men whom the Jacobins favored: J.-M. Roland de la Platière, E. Clavière, and in May, J. Servan. With the Dumouriez ministry in office, Louis XVI asked the Legislative Assembly to declare war on the Hapsburg ruler, Francis II. It did so by an overwhelming vote.

Growing suspicion of counterrevolutionary priests led to the decree of 27 May 1792 providing for deportation of nonjuring clergymen on petition of twenty active citizens followed by local administrative decision. Agitation in Paris led to the decree of 8 June 1792 calling for the concentration there of 20,000 National Guardsmen from all over the kingdom. The king vetoed both decrees. Roland handed to Louis XVI a blunt letter warning about the probable consequences of the vetoes. The king dismissed the pro-Jacobin ministers on 13 June.

The Assembly, divided, now found itself caught between opposing forces. The pure royalists around the king were more extreme than the constitutional monarchists (Feuillants and followers of the marquis de Lafayette) in the Assembly. The democrats in the sections and the Jacobin club of Paris were more extreme than the left wing of the Assembly (J.-P. Brissot, P.-V. Vergniaud, and their associates). The Assembly would not close the Jacobin club, as Lafayette demanded, nor would it vote, as the Jacobins demanded, to disapprove Lafayette's conduct in leaving his post. The Assembly attempted a policy of unity; at abbé A. Lamourette's suggestion the members embraced one another; and they joined together to declare that "*la patrie est en danger*" (11 July 1792). But the unity was temporary and factitious. In reality, the Assembly was paralyzed. It became a target of the movement for dethronement and of the insurrection of 10 August 1792.

After the insurrection, the Assembly voted to suspend the king from his duties and ordered new elections to choose a constitutional Convention. (In these elections, all men over twenty-one, if self-supporting and not in domestic service, had the right to vote.) For the interim, the Assembly continued, although fewer than 300 members (the Left) were present. It elected the council of ministers. Yielding to pressure from the insurrectionary Commune of Paris, it provided for the election of a special criminal court to judge "the crimes committed on the day of 10 August." But on 30 August 1792, regarding the Commune as illegal and arbitrary, the Assembly voted to dissolve it and order a new municipality elected; the Commune defied the Assembly. The Assembly left a legacy of division among the Revolutionaries.

H. Glagau, *Die französische Legislative und der Ursprung der Revolutionskriege, 1791-1792* (Berlin, 1896); A. Kuscinski, *Les députés à l'Assemblée Législative de 1791. Listes par département et par ordre alphabétique* ... (Paris, 1900); M. Reinhard, *La chute de la royauté, 10 août 1792* (Paris, 1969).

P. Dawson

Related entries: BERTRAND DE MOLLEVILLE; DUMOURIEZ; FEUIL-
LANTS; JACOBINS; LESSART; NARBONNE-LARA; SELF-DENYING OR-
DINANCE; 10 AUGUST 1792.

LEOBEN, PRELIMINARIES OF. See PRELIMINARIES OF LEOBEN.

LEON, ANNE-PAULINE (1768-?), leader of the Société des Citoyennes républicaines révolutionnaires. Léon was born in Paris, the daughter of P.-P. Léon,
a chocolate maker, and his wife M. Télohan. After her father's death in 1784,
she joined her mother in the management of the family business and in the raising
of her five siblings.

In an account of her political activities written in prison in 1794, Léon described her active participation in the Revolution's beginnings. She had taken
to the streets in 1789 to urge citizens to erect barricades and to seize the Bastille.
In February 1791 she organized an attack on the home of a Parisian journalist,
L.-S. Fréron, as part of her campaign against royalists and against the marquis
de Lafayette. At about the same time she began to attend meetings of the
Cordeliers club and joined the Fraternal Society of the Section of Mutius Scae-
vola, one of a number of assemblies of lower-middle-class citizens that admitted
women. On 6 March 1791 she appeared before the National Assembly to demand
the right for women to arm and train as a militia group. To deny this right to
women, she argued, would be to exclude them from the benefits of the Declaration of Rights. Her petition, which was ignored, bore the signatures of more
than 300 Parisian women. On 17 July 1791, along with her mother and their
cook, C. Evrard, she went to the Champ de Mars to sign the Cordeliers' petition
calling for the trial of the king and the reorganization of the executive. She later
reported that as a result, she was threatened with imprisonment by her section.

Armed with her pike, she came forward to participate in the attack on the
Tuileries (10 August 1792) and only reluctantly surrendered her weapon to a
male *sans-culotte*. Nine months later she urged the Jacobins to enlist women in
the fight against the counterrevolutionary Vendéans. She was one of the founders
(10 May 1793) of the Citoyennes républicaines révolutionnaires, the sole Parisian
political society to admit only women. The society's goals were to instruct women
in the law, to participate in public affairs, to aid the suffering, and to resist
arbitrary actions. Léon's militant stamp shows in the first of the society's regulations, which proclaimed the *citoyennes'* readiness to rush armed to the defense
of the *patrie*. Léon remained the society's moving force until August 1793.

During these months, the *citoyennes* provided valuable armed street support
for the Montagnards' successful campaign to purge the moderates from the
Convention (May-June 1793). On 19 May 1793 the society joined the Cordeliers
in urging the Jacobins to draft harsh laws against counterrevolutionaries and
hoarders. In June it praised the new constitution and persuaded a group of
laundresses to abandon their attempt to go over the government's head and impose
their own *taxation populaire* on soap. On 1 July the society denounced the

enragé J. Roux. At this point the *citoyennes* were still comfortable with the Montagnard leaders, but in August Léon seems to have dropped out and leadership of the society passed to C. Lacombe, who would split the society by her criticism of the Jacobin leadership and her sympathy for the *enragé* program.

Little is known about Léon's activities after she ceased to lead the Citoyennes républicaines révolutionnaires. On 18 November 1793 she married T. Leclerc, an *enragé* and editor of *L'ami du peuple*. After their marriage, both retreated into private life, with Léon giving particular attention to her mother's business affairs. Léon and Leclerc were arrested in April 1794 and held until August. In 1804 Léon was in Paris, supporting her mother and son by teaching.

M. Cerati, *Le Club des Citoyennes républicaines révolutionnaires* (Paris, 1966); D. G. Levy, H. G. Applewhite, and M. D. Johnson, eds. *Women in Revolutionary Paris, 1789-1795* (Urbana, 1979); R. B. Rose, *The Enragés: Socialists of the French Revolution?* (Sydney, 1965).

L. J. Abray

Related entries: AMI DU PEUPLE, L'; CORDELIERS CLUB; FRERON; LAFAYETTE; LACOMBE; LECLERC; ROUX; VENDEE.

LEOPOLD II (1747-92), archduke of Austria, king of Hungary, Holy Roman Emperor (1790-92). Leopold, born in 1747, was the third son of Maria Theresa (1740-80) and brother of Joseph II (1780-90) and Marie Antoinette (1755-93). Before he became the ruler of the Hapsburg territories, Leopold served for twenty-five years as grand duke of Tuscany, where he introduced many reforms. However, as emperor he undid many of Joseph II's reforms in order to restore tranquility. He ended the Belgian revolt and the war with the Ottoman Empire by the Treaty of Sistova in 1791.

Leopold initially sympathized with the Revolution in France but became concerned about the safety of the French royal family. On 5 July 1791 he issued the Padua Circular in which he proposed cooperation to restore the liberty and honor of Louis XVI, to limit the dangerous extremes of the Revolution, and to demand the release of the royal family. On 27 August Leopold and Frederick William II of Prussia (1786-97) issued the Pillnitz Declaration, which appealed to European monarchs to cooperate to enable France to consolidate the foundations of a monarchical government and agreed to use force if necessary to achieve that objective. Leopold did exert pressure on the elector of Trêves to expel the *émigrés*, whom he disliked. The French Legislative Assembly demanded on 25 January 1792 that Leopold renounce every treaty against France. The Austrian reply of 19 February was vague and restrained but did contain some unfriendly remarks against the Jacobins. However, Austria and Prussia signed a defensive treaty on 7 February. Leopold died on 1 March before the outbreak of war on 20 April.

A. Schultze, *Kaiser Leopold II und die französische Revolution* (Gottingen, 1899); A. Wandruszka, *Leopold II*, vol. 2 (Vienna, Munich, 1965).

G. D. Homan

Related entries: DECLARATION OF PILLNITZ; FRANCIS II; FREDERICK WILLIAM II.

LEPELLETIER DE SAINT-FARGEAU, LOUIS-MICHEL (1760-93), deputy to the National Assembly and the National Convention, "first Revolutionary martyr." Lepelletier was the son of Michel-Etienne, the comte de Saint-Fargeau, who was a close adviser to Louis XV. Admitted to the Paris Parlement in 1779, within ten years he had become *président à mortier*. Lepelletier was elected on 16 May 1789 to the Estates General as a deputy of the Second Estate from the city of Paris. He was active in the patriot party and served as president of the National Assembly from 21 June to 5 July 1790.

Elected on 6 September 1792 to the National Convention by the department of the Yonne, Lepelletier became a *Montagnard* and voted for the death of the king. On 20 January 1793, in an act of revenge against an aristocrat turned regicide, Pâris, a former member of the *garde de corps*, assassinated Lepelletier with a sword thrust into his side. As the so-called First Martyr of the Revolutionaries, he was buried in an elaborate ceremony at the Pantheon. Perhaps more important in death than in life, Lepelletier, along with J.-P. Marat and J.-B. Chalier, became the part of the Revolutionary triad of a cult of martyrs that was an important aspect of the subsequent dechristianization movement.

A. Soboul, *The French Revolution, 1789-1799: From the Storming of the Bastille to Napoleon* (New York: 1974).

D. M. Epstein

Related entries: DECHRISTIANIZATION; MARAT; PATRIOT PARTY; SYMBOLISM.

LESSART, CLAUDE-ANTOINE VALDEC DE (1742-92), foreign minister. Lessart began his active career as a protégé of J. Necker and was active in government financial circles. In 1790 he became controller general of finances and an important member of the Feuillant faction. His rise after 1790 was rapid; he served as minister of the interior, interim minister of the navy and colonies, minister of war, and minister of foreign affairs between 1791 and 1792.

He favored the reforms of the Revolution's early years but, like his fellow Feuillants, wanted to retain limited suffrage and a strong executive. In foreign affairs he resisted the drift to war, fearing defeat much less than the political turmoil that war would produce at home. Powerful factions, however, saw foreign war as a means of gaining domestic power. The king hoped that Austria and Prussia would defeat the Revolution and restore royal authority. J.-P. Brissot and his followers wanted a victorious conflict to compel the monarch to place and retain them in office. Ambitious generals, intending to use the prestige of victory to seize power, also advocated war. The Feuillants themselves were divided over the issue of war and peace. A portion of their members in the Legislative Assembly, and M. Robespierre in the Jacobin club, fought a losing battle against pro-war elements.

Leopold II of Austria had threatened to intervene in French affairs if the Constituent Assembly dethroned Louis XVI after the Varennes fiasco. He believed that such threats would restrain French radicals while bolstering the moderates' position within the new Legislative Assembly. The new assembly, however, was more radical in composition than the Constituent and was less experienced in foreign affairs than the earlier body. As a result Leopold's threats stimulated rather than restrained pro-war groups.

Lessart could do little to prevent the deputies from moving closer to hostilities in January 1792. The king, seeking to restrain the radicals until Austria and Prussia were ready to act, dismissed L. Narbonne, the war minister, who had earlier declared that the army was ready to fight and that the Assembly should purge the ministry of royalists and Austrian sympathizers. Since Narbonne was in league with Brissot, the Brissotin faction struck back by accusing Lessart of complicity in a plot against the constitution and obtained a decree arraigning him before the high court on charges of treason. Lessart was arrested, the remaining Feuillant ministers resigned, and the Brissotins gained control of the major ministries. On 20 April 1792 France declared war on Austria.

Lessart, meanwhile, was imprisoned at Orléans. In September 1792, he was brought to Versailles, but before any trial could take place, he perished in the September Massacres. Lessart, like Robespierre, realized the danger of going to war before securing power at home. Both men were right, but neither could prevent hostilities.

J. H. Clapham, *The Causes of the War of 1792* (Cambridge, Eng. 1899); H. A. Goetz-Bernstein, *La diplomatie de la Gironde: Jacques-Pierre Brissot* (Paris, 1912).

S. T. Ross

Related entries: BRISSOT; DECLARATION OF PILLNITZ; FEUILLANTS; FIRST COALITION; LEOPOLD II; NARBONNE-LARA; VARENNES.

LESUEUR, JEAN-FRANCOIS (1760-1837), operatic composer and teacher at the Paris Conservatory. See MUSIC.

LETTRE CLOSE. See *LETTRE DE CACHET*.

LETTRE DE CACHET (or *LETTRE CLOSE*), warrant of arrest (occasionally exile) signed by the king and countersigned by one of the secretaries of state; ordinarily written on a single sheet of paper, it was folded so that it could not be read without the breaking of the seal (*cachet*).

Written most often to an officer charged with its execution, the *lettre de cachet* was a royal order to receive in prison a specific individual and to retain him there until further notice. All expenses of the individual's incarceration were to be borne by the crown; and the document always concluded with the absolutist formula "car tel est nôtre plaisir."

The *lettre de cachet* was also used against ordinary criminals, by parents who requested royal intervention in cases involving errant sons or daughters, and by powerful nobles who wished to settle private scores against their enemies. However used, it was a potentially abusive weapon held by any minister of state who, with the monarch's assent, could incarcerate an individual for an indeterminate period of time. Its violation of judicial procedure, particularly the right to a trial, made the *lettre de cachet* a hated symbol of absolutism.

The largest number of *lettres de cachet* were issued during the reign of Louis XV; estimates for the fifty-nine-year period run from 80,000 to 150,000. These *lettres* were usually directed at what J. M. Thompson has called moral delinquencies. The comte de Mirabeau and F.-M. Voltaire, one an inveterate gambler and womanizer in his father's eyes and the other an author of alleged libelous verse, are but two examples. Jansenists, often viewed by the government as spiritually and morally corrupt, were similarly imprisoned in large number by *lettres de cachet* initiated by Cardinal Fleury.

Under Louis XVI, an estimated 14,000 *lettres de cachet* were directed mainly at political opponents of the regime. These men, articulate and persuasive with the pen, used their imprisonment to decry the patently illegal and despotic actions taken against them. Thus they succeeded in generating public sympathy for themselves while condemning an iniquitous feature of the *ancien régime*.

Denounced in many *cahiers de doléances* as an illegitimate intrusion in the life of Frenchmen, the National Assembly formally abolished the *lettre de cachet* on 15 January 1790 and ordered the immediate release of all those who had been imprisoned by it.

M. Marion, *Dictionnaire des institutions de la France aux XVIIe et XVIIIe siècles*, new ed. (Paris, 1972); J. M. Thompson, *The French Revolution* (Oxford, 1962).

B. Rothaus

Related entries: CAHIERS DE DOLEANCES; JUSTICE; NATIONAL ASSEMBLY; PARLEMENTS; PRISONS.

LETTRES DE JUSSION. See PARLEMENTS.

LEVEE EN MASSE (23 August 1793), mass conscription and requisition of the entire French population to combat advancing enemy armies. In August 1793, in order to meet the threat of the First Coalition, the French *sans-culottes* preached a mass levy of all French. They presumed that if everyone rose up at once and "like the Gauls, fell *en masse* on the hordes of brigands," speedy victory would be won. The Montagnards, who were at first reticent about a mass levy, which they felt would disorganize the commonwealth, came to support the idea, but only after transforming it into a requisition of unmarried men and widowers without children between the ages of eighteen and twenty-five. Replacements were forbidden. Married men were to forge arms; women would make tents and serve in hospitals; children would shred cloth into lint; and old men would teach hatred of tyrants and the unity of the Republic to all.

Although this requisition, which formed an integral part of the Terror, was effected without difficulty and even with enthusiasm in certain cities like Paris, it also ran into considerable opposition. Small farmers complained that with the departure of their sons, they could no longer cultivate their land. The poor denounced the rich who, by going into hiding or by buying medical exemptions from doctors, escaped obligatory service. Yet, by simultaneously employing coercive means and political propaganda, together with social measures, the Jacobins and the *sans-culottes* managed to levy, equip, and arm over 300,000 men, who, added to the preceding levies, brought the strength of the army to nearly 800,000.

J. Bertaud, *La Révolution armée* (Paris, 1979); A. Mathiez, *La victoire en l'an II* (Paris, 1916); A. Soboul, *Les Soldats de l'an II* (Paris, 1959).

J.-P. Bertaud

Related entries: FIRST COALITION; TERROR, THE.

LIGURIAN REPUBLIC, one of the sister republics of France, created from the former Republic of Genoa, 1797-1805. The Republic of Genoa enjoyed its splendor during the thirteenth and fourteenth centuries, when it contended with Venice for mastery of the eastern Mediterranean. In 1796 it still preserved its medieval institutions. It was governed by a senate, composed exclusively of patricians, which elected a doge, who had no real powers but simply executed the decisions of the aristocracy. Still, since 1792, the Republic of Genoa was one of the rare Italian states that had maintained a strict neutrality with France. The Army of Italy had even been able to borrow money at Genoa and purchase provisions and equipment there. Revolutionary propaganda benefited from these circumstances to spread in the old republic.

When C. Saliceti, the commissioner to the Army of Italy, reached Genoa in March 1796 to negotiate new loans and purchases, he was welcomed by the Genoese Jacobins. Moreover, on the eve of the Italian campaign of April 1796, Genoese territory was violated by French and Austrian armies. After N. Bonaparte's victories, Genoa was considered a rear depôt for French troops. A Genoese, the banker count Balbi, became the Army of Italy's banker, and the articles confiscated from the churches and pawnshops by the army were turned over to him to sell, with the proceeds sent to Paris.

The Genoese patriots, like other Italian patriots, wanted the formation of a centralized republic in Italy or at least, for the time being, several democratic republics. Following the formation of the Cispadane Republic (31 December 1796) and subsequently the Cisalpine Republic (effectively established in April 1797), it was difficult for Bonaparte and the French government to resist the pressure of Genoese patriots.

On 22 May 1797 an insurrection broke out at Genoa; the democrats demanded that the senate modify the republican constitution. But the patricians, with the help of the stevedores, resisted; in the course of the fighting, forty Genoese and two Frenchmen were killed. The patriots then requested help from Bonaparte; he called on the doge to free the French who had been arrested and threatened reprisals if this were not done. The senate was alarmed and immediately sent a deputation to Paris and another one to Bonaparte, at the château of Mombello near Milan. These representatives signed a convention with the general that transformed the Republic of Genoa into the Ligurian Republic and laid the bases of a new constitution (6 June 1797). Henceforth, all Genoese citizens would be equal, and the legislative power would be exercised by representatives of the people, who would elect an executive directory.

A commission of twenty-two members, chosen with Bonaparte's approval, drew up the constitution, which was completed on 11 November 1797 and approved by a plebiscite of 100,000 yeas against 17,000 nays on 2 December. The constitution was prefaced with a declaration of rights and duties analogous to the French declaration of 1795. Citizens were to elect, on the basis of universal suffrage, electors, selected from among men whose income was "more than the wages of a day laborer." These electors, in turn, elected two legislative councils that named a directory. The constitution provided for the right to public assistance and the right to education; it declared that the state would accord "special protection to industry, to commerce, to the arts, to the sciences, as well as to agriculture and to shipping." In addition, the feudal regime, which was of little importance, was abolished, but Catholicism was recognized as the state religion. The constitution also established a permanent alliance with the French Republic.

The Ligurian Republic, like the other sister republics, experienced a coup d'état. When the Ligurian directory refused to loan 800,000 francs to France in August 1798, the consul C.-G. Redon de Belleville, supported by the Genoese Jacobins, dismissed ten deputies (out of a total of thirty) from the Council of the Young. The directory transferred and even exiled the archbishop of Genoa to Novi (31 August) since he was hostile to France.

In the spring of 1799, when the French troops evacuated Italy under pressure from Austro-Russian forces, the Ligurian Republic alone escaped invasion. The French troops, commanded by A. Masséna, shut themselves up in Genoa and capitulated, after running out of provisions and munitions, only on 4 June 1800, ten days before Bonaparte's victory at Marengo. The Ligurian Republic was reconstituted and provided with a new constitution in 1802, a constitution drawn up by Saliceti and based on the constitution of the Italian Republic. After the annexation of Piedmont to France (11 September 1802), however, it appeared that the Ligurian Republic, a natural outlet to the Mediterranean, and Genoa, which was bound to become a major naval base, could not remain independent. The Ligurian Republic was annexed to the French Empire on 30 June 1805. It had lasted eight years.

G. Assereto, *La Repubblica ligure: Lotte politiche e problemi finanziari, 1797-1799* (Turino, 1975); J. Godechot, *La Grande Nation* (2d ed., Paris, 1983), and "La Ligurie à l'époque révolutionnaire et napoléonienne," in *Actes du Congrès* de la *Società Savonese di Storia Patria* (Savona, 1983); A. Ronco, *La Marsigliesa en Liguria* (Genova, 1973), *L'assedio di Genova* (Genova, 1976), and *Filippo Buonarroti e la rivoluzione en Liguria* (Genoa, 1982).

J. Godechot

Related entries: CISALPINE REPUBLIC; CISPADANE REPUBLIC; SECOND COALITION.

LINDET, JEAN-BAPTISTE-ROBERT (1746-1825), deputy to the Legislative Assembly and the National Convention, member of the Committee of Public Safety. Born at Bernay on 2 May 1746, the son of a prosperous lumber merchant, Lindet received a degree in law from the University of Paris and was appointed *procureur du roi* on 11 September 1776. During the early phase of the Revolution, he served as mayor of Bernay, as one of the commissioners appointed to establish the department of the Eure, and as *procureur-syndic* for the district of Bernay. On 20 August 1791, the Eure elected Lindet to the Legislative Assembly, where he stayed aloof from the warring factions and had an undistinguished record.

Lindet's role would be quite different in the National Convention to which he and his brother Thomas were elected in September 1792 by the Eure. He became a staunch member of the Mountain and as such displayed an implacable hostility toward those whom he believed were enemies of the Revolution and of the newly established Republic. On 10 December 1792, on behalf of the Committee of Twenty-One, he proposed to the National Convention the indictment against Louis XVI. Stating that one must not hesitate to strike down tyrants, he subsequently voted without reservation for the execution of the former monarch. As reporter for the Committee on Legislation, he recommended the establishment of a Revolutionary Tribunal. Similarly, Lindet wrote a lengthy defense of the arrest on 2 June 1793 of the Girondin deputies whom he accused of federalism and of conspiring with the enemies of the Republic.

Lindet's major role in and contribution to the French Revolution came from his service on the Committee of Public Safety. Elected to this body on 6 April 1793, he would have the longest tenure of any of its members and would demonstrate a tremendous capacity for hard work and an outstanding talent for administration.

After failing in his initial task to resolve the insurrection at Lyon and in the Eure by peaceful methods, Lindet henceforth specialized in the area of provisions and transportation for the army and in enforcement of the Law of the Maximum. He was the liaison between the Committee of Public Safety and the Subsistence Commission (established on 22 October 1793) whose function was to implement the economic dictatorship of the Terror. With a staff of over 500 employees, Lindet and the commission supervised agricultural and industrial production, imports and exports, wage and price controls, and the drafting of workers for service in nationalized munitions factories. He was also in charge of the Commission of Transports, and in the spring of 1794 he designed the so-called evacuation agencies whose function was essentially to plunder conquered territories adjacent to France. Lindet, though an unobtrusive member of the Committee of Public Safety, was therefore the directing force behind its economic policies. L. Carnot, with whom Lindet worked closely, praised the latter's efforts as essential for the military victories of the Republic.

In the spring and early summer of 1794, the Terror reached its zenith, and the Committee began to fragment into hostile factions. Lindet arranged for a grant of 2 million *livres* to the Paris Commune to provision the city in order to placate the supporters of J.-R. Hébert who was arrested and executed, but he opposed a similar fate for G.-J. Danton. He also tried unsuccessfully to restore unity within the committee. Lindet played no role in the events of Thermidor and continued to serve on the committee until he was replaced by normal rotation on 6 October 1794.

During the Thermidorian period, the policies and personnel of the Terror came under increasing attack in the National Convention. On 20 September 1794, an unrepentant Lindet defended the earlier purge of the Girondin deputies and stated that abuses of power were unavoidable in great revolutions. He also spoke up courageously but fruitlessly on behalf of his former colleagues J.-N. Billaud-Varenne, J.-M. Collot d'Herbois, and B. Barère when they were tried before the National Convention in March of 1795. But when Lindet was indicted on 28 May 1795 on charges of having participated in the uprisings of April and May and of being "a barbarian who had thirsted after 200,000 heads," he publicly broke with the Committee of Public Safety for the first time. After a strong denial of any role in the uprisings, Lindet blamed the more sanguinary measures of the Terror on M. Robespierre and L. Saint-Just for whom, he said, he had never felt any friendship. Lindet was saved by the amnesty passed by the National Convention on 24 October 1795.

Lindet's political career was not uneventful during the period of the Directory. His election to the Council of Five Hundred in 1795 was nullified on the grounds that it violated the terms of the amnesty. Lindet's election to the same body in 1798 was overturned on the grounds of irregularities. On 25 May 1797, the high court acquitted him for lack of evidence on the charge of being a member of the Babeuf conspiracy.

After marrying A.-E. Mesnil in 1798, Lindet accepted the appointment as minister of finance in July of the following year. A staunch Revolutionary republican to the end, he resigned after the coup of Brumaire and refused to serve under Napoleon. He then led the life of a successful attorney in Paris until his death on 16 February 1825. He is the only member of the Committee of Public Safety buried in the capital.

H. Dupre, *Two Brothers in the French Revolution: Robert and Thomas Lindet* (New York, 1967); A. Montier, *Robert Lindet, deputé à l'Assemblée Legislative et à la Convention, membre du Comité de Salut Public, Ministre des Finances: Notice Biographique* (Paris, 1899); R. R. Palmer, *Twelve Who Ruled: The Year of the Terror in the French Revolution* (Princeton, N.J., 1969).

D. M. Epstein

Related entries: CARNOT; COMMITTEE OF PUBLIC SAFETY; CONSPIR-
ACY OF EQUALS; COUP OF 18 BRUMAIRE; GIRONDINS; HEBERT; LYON;
9 THERMIDOR YEAR II; REVOLUTIONARY TRIBUNAL; ROBESPIERRE,
M.; SAINT-JUST; TERROR, THE.

LINDET, ROBERT-THOMAS (1743-1823), deputy to the National Assembly, National Convention, and Council of Ancients; constitutional bishop. Born
at Bernay 14 November 1743, older brother of J.-B.-R. Lindet, Thomas earned
a doctorate in theology from the Sorbonne and then served as curé in his native
town. Elected to the Estates General (17 March 1789) as deputy to the First
Estate from the *bailliage* of Evreux, he supported the aims of the Third Estate
and was a proponent of the ecclesiastical legislation of the National Assembly.
Elected bishop of Evreux on 15 February 1791, he consistently defended the
persecution of nonjuring priests. As a deputy to the National Convention from
the Eure (elected 4 September 1792), Lindet became a staunch Montagnard and
voted without reservations for the death of Louis XVI. In addition, he married,
and early in 1793 resigned his bishopric in a public defrocking ceremony.

Under the Directory, Lindet served in the Council of Ancients from 1795 to
1797, was subsequently appointed executive commissioner in the Eure, and
studied law. After his reelection to the Council of Ancients was annulled on
grounds of irregularities in May 1798, he withdrew from public life and returned
to Bernay where he practiced law. When he died there on 10 August 1823, the
Catholic church forbade a religious burial.

H. Dupre, *Two Brothers in the French Revolution: Robert and Thomas Lindet* (New
York, 1967); A. Montier, ed., *Correspondance de Thomas Lindet, pendant la Constituante et la Législative (1789-1792)* (Paris, 1899).

D. M. Epstein

Related entries: CIVIL CONSTITUTION OF THE CLERGY; LINDET, J.-
B.-R.

LIT DE JUSTICE, literally, "bed of justice," a term designating one of the
most imposing (and politically significant) ceremonies in pre-Revolutionary France.
More specifically, the *lit de justice* was an extraordinary and solemn session of
one of the sovereign or highest courts of law presided over by the king (or a
deputy) and attended by other great personages; the crown staged the occasion
to force the law court in question to register or formally ratify and legitimize
important royal legislation.

The most portentous *lits de justice* by far were usually those held by the French
kings in the Parlement of Paris, the most powerful and prestigious tribunal in
the *ancien régime* after the king's own council. The Paris Parlement, which had
originated in the medieval king's court or *curia regis*, dispensed the monarch's
highest justice in the customary absence of the monarch himself. Provincial
parlements of more recent foundation dispensed royal justice in the outlying
areas of the expanding French monarchy; nevertheless, the original parlement

in the capital maintained its huge jurisdiction over central and northern France and its preeminent status to the end of the *ancien régime*. Over the centuries, the kings had come gradually to use the parlements and certain other sovereign law courts (but above all the Paris Parlement) to register important legislation, thus legitimizing it in the eyes of the kingdom. This tradition became all the more deeply rooted as the Estates General, the only national consultative assembly, failed to take hold in the realm. However, as time went on, the Paris Parlement asserted (and was usually accorded) the right to remonstrate against legislation it regarded as injurious to the king, his subjects, or the unwritten and nebulous constitution of the kingdom. If the parlement persisted in criticizing (and refused to register) the legislation in question, the magistrate-king could return to his primal parlement and, in a splendid and solemn ceremony, reenact the role of the medieval king in his *curia regis* by quashing the judges' resistance and enforcing registration of his legislation. Most of the famous *lits de justice* took place in the Great Chamber of the parlement's Palace of Justice in Paris. The king, seated on a magnificent and cushioned throne or "bed" (whence the term *bed of justice*) and surrounded by the princes of the blood, the lay and ecclesiastical peers, and other glittering personages, had his chancellor or keeper of the seals impose his will ceremoniously on the refractory justices of the parlement. When particularly controversial public issues were involved, the parlement might risk the royal wrath by protesting the *lit de justice* itself in a subsequent parlementary session; ordinarily, however, the assertion of the royal will at a *lit de justice* terminated all formal discussion of the issue or issues in question.

Although *lits de justice* consequently marked times of tension between the crown and the Paris Parlement (and/or other sovereign law courts) from the early fifteenth century, they acquired unprecedented political significance in the 1770s and 1780s because of the weak kingship of Louis XVI, the inspiration of the American Revolution, and the fiscal dilemma of the French government. With the onset of the pre-Revolution of 1787-88, precipitated by Finance Minister C.-A. de Calonne's revelation of the government's bankruptcy to the Assembly of Notables, *lits de justice* staged in the Paris Parlement constituted milestones along the road to Revolution. The crown's insistence at the *lit de justice* of 6 August 1787 on parlementary registration of new taxation affecting all landowners sparked magisterial defiance, which led to the court's exile soon after. A subsequent reconciliation between crown and parlement was shattered by a royal session of 19 November 1787 that resembled a *lit de justice* in that the government used it to extract from the judges hasty ratification of an extension of the traditional taxes. The renewed impasse between the two sides culminated in the dramatic *lits de justice* of 8-10 May 1788, which momentarily compelled all the parlements to register drastic judicial reforms but that ultimately ignited a nationwide revolt against the government. Thus, these final solemn assemblages of king and magistrates helped to articulate critical constitutional and social issues, stimulate discussion and insubordination throughout France, and unleash revolutionary forces. Ironically, the parlements and absolute monarchy would perish together in the cataclysm precipitated in part by their confrontations.

J. Egret, *The French Prerevolution, 1787-1788*, trans. W. Camp (Chicago, 1977); J. H. Shennan, *The Parlement of Paris* (London, 1968); B. Stone, *The Parlement of Paris, 1774-1789* (Chapel Hill, N.C., 1980).

B. Stone

Related entries: ASSEMBLY OF NOTABLES; CALONNE; PARLEMENTS.

LODI, BATTLE OF. See BATTLE OF LODI.

LOGOGRAPHE (1791-92), journal published daily from 27 April 1791 until its suppression by the Legislative Assembly on 18 August 1792. The *Logographe* was owned and directed by the Feuillant leaders A. Barnave, A. Duport, A. de Lameth, and F.-L. Laborde de Méréville. They wanted the journal to become a daily habit for the upper classes. Despite the very high annual subscription rate of 72 *livres*, the *Logographe* was unable to cover its costs and had to be supported by the king's civil list. The journal employed eleven reporters, led by its chief political correspondent, E. Le Hodey. Barnave wanted the paper to avoid advocating particular policies or attacking dissident politicians. He instructed the staff to focus on a dispassionate account of the news. Le Hodey and his assistants admirably followed Barnave's advice. More than two-thirds of every issue was devoted to printing the debates of the national assembly. Le Hodey developed a peculiar shorthand system ("logographic"), which he claimed allowed him to reproduce the sessions more accurately than any other journal. The rest of the paper was devoted to foreign news, letters, book reviews, theater listings, and stock market reports. The *Logographe* was remarkably restrained from attacking Feuillant adversaries. Only in the political crises after the king's abortive flight in June 1791 did the paper include polemical articles (attacking the republican movement) on a regular basis. Curiously, however, no mention of the Feuillant Club was ever printed. In fact, the *Logographe* was mildly supportive of the Roland government and praised its minister of war, J. Servan. In June 1792 the journal even printed a letter by the radical journalist J.-A. Dulaure, which charged that T. de Lameth was about to emigrate to America. Instead of using the occasion to attack Dulaure, it merely printed a short denial by Lameth. Thus the *Logographe* was more of a financial interest established by the Triumvirate than a Feuillant party organ.

G. Michon, *Essai sur le parti Feuillant. Adrien Duport* (Paris, 1924).

G. Kates

Related entries: FEUILLANTS; SERVAN DE GERBEY; TRIUMVIRATE; VARENNES.

LOI AGRAIRE. See PEASANTRY.

LOI LE CHAPELIER. See LE CHAPELIER.

LOMENIE DE BRIENNE, ETIENNE-CHARLES DE (1727-94), archbishop, minister. Born in Paris in 1727, the younger son of an eminent noble family, E.-C. de Loménie de Brienne was designated for a career in the church. He was ordained in 1751 and earned a doctorate in theology a year later. He spent some years in minor posts but, undoubtedly aided by family connections, succeeded in gaining appointment to the prestigious archbishopric of Toulouse in 1763.

As archbishop, he was also automatically a member of the estates of Languedoc and over the years gained a reputation as an effective administrator and ecclesiastical politician with a social conscience. Probably because of his enlightened projects for relief of the poor as well as his philosophic interests generally, A.-R.-J. Turgot, A. Morellet, and J. Le Rond d'Alembert were numbered among his friends and correspondents. Besides his success as an administrator, he was master of the social graces, and his wit, conversational skills, and taste for letters all contributed to his success in the salon and probably his election to the French Academy. He was proposed for archbishop of Paris in 1780, but Louis XVI is reported to have turned him down on the grounds that the archbishop of Paris should at least believe in God. He was a close friend of the queen's *lecteur*, the abbé Vermond, and his name was several times mentioned for ministerial posts. Unfortunately, the devout Louis XVI disliked the man.

In January 1787, however, he was among the prelates named to the First Assembly of Notables. He immediately became a leader of the opposition to the controller general, C.-A. de Calonne, in the Assembly, and when Calonne failed to win the support of the Notables and was dismissed, Louis XVI, after a brief interval and urged by the queen, appointed Loménie to head the Royal Council of Finances. He now found himself forced to adopt and defend Calonne's proposals; he was unsuccessful in gaining approval from either the Notables or the Parlement of Paris when the controversial proposals were presented to it for registration in July. As though to emphasize his determination and support for Loménie, the king raised him to the rank of first minister in August. At about the same time, the Parlement of Paris tried to justify its opposition to the new tax proposals by declaring that any new taxes must have the approval of an Estates General. After an attempt at compromise collapsed, Loménie concluded that the only way to save the monarchy from financial disaster was to deprive the parlement of its traditional right to register all royal acts, including loans.

Typically, he did not attempt to do this directly by a single royal decree. In a series of ordinances offered in May 1788, Loménie proposed a fundamental reorganization of the whole judicial system. While many aspects of the proposed changes were recognized as excellent and much needed, the provision calling for the right of registration to be taken away from the Parlement of Paris and given to a new court (*Cour plenière*) whose members would be chosen directly by the king brought the entire proposal into public disfavor. Loménie and the royal government found themselves confronted by an overwhelming popular protest expressed through resolutions by various judicial and other official bodies, such as municipal officers and assemblies, spontaneous popular assemblies, and individuals expressing their disapproval in the only way they could publicly, through the printed pamphlet. Since the parlements were the chief agents for the enforcement of censorship, those supporting the parlements' cause had nothing to fear. It was this situation that encouraged the flood of pamphlets in the summer of 1788, not the decree of 5 July calling for information on the Estates General as has traditionally been maintained.

Between 8 May and 25 September when the offending May decrees were finally withdrawn, over 500 pamphlets appeared as opposed to only 150 for the whole preceding year. The vast majority were hostile to Loménie's efforts. He tried to stem the tide by issuing the edict of 5 July calling for information about procedures in past Estates Generals, but the implication that a convocation was imminent had little or no effect on popular opinion. Even the definite announcement on 8 August of the convocation of an Estates General for the following May failed to calm the public. Loménie's fall became inevitable a few days later when the treasury was forced to suspend payments on certain royal obligations for lack of cash. A desperate financial crisis was now at hand, and the king was persuaded finally that only the financial wizard J. Necker could save the day. Loménie, however, did not leave in disgrace or empty-handed. A few months earlier, the king had arranged his translation to the more remunerative archbishopric of Sens, and he now promised him a cardinal's hat, as well as valuable posts for some of his relatives.

The archbishop of Sens played no role in the Constituent Assembly but was one of seven bishops who accepted the Civil Constitution of the Clergy—at least until it was formally condemned by the pope. In the fall of 1793, he and other members of his family were arrested as suspects, and he died in confinement under mysterious circumstances in the spring of 1794 (suicide was suspected).

Although for a long time Loménie de Brienne has suffered from the opprobrium of both sides (from the Revolutionaries for having supported the monarchy and from the royalists for having opened the door to popular power by urging the king to call an Estates General), there has recently been an effort to reevaluate the man and his role. Although it is hard to gloss over his weakness and indecision, it should also be recognized that the situation was one of unprecedented difficulty. It has also been stressed that the reform program he attempted to implement would, in the long run, have redressed many wrongs and benefited many people and that even his much-maligned attempt to reduce the power of the parlements would have accomplished some of the goals achieved later by the Revolution. But even while recognizing the potential benefit of the program he sponsored, one can question whether even a beneficial policy of enlightened despotism (which Louis XVI was quite incapable of following) would have satisfied either nobles or commoners.

P. Chevallier, *Journal de l'Assemblée des Notables de 1787 par le Comte de Brienne et Etienne-Charles de Loménie de Brienne, Archevêque de Toulouse* (Paris, 1960); J.

Egret, *La Pré-révolution française* (Paris, 1962); M. B. Garrett, *The Estates General of 1789* (New York, 1935).

R. W. Greenlaw

Related entries: ASSEMBLY OF NOTABLES; CALONNE; NECKER.

LOUIS XVI (1754-93), king of France. Born Louis-Auguste on 23 August 1754, grandson of Louis XV, he became dauphin in 1765 on the deaths of his father and two elder brothers. At sixteen he was married to Marie Antoinette of Austria, who was fifteen, a union planned to bring the ruling houses of France and Austria closer, and in 1774 he was crowned king. It early became obvious that he lacked the necessary preparation, strength of will, and character to deal with disruptive factions in his court. Moreover, he did not possess the breadth of concept and the decisiveness needed to resolve the problems he had inherited and that continued into the 1780s.

The actions of Louis XVI prior to the Revolutionary decade indicate a true willingness to undertake some economic, political, and social reforms, although there appears no real understanding of the intensity of Revolutionary forces in France or the depth of discontent of people below the ranks of the nobility and upper clergy. This duality continued after the meeting of the Estates General in 1789. Characteristic of the king's approach was his speech at the *séance royale* on 23 June, after the Third Estate had declared itself the National Assembly and had taken the Tennis Court Oath.

In his preamble, the paternalistic nature of the monarch was evident when, speaking as "father of my subjects," he told of what "I" wish to do for their well-being and stated that all they have to do is "complete my work." He insisted that the three orders deliberate separately and nullified the independent actions taken less than a week earlier by the Third Estate. He emphasized that the nobility and clergy were to retain their rights and privileges and that the Estates General was to act in an advisory capacity.

Although the concessions, mostly the work of J. Necker who, incidentally, was absent, seemed generous and timely to the monarch, they were resented by the first two orders. To the activists of their time and to those looking backward, they were too little and too late. The items appearing in the speech were familiar by then: no new taxation without representation, no loans contracted except for war emergencies, allowing the Estates General to examine expenditures, strict budgeting, and reform of the system of justice and civil and criminal law. Specific proposals for the French situation included the promise to recognize renunciation of monetary privileges and abolition of the *taille* and *franc-fief*, although other property rights (tithes, *rentes*) and seigneurial rights and duties were to be retained. The Estates General was asked to propose methods of granting titles and nobility, reconciling the abolition of *lettres de cachet* with matters of national security, and reconciling the freedom of the press with the respect due to religion and the morals and honor of the citizenry. Other proposals treated the abolition of the *corvée*, the institution of the militia, the structure of the government, and the transfer of the administration of hospitals, prisons, forests, and other institutions to the provincial estates.

In closing, the king declared that all authority over the military and police was to remain as it had been under his predecessors and reminded his listeners that if they were to abandon him, he would then have to act for his people as their true representative. The concluding note was a warning that the Estates General could only make proposals and that the king's approval was needed to make them law. He dismissed the assembly and commanded it to begin its work as separate orders, thus ignoring the Tennis Court Oath (20 June) and refusing to recognize the Third Estate's claim to be the National Assembly, a decision reached on 17 June.

The fall of the Bastille on 14 July and Louis' acceptance of the Paris revolution began to erode the king's intransigence, and changes earlier resisted, temporized on, or unexpected, began to emerge. The Declaration of the Rights of Man, the adoption of the suspensive veto, the abolition or revision of privileges, serfdom, tithes, and dues, and the placing of church property at the disposal of the state—all in place by the end of 1789—marked the formal beginning of the reduction of royal power. Under mounting political and popular pressure, the royal family moved in October from Versailles to the Tuileries amid the more hostile environment of Paris.

Further erosion occurred in 1790 when noble rank was abolished and the Civil Constitution of the Clergy, along with the civil oath required of the clergy, was enacted. In June 1791 the royal family fled the Tuileries, the king leaving behind a declaration that complained that he had been reduced to a figurehead and found it impossible to govern in the fields of justice, internal administration, the military, foreign affairs, and finances. The capture of the royal entourage at Varennes, its return to Paris, and the suspension of the king by the Assembly reduced the royal family's situation from one of close surveillance to something approaching imprisonment. In September the king accepted the new constitution embodying constitutional monarchy. From that month he was playing for time, evidently hoping either for some miraculous political change internally or for rescue by the friendly ruling houses of Europe, and occasionally showing resolve by exercising the royal veto. On 10 August 1792, the attack on the Tuileries took place. The royal family fled to the Legislative Assembly, from which it was taken to its incarceration in the Temple.

The momentum for a trial of Louis, who once again was suspended as king, had been building up among Revolutionaries in the capital; inevitably such sentiment found its way into the Assembly and, after September, the National Convention. To many, it may have been the institution and not the monarch they would be judging, but the wily G.-J. Danton knew better, believing that if the king were placed on trial he would be doomed.

When the motion to try the king was finally made before the Convention, precipitous action was deemed imprudent, so the matter was referred to a special committee. Several questions of substance and procedure had to be faced, keeping in mind the impact any action might have on the rest of Europe. The possible charges had to be considered. The question of procedure had to be solved: whether the king, as citizen, would be tried by a regular court, or whether extraordinary charges and the person of the offender might warrant a special tribunal, an institution not unknown in French history.

The deputy J.-B. Mailhe, speaking for the special committee, presented its report on 7 November. On the immunity of the monarch, the committee concluded that the old constitutional provision on the inviolability of the monarch was a guarantee of the king's neutrality but that once he had breached it by his personal actions against the nation, this inviolability was forfeited; then he was personally responsible and could be tried. It was recommended that trial be by the Convention rather than by the ordinary courts. On the problem of ensuring fairness, the committee reasoned that because the Convention represented the people, to ignore the principles of justice by which it wished to abide would be suicidal. As for the proposal that the verdict of the Convention should be submitted to the people for ratification, the committee again stated that the Convention was a national body and that the people, not having heard the evidence and deliberated on it, would have been deprived of the opportunity to make a proper judgment in the case. The Convention also heard a speech by L. Saint-Just proposing that Louis be judged as an enemy alien and that he be tried for being a king, which to Saint-Just was the worst crime of all. M. Robespierre claimed that Louis' conspiracy to use armed force against the nation was sufficient to execute him without a trial.

If, from a legal point of view, the reasoning of the committee evaded some of the constitutional issues and seems less than convincing, it was put together cleverly enough to persuade the Convention, which on 3 December decided it was competent to judge the king. Most likely the discovery in the Tuileries in November of the *armoire de fer* that contained incriminating documents dealing with bribery schemes organized by Louis with the help of H.-G. R. Mirabeau, along with correspondence treating royal intrigues with foreign powers, was probably sufficient to push the Convention in the direction of a trial.

The trial began on 11 December. R.-R. Desèze, one of the king's defense attorneys, stressed the theme of inviolability, declaring that abdication seemed to be the most drastic penalty envisaged by the constitution. He also challenged the extraordinary character of the trial and the absence of regular procedure, observing that if Louis' immunity was removed, he still had the rights of a citizen, and that the Convention was acting as both prosecutor and jury. Concluding that there would be neither mitigating votes nor secret deliberations on the verdict, he contended that the Convention had already made up its mind.

B. Barère, for the prosecution, argued that although inviolability was provided for, once the king refused to apply the constitution, that protective cloak was lost. Thus the idea of inviolability and the personal guilt of Louis was submerged by the political need to discredit the monarchy in favor of popular sovereignty. The trial proper ended on 7 January. Beginning on 15 January, three questions were put to a roll call of the Convention. The first was: Is Louis guilty of conspiracy against the nation and of criminal attempts against the general security of the state? Of 745 members, 671 voted guilty, without comment, and 45 voted guilty, with comment. There were absentees but no negative votes. On the question of submitting the judgment to the people, the vote was 424 against and 283 in favor. Here the Girondins, hoping to stem the tide of the Paris Revolutionaries by rousing support in provinces, lost out, and the fortunes of the Jacobins began to rise. On 17 January the third question, that of the penalty, was put to the Convention. Of 721 voting, 387 had voted for the death penalty, but there was a question of a reprieve attached to some 26 of the death penalty votes. Thus the straight death penalty received only 361 votes against the combination of reprieve and negative votes totaling 360, too close a margin to be countenanced politically. It was therefore considered prudent to take another vote on the question of the reprieve. On 20 January, the reprieve was rejected by a vote of 380 to 310, and the execution was set for the following day.

The king, in imprisonment, judgment, and execution, was a figure of dignity. His love for his family comforted them in their captivity, and his deep and devout religious faith fortified him in his personal ordeal. C.-H. Sanson, the ever-present executioner, guillotined Louis XVI on 21 January 1793.

P. Bastid, *Les grands procès politiques de l'histoire* (Paris, 1962); C. Bertin, *Les grands procès de l'histoire de France*, vol. 4 (Paris, 1968); V. Cronin, *Louis and Antoinette* (New York, 1975); B. Fäy, *Louis XVI* (Chicago, 1968); D. Jordan, *The King's Trial* (Berkeley, 1979); C. Manceron, *Twilight of the Old Order*, trans. (New York, 1977); S. K. Padover, *The Life and Death of Louis XVI* (New York, 1963); J. M. Thompson, *The French Revolution* (Oxford, 1966).

R. L. Carol

Related entries: ARMOIRE DE FER; BARERE; BASTILLE, THE; CIVIL CONSTITUTION OF THE CLERGY; DECLARATION OF THE RIGHTS OF MAN AND OF THE CITIZEN; DROUET; GIRONDINS; MARIE ANTOINETTE; NECKER; OCTOBER DAYS; SAINT-JUST; TENNIS COURT OATH; VARENNES.

LOUIS XVII (1785-95), Louis-Charles de France, dauphin of France, declared king as Louis XVII by the comte de Provence after the execution of Louis XVI in January 1793. Louis-Charles of France was born 27 March 1785, the second son and third child of Louis XVI and Marie Antoinette. He started life as the duc de Normandie, a title he retained until he became the dauphin on the death of his elder brother on 4 June 1789. The duchesse de Polignac and the marquise de Tourzel were his governesses and the abbé Davaux his tutor, but it was his father who supervised the education of this lively and intelligent child.

On 6 October 1789, the four-year-old dauphin was in his mother's arms as the royal family faced the mob while standing on the little balcony overlooking the court of marble at the Château of Versailles. He cowered on the floor of the carriage screaming, ''don't kill mama'' as the royal family on the same day departed for the Tuileries Palace in Paris and bade goodbye forever to Versailles. Louis-Charles was disguised as a little girl when the royal family attempted to flee France in June 1791. On the third anniversary of the Tennis Court Oath, 20 June 1792, a red cap was forcibly placed on the head of smiling ''little veto,'' as the citizens of Paris marched through the Tuileries Palace. The popular uprising of August 1792 and the subsequent suspension and imprisonment of the king and members of his family were the culmination of a succession of traumatic experiences for the dauphin.

In their prison, the great tower of the Temple, the former king tutored his young son in history, geography, mathematics, Latin, and other subjects; and before his execution in January 1793, he asked the seven-year-old dauphin and other members of the family to refrain from trying to avenge his death. From Hamm, the comte de Provence, the brother of Louis XVI and now calling himself regent, proclaimed Louis-Charles king as Louis XVII; and the European monarchs, as well as the army of the prince of Condé and other French royalists, recognized him as king of France. Royalist attention centered on the ''Orphan of the Temple,'' and this made him potentially dangerous to the Revolutionary leaders; he became the symbol of the monarchical threat to the Revolution. Royalist plots to free the prisoner angered members of the Committee of General Security, and on 3 July 1793, A. Simon, a shoemaker and member of the Cordeliers club, was made Louis' guardian. The boy was separated from his mother on that date. On 6 October J. Hébert and other members of the Commune visited him, and he was induced to sign a statement in which he described an incestuous relationship with his mother. This and other accusations were used against Marie Antoinette at her trial, leading to her death sentence and execution on 16 October 1793. On 7 October Louis XVII saw his fourteen-year-old sister, Marie-Thérèse (Madame Royale) for the last time. She was released on 19 December 1795 and sent to Vienna.

In January 1794 Simon resigned as guardian, and a few days later Louis was placed in a dark barricaded room and left in complete isolation. He lived the next six months, royalists insist, with bed linen unchanged, body unwashed, minimal food, and with rats and other vermin as company. After a member of the Convention, P. Barras, visited him on 27 July 1794, Louis' situation improved. A new guardian, J. Laurent, came to see him daily. Louis was bathed and examined by a doctor. His cell was cleaned, and new clothes were provided.

In the late fall of 1794 and early spring of 1795, representatives of several foreign powers (Spain, Tuscany, Sardinia) negotiated for Louis' release from the Temple so that he could go into exile, but J.-M. Lequinio, a member of the Convention, demanded that the ''free earth be purged of the last vestige of royalism.'' J.-J. Cambacérès, in the name of the Committee of General Security, warned that ''the expulsion (exile) of tyrants almost always leads to their re-establishment.'' Thus did the Convention sign what amounted to a death decree for the boy whose physical condition was rapidly deteriorating in the spring of 1795. On 6 May Dr. Dessault examined Louis-Charles and diagnosed incurable scrofula; Drs. Pelletan and Dumangin confirmed this diagnosis. Louis died at 2:00 P.M. on 8 June 1795. On 9 June four members of the Committee of General Security came to verify his death; a number of the guards, municipal officials, and others who had known him attested that the deceased was Louis XVII. In the autopsy report, signed by Drs. Pelletan, Dumangin, and Jeanroy, it was stated that he died of infectious and incurable scrofula. On 10 June the body was buried in the cemetery of Sainte-Marguérite, but no marker was provided to identify the site. In 1814, when Louis XVIII ordered a search to be made for the remains, no trace of the body could be found. On the motion of the vicomte de Châteaubriand, the Chamber of Peers and Chamber of Deputies voted to construct a monument in his memory.

Despite overwhelming evidence that it was Louis XVII who died in the Temple, some forty pretenders (one of them black) later insisted that it was a substitute, not Louis, who died in the tower. K. W. Naundorff, the comte de Richemont, M. Bruneau, and J.-M. Hervagault were among the better-known of these claimants to the French throne. The comte de Provence, who declared himself king as Louis XVIII on the death of the ten-year-old Louis in 1795 and became king in fact in 1814, took a dim view of the pretenders; some of them were severely punished.

M. et G. de Béarn, *Louis XVII, ou la couronne du silence* (Paris, 1968); A. Castelot, *Le mystère de Louis XVII* (Paris, 1950); G. Lenôtre [pseud.], *Le roi Louis XVII et l'enigme du temple*, (Paris, 1920).

V. W. Beach

Related entries: CAMBACERES; CONDE; COMMITTEE OF GENERAL SECURITY; FOUQUIER-TINVILLE; HEBERT; LOUIS XVI; MARIE ANTOINETTE; PROVENCE; REVOLUTIONARY TRIBUNAL; 10 AUGUST 1792; TENNIS COURT OATH; VARENNES.

LOUIS-PHILIPPE (1773-1850), duc de Chartres and duc d'Orléans after his father's execution in 1793, prince of the blood, lieutenant general in the French Revolutionary army, *émigré*, and king of the French, 1830-48. Born on 6 October 1773, the eldest son of Louis-Philippe-Joseph, duc d'Orléans, Louis-Philippe received an intensive education emphasizing the liberal principles of the Enlightenment under the direction of his father's mistress, the remarkable comtesse de Genlis. In 1785, when his father became duc d' Orléans, Louis-Philippe as the eldest son assumed the title of duc de Chartres. He grew up in the family residence, the Palais-Royal, in the heart of Paris, and as a teenager met and talked with many of the men who would play leading roles during the Revolution. At the age of twelve, he was appointed colonel of the Fourteenth Regiment of Dragoons, an honor reserved for his family. Military instruction by the comte de Valence prepared him for his brief military career.

Influenced by Madame Genlis and his father, Louis-Philippe became an enthusiastic supporter of the Revolution. In 1790 he joined the Paris Jacobin club, and in June 1791, he left Paris to join his regiment at Vendôme. When France declared war on Austria and Prussia in April 1792, Louis-Philippe was present at the first exchanges of fire at Boussu and Quaraguan. After an engagement with the enemy on 30 April at Quievrain, his commanding officer, the duc de Biron, reported to the war ministry that under fire the duc de Chartres displayed heroism. In May 1792, eighteen-year-old Louis-Philippe was appointed a brigadier general, and on 11 September he was promoted to lieutenant general. At Valmy, on 20 September, Chartres distinguished himself as leader of the second line and was cited in an order of the day by General F.-C. Kellermann. A few weeks later at Jemappes, riding at the head of his men, he overran the Austrian center at a critical point in the battle and made a substantial contribution to the French victory.

Louis-Philippe was a brave and able leader of men on the battlefield, but the Revolution was becoming more radical, and the wealth and rank of his family made it increasingly suspect, despite its liberal leanings. When his fifteen-year-old sister Marie-Adélaïde returned from a leisurely visit to England in November 1792, she was declared an *émigré* and ordered to leave Paris in twenty-four hours and France in three days. The duke's enthusiasm for the National Convention (and the Republic) was rapidly waning, and he urged his father, the duc d'Orléans, to emigrate to America. But Orléans, weak and indecisive, chose to remain in Paris; as a deputy in the Convention he voted for the death of Louis XVI. Chartres, disillusioned and fearful, rejoined the army of General C. Dumouriez. At Neerwinden, he fought heroically in a losing battle, but his association with Dumouriez, who challenged the Convention and was declared a traitor, compromised him. On 5 April 1793, the nineteen-year-old Louis-Philippe and Dumouriez crossed over to the Austrian lines; Chartres' military career was over. He refused to fight against the French and, with his sister, made his way to Switzerland. His desertion was the immediate cause of the National Convention's decree (6 April) ordering the arrest of all the Bourbons still in France, and it was an important factor in turning the Convention against his father, who was tried and executed seven months later.

For a few months Louis-Philippe taught geography and mathematics in Switzerland, but he eventually continued his travels in Denmark, Norway, Sweden, Finland, and the German states. Harassed by the Directory government, he sailed (as a Danish citizen) for the United States and landed in Philadelphia on 21 October 1796. After extensive travel in the United States in the company of his brother, the duc de Montpensier, he decided to go to England and landed at Southampton in January 1800.

He made his peace with the comte d'Artois and the comte de Provence (now styling himself Louis XVIII), but at no time during the twenty-one-year exile did he bear arms against his homeland. In 1809 he married Marie-Amélie, daughter of Ferdinand IV, king of the Two Sicilies, and he returned to France after Napoleon's downfall in 1814. He occupied a seat in the Chamber of Peers, and, while remaining loyal to Louis XVIII and Charles X, entertained the more liberal members of the Chamber of Deputies and made the Palais-Royal a center of attraction for artists and writers. When Charles X abdicated in August 1830, the Chambers invited him to become king as Louis-Philippe I. After waiting in the wings for almost two hundred years, the junior branch of the Bourbons (the descendants of the second son of Louis XIII) would furnish France a king until Louis-Philippe abdicated in February 1848.

M. Castillon du Perron, *Louis-Philippe et la Révolution française*, 2 vols. (Paris, 1963); T. Howarth, *Citizen-King, The Life of Louis-Philippe, King of the French* (London, 1961); Louis-Philippe, *Memoirs, 1773-1793* (New York and London, 1977).

V. W. Beach

Related entries: ARTOIS; BATTLE OF JEMAPPES; BATTLE OF NEERWINDEN; BATTLE OF VALMY; BIRON; DUMOURIEZ; KELLERMANN; ORLEANS; PROVENCE.

LOUSTALOT, ELISEE (1761-90), publicist. Born 25 December 1761 at Saint-Jean d'Angély into a long line of barristers, Loustalot received his legal training at Bordeaux. He practiced law in his home town until 1787 when his overly aggressive prosecution of a lawsuit discredited him in the eyes of the local justices. He then migrated to Paris to become a writer. Like so many other aspirants to literary fame, he found success elusive and resorted to any job available. This marginal existence brought him into contact with L.-M. Prudhomme, a bookseller, who promoted works at and beyond the fringe of respectability. Loustalot joined his stable of writers.

When the Revolution erupted, Prudhomme founded the weekly *Révolutions de Paris*. He set the policy that the publication would support radical politics and intensively cover the local Revolution but hired journalists to perform the daily toil. Prudhomme and his first editor, A. Tournon, could not get along, and after fifteen issues the publisher turned to Loustalot. During the next forty-nine weeks, Loustalot directed the newspaper, achieving great fame for his cogent and incisive critiques. But a sudden infection struck him in early September 1790 and claimed his life on 11 September.

D. d'Aussy, "Elisée Loustalot," *Rev. de la Révo.* 11 (1888); M. Pellet, *Elysée Loustalot et les "Révolutions de Paris"* (Paris, 1872).

J. Censer

Related entries: PRUDHOMME; *REVOLUTIONS DE PARIS*.

LOUTCHISKY, IVAN VASSILIEVICH (1845-1918), Russian historian of agrarian France in the eighteenth century; professor at the University of Kiev. Although both his master's and doctoral theses dealt with the sixteenth century, beginning in the 1880s Loutchisky devoted his work entirely to the study of agrarian relations in France on the eve of the Revolution. He differed from his predecessors, who had considered the official documents of the Estates General the principal source, in that he undertook a meticulous investigation of departmental archives. There he found extremely valuable documents, especially lists of those liable to the *vingtièmes* and the *taille*. Loutchisky exploited these sources, previously unstudied, through the use of statistical methods. He presented his conclusions in two books, *La propriété paysanne en France à la veille de la Révolution, principalement en Limousin* (Paris, 1897, and Kiev, 1900) and *L'état des classes agricoles en France à la veille de la Révolution* (Paris, 1911, and Kiev, 1912).

Loutchisky, who in a number of ways continued the work of A. de Tocqueville, came to the conclusion that property ownership among the small peasantry before the Revolution was much more extensive than previously believed. He also concluded that the peasant *cens* was completely transformed into property only with the Revolution, which dealt the definitive blow to feudal rights. This idea provoked a number of objections, for example, by M. M. Kovalevsky in Russia and M. Marion in France, but eventually was generally accepted.

Loutchisky's work was highly valued in France, particularly by G. Lefebvre. On the occasion of Loutchisky's seventieth birthday, H. Sée published an article in the *Revue scientifique historique* (September, 1914) in which he wrote that without knowing Loutchisky's works, "one cannot presently engage in the social and economic history of the eighteenth century. There is no one who does not realize the importance of this work."

Nevertheless, Loutchisky underestimated the intensity of capitalist development in France on the eve of the Revolution, as well as capitalist differentiation in the countryside. His own social thought was strongly colored by democratic ideas. He was very close to P. Lavrov, the ideologist of Russian populism, and was deeply influenced by his ideas. Loutchisky sympathized with the Paris Commune of 1871; along with F. I. Uspensky, he attended the trial of the *communards*. He did not want to meet F.-A. Aulard because he had expressed a certain disdain for economic history. In 1907 he was elected to the third Duma; at first, he sat with the Cadet party but subsequently broke with it and joined the party of the popular Socialists.

An eminent teacher, as well as scholar, Loutchisky educated a number of gifted disciples, such as E. Tarlé and D. Petrouchevsky.

N. Kareyev, *Historians of the French Revolution*, vol. 3 (in Russian) (Leningrad, 1925); B. Verber, *Historiographical Problems* (in Russian) (Moscow, n.d.).

V. M. Daline

Related entries: CENS; LEFEBVRE; PEASANTRY; *TAILLE*; TARLE; TOCQUEVILLE.

LOUVET DE COUVRAY, JEAN-BAPTISTE (1760-97), writer and politician. Son of a stationer, early employed in a bookshop, Louvet seemed destined for a literary career; indeed he gained his initial fame as the author of a three-part novel, *Les amours de Chevalier Faublas* (1787-89), the heroine of which, Lodoiska, was modeled on his mistress, the wife of a Parisian jeweler. After her divorce, Louvet married his Lodoiska, a union that proved devoted and happy. A second novel, *Emilie de Varmont* (1791), not surprisingly dealt with divorce, a question that also had made its way into Revolutionary politics. Indeed, from the beginning of the Revolution, Louvet's literary efforts, especially his plays, such as *L'anobli conspirateur* (1790), an attack on royalism, and pamphlets, such as *Paris justifié*, an explanation of the *journées* of 5-6 October 1789, were increasingly directed toward Revolutionary ends. Louvet was an enthusiast for the Revolution, initially opposed to despotism and reaction, ultimately to the Montagnards, whom he persisted in believing to be royalist conspirators, and consistently and moderately republican.

Louvet actively entered Revolutionary politics as a *sectionnel* in 1791; he early and loyally attached himself to the Girondist faction. In December 1791, at the head of a deputation from his section, the Lombards, he demanded that the Assembly pass a law against *émigré* princes, a measure consistent with the Girondist policy. Girondists were quick to respond to Louvet's loyalty and to his talents as a writer. He became associated with the partisan journal *Le Sentinelle*, published with funds provided by J.-M. Roland de la Platière through the Ministry of Interior; Louvet also became editor of the *Journal des débats*. Both organs were used to support Girondist politics and politicians and became, by autumn 1792, conspicuous by increasingly immoderate attacks on M. Robespierre in particular and the Montagnards in general. In his partisan activities, Louvet was faithfully supported by his wife.

Elected to the Convention from the Loiret, Louvet carried on his invective against the Mountain; this proved increasingly impolitic, as did his support for an appeal to the people during the trial of Louis XVI. Louvet remained faithfully but indiscreetly partisan while the Girondin position deteriorated in the spring of 1793, and during the 31 May-2 June insurrection, which purged the Convention of leading Girondists, he shared their fortune. Escaping to Caen, Louvet sought unsuccessfully to stir up insurrection in Normandy; from there, he moved to Brittany and on to Guyenne, following the career of a hunted man, wandering the roads of France to avoid capture. After 9 Thermidor, the fall of Robespierre, Louvet returned to Paris, was reseated in the Convention, where he sought to bring to justice those involved in the terrorist drownings, the *noyades de Nantes* (1794), and served in the Committee on the Constitution. He was elected to the Directory's Council of Five Hundred by nineteen departments (he chose to represent Haute-Vienne), though he lost his seat in 1797. He was also elected during the Directory to the Institute (Class: literature; Section: grammar).

As a means of renewing private life, Louvet and Lodoiska opened a bookshop in the Palais Royal, but in the shifting political tides of post-Thermidor Paris, they were to find no peace. Louvet's Revolutionary career and republican enthusiasm were abhorrent to many, and he and his wife were menaced and insulted and their shop was attacked. They moved their business to the faubourg Saint-Germain, where harassment continued and where he died, aged thirty-seven, on 25 August 1797. His Lodoiska, in an act as romantic as any in Louvet's novels, took poison in despair, but survived.

J.-B. Louvet, *Paris justifié contre M. Mounier* (Paris, 1789); J.-B. Louvet de Couvray, *Mémoires* (Paris 1823); J. M. Thompson, "Louvet," in *Leaders of the French Revolution* (London, 1929).

C. A. Le Guin

Related entries: GIRONDINS, MONTAGNARDS; 9 THERMIDOR YEAR II; *NOYADES DE NANTES*; ROBESPIERRE, M.; ROLAND DE LA PLATIERE, J.-M.; THERMIDORIAN REACTION.

LUCKNER, NICOLAS, COMTE DE (1722-94), marshal of France. Born in Cham, Upper Palatinate, as a member of a noble family, Luckner entered the Bavarian army in 1737 and served in the war against the Turks (1737-39). In 1745 he entered the service of the Dutch Republic. During the Seven Years War, he fought in the Hanoverian army and participated in the battle against the French at Rossbach (1757). In 1763 he volunteered his services to France. He received the rank of lieutenant general and in 1778 the title of baron; in 1784 he became a count. He supported the Revolution and became marshal of France in 1791. In the same year, he was made commander of the Army of the Rhine, serving in that capacity until May 1792. The *"Chant de l'armée du Rhin,"* later known as the *"Marseillaise"* was dedicated to him by the composer J.-C. Rouget de Lisle (1760-1836).

In July 1791, as commander of the Army of the North, he invaded Belgium, seizing Courtrai and Menin, but was forced to retreat within a few days. A year later Luckner and the marquis de Lafayette agreed on the *chassé-croisé* plan by which most of the troops were to concentrate along the eastern border. However, it was Lafayette's intention to use his troops to march on Paris and crush the Jacobins, a venture to which Luckner might not have agreed. Luckner was called to Paris to explain and defend his actions before the Legislative Assembly. Cleared of complicity, he was given a brief command of the Army of the Center and then appointed to the nominal position of generalissimo of the Army of the Reserve. He was called to Paris in September 1792 and allowed to retire. Arrested during the Terror in October 1793, he was executed on 4 January 1794. Luckner was a brave and energetic soldier but not very competent. One of his direct descendants was Count F. von Luckner (1881-1966), commander of a German World War I raider.

R. W. Phipps, *The Armies of the First French Republic*, vol. 2 (London, 1929); G. Six, *Dictionnaire des généraux et amiraux français de la Révolution et de l'Empire*, vol. 2 (Paris, 1934).

G. D. Homan

Related entries: LAFAYETTE; *"MARSEILLAISE"*; ROUGET DE LISLE.

LUKIN, NIKOLAI MIHAILOVICH (1885-1940), Soviet historian. Lukin, a teacher's son, studied at Moscow University where he completed his thesis on the fall of the Girondins. A disciple of R. J. Wipper and D. M. Petrushevsky, he was appointed lecturer in history at this university in 1915. He had become a Bolshevik in 1904 and worked for party newspapers in 1917 and 1918 under the pseudonym Antonov. After the October Revolution, he was promoted to professor; in 1929 he became a member of the Soviet Academy of Sciences and in 1932 editor of the historical review *Istorik-marksist*.

His *Maximilien Robespierre* (1919) was the first Russian monograph on the Incorruptible. In 1926 he published a collection of documents, *Le gouvernement révolutionnaire au temps de la Terreur*. While working in Paris archives during the 1920s, he developed a keen appreciation for the research of A. Mathiez and G. Lefebvre. In the 1930s he became the first historian to analyze systematically Lenin's views on the French Revolution.

Lukin became the leader of the Moscow school of historians of the French Revolution, and in 1931 he edited and wrote an introduction to a selection of the best papers of members of this group in *The Class Struggle in France during the Great French Revolution* (in Russian). In 1937 he published the reports of J. M. Simolin, the Russian ambassador to France during the Revolution. He also engaged in discussion of the interpretations of famous historians of the Revolution, such as J. Jaurès, F.-A. Aulard, and P. Kropotkin, among others.

Lukin succeeded in combining a thoroughly scrupulous approach to facts and sources with a genuinely dialectical methodology based on Marxist principles.

V. A. Gavrilichev, *N. M. Lukin: His Role in the Development of Soviet Historiography of the Great French Revolution* (in Russian) (Moscow, 1965); N. M. Lukin, *Selected Works* (in Russian), vol. 1 (Moscow, 1960); A. Z. Manfred, ''Nikolai Mihailovich Lukin'' in *Europe in Modern Times* (in Russian) (Moscow, 1966).

V. M. Daline

Related entries: AULARD; JAURES; LEFEBVRE; MATHIEZ.

LYON, one of the greatest cities of France, center of the silk industry, and major commercial *entrepôt*; rent by bitter local and national divisions throughout the Revolution. On the eve of the Revolution, Lyon was the chief city of the generality and see of the primate of the Gauls, but a capital without provincial estates, a university, or even a parlement. It was an important commercial center, with four annual fairs, and a major banking center. For a long time, these activities had provided it with numerous contacts and made it a focal point for the exchange of ideas. Its manufactures were sold in Spain, Germany, and even Russia. With nearly 200,000 inhabitants, the city was overpopulated, and economic crises flooded Lyon with people seeking work or assistance. The manufacture of silk cloth tended to connect the city with the rural areas around it, in Burgundy and the Auvergne, where it put out weaving; it was tied to the Midi by its need for provisions, to Germany, Italy, and Spain by its trade, and to Switzerland and the Comtat Venaissin by the smuggling of salt, tobacco, and books. A kind of turntable, Lyon was the center of a modest province, whose influence was limited by the nearness of Dijon, Grenoble, and even Bourg.

Severe crises raged periodically through its vast international market, and the absence of precise boundaries was both its strength and its weakness.

Lyonnais society counted few aristocrats but included a numerous and enlightened clergy and, above all, a business middle class that was tied to men of the law and the liberal professions. The lesser nobility of recent date and the upper bourgeoisie mixed easily. This elite shared many currents of thought. Catholicism there was strongly Jansenist, and Protestantism was kept vigorous by the proximity of Geneva, Lausanne, and the Cévennes. Learned societies, literary societies, and academies were numerous and dynamic. In the later eighteenth century, the Lyonnais eagerly welcomed sentimentalism; they had tired of rationalism and allowed themselves to be won over by the mystical Freemasonry of M. de Pasqually, L.-C. de Saint-Martin, and J. B. Willermoz. A new crisis of conscience gripped this society, already shaken by the difficulties of the silk industry, social tensions, and political debates.

The creation of a provincial assembly in 1787 marked the beginning of the pre-Revolution here. The *sénéchaussée* of Lyon took the side of the parlements, which were under attack from the king's ministers, and some officials opposed the creation of the ephemeral *grand bailliage*. During the drawing up of the lists of grievances (*cahiers de doléances*) for the Estates General, communities in the generality complained of the despotism of the chief city and criticized its bourgeois who appropriated land. Beaujolais demanded its autonomy; the same complaints were voiced by villages in the Forez and even in the Lyonnais, and local nobles supported the demands of the Third Estate directed against Lyon.

Despite this, in January 1790 the Constituent Assembly created the department of the Rhône-et-Loire, one of the largest and most populous departments, corresponding to the former generality of Lyon. The three provinces (Lyonnais, Beaujolais, and Forez) wanted to rotate government sessions among the district capitals and multiplied their complaints against what they called the aristocracy of the city of Lyon. The consular bourgeoisie thus found itself isolated, and neither the provost of the guilds (*prévôt des marchands*), L. Tolozan de Montfort, nor the first alderman (*premier échevin*), J.-P. Imbert-Colomès, was elected a deputy of the Third Estate. The silk workers chose D. Monnet, who had been the leader of the opposition to the merchant-manufacturers during the rebellion against the *tarif* (a fixed rate for piecework) in 1786.

Excitement gripped the city from the meeting of the Estates General, and a split occurred between the workers and a bourgeois guard of sorts, composed of some nobles, sons of wholesale merchants, and merchant-manufacturers but also including some of their employees. From July 1789 to July 1790, disturbances broke out several times over the *octrois* (tolls on goods entering the city) in a very strained social and economic climate. The proximity of Switzerland, Turin, and Piedmont, where *émigrés* were assembling, encouraged Imbert-Colomès and some of his friends to make Lyon a stronghold of royalism. An aristocratic club planned to bring Louis XVI to Lyon, but in order to forestall the monarchists, the patriots seized the arsenal in February 1790. Colomès appealed to Swiss troops, failed in this attempt, and had to flee the city. The former *consulat* was replaced in April by moderate bourgeois of a Rolandist (after J.-M. Roland de la Platière) tendency. In July a new uprising against the *octrois* allowed the minister F.-E.-G. Saint-Priest to summon troops to Lyon. The royalist conspiracy developed in Beaujolais, with the complicity of the comte d'Artois, as well as in the Velay, Gévaudan, and Vivarais. An insurrection would permit the king to come to Lyon. The attempted flight of the royal couple to the East, on the proposition of the marquis de Bouillé, put an end to these plans. The Lyonnais conspirators were arrested or forced to flee. Discouragement reigned in the ranks of the counterrevolutionaries.

The electoral system was based on property; ownership allowed the social elite that favored the reforms to carry the election; only a third of those eligible were shopkeepers and artisans; those employed in manufacturing were still excluded; and the body politic remained in the image of Old Regime society. Tensions were further aggravated by the religious policy of the Constituent Assembly. The Civil Constitution of the Clergy aroused the opposition not only of the canons of Lyon and the archbishop, who emigrated, but also of popular elements. During all of 1792, the church of Saint-Nizier was the scene for confrontations between refractory priests, supported by their faithful, and members of the sections and the Jacobins. Meanwhile, the Revolution was accepted by all the dominant groups of Lyon; thanks to Roland, who had entered the ministry, and to Madame Roland, the Egeria of the Brissotins, Girondin influence won over many notables on the municipal and departmental councils. Both merchants and workers hoped for economic recovery, the reopening of European markets to Lyonnais fabrics, and the establishment of a constitutional monarchy. Soon the monarchists became concerned by Girondin successes, while the issuing of *assignats* frightened the notables. In turn, the violent and daring language of newspapers, songs, and the theater, as well as the propaganda of M.-J. Chalier, disturbed the Girondins.

After the king's death, the political balance was modified somewhat, but in Lyon the same citizens continued to dominate the new bodies; the mayor, L. Vitet, as well as the principal municipal officials and the judges of the district tribunal, were all Girondin moderates. After the establishment of universal male suffrage, the sections, which corresponded to the different neighborhoods and were sometimes affiliated with the Jacobin club, intensified their activity. In the section assemblies, moderate republicans retained the majority, a peculiar Lyonnais phenomenon. In November 1792 the merchant A. Nivière-Chol, a Girondin, was elected mayor; but his rival, Chalier, who was devoted to the Montagnard ideal, became the idol of a minority of workers. In a climate of agitation, the mayor resigned twice. Several moderate sections attacked the Temple of Liberty and tried to destroy the Liberty Tree. These excesses and the foreign situation favored Jacobin propaganda; Chalier was elected president of the district tribunal, and a friend of his became mayor. The majority of the sections and the General Council of the department, however, opposed the policy of the Montagnards.

Alarmed, the moderates of every tendency mobilized; on 29 May 1793, at the very time when the Parisian Montagnards were indicting the Girondins, Lyonnais moderates, who retained control of the military forces and took advantage of significant popular support, arrested the Jacobin leaders, imprisoned Chalier, and announced the dissolution of the municipal government. While proclaiming its devotion to the Republic, Lyon entered into rebellion against the National Convention.

From June to August, the men who controlled Lyon sought, in vain, to reassure the envoys of the Convention who feared the spread of such federalist revolts. In June the entire southeast, hostile to the dominance of Paris, sent its congratulations and offered its services to the Lyonnais. In Lyon, Jacobins were massacred, Chalier was executed, and the defense of the city was organized. Soon the situation became delicate, and some moderates, frightened by their own boldness, drew back. The army of Lyon was forced to accept any and all recruits and to entrust command to the comte de Précy, a former colonel of the Royal Guard. Without doubt, some laborers, silk workers, and servants participated in the rebellion, but the Lyonnais front against Paris and the Mountain was not homogeneous. Lyon appeared to be the seat of a new monarchist conspiracy, for even though the revolt was of Girondin inspiration, the defense of Lyon, from 8 August to 9 October 1793, was in fact directed by royalists.

From the second half of July the armed forces of the Convention, under the command of F.-C. Kellermann, encircled the city; later the shelling demoralized the inhabitants. At the beginning of October, the authorities handed over the city, while Précy's army tried to flee to Switzerland. When the army of the Convention entered Lyon, the population was debilitated. The department of the Rhône-et-Loire was dismembered; the districts of Saint-Etienne, Roanne, and Montbrison formed the department of the Loire. The punishment was pitiless. On 12 October the Convention proclaimed, "Lyon made war on Liberty; Lyon is no more." The city was to be destroyed and a new city established under the name Commune-Affranchie.

G.-A. Couthon symbolically broke the "arrogant facades" of the place Bellecour, while the Revolutionary Tribunal began reprisals. J.-M. Collot d'Herbois and J. Fouché set the Red Terror in motion in November 1793; suspects were executed with grape-shot by the hundreds in the plain of Brotteaux. There were more than 2,000 victims, mostly from the popular classes. Even the Jacobins were shocked by the spirit of the Revolutionary army that undertook the repression. This violence left a lasting impression on the collective memory of the Lyonnais and strengthened their anticentralist tendencies. The surrounding provinces and the battered city would welcome 9 Thermidor as a deliverance.

The representatives on mission could not continue a repression that was antagonizing the entire population and risking a rebirth of counterrevolutionary tendencies. In August 1794 the popular society was dissolved. It became necessary to strike a balance between Jacobin tendencies, which were marked by social demands, and an active counterrevolutionary minority that dared not show itself openly. During the winter of 1795, when misery was at its height, a White Terror broke out. The sons of merchants, of military men, and even some *émigrés* formed networks, and assassinations became more and more numerous. These *muscadins*, perhaps brought together in the Company of Jesus, who were helped by refractory priests and deserters from the Army of Italy, avenged the shootings of Brotteaux. In May 1795 they started a massacre in the prisons; the victims were the *Mathevons*, the Jacobin collaborators of Chalier. The aldermen of 1789 and the officers of Précy's army then prepared public opinion for a monarchist restoration in favor of Louis XVII. On the youth's death, many Lyonnais went into mourning.

Disturbed by all this, the Convention suspended the administrators of Lyon and new representatives on mission put an end to the White Terror in July 1795. Lyon was then in a dramatic state of ruin and misery. Everything converged to aggravate the crisis under the Directory; peasants refused to deliver grain that would be paid for in *assignats*, and insecurity became endemic. The celebrated affair of the courier of Lyon was an example of the frequency of brigandage. A courier, entrusted with 7 million *livres* in *assignats* earmarked for the Army of Italy, was attacked in the Seine-et-Marne on 27 April 1796, and the subsequent trial resulted in a miscarriage of justice.

The Lyonnais were tired of a Republic incapable of repressing violence and of restoring business. Apathy reigned, and notables regained political positions; for example, Imbert-Colomès and C. Jordan were elected deputies for the department of the Rhône in 1796 but were purged in September 1797. The political struggles of the Directory, the intrigues of royalist agents, the permanence of troubles explain the ease with which the coup d'état of Brumaire was accepted by this spiritless city, rent by Revolutionary commotions.

R. Cobb, *L'Armée révolutionnaire parisienne à Lyon (frimaire-prairial An II)* (Lyon, 1952) and "La Commission temporaire de Commune-Affranchie," *Cah. d'hist.* (1957); M. Fridieff, *Les origines du réferendum dans la Constitution de 1793* (Paris, 1931); R. Fuoc, *La réaction thermidorienne à Lyon (1795)* (Lyon, 1957); J. P. Gross, *Saint-Just: Sa politique et ses missions* (Paris, 1976); E. Herriot, *Lyon n'est plus*, 4 vols. (Paris, 1937-40); A. Latreille, *Histoire de Lyon et du Lyonnais* (Toulouse, 1975); C. Riffaterre, *Le mouvement anti-jacobin et anti-parisien à Lyon* (Lyon, 1928); L. Trenard, *Lyon de l'encyclopédie au préromantisme*, 2 vols. (Paris, 1958); E. Vingtrinier, *La Contre-Révolution, 1789-1791* (Paris, 1924).

L. Trenard

Related entries: ARMEES REVOLUTIONNAIRES; ARTOIS; BOUILLE; CIVIL CONSTITUTION OF THE CLERGY; COMPANIES OF JESUS; COUNTER-REVOLUTION; *EMIGRES*; FEDERALISM; GIRONDINS; *MUSCADINS*; 9 THERMIDOR YEAR II; PARLEMENTS; PROVINCIAL ASSEMBLIES; WHITE TERROR.

M

MABLY, GABRIEL-BONNOT, ABBE DE (1709-85), *philosophe*. The abbé de Mably, one of the minor *philosophes* of the pre-Revolutionary period, was born at Grenoble on 14 March 1709. The abbé de Condillac, who became the foremost French exponent of the sensationalist psychology, was a brother, and the Mably family was allied with the family of Madame de Tencin and the cardinal de Tencin. It was because of these connections that Mably, after finishing his studies at the collège de Lyon, came to Paris and completed his education at the seminary of Saint-Sulpice. He entered the clergy and retained for the rest of his life the title of abbé, but he never advanced beyond the subdiaconate.

Mably's career began in the world of Madame de Tencin's salon in Paris and continued in the world of diplomacy. When cardinal de Tencin entered the ministry of Louis XV, Mably became his private secretary. During this period he drafted state documents, played a prominent role in diplomatic negotiations in the 1740s, and published a collection of international treaties in 1748.

By this time, however, he had broken with the cardinal and had retired from public life. He declined nomination to the French Academy when his writings later made this honor seem appropriate to his friends and devoted the rest of his years until his death on 23 April 1785 to a simple life of study, reflection, and writing.

His classical education had set the tone and provided the themes for much of his work. The austere morality preached by the Greek and Roman authors to which he had been introduced at school, and the simplicity of the Sparta of Lycurgus as described by Plutarch were constantly on his mind as he wrote in book after book on the necessary relationship between morality and politics and the ideal of the Spartan way of life.

His writings, which made up fifteen volumes in his collected works, included studies in diplomatic history, observations on Greek and Roman history, the history of France, the writing of history, observations on the constitutions of the newly established American states, and recommendations for reorganizing the government of Poland.

In 1763 he published what was to become his most frequently republished and quoted work. The *Entretiens de Phocion sur le rapport de la morale avec la politique*, presented as newly discovered dialogues dating from the period of Athenian decline, is probably his best work, setting forth his basic thesis that the happiness of mankind must be based on public morality rather than on the advance of enlightenment and civilization.

In 1776 appeared his *De la législation ou principes des lois*, which developed in detail his radical ideas concerning equality. Natural law, he wrote, requires equality, which necessarily includes economic equality. Private property in land, which Lycurgus had been wise to abolish in Sparta, has led to a decline in happiness, for happiness does not come from riches. This attack on private property is the basis for the traditional listing—not quite logically—of Mably, along with A. Morellet, as one of the pioneer exponents of communism. But today, Mably wrote, there is no hope of achieving this equality, except perhaps in America or Africa. One can and should, however, by legal reforms restrain avarice and restrict the advance of commerce and luxury. This is a familiar theme in Mably's writings.

His most important work to be considered in relation to his supposed influence on the French Revolution was his *Des droits et devoirs du citoyen*, written in 1758 during the continuing conflict between the parlements and the king. Here, as in his writings on French history, he voiced harsh criticism of royal despotism and asserted the right to resist oppression. But instead of siding with the parlements, he advocated reviving the Estates General, which should draft a fundamental law for, in effect, a limited, constitutional monarchy, which should also pass laws designed to guarantee the greatest possible equality.

This work, which was to become so pertinent a generation later, reappeared in three separate editions in 1789 and in his collected works published the same year. He had the glory of predicting and accelerating the Revolution, proclaimed a writer in the *Moniteur* in 1790. He was quoted in the legislature but not as often as the other *philosophes*. Commentaries on his principles were published. His collected works appeared again in 1793, in the Year III and the Year V. L. Saint-Just possessed a copy of one of Mably's works at the time of his execution, and M. Robespierre's small library contained at the time of his overthrow a copy of the *Droits et devoirs du citoyen*. While Robespierre never cited Mably in his speeches, he had spoken in Mablyian terms of the extremes of poverty as a cause of social ills and crimes. His project for the Cult of the Supreme Being parallels in important respects Mably's ideas concerning the need for a public cult. G. Babeuf had read Mably on the evils of private property and cited Mably in his defense at his trial in 1797.

During the Thermidorian Reaction, his friends and executors formally requested that Mably be awarded the honors of the Pantheon, which had been accorded F.-M. Voltaire and J.-J. Rousseau, and a motion for this was made in the Convention, but nothing came of it.

Collection complète des oeuvres de l'abbé de Mably (Paris, 1794-95), 15 vols., especially "Elogie historique de l'abbé de Mably," l'abbé Brizard, vol. 1; "Mably," *Biographie universelle (Michaud) ancienne et moderne*, vol. 25; H. Sée, *L'évolution de la pensée politique en France au XVIIIe siècle* (Paris, 1925).

G. H. McNeil

Related entries: BABEUF; CONSPIRACY OF EQUALS; CULT OF THE SUPREME BEING; ENLIGHTENMENT.

MACDONALD, JACQUES-ETIENNE-JOSEPH-ALEXANDRE (1765-1840), duke of Tarentum, general, and marshal of the empire. Born of a noble Scottish immigrant family on 17 November 1765, Macdonald received an aristocratic education. At the age of nineteen, he entered the *Légion de Moillebois* with the rank of second lieutenant. After serving in Holland (1785), he returned to France and joined the Dillon (Irish) Regiment. Despite his aristocratic origin, Macdonald remained in France and in the army when the nation was torn by revolution. He served as *aide-de-camp* to Generals P.-P. Beurnonville and C. Dumouriez and fought at Jemappes. Promotions came rapidly, and by the end of the summer of 1793, he held the rank of brigadier general. Following the Battle of Hondschoote, he was promoted to general of division (1794). Between 1795 and 1798, he served in Holland and with the armies of the Sambre-et-Meuse and the North. The next two years were spent in Italy. He was first governor of Rome and then, following the formation of the Second Coalition, commander of the Army of Naples. He won the Battle of Modena, then was defeated at Trebbia, and finally was forced to evacuate Italy.

General Macdonald joined the Army of the Rhine late in 1799 as General J.-V. Moreau's second in command, a position he still held at the end of the war of the Second Coalition. Four years later, he spoke out in Moreau's defense when the latter was accused of conspiracy. As a result of this loyalty to his former superior, Macdonald spent the next three years out of the emperor's favor. He was not employed by Napoleon in the campaigns of 1805, 1806-7 or in the Spanish expedition of 1808. By 1809, however, he commanded a corps under Prince Eugène in Italy. When the Army of Italy took the field at Wagram, Macdonald fought under the eyes of the emperor. It was his corps that broke the Austrian center and led to the French victory. A grateful Napoleon gave him a marshal's baton on the battlefield (12 July 1809). Other honors and rewards followed quickly: the Legion of Honor, a large annuity from Italian lands, and the title of duke of Tarentum.

His brief service in Spain in 1811 was uneventful, and the following year he commanded the Tenth Corps of the Grand Army, which invaded Russia. Macdonald's corps formed the extreme left wing of the French army. It advanced in the direction of St. Petersburg as far as Riga. After an unsuccessful siege, the Tenth Corps joined the retreating army as the Russian campaign turned into a disaster. He commanded the Eleventh Corps in the campaign of 1813. He fought at Merseburg, Bischofswerda, and Bautzen before he was defeated by General G. L. von Blücher in Silesia and later served at Leipzig. He was active in the campaign of 1814. Together with Marshals M. Ney and A.-F.-L.-V. Marmont he negotiated the abdication of Napoleon in April and took service with Louis XVIII. During the Hundred Days Macdonald retired to his estate and remained inactive. After serving the Bourbons during the Restoration, he supported the Orléans monarchy of Louis-Philippe until his death in 1840.

L. Chardigny, *Les maréchaux de Napoléon* (Paris, 1946); J.-E.-J.-A. Macdonald, *Souvenirs* (Paris, 1892); R. W. Phipps, *The Armies of the First French Republic and the Rise of the Marshals of Napoleon I*, vol. 5 (Oxford, 1935-39); G. Six, *Les généraux de la Révolution et de l'Empire* (Paris, 1947).

J. G. Gallaher

Related entries: BATTLE OF HONDSCHOOTE; BATTLE OF JEMAPPES; DUMOURIEZ; MOREAU; SECOND COALITION.

MAILLARD, STANISLAS-MARIE (1763-94), Parisian political figure, crowd leader, best known for his participation in the taking of the Bastille, the women's march to Versailles, and the September 1792 Massacres. Maillard was a discharged soldier from a small town in Normandy who served for a time as a court attendant in Paris but never really established himself in a stable occupation. He was brave and decisive enough, and his intelligence and oratorical gifts were such that he was able to step forward among the leaders in popular uprisings. There is an engraving of Maillard's crossing of a plank held by his comrades over the Bastille moat to accept the terms of surrender from a crack in the still-closed drawbridge. It is known that one man had fallen in the attempt; whether Maillard was the one who succeeded is uncertain, but he did become known as the hero of the occasion and he was one of those who arrested B. de Launey, the commander of the fortress. It was Maillard who drew up one of the still extant lists of *Vainqueurs de la Bastille* approved by the Constituent Assembly.

As the October Days began—it was the morning of the fifth—Maillard was in the streets at the head of a detachment of Bastille Volunteers. The occasion was to be one in which bread and politics, spontaneity and conscious leadership were mixed, as Parisian demonstrators invaded the Hôtel de Ville, threatened the city authorities, and then marched to Versailles. At first there were crowds dominated by women; later there were Parisian National Guards, only with difficulty controlled by the marquis de Lafayette, and increasing numbers of hangers-on. In these confrontations at the Hôtel de Ville and later at Versailles, Maillard was highly visible. He helped restore order at the Hôtel de Ville and, whether to that end or from political motives, he led the women's march to Versailles, where he acted as their spokesman when they invaded the National Assembly. We have it from A. Barnave that he spoke crudely and emotionally but seemed sincere in demanding bread for Paris, apologies from the king's bodyguard for insulting the tricolor, abolition of aristocratic distinctions, and liberty for the nation. Others report that he demanded removal of the Flanders Regiment from the Paris region. After a delegation of women had visited the king and been promised food deliveries, Maillard returned to Paris with the delegates in carriages provided by the court. He was therefore not a participant in the disorders of that night or the royal procession to the city the next day. It is clear that his reputation won in July had been enhanced by the October Days, but his understanding of the political manipulations on that occasion is less easy to determine. The Revolution was to provide many such cases of neighborhood leaders whose influences on crowd behavior seconded the policies of higher-ups.

Maillard's availability was continuous after 1789 and he seems to have enjoyed minor celebrity in the cafés. J.-P. Marat once accused him of serving the moderate Lafayette faction but later recanted. J. Michelet found Maillard among the signers of the Champ de Mars petition. During the September Massacres in 1792, Maillard was sent by the Paris Commune's Committee of Surveillance to set up a tribunal at the Abbaye prison at Saint-Germain-des-Près, where priests and other suspects were being killed by uncontrolled crowds. When Maillard arrived, he improvised a people's court, interrogated the remaining prisoners one by one, and while delivering more than half of them to the volunteer executioners, saved the lives of the rest. His actions gave a semblance of legality to an atrocity, but as in the case of the women's march in 1789, Maillard was to some extent tempering a bad situation, although again his motives and his place in the network of political relationships remain obscure.

During the National Convention period, Maillard continued to be a minor political figure associated with leaders of the *sans-culottes*. He was employed briefly for police work by the Committee of General Security, but during the Terror he was attacked along with the so-called ultra-revolutionaries during their struggle with the Dantonists. He was accused of swindling and brutality, charges he denied. He was twice arrested and twice freed (October-November 1793 and December-February 1793-94), but by this time he was ill with tuberculosis. He escaped the purge of the Hébertists but died in mid-April 1794.

P. Caron, "Indications biographiques," *Révo. française* 85-86 (1932-33); J. Egret, *La Révolution des notables. Mounier et les monarchiens. 1789* (Paris, 1950); G. Rudé, *The Crowd in the French Revolution* (Oxford, 1959); A. Sorel, *Stanislas Maillard, l'homme du 2 septembre 1792* (Paris, 1862); G. Walter, "Maillard (Stanislas-Marie)," in "Personnages," *Michelet, Histoire de la Révolution française*, ed. G. Walter, vol. 2 (Paris, 1952).

P. H. Beik

Related entries: BASTILLE, THE; FLANDERS REGIMENT; LAUNEY; INDULGENTS; OCTOBER DAYS; PRISONS; SEPTEMBER 1792 MASSACRES.

MAINMORTE. See SERFDOM.

MAINZ, REPUBLIC OF. See REPUBLIC OF MAYENCE.

MALESHERBES, CHRETIEN-GUILLAUME DE LAMOIGNON DE (1721-94), magistrate and ex-minister.

Born into an ancient noble family with a distinguished lineage of judicial service in the Parlement of Paris, Malesherbes was the son of G. de Lamoignon de Blancmesnil (1683-1772), chancellor of France from 1750 to 1768. He was educated at the Jesuit collège of Louis-le-Grand and by the prominent Jansenist magistrate R. Pucelle. In 1749 he married M.-F. Grimod de la Reynière, daughter of a farmer general. Before her suicide in 1771, they had two daughters, Antoinette-Thérèse-Marguérite (1756-94), who was guillotined with her father, and Françoise-Pauline de Montboissier (1758-1827), who emigrated during the Revolution. One granddaughter married the brother of F.-R. Chateaubriand and another was the mother of A. de Tocqueville.

Malesherbes began his public career in 1741 as deputy to the eminent *procureur général*, G.-F. Joly de Fleury, and joined the parlement as a magistrate three years later. He subsequently succeeded his father as First President of the *cour des aides* (1750-75), the court with jurisdiction over cases involving tax matters, and served concurrently as director of the book trade (1750-63). In the latter capacity, Malesherbes conscientiously supervised royal censorship operations during a critical period in the history of the French Enlightenment. Although he protected D. Diderot's *Encyclopédie* and played an instrumental role in the publication of J.-J. Rousseau's *Emile*, he was not consistently partial to the *philosophes* in discharging his duties. While advocating liberalization in his memoirs of 1758 (published in 1809) on the administration of the book trade, he also supported restrictions against immoral, libelous, irreligious, and seditious works.

Under Malesherbes' leadership, the *cour des aides* joined the parlement in resisting royal tax legislation. Since he opposed the abolition of judicial venality, Malesherbes condemned Chancellor R.-N. Maupeou's suppression of the parlement as an act of ministerial despotism and called for the convocation of the Estates General in his defiant remonstrances of 18 February 1771. The *cour des aides* was subsequently suppressed, and Malesherbes spent the next three years in exile from the capital at his country estate. After Louis XVI reestablished the courts on his accession to the throne, Malesherbes drafted the monumental remonstrances of 6 May 1775, denouncing injustices in the system of tax collection as symptomatic of the maladministration of the kingdom. He urged the new monarch to protect citizens against arbitrary abuses of authority and to restore national confidence in the crown by summoning the Estates General.

At the request of Louis XVI, Malesherbes relinquished his judicial office and reluctantly accepted the position of secretary of state for the king's household in the Turgot ministry in July 1775. During his ten months at court, he concerned himself with such problems as the reduction of royal expenditures, the restriction of *lettres de cachet*, and the toleration of Protestants. In the decade following his resignation in May 1776, he composed a number of memoirs on the last of these questions, most notably the works on Protestant marriages written in 1785-86 (published in 1787). Returning to the royal council without portfolio in 1787 during the Loménie de Brienne ministry, Malesherbes collaborated with the

Protestant spokesman J.-P. Rabaut Saint-Etienne and other partisans of toleration. He was the principal architect of the edict of 17 November, which assured the civil status of non-Catholics without granting them freedom of worship, although Malesherbes himself was inclined to concede more extensive liberty. He left the government in August 1788 without completing his work on the condition of French Jews.

Although Malesherbes played no public role in the Revolution until his involvement in the trial of Louis XVI, he recorded his reflections on a number of topical subjects in the years 1788-89. In the "Memoir on the Present State of Affairs" submitted to the king shortly before his resignation, he criticized the recent suppression of the parlement effected by his cousin, the keeper of the seals, C.-F. Lamoignon, but he now renounced the doctrine of intermediary bodies, which he had invoked in the remonstrances of the *cour des aides*. Elaborating on a proposal formulated after his first term in the ministry, Malesherbes called for a representative national assembly to replace the traditional Estates General and supported the doubling of the Third Estate, as well as the vote by head rather than by order. Recommending the adoption of a constitution to guarantee the rights of citizens and ensure consent to taxation, he contended that royal authority derived from the nation and not from divine right. As a confirmed monarchist, however, he later opposed constitutional provisions that deprived the king of political independence of the assembly.

In another memoir of 1788 (published in 1809), he advocated almost unlimited liberty of the press in order to promote the enlightenment of the public and its representatives. Countenancing anonymous writings as a means of exposing abuses, he now made prior censorship voluntary and retained strict sanctions only against defamatory and licentious works. Malesherbes also drafted memoirs against the misuse of *lettres de cachet* and the penalty of *dérogeance* inflicted on nobles who engaged in trade. Soon disillusioned with the course of events in Paris, he spent most of his time during the Revolutionary years in the country, where he pursued his lifelong interest in natural history and composed several volumes on botany and agronomy.

Unwavering in his loyalty to the crown, Malesherbes wrote to the president of the Convention on 11 December 1792 to offer his services in Louis XVI's impending trial. For the next month, he visited the royal prisoner daily in the Temple. He worked with the king's other lawyers, F.-D. Tronchet and R. de Sèze, on the defense that the latter presented on 26 December, and it was he who informed Louis XVI of the Convention's sentence on 17 January. Malesherbes himself was arrested at his estate a year later, on 20 December 1793, over the protests of the local population. Condemned by the Revolutionary Tribunal for alleged counterrevolutionary offenses (conspiring with *émigrés* for the restoration of the *ancien régime* and conniving with W. Pitt in the defense of Louis XVI), he was executed, along with members of his family, on 22 April 1794.

J. M. S. Allison, *Lamoignon de Malesherbes, Defender of the French Monarchy, 1721-*

1794 (New Haven, 1938); P. Grosclaude, *Malesherbes témoin et interprète de son temps* (Paris, 1961); D. P. Jordan, *The King's Trial: The French Revolution vs. Louis XVI* (Berkeley, 1979); G. A. Kelly, "The Political Thought of Lamoignon de Malesherbes," *Pol. Theo.* 7 (1979) and *Victims, Authority, and Terror: The Parallel Deaths of d'Orléans, Custine, Bailly, and Malesherbes* (Chapel Hill, 1982).

J. Merrick

Related entries: DIDEROT; *ENCYCLOPEDIE*; ENLIGHTENMENT; *LETTRE DE CACHET*; LOMENIE DE BRIENNE; LOUIS XVI; RABAUT SAINT-ETIENNE; TRONCHET.

MALLET DU PAN, JACQUES (1749-1800), Swiss journalist, witness, and participant-historian of the French Revolution. As author of the political section of the weekly *Mercure de France*, Mallet du Pan—the *du Pan* was his mother's family name—worked in Paris from 1784 to 1792. A citizen of Geneva, son of a Protestant pastor, Mallet had been a protégé of F.-M. Voltaire and had contributed to S.-N.-H. Linguet's publications before joining the *Mercure*. In the 1780s he became known as a critic of the Enlightenment, although he always claimed to distinguish between scientific thinking and radical simplifications. Mallet admired A. Smith, was skeptical of physiocracy, praised J. Adams but was cool toward the American Revolution. In January 1789, he published a long and favorable review of J.-L. Delolme's *Constitution de l'Angleterre*. Notwithstanding his success, Mallet remained an outsider who was critical of the French national character. Pessimistic about French prospects on the eve of the Revolution, he was appalled by its outbreak; yet despite his posture as an impartial Swiss republican, he in fact supported the Revolution's early Anglophile phase and formed lasting friendships with J.-J. Mounier, P.-V. Malouet, and a few others who shared his belief in the balancing of crown, aristocracy, and influential commoners against each other and together against the weight of the whole people. This Revolutionary strategy, which called for two legislative chambers and an absolute royal veto, was to become the basis for later counterrevolutionary efforts by Mallet and his friends.

After the defeat of the Anglophile program in 1789, Mallet du Pan came to see the Revolution as a loss of equilibrium and a resulting unregulated struggle of factions, whose appeals for popular support were leading to political and social leveling that menaced all of Europe. By April 1792 when, shortly before the declaration of war, he wrote his last article for the *Mercure*, he was thinking in terms of a combined French and European solution to the crisis. Circumstances very soon involved him in the search for such a remedy. Just as Mallet's position in Revolutionary Paris was becoming untenable, Louis XVI's advisers used the journalist's return to Geneva as cover for a secret mission to the king's *émigré* brothers and the Hapsburg and Hohenzollern rulers. It was hoped that the war would smother the Revolution, but to this end it was essential that the behavior of the great powers be kept from looking like an international counterrevolutionary crusade sponsored by the French royal family. Mallet was to explain this point of view, and he did so, leaving Paris on 21 May and concluding his interviews on 18 July 1792, after delivering to the Austrian and Prussian monarchs a memorandum he apparently thought would contribute to a moderate settlement. He seems never to have doubted that Louis XVI's intentions were similar to his own. Stronger forces prevailed at the French court and in the emigration, and the outcome was the Brunswick Manifesto of 25 July 1792.

Thereafter French military successes forced Mallet and his family to retreat from Geneva to Lausanne and finally, in the fall of 1793, to Berne, where for the next four years he conducted a confidential information service on French affairs subsidized by various European courts. This intelligence gathering was based on contacts in France and abroad and involved not only reporting to his sponsors but also, by his own choice, explaining the Revolution to them and pointing out their mistakes. Periodically he also tried to influence events with pamphlets aimed at the literate public. It had indeed been such a pamphlet, his *Considérations sur la nature de la Révolution de France et sur les causes qui en prolongent la durée* (London and Brussels, 1793), that had attracted wide attention and helped launch his career as an agent and self-appointed mentor of the counterrevolution. Although these activities were Mallet's livelihood, they were also his vocation; he was by nature a moralist and social critic, saw himself as a witness to history, and aspired to literary excellence beyond the demands of the moment. Mallet's activities finally cost him his refuge in Berne, from which he was driven in 1797 by pressure from the French government and its rising star, General N. Bonaparte, for supporting royalist maneuvers within France—those that occasioned the Directory's coup of 18 Fructidor (4 September 1797). From 1798 until his death, Mallet lived in England, where he published the *Mercure britannique* along lines similar to those of the *Mercure de France*.

Mallet du Pan's secret reports about the French Revolution, amounting to almost week-by-week commentaries, remained for half a century unknown to the European public, until collections of his papers began to appear. Mallet's appeals to contemporaries, apart from the two *Mercures*, were hasty responses to particular crises. None was as successful as the *Considérations*, but all bore Mallet's trademark of extravagant language, disdain for positions to the right or left of his own, and occasional brilliant passages of analysis. One example is the *Correspondance politique pour servir à l'histoire du républicanisme français* (Hamburg, 1796), a fragment of a projected major work, rushed into print as a warning against complacency in the Directory era. Mallet's return to journalism after his expulsion from Berne and move to England produced the thirty-six numbers of the *Mercure britannique*, a monumental one-man performance. Also published in English translation, the *Mercure britannique* was less violent in tone than the pamphlets and more contemplative than the secret reports. Mallet was in poor health, but his powers of imagination and analysis were as strong as ever. It fell to him to write the obituary of the Switzerland he had known, to sum up his views on the Enlightenment, and finally to interpret Bonapartism, which he denounced as a falsification of representative government while acknowledging Napoleon's extraordinary ability, not least in the field of counter-revolutionary pacification.

Mallet remained loyal to Louis XVIII although he considered the king's prospects poor and his cause badly served by reactionary advisers. Mallet's own counterrevolution, at one with his basic conception of the Revolution, had always been extremely demanding of patience and conciliation in the defining of ends, even though he had sought force as a means. He had only occasionally weakened in his pursuit of this ideal.

Mallet's aims anticipated the Restoration era. What is perhaps more interesting is that Mallet's position was basically nonrevolutionary and amounted to an effort, first to avoid, then to defeat, the Revolutionary process. His notations concerning men and events were to be prospected by many historians, and his appreciation of social forces and ideological currents was to influence interpretations as dissimilar as those of H.-A. Taine and G. Lefebvre.

F. Acomb, *Mallet Du Pan (1749-1800): A Career in Political Journalism* (Durham, N.C., 1973); *Correspondance inédite de Mallet du Pan avec la Cour de Vienne (1794-1798), publieé d'après les manuscrits conservés aux Archives de Vienne par André Michel*, 2 vols. (Paris, 1884); B. Mallet, *Mallet du Pan and the French Revolution* (London, 1902); N. Matteucci, *Jacques Mallet-du-Pan* (Naples, 1957); *Mémoires et correspondance de Mallet du Pan pour servir à l'histoire de la Révolution française, recueillies et mis en ordre par A. Sayous*, 2 vols. (Paris, 1851).

P. H. Beik

Related entries: ANGLOMANES; BRUNSWICK MANIFESTO; COUP OF 18 FRUCTIDOR YEAR V; MALOUET; MOUNIER.

MALMESBURY, JAMES HARRIS, FIRST EARL OF (1746-1820), British diplomat. The eldest son of J. Harris of Salisbury (writer, grammarian, member of Parliament), young James had every opportunity for a good education, but he had been overindulged at Winchester and had spent more time drinking claret and playing cards with commoners than attending lectures at Oxford. Without graduating from Oxford, he left for the Continent in 1765 to study Dutch culture and language at Leyden and to visit Prussia, Poland, and France. He remained on the Continent for most of the next thirty-two years, serving as secretary of the embassy at the court of Madrid in 1767, minister to the court at Berlin, 1772-76, ambassador to the court at St. Petersburg, 1777-84, and ambassador at the Hague, 1784-88.

His greatest success was achieved at the Hague during the crisis of 1787 when he helped to defeat the patriots, to restore the stadtholder, and to reassert British influence in the United Provinces. With the support of W. Pitt and an ample supply of secret service money, he aggressively undermined the party of the Patriots and supported the stadtholder. When France aided the patriots, Britain urged Prussia to clear the provinces of republican forces, and Pitt threatened France with war if it intervened. Economically embarrassed and politically fractured at the time of the first Assembly of Notables, France had no choice but to acquiesce to Anglo-Prussian pressure. The resulting Triple Alliance of 1788 was the culmination of British, Dutch, and Prussian cooperation. Harris, who played a role in the drafting of the treaty, was supplied with funds to secure its approval in Holland. For his efforts he was created Baron Malmesbury in 1788 and received the Prussian Order of the Black Eagle. It was his only moment of diplomatic glory.

Concurrent with his diplomatic responsibilities, Harris served in Parliament, taking over the family seat at Christchurch after the death of his father in 1780. By conviction a Whig, he held great admiration for C. J. Fox and consistently supported him throughout the 1780s. Returning to England in 1788 during the regency bill crisis, he voted for Fox and against Pitt. When George III recovered from his illness, Pitt, who always rewarded his supporters and punished his opponents, removed Harris, by now Lord Malmesbury, from diplomatic service for the next four years. It was not until the end of 1793, when the old Whigs, including Malmesbury, shifted their allegiance from Fox to Pitt, that the latter again used Malmesbury on a diplomatic mission. In November he sent Malmesbury to Berlin to persuade Frederick William II to honor the Triple Alliance by supporting Britain and Holland in the French War. When Malmesbury failed, Pitt recalled him in 1794.

On two occasions, Pitt sent Malmesbury to France to negotiate a peace settlement. At the first conference in Paris in October 1796, Malmesbury found himself in an impossible situation because neither Britain nor France was willing to make any territorial concessions. Pitt's ministry insisted that the Belgic provinces be returned to Austria and that Cape Colony, Ceylon, and Trinidad be retained by Britain. The Directory categorically rejected these conditions and on 19 December ordered Malmesbury to leave France. During the second attempt at Lille in the summer of 1797, when Britain was at its lowest prestige in the war, the climate was more favorable because Austria was virtually out of the war, Britain was willing to cede the Belgic provinces to France, and the political shift in the Directory from Left to Right softened France's demands. The only important unresolved issue was Britain's request for some territorial indemnity. Pitt wanted the Cape Colony, Trinidad, and Ceylon, although he considered Ceylon negotiable. France, in contrast, insisted that Britain must surrender all of its colonial conquests. The coup d'état of 18 Fructidor ended any possibility of a settlement, and once again the Directory expelled Malmesbury.

This mission concluded Malmesbury's public life. Increasing deafness and old age forced him into retirement. Although he had little to show for his diplomacy since 1788, he was considered one of the most distinguished members in the diplomatic corps. For his services he was created the first earl of Malmesbury and Viscount Fitzharris.

A. Cobban, *Ambassadors and Secret Agents, the Diplomacy of the First Earl of Malmesbury at The Hague* (London, 1954); Third Earl of Malmesbury, ed., *Diaries and Correspondence of James Harris, the First Earl of Malmesbury*, 4 vols. (London, 1844);

Official Copies of the Correspondence of Lord Malmesbury to the French Republic and the Executive Directory of France. . . .relative to the Negotiations for Peace (London, 1796).

H. V. Evans

Related entries: ASSEMBLY OF NOTABLES; COUP OF 18 FRUCTIDOR YEAR V; DIRECTORY; FOX; FREDERICK WILLIAM II; PITT; WILLIAM V.

MALOUET, PIERRE-VICTOR (1740-1814), naval intendant, moderate monarchist, *émigré*. Born in Riom 11 February 1740, son of a local bailiff, Malouet turned to legal study and government service after his early hopes of literary fame as poet and dramatist were disappointed. From 1758 he filled a variety of positions in the French government, including a brief and disillusioning stint in an administrative assignment with marshal de Broglie's army during the Seven Years War. From 1767 to 1773 he held administrative posts in Santo Domingo, where he married and acquired considerable property. Service in Guyana between 1776 and 1778 and capture and brief imprisonment by the British during his return impaired his health and brought temporary retirement. He resumed government service in 1780 and in 1781 was appointed naval intendant at Toulon, where he remained until his election to the Estates General as deputy of the Third Estate from his native area of Riom.

An experienced official of the *ancien régime*, Malouet recognized the need for reform but believed that it should issue from strong monarchical initiative. He favored establishment of a legislature but feared that its actions would become too extreme unless restrained by proper organization. Along with J.-J. Mounier and others, he championed a bicameral legislature, somewhat on the English model, though his conception of the upper (more conservative) chamber was considerably different from theirs. Such views he expressed in pamphlets and in numerous speeches to the Constituent Assembly. He spoke out for practical reform and denounced metaphysical and misleading assertions such as found in the Declaration of the Rights of Man and of the Citizen. While denying that he supported Negro slavery, he argued against interference from Paris in colonial property rights, predicting that only chaos and violence would follow such interference. Malouet was active in the Naval Committee of the Assembly and delivered several substantial reports on the funding and organization of the navy. As a political moderate, he was subjected to attacks from Right and Left. The general course of reform went too far for him, but, unlike Mounier, he retained his seat in the Assembly throughout its existence, despite the unpopularity engendered by pronouncements against various parts of the Constitution of 1791 as they were being formulated. Indeed, on 8 August 1791, he was not allowed by the majority in the Assembly to complete his generally critical remarks of the constitution. Outside the Assembly, Malouet was a leading founder of two political clubs: the Impartials in 1790 and, after its demise, the Society of Friends of the Monarchical Constitution in 1791. Neither had significant influence.

After the Constituent Assembly, Malouet was busy with schemes to undo its handiwork. He even formulated plans to overturn the constitution by force, but their impracticality induced him to consider emigration. Unexpected circumstances kept him in France until 10 August 1792. Then, fearing for his life, he escaped to England where, for the next eight years, he held a prominent but rather unpopular place among the large group of *émigrés* in London. He sought unsuccessfully to have a part in the defense of the former king in the fall of 1792 and was active in efforts to assist proprietors in Santo Domingo, where, as he had predicted, disorder and bloodshed had led to full-scale revolt. He even launched a scheme for invasion of the island by armed forces under F.-C.-A. de Bouillé, but the plan had to be abandoned when expected British support fell by the wayside.

In 1801 Malouet was among the many *émigrés* returning to France during the Consulate. Although briefly imprisoned, he was granted unmolested residence. On 3 October 1803 Napoleon brought him out of obscurity by assigning him the post of commissioner general of the navy at Antwerp, a post he filled commendably until 1810, when Napoleon honored him by appointment to the Council of State and the title of baron. The emperor's opinion of him changed abruptly in 1812 when Malouet opposed the Russian campaign and was forced to retire. The restoration of Louis XVIII brought Malouet an honor he had long before desired, that of appointment as minister of the navy on 13 May 1814. He was not long to enjoy it, however; he died on 7 September 1814.

P.-V. Malouet, *Collection de mémoires et correspondances officielles sur l'administration des colonies*, 5 vols, (Paris, 1802) and *Mémoires de Malouet*, 2 vols. (Paris, 1874); J. R. Vignery, "Political Ideas of Pierre-Victor Malouet, 1789-1791" (Master's thesis, University of Kansas, 1957).

A. Saricks

Related entries: BOUILLE; CONSTITUTION OF 1791; DECLARATION OF THE RIGHTS OF MAN AND OF THE CITIZEN; MOUNIER; SOCIETY OF 1789.

MANDATS TERRITORIAUX (1796-97), legal tender issued by the Directory government to replace the worthless *assignats*. On 23 December 1795, the Directory government took steps to replace the paper money called *assignats* with a new legal tender, the *mandats territoriaux*. The *assignats* were a dismal failure as currency, carrying less than 1 percent of their original value. The assurances of their creators had proved false; the *assignats* had not resisted fluctuation because of their basis on real property. Although they were allegedly at par with specie when they were issued, by December 1795, 24 *livres* of metallic currency could purchase 3,575 *assignats*. By March 1796, 7,200 *assignats* could be purchased with the same 24 *livres* in specie.

The Law of 2 Nivôse Year IV (23 December 1795) sought to replace the old, valueless paper money with a stable form of legal tender. Based on the principles of the physiocrats, land was to provide value for the new currency, as had been the case originally with *assignats*. Since domains were fixed, it was believed that the new paper currency would be at par with specie.

Returning to 1790 valuations as the economic benchmark, *assignats* could be exchanged for *mandats* at the rate of thirty to one. Eight hundred millions in *mandats* therefore would retire the *assignats* in circulation. The total issue of *mandats*, however, was to be 2,400 million to allow the government a surplus to be used as needed. The new bills were scheduled for issue in April 1796.

The *mandats* were no more successful than their predecessors. From the beginning, they had been based on faulty economic reasoning. It was believed that they would retain their face value because they were consistent with the property on which they were based. The proponents, however, failed to realize that property values had decreased by more than half during the previous six years. "The *mandat*," wrote historian A. Thiers (1838), "was worth as much as the land, but it could not be worth more." The *mandat*, therefore, never could have maintained its value compared to gold or silver. On the first day of issue, in fact, 100 *livres* in *mandats* were quoted at 18 *livres* in specie. Fluctuating wildly, by September they had fallen to 5 percent of their face value, and they continued to fall. The government, which was unable to control the economy, chose to allow payments in any form, and specie, which had previously been hoarded, appeared again in the marketplace.

On 21 May 1797, the *mandats territoriaux*, along with any remaining *assignats*, were demonetized. The government returned to specie, ending the disastrous fling with paper currency.

H. Higgs, "Revolutionary Finance," *The Cambridge Modern History*, vol. 8 (Cambridge, 1904); J. Lafaurie, *Les assignats: Et les papiers-monnaies émis par l'Etat au XVIIIe siècle* (Paris, 1981); A. Thiers, *Histoire de la Révolution française*, 10 vols. (Paris, 1838).

S. Conner

Related entries: ASSIGNATS; DIRECTORY.

MANIFESTO, BRUNSWICK. See BRUNSWICK MANIFESTO.

MANUEL, PIERRE-LOUIS (1751-93), *procureur-syndic* of the Paris Commune from 1791 to his election as deputy to the Convention. Manuel was the son of a porter of the collège des Doctrinaires in Montargis, department of the Loiret. Despite his humble origin, he was intelligent and ambitious enough to become a private tutor to a Parisian banking family and later a *commis* to a book dealer before beginning his life as a man of letters. In 1783 he published *Essais historiques, critiques, littéraires, et philosophiques* and three years later *Coup d'oeil philosophique sur la règne de Louis*, which resulted in his arrest and confinement for three months in the Bastille. His four-volume memoirs were commended by the marquis de Condorcet, who had called them distinguished, singling out especially Manuel's discussion of public education.

Politically, Manuel was a Girondist, but this did not prevent him from playing an important role as a representative to the General Council, member of the Paris Commune's Conseil de Ville and of its police administration, and *procureur*. He was popular among patriots until the more radical politics of the Mountain left him hopelessly behind.

In 1786, for instance, he had published a brochure entitled *Lettre d'un garde du roi* in which he satirized cardinal de Rohan and J. de Luz comtesse de La Motte in the notorious affair of the queen's necklace, and a few weeks before the fall of the Bastille, he had warned the comte d'Artois that the people were opposed to the threat of soldiers, under which the Estates General was laboring. In a defense of J. Necker he compared him to Varrus who, after Cannae, "did not despair of the state," one of the allusions to classical literature and to Greek and Roman statesmen that appeared constantly in his works. Warning Artois of a possible civil war, he had proceeded to attack those prelates, nobles, and priests who separated themselves from the people and who "belittled the majesty of the communes." And, in a letter to his co-citizens written shortly after, he asserted that "it is within the communes that *Spartacists* may be found."

In his publication of *Lettres originales de Mirabeau écrites du donjon de Vincennes...*, he not only defended the honesty and sincerity of Gabriel (Mirabeau) and the love for his inamorata, Sophie, but stressed the virtue of love and the affections of the heart, which he found superior to the endowments of the intellect—quite in the Romantic tradition of J.-J. Rousseau. Manuel revealed that he had been able to acquire these letters, which filled four small volumes, by gift, purchase, and discovery.

In his publications and orations, Manuel remained true to the principles of 1789, which he cherished and championed. The liberties won by the people in 1789 aroused his warm sentiments and devotion. Above all, he was opposed to censorship and championed the principle of liberty of the press. In his *La police de Paris dévoilée* (1790), Manuel gave numerous illustrations of classical works being censored and destroyed and confessed that had it not been for the smuggling of forbidden books across the Dutch and Swiss borders, many well-known authors would have been unknown to Frenchmen.

His devotion to liberty, however, did not go beyond the principles of 1789, and he warned his audience in several speeches delivered in August 1789 that they should fear anarchy because "it can do more damage than a tyrant." After the royal family's abortive flight to Varennes, he began calling the king *Louis-le-perjure* and insisted that sovereignty belonged to the people, not to the monarch.

On 21 August 1792, Manuel announced to the Legislative Assembly that the Venetian ambassador was shortly to leave Paris and questioned whether this should be permitted when it was not at all certain that French envoys would be respected by the several courts of Europe, a not-too-subtle suggestion for the taking of hostages. When negotiations between C. Dumouriez and Prussian envoys seemed promising, the Executive Council asked Manuel to prepare written proof that the motions of the Commune relating to the confinement of the royal family in the Temple were concerned with securing a decent existence for Louis and his family. Nothing came of this, of course.

Elected as a deputy to the National Convention, Manuel proposed unsuccessfully on the first day of its tenure that a mansion be maintained as the exclusive residence for the president of the Assembly, whom he termed president of France, and that he be surrounded with marks of honor and distinction, a proposal out of keeping with Manuel's earlier democratic sentiments. Interestingly, in one of his letters written during the early stages of the Revolution, he had opposed sharply any demonstration of deference to elected officials and had urged their surveillance so that justice would be done.

When the Girondins hesitated bringing the king to trial by proposing that proper legal forms be established first, Manuel attempted to postpone even this consideration as being too rapid a move. Instead he suggested that the question of abolishing the monarchy be submitted to the people in their primary assemblies, a proposal that intensified the growing division between the Mountain and the Gironde. Addressing the Convention on the question whether that body had the right to try Louis, he began with the declaration that only slaves could ask if the king were judgeable. Being a king, Louis was guilty by that fact alone. This radical position continued as he denounced the role of kings with appropriate allusions to classical times. He concluded, however, that although Louis was guilty and was indeed "perfidious," he should be left to live, "in order to inspire disgust with royalty." He favored forgiving him the vices and ills of his birth and hoped to reeducate him. His last sentence declared, "A dead king is no less a man."

After the execution of the king, Manuel left Paris for his native region, where he hoped to continue his literary career. He was arrested in August 1793 by the local Revolutionary committee, brought to Paris where he appeared before the Revolutionary Tribunal, was condemned, and guillotined on 24 Brumaire Year II (14 November 1793).

P.-L. Manuel, *Lettre d'un garde du roi* (Paris, 1786), *La police dévoilée*, 2 vols. (Paris, 1790), *Les lettres de P. Manuel, l'un des administrateurs de 1789, sur la Révolution, recueilliés par un ami de la constitution* (Paris, 1791), *Lettres originales de Mirabeau écrites de donjon de Vincennes pendant les années 1777, 1778, 1779, and 1780*, 4 vols. (Paris, 1792), and *Opinion de P. Manuel sur la première question: pour le jugement de Louis XVI* (Paris, 1792).

M. Slavin

Related entries: BASTILLE, THE; GIRONDINS; MIRABEAU; PARIS COMMUNE.

MARAT, JEAN-PAUL (1743-93), radical, editor, Montagnard deputy to the National Convention. Marat was one of the foremost radicals of the Revolution. He is notorious for his denunciations of conspirators, his calls for popular violence, and his advocacy of a dictatorship. His detractors claim he provoked suspicion and bloodshed, whereas his admirers see him as a selfless friend of the people and prophet.

Marat was born in Boudry, near Neuchâtel (Switzerland), on 24 May 1743 into a lower-middle-class Calvinist family. He received his early education at home but at sixteen went to France to study medicine. In 1765, he settled in Great Britain, where he acquired a medical degree and became a prosperous physician and writer of philosophical treatises. In his *Chains of Slavery* (1774), he unmasked the despotism of kings while demonstrating his concern for liberty, human rights, and popular sovereignty. In 1777, he returned to France, where he became the doctor to the comte d'Artois' bodyguard. He devoted himself to medicine and science. In his *Plan de législation criminelle* (1780), he revealed his concern for the poor. Before 1789, Marat was a liberal and democrat concerned with alleviating poverty, but politics did not preoccupy him. An understanding of his future behavior must be sought in his temperament as well as his ideas. Marat's *amour de la gloire* led him to seek public recognition, but he had a persecution complex. When he failed to gain admission to the Academy of Sciences, he blamed a conspiracy of academicians. Disappointed, he found an outlet in the Revolution.

Marat expected cooperation between the king and the Third Estate to produce reform. In February 1789 he advocated a constitutional monarchy, a declaration of rights, abolition of tax exemptions and hunting privileges, and a more humane criminal code. He called on the deputies to meet in common and vote by head. He played a minor role in the fall of the Bastille. In August he proposed universal male suffrage, recall of deputies, and popular referenda. While upholding private property, he argued that the poor had the right to subsistence. Conspicuous inequalities of wealth should be eliminated by confiscating the property of the rich. He opposed J.-J. Mounier's proposed bicameral legislature and royal veto.

In September 1789 Marat published a newspaper, *L'ami du peuple*. Disappointed in the king and the Assembly, he placed his faith in the people. Setting himself up as a monitor, he censured the enemies of the Revolution. When he suspected that the ministers were in league with an aristocratic faction in the Assembly, he called for popular action. Pursued by the police for inciting the insurrection of 5-6 October, he was forced to hide, the first of many times. In January he fled to England.

When the plots that Marat suspected materialized, he demanded popular executions. Popular justice was only a defensive reaction to counterrevolutionary provocations. Only by force could aristocratic plots be forestalled and a massacre of patriots prevented. Marat called for a large number of heads, varying from 500 to 100,000. In July 1790 he argued that if 500 or 600 heads were cut off, millions of lives would be saved. In September he claimed that if 500 heads had been cut off when the Bastille was taken, the Revolution would have triumphed. But now 10,000 heads would scarcely suffice. On 27 May 1791 he declared that 50,000 heads might be necessary.

Marat was unique in his early and frequent calls for a dictator. He believed that popular insurrection could not succeed without a leader. He called on the people to choose a dictator and follow him until the counterrevolution was crushed. He demanded either a military tribune or a supreme dictator, who would serve only temporarily. First mentioning a dictator on 5 October 1789, during his stay in England, he called for a supreme dictator. In September 1790 he demanded a military tribune. The flight to Varennes (20 June 1791) prompted him to call for a military tribune or a supreme dictator.

Although Marat lost faith in Louis XVI and the monarchy, his views underwent a convoluted evolution. Accepting the idea that a republic was impracticable in a large country, he favored a very limited monarchy. But in September 1790 Marat questioned the value of monarchy for France. In November he urged the next legislature to proscribe monarchy. In February 1791 he again advocated a very limited monarchy. When the king fled on 21 June 1791, Marat demanded his execution and the creation of a regency. It was only when France became a Republic (22 September 1792) that Marat became a republican.

Marat's early faith in the Assembly gave way to indignation. His outrage at the deputies for their role in the Champ de Mars "massacre" (17 July 1791) led him to call for their deaths. His contempt for the constitution was based on ideological principles. He rejected the distinction between passive and active citizens and opposed the *marc d'argent* qualification for deputy. Like the *sans-culottes*, he believed in direct democracy. He placed his faith in the people acting through electoral assemblies, patriotic clubs, or an insurrection. He demanded that the lot of the poor be ameliorated. He proposed a progressive income tax. Although he regretted that more of the national lands did not go to the poor, he opposed an agrarian law. Advocate of a free market economy, he believed in a welfare state, not socialism.

Marat opposed the war. He advocated guerrilla warfare in case of invasion. Forced into hiding on 3 May 1792 for urging the troops to kill perfidious generals, Marat's role in the insurrection of 10 August was limited to a few appeals for action against the king and all traitors. Although he has been accused of being the guiding hand behind the September Massacres (2-6 September 1792), his role has been exaggerated. On 19 August he exhorted the people to rise up and kill traitors, especially the Swiss officers in the Abbaye prison. On 2 September Marat was appointed to the Paris Commune's Comité de Surveillance and signed its circular letter of 3 September urging the departments to imitate Paris, but responsibility for the bloodshed was collective.

Marat's popularity at this time is attested to by the fact that he was elected a deputy from Paris to the Convention. A leading Montagnard, he was the object of violent attacks by the Girondins. Denounced for advocating a dictatorship and instigating the September Massacres, he was accused of demanding 200,000 heads. He called for the speedy trial and execution of Louis XVI. When some Girondins appealed for leniency, Marat was convinced they had defected to the king. Marat was accused of instigating the Parisian food riots of 25 February 1793 by inciting the people to pillage the shops and hang a few hoarders. The defection of C. Dumouriez in early spring 1793 convinced Marat that the Girondins were conspiring with that general. On 13 April the Convention voted to send Marat before the Revolutionary Tribunal, but he was unanimously acquitted. Marat obtained his revenge on the Girondins by the insurrection of 31 May-2 June 1793, in which he played an important role. He called for the suppression of the Commission of Twelve and the purge of the twenty-two Girondins named in the section petitions. While urging the sections to arm, he rejected the *Enragé* demand for the dispersal of the Convention. Due to illness, Marat curtailed his activities after 2 June. Nonetheless, he called for the trial of the Girondins and a purge of all ex-nobles from public office. His last efforts were devoted to strengthening the Committee of Public Safety, which he criticized for moderation.

Marat was a valuable asset in the Mountain's campaign to crush the *Enragés*. Competing with the latter for the support of the *sans-culottes*, Marat tried to align the popular movement with the Mountain. On 4 July 1793 he assailed J. Roux, J.-F. Varlet, and J.-T.-V. Leclerc as counterrevolutionaries. He rejected their economic program. Opposing the maximum, he preferred the punishment of hoarders. Rejecting the *cours forcé* of the *assignats*, he advocated withdrawing large quantities from circulation.

When C. Corday's dagger struck him down in his medicinal bath on 13 July 1793, Marat was dying from skin and lung diseases. Envisioning herself as a modern Judith, the young Norman noble sought to rid France of an oppressor. The result was exactly the opposite, for Marat's murder hastened the execution of the Girondins and the establishment of the Terror and the Revolutionary government. As a "martyr to liberty," Marat became the object of a popular cult. The Cordeliers club hung his embalmed heart from its ceiling and buried him in its garden. The Convention voted his burial in the Pantheon in November. Since the Cordeliers and J.-R. Hébert claimed to be his heirs and *maratisme* became synonymous with ultraterrorism, the Mountain was ambivalent toward his memory. Marat was "Pantheonized" only on 24 September 1794. In the anti-Terrorist wave after Thermidor, Marat's reputation was denigrated, and his body was removed from the Pantheon in February 1795.

Marat left an ambiguous legacy. Champion of popular sovereignty and radical revolution, he devoted his last efforts to denouncing the *Enragés*, rejecting the maximum, calling for an end to the permanence of the section assemblies, and strengthening the Revolutionary government. Marat was politically akin to the Montagnards. He pointed the way to Babouvism, with its call for a dictatorship of a revolutionary elite. Unlike G. Babeuf, Marat wanted a one-man dictator and he never advocated the abolition of private property.

L. Gottschalk, *Jean Paul Marat: A Study in Radicalism* (New York, 1967); J. Massin, *Marat* (Paris, 1960).

M. Edelstein

Related entries: ACTIVE CITIZEN; *AMI DU PEUPLE, L'*; BABEUF; CHAMP DE MARS "MASSACRE"; CORDAY D'ARMANS; CORDELIERS CLUB; MOUNIER; OCTOBER DAYS; PASSIVE CITIZEN; SEPTEMBER 1792 MASSACRES.

MARATS, LES, radical group controlling city government in Nantes. See *NOYADES DE NANTES*.

MARC D'ARGENT (29 October 1789), qualification for election as deputy to the Legislative Assembly. The electoral provisions of the Constitution of 1791 differentiated between active citizens (approximately 4.3 million) who had the right to vote and passive citizens (approximately 3 million) who did not. To qualify as an active citizen, Frenchmen had to be at least twenty-five years old and to have paid in annual direct taxes a sum equivalent to the value of three days' labor in their locality. The enfranchised met in primary assemblies to select electors whose annual direct tax payments had to equal the local value of ten days' labor. Only about 50,000 Frenchmen could meet the qualifications for electors, who then assembled to elect deputies for the Legislative Assembly. To be eligible for election as a deputy, the decree of 29 October 1789 stipulated that one had to be a landholder who paid in annual direct taxes the equivalent of a *marc d'argent* (silver mark), which was worth approximately 52 francs or fifty-four days' labor.

These electoral regulations, mainly the work of the abbé Sieyès, established a political monopoly for the wealthier classes in French society. Although the National Assembly on 27 August 1791 eliminated the requirement of the *marc d'argent*, the only elections for the Legislative Assembly had already taken place. The Constitution of 1791 established the pattern for the indirect election of national legislatures that many subsequent French constitutions would incorporate.

P. Campbell, *French Electoral Systems and Elections, 1789-1957* (London, 1958).

D. M. Epstein

Related entries: ACTIVE CITIZEN; PASSIVE CITIZEN; SIEYES.

MARECHAL, PIERRE-SYLVAIN (1750-1803), journalist, writer, leader in Babeuf's Conspiracy of Equals. A writer affiliated with the Bibliothèque Mazarine, Maréchal was steeped in the works of classical antiquity and the ideas of J.-J. Rousseau. At first he published moralistic stories and later some bacchic songs, and, above all, antireligious lampoons. His *Almanach des honnêtes gens (Almanac for Respectable People)* outlined a Revolutionary calendar, which earned him three months in jail. In his later books, he preached communalist and libertarian ideas.

When G. Babeuf came to Paris in February 1793, he came to Maréchal to obtain work. The latter was then editor of the *Révolutions de Paris* of Prudhomme. When imprisoned, Babeuf asked Maréchal to plead his case and was, thanks to him, freed on two occasions. Maréchal published in this newspaper (no. 40) his article, "The Opinion of One Man on the Strange Case Brought against the Tribune of the People." Subsequently Maréchal took part in the secret directing committee of the Babouvist movement, composed the "New Song for the Use of the Faubourgs," and, above all, drew up the Manifesto of the Equals, although its libertarian principles were not accepted unanimously by the conspirators. Following the repression of the Conspiracy of Equals in 1796, Maréchal escaped the final stage of the plot because the traitor, G. Grisel, did not know him, and consequently he was not brought before the high court of Vendôme as were the other leaders of the movement.

Outside of his numerous publications, practically nothing more was heard of Maréchal, and he did not maintain contact with those Babouvists who were acquitted, such as F.-L.-F. Lepelletier and P.-A. Antonelle. He published a twelve-volume series, The Antiquities of Herculaneum, and some antireligious pamphlets. In 1800 he published his *Dictionary of Ancient and Modern Atheists*, which created such a scandal that *The Antidote to the Dictionary of Atheists* was published to rectify Maréchal's assertions.

A simple and kindly man of innocent morality, this scholar, artist, and libertarian left behind him important work that has become somewhat obsolete. M. Dommanget (1950) called him "a sage molded by antiquity."

M. Dommanget, *Sylvain Maréchal, l'égalitaire, "l'homme sans Dieu"; Sa vie, son oeuvre (1750-1803)* (Paris, 1950) and ed., *Sur Babeuf et la Conjuration des Egaux* (Paris, 1970); R. Legrand, *Babeuf et Ses Compagnons de Route* (Paris, 1981).

R. Legrand

Related entries: ATHEISM; BABEUF; CONSPIRACY OF EQUALS; PRUDHOMME; *REVOLUTIONS DE PARIS*.

MARET, HUGUES-BERNARD (1763-1839), writer. See *MONITEUR UNIVERSEL*.

MARIE ANTOINETTE (1755-93), queen of France. Marie Antoinette, daughter of Emperor Francis I and Maria-Theresa of Austria, was married to the dauphin Louis-Auguste of France in 1770, when she was fifteen and he was sixteen years old, as a move to strengthen relations between the ruling houses of the two countries. On becoming queen in 1774, she was cheered and respected initially as the wife of the monarch, but her popularity among Frenchmen was neither very great nor longstanding; the appellation *l'Autrichienne* characterized her as an outsider. Her caprices and expenditures, intrigues and ostentation, her acting in the royal manner, were all part of court behavior as she knew it. Unfavorable news and gossip about her vanity and gambling, and her flirtations, especially with Count Fersen, spread rapidly. Even matters in which she was innocent, such as the diamond necklace affair, in which the favor-seeking cardinal de Rohan was duped, further tainted her reputation. With the coming of the Revolution, her inept involvement in plots to save the monarchy and defeat any new regime and her attempts to save her husband and family, such as the flight to Varennes, deepened the suspicion and hatred of her. As the tempo of Revolutionary fervor increased, so did the number of pamphlets vilifying the queen.

It has been contended convincingly that Marie Antoinette had no deep understanding of either France or its people, and, like her royal husband, she could comprehend neither the nature of the problems and crises of the times nor the forces they had unleashed. In trying to delineate her role, perhaps it was H. Belloc (1924) who put it most succinctly: "She exasperated the Revolution."

The transfer of the royal family from Versailles to Paris in October 1789 became a virtual imprisonment as troops of the National Guard replaced those loyal to the king at the Tuileries. By 1791, when their situation had become increasingly precarious, the two sovereigns, using H. A. von Fersen as their chief agent, planned the flight of the royal family on 20 June, which ended in their capture at Varennes. Through the fall and winter of 1791, the queen remained in secret contact with the moderates, chiefly through A. Barnave, resorting to letters in cipher or invisible ink. Fersen, now abroad, represented her interests in Austria and Prussia. When war against Austria was declared in April 1792, the intense nationalism it engendered in France made the Austrian-born queen a subject of renewed attacks.

On 20 June 1792, when the first invasion of the Tuileries occurred, the queen and her children were safely barricaded and guarded while the king appeased the invaders by appearing at a window in a red Revolutionary cap and toasting the nation from a bottle of red wine offered to him. The respite was brief; 10 August saw the second and more fateful attack by heavily armed forces from the Paris sections. For protection, the royal family left the Tuileries for the Legislative Assembly. From there the route began for Marie Antoinette to the Temple, the Conciergerie, and the guillotine.

The life of the royal family in the Temple was one of close confinement, accompanied by petty harassments over such matters as clothing and bed linens and calculated cruelties such as forcing the queen to the window to view the head of her friend, the princesse de Lamballe, carried by on a pike. The king was separated from his family before his trial and sentencing. Their last meeting with him occurred on the night before he went to the scaffold on 21 January 1793.

In July, the Convention decreed that the queen be separated from the dauphin. A month later she was moved from the Temple to a narrow cell in the Conciergerie, a prison that usually signified death for its inmates. There was one aborted attempt at escape, engineered by the chevalier Gonsse de Rougeville, who had arranged for her safety in the first attack on the Tuileries.

When she was eventually brought to trial on 14 October, A.-Q. Fouquier-Tinville, the public prosecutor, made certain that Marie Antoinette did not emerge as a martyr. He compared her to Messalina and other infamous women of history. After attacking her morals and character, he presented the charges: intelligence with the enemy, sending of large sums of French money to *émigrés* for counterrevolutionary purposes, the Champ de Mars "massacre," the flight to Varennes, ordering the Swiss Guard to fire on Frenchmen during the 10 August invasion of the Tuileries, and various malign influences on her husband. He concluded his accusation with an unanswerable charge of treason, for during the Austrian war she had written to her nephew Francis II informing him of French battle plans, particularly warning him of a C. Dumouriez-led attack on Savoy and another around Liège to be commanded by the marquis de Lafayette. C.-F. Chauveau-Lagarde, the queen's attorney, sought to delay the trial in order to respond to the long indictment. A letter requesting this was signed by the queen, given to Fouquier, and he passed it along to M. Robespierre, who ignored it.

The queen's conduct at the trial was calm and contained throughout the hearing of general and particular charges leveled at her by witnesses. When J.-R. Hébert accused her of committing incest with the dauphin, she replied with dignity and even aroused some sympathy. Fouquier shrewdly buried this charge. When the sessions ended, she spoke briefly, disclaiming the charges and stating that she had only done her duty as the wife of the king. M.-J.-A. Herman, the presiding judge, put the questions to the jury to decide: did the queen commit treason by conspiring with and supporting the enemies of France, and had she been involved in plotting a civil war? The jury found her guilty on both counts; and she was sentenced to death. On the morning of 16 October 1793, a few hours after her judgment, Marie Antoinette mounted the scaffold and was executed by C.-H. Sanson, who had beheaded her husband.

H. Belloc, *Marie Antoinette* (New York, 1924); C. Bertin, *Les grands procès de l'histoire de France*, vol. 2 (Paris, 1966); A. Castelot, *Marie Antoinette* (London, 1957); V. Cronin, *Louis and Antoinette* (New York, 1975); J. E. Hearsey, *Marie Antoinette* (New York, 1973).

R. L. Carol

Related entries: CHAMP DE MARS "MASSACRE"; FERSEN; FOUQUIER-TINVILLE; LOUIS XVI; LOUIS XVII; OCTOBER DAYS; PRISONS; 10 AUGUST 1792; VARENNES.

MARIE-CAROLINE (1752-1814), queen of Naples, older sister of Marie Antoinette. See PARTHENOPEAN REPUBLIC.

MARIE-LOUISE OF PARMA (1751-1819), wife of Charles IV of Spain. See CHARLES IV.

MARIE-THERESE OF SAVOY (1757?-1805), wife of the comte d'Artois. See ARTOIS.

"MARSEILLAISE, LA," France's stirring national anthem written during the night of 25-26 April 1792 by J.-C. Rouget de Lisle (1760-1836), an army captain of aristocratic lineage in the Royal Engineer Corps. While posted in the frontier city of Strasbourg, Rouget de Lisle had become friendly with several notable local musicians as well as Baron Dietrich, the popularly elected mayor. The young officer was caught up in the war fever that swept France during the winter and spring of 1792. This growing sentiment, evident in Strasbourg and elsewhere throughout the country, led the Revolutionary government in Paris to declare war on Austria on 20 April 1792. News of the declaration reached Strasbourg

five days later. The Strasbourg garrison, part of the *Armée du Rhin*, was then mobilizing in anticipation of an offensive against the German states across the Rhine.

On the evening of 25 April, Dietrich, like Rouget an early supporter of the Revolution, was hosting a party at the city hall for some of the army's officers. As the evening wore on and as the mayor's guests became freer with wine, Dietrich, regarding the main square of Strasbourg where elements of the army were camped, is said to have commented, to himself at first, that he was dismayed that the army then mobilizing in defense of liberty, equality, and fraternity had no marching song particularly its own.

Then turning to Rouget de Lisle, whose amateur musicianship the mayor knew and respected, Dietrich specifically charged the young officer to write such a song. The young captain left immediately for his quarters. He said later that the music and the lyrics (based on political pamphlets and placards he had seen all over Strasbourg) came to him effortlessly and simultaneously.

When he awakened at dawn, he was unable to judge the merits of his work, which he entitled originally "War Song of the Rhine Army." He took the manuscript to Dietrich who, in spite of the early hours, sang the song accompanied by his wife on the piano. Extremely pleased with Rouget de Lisle's achievement, the mayor arranged immediately for the unsigned manuscript to be printed and distributed among the garrison and populace of Strasbourg by the city council.

By the end of the summer of 1792, Rouget's passionate march-hymn was known all over France. The name *"Marseillaise"* came about when a battalion of volunteers from Marseille sang the song as they participated in the storming of the Tuileries on 10 August 1792, when Louis XVI was overthrown. From that time, the song has been known as the *"Marseillaise,"* although it officially became the French national anthem only on 14 March 1879 after the consolidation of the Third French Republic.

E. A. Arnold, Jr., "Rouget de Lisle and the 'Marseillaise,'" in *Pro. of the WSFH* (1978); C. Pierre, *Les hymnes et chansons de la Révolution* (Paris, 1904); J. Tiersot, *Rouget de Lisle, son oeuvre, sa vie* (Paris, 1892).

E. A. Arnold, Jr.

Related entries: DIETRICH; ROUGET DE LISLE; 10 AUGUST 1792.

MARSEILLE, the third largest city and, according to some authorities, the premier port of France in 1789. Its population in 1789 of 105,000 included 1,000 ecclesiastics, a varied middle class, seventy-four guilds of artisans, and a colorful waterfront element of dockers, sailors, and fishermen. The nobility was inconsequential. Politically, culturally, and economically, Marseille was dominated by wealthy merchants *(négociants)*, who constituted 3 percent of the inhabitants.

Bread shortages and popular indignation over taxes led to the first outbreak of violence in 1789. On 23 March a mob sacked the residences of the intendant and tax farmer general, and forced some municipal oligarchs to flee. Royal authority was not restored until May when the marquis de Caraman arrived with Swiss mercenaries. After further disturbances in July-August, E.-F.-A.-B. Sanchon de Bournissac, the provost general of Provence, made wholesale arrests.

H.-G. R. Mirabeau intervened on the behalf of those imprisoned, and the National Assembly divested Bournissac of his powers (8 December 1789), effectively ending the Old Regime in Marseille. On 28 January 1790, a municipal government, filled with patriots, was elected. A National Guard was established the next month. On 11 April 1790, a large group of citizens founded a Jacobin club (Patriotic Assembly of Friends of the Constitution). Some of its members seized Fort Notre-Dame-de-la-Garde by surprise in the night of 29-30 April. The following day, Forts Saint-Jean and Saint-Nicolas, which had been the strongholds of Caraman and Bournissac, were taken over by national guardsmen.

A power struggle followed between the club and the National Guard commandant, J.-F. Lieutaud. At stake was control of the guard, an army of 14,000 men. The municipal government, composed largely of clubbists, had Lieutaud imprisoned in the fall of 1790. For the next two years, the club and the municipal officials worked in tandem to propagate Revolution in the southeast. On 26 February 1792, for example, some 8,000 Marseillais disarmed a Swiss regiment at Aix and purged the Directory of the Bouches-du-Rhône. In March, an army from Marseille overthrew the counterrevolutionary Chiffonists of Arles. Immediately afterward it marched into the Vaucluse to organize this newly annexed region.

Marseille had become a hotbed of republicanism by 1792. In June, a 500-man republican force was organized to go to Paris. This battalion on 10 August led the assault on the Tuileries that ended the reign of Louis XVI. During its march from Marseille to Paris in July, its members popularized J.-C. Rouget de Lisle's recently composed *"Chant de guerre de l'armée du Rhin,"* known forever afterward as *"La Marseillaise."*

The fall of the monarchy in Paris coincided with major outbreaks of lawlessness in Provence. Between 23 July and 8 September, more than a dozen counterrevolutionaries were murdered in the streets of Marseille. On 22-23 August, a band of men forcibly transferred the departmental government from Aix to Marseille. The electoral assembly of the Bouches-du-Rhône department, which met at Avignon in early September, was also intimidated by Marseille. Five Marseillais were chosen as deputies to the National Convention.

Marseille was profoundly shaken by the Girondin-Montagnard factionalism of 1792-93. Bread shortages and the paralysis of trade caused by naval warfare and the depreciation of *assignats* exacerbated the political crisis. In January 1793 pro-Montagnards seized control of the club. They demanded forced loans on the rich, the incarceration of suspects, and a third insurrection to purify the Convention of Girondin deputies. On 19 March, at the club's instigation, the disarming of suspects took place. In early April, the club persuaded the Montagnard representatives on mission, M. Bayle and J.-A. Boisset, to arrest the mayor.

A revolt against the club's dictatorship began in the same month. The thirty-two sectional assemblies, which had previously been sparsely attended, were suddenly flooded with moderate republicans and crypto-royalists. All classes were involved in the insurrection, but there were disproportionately large percentages of *négociants*, landlords, and lawyers. The *sectionnaires* formed a governing body called the general committee. It ordered Bayle and Boisset to leave the city (28 April), arrested the principal Jacobins (14-20 May), closed the club (3 June), and, after learning of the purge of the Girondins in the Convention, severed ties with the central government (6 June). In August, after the sectionalist army had suffered a succession of defeats at the hands of a government force under General J.-F. Carteaux, the general committee offered to open the city to the English Admiral S. Hood. Before this supreme act of treason could be consummated, however, Marseille fell (25 August 1793) to Carteaux.

The entry of the governmental army inaugurated the Terror. Although the club was reestablished, real power rested in the hands of representatives on mission from Paris. P. Barras and L.-M.-S. Fréron, the most celebrated, arrived on 12 October 1793. Punishment of traitors was not enough for these proconsuls. Buildings were destroyed, Marseille was called *Ville-Sans-Nom*, and consideration was apparently given to blocking the harbor with stones. Protests by local citizens resulted in the recall of Barras and Fréron on 23 January, 1794. They were replaced by E. Maignet, a dour but honest Montagnard.

A Revolutionary tribunal was set up in the first days of the Terror. It operated for about six months, judging 975 individuals and condemning 289 to death. Fréron replaced it briefly with a military commission of five judges (non-Marseillais) who judged 218 people and executed 123. The Revolutionary tribunal, staffed by local Jacobins, concentrated on eliminating leaders in the sectionalist revolt. As Fréron had intended, however, the military commission waged a kind of economic terror, sending many wealthy merchants to the guillotine for minor offenses.

After Thermidor, the conservative deputies, F. Auguis and J.-J. Serres, arrived. They purged the club (26 September 1794) and permitted the reopening of churches and the return of *émigrés*. By 1795 bands of royalists called Companies of the Sun roamed the streets attacking republicans. The worst incident of violence occurred on 5 June when a mob murdered more than 100 imprisoned terrorists. In the autumn, Fréron, now the soul of moderation, returned as a commissioner of the Directory. His policies antagonized the extreme Left and Right, however, and led to his recall in March, 1796. Under his replacement, General A. Willot, former *émigrés* and nonjuring priests enjoyed nearly complete freedom of action. The years 1798-99, in which Marseille was governed by a succession of military men, were checkered with royalist plots. Antirepublican sentiment fed on economic discontent. The Revolution had ruined the city's commerce.

A. Chabaud, "Essai sur les classes bourgeoises dirigéants à Marseille en 1789," *Documents relatifs à la vie économique de la Révolution* (Besançon, 1942); M. L.

Kennedy, *The Jacobin Club of Marseilles, 1790-1794* (Ithaca, 1973); C. Lourde, *Histoire de la Révolution à Marseille et en Provence depuis 1789 jusqu'au Consulat*, 3 vols. (Marseille, 1838-39); P. Masson, *Le commerce de Marseille de 1789 à 1814* (Paris, 1919); W. Scott, *Terror and Repression in Revolutionary Marseilles* (New York, 1973).

M. Kennedy

Related entries ASSIGNATS; BARRAS; COMPANIES OF THE SUN; FEDERALISM; FRERON; GIRONDINS; "*MARSEILLAISE, LA*"; MONTAGNARDS; 9 THERMIDOR YEAR II; ROUGET DE LISLE; TERROR, THE.

MASSACRES, SEPTEMBER. See SEPTEMBER 1792 MASSACRES.

MASSENA, ANDRE (1758-1817), duc de Rivoli, prince d'Essling, marshal of France. Probably Napoleon's greatest marshal, Masséna was born near Nice (6 May 1758) of humble parentage. Orphaned at six and informally educated by relatives, he ran away to sea as a cabin boy at the age of thirteen. Four years later he joined the Royal Italian regiment and was promoted after fourteen years of service to the highest noncommissioned rank. Unable to advance further due to his humble origins, he resigned, married the daughter of a doctor, and became a grocer.

When the Revolution erupted, Masséna first joined the National Guard of Antibes and then a volunteer unit at Var, in which he was soon elected lieutenant colonel. He served with distinction in the Maritime Alps and was promoted to general of brigade in the Army of Italy. He took part in the siege of Toulon (December 1793), where he led attacks on Forts Catherine and Lartigne. Thereafter he was given the right wing of the Army of Italy, and he captured Saorgio (29 April) and the Col de Tende (8 May 1794). In 1794 Masséna exercised semi-independent command under General B. Schérer and achieved his first major victory at Loano (23-24 November). In March 1796, Napoleon rather than Masséna was given command of the Army of Italy. Nevertheless, Napoleon appreciated Masséna's martial abilities and appointed him to command the advance guard of the army. Masséna's division played a decisive role in Napoleon's first victories of Montenotte (12 April), Dego (14 April), and Mondovi (21 April) when the Sardinians were forced out of the war.

During Napoleon's major battles in Lombardy and Venetia, Masséna's contributions were vital for the success of the campaign. At Lodi (10 May) Masséna successfully led his troops across the bridge against the Austrians, opening Lombardy to the French invasion; at Castiglione (5 August) and Bassano (8 September) his division shared the brunt of the fighting; at Arcola (15-17 November) his troops were instrumental in the victory; and his timely arrival at Rivoli (14 January) won the battle and forced the surrender of Mantua. In pursuing the Austrians in 1797, Masséna's advance guard drove the enemy through Tarviso Pass (23 March) to Klagenfurt (28 March), up the Mur to Leoben where an armistice was negotiated. In recognition of Masséna's achievements, not only was he dubbed *l'enfant chéri de la victoire* by Napoleon, but he was sent to Paris with the victory dispatches (23 April 1797). The members of the Directory honored Masséna, but instead of rewarding him with command of the Army of Italy, they gave it to General A. Berthier. In 1798 he was ordered to assume command of the starving French troops occupying Rome. Despite his efforts, he could not prevent the looting, rioting, and mutinous behavior among his troops, and he was ultimately recalled and ordered home. In August 1798 he was assigned to the Army of Mayence, and in December he was given command of the Army of Helvetia, probably the most important command of his career.

Over a period of months, his forces were increased until he had collected some 80,000 men to face Austro-Russian forces of 50,000 men in the vicinity of Zurich, who were supported by an additional 30,000 Russians under the illustrious Russian general A. Suvórov, marching from Italy to unite the allied armies for the invasion of France. The Battle of Zurich (25-28 September 1799) began at Dietikon and along the Linth; within two days, the Austro-Russian forces at Zurich had been decisively defeated. Masséna then turned against Suvórov, boxing him up in the Linthal valley where his army lost 5,000 men and most of its baggage. This was undoubtedly Masséna's most brilliant victory. His determination, leadership, and incisive action saved France from imminent invasion and had a major impact on the dissolution of the Second Coalition.

With the return of Napoleon from Egypt and the coup d'état of 18 Brumaire, Masséna was appointed to command the exhausted Army of Italy, blockaded at Genoa. He assumed command (7 December 1799) and began to reorganize his army as the Austrians tightened the blockade. Masséna held the city for almost three months until starvation forced him to sign a convention for the evacuation of the city. Nevertheless, Masséna's determined defense forced the Austrian general, M. Melas, to detach 25,000 troops to besiege Genoa, thereby setting the stage for Napoleon's victory at Marengo (14 June 1800).

With his health seriously impaired after the grueling siege of Genoa, Masséna returned home to Reuil, where he remained in retirement for the next five years. He became a member of the Legislative Body and as a committed republican voted against Napoleon's life consulate; nevertheless, Napoleon named him a marshal of France in May 1804. As commander of the Army of Italy in 1805, Masséna, with inferior forces, successfully engaged Archduke Charles' Austrian army in Italy, contributing strategically to Napoleon's victorious Austerlitz campaign. In 1806 he was given a corps in the new Army of Naples in order to subdue the Kingdom of Naples for J. Bonaparte. After resistance had been crushed in Naples, Masséna was given the Seventh Corps of the Grand Army and posted at Pultusk north of Warsaw until the war of the Fourth Coalition was ended (July 1807).

During the Austrian campaign of 1809, Masséna's corps formed the right wing of the French army. At the bloody battle of Aspern-Essling (21-22 May), Masséna and Marshal J. Lannes, cut off by the Danube, successfully held off most of the Austrian army, and at Wagram (6 July) an injured Masséna commanded his corps from a carriage. For his contribution in the campaign, Napoleon later awarded Masséna the title of prince d'Essling and gave him the castle of Thouars.

On his return to France Masséna settled down to recuperate from the physical rigors of the campaign. However, despite his protests, he was given command of the Army of Portugal (April 1810) and ordered to drive the Anglo-Portuguese army into the sea. After the frontier fortresses of Ciudad Rodrigo (10 July) and Almeida (27 August) were besieged and captured, Masséna invaded Portugal and advanced to Bussaco, where he fought the duke of Wellington's army (27 September 1810). Unable to seize the Sierra de Bussaco, he turned the Allied position at Sardao and pursued Wellington to within nineteen miles of Lisbon, only to be halted by the lines of Torres Vedras. Despite unsuccessful appeals to Napoleon for men and supplies, Masséna remained before the lines until 5 March when he began his retreat to the Spanish frontier, closely pursued by Wellington. Masséna made one last unsuccessful attack on Wellington at Fuentes de Onoro (3-5 May) and then was relieved of command and recalled to France in disgrace. Broken in health and blamed for defeat by Napoleon, Masséna never again commanded an army in the field.

During the Restoration he was made a peer by Louis XVIII and given command of the Eighth Military District at Marseille. When Napoleon returned to France in March 1815, Masséna hesitantly acknowledged Napoleon's restoration but played no active role in his military organization. Yet soon after the Bourbons returned to France, he was disgraced and retired to Nice where he died on 4 April 1817.

With the exception of Napoleon, Masséna was the most distinguished French general of his day. Although not a brilliant tactician, in times of crisis his martial abilities were at their peak, and he could inspire his men to do what appeared impossible. His brilliant victories in Italy, Switzerland, and Austria rank him among the greatest soldiers of France. Indeed, the duke of Wellington, his most implacable enemy, acknowledged Masséna as second only to Napoleon as a field commander.

E. Gachot, *Histoire militaire de Masséna, La troisième campagne d'Italie (1805-1806)* (Paris, 1911) and *Histoire militaire de Masséna, La siège de Gênes (1800)* (Paris, 1908); L. Hennequin, *Zurich, Masséna en Suisse* (Paris, 1911); D. Horward, *The Battle of Bussaco: Masséna vs. Wellington* (Tallahassee, Fla., 1965); J. B. Koch, ed., *Mémoires de Masséna redigés d'après les documents qu'il a laissés*, 7 vols. (Paris, 1848-50); J. H. Marshall-Cornwall, *Marshal Masséna* (London, 1965); J. J. Pelet, *Mémoires sur la guerre de 1809*, 4 vols. (Paris, 1824-26).

D. D. Howard

Related entries: BATTLE OF LODI; BATTLE OF ZURICH; PRELIMINAR-IES OF LEOBEN; SECOND COALITION; SUVOROV-RYMNIKSKII; TOULON.

MASSIAC, CLUB. See SAINT-DOMINGUE.

MATHIEZ, ALBERT-XAVIER-EMILE (1874-1932), historian, teacher, and journalist, specializing in the history of the French Revolution. Born to a modest peasant family living in rural Franche-Comté, Mathiez early showed intellectual promise. With the aid of scholarships, he attended secondary schools at Lure and Vesoul before entering the Lycée Lakanal at Sceaux. Admitted to the Ecole Normale Supérieure in 1893, he first spent a year fulfilling his military obligations, doing garrison duty at Belfort. At the Ecole Normale he studied under G. Bloch, G. Monod, and E. Bourgeois, becoming an *agrégé d'histoire* in 1897. With his friend C. Péguy, he also became an ardent socialist. Mathiez began his teaching career at Montauban in 1898 but was transferred summarily the next year because of his strong temperament and enthusiastic republicanism. In 1900 he was awarded a residential scholarship at the Fondation Thiers, where he started work on his doctoral dissertation under F.-A. Aulard. With Aulard's encouragement, he published numerous articles on religious and political history in *La Révolution française*. Mathiez also helped to found the Société d'histoire moderne, and served as its first secretary. In 1901 Mathiez left the Fondation Thiers to marry and resume teaching, first at Châteauroux and then at Caen, presiding over the local chapter of the Ligue des Droits de l'Homme. Promoted to the Lycée Voltaire in Paris (1906), he remained there for five years during which he received his doctorate from the Sorbonne. His principal thesis, *La Théophilanthropie et le culte décadaire, 1796-1801*, studied Revolutionary religion, while his secondary thesis, *Les Origines des cultes révolutionnaires*, applied a Durkheimian explanation to the new cults born during the Revolution. Rising to the University of Besançon (1911-19) and the University of Dijon (1919-26), he sought unsuccessfully to replace Aulard when the latter retired in 1922. But four years later Mathiez secured a lectureship at the University of Paris, only to have his career cut short when he suffered a fatal stroke in his classroom.

Mathiez' early work was largely devoted to religious history, as exemplified by his *La Révolution et l'Eglise* (1910) and *Rome et le clergé français pendant la Constituante* (1911). His fame, however, is linked to his enthusiastic defense of M. Robespierre, whom he sought to rescue from calumny and misunderstanding. In 1907 Mathiez founded the Société des Etudes Robespierristes and its journal, *Annales révolutionnaires* (after 1924 *Annales historiques de la Révolution française*). He broke publicly with Aulard in 1908, conducting a one-sided attack on his former mentor for nearly a quarter-century. Although a socialist and antimilitarist in 1914, Mathiez became a Jacobin patriot at the outbreak of World War I and volunteered for military service despite blindness in one eye. Writing in various newspapers, he attacked German militarism abroad and defeatism at home, while encouraging French hopes for ultimate victory by drawing parallels with the wars of the Revolution. His articles were collected in *La victoire en l'an II* (1916) and *La monarchie et la politique nationale* (1917). Mathiez' wartime experiences with inflation, scarcity, and governmental controls over the economy led him to investigate similar conditions during the 1790s, research later incorporated into his *La vie chère et le mouvement social sous la Terreur* (1927).

The Russian Revolution of March 1917 encouraged him to believe that the work of the French Revolution was continuing and that the new democratic republic would pursue the war against Germany. Disillusioned with A. Kerensky, Mathiez hailed the October Revolution organized by V. Lenin with enthusiasm, seeing the Bolshevik leader as a new Robespierre. Mathiez subsequently joined the French Communist party in 1920. Contributing to the party newspapers *L'Humanité* and *L'Internationale*, he combined historical scholarship with sharp attacks on the ruling conservatives. By 1923, however, he had left the party, complaining of its domination by Moscow. He returned to the socialist ranks and for a time was an avowed Marxist. In homage to J. Jaurès, Mathiez republished the *Histoire socialiste de la Révolution française* (8 vols., 1922-24). His own writings were translated into Russian and he was elected a corresponding member of the Academy of Sciences of the U.S.S.R. But his attitude toward the Soviet Union changed dramatically in 1930 following the arrest of the Russian historians E. Tarlé and S. F. Platonov, as well as evidence of Stalin's growing authoritarianism, which he denounced.

At his death, Mathiez left incomplete a general history of the Revolution: *La Révolution française* (3 vols., 1922-27), *La Réaction thermidorienne* (1929), and *Le Directoire* (1934). Many of his articles were collected in *Etudes robespierristes* (2 vols., 1917-18), *Robespierre terroriste* (1921), and *Autour de Robespierre* (1925), which depicted his hero as thoroughly honest and a staunch defender of popular democracy and social justice. In contrast, his studies of Robespierre's rival, *Danton et la paix* (1919) and *Autour de Danton* (1926), characterized him as immoral, corrupt, a defeatist, and a secret royalist. His other studies include *Girondins et Montagnards* (1930), a history of party rivalries during the period of the Convention, and *Le Dix août* (1932), a popular account of the overthrow of the monarchy in 1792. Mathiez' historical scholarship is marked by his numerous finds in the archives and his vibrant and lucid style.

J. Friguglietti, *Albert Mathiez, Historien révolutionnaire (1874-1932)* (Paris, 1974); J. Godechot, *Un Jury pour la Révolution* (Paris, 1974).

J. Friguglietti

Related entries: AULARD; JAURES; TARLE.

MAURY, JEAN SIFFREIN (1746-1817), cleric and counterrevolutionary. Maury was born in the Comtat-Venaissin, the papal enclave, the son of a cobbler. Despite his later eminence, he never gave up the rough plebeian manners of his origins. Educated at Avignon and Paris, ordained in 1770, he quickly won renown as a preacher. His *Essai sur l'éloquence* (1777) won him election to the Académie Française.

In 1789, the clergy of Péronne named Maury a deputy to the Estates General, and there his oratorical and debating skills brought him to prominence as a vigorous opponent of the nationalization of church property and the Civil Constitution of the Clergy. As relations between Left and Right grew increasingly bitter in 1791, Maury's opposition to the Revolution's course became even more outspoken.

One of the last ecclesiastical deputies of the Right to leave the Assembly, he emigrated in late 1791. On Maury's arrival in Rome, Pius VI named him titular bishop of Nicea and in 1792 sent him as papal nuncio to Frankfurt, where the imperial electors were meeting to choose Leopold II's successor. The appointment of Maury was a clear signal to the Revolutionary leadership in Paris that the papacy was now wholly committed to the destruction of their regime.

In 1794, Pius VI named Maury bishop of Montefiascone and a cardinal. He remained in the Papal States, administering his diocese and advising the pope, until the French invasion of 1798. In 1800, he made his way to Venice and participated in the conclave that elected Pius VII. He was also functioning as ambassador of the Bourbon pretender, the future Louis XVIII. The new pope did not value Maury's advice as his predecessor had done, and in 1806 Maury returned to Paris to serve the Napoleonic empire. His reasons may have been in part frustration at his own diminished role in papal councils, but he may have believed quite sincerely that Napoleon was the new Charlemagne who would restore the church's authority in the world.

As the emperor's relations with the papacy worsened, Maury continued to serve him faithfully. In 1810, he agreed readily to take on the administrative functions of archbishop of Paris, an act that earned him an angry rebuke from Pius VII, then a prisoner at Savona. When the pope was brought to Fontainebleau three years later, Maury was the only one of the cardinals who had rallied to Napoleon whom he refused to see.

At the Bourbon restoration, his one-time *émigré* colleagues would have nothing to do with him. Maury returned to Rome, where he was imprisoned for six months and deprived of his diocese. After several years of obscurity, he died in a Roman monastery in 1817.

Maury had been one of the ablest and most intelligent critics of the actions of the National Assembly. His coarse but effective style, the mixture of idealism and self-serving that motivated his political actions, and his final humiliation all recall P. Laval's transition from socialist to German collaborator in the twentieth century.

E. Hales, *Revolution and Papacy, 1769-1846* (South Bend, Ind., 1966); A. Latreille, *L'église catholique et la Révolution française*, 2d ed. (Paris, 1970); J. Maury, *Correspondance diplomatique et mémoires inédits*, ed. A. Ricard (Paris, 1891).

C. Garrett

Related entries: CIVIL CONSTITUTION OF THE CLERGY; PIUS VI.

MAXIMUM, LAW OF THE. See LAW OF THE MAXIMUM.

MAYENCE, REPUBLIC OF. See REPUBLIC OF MAYENCE.

MEDICINE. The guillotine functioning on the place de la Révolution on 21 January 1793 did more than end the French monarchy in the person of Louis XVI. That instrument of death, and the forces it represented, paradoxically helped create a new status and potential for the healing arts in France and across Europe, sweeping away the baroque edifice of Old Regime medicine to allow the new and vigorous development of the French clinical school.

Dr. J.-I. Guillotin's machine performed with a professional precision in the formerly artisanal and inexact business of execution. Its blade, following a trajectory calculated by the surgeon A. Louis during weeks of experimentation on corpses, dispatched the mighty and the meek alike in an awe-inspiring demonstration of equality before the law: both nature's mechanics and man's new laws of society. Both Louis XVI and A. Lavoisier, the most exalted folkhealer in the kingdom and the aristocratic scientist, perished thus. In a very analogous way, the new medicine and medical elite, invigorated by an infusion of Enlightenment science and optimism and preferring the surgeon's skills to the classics of Galen, scored victories over folk medicine and the traditional medical elite. The very recesses of the human body and the forms of illness concealed within could be exposed by this political and social triumph. The power thus gained has never been relinquished, and the blows that first celebrated it must be counted as some of the most significant in the history of modern medicine.

The victory of the French Revolution and its supporters promoted currents of reform that were already struggling against outmoded political and institutional structures. The upper strata of the Old Regime medical profession—the hospitals, the corporations, and especially the university faculties, all dominated by privileged secular and religious orders—had already been undermined and partially circumvented by new institutions well before the fall of the Bastille. Foremost among these was the Royal Society of Medicine, organized originally in 1776 on the advice of A.-R.-J. Turgot to coordinate a nationwide investigation of epidemic and epizootic disease. While the society never accomplished its ambitious goals of determining the origins of such diseases, it did provide an institutional base for mobilizing and promoting a grander professional self-consciousness, based on duty, sacrifice for humanity, and education in the ideals and methods of Enlightenment science.

In the heady atmosphere of the early Revolution, the reaction against established forms went so far as to abolish most institutions of organized medicine. The three pillars of the Old Regime profession—the hospitals, the corporations, and the faculties—were abolished between 1789 and 1794. The hospitals came under attack early because of their usual close association with religious orders. In November 1789, all property of religious orders was placed at the disposal of the state; remaining hospital property was nationalized, and, in principle at least, all care of the indigent, ill, and infirm was assumed by the state. The corporations were dissolved with the passage of the Le Chapelier law in 1791, and by August of the following year, the universities and medical societies had lost any semblance of normal existence.

This early Revolutionary period, encompassing the National Assembly, Legislative Assembly, and the National Convention, did not aim merely at destruction. A great deal of thought was expended on theories for reorganizing medical care and charity, especially in the work of the Committee of Mendicity from 1790 to late 1791. Under its able chairman, the duc de la Rochefoucauld-Liancourt, the committee outlined a program of domiciliary care supported by resident, publicly paid medical staff guaranteeing the right of every citizen to adequate medical care. Nationwide organization of hospitals and freedom of entry to the medical profession would increase the number of healers and provide more accessible and more effective health care for the whole population. Unfortunately, the press of political disorder, financial need, and continuing military expenditure relegated the committee's program to the status of ideal rather than actuality.

In the countryside, little attention was paid to these grand schemes. By and large, medical care continued in the same forms it had assumed under the Old Regime. Surgeons, augmented by health officers, continued their practices in the smaller towns, treating all manner of accidents and indispositions. Those more exalted practitioners, the physicians, clung to the larger towns wherever those with the means and the taste for university training in medicine demanded their services. Local folkhealers maintained the large, though illegal, share of healing duties they had held under the Old Regime.

Only three differences distinguished the Revolutionary from the preceding periods in terms of medical care. Itinerant and widely reputed folkhealers, the charlatans most often decried by physicians of the period, probably had greater freedom to practice without fear of official repression. Greater care was taken by a department's administration to send physicians into the countryside to treat epidemics, but, as a result of the army's appetite for medical personnel, fewer orthodox healers actually resided outside the larger towns. Thus the complaints of charlatans invading the countryside, which fueled the drive for greater professionalism and licensure after Thermidor, probably had a real basis in a growing contact between physicians and folkhealers in the Revolutionary period.

The reconstruction of the French medical profession and the institutions through which it would later operate began with Thermidor. The ideals of domiciliary care and free entry to the profession were gradually abandoned in favor of guarantees of competence and the centralized licensure and education those guarantees implied. Medical education was reestablished on 4 December 1794, with both theoretical and practical studies at three universities: Paris, Strasbourg, and Montpellier. National control of the hospitals was reversed in September of the following year; they returned to private and communal control and to the service of the new medical elite. Societies of Health and Medical Emulation appeared in 1796, with the purpose of uniting progressive and educated physicians throughout the nation. Qualifications, rather than freedom of entry to the profession, gradually returned to vogue.

These currents of professional self-definition reached fruition in the Law on

Medical Practice of 11 March 1803 (19 Ventôse Year XI). The health officers of the early Revolution were institutionalized under the supervision of medical juries, or committees of local physicians chaired by a university medical professor, in each department. They were to treat the simple indispositions of the countryside with their less rigorous education and lower fees. True physicians, products of the new university system, could practice anywhere in the nation and were bid to supervise health officers in major surgical operations. The remaining surgeons who had practiced under the Old Regime were assimilated with the health officers. Thus was the traditional dual-level hierarchy of the medical profession, as well as the implicit subordination of medical practice in the countryside, perpetuated through the nineteenth century.

Relieved of the weight of outmoded institutions, promoted by the victory of Enlightenment science, institutionalized in reinvigorated universities and teaching hospitals, and protected by licensure, the French medical profession could peer with new eyes into the mysteries of the human body. From England, from the Germanies, and especially from the new United States came students to study at the side of R.-T.-H. Laennec or Louis in the most creative center of medical research in the early nineteenth century: Paris. The blood of the hereditary folk healer mingled with that of a thousand anonymous corpses, reflecting the political and social triumph founding modern scientific medicine.

E. Ackerknecht, *Medicine at the Paris Hospital, 1794-1848* (Baltimore, 1967); F. Dreyfus, *L'assistance sous la Législative et la Convention (1792-95)* (Paris, 1905); M. Foucault, *The Birth of the Clinic*, trans. A. M. Sheridan Smith (New York, 1975); J. Leonard, *Les médecins de l'ouest au 19ᵉ siècle* (Paris, 1976); G. Rosen, "Hospitals, Medical Care and Social Policy in the French Revolution," in G. Rosen, ed., *From Medical Police to Social Medicine* (New York, 1974); D. M. Vess, *Medical Revolution in France, 1789-1796* (Gainesville, 1975).

J. V. Spears

Related entries: GUILLOTINE; LE CHAPELIER; 9 THERMIDOR YEAR II; SCIENCE.

MEHEE DE LA TOUCHE, JEAN-CLAUDE-HIPPOLYTE (1760–1826), editor of *L'ami des citoyens*. See TALLIEN.

MEHUL, ETIENNE-NICOLAS (1763–1817), operatic composer, writer of first *opéras comiques*. See MUSIC.

MENOU, JACQUES-FRANCOIS, BARON DE (1750-1810), general. Born in Boussay-de-Loches, Touraine, Menou received the education of a provincial nobleman and entered the army. Having risen through the ranks, he was *maréchal de camp* (major general) on the eve of the French Revolution, when he was elected by the nobility of Touraine to serve in the Estates General. As a member of the National Constituent Assembly, he was a monarchist who opposed a state religion, supported liberty, and believed that the power to make war and peace should be in the hands of the nation rather than the monarch. As a soldier he supported reforms in the army and the peacetime draft of 100,000 men in 1791. Menou's liberalism, which grew during the years of the Revolution, enabled him to remain in the army under the Republic. He was second in command of the garrison of Paris in 1792, and in 1793 he fought in the Vendée. By 1795 he commanded the Army of the Interior. On 13 Vendémiaire General Menou yielded his command to General N. Bonaparte, who subdued the rightist insurrection. Menou's somewhat questionable conduct in connection with the Vendémiaire uprising resulted in his receiving minor commands in the interior for the next two and one half years.

In 1798 Menou joined the Egyptian expedition and sailed with Bonaparte to the land of the Nile where he took an active part in the campaign. While in Egypt he married, adopted the Moslem religion, and added "Abdallah" to his name. When General J.-B. Kléber was assassinated, after being left in command of the expedition when Bonaparte returned to France (1799), General Menou, as senior officer, succeeded him. Following his undistinguished handling of affairs, he presided over the evacuation of Egypt and the return of the remnants of the army to France. Napoleon, who had little respect for Menou's military abilities, used him in an administrative capacity in Italy under the Empire. He was named administrative general of Piedmont in 1803 and then governor general of Tuscany in 1808. The following year he became governor general of Venice, where he died in 1810.

F. Rousseau, *Kléber et Menou en Egypte, depuis le départ de Bonaparte, août 1799-septembre 1801* (Paris, 1900); G. Six, *Les généraux de la Révolution et de l'Empire* (Paris, 1947); J. d'Yvray, *La vie aventureuse du général Menou* (Paris, 1938).

J. G. Gallaher

Related entries: EGYPTIAN EXPEDITION; KLEBER; 13 VENDEMIAIRE YEAR IV.

MERCURE NATIONAL (1789-91), newspaper. For convenience, historians have labeled the succession of journals that L. de Kéralio (1758–1822) edited the *Mercure national*. In actuality, Kéralio, one of the best-known female journalists of the Revolution, called her first periodical (begun 13 August 1789) *Journal d'état et du citoyen*. Assisted initially only by her father, she added in December 1789 a number of collaborators, including F. Robert (1763–1826), her future spouse, and altered her journal's title to *Mercure national ou journal d'état et du citoyen*. A merger in September 1790 with A. Tournon's *Révolutions de l'Europe* brought about several more changes. Some participants left, and the new editors, apparently dominated by Robert, selected two titles in two weeks, settling finally on *Mercure national et révolutions de l'Europe*. One later shift occurred as Robert and the now Madame Robert shed all past coworkers, located still another partner, P. Lebrun-Tondu, and renamed their product *Mercure national ou journal politique de l'Europe*.

Through all these vicissitudes and different renditions of the *Mercure national*, some characteristics persisted. The journalists promulgated the boldly Revolutionary ideas of the Cordeliers, but their newspaper maintained a relatively restrained tone. The publicists avoided character assassination and tended to focus on less controversial affairs, such as National Assembly debates. This restraint possibly stemmed from their background. Although the journalists' personal proclivities led them to embrace radical notions, they were reasonably wealthy. Perhaps their comfortable life moderated the stridency, if not the content, of their convictions.

L. Antheunis, *Le conventionnel belge François Robert (1763-1826) et sa femme Louise de Kéralio (1758-1822)* (Wetteren, 1955).

J. Censer

Related entries: CORDELIERS CLUB; LEBRUN.

MERCURE NATIONAL ET REVOLUTIONS DE L' EUROPE. See *MERCURE NATIONAL.*

MERCURE NATIONAL OU JOURNAL POLITIQUE DE L' EUROPE. See *MERCURE NATIONAL.*

MERCY-ARGENTEAU, FLORIMOND-CLAUDE, COMTE DE (1727-94), Austrian diplomat, born in Liège. After studying at the Royal Military Academy in Turin, Mercy entered the Austrian diplomatic service and took part in Prince Kaunitz's mission to Paris, which led to the Franco-Austrian alliance of 1756. He thereafter served as Austrian minister in Turin and ambassador in St. Petersburg.

In 1766 Mercy was appointed ambassador to Paris, where he played a leading role in negotiating the betrothal of the Austrian archduchess Marie Antoinette to the dauphin Louis. When Marie Antoinette departed for Paris in 1770, her mother, Empress Maria Theresa, instructed her to put her full confidence in Mercy. Thereafter Mercy sent the empress frequent, detailed reports on her daughter and received from her voluminous advice, which he conveyed to the young dauphine. When Louis XVI succeeded to the throne in 1774, Mercy became one of the most powerful men in France since he had the new queen's ear. He did not hesitate to use his unique position of confidence to intervene in France's internal affairs, to Austria's advantage; and he used this influence in support of E.-C. de Loménie de Brienne and later of J. Necker.

Following the outbreak of the Revolution, Mercy at first counseled moderation and sought to reconcile the royal couple and H.-G.-R. Mirabeau through his Belgian compatriot, the comte de La Marck. Louis XVI and particularly Marie Antoinette were, however, increasingly inclined to heed more reactionary advice. Although they were persuaded to meet secretly with Mirabeau in July 1790, they placed no confidence in him. Marie Antoinette meanwhile strove to influence Mercy into adopting a more uncompromising opposition to the Revolution and, through him, the court of Vienna.

Mercy was recalled from Paris by Emperor Leopold II to serve as his pleni-potentiary at the Congress of the Hague (1790) for the pacification of the re-bellious Austrian Netherlands, over which he was then appointed governor general. Here he sought to counterbalance the conservative Estates party, which he considered responsible for the rebellion against Austrian rule, by playing off against it the more democratic Vonckist faction, which he nevertheless mistrusted because of the influence of the French Revolution.

Marie Antoinette, in collaboration with the baron de Breteuil, the marquis de Bouillé, and the Swedish count A. von Fersen, secretly planned the escape of the royal family from Paris, beginning in the winter of 1790-91. She wrote repeatedly to Mercy, urging him to use his influence to impress on Leopold II the danger to all thrones posed by the French Revolution and to secure his firm commitment to intervene. As Austria was then at war with Turkey, Mercy could only counsel patience, although Leopold finally did agree to provide help on the eve of the flight of the royal family in June 1791.

After the failure of the escape attempt at Varennes and the return of the royal family to Paris in captivity, Mercy's opposition to the Revolution became implacable. Although also mistrusting the motives of the *émigrés* in Coblentz, he dissuaded Vienna from recognizing a regency under the comte de Provence. Following the outbreak of the War of the First Coalition (1792–97) in April 1792, Marie Antoinette urged through Mercy that Austria and Prussia issue a threatening declaration to discourage French opposition and to protect the royal family (the Brunswick Manifesto). In endorsing such a declaration, Mercy recommended to Vienna that most of France be partitioned among the neighboring powers.

Mercy was forced to flee Brussels ahead of the French invasion in the fall of 1792 and take refuge in Germany, where he was involved in various attempts to save the French royal family. In July 1794 he was appointed Austrian ambassador extraordinary to London, to negotiate a renewed allied offensive against the French, but he died only a few days after arriving there. For nearly three decades he had been the key figure in Austro-French relations.

A. von Arneth, ed., *Marie Antoinette, Joseph II und Leopold II. Ihr Briefwechsel* (Leipzig, 1866); A. d'Arneth and J. Flammermont, eds., *Correspondance secrète du comte de Mercy-Argenteau avec Joseph II et le prince de Kaunitz*, 2 vols. (Paris, 1889–91); A. d'Arneth and A. Geffroy, eds., *Correspondances secrètes de Marie-Thérèse avec le comte de Mercy*, 3 vols. (Paris, 1874); C. de Pimodan, *Le comte F.-C. de Mercy-Argenteau* (Paris, 1911).

H. A. Barton

Related entries: BOUILLE; BRETEUIL; BRUNSWICK MANIFESTO; FERSEN; FIRST COALITION; LA MARCK; LOMENIE DE BRIENNE; MIRABEAU; NECKER; PROVENCE; VONCK.

MERLIN DE DOUAI, PHILIPPE-ANTOINE, COMTE DE (1754–1838),

deputy to the Estates General, the National Convention, and the Council of

Ancients; minister, director, and noted legal expert. Born in the northern village of Arleux in 1754, the son of a farmer, Merlin studied law in Douai and was received as an *avocat* in the Parlement of Flanders in 1775. Before the Revolution, Merlin established his reputation as a contributor to legal studies and as an attorney in celebrated cases.

In 1789 he was elected to the Estates General from the *bailliage* of Douai, and he soon made a name for himself as one of the foremost legal experts in the Constituent Assembly. He wrote the report on the abolition of the feudal regime, was a member of the committees on the constitution and on the sale of national properties, and proposed much of the new legislation regarding the family. In 1792 the department of the Nord elected him to the National Convention where he voted for the death sentence in the trial of Louis XVI. Despite his active participation in the committee on legislation, Merlin never felt comfortable with the Jacobin leadership and supported the overthrow of M. Robespierre.

After 9 Thermidor, Merlin was elected to the Committee of Public Safety where he played an important role in both internal politics and foreign affairs. He was also the chief author of the Convention's criminal code, which remained in force until 1811. Many of its provisions were incorporated into the Napoleonic criminal code. In 1795 Merlin was elected to the Council of Ancients, but he gave up his seat to become minister of justice. After a brief stint organizing the newly created Ministry of Police, he returned to the Justice post. Merlin was elected to the Executive Directory after the coup of 18 Fructidor Year V (4 September 1797). As minister and as a director, Merlin was known for his rigorous repression of both rightist and leftist organizations. Four months before Bonaparte's coup d'état, Merlin was forced to resign and return to private life. The majority of members in the legislative councils increasingly resented the interference of the directors in internal politics, and they blamed the directors for the failures of republican foreign policy.

During the Consulate and Empire, Merlin served as *procureur général* for the Tribunal de Cassation, the supreme court. Napoleon made him a count in 1810. When the Bourbons returned for a second time in 1815, Merlin was forced into exile in Belgium. He came back after the revolution of 1830 and died in Paris in 1838.

Merlin served the Revolution in many different capacities. Between 1789 and 1799 he was a deputy three times, a civil court judge in Paris, minister, and director. He never was a very popular politician, but he earned enormous respect as a jurist and legislator. From the Old Regime through the Empire, Merlin worked tirelessly to shape the French legal code, to fashion a new legal system, and to reconcile old and new legal forms. He was a reformer but also a compiler and a commentator on the law. It was this interest and skill at interpreting the many changes in the legal system that distinguished him as a Revolutionary jurist.

A. Cocâtre-Zilgien, "Merlin de Douai et le droit public de la monarchie française,"

Rev. hist. de dr. franç. et étr. 38 (1960); R. Falco, "Philippe-Antoine Merlin de Douai," *Révo. française* 17 (1939); L. Gruffy, *La vie et l'oeuvre juridique de Merlin de Douai* (Paris, 1934).

L. A. Hunt

Related entries: BAILLIAGE; BIENS NATIONAUX; COMMITTEE OF PUBLIC SAFETY; COUNCIL OF ANCIENTS; COUP OF 18 BRUMAIRE; COUP OF 18 FRUCTIDOR YEAR V; DIRECTORY; 9 THERMIDOR YEAR II.

MERLIN DE THIONVILLE, ANTOINE-CHRISTOPHE (1762-1833), deputy to the Legislative Assembly, the Convention, and the Council of Five Hundred and representative on mission. Merlin came from a bourgeois family of Thionville where his father served as a judicial officer. After a brief training for a career in the church, Merlin turned to the study of law and in 1788 became an *avocat* with the Parlement of Metz. He welcomed the Revolution enthusiastically and during its first two years helped consolidate it in Thionville through his service as a municipal official and officer in the National Guard.

His career as a deputy spanned the most turbulent years of the Revolutionary decade. Voters of the Moselle department elected him to the Legislative Assembly in 1791 and to the National Convention the following year. He sat on various committees and shortly after Thermidor served on the Committee of General Security and as president of the Convention.

A man of action rather than a parliamentarian, Merlin is best remembered for the missions he undertook for the Legislative Assembly and the Convention. With foreign invasion imminent and the nation in crisis following the insurrection of 10 August 1792, the Legislative Assembly sent Merlin to the departments of the Somme, Aisne, and Oise to raise troops and arouse the patriotism of the population. The Convention sent him on three missions, the first and most celebrated of which was to the Army of the Rhine in the first half of 1793. In addition to providing for the needs of the army, Merlin propagandized vigorously first to revolutionize and later to annex to France the area on the left bank of the Rhine occupied by this army. When his propaganda failed to convince the hostile population, he did not hesitate to use force to bring about an affirmative result in a plebiscite on the question of annexation. When Mainz, the chief city in the area, fell under siege by the Prussians in June 1793, Merlin became the soul of the French defense. He supervised the strengthening of the city's fortifications, encouraged the Republican soldiers to hold firm, and set an example to them by participating courageously in the combat. The garrison withstood the assault for nearly two months but was forced to capitulate on 24 July. By this time the Republic was again threatened by its enemies within and without, and in the new crisis that led to the Terror, there were accusations that various political and military leaders were in collusion with the enemy. Merlin and the officers who had commanded in Mainz were charged with not having done enough to hold the city, but Merlin, now back in the Convention, refuted the charge and won from the deputies a commendation for the army's role during the siege.

From September to November 1793, Merlin was in the Vendée, where civil war raged between Republicans and royalists and in 1794-95 he was again with the Army of the Rhine. Under the Directory and the Consulate, Merlin's political influence diminished. He represented the Moselle in the Council of Five Hundred until May 1798 and then held administrative posts until his withdrawal from public affairs in 1802 when N. Bonaparte made himself consul for life. Merlin returned briefly to the political scene in 1814 when he tried unsuccessfully to raise a force to resist the Allied army then invading France. He died in Paris in 1833.

Merlin has been praised by historians for his patriotism, courage, zeal for the Revolution, and humanity toward the enemies of the Revolution during the periods of the worst excesses. He has also been condemned for his unprincipled political conduct. At the outset of his parliamentary career in 1791, the impetuous Merlin established a reputation as one of the violent deputies on the extreme Left. He joined the Jacobins and became noted for his attacks on the court, the *émigrés*, and refractory priests. He participated in the attack on the Tuileries on 10 August 1792 and later the same month demanded that wives and children of *émigrés* be seized as hostages. In the Convention he sat with the Mountain, defended M. Robespierre against his enemies, and as early as October 1792 demanded the execution of the dethroned king. When the Convention was judging the king in January 1793, Merlin was in Mainz, but he sent a letter asking for the death sentence. At the time of Robespierre's downfall in July 1794, however, Merlin changed course abruptly and became an ardent Thermidorian. In the following months he harassed his former Jacobin friends, labeled them "butchers," proposed the closing of their clubs, and urged the deportation of Jacobins who had held important positions during the Terror. Merlin has also been harshly judged for his personal conduct. He aroused suspicion because of the rapidity with which he accumulated money after he became a legislator, while his ostentatious display of wealth fell far short of the standards expected of a republican and representative of the people. The reputation of the courageous patriot was thus tarnished by political opportunism and personal failings.

A. Kuscinski, ed., *Dictionnaire des conventionnels* (Paris, 1919); R. Merlin, *Merlin de Thionville d'après des documents inédits*, 2 vols. (Paris, 1927).

J. P. McLaughlin

Related entries: COMMITTEE OF GENERAL SECURITY; DOCTRINE OF NATURAL FRONTIERS; LAW OF 14 FRIMAIRE; 9 THERMIDOR YEAR II; REPRESENTATIVES ON MISSION; REPUBLIC OF MAYENCE; THERMIDORIAN REACTION; VENDEE.

MERVEILLEUSES, ironical name given to the most prominent leaders of female fashion, in the Thermidorian and Directory periods. Parisian ladies' dress styles during this time, promoted by the journal *La magasin des modes*, were inspired by both neoclassical simplicity and a snobbish Anglophilism (although the latter characteristic was more marked among the *merveilleuses'* male partners, the *incroyables*). The so-called antique style favored a simple white tunic of muslin, worn with bare arms, sandals, no stockings, and gold rings on the toes. Madame Récamier, the banker's wife whose portrait was painted by J.-L. David, wore such white tunics with a thread of gold. This Greek-inspired style also favored a high waist, gathered by a blue or black belt, which served to hold a fan. The more extravagant dressers, often associated with the *nouveaux-riches*, earned the title *merveilleuses*. Madame Hamelin, wife of a government contractor, was seen in a costume that was topless save for a thin veil. In addition, there was a vogue for *chapeaux à l'anglaise*, some of which were decked in flowers, plumes, and ribbons.

This parade of fashion was partly a self-conscious reaction against the puritanical social mores associated with the Terror. At the infamous *Bal des Victimes*, entrants had to provide the death certificate of a relative killed during the Revolution. Immediately after 9 Thermidor Year II, there was a brief vogue for the wig, a symbol of *ancien régime* society; and L.-S. Mercier reports a brisk trade in blonde wigs, conducted by ex-nuns.

The most notorious leader of Paris fashion in the later 1790s was Madame Tallien. Formerly Thérèse Cabarrus, daughter of a banker in Spain, she married the *conventionnel* Tallien in the Year III and gave birth to a daughter named Thermidor. She subsequently became the mistress of the director P. Barras and then the contractor G. Ouvrard, who were financially well capable of indulging her exacting taste in dress and entertainment. Her appetite for extravagant clothes and lavish furnishings was matched only by J. de Beauharnais, of whom Barras cynically remarked that she would have drunk gold out of her lover's skull.

J. Godechot, *La vie quotidienne en France sous le Directoire* (Paris, 1977); L.-S. Mercier, *Le nouveau Paris* (Paris, 1798); R. A. Weigert, *Incroyables et merveilleuses* (Paris, 1955).

M. Lyons

Related entries: BARRAS; CABARRUS, J.-M.-I.-T.; DAVID; 9 THERMIDOR YEAR II; RECAMIER; TERROR, THE.

MESMER, FRIEDRICH-ANTON (1734-1815), scientist. Born in a village in Swabia, the son of an impecunious forester, Mesmer received a thorough education in the schools and universities of Bavaria and Austria, probably on scholarship in preparation for the priesthood. In the process, he came in contact with the magical-mystical tradition of such figures as J. B. van Helmont, Paracelsus (T. B. von Hohenheim), and A. Kircher. In 1759 he went to the University of Vienna to study law and then switched to medicine. He received his doctorate in 1766, having presented a thesis that speculated on the currently popular question of the existence of invisible fluids that behaved in conformity with Newton's laws of planetary motion. The next year he joined Vienna's medical faculty, one of the most respected in Europe. Influenced also by the Hapsburg court astronomer who practiced healing by the use of magnets and by the activities of the Bavarian exorcist, J. J. Gassner, Mesmer now began to develop a theory of healing based on the magnetic attraction of these invisible fluids in the body. His marriage to a wealthy widow gave him an entry into Viennese society.

What appears today to be a bizarre muddle of occultism and credulity was seen by many in the eighteenth century as an entirely plausible extension of the work of the great Newton. Mesmer's techniques seemed to be especially effective on young female hysterics. Mesmer saw patients in his town house–clinic, engaged in his researches, and pursued his love of music. The Mozarts were close friends.

Despite the apparent success of his clinic and a decade of lecture demonstrations of his theories of animal magnetism throughout the German Catholic world, Vienna's medical establishment became openly hostile. In 1778 Mesmer left Vienna for Paris, where he launched a campaign to force French scientific bodies to acknowledge his great medical discovery. In this he failed completely, in part because his theory of curing through touch, seeking poles for the infusion of those mesmeric fluids that would restore the body's natural harmony, was diametrically opposed to the conventional practices of bleeding and purging. Despite his followers' recording and documenting of hundreds of apparent cures (Mesmer himself wrote only two pamphlets in his own behalf), in 1784 a royal commission including A. Lavoisier, J.-S. Bailly, and B. Franklin declared that Mesmer's fluid did not exist. Mesmer left France, and after traveling through England, Austria, Germany, and Italy, he lived quietly in Switzerland for the last thirty years of his life. Mesmerism, especially through the Puységur brothers' techniques of hypnotism that entirely dispensed with the invisible fluids, would be an intellectual force for another century, but as a scientific theorem mesmerism was without further significance.

Mesmer's importance for the French Revolution, as R. Darnton has shown, lies less in Mesmer himself than in the sociopolitical program that some French followers built on his foundations. Led by the Lyon lawyer N. Bergasse, they erected an elaborate theoretical system and a pseudo-Masonic network of Sociétés de l'Harmonie Universelle. In 1785, the Bergasse faction was expelled for challenging Mesmer's authority and pressing for a more extensive propaganda campaign. Meeting at the home of the banker G. Kornmann, the dissidents moved steadily in the direction of direct political activism for the sake of generating a revolution that would produce in France a harmonious society, whose outlines owed as much to J.-J. Rousseau's ideas as they did to Mesmer's. A large number of important future Revolutionaries had their sensibilities shaped in part by the activities and speculations of the Kornmann group.

With the coming of the Revolution, reality rapidly outran theory, and those who had been Revolutionaries for the sake of mesmerism or mesmerists for the sake of Revolution found themselves utterly divided. The splintered movement survived, to be absorbed into a variety of nineteenth-century philosophical systems, but in the decade before the Revolution, it had offered a faith that a new age was dawning in which all of society was to be transformed.

R. Darnton, *Mesmerism and the End of the Enlightenment in France* (Cambridge, Mass., 1968); *Dictionary of Scientific Biography*, ed. C. C. Gillispie (New York, 1974); F. Rausky, *Mesmer ou la Révolution thérapeutique* (Paris, 1977).

C. Garrett

Related entries: BAILLY; BRISSOT DE WARVILLE; CARRA; LAFAYETTE; LAVOISIER; LYON; MARAT.

METRIC SYSTEM. See LEGENDRE.

MIDI, FEDERAL REPUBLIC OF THE. See COUNTERREVOLUTION.

MILES, WILLIAM AUGUSTUS (1753?-1817), political writer, British intelligence agent in Liège (1785-90) and Paris (1790-91). From the publication of his first "Selim" letters in 1770 to his last "Hampden" letters in the *Independent Whig* (1817), Miles lived by the power of his pen. After serving in the navy in the American Revolution, he settled near Liège, where he published letters under the signatures of "Neptune" and "Gracchus" in the *London Morning Post*. The letters, which supported W. Pitt and condemned the Whigs, created a greater stir than anything since the appearance of the Junius letters. When Miles offered his services as an intelligence agent on the Continent in 1785, Pitt accepted his offer and paid him 250 pounds per year. His intelligence reports are still extant in the Public Record Office.

During the Nootka Sound controversy in 1790, Miles moved to Paris, joined the Jacobin club and the Society of 1789, wrote countless letters on the Revolution, and became known as Pitt's secret agent. On his return to London in April 1791, Pitt discontinued his services as a confidential agent but paid him 500 pounds per annum to support his government in the newspapers.

When war between Britain and France appeared to be imminent in the winter of 1792, French emissaries used Miles to contact Pitt's ministry. Through letters to P.-H. Lebrun, French minister of foreign affairs, Miles sought unsuccessfully to preserve the peace during the last-minute missions of H.-B. Maret in London and C. Dumouriez in Holland.

Miles continued to support Pitt until 1797. Thereafter the increasingly conservative prime minister and the liberal pamphleteer parted company. Miles now attacked Pitt as a spineless coxcomb who had needlessly flung England into war in 1793 when George III ordered him to fight France or resign. This turnabout and unproved thesis was reiterated in Miles's *Letter to the Prince of Wales* (1808), in his unfinished "History of the French Revolution," and in several Whig histories of the Revolution.

H. V. Evans, "William Pitt, William Miles, and the French Revolution," *Bull. of the Inst. of Hist. Res.* 43 (November 1970); C. P. Miles, ed., *The Correspondence of W. A.*

Miles on the French Revolution, 2 vols. (London, 1890); The Miles MSS in the possession of M. Claude Waddington (Paris), a direct descendant of W. A. Miles.

H. V. Evans

Related entries: LEBRUN; NOOTKA SOUND CONTROVERSY; PITT; SOCIETY OF 1789.

MIRABEAU, HONORE-GABRIEL RIQUETTI, COMTE DE (1749–91), foremost orator of the National Constituent Assembly, Jacobin, secret agent of the monarchy. Mirabeau's pre-Revolutionary career had an enormous effect on his future. He was born on 9 March 1749, the son of M.-G. de Vassan and the marquis de Mirabeau, a celebrated political and economic theorist. His eight years in prison as a profligate youth, due mainly to *lettres de cachet* obtained by his father who detested him, and his subsequent career as a hired pamphleteer on the Paris *Bourse*, gave him an unsavory reputation in Paris and at court. Also, by subjecting J. Necker's past record to a series of scathing denunciations, Mirabeau created in the finance minister an unalterable opposition to any alliance with him. Rejected by his own order, Mirabeau was overwhelmingly elected to the Estates General as a deputy of the Third Estate from Aix-en-Provence.

Mirabeau's Revolutionary career can be divided into three stages. During his most famous demagogic activity from May 1789 to March 1790, he became the most feared orator of the National Assembly. Although his disreputable past at first caused him to be held in general opprobrium by the deputies, his influence in the Assembly and in Paris underwent a dramatic change during the tumultuous events of June and July 1789. His famous speech at the royal session of 23 June 1789, in which he challenged the master of ceremonies to remove the deputies by force, and his savage attack on the government following the encirclement of Versailles and Paris with troops in July established his reputation as a dauntless tribune of the people. Mirabeau also assiduously cultivated popularity within the Parisian electoral districts but was rebuffed in his attempt to establish an alliance with Necker and A.-M. Montmorin, the foreign minister.

The primacy of Mirabeau's political ambitions over any ideological considerations explains his role during the October Days. The National Assembly's acceptance of his motions to reject Louis XVI's plea for aid and to follow the royal family to Paris made both the king and the Assembly virtual prisoners of the Paris *menu peuple*, over whom Mirabeau exercised a great deal of influence. Mirabeau may also have participated at that time in the abortive conspiracy to make the duc d'Orléans either regent or lieutenant general of the kingdom.

Less than a month later, aware of the strong opposition to him at court and convinced that his best avenue to a ministerial post was through the legislature, Mirabeau decided that the time had come to establish a parliamentary ministry that would guarantee effective cooperation between the executive and legislative branches of government. But largely out of fear and distrust of him, on 7 November 1789 the Assembly voted by a large margin to exclude all deputies from the ministry and other governmental positions during the present legislative session.

Mirabeau's career changed dramatically during its second stage from March to October 1790, when he eagerly seized on the opportunity for a secret alliance with the monarchy. Louis XVI offered generous monetary rewards to Mirabeau for his support of royal interests in the Assembly and for his advice on matters pertaining to the Revolution. Demonstrating no thought of having prostituted himself, Mirabeau boasted of having finally contrived a means of making his ideas triumph at court.

During the summer and fall of 1790, Mirabeau submitted various plans of action to the court, most of which foundered on the king's indecision. For example, after Mirabeau had maneuvered Necker's resignation, the monarch did not follow his recommendation to select a new ministry from the Assembly and present the legislature with a fait accompli. Angered over the consistent rejection of his advice, Mirabeau decided to resume the role of demagogue in order to refurbish his popularity and to show the court their need of him.

In the third stage of Mirabeau's career, from October 1790 to April 1791, he reached the pinnacle of his power with the Left and his most cooperative stage with the monarchy. During the fall and winter of 1790-91, the former riding school of the Tuileries rang with Mirabeau's demagogic speeches, which ranged from a vigorous defense of the mutineers in the French fleet at Brest to a vicious denunciation of the nonjuring clergy. These speeches not only won him unstinted praise from the galleries of the Assembly and from many of the Paris sections but were instrumental in his surge to power at the Jacobin club, where he was elected president on 30 November 1790, and then reelected to an unprecedented second consecutive term. On 29 January 1791, he achieved a major goal with his election as the forty-fourth president of the National Assembly. In vehement reaction, the court accused him of base betrayal.

Nevertheless, Mirabeau's relations with the monarchy underwent a profound change when Montmorin, in December 1790, sought an alliance with him. Montmorin hoped to restore his own credit at court through a plan to revitalize the monarchy, which Mirabeau agreed to devise. Mirabeau proposed the establishment of a series of secret agents, unknown to each other, who would operate within the National Assembly, Paris, and the provinces. The major step in his plan was the king's escape from Paris to the eastern frontier, where he would declare the abolition of the National Assembly and the establishment of a new legislative body. Although feeling that Mirabeau had greatly exaggerated the dangers facing the monarchy, Louis XVI, under pressure from the queen, released funds through Montmorin's office for the implementation of the cabal.

The conspiracy underwent a rapid development. Mirabeau hired journalists and publicists to influence public opinion and won over P.-V. Malouet who promised him the support of fifty other deputies of the Assembly. The marquis de Bouillé, commander of the northeastern frontier, pledged commitment to Mirabeau's plan, and A.-O. Talon, a lieutenant of the Paris Châtelet, succeeded in infiltrating the Paris police. The king's public image started to improve and there was less vilification of the queen. Yet, just at this moment, when Mirabeau was convinced that his plan was succeeding, he fell ill and died on 2 April 1791.

Two important conclusions emerge from an analysis of Mirabeau's role in the French Revolution. First, prior to his death, considerable progress had been made in Paris and in the National Assembly with the conspiracy that ended with his demise. Second, ambition rather than venality or ideology was the keynote in Mirabeau's Revolutionary career. He wanted above all else to play a leading role in the momentous events that were reshaping France but was unable to obtain a post in the ministry. The duplicity of his conduct, as evidenced by a continuous pursuit of all possible avenues toward political power, engendered a grave distrust in him by others and created an infinite circle of frustration instead of an efficacious path toward his goal.

A. de Bacourt, ed., *Correspondance entre le comte de Mirabeau et le comte de La Marck pendant les années 1789, 1790, et 1791*, 2 vols. (Brussels, 1851); D. M. Epstein, "The Role of Mirabeau in the French Revolution" (Ph.D. dissertation, University of Nebraska, 1967); P. Guilhaume, *Mirabeau* (Paris, 1982); L. and M. Loménie, *Les Mirabeau: Nouvelles études sur la société française au XVIIIᵉ siècle*, 5 vols. (Paris, 1889-91); L. de Montigny, ed., *Mémoires biographiques, littéraires et politiques de Mirabeau: Ecrits par lui-même, son père, son oncle et son fils adoptif*, 8 vols. (Paris, 1834); O. J. G. Welch, *Mirabeau: A Study of a Democratic Monarchist* (London, 1951).

D. M. Epstein

Related entries: BOUILLE; CLAVIERE; DUMONT; MALOUET; MONTMORIN DE SAINT-HEREM; NECKER; OCTOBER DAYS; TALON.

MIRANDA, FRANCISCO DE (1750-1816), general, Revolutionary. After his childhood years in Caracas, Miranda began his young adult life as an apparently loyal servant of the Spanish crown. He sought and received a commission in the Spanish army, serving in Spain and the Mediterranean from 1771 to 1780. In 1780 he sailed with Spanish troops sent to attack English strongholds along the Gulf of Mexico and in the Caribbean. He rose to the rank of lieutenant colonel but in 1782 was arrested for being rebellious. Miranda had already entered into seditious correspondence with South American malcontents, and he had become interested in the newly independent United States. He escaped Spanish justice in Havana and toured the new nation from June 1783 to December 1784. Leaving Boston, he sailed for Europe. Constantly under the shadow of Spanish persecution, he traveled extensively, reaching Russia where he gained the favor and protection of Catherine II.

These wanderings ended when he arrived in Paris in March 1792. Miranda came with letters of introduction to J.-P. Brissot, J. Pétion, and others of the Girondist faction. After war began in April, they asked him to aid the French in the struggle, to which he agreed, although he insisted that the French consider their support of a liberation movement in South America. Through Girondist influence, he received a commission as a major general. Sent to join the army under General C. Dumouriez in early September, Miranda commanded troops at Valmy. He then went north with the army. While not at Jemappes, he did play a conspicuous role in the subsequent conquest of the Austrian Netherlands. He captured Antwerp and commanded the siege of Maastricht. Before this siege was successful, however, the Austrians reentered the Netherlands. At the Battle of Neerwinden on 18 March 1793, Miranda commanded the left wing of the army. The retreat of Miranda's troops doomed the French to defeat that day. Dumouriez soon charged Miranda with incompetence and disloyalty. There is no reason to see Miranda as a great military commander, but it is important to realize that the battalions in his wing were new levies and hardly reliable. Dumouriez also had other reasons to attack Miranda, since Miranda would have nothing to do with Dumouriez' treasonous schemes. On 21 March Miranda was sent to Paris in order to answer to the Revolutionary Tribunal.

He was acquitted in May but never exercised command again after Neerwinden. His active involvement in French affairs was at an end. In July 1793 he was again arrested, this time because his Girondist associations compromised him in the eyes of the Committee of Public Safety. Released in January 1795, he soon ran afoul of the government and was placed under arrest and subjected to police surveillance in November of that year. After the coup of 18 Fructidor, Miranda's name appeared on the list to be transported to Guyana, so he wisely fled France in January 1798.

Going to England, he tried unsuccessfully to gain support for a South American rising. Returning to France in October 1800 he was ejected five months later. Between that time and 1812 he launched a premature and unsuccessful invasion of Venezuela, met S. Bolivar, and with him took part in a more successful rebellion in 1810. Indeed, in April 1812 Miranda was appointed chief of the rebel army. Faced, however, by a superior Spanish force and weakened by crumbling support, Miranda concluded an armistice that Bolivar believed treasonous. Miranda was betrayed into Spanish hands in July 1812. Sent to Spain, he died in a Cadiz prison in 1816.

Miranda was more a revolutionary than a general. His peripheral commitment to the American Revolution, his direct involvement in the French Revolution, and his lifelong dedication to Latin American independence make his life a microcosm of what some have called the Atlantic revolution.

R. R. Palmer, *The Age of the Democratic Revolution*, 2 vols. (Princeton, 1959-64); C. Parra-Perez, *Miranda et la Révolution française* (Paris, 1925); W. S. Robertson, *The Life of Miranda*, 2 vols. (Chapel Hill, N.C., 1929).

J. A. Lynn

Related entries: BATTLE OF NEERWINDEN; BATTLE OF VALMY; BRISSOT DE WARVILLE; COMMITTEE OF PUBLIC SAFETY; DUMOURIEZ; GIRONDINS; PETION DE VILLENEUVE.

MOMORO, ANTOINE-FRANCOIS (1756-94), leading member of the Cordeliers club and dechristianizer. Momoro was born in Besançon of an old Spanish family. Arriving in Paris as a young man, he became a skilled printer and successful book dealer. His *Traité élémentaire de l'imprimerie ou le manuel de l'imprimeur* (1786), which went through several editions, was composed in the form of a dictionary and defined the technical terms and processes used in printing. When the Revolution began, he joined the Cordeliers, becoming secretary of the club and editor of its journal. On 10 June 1791 he was elected secretary of his section's primary assembly (Théâtre français, later Marat) and on 2 July became an elector.

After the king's unsuccessful flight to Varennes, he joined with the Amis de la Verité (Cercle Social) opposing Louis' reinstatement, and immediately after the Champ de Mars "massacre" he drafted an indignant report in which he held the marquis de Lafayette responsible for the event. As a result, he was imprisoned in the Conciergerie on 9-10 August 1791 and was not released until 15 September. He was bitter when he left prison, resenting both his arrest and his loss of a livelihood.

After the overthrow of the monarchy on 10 August 1792, Momoro was elected (21 August) to the administration of the Paris department and to its directory. Nine months later he was assigned to the Vendée as one of the commissioners of the Executive Council where he signed C.-P. Ronsin's and J.-A. Rossignol's letter to the Committee of Public Safety regarding the steps that ought to be taken for the defense of Saumur. In a letter to F.-N. Vincent he accused a number of government agents of treason and urged that nobles be purged from the army. While on his mission in the Vendée, he was accompanied by his wife, M.-F.-J. Fournier, whom he had married in 1786 and treated like a *grande dame,* an action resented by several of his future enemies. She was to preside as the goddess of liberty during the celebration of the Cult of Reason in the fall of 1793.

His ideas were more radical than those of the leading Jacobins, as may be seen in his addresses, petitions, and public statements. In May 1793 Momoro examined the rights of property in *Opinion sur la fixation du maximum du prix des grains* and concluded that the products of the soil belonged to society rather than to individual owners. When popular societies came under attack by the Jacobins, he made the sensible reply that although it was true in some sections intriguers had abused the privileges accorded to popular clubs, the right to meet in these bodies was sacred.

On 14 Ventôse Year II (March 1794), the Cordeliers had veiled the Declaration of the Rights of Man in protest against the policy of compromise with the Jacobins of the right (the Indulgents, as A. Mathiez termed them). The following day, after an epic campaign by the government for victory in the war, Momoro appeared at the head of a delegation from his section with loaves of saltpeter to donate to the Convention. In presenting his gift, he reminded the deputies that his section possessed an inexhaustible source of moral saltpeter whose explosions had so often served the cause of liberty and of equality. None of this could have endeared him to the government.

The intemperate remarks of J.-B. Carrier and J.-R. Hébert, calling for a holy insurrection and supported by Momoro, Vincent, and others, alarmed the government. Although the visit of a delegation of Jacobins led by J.-M. Collot d'Herbois seemed to heal the breach between them and the Cordeliers, when Collot asked to see the *procès-verbal* of the meeting at which threats of insurrection had been made, Momoro, who presided, evaded a forthright answer. Instead, he offered the excuse that several amendments had been made during the session and were not yet incorporated into the minutes and that the complete *procès-verbal* would be published after it had been adopted definitively by the society. That his own sentiments were quite different may be gleaned from a document found among his papers after his arrest. In it he denounced the perfidious system created by cowardly men who because they lacked vigor, made it criminal to have it, and who did not want to be reminded of the principle of liberty and equality which they openly violated.

Momoro was arrested during the night of 23-24 Ventôse (13-14 March), and his premises were searched the following day, yielding nothing suspicious. The denunciations received by the Revolutionary Tribunal accused him of conducting the general assembly of his section despotically whenever he presided and of threatening those who opposed him. Others claimed that during the session of the section Marat on 15 Ventôse, when a motion for insurrection had been made, a citizen, recognizing the danger of such a proposal, asked for the floor to read a report on the state of provisions, but Momoro, as chairman of the session, attacked him for wanting to turn away the discussion from the larger objectives of the meeting. Momoro knew that he was doomed and took his farewell in a letter to his wife, who had also been arrested. He was executed with the leading Cordeliers on 4 Germinal Year II (24 March 1794).

Ann. hist. de la Révo. française 3 (1926); A. Mathiez, *Le club des Cordeliers pendant la crise de Varennes et le massacre du champs de mars* (Paris, 1910); A.-F. Momoro, *Rapport sur l'état politique de la Vendée fait au Comité de salut public de la Convention Nationale, au Conseil exécutif et au département de Paris* (Paris, s.d.), *Rapport sur les événemens de la guerre de la Vendée et le plan d'oppression dirigé contre les chauds républicains...fait à la société des Cordeliers* (Paris, 1794), and *Traité élémentaire de l'imprimerie ou le manuel de l'imprimeur* (Paris, 1786).

                                                                          M. Slavin

Related entries: CARRIER; CERCLE SOCIAL; CHAMP DE MARS "MASSACRE"; COLLOT D'HERBOIS; CORDELIERS CLUB; DECHRISTIANIZATION; HEBERT; INDULGENTS; PRISONS; SECTIONS; VARENNES.

MONARCHIENS, derogatory term applied to those coalitions of groups during the early Revolution that supported the concept of a representative monarchy. The term is commonly applied first to that faction of the patriot party, led by J.-J. Mounier, that supported in the constitutional debates of 1789 a second legislative chamber and greater royal authority than available under the suspensive veto. These proposals appeared in early 1789 in Mounier's pamphlet *Nouvelles observations sur les Etats-Généraux*. Mounier found himself joined by such liberal nobles as T.-G. Lally-Tollendal, S. Clermont-Tonnerre, and P.-V. Malouet.

In his report to the National Constituent Assembly on 9 July, Mounier urged that the body proceed first to determining the precise form of government rather than preoccupying itself with individual issues. Shortly after the Assembly's votes on 10-11 September against his views on the government, Mounier resigned and was followed by Lally-Tollendal and other *monarchiens*.

In December 1790, a new organization was founded under the leadership of Clermont-Tonnerre under the title Amis de la Constitution monarchique, taking for their motto Liberty and Fidelity. Following the flight to Varennes, the society and its journal disbanded.

C. Du Bus, *Stanislas de Clermont-Tonnerre et l'échec de la Révolution monarchique (1757-1792)* (Paris, 1931); J. Egret, *La Révolution des Notables: Mounier et les Monarchiens, 1789* (Paris, 1950); D. M. Epstein, "*Les Impartiaux* and *Le Club Monarchique*: A Study of the Failure of the Constitutional Monarchists During the French Revolution," *Red Riv. Val. Hist. J. of W. Hist.* 3 (1978); *Journal* [de la Société] *des Amis de la Constitution monarchique*, 18 décembre 1790-18 juin 1791.

R. R. Crout

Related entries: CLERMONT-TONNERRE; LALLY-TOLLENDAL; MALOUET; MOUNIER; PATRIOT PARTY; SUSPENSIVE VETO.

MONGE, GASPARD (1746-1818), scientist, academician, and educator. Born the son of a modest merchant at Beaune, Monge was destined to become one of the leading scientific figures of the age. The young Monge received an excellent education at the Oratorian collège at Beaune and at the collège de la Trinité at Lyon. He early showed a strong aptitude for science and mathematics, such that he was permitted to teach a course in physics at Lyon. Monge's work in mapping his native town soon brought him to the attention of an officer at the Royal Engineering School at Mézières in 1765. Admitted to the school, he studied draftsmanship and the building of model fortresses. His introduction of descriptive geometry into plans for fortifications won him a permanent position at the school, where he would teach until 1784. Already by 1775 he had attained the rank of royal professor of mathematics and physics. Five years later he was admitted to the prestigious Academy of Sciences as a result of his experimental work. Most of Monge's scientific papers dealt with problems in mathematical theory and applications of descriptive geometry to practical military questions. Monge also turned his attention to chemistry and physics, conducting numerous experiments. Appointed an examiner of naval cadets in 1783, he found that his new position required long absences from his teaching post at Mézières, which he felt compelled to give up the next year. Between 1784 and 1792 he continued his tours of inspection of naval schools while maintaining his scientific endeavors and presenting numerous papers to the Academy of Sciences.

Although the Revolution had begun in 1789, Monge played no active role in the turbulent political events of the day. Instead, he continued his scientific work without a break. In 1790, along with several other leading scholars, he was named to a Central Commission on Weights and Measures, which helped to prepare the way for the metric system. But after the fall of the monarchy in August 1792, Monge was unexpectedly named minister of the navy by the Legislative Assembly, at the recommendation of the marquis de Condorcet, because of Monge's abilities and familiarity with naval questions. He held the position until April 1793, when physical exhaustion and political criticism forced him to resign. During his brief ministry, he labored strenuously to reorganize and rearm the weakened French fleet, as well as to expand production of arms and munitions production.

Now free to return to his scientific work, Monge threw himself into the war effort on behalf of the embattled Republic. During the Terror he, along with A. Fourcroy and C.-L. Berthollet, succeeded in developing a process to use bronze from confiscated church bells to make cannon, as well as inventing methods to manufacture high-quality steel and means to gather and refine saltpeter for producing gunpowder. At the same time, Monge strove to develop improved forms of higher education to train military and civil engineers. In March 1794 he was named to serve on a commission charged with establishing a Central School for Public Works, the predecessor of the modern Ecole Polytechnique. From November 1794, when the first classes met, to March 1795, Monge lectured on descriptive geometry to the new generation of engineers. He also helped to found the Institut National in 1795-96, a body intended to replace the old Academy of Sciences abolished in August 1793.

Monge was not destined to remain an academic, however. In May 1796 he was designated by the Directory to serve on the Commission of Sciences and Arts in Italy. There he was to inspect and preserve artistic and scientific objects captured by the republican armies under N. Bonaparte. His work as a commissioner took him throughout the Italian peninsula. As a result, he became friendly with Bonaparte, who, because of his knowledge of Monge's earlier scientific studies, received him warmly. When French military victories over the Austrians resulted in the Treaty of Campoformio in October 1797, Monge and his colleague Berthollet were charged with transmitting the treaty to the Directory, along with a vast collection of art objects confiscated by the French.

After seventeen months abroad, Monge resumed his teaching and assumed the directorship of the Ecole Polytechnique, to which he had been named in September 1797. After only three months in Paris, he was once more chosen to carry out a mission to Italy, this time to serve as a political commissioner in Rome where he was to conduct an inquiry into the murder of the French representative, L. Duphot. Monge's mission took on greater importance when he helped to establish the Roman Republic, replacing the papacy of Pius VI, who fled the city. In Rome Monge concerned himself chiefly with such questions as the establishment of a scientific society and the selection of artworks to be sent back to France.

While in Italy, Monge was approached by Bonaparte to help organize an expedition to Egypt that the general was preparing, specifically to select maps, reports, and other information needed for the adventure. Bonaparte also pressed Monge to take part in the expedition. At first unenthusiastic, the middle-aged scholar eventually consented. Meanwhile, Monge learned that he had been elected, without any campaigning on his part, to the Council of Ancients by three departments and to the Council of Five Hundred by his native Côte-d'Or. He could not participate in the legislature, for he was already preparing to leave for Egypt.

Sailing from Civita Vecchia in May, Monge joined Bonaparte's fleet off Malta. He participated in the capture of Alexandria in July and then made the difficult march across the desert to Cairo. There he was given important assignments by Bonaparte, including the establishment of a printing press, the creation of the Institute of Egypt (which he headed), the administrative reorganization of the country, and the tracing of the ancient Roman canal between the Nile and the Red Sea. Monge accompanied Bonaparte on his military expedition into Palestine and Syria from February to June 1799. He suffered severely from dysentery and survived largely because Bonaparte ordered that he receive good care.

Returning to Egypt after the failure of the expedition, Monge resumed his scientific and administrative activities. These ended abruptly when Bonaparte secretly departed from Egypt in August, leaving most of his troops behind but taking along a select group, including the valuable Monge. The two ships that carried them back to France escaped capture by the British fleet and arrived off the French coast in October. After twenty months away from home, Monge eagerly returned to Paris, where he resumed his duties as director of the Ecole Polytechnique.

In November Bonaparte overthrew the Directory in the coup of 18 Brumaire. He soon rewarded the scientist who had shared so many adventures with him by naming Monge to the Conservative Senate. Loyal to the first consul, later the emperor, Monge was elevated to the Legion of Honor in 1804, chosen president of the Imperial Senate in 1806, and named comte de Pélouse in 1808. Meanwhile he pursued his scientific experiments, publishing various treatises on mathematics.

The last years of the Empire saw a deterioration in Monge's health, but he did not suffer politically when the Bourbons were restored in April 1814. He continued to participate in the work of the Institut until Napoleon returned from exile during the Hundred Days. Monge compromised himself by renewing his friendship with the emperor and accepting a peerage. Fearing reprisals from the monarchists after the Second Restoration, the elderly scientist fled to the Netherlands in October. Returning to Paris after a five-month exile, Monge found himself expelled from the Institut and dismissed from the Ecole Polytechnique. Exhausted and disheartened, he died in October 1818.

P. V. Aubry, *Monge, le savant ami de Napoléon Bonaparte, 1746-1818* (Paris, 1954); C. Richard, *Le comité de salut public et les fabrications de guerre sous la Terreur* (Paris, 1922); R. Taton, *L'oeuvre scientifique de Gaspard Monge* (Paris, 1951).

J. Friguglietti

Related entries: CONDORCET; EDUCATION; EGYPTIAN EXPEDITION; ROMAN REPUBLIC; SCIENCE; TREATY OF CAMPOFORMIO.

MONITEUR UNIVERSEL, newspaper founded by Charles-Joseph Panckoucke and the best known journal of the Revolutionary period. The French Revolution caused immense problems for Panckoucke (1736-98), the magnate of periodical publishing in the Old Regime. Before 1789 he had employed many legal advantages together with consummate business acumen to reduce competition substantially. But a rich political life emerged, creating unprecedented types of news that no Panckoucke journal was ready to cover. Furthermore, in May 1789 the authorities lifted restrictions on other publicists, who hurried to report these exciting events. Far more committed to his business interests than to the new freedoms, Panckoucke endeavored to improve his competitive position by acquiring a new legal advantage. On 23 May 1789 he requested permission from the Estates General to become the official publisher of their debates, resolutions, and other proceedings. Despite the representatives' rejection of his proposition, this idea gave birth to the *Moniteur*.

Although denied a monopoly, Panckoucke knew that, to contend with his opposition, he must thoroughly report news from Versailles, Paris, and elsewhere. He added a political correspondent to one of his papers, the *Mercure de France*, and he published a summary of the Estates General's activities as a supplement to his journal, the *Gazette de France*. On 24 November 1789 Panckoucke greatly extended his efforts by releasing the first issue of the daily *Gazette national ou moniteur universel*. Endeavoring to provide unofficially what he would have liked to do with official sanction, he envisioned the *Moniteur* as the paper of record for the Revolution. He intended this publication to include reports on the National Assembly and governmental administration, as well as international news, information on cultural and economic life, and advertisements. Commentary was to be minimal. Despite the breadth of this project, for a variety of reasons it was not at first well received. In February 1790 Panckoucke overcame this difficulty by attracting H.-B. Maret (1763-1839) to write the accounts of the National Assembly.

Maret's ability to record speeches verbatim allowed him to make a significant contribution to the *Moniteur*. At the beginning of the Estates General, no special arrangement for reporting speeches existed, so correspondents had to struggle to comprehend the remarks. Maret seems to have had an uncanny memory and a sophisticated system of abbreviations for following the interchanges. From the start, many demanded his accounts, and from September 1789 he edited his own journal. In February 1790, Panckoucke persuaded Maret to publish his reports simultaneously in the *Moniteur*. Also at this time the journalist began to cast the debates in the form of dialogues instead of synopsized arguments, and this added power to the accounts. His accurate descriptions made Panckoucke's journal indispensable, giving it the reputation of the most reliable source for news.

With Maret on the staff, circulation rapidly reached a high level; 8,500 subscribed by 1792. Relatively expensive, the journal cost 72 *livres* in Paris, 84 in the provinces, and single issues sold for 6 *sous*. The staff of the periodical was large and constantly renewing itself. Even after Maret resigned, his successors preserved his techniques.

The *Moniteur* adapted well to the increasing radicalization of the Revolution. As new governments came into power, the newspaper simply reported the activities of each. Monarchist until 10 August 1792, the *Moniteur* parroted Girondist views until June 1793 and Jacobin ideas during the Terror. The paper's format, which emphasized reporting over editorializing, made these shifts easy. Furthermore, Panckoucke, though he believed in a constitutional monarchy, faithfully pursued his business interests, never allowing ideology to alter his procedures. This dutiful acceptance of the ruling group guaranteed survival, and indeed governments came to rely on the *Moniteur*. A succession of leaderships subsidized the newspaper. In 1794 Panckoucke relinquished the journal to his son-in-law I. Agasse, who followed the same politically prudent policies. Governments trusted the *Moniteur* so much that in 1800 it became, as Panckoucke had originally desired, the official French newspaper especially designated by the government to publish all its laws, regulations, and pronouncements. It held this position, with a short interruption in 1814, until it ceased publication in 1869.

E. Hatin, *Histoire de la presse*, vol. 5 (Paris, 1860); S. Tucoo-Chala, *Charles-Joseph Panckoucke et la librairie française, 1736-1798* (Pau and Paris, 1977); G. B. Watts, "Charles-Joseph Panckoucke, l'Atlas de la librairie française," *Stud. on Voltaire and Eighteenth Cent.* 68 (1972).

J. Censer

Related entries: AMI DU PEUPLE, L'; AMI DU ROI; CHRONIQUE DE PARIS; MERCURE NATIONAL; REVOLUTIONS DE FRANCE ET DE BRABANT.

MONTAGNARDS, left-wing deputies in the National Convention (1792-95), frequently characterized in relation to their conflict with the Girondins and their support for the government of the Terror. The original members of the Mountain chose the highest seats in the Manège where the Convention met in 1792, but they were also later referred to in an allegorical sense ("Moses sought his laws on a mountain; so too the Mountain of the Convention will give laws to France.")

The group nicknamed the Mountain gradually crystallized between 1791 and mid-1793 in response to pressures imposed by a series of political crises and partly in opposition to the political views being expressed by the so-called Girondins. During 1791-92, a number of both future Girondins and future Montagnards belonged to the Jacobin club, within which a conflict originating in M.

Robespierre's disagreement with J.-P. Brissot over the prospect of war became more serious as the crisis of the monarchy reached its climax. After the monarchy fell, there was complete estrangement between Robespierre, associated with the Revolutionary Paris Commune, and Brissot and his allies in the Legislative Assembly. In September 1792, the election of the Parisian delegation to the Convention took place in the Jacobin club (possibly because of its size and convenience) at the same time as the September Massacres. Brissot, A. Kersaint, and the marquis de Condorcet lost the Parisian seats they had held in the Legislative, although they were reelected elsewhere, whereas M. Robespierre, G.-J. Danton, and J.-P. Marat were chosen as members of a delegation dominated by the left wing of the club in alliance with the Cordeliers; in addition, Robespierre had endangered the lives of Brissot and J.-M. Roland de la Platière by trying to have them arrested while the massacres were proceeding. Henceforth, Brissot and his friends saw nearly all the Parisian deputies as tools of the Paris Commune and the club as a vehicle for bloodthirsty radicalism; by the end of October, some leading Girondins had been expelled from it, and others had resigned. Traditionally, those remaining in the club were to form the core of the Montagnard group, but it should also be noted that some conspicuous Montagnards, of whom L. Carnot was one, never joined it, and that attachment to the group went beyond the club's boundaries.

Both at this time and later, the Girondins consistently described the Montagnards as a small faction, closely linked with Paris and sympathetic to Parisian radical attitudes. The question of Paris was indeed central but not quite in the sense implied. Few Montagnards actively approved of the massacres, and the Parisian right to intervene in national politics was so little conceded that in 1794 it was the Montagnard Committee of Public Safety that brought the Commune under effective control. The Montagnards from the Parisian delegation were a total of 20 or 21 in a Convention of 749 and contributed only three members to the Committee of Public Safety, whose other 9 deputies had been elected by 9 different departments. The response of leading Montagnards to the grocery riots of February 1793, the long delay between the first maximum in May and the general maximum in September, and the way the latter was administered suggest that Parisian economic grievances were not always understood or Parisian remedies automatically accepted.

There were connections, nevertheless, established before the Convention met, between leading Montagnards and the Commune, and debates in the Jacobin club were open to the public. The temper of the Montagnards was democratic, as their 1793 constitution showed; the constitution also reflected concern for the poor and an acceptance of the right to work, combined with the principle of private property and a modest egalitarianism, which chimed well enough with *sans-culotte* attitudes. The great majority of Montagnards were fully aware of the political danger of Parisian assertiveness, especially if it could be seen as threatening the independence of the Convention. What they refused to do was to rate this as the most serious danger of early 1793 or to contemplate taking the risk of calling in departmental help to protect the Convention against the capital. This they saw as suicidally divisive. In any choice between a policy that might be tainted by Parisian-type republicanism and a policy that might give openings to provincial royalism, the Montagnards took the risk of leaning toward the Republic, even if as a consequence they might be labeled *septembriseurs*.

How numerous the Montagnards were when the Convention first met is hard to estimate, although some deputies, such as G.-A. Couthon, were already being influenced toward them by the intemperate attacks on the Commune in general, and Robespierre, Danton, and Marat in particular, by which the Girondins drove their opponents closer together than they might otherwise have been. With the king's trial, some of the issues began to clarify. The Girondin proposal of a referendum was seen as politically irresponsible and was soundly defeated. Among the victorious regicides were some who showed Parisian-type bloodlust, but many more saw the outcome as a just one, even if it were approved in Paris. The trial was significant in that not only were the future Montagnards virtually all regicides, but also the regicides were eventually very largely Montagnard. Moreover, from this point on regicides controlled the executive committees, supplied the majority of deputies on mission, and sponsored the greater part of important legislation. There was in fact a Montagnard government, if such a thing could be said to exist, on the national level. On the local level, the Parisian-Girondin enmity continued; Girondin efforts to rally provincial support could hardly be prevented; there seemed no solution to a dangerous problem except interference with the Convention's membership, which few Montagnards were willing either to commit or permit. The eventual Parisian rising was tolerated rather than approved and was indeed rejected by some—P.-J. Cambon, for example—who became closely associated with the government of the Terror.

The Montagnard regime, which emerged to cope with a frightening emergency, took shape slowly and commanded support from a range of very different deputies. How close any of these came to having socialist principles can still be a matter of contention; at the other extreme, R. Lindet and B. Barère can hardly be called social radicals. The variety of opinion was well illustrated within the Committee of Public Safety itself. Among the Montagnards more generally, disparities of outlook were complicated by jealousies and ambitions—for example, among deputies on mission, by rivalries between the executive committees and friction between them and their colleagues, by the venality of some who feared retribution, and by conflicts of temperament as well as by differing political judgments. Outside the Convention but working with men within it were politicians from the Commune and the Cordeliers. The opaque and confusing evidence gives occasional glimpses of a vast jungle of intrigue. As the crisis passed in late 1793, there were a series of Montagnard conflicts, producing first, the myth of a foreign plot (but financial intrigue was real enough), and then the fall and execution of the two factions of Hébertists and Dantonists. As the war swept toward the victory of Fleurus (June 1794), Robespierre grew increasingly isolated and conspicuous, and his intentions became a crucial problem. He was a central figure on the Committee of Public Safety, the orator of a future democratic Republic, but ardent dechristianizers now feared his Cult of the Supreme Being, Danton's sympathizers feared his puritanism, returning terrorists feared inquiry, and the purpose of the new Police Bureau and the Law of 22 Prairial was uncertain. To conflict between the executive committees was added serious division within the Committee of Public Safety itself. Never a monolith, the Mountain disintegrated, and with the help of its renegades, the Thermidorian regime emerged.

After Thermidor, those who clung to left-wing ideals or who opposed Thermidorian vengeance against real or suspected terrorists were a beleaguered minority. For a while they still staffed the committees, and, despite the closing of the Jacobin club (November 1794), there were still a hundred left in 1795, but the Germinal-Prairial risings (April-May 1795) were the excuse for the final onslaught, which brought for many deputies arrest, suicide, exile, or flight. Even the Two-thirds law brought few of them into the Directory's legislature, and they were not again a major force in national politics, though the last phase of the Directory saw a brief neo-Jacobin revival. About two-thirds of the survivors followed their parliamentary careers with civil service posts. The proportion serving Napoleon was virtually the same as that in the Convention at large; it does not seem that regicides were especially likely to seek security in the Empire. Among those still living in 1816, a high proportion were exiled.

The number of Montagnards in the Convention has long been underestimated, perhaps because of Girondin insistence that the Montagnard regime was the domination of a small minority over the great majority of deputies and perhaps also because after Thermidor it was in no one's interest to argue that Montagnard policies had had a substantial measure of support. The lack of party organization and the divergence of attitudes among recognized members of the group make it necessary for historians to establish their own criteria; hence, there is never likely to be complete agreement on the size of the group or the identity of its members. Nevertheless, recent research suggests a considerable amount of consensus.

It can be argued that to be acceptable as a Montagnard, a deputy should be (1) reputed to have sat with the Mountain or (2) identifiable, at least until the end of 1793, as a member of the Jacobin club of Paris, or (3) both a supporter of a Montagnard line in the *appels nominaux* of January-June 1793 and willing to appear as a supporter of the regime in 1793-94. Category 3 would exclude time-servers and waverers who accepted Montagnard leadership only after the events of mid-1793 made it seem pointless to oppose it and could also ensure that little-known deputies classified as Montagnard did have to go through the catalytic experience of the king's trial. Thus *suppléants* and deputies who did not reach Paris until after 21 January 1793 can be eliminated, though their left-wing attitude may have been deeply held, and so can deputies on mission in January, unless their allegiance is otherwise attested. Those who died, resigned, or otherwise left the Convention by mid-1793 can also be excluded.

Using these criteria, the total number of Montagnards would be 302: 73 men sitting with the Mountain, although not known as members of the Jacobin club, 142 identifiable Jacobins, and 87 deputies who combined left-wing voting with later support for the Montagnard regime. A different estimate has lowered this figure to 258 (57 sitting with the Mountain, 137 Jacobins, 64 others), but would raise it to 267 by adding 9 supposed Montagnards who did not reach the Convention until after the death of the king. This would reduce the size of the Mountain by about 15 percent, leaving it still very much larger than the Gironde and only slightly smaller than the Plain, whose Montagnard-sympathizing left wing would be somewhat increased. The classification of the deputies in dispute depends on personal judgment and on the weight attached to small, sometimes contradictory pieces of evidence. One difficulty about a minimum-sized Mountain is that this makes the voting patterns of 1793 totally consistent, with no room for a few mavericks who, despite a generally Montagnard outlook, may genuinely have believed that it would be politically wiser to let Louis live or who thought Marat was a public danger. But small details of disagreement seem less important than the fact that independent inquiries have agreed on the existence of a very substantial body of Montagnards, more than a third of the whole Convention, and that general conclusions about the characteristics of the Mountain are unaffected—are indeed strengthened—by the removal of marginal candidates.

Whether one considers the larger number or the smaller, it is not easy to distinguish the Mountain from the rest of the Convention on social grounds alone. The social background of deputies of all political outlooks was fairly uniform and so was the range of occupations, although, interestingly, a reduction in Montagnard numbers eliminates a few men of undoubtedly lower-class background. If the Montagnards sympathized with the *sans-culottes*, the poorest members of the Convention were not necessarily Montagnard. In geographical origin, there was some bias toward the northern and eastern, rather than the southern and western, departments, but if the Parisian delegation is omitted, this was a bias of 60 percent against 40 percent, which is not extreme. (Among the 48 deputies who were actually Parisian, as against the 24 elected to represent Paris, 27 at most were Montagnard and 13 were Girondin; the city was not politically of one mind, as May 1793 fully demonstrated.) Like the leadership—but not the followers—among the Girondins, the Jacobins among the Montagnards came disproportionately from urban backgrounds, but this is not the most striking difference between the Mountain and the rest of the Convention. What distinguished the Montagnards as a group were age and previous political experience.

In the Convention as a whole, two-thirds of the deputies were, in January 1793, under forty-five years old. For the Mountain, the figure was 72.5 percent; for the rest of the Convention, less than 63 percent. Over 52 percent of the Montagnards, fewer than 40 percent of their colleagues, were under forty; and the Montagnards were unique in having their heaviest concentration of membership in the 35 to 39 age bracket, a characteristic mirrored among the membership of the Committee of Public Safety, whose average age was just over 36. The Girondin leaders were on average even younger than the Montagnards, but they did not attract a following of their own kind—rather, they were backed by the middle-aged—whereas the pattern among the Montagnards, whatever the degree of their commitment, was surprisingly uniform.

The other striking characteristic of the Mountain as a whole is the amount of support it attracted from the ex-deputies of the Legislative Assembly, who provided something like 40 percent of its members. It had a very low proportion of the completely inexperienced, and setting aside the ex-Constituents, who by 1793 were wary of commitment, it could be said that the higher the level of political experience, the more likely it was that the deputy would be Montagnard. Given the origin of the Gironde among the deputies of the Legislative and the presumed Montagnard base in the Paris Commune, this is not quite what one might expect, but it was so. France's first constitutional legislature was a nursery of Montagnards-to-be, and the prototype Montagnard, could there be such a person, would be not a radical Parisian *littérateur* like P.-F. Fabre d'Eglantine but a provincial lawyer-deputy like Couthon.

M. Bouloiseau, *La République jacobine* (Paris, 1972); A. Kuscinski, *Dictionnaire des conventionnels* (Paris, 1916-20); A. Mathiez, *La Révolution française* (Paris, 1927); A. Patrick, *The Men of the First French Republic* (Baltimore, 1972); G. Rudé, *Robespierre: Portrait of a Revolutionary Democrat* (London, 1975); A. Soboul, *The French Revolution*, trans. (London, 1973) and ed., *Girondins et Montagnards* (Paris, 1980).

A. Patrick

Related entries: BRISSOT DE WARVILLE; CARNOT; CONSTITUTION OF 1793; CORDELIERS CLUB; CULT OF THE SUPREME BEING; GIRONDINS; HEBERTISTS; INDULGENTS; JACOBINS; LAW OF 14 FRIMAIRE; LAW OF THE MAXIMUM; LAW OF 22 PRAIRIAL; REPRESENTATIVES ON MISSION; *SANS-CULOTTES*; TWO-THIRDS LAW.

MONTESQUIEU, CHARLES-LOUIS DE SECONDAT, BARON DE LA BREDE ET DE (1689-1755), writer, historian, political philosopher. Born at La Brède, near Bordeaux, on 18 January 1689, of a family with roots well established in both the sword and the robe nobility, Montesquieu was educated by the Oratorians at the renowned collège de Juilly. In 1709, after a brief period of legal study in Bordeaux, he was drawn to Paris, where he encountered some of the more daring thinkers of the last years of Louis XIV's reign and acquainted himself with the heterodox ideas that were then finding clandestine expression. Recalled to Bordeaux on his father's death in 1713, he entered on the life of a seigneur and provincial landowner, producing for the lucrative Bordeaux wine trade. His fortune was enhanced in 1715 by an advantageous marriage (to a wife who retained her Huguenot faith) and extended in 1717 by the inheritance of the prestigious office of *president à mortier* in the Parlement of Bordeaux. Thus firmly established in the two principal occupations of the Bordelais noble elite— wine production and the magistracy—Montesquieu naturally joined its more intellectual members in the Academy of Bordeaux, to which he offered several early papers, principally on scientific topics.

The *Lettres persanes*, the book that was to establish Montesquieu's literary reputation and forge the link between literature and social criticism that became a defining characteristic of the French Enlightenment, was published anonymously (as were his other major works) in Amsterdam in 1721. It immediately enjoyed an enormous success. Its shimmering literary brilliance and satirical wit gave expression to an explosion of ideas and discontents that had accumulated in the last years of Louis XIV's reign and now burst forth in the freer air of the Regency. While the satire of the *Lettres persanes* amused, it also pricked established allegiances. Through the eyes of Montesquieu's Persians, Frenchmen saw the pope as ''an old idol worshipped out of habit,'' their late king as ''a great magician,'' and their laws and customs as an offense to human reason. While its harem scenes titillated, they also raised fundamental questions about the nature of human sociability and the relationship between natural virtue and institutionalized practices—not only in Persia but in France. Exploiting the potential of the epistolary form for ''joining philosophy, politics and ethics to a novel, and linking the whole together by a secret and, in some respects, hidden chain,'' Montesquieu also offered a sustained critique of the drift of the French monarchy towards despotism.

The success of the *Lettres persanes* gained Montesquieu ready acceptance in court circles and in the salons of the capital, and he may also have participated in the reform-minded discussions of the Club de l'Entresol. Nor did his earlier jibes at the Académie française prevent his admission to that body in 1728. Shortly after, having earlier sold his parlementary office to free himself for such travels, Montesquieu embarked on a lengthy tour of Europe with extended stays in Italy and England (where, during his two-year visit, he was elected to the Royal Society and became a Freemason). It was during this period that his understanding of English politics was formed, shaped by observation and by the opposition views of H. Saint-John viscount Bolingbroke.

The importance of classical republican themes in English political debate seems also to have rekindled Montesquieu's interest in Roman history. On his return to France, he began work on his *Considérations sur les causes de la grandeur des Romains et de leur décadence* (1734). Like N. Machiavelli, to whom this work owes much by way of inspiration, Montesquieu offered a bold exploration of the relationship between civic virtue and republican government, between political liberty and factional conflict, between military expansion and moral corruption, between general and particular causes in political life. The *Considérations* laid the historical basis for Montesquieu's claim in *De l'esprit des lois* that political virtue is the principle of republican government and gave powerful impetus to the tradition of classical republicanism that was to shape the consciousness of the French Revolutionaries so profoundly.

In 1748, Montesquieu published *De l'esprit des lois*, the massive study of the nature of political and legal forms and of their sociological determinants with which he claimed to have wrestled for twenty years. Clerical attacks did little to impede its recognition throughout Europe (and America) as a classic expression of the new spirit of enlightenment in search of principles of reason, humanity, and moderation in human affairs. Nor was any other work to shape the language of eighteenth-century political thought more profoundly. Montesquieu offered a new typology of the forms and principles of government, in which monarchy— constituted by the existence of ''intermediary powers,'' which served to maintain the fundamental laws, and sustained by the sentiment of honor—appeared as the moderate, tempered form appropriate to modern societies, in contrast to the self-destructive regime of a despotism (in which all lived in fear under the arbitrary will of the despot) or the free exercise of popular sovereignty in the ancient republics (which depended upon the rigorous demands of civic virtue). In doing so, he articulated the principles of an aristocratic liberalism that provided the essential terms of parlementary, constitutionalist opposition to arbitrary royal authority in France until the Revolution. *De l'esprit des lois* also propounded a powerful interpretation of the nature of the English constitution in terms of a theory of balanced government and the separation of legislative, executive, and judicial powers, a theory that was to inform the constitutional debates of revolutionary assemblies in both America and in France. Concluding his work with a lengthy contribution to the historical debate over the nature and origins of the early French constitution, Montesquieu offered a modified version of the *thèse nobiliaire* and developed a comprehensive analysis of the emergence of feudalism.

Montesquieu died in Paris on 10 February 1755. During the French Revolution, his authority was particularly strong before 1791 and among those who favored a balance of powers under a monarchical regime. But there are still echoes in the discourse of the Terror of his insistence that virtue must be the spring of republican government.

L. Althusser, *Politics and History* (London, 1972); E. Carcassonne, *Montesquieu et le problème de la constitution française au XVIIIe siècle* (Paris, 1926); C. L. Montesquieu, *Lettres persanes*, ed. P. Vernière (Paris, 1960); M. Richter, *The Political Theory of Montesquieu* (Cambridge, 1977); R. Shackleton, *Montesquieu: A Critical Biography* (Oxford, 1961); P. Vernière, *Montesquieu et l'esprit des lois ou la raison impure* (Paris, 1977).

K. Baker

Related entry: ESPRIT DES LOIS, L'.

MONTESQUIOU-FEZENSAC, ANNE-PIERRE, MARQUIS DE (1739-98), writer and general. Montesquiou-Fézénsac was born in 1739 to a noble family of the Périgord. In 1761 he was appointed colonel of the Regiment du Vaisseau and in 1771 became the first equerry to the comte de Provence. Through this position he became a close friend of the comte. In 1788 Montesquiou-Fézénsac was given command of an infantry division and, later in the same year, led an army division in Alsace.

In 1789 he was elected to the Estates General as a representative of the nobles from the *bailliage* of Meaux. Although a close friend of Provence and presumably an advocate of his viewpoint, Montesquiou-Fézénsac proposed that the nobles should surrender their privileges in taxation. Because of his willingness to speak out on matters of taxation and finances, in 1789 he was selected for the Committee of Finances in the National Constituent Assembly, and soon became its *rapporteur*. In April 1792 he was promoted to lieutenant general and a month later was dispatched to the marquis de Lafayette's army. In the same year an *Armée du Midi* was created whose jurisdiction extended from Lake Geneva to Bordeaux. Montesquiou-Fézénsac, stationed in Lyon, was selected by C. Dumouriez as commander.

In September this army crossed the Italian frontier to Savoy, where it was received enthusiastically by the native population. On 28 September Montesquiou-Fézénsac informed the National Convention that the Savoyards had asked to form the eighty-fourth department of the Republic. Girondins were divided over this issue, and Montesquiou-Fézénsac sanctioned the formation of new political clubs as well as a national assembly of Allobrogians. These incidents alarmed Geneva's aristocrats, and they appealed for aid from the cantons of Zurich and Berne, each of which sent reinforcements to the Genevan nobility.

The Executive Council in France, on receiving the Convention's approval, ordered Montesquiou-Fézénsac to enter the city and ask the administration of Geneva to withdraw its forces. Instead of entering Geneva, however, Montesquiou-Fézénsac negotiated a treaty by which the Genevan aristocrats agreed to the dispersal of the Swiss troops. The Convention refused to ratify this treaty, however, and in November 1792 accused him of compromising the Republic's dignity. Choosing not to face a trial, Montesquiou-Fézénsac withdrew to the canton of Zurich, where he remained until after 9 Thermidor. In 1795 he had his name struck from the list of *émigrés*. Returning to France in 1797, Montesquiou-Fézénsac became a member of the Constitutional Circle, which opposed the Clichyens. He died in Paris in 1798, but not before he had published *On the Administration of Finance in a Republic*.

R. W. Phipps, *The Armies of the First French Republic and the Rise of the Marshals of Napoleon I*, vol. 3 (London, 1931); A. Soboul, *The French Revolution*, trans. (New York, 1962).

N. Chaudhuri

Related entries: CLUB DE CLICHY; DUMOURIEZ; GIRONDINS; PROVENCE.

MONTGOLFIER, JACQUES-ETIENNE (1745–99), manufacturer, engineer, scientist. A younger brother of J.-M. Montgolfier, Jacques-Etienne excelled as a youth in mathematical studies in Paris and then trained under J.-G. Soufflot for an architectural career. Before he was thirty, his father summoned him to Annonay, south of Lyon, to head his paper factory, and here Jacques-Etienne contributed such inventions as vellum paper, resembling parchment. Shortly, his earlier fascination with the possibilities of lighter-than-air balloons infected

Joseph-Michel also. At first they apparently believed that the smoke rising from a fire beneath an inflating balloon manifested the presence of a special gas lighter than air rather than understanding that the expansion, and hence the lightening, of heated air itself impelled the balloon upward. In any case, the brothers soon created and demonstrated the first hot-air balloons. Their partnership seems to have been a fully equal one. Both brothers were honored by the government, both resumed and further improved the manufacture of paper, and together they invented the hydraulic ram; neither participated directly in the further development and experimental military use (1794) of hot-air balloons. During the Terror, Jacques-Etienne was the object of several denunciations but was saved from arrest by faithful employees. A heart ailment led to his semiretirement in Lyon, and death came on a trip to Annonay.

Biographie universelle ancienne et moderne, Nouvelle édition, 1843-65, s.v. ''Montgolfier, Jacques-Etienne''; C. C. Gillispie, *The Montgolfier Brothers and the Invention of Aviation, 1783-1784* (Princeton, 1983); C. V. Glines, ed., *Lighter-than-Air Flight* (New York, 1965); L. T. C. Rolt, *The Aeronauts: A History of Ballooning, 1783-1903* (New York, 1966).

H. S. Vyverberg

Related entries: MONTGOLFIER, J.-M.; SCIENCE.

MONTGOLFIER, JOSEPH-MICHEL (1740-1810), manufacturer, engineer, scientist. Son of a paper manufacturer in Annonay, Montgolfier continued his youthful interests in chemistry and technology by simplifying and improving the paper-making process. With his brother Jacques-Etienne, he experimented (1782-83) with lighter-than-air balloons. On 5 June 1783 came the first public demonstration with a large paper and cloth balloon filled with hot air from a fire of straw and wool; it rose over a mile. In September an ascension was staged at Versailles for king and court, with a basket suspended from the balloon to hold three live animals, which survived the two-mile trip. On 21 November 1783 came the first manned free flight by a *montgolfière*, or hot-air balloon (as distinguished from the hydrogen balloons introduced shortly after the Montgolfiers' early balloons). In the November flight J.-F. Pilâtre de Rozier and the marquis d'Arlandes stood on a platform around the soaring balloon from which they fed the fire in a container and sponged incipient conflagrations elsewhere. Montgolfier contributed further inventions and innovations in several fields, including (with Jacques-Etienne in the 1790s) a hydraulic ram for raising water levels without employing pistons. He maintained a low profile during the Revolution, though aiding several potential victims of the Terror. Manned *montgolfières* served (1794) for observation of the enemy at the siege of Charleroi and the battle of Fleurus. Montgolfier was later decorated by Napoleon and in 1807 became a member of the Institut National.

Biographie universelle ancienne et moderne, Nouvelle édition, 1843-65, s.v. ''Montgolfier, Joseph-Michel''; C. C. Gillispie, *The Montgolfier Brothers and the Invention of Aviation, 1783-1784* (Princeton, 1983).

H. Vyverberg

Related entries: BATTLE OF FLEURUS; MONTGOLFIER, J.-E.; SCIENCE.

MONTMORIN DE SAINT-HEREM, ARMAND-MARC, COMTE DE

(1745-92), ambassador, foreign minister. Born in Paris on 13 October 1745, the descendant of a distinguished aristocratic family originally from the Auvergne, Montmorin officially entered public life in 1768 when he was attached as *menin* to the retinue of the dauphin. Six years later, on the dauphin's accession to the throne as Louis XVI, Montmorin was appointed minister to the archbishop of Trêves and in 1777 was named ambassador to Spain.

At the court of Charles III, he successfully initiated and implemented French foreign policy by obtaining Spanish aid against England in the War for American Independence. Through this endeavor, Montmorin gained a reputation among his diplomatic colleagues for exceptionally clear-sighted and well-conceived diplomacy. His Spanish mission concluded, Montmorin requested relief from his post and returned to France in 1783, where Louis created him *commandant* of Brittany and granted him a royal pension in recognition of his decade in diplomacy. Over the next three years, Montmorin and his wife, the former Louise de Tanes, earned the respect of the Bretons for efforts in their behalf. He succeeded C.-G. Vergennes as foreign minister on 14 February 1787.

Named to this post barely a week before the first Assembly of Notables convened, Montmorin played no important role in that body's deliberations. His attention instead was directed to the United Provinces where French partisans, so-called *patriotes*, feared an impending Prussian invasion. To forestall this event, Montmorin recommended enthusiastically to the royal council that military aid be given the *patriotes*. Despite his warm advocacy, Montmorin was deterred by the collapse of French finances and the knowledge that Austria, France's nominal ally since 1756, was unable to provide needed support. Montmorin was thus forced to withdraw his offer of aid and saw French prestige in the United Provinces reach a nadir. Montmorin's apparent breach of diplomacy also served to weaken traditional bonds with Sweden, Poland, and Turkey, states dependent historically on French military and financial support.

Foreign policy, however, became secondary to Montmorin as the internal fiscal and political crisis heightened in France. In mid-August 1788, with the appointment of J. Necker as comptroller general of finances, he became involved, despite his official position, almost exclusively in domestic issues. On 27 December 1788, he supported Necker's policy of doubling the representation of the Third Estate to the future Estates General, and on 22 June 1789 he submitted a *mémoire* to the council that urged acceptance of additional recommendations by Necker calculated to permit the government to seize the initiative from the Third Estate in the Revolution: eligibility to high office on the basis of talent, a bicameral legislature, and joint deliberations of the Estates on all matters of general interest.

Louis rejected this plan on 23 June at a specially convened royal session of the Estates, asserting instead a much less conciliatory program sponsored by court reactionaries. The monarch's further displeasure toward his ministers was seen on 11 July when he dismissed Montmorin and the entire Necker ministry.

Three days later Paris, apprehensive of a troop concentration in the Versailles-Paris region, rose up in a spontaneous popular movement, which led to the attack and seizure of the notorious Bastille. The events of 14 July led to the consolidation of power by the National Constituent Assembly and, three days later, to the restoration of Montmorin and the others to office. Until September 1790, when Necker was dismissed permanently, Montmorin worked with him in a futile effort to persuade the king to accept reform. Montmorin may, in fact, be identified with the constitutional moderate party during this early phase of the Revolution, and he counted among his closest friends the anglophile P.-V. Malouet.

After Necker's forced retirement, Montmorin became the most prominent figure in the ministry, but with no significant base of support inside or outside the National Assembly, his potential for political leadership was severely circumscribed. His aristocratic background also made him suspect in the eyes of radicals and journalists, and he was vilified particularly in the pages of J.-P. Brissot's *Patriote français*, a widely read journal. The combined lack of a solid political base in addition to constant public attacks on him drove Montmorin into political alliance in December 1790 with the comte de Mirabeau in an effort to sustain a tottering crown.

Mirabeau defended Montmorin's policies consistently in debate before the Assembly and at the Jacobins, and both men formulated extensive plans to preserve the best features of constitutional monarchy for Louis XVI. Despite their efforts, however, they could neither moderate the reactionary tendencies of the crown nor gain the total confidence of the king and queen. Within a month of Mirabeau's early death (2 April 1791), the royal couple had concluded that their lost authority could be restored only if they escaped from France and then returned at the head of an interventionist foreign army.

The ill-fated flight of 21 June 1791, which ended at Varennes, was the result of this deep-set conviction. Traveling under aliases, on a passport issued unwittingly by Montmorin, the royal family was intercepted within a day of its departure and was returned to Paris on 25 June. Because he had signed the passport, Montmorin was suspected immediately of being in collusion with the flight. He was, however, cleared of all complicity by an investigative committee of the Assembly, and his conduct was declared irreproachable. Despite this legislative clearance, his credibility suffered immeasurably.

Even before the king's attempted flight, a campaign of character assassination had been directed at Montmorin. Indeed, within a week of Mirabeau's death, the foreign minister was accused by the Assembly's Diplomatic Committee of harboring obstructionist and royalist views. Such accusations became more strident after 21 June, and some even alleged that Montmorin was in the pay of foreign powers. He remained in office nonetheless, drafting Louis' speech in September accepting the constitution and serving for several weeks under the newly elected Legislative Assembly. He was replaced by A. de Valdec de Lessart in early November 1791.

From the date of Montmorin's resignation until his death eleven months later, he worked untiringly as special adviser to the king and queen. Along with such political figures as P.-V. Malouet and A.-F. de Bertrand de Molleville he offered careful and constructive advice, which the royal couple totally ignored. With the possibility of war becoming more likely in the mid-spring of 1792, Montmorin's record as foreign minister was scrutinized at the Assembly and the Jacobins, where members were calling for his public hanging. And when war finally occurred and the French armies suffered immediate reversals, his policies were bitterly assailed.

In July 1792, Brissot and A. Gensonné publicly accused Montmorin of being a chief of the so-called Austrian Committee. Unsubstantiated in open court, these charges nevertheless received much public exposure, suggesting that Montmorin had become a lightning rod for Brissot's implacable hostility. By this date, Montmorin was convinced he was a marked man. Following the successful popular assault on the Tuileries on 10 August 1792, Montmorin went into hiding. He was arrested eleven days later in the faubourg Saint-Antoine at the residence of a laundress where he had been secreted by friends. Despite an able defense before the *comité des recherches* and the Assembly itself, he was indicted on 31 August, sent to the Abbaye prison, and was hacked to pieces there two days later by a mob in the course of the September Massacres.

A.-F. Bertrand de Molleville, *Mémoires secrets pour servir à l'histoire de la dernière année du règne de Louis XVI, roi de France*, vol. 1 (Paris, 1797); F. Masson, *Le département des Affaires étrangères pendant la Révolution: 1787-1804* (Paris, 1903); R. B. Morris, *The Peacemakers: The Great Powers and American Independence* (New York, 1965); J.-L. Soulavie, *Mémoires historiques et politiques du règne de Louis XVI depuis son mariage jusqu'à sa mort*, vol. 6 (Paris, 1801); A. Stern, *La vie de Mirabeau*, trans. M. H. Busson, vol. 2 (Paris, 1896).

B. Rothaus

Related entries: ASSEMBLY OF NOTABLES; AUSTRIAN COMMITTEE; BASTILLE, THE; BERTRAND DE MOLLEVILLE; BRISSOT DE WAR-VILLE; JACOBINS; LESSART; LOUIS XVI; MALOUET; MIRABEAU; NECKER; "RESULT OF THE COUNCIL"; SEPTEMBER 1792 MASSA-CRES; VARENNES; VONCK.

MOREAU, JEAN-VICTOR (1763-1813), general. Born in Morlaix the son of a Breton lawyer, the young Moreau seemed destined to follow his father's career. But he early yearned for the more exciting life of a soldier. Having enlisted in a regiment, he was bought out by his father and sent to study law at Rennes. Winning great popularity among his fellow students, he used his influence in 1788 to calm the angry population of the town after royal troops were sent to disperse the Parlement of Rennes. His soldierly abilities were put to the test in January 1789 during the turbulence accompanying the convocation of the Estates General. He led the law students against the Breton nobles and besieged them in their hall. The nobles were forced to fight their way out at sword's point.

Later that same year, Moreau gladly abandoned his studies to join the newly organized National Guard, raising a volunteer company of cannoneers and becoming its captain. He later transferred to the regular army and rose to the rank of senior lieutenant colonel of a battalion of volunteers by September 1791. With the outbreak of the war against Austria and Prussia, Moreau saw service in the Army of the North under Generals C. Dumouriez and F.-M. Chesnon de Champmorin. Showing conspicuous courage, he took part in the Battles of Stephenswerth and Neerwinden in 1793. As a reward, deputies on mission raised him to the rank of brigadier general in December, the position being officially confirmed in 1794 when he was attached to General J.-C. Pichegru, new commander of the Army of the North. Promoted to command the second division, Moreau fought at Menin, Tourcoing, and Nieuport, battles that drove the Allies from the Low Countries. His brilliant campaigning, which led to the conquest of Holland in 1795, brought him command of the Army of the North and then the Army of the Rhine and Moselle in 1796.

Taking the offensive against the Austrians, Moreau crossed the Rhine and scored impressive victories in southern Germany. But by October 1796 he was compelled to withdraw into France and remain on the defensive. He was subsequently given joint command of the Army of the Rhine and Moselle and the Army of the Sambre and Meuse. At this point, his political sentiments jeopardized his military career. Never an ardent republican, he had been angered when his father, a judge of the tribunal at Morlaix, was guillotined for royalism during the Terror. While advancing into Germany in April 1797, Moreau's forces seized a wagon belonging to the Austrian general baron Klinglen. Its contents revealed compromising correspondence between his friend Pichegru and French *émigrés*. Moreau failed to communicate these letters to the Directory until September, following the antiroyalist coup of 18 Fructidor and the arrest of Pichegru. Moreau may have felt it rash to denounce a fellow general at a time when royalists seemed about to seize power. But once the royalists were defeated, Moreau hastened to transmit the information to the director F. Barthélemy in order to cover himself. Suspected of royalist sympathies, Moreau returned to Paris and was placed on the inactive list.

In September 1798, however, he was recalled to duty and named general of infantry in the army of Italy, fighting under General B.-L.-J. Schérer. Succeeding Schérer as commander, Moreau suffered a serious defeat at the hands of the Austrians at Cassano (April 1799) but recovered to score a victory at San Giuliano two months later. In July Moreau was placed under the orders of B.-C. Joubert, only to regain full control of the Army of Italy when Joubert was killed at Novi. Ordered transferred to the Army of the Rhine in September, Moreau went to Paris where he met with N. Bonaparte, newly returned from his Egyptian expedition and plotting to overthrow the Directory. Throwing in with the conspirators, Moreau was put in charge of guarding the directors L.-J. Gohier and J.-F. Moulin during the coup. After the success of 18 Brumaire, Moreau's fortunes rose once more. Assuming command of the Army of the Rhine in November 1799, he engaged in two victorious campaigns in southern Germany in 1800, winning the battle of Hohenlinden against the Austrians. Retiring from active duty in September 1801, he was later rewarded with the Legion of Honor. But his lingering royalist sympathies led him to conspire with Pichegru against Napoleon. As a result, Moreau was arrested, imprisoned, and removed from the ranks of the army.

Going into self-imposed exile in the United States from 1804 to 1813, he was summoned by Czar Alexander I to advise the Allies in their struggle against Napoleon. After meeting with the Allied commanders in Prague, Moreau went to Saxony, where he was critically wounded by French fire at the Battle of Dresden (August 1813). He died five days later at Lahn in Bohemia.

J. Godechot, "Moreau et les papiers de Klinglen," *Ann. hist. de la Révo. française* 9 (1932); R. W. Phipps, *The Armies of the First French Republic and the Rise of the Marshals of Napoleon I,* 5 vols. (Oxford, 1926-39).

J. Friguglietti

Related entries: BARTHELEMY; BATTLE OF NEERWINDEN; BATTLE OF TOURCOING; COUP OF 18 FRUCTIDOR YEAR V; DUMOURIEZ; GOHIER; MOULIN; PICHEGRU.

MORRIS, GOUVERNEUR (1752-1816), U.S. minister to France. The witty and cynical "great lover with the wooden leg," Gouverneur Morris was U.S. minister to France from 1792 to 1794. Born in the colony of New York on 31 January 1752 into a wealthy and prominent family, Morris was linked to France through his mother's Huguenot ancestors. Trained as a lawyer, during the American Revolution he served in the New York State Congress, the Continental Congress, and worked (1781-85) for R. Morris (no relation), the superintendent of finance. R. Morris sent him to Europe in 1789 to handle a variety of public and private financial transactions for the new government and some of its citizens. A member of the emerging Washington-Hamilton faction, Morris approved of the French Revolution as long as it headed toward a constitutional monarchy. For him, democracy would lead to wholesale corruption as the propertyless masses would sell their votes to the highest bidder. Greatly admired for his wit in Paris, he became a member of Madame G. de Staël's salon and, for several years, shared C.-M. Talleyrand's mistress, A. de Flahaut.

President G. Washington nominated him to be minister to France late in 1791. After a bitter fight, he was approved by the Senate on 12 January 1792 and charged with the task of improving Franco-American relations, which had been deteriorating because of disputes over the West Indies trade, spoliations, and debts. He worked tirelessly, if ineffectively, on these matters in Paris. Distrusted by the French government almost as much as he was distrusted by the Jeffersonians, Morris gave refuge to royalists and even submitted escape plots to Louis XVI. So close was he to the king that Louis entrusted him with a good portion of his fortune, which Morris ultimately delivered to the royal heirs in Austria.

As early as February 1793, the French demanded his recall. From that point through 1794, they contracted almost all of their diplomatic business through

Philadelphia and their own envoy, E. Genêt. Despite this humiliation, Morris maintained his post in Paris even during the Terror when all other accredited diplomats were ordered home. He was finally recalled in 1794 in a celebrated exchange of recalls that sent the by-then infamous Citizen Genêt back to France. Morris was replaced by J. Monroe, an American much more favorable to republicanism.

Morris remained in Europe until 1799, serving a period (1796-97) as a secret agent for British Foreign Secretary Lord Grenville. After his return to the United States, he represented New York in the Senate (1800-02), and then retired to private life until his death on 6 November 1816.

His intelligent and perceptive diaries of his experiences in Europe during the decade of Revolution have been used with profit by several distinguished historians. A brilliant cosmopolitan who was at home on two continents, Morris never joined the first rank of American leaders during the era, perhaps because of his merciless wit and perceived association with ultraconservative causes.

B. C. Davenport, ed. *The Diary and Letters of Gouverneur Morris*, 2 vols. (New York, 1939); H. Swigget, *The Extraordinary Mr. Morris* (Garden City, 1952); D. Walther, *Gouverneur Morris, Witness of Two Revolutions* (New York, 1934).

M. Small

Related entries: GENET; GRENVILLE; JEFFERSON; STAEL-HOLSTEIN.

MOULIN, JEAN-FRANCOIS, BARON (1752-1810), general and director. The son of a *marchand épicier*, Moulin was born in Caen in March 1752. Educated at the Jesuit collège there, he first entered the Twenty-ninth Infantry Regiment for seven months in 1768-69. Thereafter he served as a geographer in the Ponts et Chaussées in Saint-Mâlo and Calais, until 1785 when he transferred to the intendance of Paris as an engineer. This post vanished with the Revolution, but his sympathies were very much with the new order even so. In July 1789 he volunteered for the National Guard as a private and rose to be a noncommissioned officer and, finally, an officer. By 1791 he held staff office under J.-B.-D. Rochambeau, and from August 1792 he was adjutant general to the Parisian National Guard.

In the spring of 1793 he became a temporary *chef de bataillon* of an infantry regiment and campaigned with it in the Army of the West against the Vendéans. It was in this campaign that his younger brother, whose career had been almost identical to his, committed suicide rather than fall into enemy hands. He himself performed bravely preventing the evacuation of Saumur from becoming a rout and winning victories at Doué and Vihiers. These won him promotion in the field to general of brigade in September 1793. He also served as governor of Saumur on its recapture and was promoted to general of division at the end of November. His career was then briefly halted by his decision to release prisoners who had surrendered to him after the fall of Le Mans in December 1793. For this alleged breach of orders, J.-B. Carrier had him imprisoned in Nantes. He was soon released as a result of a public outcry, including the intervention of the Jacobins, of which he was a member, and other representatives in the west. After further service in the west against J.-G. Puisaye, he was made commanding general of the Army of the Alps from December 1794. In this capacity he inflicted a number of checks on the Piedmontese, but ill health made him transfer to a post as military governor in Lyon in October 1795. He later held a similar position in Strasbourg and joined in the campaign on the Rhine front, playing a large and distinguished part in the recapture of Kehl in September 1796.

The following year he was destined for a command in Holland, but the Directory instead made him head of the Seventeenth Military Region around Paris in Frimaire Year VI, and although he refused election that year to the legislature, he proved himself politically by his vigorous treatment of *émigrés*. In 1798 he was given command of the Army of England and again returned to campaigning against the *chouans* in the west. This service was interrupted by a trip to Belgium to repress the Catholic revolt there in the autumn of 1798. The following summer he was elected a member of the directory in replacement of L.-M. La Revellière-lépeaux, since he was the least offensive and ambitious of the available generals. In office he supported P. Barras against E.-J. Sieyès, who had been opposed to his nomination, and contested both the closure of the Manège and the replacement of J.-B.-J. Bernadotte as minister of war by E.-L.-A. Dubois-Crancé. When it came to Brumaire, he was one of the few directors to envisage opposition to N. Bonaparte, considering a call for troops to come from Italy and the possible arrest of Bonaparte. Even so he caused less concern to the conspirators than did L.-J. Gohier. Moulin refused to resign from his office even though abandoned by Barras and Gohier, and he found himself placed under house arrest in the Luxembourg by J.-V. Moreau. Two days later he escaped, but the only punishment inflicted on him was to place him on the inactive list.

He also remained under surveillance for some time since he maintained his old links with the Left, but eventually poverty led him to come to terms with the new order. Although he failed to gain compensation for his lost position as a director, he was eventually placed again on the active list. He served in Antwerp, Mayence (Mainz), Elbing, Mézières, and Augsburg until the stress and strain of campaigning forced him to return home to France in March 1810. He died a few days after his return to Pierrefitte (Seine), his adopted home town, where he had bought an estate under the Empire. The Empire also had rewarded him with the Legion of Honor in 1807 and the rank of baron two years later.

G. Buffy, "Le général Moulin," *Revo. française* 50 (1906); G. Uzereau, "Moulin," *Anj. hist.* 25 (1925).

C. Church

Related entries: BARRAS; BERNADOTTE; CARRIER; *CHOUANNERIE*; COUP OF 18 BRUMAIRE; DUBOIS-CRANCE, GOHIER; PUISAYE; ROCHAMBEAU; SIEYES.

MOUNIER, JEAN-JOSEPH (1758-1806), constitutional monarchist. Son of a wealthy Grenoble cloth merchant, Mounier gained prominence as a leader of the Revolution of 1788 in Dauphiné and as one of the more influential leaders of the Estates General and the National Constituent Assembly in the summer of 1789. In many ways he typified the early Revolutionary leadership. A well-educated and respected lawyer, his father's wealth enabled him to purchase a royal judgeship, which carried with it the title *écuyer*. In spite of his education and wealth, however, his common birth excluded him from the ranks of the *parlementaires*.

After the government's financial crisis and subsequent disputes led to the outbreak of rioting in Grenoble in May 1788, Mounier was elected secretary of the Assembly of Grenoble, which met in June, and had an important role in writing some of the most important documents that emerged from the Dauphinois revolution. He led the three orders of Dauphiné to accept such Revolutionary programs as the doubling of the Third Estate and vote by head in the Estates General.

Mounier's role in the revolt in Dauphiné and his book-length political pamphlet, *Nouvelles observations sur les Etats Généraux de France* brought him nationwide attention in the months preceding the meeting of the Estates General in May 1789. He came to the Estates General as a representative of the Third Estate of Dauphiné and as one of the nation's most outspoken opponents of privilege and monarchical absolutism. His ideal was the English constitution. His goal was to give the Third Estate a voice in running France, to abolish the fiscal, political, and legal privileges of the nobility, opening careers to talent (without abolishing the nobility as an order), to terminate provincial and other local privileges, and to adopt a written constitution that would establish in France a constitutional monarchy on the English model.

As long as he thought the Revolution was taking France toward his ideal government, Mounier was a Revolutionary. He was the proposer of the Tennis Court Oath; he rejoiced at the 14 July uprising and the storming of the Bastille; and his wording for the first three articles of the Declaration of the Rights of Man was accepted by the Assembly. In these articles, the basic ideas of liberty, equality before the law, and popular sovereignty were stated.

Although Mounier advocated the principle of popular sovereignty, he was not a democrat. He opposed allowing the people to exercise their sovereignty directly. Likening democracy to the tyranny of the multitude, he sought to contain popular influence on government within narrowly defined boundaries.

Like most other members of the National Assembly, Mounier advocated a parliamentary monarchy with a written constitution, but compared to most of his colleagues he was a moderate. He favored giving the king an absolute veto over legislation and establishing a bicameral legislature with an aristocratic upper house interposed between king and popular representatives. The members of the upper house would come from a newly created hereditary peerage, distinct from the traditional nobility, supplemented by the princes of the blood royal, the marshals of France, and other notables. The peers would be chosen by the king from among the most distinguished noblemen and the most meritorious commoners. One has the impression that Mounier was in favor of an aristocracy as long as men like himself had a chance to be part of it.

This last point explains how Mounier reconciled his advocacy of a partially aristocratic government with his abhorrence of privilege. He was not opposed to social distinctions per se. He was opposed to a small, exclusive, highly privileged group nobility. To Mounier all men of merit should be able to enter the upper crust.

Mounier's moderation soon departed from the mainstream of the Revolutionary movement. Late in the summer of 1789, the proposals of the Committee on the Constitution, of which Mounier was an influential member, met with a cool response both within and outside the National Assembly. In Paris Mounier was often referred to as "Monsieur Veto" for his advocacy of the absolute veto. By mid-September the Assembly had voted down all of his constitutional proposals and had decided to create a unicameral legislature and give the king a suspensive veto.

Though defeated, Mounier was elected president of the Assembly at the end of September. He was still respected by his colleagues. It was during his term as president that the market women of Paris and their cohorts, followed by the marquis de Lafayette and the National Guard, marched on Versailles. Mounier led a delegation from the Assembly belatedly to obtain the king's reluctant assent to the Declaration of Rights and the abolition of feudalism. When this failed to appease the crowd, which began demanding that the king return with them to Paris, Mounier advised Louis to use force against them if necessary. The king declined this advice and finally agreed to allow the mob to take him back to Paris.

Disgusted with this turn of events, Mounier left his deputy's post, without the formality of resignation, and returned to his native Dauphiné to mount resistance against the popular despotism, which he thought was now ruling France. Mounier was unsuccessful in his efforts to rally the Dauphinois behind him, and local radicals began to threaten his safety. In May 1790 he fled across the border to Savoy, beginning a long exile that took him to Switzerland, England, Italy, and Germany.

Germany was where Mounier spent most of his time. He always refused to remain in a country at war with France, and he remained a moderate, rejecting the excesses of both the Right and the Left. In his writings of this period, he continued to advocate the principles that had characterized his Revolutionary program in 1789 and was completely out of sympathy both with the Revolution as it had developed after 1789 and with the idea of restoring the Old Regime.

In 1795 the duke of Saxe-Weimer put his castle of Belvedere at Mounier's disposal to establish a school for preparing young people for careers in public service. Evidently Mounier's reputation as a man of learning and wise moderation had become well known. Mounier taught history and philosophy here from 1795 to 1801. During this period he associated with men such as F. Gentz, K. A. Boettiger, J. G. Herder, and J. W. Goethe.

The efforts of family and friends enabled Mounier to return home with the permission of the Consulate in October 1801. Shortly after, Napoleon appointed him prefect in the department of the Ille-et-Vilaine. In February 1805 the emperor called him to the Council of State, where he served until his death in January 1806 at a little over forty-seven years of age.

Mounier typified the Revolutionary of 1789: a lawyer and minor official of the Old Regime prevented by social barriers from reaching the highest positions; a liberal, constitutional monarchist who sought a society in which merit would receive recognition. The latter point, indeed, was the keystone of his thought and was the subject of his last pronouncement on the Revolution, a speech he delivered to the Lycée in Rennes. "Careers open to talent," the destruction of excessive privilege—this to Mounier was the lasting gain of the Revolution.

F.-A. Aulard, ed., "Un discours de l'ex-constituant Mounier, sur l'instruction publique, en l'an XII," *Revo. française* vol. 55 (1908); J. Egret, *La Révolution des notables: Mounier et les monarchiens, 1789* (Paris, 1950); J.-J. Mounier, *Considérations sur les gouvernements, et principalement sur celui qui convient à la France* (Versailles, 1789), *De l'influence attribuée aux philosophes, aux franc-maçons et aux illuminés sur la Révolution de France* (Tubingen, 1801), *Exposé de la conduite de M. Mounier, dans l'Assemblée Nationale, et des motifs de son retour en Dauphiné* (Grenoble, 1789), *Nouvelles observations sur les Etats-généraux de France* (n.p., 1789), and *Recherches sur les causes qui ont empêché les François de devenir libres, et sur les moyens qui leur restent pour acquéir la liberté* (Geneva, 1792).

T. A. DiPadova

Related entries: BARNAVE; DAUPHINE; GRENOBLE; *MONARCHIENS*; OCTOBER DAYS; TENNIS COURT OATH.

MOUNTAIN. See MONTAGNARDS.

MUNICIPAL REVOLTS (1789), series of uprisings in the towns announcing local support for the Revolution. The Revolution of 1789 had four major parts: the constitutional revolution initiated by the decision of the Third Estate to call itself the National Assembly, the Parisian uprising that culminated in the attack on the Bastille, the peasant revolts against seigneurial rights, and the municipal revolts in the provinces. All four were necessary to the success of the Revolution; constitutional crises, city riots, and peasant revolts had occurred during the monarchy, but they rarely coincided.

Municipal revolts, in particular, were unique to 1789. Never before had so many French cities and towns acted in concert in the name of a fundamental transformation of local and national politics. Within a few days of the fall of the Bastille in Paris (14 July 1789), almost every city and major town of France experienced its own version of revolution. Never again would the towns of the provinces react to national events with such unanimity. Only a few cities joined the federalist revolt of 1793, and in 1848 and 1870 most towns worked to defeat the revolution in Paris.

Although the fall of the Bastille was the signal for uprisings in most French cities, it was not the first example of municipal revolt in 1789. In March, food riots and demonstrations disrupted the local meetings held to elect delegates to the Estates General in several towns, most notably in Reims, Toulon, and Marseille. In Marseille, the result was the establishment of the first Revolutionary committee, known as the Council of the Three Orders, which was dominated by representatives of the Third Estate. The revolt in Marseille did not inaugurate a national movement, however, because it took place while other cities were preoccupied with their own elections for the Estates General. The king and his ministers dispatched several thousand soldiers to suppress the agitation in Marseille, which had its center in the local militia.

The Paris revolt of July succeeded because it occurred at a critical juncture of national socioeconomic and constitutional crises. The people of Paris armed themselves to defend the city against an aristocratic conspiracy that they believed was being organized by the reactionary court faction. At the same time, they were protecting the deputies of the Third Estate who were working to establish their authority over the entire nation. The king's decision to invest Paris with troops provided the fuel; his exile of the popular minister J. Necker was the spark. Once under way, the fire could not be contained either in Paris or within the nation at large.

Frequently it was the arrival of news from Paris that touched off riots in provincial cities. Yet provincial towns and cities also followed their own timetables. The town council in Rouen set up a special committee at the same time that their counterparts in Paris acted. Some towns seven or eight days' ride from Paris organized Revolutionary committees before those only one or two days away. Between 13 and 26 July, twenty of the thirty largest towns in France set up such committees, and six more did so in August. Most committees were introduced in response to food riots and mass demonstrations directed at city hall. In Strasbourg, for example, an angry mob demolished the building in which the city council met.

The committees were the most distinctive feature of the municipal revolts. Their chief responsibilities were control of local food supplies and organization of town militias. In many places, the committee eventually absorbed or replaced the previous town council. Elsewhere the committees shared control of town affairs with the council. Several cities, such as Paris, had more than one committee in 1789. Everywhere, however, it was the installation of a committee, often called a permanent committee, that marked the town's active support of the Revolution emanating from Paris. Most of the original committees were composed of the electors for the Third Estate, the delegates chosen by town meetings to attend the *bailliage* meetings, which elected deputies to the Estates General. Most subsequent committees were elected by the townsmen in special elections called for that purpose.

The social composition of the Revolutionary committees varied from town to town. In Paris, over half of the members came from the liberal professions. In the textile towns, many of the committeemen were merchants. Political attitudes counted more than profession, however, for townspeople were eager to show their support for the Revolution. Officials closely identified with the Old Regime were for the most part rejected as unsuitable for the new order, but liberal nobles were welcomed on the committees.

Although most towns did eventually install committees, local sentiment was not always unanimous. Many town councillors resented the ambitions of the newcomers, and in a handful of places they actively resisted the formation of Revolutionary committees. Grenoble and Lille had committees for only a few days in July; Toulouse and Clermont-Ferrand never introduced committees at all. The first committee in Troyes was dominated by Old Regime officials, and it agreed to hold elections for a successor only when confronted by an armed crowd. A few days later, the mayor of the Old Regime council was murdered in a wild riot. In response, the *bailliage* court of the town declared the committee illegal and recalled the former town council to its functions. In other towns, the committees also aroused hostility, but this did not usually have such tragic consequences.

Violence accompanied the municipal revolts in many places. Food riots and demonstrations usually started urban movements, and they continued to punctuate local politics until October. The Great Fear or rural panic of the summer fueled apprehension in many towns. By the autumn, nevertheless, most committees had gained control of the local situation, and with or without the former town councillors, they successfully ran local affairs until the elections of early 1790. During the summer and fall of 1789, the National Assembly was too busy trying to consolidate its position in the capital to pay much attention to local affairs. The Assembly decreed the abolition of the feudal regime in August in order to satisfy peasant demands. Then it turned to drafting the Declaration of the Rights of Man and of the Citizen. Not until December did it pass laws to set up local elections for new municipal governments. Until the end of the year, consequently, local committees had free rein. Most large cities tried to follow the example being set in Paris, but again and again they were forced to improvise and adapt to local conditions. As a result, the provincial towns enjoyed considerable autonomy in this period, and many townspeople received their first education in Revolutionary politics.

The experience of the towns was much more uniform after the elections of 1790. The National Assembly standardized the electoral process and made provision for identical administrations across the country. The municipal revolts had confirmed the townspeople's desire for local elections of officials, and the National Assembly recognized their impact by establishing relatively autonomous local governments. Once they were integrated into a national network, however, the towns lost most of their initiative. After 1789, as a consequence, municipal revolts, when they occurred, were usually directed against the central government.

Z. Harsany, "Metz pendant la Révolution," *Mém. de l'Acad. Natl. de Metz*, 5th series, vols. 6-7 (1959-62); L. Hunt, "Committees and Communes: Local Politics and National Revolution in 1789," *Comp. Stud. in Soc. and Hist.* 18 (1976) and *Revolution and Urban*

Politics in Provincial France: Troyes and Reims, 1786-1790 (Stanford, 1978); G. Lefebvre, *The Coming of the French Revolution*, trans. R. R. Palmer (Princeton, 1947); M. Lhéritier, "La Révolution municipale: point de départ de la Révolution française," *Révo. française* 18 (1939); D. Ligou, "A propos de la Révolution municipale," *Rev. d'hist. écon. et soc.* 34 (1960) and *Montauban à la fin de l'Ancien Régime et aux débuts de la Révolution, 1787-1794* (Paris, 1958).

L. A. Hunt

Related entries: BASTILLE, THE; GREAT FEAR; MARSEILLE; NECKER.

MURAT, JOACHIM (1767-1815), French cavalry general, grand duke of Berg, king of Naples. The son of an innkeeper at La Bastide-Fourtunière (Lot), Murat was born on 25 March 1767. Having attended the collège of Cahors on a scholarship, he was destined by his family for the priesthood, but he gave up his theological studies to enlist in the Twenty-third Light Cavalry in February 1787. Ousted after two years for insubordination, he led an aimless life (for some time heading a mounted squadron of poachers, an activity that got him denounced to a Revolutionary committee of surveillance at Amiens, but he was cleared) before entering the Constitutional Guard of Louis XVI in 1791. He left this unit because it was too aristocratic and joined the Twenty-first Regiment of Light Cavalry as a second lieutenant on 30 May 1792. After participating in the Argonne campaign, he conducted himself so well in the western Pyrenees that he was promoted to captain. After 9 Thermidor he was discharged for his Jacobinism and was without employment.

N. Bonaparte used him to bring up the decisive cannons on 13 Vendémiaire, as a result of which Murat became a colonel and (at his own suggestion) Bonaparte's aide-de-camp on the first Italian campaign, where he performed brilliantly. He became a brigadier general in Pluviôse Year V and a general of division in Egypt, from which he returned with Bonaparte in 1799.

His contribution to the coup of Brumaire, when he led sixty grenadiers into the meeting room of the Council of Five Hundred and dispersed the legislators, won him the hand of Bonaparte's sister Caroline in January 1800 and command of the Consular Guard. In the second Italian campaign, he was commander of the advance guard and fought well at Marengo. Governor of the Cisalpine Republic, he forced the Neapolitans to leave the Papal States and sign the Treaty of Florence. The department of the Lot sent him to the Legislative Body in October 1803. He became governor of Paris in January 1804 and as such constituted the military commission responsible for the execution of the duc d'Enghien. After the Empire was established, Murat became one of the initial marshals, a prince, and grand admiral, and also received the grand eagle of the Legion of Honor in February 1805.

Murat performed well in the campaign of 1805—at Ulm and Austerlitz he led admirable cavalry charges and took a bridge west of Vienna by a ruse—although M. Kutusov did deceive him with respect to the location and aims of his army. On 15 March 1806 he became the first ruler of the Grand Duchy of Berg, which he tried to enlarge. He put taxation on a permanent basis and wanted to reorganize completely the system of justice. Overall, his subjects benefited from his rule.

He rejoined the Grand Army for the fall campaign of 1806, staying with it from Jena through Tilsit. After Jena he pursued G. L. von Blücher to Lübeck and at Eylau led one of the finest cavalry charges ever executed.

In 1808 he was commander in chief in and lieutenant general of Spain, where he imposed martial law and rigorously suppressed the Madrid insurrection of 2 May. His appointment as king of Naples on 1 August did not soothe his disappointment at being passed over for the Spanish throne. From this time on, he and Caroline were bitter toward Napoleon and perhaps even disloyal. As king of Naples, he seized Capri, but his expedition against Sicily, a failure, brought reprimands from Napoleon. His reign did introduce most of the reforms Napoleon had instituted or retained in France. Abolition of feudalism, however, led to even greater concentration of land in the hands of the ex-barons. Murat began a cadastral survey and lowered the tariff to revenue levels, and Neapolitan prosperity increased after 1810 when imperial trading licenses became available. Murat saw his first loyalty as being to the Neapolitans and thus found himself at adds with Napoleon on many issues, one of which was the matter of French officials and troops in Naples. Especially after the birth of Napoleon's son, Murat became more nationalistic; he worked secretly with the Freemasons and perhaps with the Carbonari. By offering amnesty to all but the leaders of the numerous bands of brigands, he got most of the bands to dissolve.

Murat furnished a contingent for the Russian campaign of 1812, and he became a cavalry commander of the Grand Army. After the retreat from Moscow had been decided, Kutusov surprised Murat's forces. During the retreat, Murat commanded the "sacred squadron" that protected Napoleon. When Napoleon left the army, he named Murat commander in chief. Murat in turn left, on 17 January 1813, to attend to dynastic interests in Naples. In the summer of 1813, he rejoined Napoleon in Saxony but returned to Naples in November after the Battle of Leipzig. In the following January, he signed treaties of alliance with Great Britain and Austria; the Austrian alliance let him retain his royal title and gain half a million subjects from the Papal states in return for military aid against the French. In February and March, he contributed to the defeat of E. de Beauharnais in northern Italy.

When Napoleon returned from Elba, Murat marched north, occupying several cities. Knowing that the viscount Castlereagh and prince Metternich were now planning his downfall, on 30 March 1815 he issued from Rimini a manifesto calling on all Italians to strive for independence. When he lost decisively at Tolentino, the Bourbons regained the throne of Naples, and Murat was forced to go to France. There he offered his services to Napoleon, who may have thrown away victory at Waterloo by understandably rejecting a man who had let him down in 1812 and 1813 and betrayed him in 1814, even though that man was the best cavalry leader in Europe.

The White Terror of the Second Restoration caused Murat to go to Corsica.

There he was persuaded to try an invasion of the kingdom of Naples. Initially his expeditionary force consisted of six ships and 250 men; by the time he landed, he had only one ship and about 30 followers. In a few hours he was a prisoner of war. An improvised military commission rapidly imposed the death sentence. After just enough time for last rites and a farewell letter to his wife and children, Murat was executed by a firing squad on 13 October 1815 at Pizzo, Naples.

Murat was noted for his swagger and his love of fancy uniforms. Extremely able on the field of battle (though not in staff work, logistics, or strategy), in government he showed little wisdom. This last fact did not prevent him, goaded by his wife, from being ambitious.

K. M. Baker, ''Prince Joachim Murat as the Grand Duke of Berg'' (Master's thesis, Louisiana State University, 1966); D. Chandler, *The Campaigns of Napoleon* (New York, 1966); O. Connelly, *Napoleon's Satellite Kingdoms* (New York, 1965); J. P. Garnier, *Murat, roi de Naples* (Paris, 1959); A. Valente, *Gioacchino Murat e l'Italia meridionale* (Turin, 1941).

R. B. Holtman

Related entries: BONAPARTE, N.; CISALPINE REPUBLIC; COUP OF 18 BRUMAIRE; 9 THERMIDOR YEAR II; 13 VENDEMIAIRE YEAR IV.

MUSCADINS, young dandies of the Thermidorian Reaction, otherwise known as *incroyables, collets noirs*, the *jeunesse dorée*, and *Fréronistes* (followers of the *conventionnel* L.-M.-S. Fréron). The *muscadins* probably derived their name from their liberal use of musk perfume, but they were more obviously distinguished by their taste in dress. They favored a long jacket with wide lapels and a black velvet collar, signifying a state of mourning for the beheaded king. They often wore seventeen buttons, a sartorial reference to Louis XVII. They wore tight breeches and boots, and they carried a stick weighted with lead, euphemistically known as the *pouvoir exécutif*, which they put to aggressive use during innumerable street brawls in the Year III. They sometimes carried a monocle, which came to symbolize their insolent and disdainful attitude toward the lower classes. They wore their hair in ringlets. They had their own affectations of speech, and their own hymn (*''Le réveil du peuple''*). The Parisian set dined regularly at the café de Chartres and the restaurants of the Palais Royal, even during the famine and starvation of 1795.

The *muscadins* were most frequently students, merchants' and lawyers' clerks, and sons of bourgeois placed in the public administration to escape conscription. The politically active *muscadins* of Paris have been numbered at between 2,000 and 3,000, and their strength lay chiefly in the northwestern sections of Le Pelletier, Butte-des-Moulins, Tuileries, Piques, Guillaume-Tell, Halle-au-Blé, Brutus, and Muséum. This was the area around the Palais Royal and the Stock Exchange, where the *muscadins* were associated with currency speculation. It was also an area deeply implicated in the royalist rising of Vendémiaire Year IV.

The *muscadins* were responsible for the harassment of ex-terrorists on the streets and in the theaters of the larger cities, as well as from the public gallery of the Convention. Egged on first by Fréron but then principally by J. Rovère, they forced the pace of the Thermidorian Reaction, influencing the closure of the Jacobin club of Paris and the removal of J.-P. Marat's remains from the Panthéon.

Their extravagant tastes, however, their refusal to join the army, and their patronage of expensive restaurants at a time when people were dying from starvation made the *muscadins* the object of popular detestation. They may, therefore, have helped to provoke the popular Parisian rising of Germinal and Prairial Year III. The Convention employed the *muscadins* as its praetorian guard, but in Prairial, they were no match for the serried ranks of the workers of the faubourg Saint-Antoine.

Once the Convention had crushed the last *sans-culotte* rising in Prairial Year III, it could dispense with its embarrassing alliance with the *muscadins*, who were beginning to express openly royalist sentiments. From then on, the *muscadins* were doomed as a political force. The café de Chartres was closed in Messidor Year III, and J.-M. Souriguères de Saint-Marc, author of *"Le réveil du peuple,"* was arrested. In Vendémiaire Year IV the northwestern sections of Paris attempted to resist the Two-thirds Law, which perpetuated two-thirds of the *conventionnels* in power under the new constitution. Troops led by General N. Bonaparte helped to defeat this rising, in which many *muscadins* were involved.

The *muscadins* were a group distinguished by their youth, mainly bourgeois social origin, provocative manners, and emblematic dress. They played a political role in the Year III as the militant wing of the antiterrorist reaction, but Vendémiaire Year IV was their day of reckoning with the Thermidorian Convention.

F.-A. Aulard, *Paris pendant la réaction thermidorienne et sous le Directoire*, 5 vols. (Paris, 1898-1902); G. Duval, *Souvenirs thermidoriens*, 2 vols. (Paris, 1844); F. Gendron, *La jeunesse dorée: épisodes de la Révolution française* (Québec, 1979).

M. Lyons

Related entries: FRERON, *JEUNESSE DOREE; MERVEILLEUSES*; ROVERE; *SANS-CULOTTES*; 13 VENDEMIAIRE YEAR IV; TWO-THIRDS LAW.

MUSIC. In an article in *La France musicale* of August 1841, the French Revolution was described as "a great lyric drama, words by M.-J. Chénier, music by Gossec, decoration by David." This obvious exaggeration contains some truth. Music and the arts were used by the Revolutionary leaders to influence and inspire the populace to support and defend the cause of the Revolution. It was for this reason, and not for any desire to raise the cultural level of the masses, that the government supported the arts. Music had often had a religious or political function; now, during the Revolution it was directed primarily at influencing the emotions of the mob. Although the purely aesthetic quality of the music is not the highest, many of the innovations of the 1790s have had a lasting effect on the course of nineteenth century music. The following brief summary of the state of French music to 1789 will provide a background for the innovations of the Revolution.

- *Opéra*. Paris in the eighteenth century was one of the leading musical centers of the world. Its singers and instrumentalists were the best. In the 1770s the Académie Royale de Musique, popularly known as the Opéra, had been revitalized by the reform operas of the Austrian C. W. Gluck (1714-87). Important new operas premiered there under the influence of Gluck's reforms: *Didon* (1783) by N. Piccinni (1728-1800); *Dardanus* (1784) and *Oedipe à Colone* (1786) by A. Sacchini (1730–86); *Les Danaïdes* (1784) and *Tarare* (1787) by A. Salieri (1750-1825).

- *Opéra-Comique*. Operas on less serious subjects were given by the Opéra-Comique. While retaining the tradition of spoken dialogue, these works had developed into sophisticated musical dramas. Among the most successful were *Tom Jones* (1765) by F.-A.-D. Philidor (1726-95); *Le Déserteur* (1769) by P.-A. Monsigny (1729-1817) ; *Nina* (1786) by N. Dalayrac (1753-1809); *Le tableau parlant* (1769), *Zémire et Azor* (1771), *L'amant jaloux* (1778), and *Richard Coeur de Lion* (1784) by the most important composer of this genre, A.-E.-M. Grétry (1741-1813). Whereas the subjects at the Opéra were on remote and serious classical themes, the Opéra-Comique's concerned everyday life and people and accordingly emerged as the most important operatic form during the Revolution.

- *Concerts*. The most important eighteenth century concert series, the Concert Spirituel of Paris, came to an end during the early days of the Revolution. After sixty-five years and some 1,280 concerts, the last concert was held on 13 May 1790. As the Opéra had a virtual monopoly on all musical performances in France, it was by special permission that these concerts could be given during Lent, Christmas, and at other times when the opera house was closed. These concerts were distinguished by the excellence of the orchestra and soloists. Major works by the leading composers of France and Europe were performed. The success of these performances helped establish a flourishing French symphonic school, of which the leading composers were F. Devienne (1759-1803), F.-J. Gossec (1734-1829), C. Pleyel (1757-1831), J.-B.-S. Bréval (1756-1825) and J.-B. de Saint-Georges (1739-99). Unfortunately, this impetus for writing instrumental music was lost during the Revolution, and as a result, French instrumental music suffered a major decline, from which it did not recover until late in the nineteenth century.

- *Sacred Music*. Many large-scale motets and masses were written during the late eighteenth century for the court chapel and the great churches of France. One of the most famous was the *Messe des morts* (1760) by Gossec, which retained its popularity throughout the eighteenth century and was performed even during the Revolution.

Music for the French Revolution. In the winter of 1790, as the Revolutionary fever spread throughout France, meetings of patriots were held in which a mass was said, patriotic speeches were given, and songs and military music performed; the purpose was to arouse the Revolutionary spirit. The success of these largely spontaneous affairs suggested to the leaders in Paris that a grand festival to celebrate the Fédération would be effective propaganda. On 5 June 1790 the National Assembly set 14 July, the first anniversary of the fall of the Bastille, for a grand Fête de la Fédération to be held in Paris. Frantic preparations began immediately to prepare the Champ de Mars for the ceremony, to make the decorations, and to compose the music for the occasion. Thousands of volunteers, often singing the popular Revolutionary song "Ah! ça ira, ça ira," worked day and night to prepare the field. Gossec, assigned to compose a *Te Deum*, completed the score on 6 July with only a week's time to copy parts and rehearse the singers and instrumentalists.

The preceremony began at Notre Dame with the performance on 13 July of an oratorio, *La prise de la Bastille, hiérodrame tiré des Livres Saints* by M.-A. Desaugiers (1742-93). Later, a parade of the representatives and soldiers from the various departments of France passed in review before the king. On 14 July the soldiers, 50,000 strong, joined by 300,000 citizens, marched to the Champ de Mars to witness the Fête de la Fédération ceremony. In the center of the field a large altar was erected and decorated with the tricolor. The king and the royal family were on a pavilion before the Ecole Militaire. Mass was celebrated by a member of the Assembly, the bishop of Autun, C.-M. Talleyrand. Music was performed during the Mass and included a chorus from Sacchini's opera *Dardanus*. After the Mass, the marquis de Lafayette mounted the platform and pronounced the *serment civique* of the Fédération followed by similar oaths by the president of the Assembly and the king. Then was performed the *Te Deum* composed especially by Gossec for the occasion. It was scored for three-part chorus, piccolos, oboes, clarinets, trumpets, horns, violas in pairs, three trombones, bassoons, serpent, and percussion. The vocal setting of the traditional Latin text was in a simple chordal style. The *Te Deum*, approximately twenty minutes in length, was sung by 1,200 voices, accompanied by 300 winds, including 50 serpents (a bass wind instrument), and 300 percussionists. At the conclusion of the *Te Deum*, the traditional *Domine salvum fac* was sung. However, for this occasion, the phrases "God save the people, God save the law," were added to the traditional "God save the king." The work concluded with a most unusual coda for percussion alone. After the long official ceremony ended, the populace continued their celebration with dancing in the streets and singing of the popular "Ah! ça ira! ça ira!" This song, the most popular song before the "Marseillaise," was a setting of a Revolutionary text to a popular instrumental piece called *Carillon national*.

Gossec was later criticized for using the Latin religious text for the *Te Deum* instead of a French text, which would have shown more nationalistic fervor. The short time available was insufficient to write a new text and set it to music, but the Latin text was also used symbolically to express the hope that the people, the clergy, and the monarchy could work together for the rebirth of the nation.

Latin, however, was not used again, and the subsequent fêtes became more and more secular and pagan.

The next important musical work was Gossec's *Marche lugubre* for the ceremony in the Champ de Mars on 20 September 1790 in honor of the officers killed in the military revolt in Nancy. Scored for wind and percussion (including the tam-tam, a form of gong), the lugubrious roll of the drums and gong with the tortured sounds of the winds engendered, according to contemporary accounts, a religious terror in the souls of the listeners. The dissonant harmony and instrumental color, so different from the typical eighteenth-century style, must have produced a startling effect. The *Marche* was played for other important occasions, including the funeral of H.-G. R. Mirabeau (4 April 1791) and the removal of F.-M. Voltaire's body to the Panthéon (11 July 1791) (for which occasion Gossec also composed a hymn to the text of M.-J. Chénier), and for the funeral of General L.-L. Hoche (1 October 1797).

With the *Te Deum* and *Marche lugubre*, Gossec established a model for the ceremonial music of the Revolution: text set strophically, sung by a three-part male chorus, with or without soloists, and accompanied by massed winds and brass. The success of the early festivals and ceremonial processions attracted the full support of the National Assembly. According to the catalog of C. Pierre, between 1790 and 1802, 2,337 pieces of music were written for or about the Revolution (167 hymns, 2,090 *chansons*, and 80 pieces of military music for winds). In most cases both text and music were composed for the occasion. M.-J. Chénier (1762-1811), brother of André, was principal poet of the Revolution, and twenty-eight of his poems were set to music. All of the major composers in France participated in Revolutionary composition: Gossec (1734-1829), thirty-five pieces; J.-F. Lesueur (1760-1837), eighteen; E.-N. Méhul (1763-1817), fourteen; G.-M. Cambini (1746-1825), eleven; C.-S. Catel (1773-1830), eleven; L.-C. Cherubini (1760-1842), ten; D. Steibelt (1765-1823), six; J.-P.-E. Martini (1741-1816), four; Pleyel (1757-1831), three; J.-C. Rouget de Lisle (1760-1836), three; and Grétry (1741-1813), three. Many of these works are available in the various editions of Pierre.

Written for grand outdoor performances, the music was fairly simple in form and texture—no learned fugues, complicated harmony, or rhythm—for practical considerations demanded straightforward music suitable for massed performance with little rehearsal. Yet in the best of these pieces there is a certain excitement and grandeur. With their massed sound, they created a sonority unique and quite different from the typical refined French instrumental sound of the eighteenth century.

Space does not permit more than a brief mention of the important later fêtes and the titles of some of the important musical compositions written for the occasions: (1) the Fête de la Liberté (15 April 1792), *Choeur à la liberté* and *Ronde Nationale* with text by Chénier and music by Gossec; (2) Fête de la Fédération (14 July 1792), *"Chant du 14 juillet"* and *"Hymne à la liberté"* by Chénier and Gossec; shortly after this festival the *"Chant de guerre de l'armée du Rhin''* (*"La Marseillaise"*), with words and music by Rouget de Lisle, took Paris by storm; (3) Fête de la Raison (10 November 1793) and *"Hymne à la liberté"* by Chénier and Gossec; (4) Fête de l'Etre Suprême (8 July 1794), organized by the painter J.-L. David on the plan of M. Robespierre, including two *"Hymnes à l'Etre Suprême"* by Chénier and Gossec, soon after which in the same year appeared the famous *"Chant du départ,"* text by Chénier and music by Méhul, which was performed at nearly all the official ceremonies between 1784 and 1800; (5) Fête de la Reconnaissance et Victoire (29 May 1795), *"Hymne à la victoire,"* with text by C. de Flins des Oliviers and music by Cherubini, and a *"Chant martial"* by Gossec.

The great Paris Conservatory of Music was established by the National Convention on 3 August 1795 in recognition of the need for more trained musicians to participate in the grand official ceremonies. The conservatory consolidated two earlier institutions, the Ecole Royale de Chant, established under Gossec's direction in 1784 to train instrumentalists and singers for the opera, and the Ecole Gratuite de Musique de la Garde Nationale Parisienne, founded in 1792 by B. Sarrett (1765-1858) to train military musicians. At the new conservatory, tuition was free to talented students. The five greatest musicians of the Revolution—Gossec, Méhul, Grétry, Lesueur, and Cherubini—were named inspectors. From the beginning, the most distinguished musicians of France have been on its faculty, and its graduates continue to number among the greatest musicians of the world. The Paris Conservatory served as a model for other national conservatories of music.

Opera during the Revolution. The Revolution popularized both theater and opera. The less sophisticated audience forced librettists and composers to strike out in new directions. As a result, the Opéra, formerly closely tied to the court, went into a decline and offered only old standard favorites. The Opéra-Comique became the center of innovations. Plots praised the oppressed, and tyranny in any form was exposed. One of the most popular themes was the rescue of the unjustly imprisoned. While the first of the rescue operas dates from the pre-Revolutionary period, Grétry's opéra-comique, *Richard Coeur de Lion* (1784), became the most popular subject of the 1790s. Leading French opera composers of the time, Cherubini, Méhul, and Lesueur, all wrote rescue operas. Many of the librettos—for example, Cherubini's *Les Deux Journées* (1800)—were based on actual occurrences. The best known of these composers today, Cherubini, achieved his first success with *Lodoïska* (1792), which fits the Revolutionary mold. *Lodoïska* is a pioneering musical work in that it reflects the intensity of the drama within the music. Cherubini wrote his most important operas during the Revolution, including *Eliza* (1794) and *Médée* (1797); all include spoken dialogue. Cherubini adapted his style to the demands of the French language; however, his musical style was fuller and richer in harmonic treatment and orchestration than that of any of his predecessors. He expanded the musical numbers and shortened the spoken dialogue, thus creating a more concise and dramatic style, one that was greatly admired and copied by L. van Beethoven, especially in *Fidelio*, the masterpiece of rescue operas. The greatest operatic successes of Méhul (*Joseph*, 1807) and Lesueur (*Ossian*, 1804) occurred after the Revolution.

In the first decade of the Consulate and Empire, ceremonial music was neither as important or as innovative as during the Revolution. Napoleon's favorite composer was the Italian opera composer G. Paisiello (1749-1801).

The French Revolution had a major impact on the course of music history. Many scholars believe that the Romantic period began with French Revolutionary opera. French nineteenth-century opera absorbed many of the musical innovations of the grand, open-air pageants of the fêtes. The grand sweep of the large massed orchestras and choruses found its way into the opera house and even into the concert hall. This influence is seen in the finale of the Ninth Symphony of Beethoven, the operas of K. M. von Weber, the *Requiem*, the *Te Deum*, and, in particular, the *Symphonie funèbre et triomphale* of H. Berlioz. The spectacular effects of the fêtes also appeared in the opera house through the works of Cherubini, Méhul, and Lesueur and were later used to grand effect by G. Meyerbeer, who in turn influenced G. Verdi and R. Wagner.

W. Dean, "Opera under the French Revolution," *Pro. of the Roy. Mus. Assoc.* 94 (1967-68); E. J. Dent, *The Rise of Romantic Opera* (Cambridge, 1976); J. Ehrard and P. Viallaneiz, eds., "Les fêtes de la Révolution: Colloque de Clermont-Ferrand (juin 1974)," in *Bibliothèque d'histoire révolutionnaire*, 3d ser., no. 17 (Paris, 1977); P. H. Lang, "French Opera and the Spirit of the Revolution," *Stud. in Eighteenth Cent. Cult.* 2 (1972); C. Pierre, *Les hymnes et chansons de la Révolution* (Paris, 1904), *Musique de fêtes et cérémonies de la Révolution française* (Paris, 1899), and *Musique exécutée aux fêtes nationales de la Révolution française* (Paris, 1893-94); J. Tiersot, *Les fêtes et les chants de la Révolution française* (Paris, 1908).

A. C. Minor

Related entries: "*CA IRA*"; CHENIER, J.; DAVID; "*MARSEILLAISE, LA*"; ROUGET DE LISLE.

MUTINY OF NANCY (August 1790), the most serious of the numerous military disorders that occurred in more than one-third of the units of the Royal Army during 1790. Nancy, in Lorraine, was among the many cities and towns in the region that customarily contained a substantial garrison. In the summer of 1790, three regiments were quartered there: The King's Own (Du Roi) Infantry, the Mestre de Camp Général Cavalry, and the Châteauvieux Swiss. Since the beginning of the Revolution, soldiers in these units had established ties with local pro-Revolutionary elements, by participation in the federation ceremony on 19 April 1790, by membership in the Jacobin club, and through socializing with radical members of the National Guard. In addition, some enlisted men of the King's Own Infantry had established a soldiers' committee, which corresponded with similar organizations in other units. These developments intensified divisions within the city and within the garrison. Officers insulted, harassed, discharged, and arrested a number of their subordinates, particularly those associated with the soldiers' committee. Simultaneously, young noble officers instigated quarrels with National Guardsmen.

On 6 August 1790 the National Constituent Assembly outlawed any deliberating associations within regiments and ordered an audit of all unit funds. The first decision vindicated the officers of the Nancy garrison who had, on 19 July, outlawed the soldiers' committee on their own authority. The second, however, justified complaints that this committee—and others like it throughout the army—had been making about financial malfeasance by their officers. On 9 August soldiers of the King's Own Infantry took matters into their own hands, confining the officers to their quarters and forcing the regimental quartermaster-treasurer to hand over 150,000 *livres* that they maintained was due them. The next day, a delegation of soldiers from the Châteauvieux regiment presented similar complaints to their superiors. The Swiss officers responded by ordering two soldiers to be whipped publicly. This act outraged the French troops and many sympathetic civilians, who forced the soldiers' release and the distribution of 27,000 *livres* to the men. The garrison commandant pressed the civil authorities to declare martial law, but they refused since so many citizens supported the troops' position. On 14 August the men of the cavalry regiment pressured their officers into handing over some of the 48,000 *livres* that they demanded.

The central government, urged by the marquis de Lafayette, ordered the garrison to return to discipline and threatened to charge the soldiers with high treason if insubordination continued. On 20 August the soldiers signed a declaration of submission to the Assembly and the king. Four days later, the marquis de Malseigne arrived in Nancy to investigate conditions within the garrison there. Almost immediately he so abused and insulted the troops that they drove him to barricade himself in the commandant's quarters. On 28 August Malseigne escaped to Lunéville and attempted to rally the troops stationed there to attack their comrades in Nancy, but they refused and turned him over to the mutineers. Meanwhile, Malseigne's conduct had convinced the soldiers at Nancy, and many civilians as well, that rumors of an aristocratic plot were in fact true; they arrested the officers and prepared to defend themselves.

In the meantime, the Assembly had deputized the marquis de Bouillé, the military commander of the entire region, to gather an army and crush the Nancy mutiny. Bouillé arrived outside the gates of Nancy on the evening of 30 August with a force of nearly 4,500 men, many of them from foreign regiments in his command. To a delegation sent out by the municipal officials and the troops, Bouillé demanded the immediate release of the imprisoned officers and the unconditional surrender of the mutineers. On 31 August the soldiers agreed. When the advance guard of Bouillé's forces began to enter one of the city gates, however, they were fired on. The Swiss soldiers, who manned this sector, and unidentified snipers put up a determined resistance, and Bouillé was unable to take over the city until nightfall.

Repression was swift and harsh. The three regiments who participated in the mutiny were transferred to other localities within hours. The local National Guard was temporarily disbanded. The Jacobin club was closed, despite the absence of evidence linking it to the violence. The Swiss soldiers, who enjoyed no protection under either French military or French civil law, were most severely punished: one man was broken on the wheel, twenty-two were hanged, forty-one were condemned to the galleys for thirty years, and seventy-four received lesser punishments. In addition, scores of soldiers from the other two regiments and civilians were imprisoned. Subsequently the two French regiments were removed from the army rolls.

In the aftermath of this affair, there was a marked decline in the incidence of insubordination within the regular army, thus accomplishing the government's immediate aim. On the other hand, the treatment of the Nancy garrison widened the growing divisions between officers and men in the line army, and there would be a new wave of insubordination among the troops the following spring, a movement intensified by the king's attempted flight in June. Furthermore, the differences within the military establishment more and more were being defined in political terms that depicted a struggle between patriot soldiers and aristocrat officers. Within a year of the Nancy mutiny, such discord would lead to the nearly complete collapse of the regular army.

W. C. Baldwin, "The Beginnings of the Revolution and the Mutiny of the Royal Garrison in Nancy: *L'affaire de Nancy*, 1790" (Ph.D. dissertation, University of Michigan, 1973); F.-C.-A. Bouillé, *Mémoires du Marquis de Bouillé* (Paris, 1821); G. Bourdeau, "L'affaire de Nancy—31 aout 1790," *Ann. de l'Est* 12 (1898); L. de Chilly, *Le premier ministre constitutionnel de la guerre, La Tour du Pin: Les origines de l'armée nouvelle sous la Constituante* (Paris, 1909); S. F. Scott, *The Response of the Royal Army to the French Revolution: The Role and Development of the Line Army, 1787-1793* (Oxford, 1978).

S. F. Scott

Related entries: BOUILLE; FEDERATION; LA TOUR DU PIN GOUVERNET; VARENNES.

N

NANCY, MUTINY OF. See MUTINY OF NANCY.

NAPOLEON I. See BONAPARTE, NAPOLEON.

NARBONNE-LARA, LOUIS, COMTE DE (1755-1813), general, diplomat, minister of war. Born in Colorno, Parma, to a maid of honor of Louis XV's daughter, Elisabeth, Narbonne was the son of either a Spanish nobleman, F. de Narbonne-Lara or, as was alleged, of Louis XV himself. He early returned to France with his mother, who became lady-in-waiting to Madame Adélaïde, eldest daughter of Louis XV, and was brought up at court until he attended the collège de Juilly, where he acquired his formal education, proved proficient in European languages, and specialized in jurisprudence and diplomacy. He was a popular young man, graceful and amiable, at ease in good society, where he was much favored. By virtue of his literary taste and linguistic facility, Narbonne was equally at home among distinguished men of letters and among courtiers and politicians. Through C.-G. Vergennes he had access to the Ministry of Foreign Affairs, where he continued to pursue his interest in foreign relations and diplomacy. Being a partisan of J. Necker, Narbonne naturally attracted the friendship of Necker's daughter, Madame de Staël, a relationship that united the worlds of literature and politics.

Narbonne chose the army as his profession and by age twenty-five was a colonel, successively, of the Angoumois and Piedmont regiments. In 1790, after the outbreak of Revolution, he was named commandant of National Guard units in the department of the Doubs (1790). Relying on persuasion more than force and discipline, he found it difficult to maintain order in the untranquil early months of the Revolution, and he consequently found himself under attack, particularly in the radical press. By preference, he was loyally and sincerely attached to the House of Bourbon, and as a trustworthy monarchist, he was selected for the delicate task of accompanying Louis XVI's aunts, troubled because of their religious opinions, to Rome in February 1791. In the course of the trip, the party was stopped and detained at Arnay-le-Duc. Narbonne escaped to Paris where he obtained a decree permitting the princesses to continue their journey. He returned from Rome at the time of the flight to Varennes (21-25 June 1791), the king's abortive effort to flee his kingdom and the Revolution; he was nominated field marshal but refused the promotion until Louis XVI accepted the Constitution of 1791 and thus retained his throne.

Such was Narbonne's service and loyalty to the crown and such were his connections that he was named minister of war by Louis XVI soon after the opening of the Legislative Assembly, reputedly with the support and by the influence of Madame de Staël. Narbonne may have been too much the courtier to be minister of war during the critical autumn and winter of 1791-92, a time when belligerent pressures accelerated the drift toward war, but he showed great vigor and some capacity in his job. Dedicated to the safety of France and the maintenance of the Bourbon dynasty, his political predilection was royalist, but he was astute enough to know that he must disarm and win the confidence of the more bellicose factions, which he attempted to do by charm and prodigious activity, directing fortifications along the frontier, giving marshals' batons to J.-B.-D. Rochambeau and N. Luckner, naming them, with the marquis de Lafayette, as commanders of three armies, totaling 150,000 men, to be stationed along the frontiers in campaign readiness. His dedication to military preparedness suited the belligerent purposes of the Girondists, though not all of his plans or reports on the military situation to the Legislative Assembly were well received. On 23 January 1792, he threatened resignation if his plans were not approved; but to some of these ideas, such as the proposal to offer the command of the French armies to the duke of Brunswick, generally considered the premier military figure in Europe, the Assembly remained firmly opposed.

Narbonne not only had to struggle against opposition in the Assembly but against adversaries in the ministry, where he met opposition of a particularly persistent kind from A.-F. Bertrand de Molleville, minister of marine. Believing that the safety of the constitutional monarchy lay in harmony among the king's ministers and in reasonable agreement between them and the Assembly, Narbonne became discouraged by ministerial squabbles and by a growing lack of rapport with the Girondist-dominated Assembly, whose leaders were interested in taking control of the ministry as a means of hastening war with the Holy Roman Empire, from which they hoped to benefit. Accordingly, despite public popularity, Narbonne resigned (10 March 1792), an act that gave the Girondists the political opportunity for which they had been waiting. Narbonne joined the Army of the North. At the king's request, he returned to Paris, just in time for the insurrection of 10 August, which toppled the monarchy. Under suspicion for his loyalty to the Bourbons and criticized for his conduct as minister of war, Narbonne was indicted by the Assembly but managed to escape to London, with help again from Madame de Staël. He sought, unsuccessfully, to acquire a safe conduct so as to appear before the Convention on behalf of Louis XVI during the king's trial. As a substitute, he addressed a *Mémoire justificative* to the Convention, stressing ministerial, not royal, responsibility. This act of loyalty led to further vilification of Narbonne.

After England declared war on France (February 1793), Narbonne returned to the Continent, first to Switzerland and then to Swabia and Saxony. Not long after Brumaire, he returned to France (in 1801); at length, he also resumed his military career in Napoleon's service, as lieutenant general of a division in 1809. He became an aide-de-camp to the emperor in time to accompany him on the Russian campaign, where his courage and gaiety attracted Napoleon's attention. Napoleon assigned Narbonne to a variety of diplomatic and administrative positions. He was variously governor of Raab, of Trieste, and of Torgau; he was minister plenipotentiary to the Bavarian court; he was appointed ambassador to Vienna in 1813, where he had to deal, unequally and unsuccessfully, with C. von Metternich during the period when Austria defected from Napoleon's camp; he took part in the abortive peace talks at Prague (June-August 1813). Well might Napoleon express high esteem for Narbonne at the time of his death (7 November 1813) at Torgau in Saxony.

E. Dard, *Le Comte de Narbonne, 1755-1813* (Paris, 1943); C. Léon, *M. de Narbonne, ministre de la guerre* (Paris, 1938); L. Narbonne-Lara, *Compte de l'administration de M. de Narbonne* (Paris, an IV).

C. A. Le Guin

Related entries: BERTRAND DE MOLLEVILLE; COUP OF 18 BRUMAIRE; LUCKNER; NECKER; ROCHAMBEAU; STAEL-HOLSTEIN; 10 AUGUST 1792; VARENNES.

NATIONAL AGENTS. See *AGENTS NATIONAUX.*

NATIONAL CONSTITUENT ASSEMBLY (June 1789-30 September 1791), legislative body during first period of the Revolution. The opening of the Estates General, which took place at Versailles on 5 May 1789, included 291 members of the First Estate or clergy, 270 nobles or members of the Second Estate, and 578 deputies of the Third Estate, almost half of whom were lawyers. The following six weeks were among the most critical of the Revolution. The Third Estate, in order to control the Assembly and counting on support from the lower clergy and liberal nobility, wanted to establish voting by head in a unified body rather than following the tradition of each order meeting separately and casting one bloc vote.

On 10 June, the Third Estate invited the other two orders to meet with it for a common verification of credentials and on 17 June boldly transformed itself into a National Assembly. Three days later, the deputies, finding their meeting hall closed by royal orders, adjourned to a nearby tennis court where all save one took an oath not to separate until a constitution was firmly established.

In response, at a royal session on 23 June 1789, Louis XVI nullified all of the resolutions taken by the National Assembly and commanded the three estates to resume their separate meetings. But when the Third Estate defied him, the king gave way and on 27 June ordered the deputies of the clergy and nobility to take their places in the National Assembly, which on 9 July added the word *constituent* to its title (henceforth the National Constituent Assembly will be referred to as the Constituent). Thus, within eight weeks, the Third Estate had gained control of the Estates General and had transformed it into a powerful constitution-making body.

Still, the Constituent was not yet secure, for in late June Louis XVI ordered some 20,000 troops, many Swiss and German mercenaries, to the Versailles-Paris area. The Paris uprisings of 13-14 July 1789 induced the frightened king to dismiss the troops, thereby saving the Constituent from probable dissolution by force.

The Constituent soon had to face a crisis emanating from the countryside. The deputies viewed with alarm the widespread peasant insurrections of the spring and summer of 1789, but fearing that repression of the peasantry might encourage counterrevolution, the deputies opted instead, on 4 August, to abolish in part feudal privileges. (Supplementary decrees were enacted on 5-11 August 1789 and 15 March and 3 May 1790.) While serfdom and feudal rights relating to personal servitude were abolished without compensation, those relating to land or property were to be redeemed by monetary payments. The peasants, however, ignored this distinction and simply stopped paying them.

In a statement of principles to be followed in the writing of the constitution, the Constituent on 27 August passed the Declaration of the Rights of Man and of the Citizen. Among its provisions were equality before the law, freedom from arrest without due process, freedom of speech and press, and (reflective of the values of the bourgeois deputies) the inviolability of property rights. In another major action, after a series of heated debates, on 10-11 September 1789, the Constituent voted for a unicameral legislature and for a suspensive veto that enabled the king to delay passage of a law for two legislative sessions or for four years.

The decision of Louis XVI to again summon troops to his side led to the October Days, the march on Versailles on 5 October 1789 by several thousand Parisians. This action resulted in the king's assent to the August decrees and the forcible return of the royal family to Paris on 6 October. As consequences of the October Days, another potential attempt at counterrevolution had been defeated, the moderates in the Assembly (many of whom now emigrated) had been vanquished, and the monarch, and to a degree the Constituent, had become virtual prisoners of the Parisian radicals.

The most serious problem faced by the Constituent after 6 October was a severe financial crisis. Its solution was to vote, on 2 November 1789, to confiscate or nationalize the properties of the Catholic church, while assuming responsibility for clerical debts, salaries, and the maintenance of worship; this was amplified by decrees of 17 March and 17 April 1790. To liquidate these confiscated properties (*biens nationaux*), the Constituent created *assignats*, 5 percent interest-bearing treasury bonds to be issued to state creditors who could exchange them for church lands.

The *assignats*, which spurred inflation and fell steadily in face value, were an economic failure. Among the reasons were the Constituent's decision on 17 April 1790 to make *assignats* legal tender; an increase in the amount of *assignats* authorized for issuance from the original 400 million to 1.8 billion; and recirculation of *assignats* exchanged for land instead of destroying them as originally intended. However, the *assignats* were a success as a political expedient designed to tie the purchasers of the *biens nationaux* (mainly the bourgeoisie and wealthy peasants) to the success of the Revolution.

The policies of the Constituent reflected the desire of the bourgeois deputies to transform the country from a society in which status and power were founded on birth to one based on talent and wealth. Hence the Constituent abolished control by corporations over trade and commerce, and passed the Le Chapelier law, which in essence prohibited strikes and unionization.

These same values were reflected in the Constitution of 1791, the Constituent's major contribution to the French Revolution. Reflecting their distrust of the monarchy, the deputies severely limited royal authority: the king could no longer initiate legislation or prorogue the legislature, nor could his suspensive veto apply to constitutional or fiscal matters. Legislative consent was required for declarations of war or the signing of treaties, and the ministers, who were accountable to the legislature, had to countersign royal decrees. The act of 7 November 1789, which forbade deputies to serve in the ministry (aimed primarily at H.-G. R. Mirabeau), seriously impaired the ability of the executive and legislative branches to work in harmony. The king also lost most of his control over the provinces with the elimination of powerful royal officials such as the intendants.

The future Legislative Assembly, whose 745 deputies were to be elected for a two-year term, was given a virtual monopoly of political powers: its deputies would have parliamentary immunity, it alone could initiate legislation, it would exercise full control over national finances and possess the right to establish or abolish public offices, and, through its committee structure, it would largely control the actions and policies of the executive branch.

The electoral provisions of the Constitution of 1791, mainly the work of the abbé Sieyès, clearly illustrate the plutocratic orientation of the deputies. The Constituent divided the adult male population into two basic categories: passive citizens, including domestic servants, who did not have the right to vote (approximately 3 million), and active or voting citizens (about 4.3 million), who had to be at least twenty-five years of age and to have paid the equivalent in direct taxes of three days' labor in their locality. The enfranchised met in primary assemblies to select electors (50,000 out of the 4.3 million who could qualify) whose annual tax payments had to equal the local value of ten days' labor. The electors then chose the deputies to the Legislative Assembly (landholders who paid in annual direct taxes the equivalent of a silver mark, about 52 francs).

The Constituent replaced the chaotic structure of the *ancien régime* with a rational administrative system that consisted of eighty-three departments. These were subdivided in turn into districts, cantons, and communes. The departments assigned each district's tax quota and administered hospitals, prisons, poor relief, and public works projects. The districts allocated the tax burden among the communes, compiled the lists of active citizens, and organized the sale of nationalized properties. The cantons had no administrative responsibilities but served as judicial sites for justices of the peace. At the local or communal level, the *corps municipaux* had extensive powers, such as the assessing and collecting of local taxes and the maintenance of order, which included the right to declare martial law and to call out the National Guard. These changes accelerated the rapid decentralization of power in France.

Judicial reform paralleled that of administration. The Constituent established a new, graduated system of tribunals in both civil and criminal cases, abolished the sale of legal offices, and introduced the elective principle for judges. In criminal proceedings, there were two juries: a grand jury, which decided if sufficient grounds existed for prosecution, and a petty jury, which decided on guilt or innocence. Practices of the past, such as the use of torture to elicit confessions and the branding of convicts, were abolished.

The high court of the nation was to try offenses committed by the ministers or other high officials and to hear cases affecting national security. The national legislature decided what cases to bring before the high court and chose its two *grande procurateurs* (prosecutors) from among its own members. The most striking aspect of the judicial reorganization was its almost total separation from the crown.

In its reorganization of France, the Constituent committed its most serious blunder in the area of church reforms. Wishing to establish a national church independent of foreign influences and without the social inequities of the *ancien régime*, the Constituent passed, on 12 July 1790, the Civil Constitution of the Clergy. This act provided for the reduction of dioceses from 139 to 83 to conform to the number of departments; the election of bishops by the electors of the departments and of parish priests by the active citizens of the communes irrespective of their religious affiliation; the canonical investiture of bishops by French metropolitans instead of by the pope; the abolition of annates; payment and restructuring of clerical salaries; and the requirement of a clerical oath of loyalty to the king and constitution.

The deputies had not anticipated the strong negative reaction to the Civil Constitution. Even the curés, who had generally supported the Revolution, expressed doubts about the authority of the state to reform the church without papal approval. Angered by the growing resistance of the clergy, the Constituent decreed on 20 November 1790 that all priests had to take the required oath to support the constitution, on penalty of forfeiture of office. Only seven bishops and less than half of the parish priests took the oath, and many of them retracted it when Pope Pius VI, on 10 March 1791, condemned the new ecclesiastical laws. With the peasants generally supporting their nonjuring clergy, the result was a bitter schism in French religious and political life, which lasted until Napoleon's Concordat with the papacy in 1801.

The religious conflict was the final straw for Louis XVI who, with his family, failed in an attempt to flee from France in June 1791, the so-called flight to Varennes. The return of the royal family to Paris on 25 June as virtual prisoners brought into the open the breach between the moderate and extreme elements of the Left in the Constituent. The Triumvirate of A. Barnave, A. Duport, and A. de Lameth wanted to halt the Revolution and preserve its gains from both counterrevolution and from radical egalitarianism. A major product of the breach was the Self-Denying Ordinance of 16 May 1791, which, by prohibiting deputies of the Constituent from being elected to the next legislature, would deprive that future assembly of any men with legislative experience.

The flight to Varennes also brought to the forefront of French politics the issue of republicanism. Although the Constituent had suspended the king from office after learning of his flight, the Triumvirate, playing on the deputies' fears of republicanism, persuaded the Assembly to adopt the convenient fiction that Louis had been kidnapped. Similar fears of republican radicalism prompted the Constituent to declare martial law and suppress, on 17 July 1791, a demonstration at the Champ de Mars where the Cordeliers Club had placed a petition demanding the trial of the king and a new government. However, the Triumvirate failed to restore monarchical authority through constitutional revisions, largely because the deputies of the Right would not cooperate with it. The Triumvirate also failed to win any real trust or cooperation from the king and queen, each of whom continued to urge other European monarchs to organize armed intervention to restore the prerogatives of the French monarchy. Nonetheless, on 13 September 1791, Louis XVI formally accepted the constitution, and the Constituent dissolved itself on 30 September.

In recent interpretations, some historians have tended to demean the role of the Constituent. Charging that it had lost popular support due to its narrow class interests, they assert that the Constituent was a thoroughly discredited body by the time of its adjournment. These critics mock the naive belief of the deputies that the Revolution was over and stress the fact that the new government would last less than a year. Such interpretations ignore the basic accomplishments of the Constituent, especially in the areas of administration and in the establishment of political and civil rights. The Constituent wrought such profound changes in the French state that no subsequent government could restore the *ancien régime*.

A.N., Series A., ADxviii, AF¹, Ba, B 1, C 11, D, S. Y; A.P., 82 vols. (Paris, 1914); *B.N., département des manuscrits: Nouvelles Acquisitions françaises; Collection des mémoires relatifs à la Révolution française, publiée par MM. Berville et Barrière*, 60 vols. (Paris, 1820-28); *Collection générale des décrets rendus par l'Assemblée nationale* (Paris, An IV); R. K. Gooch, *Parliamentary Government in France: Revolutionary*

Origins, 1789-1791 (Ithaca, N.Y., 1960); *Réim. de l'Ancien Moniteur*, vols. 1-9 (Paris, 1863-70); E. Thompson, *Popular Sovereignty and the French Constituent Assembly, 1789-1791* (Manchester, Eng., 1952).

D. Epstein

Related entries: ACTIVE CITIZEN; BASTILLE, THE; *BIENS NATIONAUX*; CHAMP DE MARS "MASSACRE"; CORDELIERS CLUB; 4 AUGUST 1789; GREAT FEAR; *MARC D'ARGENT*; MIRABEAU; OCTOBER DAYS; PASSIVE CITIZEN; SELF-DENYING ORDINANCE; TRIUMVIRATE; VARENNES.

NATIONAL CONVENTION (1792-95), the body elected in September 1792 to draft a new constitution after the fall of the monarchy on 10 August. The Convention sat from 20 September 1792 until 5 Brumaire Year IV (26 October 1795). Its deputies conducted the trial and ordered the execution of Louis XVI.

During its unexpectedly long life, it faced, in addition to the financial, religious, and economic problems inherited from its predecessors, other intertwined problems more particularly its own: (1) its relationship with the Paris Commune and the Parisian *sans-culotte* movement; (2) internal political struggles, first between so-called Girondins and Montagnards, then between various Montagnard groups, and finally between the surviving Montagnards and the reactionaries of the Thermidorian period (July 1794-October 1795); (3) the waging first of Revolutionary foreign war and then of foreign and civil war simultaneously; (4) the drafting of a republican constitution, a task in fact carried out twice (1793, 1795); and (5) the creation of an emergency system of government to bridge the gap until a constitutional republican regime could be installed.

During its first two years, the combination of pressures produced the astonishing phenomenon of the total organization of the nation for Revolutionary war, which reached its peak during the Terror (July 1793-July 1794), an achievement that, despite the imperfections of eighteenth-century machinery, was unparalleled in Europe until the Bolshevik regime of 1918. It was the Convention that ensured the survival of the Revolutionary Republic. Amid their other preoccupations, the deputies continued the work of earlier assemblies in the fields of social welfare and cultural institutions, and some of their creations here still stand.

The Convention was the first body in France to be elected by virtual universal male suffrage. In spite of this franchise, a large electoral turnout was unlikely since the primary assemblies, gathering less than a year after the last elections, were to meet late in August when many of the (mainly rural) voters might not feel inclined to make the necessary journey, especially at short notice and during a war crisis when the enemy had already crossed the northern and eastern frontiers. Exactly how many primary votes were cast will probably never be known; estimates range from about 25 percent of the electorate downwards, with local variations. Many royalists may have stayed away, and in Paris they were certainly excluded if they could be identified, but in parts of France there is evidence that although outnumbered, they participated. Except in parts of southern and western

France, where electoral cooperation was limited, they seem always to have formed a small minority. At the secondary assemblies that actually chose the deputies, the electors were for the first time entitled to a modest removal allowance, and perhaps for this and other reasons, their attendance—again with some regional variation—was very good in general; two assemblies even regathered after having had to flee before invading armies. The obvious illiteracy of many electors, and the concern often expressed for the harvest, suggest that a large number were of rural background.

Adult male suffrage or not, the deputies were still drawn overwhelmingly from the bourgeoisie, with lawyers by far the largest occupational group. The range of occupations included clergy (pastors as well as constitutional priests), doctors, engineers, soldiers, and sailors; approximately one deputy in eleven was a man of business, and one in twenty was some kind of farmer. The number of nobility, understandably small, nevertheless included eight marquises and the duc d'Orléans. The clerks and artisans were a very small handful. But even if the social range was much the same as in 1791, it was not quite the same; N. Pointe the munition worker, Armonville the wool carder, Viquy the corset maker, Montégut the grave digger, and a few others like them introduced a new element into national politics. About a quarter of the deputies had been patriotic (left-wing) members of the preceding Legislative Assembly, reelected in absentia and usually at the head of the poll. A much smaller group (83 against 191) were ex-Constituents who had managed to retain their reputation. The rest were a mixture of local officials, judges, justices of the peace, some journalists and activists, and finally a small minority (under 10 percent) quite inexperienced in public life. The Convention was not elderly; two-thirds of the deputies were under forty-five and nearly 46 percent were under forty. A somewhat disproportionate number came from large cities, and fewer than 30 percent had lived only in the countryside.

Among the 749 deputies, there were no formal political parties, and the groups that developed found such unity as they possessed in general sympathies rather than in sharply defined principles. A little more than a quarter openly approved the anti-Parisian stance of the Girondin leaders. The remainder were divided, in roughly equal proportions, between Montagnards, who approved a generally left-wing line from January 1793 on and later supported the government of the Terror, and deputies of the Plain, who without aligning themselves clearly with either of the other groups gave what backing they chose to particular activities. These divisions were personal rather than social, though they may have had some geographical background; Montagnards from northern and eastern departments outnumbered those from the south and the west by three to two, whereas the Girondins came disproportionately, though by no means entirely, from southern, western, and coastal departments. Age and political experience also seem relevant. Older deputies were more likely to be conservative—the young Girondin leaders got their rank-and-file support from men much older than themselves—and (ex-Constituents aside) the level of potential support for the Mountain rose with the level of political experience; as a group, the ex-Legislatives were the most radical in the Convention.

All of the Convention's major problems were in some sense aspects of one problem: how to establish and maintain the unity and sense of direction needed if the Republic were to survive. Among the *conventionnels*, the Republic itself was accepted, and royalist sympathies were rare. Parisian-type republicanism was another matter. The deputies found it hard to agree on a policy that would both preserve the Convention's independence in the face of a growing conflict between some of its deputies and the Paris Commune and avert the danger of a Parisian attack on the Convention.

Relations between the capital and the legislature, likely to be difficult in any case after the Commune's unauthorized dethronement of the king, were exacerbated because the quarrel between the Girondin leaders and the Parisian radicals had been carried over from the Legislative Assembly into the Convention and there intensified by bitter Girondin attacks on the Commune and on individual members of the (mainly Montagnard) Parisian delegation, of whom G.-J. Danton, M. Robespierre, and J.-P. Marat were indiscriminately treated as if they epitomized the violence of the September Massacres. There were, of course, many elements in all this; for example, J.-P. Brissot and Robespierre had been at odds since the 1791-92 argument over the desirability of war. In more general terms, the *sans-culottes* were pressing not only for Revolutionary justice but for a degree of economic regulation acceptable in early 1793 to a very few *conventionnels*; and the *sans-culotte* claim that, as the local representatives of the sovereign people, they had the right to exert pressure on the Convention itself was equally unacceptable. Whatever the Montagnard sympathy for *sans-culotte* grievances, whatever the Montagnard hopes for a democratic republic, there was little sympathy for Parisian intervention in national politics, and on this the great majority of the *conventionnels* were at one. But should action be taken to discipline the Parisians before, or after, the Republic was otherwise secure? This was a question of priorities. The Girondins, having reason to feel personally threatened by Paris, tried to rally provincial support, a dangerously divisive thing to do, and this made them more suspect than ever. It seems very unlikely that they could have gained majority support for the direct attack on the Commune toward which they were moving in May 1793 after the mismanaged impeachment of Marat; and yet it is doubtful whether the Convention, left to itself, would ever have voted for their removal. While they remained, their anti-Parisian activity naturally continued, and agitation in Paris increased. This left a dilemma that the Montagnards, though already dominant in most respects, could not resolve. The Parisian rising of 31 May-2 June 1793 provided the solution, but the outbreak of federalist revolt and the widespread if short-lived protests against Parisian presumption showed how intractable the problem was.

Surrenders to the *sans-culottes* were in fact limited. A second invasion of the chamber on 5 September brought J.-N. Billaud-Varenne and J.-M. Collot d'Herbois to the Committee of Public Safety, plus concessions on economic policy and some intensification of Terror, but the effectiveness of these changes seems to have been related to their congruity with general Convention policy. The *armées révolutionnaires* did not last long, whereas the general maximum was followed by a national food commission and became part of a general system of regulation modified as the government, rather than the *sans-culottes*, saw fit. The intensified Terror of late 1793 was most savage in the provinces and can logically be seen as a response to the civil war crisis of the summer. As the Republic grew more secure, the government's hold on Paris tightened, and such independence as the Commune had had was lost long before the Thermidorian reconstruction of August 1794. Despite the many claims of early 1793 that right-wing deputies were in danger from the Paris mob, no such deputy was ever murdered in Paris; L.-M. Le Pelletier was killed by a royalist and Marat by C. Corday, and J. Féraud, who did die at his post in 1795, was hardly right wing and is said to have been murdered in mistake for L.-M.-S. Fréron.

As a body, the Convention was both more and less united than might appear. The king's trial, forcing deputies to choose among their Revolutionary principles, was an agonizing experience that deepened some kinds of divisions but probably did not create any; and the impressive willingness of deputies to shoulder their responsibilities, unexpected by P.-V. Vergniaud and Brissot, was in its way a pointer to what happened under the Terror. Had some Girondins not fled Paris to encourage civil war, the regime of 1793-94 might have been broader based than it was. During the Terror, the Montagnards had the cooperation of perhaps two-thirds of the assembly, a respectable figure under the circumstances. But when the emergency waned, differences of attitudes among the Montagnards themselves began to appear, since to plan an end to Terror involved some vision of the future and here ideas varied. As over the king, divisions became ideological as well as (unavoidably) practical. Amid the darkening intrigues of 1793-94 that accompanied the fall of the Montagnard factions and led up to Thermidor, it is hard to say precisely whose hand was against whom, but it seems clear that Robespierre's vision, whatever it was, was too demanding to be acceptable. The regime collapsed when dissident Montagnards sought support in the rest of the Convention to bring down Robespierre, converted into a symbol of Terror, and his supporters. The Thermidorians after Thermidor (27 July 1794) were an amalgam of renegade Montagnards, men from the Plain, and revitalized or returning Girondins. With a philosophy of survival rather than democratic enthusiasm, they were nevertheless vindictive and were unable or unwilling to control the excesses of provincial right-wing reaction or to return to the discipline that might have prevented the slide downhill to the inflationary disasters of 1795-96. For this, the restraints imposed by the Terror would have been needed; but after Thermidor, the thought of a return to Montagnard-type Terror was inconceivable.

Despite their great differences, the constitutions of 1793 and 1795 reveal how far the emergency government of 1793-94 outraged the normal principles of the *conventionnels*. This was recognized. The creation of committees of the legislature exercising almost dictatorial powers and of a Revolutionary Tribunal with special judicial procedures lay outside the normal apparatus of government, which in many ways continued to function for normal purposes. The Convention governed through committees drawn from its own membership because there was little alternative, but the pronouncement of 19 Vendémiaire Year II (10 October 1793) that "the *provisional* government of France is *revolutionary* until the peace" (italics added) indicated a situation accepted as exceptional by Montagnards and others alike. The Constitution of 1793, accepted by referendum but shelved until the crisis ended, was democratic, and although it safeguarded the principle of property, it showed thought for the poor; by contrast, the Constitution of 1795, with its property franchise, checks, and balances, reflected the fears and hostilities of 1793-94; but neither constitution had a strong executive, and each assumed as axiomatic the division of powers so strikingly abandoned in 1793.

The Convention constructed its committees, of which those of Public Safety and General Security were the most famous, as need arose, and used deputies on mission, with almost plenary powers, to tie the country together though in theory retaining ultimate control itself. Even a brief glance at the committees' duties and membership suggests the amount of humdrum work needed and also the breadth of participation, which after the Terror shifted only gradually into new hands. The turning point in the exclusion of the Montagnards came in Germinal-Prairial (April-May 1795) rather than earlier and cost the Convention energy and experience that it could ill afford to lose, especially since after Thermidor there was a continuous monthly rotation of committee posts—beneficial perhaps for the spread of responsibility but not for the development of consistent and creative policy in difficult times. What is nevertheless notable overall is the steady contribution of almost unknown deputies and the Convention's relatively egalitarian attitudes. The independence of deputies on mission, which created problems for the Committee of Public Safety, was a symptom of their pride in their individual status as representatives of the people, among whom, in principle, one had no more standing than another. .

Beyond the Convention's central success, which was survival, there were successes and failures. The religious problem was too difficult; neither radical dechristianization, bringing with it a new calendar, nor Robespierre's Cult of the Supreme Being, nor the disestablishment of the constitutional church could extinguish the disorders inherited from 1790. Neither the creation nor the abandonment of the maximum secured an adequate bread supply at reasonable prices, and in 1795 the worst famine of the Revolution was yet to come. The *sans-culotte* movement was not accepted as legitimate but found its last flare of protest suppressed in Germinal-Prairial; G. Babeuf's defiant conspiracy still lay in the future. The Montagnard dream of democracy was repudiated, and the Montagnards themselves became a discredited minority. But the war had developed into a succession of victories; the Vendéan civil war, already nascent in 1792, was contained and other rebellions suppressed; the conscription to which the Republic had been forced in 1793 and which had provoked the Vendéan rising, produced the first national revolutionary army in Europe. Nor were other aspects of revolution forgotten. Under the Convention, the new metric system took shape, the Bibliothèque nationale and the Archives nationales were organized, a whole structure of higher education was devised, and—in spite of the collapse of more generous Montagnard plans—a start was made on a national system of primary education. Work on the new legal code was continued; the remnants of the seigneurial system were finally buried, with some loss to bourgeois landowners. Inflation continued, and there was still no adequate tax system. But the successes were not negligible.

The Convention had been elected to draw up a new constitution. That its 1795 Constitution was to operate for only four stormy years was largely the result of the experiences of 1792-95. By 1795, the Republic was more divided than in 1792, with bloody memories of Terror and right-wing reaction too widespread for any electorally based regime to be secure. (It was under the Directory, not in 1792, that schismatic electoral assemblies were common.) Significantly, the *conventionnels* sought to give their constitution a better chance by insisting that they themselves provide two-thirds of the first legislature; this produced both a right-wing rising in Paris, the first of the Revolution, and a refusal by the electorate to approve enough reelections. Like the Constituent, the Convention left behind an unworkable constitution. Its memory has been shadowed by this, and, more important, by the Terror, and by the king's execution, which royalists never forgave; in 1816 nearly all the surviving regicides were driven into exile. Yet the deputies in exile were proud, and some refused invitations to return to France. Many regretted the excesses of the Terror, but few of the regicides regretted the death of Louis XVI. On his own deathbed in 1824, L.-B. Genevois, no Montagnard, looked forward to the day when Bourbons would again be driven from the soil of France. The legacy of the Convention was the memory of a victorious Republic.

A. Kuscinski, *Dictionnaire des conventionnels* (Paris, 1916-20); G. Lefebvre, *La Révolution française* (Paris, 1951) and *Les Thermidoriens* (Paris, 1960); R. R. Palmer, *Twelve Who Ruled: The Year of the Terror in the French Revolution* (Princeton, 1941); A. Patrick, *The Men of the First French Republic* (Baltimore, 1972); A. Soboul, *Les sans-culottes parisiens en l'an II* (Paris, 1958) and, ed., *Girondins et Montagnards* (Paris, 1980); M. J. Sydenham, *The Girondins* (London, 1961).

A. Patrick

Related entries: ARMEES REVOLUTIONNAIRES; BABEUF; CALENDAR OF THE FRENCH REPUBLIC; CONSTITUTION OF 1793; CONSTITUTION OF 1795; CULT OF THE SUPREME BEING; DECHRISTIANIZATION; FEDERALISM; GIRONDINS; LAW OF 14 FRIMAIRE; LAW OF THE MAXIMUM; MONTAGNARDS; REVOLUTIONARY TRIBUNAL; *SANS-CULOTTES*; THEORY OF REVOLUTIONARY GOVERNMENT; TERROR, THE; THERMIDORIAN REACTION; VENTOSE DECREES.

NATIONAL GUARD, a confederation of local citizen-soldier organizations formed to promote order and security. In late June 1789, the refusal of a number of companies of French Guards to act against the Paris population led the king to call regular troops from the east and north. The arrival of these 30,000 soldiers on 7 July posed a menacing threat to the independence of the National Constituent Assembly. On 8 July H.-G. R. Mirabeau denounced the danger that the troops posed, and on 10 July the electors of the city of Paris prepared a proposal for the immediate assembly of the traditional *milice bourgeoise*. The National Assembly on 9 July urged the king to remove his troops from the Paris area, a request he rejected. The attack of the Royal German contingent on a Parisian crowd in the place Louis XV enraged the city. Three days later the government of Paris was replaced by a Permanent Committee, which asked the National Assembly to obtain the king's permission to reestablish the *milice bourgeoise*. On the next day, 13 July, a force of 48,000 was ordered by the committee under the command of the marquis de La Salle.

The violence of 14 July led a number of deputies from the National Assembly to come to Paris the following day. That day Louis XVI conceded its organization and attempted to have his generals assume its command, but the municipal Assembly of Electors gave the title of colonel général de la Milice bourgeoise to the marquis de Lafayette. The king confirmed their appointment on 17 July. To regularize its organization, a *comité militaire* was established with delegates from the sixty districts. By 31 July it approved a set of temporary regulations.

Prior to this, similar turmoil throughout the provinces had led other localities to establish or activate other militia forces, but these largely reflected local conditions. In a decree of 10 August 1789, the National Assembly placed responsibility for the maintenance of local order in the hands of the municipalities. At first, the structures of these local National Guards continued to reflect local conditions. In a 29 October letter to the municipality of Epernay, Lafayette approved the necessity for local rules on a provisional basis. But as events proceeded, the National Assembly began to establish an overall structure. In December 1789 and the following February, it decided on the incompatibility of holding office in the municipality and the Guard, and the Law of 2 February ordered all militia, Guards, and volunteer units to submit to local civil authority.

During the summer of 1789, a cooperation evolved among Guard units in neighboring towns and provinces. The militia of Angers suggested in August 1789 that all units establish a regular correspondence among themselves and with Paris, and it urged that the Paris commander assume command of all such organizations throughout the realm. The theme of cooperation was echoed in November at Bourg d'Etoile: "We are no longer Dauphinais, You are no longer Languedocians, We are Frenchmen."

In the months that followed, a consistent program seemed to appear in these local *fédérations*, the fraternalism of the participants, their commitment to the anticipated constitution, and the threat to all who might threaten it—at home or abroad. The publication of a journal for the Guard, *La cocarde nationale*, provided one national forum for these ideas. On 15 May 1790 the Paris Commune announced its intention to invite representatives of all municipal National Guard units and line troops to gather in Paris on 14 July. On 8 June the National Assembly endorsed the project. Yet almost on the eve of that event, the Assembly passed important legislation defining the National Guard, limiting its membership to those who had paid taxes equal to three days' employment, and excluding units that favored aristocracy. Although all the regional *fédérations* of the spring and summer were not without incident, the general *fédération* held in Paris was a model of organization.

In the months that followed the *fédérations*, the political and religious differences that had been largely set aside in the show of unity began to assert themselves. Local turmoils stressed loyalties to the National Guard units and posed a significant threat to their *esprit*. Significant among these was the king's flight to Varennes, which severely undercut the supporters of constitutional monarchy. To underplay these dissensions, the National Asssembly voted on 28 July 1791 that there could be no further special *fédérations*.

In its decrees of 28 July and 29 September 1791 the National Assembly settled on the definitive regulations of the National Guard. Most important, its mission was defined as civilian and nonmilitary; its functions were limited to reestablish local order and maintain obedience to the law. The National Guard of Paris would no longer have a distinct commanding officer, but six *chefs de légion* would alternately exercise command for one month. By the decree of 29 September, orders were the prerogative of the municipal leadership.

With its influence on the shaping of events largely curtailed and its role in defense of an abstract constitution fulfilled, the National Guard steadily lost influence. With the mobilization of the army shortly after, it lost much political significance. When Napoleon took control after Brumaire, he suppressed the organization.

G. Carrot, "Une institution de la nation: La Garde Nationale (1789-1871)" (Thèse de 3e cycle, Université de Nice, 1979); *La cocarde Nationale* (Paris, 1790); C. Comte, *Histoire de la garde nationale de Paris* (Paris, 1827); R. R. Crout, "The National Guard as a Revolutionary Network," *Proc. of the Cons. on Revo. Eur.* 13 (1984).

R. R. Crout

Related entries: AMALGAM, THE; LAFAYETTE; VARENNES.

NATIONAL VOLUNTEERS, term used to describe the recruits raised in various levies of troops by Revolutionary governments between 1791 and 1793 who served in units distinct from the regular, or line, army. During the first half of 1791, some people brought up the idea of a Revolutionary militia, drawn from the National Guard for the purpose of defending the fatherland against foreign enemies. At a few places, such as Clermont-Ferrand, registers were opened and volunteers inscribed. On 13 June the National Assembly, disturbed by the formation of a counterrevolutionary army, decided on a free conscription of volunteer National Guardsmen to reinforce the regular troops.

The enforcement of this measure was precipitated by the king's flight (20-21 June). The Constituent Assembly then decreed the establishment of battalions of volunteers, independent of the existing army, that would be composed of National Guardsmen who volunteered for one year's service. These volunteers would receive double the pay of the regular soldiers, wear the uniform of the National Guard, and elect their own officers. At first fixed at 26,000 men, their number would soon exceed 100,000.

Levied by department, these battalions, due to their regional origin, possessed a considerable homogeneity that the later volunteers of 1792 would not know. As one officer remarked, the volunteers did not leave their homes without keen regrets, but they found in the midst of their units the same customs and language. The battalions were like second communities whose glory was the business of each citizen-soldier.

These volunteers were young (80 percent were younger than twenty-five years old) and came from the artisanate (66 percent), the bourgeoisie (11 percent), and the peasantry. Men of influence—bourgeois and nobles, sometimes mixed—officered them. These leaders had been noncommissioned and commissioned officers in the Royal Army and were familiar with the art of war. They knew how to establish discipline. Only a tenacious legend has too long represented these men as marauders sowing disorder in the army; in fact, their training and discipline were on a level with those of regular troops, and the panics that accompanied the beginning of operations were not always their fault.

Quite different were the levies of 1792, which coupled to the bourgeois army of 1791 an army of *sans-culottes*. The Law of 12 July 1792 levied 50,000 recruits for the line army and created forty-two new battalions of volunteers. These too were young men, but their origins were more rural than the volunteers of 1791, and many were poor peasants. For example, in the department of the Manche, 68 percent were peasants, of whom nearly 20 percent were servants, wage earners, and day laborers. Their officers were often former military men but without the extensive service and ability of those of 1791. They were also less capable of enforcing obedience. The volunteers of 1792, drawn from the world of wage earners close to that of the *sans-culottes*, were, like the latter, quick to denounce leaders and a discipline that they claimed was a legacy of former times. Politically radicalized by the struggles of 1792, for a time they imposed on the army a style of direct democracy, which displeased both the "blues" (volunteers) of 1791 and the "whites" (regulars). These rumblings of the courageous poor, however, let everyone know that they were the advance guard of the active masses of France, defending their new possession: equality with liberty. Their enthusiasm often made up for their lack of military experience.

Besides these battalions, other volunteer units served in the French army: the *fédérés* who played a decisive role on 10 August 1792 and the foreign legions and free companies levied by French and foreign patriots. The volunteers of both 1791 and 1792 felt that, as essentially citizens, they had fulfilled their contract with the nation by completing one campaign. In the winter of 1792, they left their battalions en masse. To meet the enemy coalition in February 1793 the National Convention ordered a levy of 300,000 men. All men between eighteen and forty years of age were eligible, but voluntary enlistment was maintained. In the event that there was an insufficient number of volunteers, citizens would be responsible for making up the difference and for adopting the most convenient method to achieve this. Thus, some proceeded to the election of volunteers; in some places communities used elections to get rid of patriots, while in other places they got rid of counterrevolutionaries. Finally, most departments, following the example of the Hérault, designated, with the aid of a committee appointed by commissioners of the Convention, those citizens whose *civisme* and physical condition made them most fit to go to the frontiers. This levy, which led to revolts—and not only in the Vendée—took time to organize, and by May fewer than 100,000 had departed. These contingents were composed of young men, but there was a much larger minority of adolescents and older men than earlier. The physical condition of these volunteers was often poor. And a large majority of them were of very humble extraction. In the Seine-et-Oise department, for example, 65 percent were peasants, and more than half were day laborers, threshers, cowherds, shepherds, and muleteers. Their officers rarely had had military training.

Thus, the Republic had several armies serving side by side that differed in recruitment, discipline and spirit, pay and uniform, leadership, and military experience. The Amalgam now was a vital necessity for the nation and the Revolution.

J. Bertaud, *La Révolution armée* (Paris, 1979); A. Mathiez, *La victoire en l'an II* (Paris, 1916); A. Soboul, *Les soldats de l'an II* (Paris, 1959).

J.-P. Bertaud

Related entries: AMALGAM, THE; FIRST COALITION; COUNTERREVOLUTION; 10 AUGUST 1792; VARENNES.

NATURAL FRONTIERS, DOCTRINE OF. See DOCTRINE OF NATURAL FRONTIERS.

NECKER, JACQUES (1732-1804), Genevan-born banker and minister of finance for Louis XVI. During his first ministry as director general of finances (1776-81), Necker established a reputation as a genius in financial administration. He was able to raise money by loans to finance the American Revolution, in striking contrast to the fiscal weakness of France during the Seven Years War. Taxes were not greatly increased, enabling the government to avoid another confrontation with the sovereign courts led by the Parlement of Paris.

The additions to the fixed obligations of the government incurred by the loans were met by reforms in the administration of finances which reduced expenditures. Yet the reforms were strongly resented by the financial companies and by the *grands* who suffered a loss in long-established privileges. A violent pamphlet campaign launched against him led Necker to demand unequivocal support by the king against his enemies. When the king refused to meet his specific requests, Necker resigned on 19 May 1781, to the great dismay of a wide sector of the public.

Over seven years later, on 25 August 1788, Necker was again appointed director general of finances. On 27 August he was made minister of state, one of the demands that he had presented to the king in May 1781 and had been refused. It was with great personal reluctance that Louis XVI consented to the return of the Genevan banker to the helm of his finances, but the circumstances in the summer of 1788 seemed to admit no alternative. On 16 August 1788 the ministry of E.-C. de Loménie de Brienne suspended amortization payments on the government debt and announced that *rentes* and other interest payments would be made partly in government paper notes. It was a declaration of partial bankruptcy. Creditors feared that worse was to come. Yet the financial crisis was only a symptom of a deeper political crisis. The absolute monarchy was confronted with what appeared to be the united opposition of a nation demanding some means of expressing its own will, particularly on fiscal matters. Necker appeared on the scene as a mediator between the king and the nation.

On 8 August the king had announced, as a gesture of appeasement, that the Estates General would be convened no later than 1 May of the following year. Most of the attempted reforms of the Brienne ministry were abandoned, and the Parlement of Paris resumed its role of spokesman for the nation in the absence of the traditional estates. At the outset of his second ministry, Necker believed that the political situation had changed completely from the time of his first ministry. Now, in August 1788, there could be no thought of reform by the government alone. The Estates General, the organ of an aroused and powerful public opinion, inevitably would become the vehicle for all reforms. Necker looked forward with eagerness to the event. He knew how difficult it had been under the *ancien régime* to get even the most modest reforms approved by the ministry and the king. Now all was in movement, change was irresistible, and Necker, who had always been an opponent of despotism, welcomed it. The principal task he saw for himself was to direct this momentous force. He had always admired the British constitution, whose strong executive worked in fruitful collaboration with the representatives of the nation in Parliament. It was this collaboration that he believed to be the secret of British power, and it was the British type of monarchy that he hoped would issue from the Estates General. Necker expected that the Estates General, imbued with patriotism, would work in harmony with the government, whose king and first minister were motivated by the same sentiments. It was an expectation and a hope that was to be disappointed in the events that followed.

The story of Necker's attempt to direct the torrent of Revolution falls into two parts, conveniently labeled his second ministry and his third ministry. The foremost preoccupation of his second ministry (25 August 1788-11 July 1789) was to find a suitable way of organizing the Estates General to carry out its mission. In this task he was continually thwarted by conservatives who refused to permit what Necker considered necessary for a truly representative assembly, the powers needed to represent the nation. Necker's popularity with public opinion continued to wax during his second ministry. It was his dismissal by the king on 11 July 1789 that ignited the July uprising in Paris. The success of the popular urban Revolution forced the king to recall Necker and ushered in his third ministry (29 July 1789-8 September 1790). On his return to Paris, Necker found the political atmosphere completely transformed. His enemies were no longer on the Right but on the Left. The National Assembly that greeted the returned hero with acclamation in July steadily turned against him in the months that followed. By September 1790, he announced his resignation from the government to a completely indifferent and even hostile Assembly. It was one of the most dramatic reversals in fortune ever seen. The popular idol of the July Days now slinked out of the country, his life and liberty threatened on his passage through eastern France to Switzerland.

The issues that arose in both ministries are' well known. The conservative, aristocratic forces wanted an Estates General organized according to medieval practices, with the three estates having the same number of deputies and organized separately, the vote taken by order. This meant a veto power for each of the three estates. Necker succeeded in getting the ministry to support him on the matter of doubling the number of deputies of the Third Estate. But he failed to win the assent of all his colleagues or of the king on the matter of organization of the Estates General. The king, influenced by the hard liners in his family and in the council, attempted at the royal session of 23 June 1789 to set aside the act of the Third Estate declaring itself to be the National Assembly, representing the French nation and calling on the deputies of the other two orders to join it. Necker did not attend the royal session, having argued for a more conciliatory compromise for the Third Estate. He believed that a compromise was possible by having the estates meet in common to deliberate on matters that all were agreed on, chiefly the principles of fiscal equality and the abolition of tax exemptions. Necker placed the blame for the failure of his compromise on the obtuseness and lack of political sense of the nobility.

After the July Days, when Necker returned to Paris, he found the executive authority of the royal government severely impaired. The National Assembly was assuming the absolute powers of the former despot, a function that it was ill suited to assume, especially in view of the rising tide of the democratic movement led by Paris. Necker was a liberal, not a democrat. He believed in the necessity of a social hierarchy for stability of government. The Revolution simply passed him by.

J. Egret, *Necker. Ministre de Louis XVI, 1776-1790* (Paris, 1975); H. Grange, *Les idées de Necker* (Paris, 1974); J. Necker, *De l'administration de M. Necker par lui-même* (Lausanne, 1791) and *De la Révolution française* (n.p., 1796).

R. D. Harris

Related entries: ASSEMBLY OF NOTABLES; BASTILLE, THE; *COMPTE-RENDU*; LOMENIE DE BRIENNE; LOUIS XVI; *RENTE*.

NEERWINDEN, BATTLE OF. See BATTLE OF NEERWINDEN.

NEY, MICHEL (1769-1815), duc d'Elchingen, prince de la Moskowa, marshal of France. Ney was born in Saarlouis (10 January 1769) the son of a cooper, and trained as a notary. Dissatisfied with his profession, he went to work in an ironworks but in 1787 turned to the military and enlisted in a regiment of French hussars. After five years of service, he had become a sergeant major, but his promotions became more frequent when the Revolution broke out, and he was attached to the staffs of General F. Lamarche and General J. Kléber.

He served at Valmy and Jemappes with the Fourth Hussars, and under Kléber's direction carried out independent operations with a column of 500 men (May 1794). He served with distinction in most of the battles in which the Army of the Sambre and Meuse was engaged (1795-96) and was promoted to general of brigade (1 August 1796). In the thick of the fighting at Neuwied and Kirchberg (April 1797), he was captured at Giessen (21 April), but he was exchanged within a month. After his active role in the capture of Mannheim, he was promoted to general of division and given command of the light cavalry of the armies of both Helvetia and the Danube (4 May 1799). After recovering from a severe wound received at Winterthur (27 May 1799), he joined the Army of the Rhine and served in the fighting across southern Germany. As a divisional commander, Ney played a vital role in the decisive victory at Hohenlinden (3 December 1800), which ended the War of the Second Coalition.

Given command of French troops in Helvetia and made minister plenipotentiary in Switzerland, Ney subdued the rebellious Swiss cantons and signed the Act of Mediation (19 February 1803), ending the insurrection and civil war. Ney organized and trained the future Sixth Corps of the Grand Army at Montreuil, and he was made a marshal of France in May 1804.

In the war of the Third Coalition, Ney won the key battle of Elchingen (14 October 1805), which sealed the fate of the Austrian army at Ulm (21 October). He commanded the Sixth Corps at Jena and while pursuing the defeated Prussian forces took 14,000 men and 800 cannons at Erfurt and 23,000 prisoners and 800 more cannons at Magdeburg. After moving into Poland, Ney's outposts were in constant contact with the Russian army. He played a decisive role in the Battle of Eylau (5 February 1807); he resisted 70,000 Russians at Gutstadt with 14,000 men and led a major attack on the Russians at Friedland.

Transferred to the Army of Spain in 1808, Ney and the Sixth Corps took part in the pursuit of Sir J. Moore to Corunna and subdued Galicia for the French. Attached to the Army of Portugal (April 1810), commanded by Marshal A. Masséna, Ney successfully conducted the sieges of Ciudad Rodrigo (10 July 1810) and Almeida (27 August 1810). He defeated Wellington's Light Division in the bitter Battle of the Côa (24 July 1810) and directed one of the attacks on the Anglo-Portuguese army at Bussaco (27 September 1810). Although the Army of Portugal reached the lines of Torres Vedras, within nineteen miles of Lisbon, it was forced by famine to withdraw from Portugal in March 1811. During the retreat, Ney fought a series of brilliant rearguard actions against Wellington at Pombal, Redinha, Casal Nova, and Corvo, and he was overtaken only once, at Foz de Arouce. During the retreat, Ney and Masséna became involved in a bitter controversy, which resulted in Ney's removal from the army for insubordination (23 March 1811).

Although Ney was sent back to Paris in disgrace, Napoleon gave him command of the Third Corps in preparation for the invasion of Russia (June 1812). Ney led his corps in battle at Smolensk (17 August) and Borodino (7 September), for which he later was made the prince de la Moskowa. During the retreat from Moscow, Ney was given command of the rear guard after the Russian attack at Viasma (3 November). Separated from the main army at Smolensk, Ney's force was attacked by a Russian army at Krasnoi, but on the advice of Colonel J. Pelet he outflanked the Russian army at Shirokorenyay and escaped to rejoin Napoleon at Orsha. Commanding the rear guard beyond the Beresina, Ney parried the Russian attacks until Kovno was reached.

In the Saxon campaign, he led the attack at Gross Gorshen near Lützen (2 May 1813) and effectively commanded the left wing of the army at Bautzen (22 May) and Dresden (26 August), but he was defeated by G. L. von Blücher and J.-B.-J. Bernadotte at Dennewitz (6 September) in his drive on Berlin. Ney fought and was wounded in the Battle of Leipzig (16-18 October) but returned to fight in almost every major engagement of the 1814 campaign in France. Following Napoleon's abdication, Ney accepted the Bourbons.

When Napoleon returned from Elba, Ney was sent to halt him, but he joined the emperor at Lons-le-Saulnier. Before the Belgian campaign, Ney was given the left wing of the army in time to contain Wellington at Quatre Bras (16 June 1815), while Napoleon defeated Blücher at Ligny. In command of the attack at Waterloo (18 June 1815), Ney had four horses shot from under him during the battle; he finally carried the center of Wellington's line at La-Haye-Sainte at 6:00 P.M. but the Prussians soon arrived with reinforcements to overwhelm the French army. Ney fled first to Paris and then to the Valais where he sought refuge at the château de la Bessonie, but he was recognized and arrested (3 August 1815).

Returned to Paris, Ney was brought before a military court; however, its head, J. Jourdan, declared the court without jurisdiction. Ney was then tried before the Chamber of Peers. He was convicted of treason and condemned to death by a vote of 137 to 23. The following morning he was shot by a firing squad (7 December 1815) at the place de l'Observatoire and buried at the cemetery of Père Lachaise.

Ney was a volatile, impatient, and often argumentative subordinate; nevertheless, he was a charismatic commander, an excellent tactician, a brilliant rearguard commander, and one of the most able and courageous field commanders that France has ever produced. Napoleon described him accurately when he dubbed him the ''bravest of the brave.'' There have been efforts by a small group of writers to establish the fact that Ney was not shot in Paris but escaped to the United States and appeared in North Carolina as P. S. Ney, a schoolteacher. Despite circumstantial evidence supporting this thesis, the facts indicate that Ney died on 7 December 1815.

A. H. Atteridge, *The Bravest of the Brave, Michel Ney, Marshal of France, Duke of Elchingen, Prince of the Moskowa, 1769-1815* (London, 1912); L. Blythe, *Marshal Ney: A Dual Life* (New York, 1937); H. Bonnal, *La vie militaire du maréchal Ney, duc d'Elchingen, prince de la Moskowa*, 3 vols. (Paris, 1910-14); G. Garros, *Ney, le brave des braves* (Paris, 1955); M. L. F. Ney, *The Memoirs of Marshal Ney, Published by His Family*, 2 vols. (Philadelphia, 1934).

D. D. Horward

Related entries: BATTLE OF JEMAPPES; BATTLE OF VALMY; KLEBER; MASSENA.

NICE, capital of a county of the same name and a possession of the House of Savoy in 1789. The official language was Italian; the spoken tongue, Nissard. Tourists, particularly English families, had already begun to winter there, and the construction of a new port in the 1750s had augmented trade. Nonetheless, Nice was by no means an important industrial and commercial center. Its 20,000 to 28,000 inhabitants were mainly artisans and farmers. Several hundred ecclesiastics were attached to the cathedral chapter, hospitals, and religious houses. The nobility was an open class. Ascension into its ranks was common, and its members engaged in trade.

French exiles began to arrive in Nice in August 1789. For three years, the city remained an *émigré* asylum. Most of the expatriates were nobles from Provence and the Comtat-Venaissin, but according to one count, 400 nonjuring priests were in residence by the spring of 1792. A small nucleus of French sympathizers also existed and, as early as 1790, had established contact with Revolutionaries in Marseille, Toulon, and Aix.

On 29 September 1792, after the rupture of diplomatic relations between France and Piedmont-Sardinia, the French army of the Var under General J.-B.-M. d'Anselme took the city without a fight. On the eve of Anselme's entry, some 10,000 residents fled in panic for Piedmont. The exodus was followed by days of pillaging in which townspeople and the undisciplined troops of Anselme were involved.

A popular society and provisional municipal government were formed by P. Barras, a representative on mission, in the first days of the occupation. The provisional government sent two deputies to Paris to demand the absorption of Nice into France. A plebiscite, ordered by the Convention, resulted in a vote in favor of union. The decrees of 31 January-4 February 1793 declared the county to be the eighty-fifth department and gave it the name Alpes-Maritimes. The two representatives on mission charged with organizing the department, H. Grégoire and G.-M. Jagot, completed their task between 1 March and 9 May 1793.

The Terror, which began with the arrival of A. Robespierre and J.-F. Ricord on 2 September 1793, was relatively mild. A guillotine was set up on the place d'Egalité, where eight people were executed. Church property was confiscated and worship suspended for a few months. Even so, dechristianization was less severe than elsewhere, and the Catholic faith enjoyed a rapid resurgence after Thermidor.

Not until 11 May 1794 was the mountainous eastern part of the county of Nice liberated from the enemy. In the intervening period and for several years after, the city was the headquarters of a French army. Napoleon was stationed here in 1794 and returned in 1796 as commander of the Army of Italy.

By 1795 a swing to the Right had commenced. A gilded youth appeared on the streets, and L.-E. Beffroy de Beauvoir and A.-M. Chiappe, representatives who arrived in March, arrested fifty-six terrorists. During the Directory, political life was dominated by a corrupt clique headed by A. Gastaud. Laws relative to refractory priests were not applied, and royalist bands roamed freely in rural parts of the county.

M. Bordes, *Histoire de Nice* (Paris, 1976); J. Combet, *La Révolution dans le Comté de Nice et la principauté de Monaco, 1792-1800* (Paris, 1925); G. Doublet, "L'émigration française à Nice de 1789 à 1792," *Nice hist.* 31-32 (1928-29).

M. Kennedy

Related entries: AVIGNON; BARRAS; DECHRISTIANIZATION; *JEUNESSE DOREE*; MARSEILLE; ROBESPIERRE, A.

NILE, BATTLE OF THE. See BATTLE OF THE NILE.

NIMES, BAGARRE DE. See BAGARRE DE NIMES.

9 THERMIDOR YEAR II (27 July 1794), date of the overthrow of M. Robespierre and his close associates and the beginning of the Thermidorian Reaction against the policies of the Revolutionary government of the Year II. On 8 Thermidor, Robespierre had called for a purge of the government committees but refused to name his proposed victims. On the following day, L. Saint-Just began a speech that denounced a new conspiracy within the government. The rebellion of the *conventionnels* began when J.-L. Tallien interrupted Saint-Just and sparked off speeches attacking the Robespierrists by members of the governing committees, J.-N. Billaud-Varenne, B. Barère, and M.-G.-A. Vadier. Robespierre was accused of exerting a tyrannical domination over the government, arbitrary police measures, promoting his acolytes to positions of power, and dividing the Convention. Although Robespierre attempted to answer these accusations, he was continually shouted down by cries of *"A bas le tyran!"* The Convention ordered the arrest of F. Hanriot, commander of the Parisian National Guard, and then of Robespierre himself, Saint-Just, and G. Couthon. Robespierre's younger brother, Augustin, and the *conventionnel* P.-F.-J. Lebas demanded to be included in this new proscription, and they were.

Robespierre still had support in the Commune of Paris, and on the night of

9-10 Thermidor, his armed supporters succeeded in releasing him and his followers from their various places of detention. They were taken to the Hôtel de Ville, while the Convention, now in permanent session, declared them outlaws.

The Paris Commune, however, was unable to muster enough forces in the capital to resist the National Convention. Its difficulties were compounded by the drunkenness and incompetence of Hanriot. The Convention, led by J.-M. Collot d'Herbois, Barère, and H. Voulland, gathered its forces and put them at the disposal of P. Barras. In the early hours of the morning of 10 Thermidor, L. Bourdon led National Guardsmen loyal to the Convention into the Hôtel de Ville and arrested or rearrested most of the rebels. Lebas had shot himself; the younger Robespierre had thrown himself out of a window; Couthon had fallen (or had thrown himself) down a staircase and was badly injured. Robespierre himself had apparently attempted to commit suicide but had only succeeded in shooting himself in the jaw. (The gendarme Méda made a dubious claim to the glory of shooting Robespierre.) On the evening of 10 Thermidor Year II, the Robespierre brothers, Saint-Just, Hanriot, and several members of the rebel Paris Commune were guillotined. Altogether 108 suspects were executed as accomplices of Robespierre in the day immediately following 9 Thermidor.

On 9 Thermidor Year II, the Revolutionary government was overthrown not by a popular rising but by a minority of Montagnard deputies who carried out a parliamentary coup d'état. The Paris Commune found that it could not call on popular intervention to save the Robespierrists. Of the forty-eight Revolutionary Committees of the Paris sections, only ten persisted in their support for Robespierre long enough to compromise themselves. The inertia of the Parisian popular movement on 9-10 Thermidor had been related to the publication of a new wage maximum by the Paris Commune on 5 Thermidor, which meant an actual reduction in wages in many trades. A wider cause of popular apathy was the fact that the Revolutionary government itself had executed many leading popular militants and had reduced the independent initiative of the sections. Furthermore, Robespierre had always justified the Revolutionary government in the name of the war effort, but military successes now made exceptional measures of repression seem superfluous in the eyes of the deputies of the Plain.

The deputies who rallied against Robespierre on 9 Thermidor were afraid of a new purge. This seemed a possibility ever since the Law of 22 Prairial had made the workings of the Revolutionary Tribunal faster and more ruthless. A new purge seemed even more likely after Robespierre's speech of 8 Thermidor, which, without being explicit, had made the deputies very apprehensive.

The Montagnard deputies who felt threatened, however, were only very loosely united. They included ex-Dantonists, like F.-L. Bourdon de l'Oise who criticized the Revolutionary Tribunal, and J.-A. Thuriot de la Rosière, who interpreted 9 Thermidor as G.-J. Danton's posthumous revenge. The Thermidorians, however, also included members of the government committees who had been instrumental in sending Danton to the guillotine. Several representatives on mission returning from the provinces, like Tallien, J. Fouché, and L.-M.-S. Fréron, felt threatened, either because the government suspected them of corruption or because Robespierre condemned their extremist policies and their promotion of the dechristianization campaign.

Within the committees of Public Safety and General Security, many individual quarrels had poisoned political discussion in the weeks preceding 9 Thermidor. Saint-Just and L. Carnot, for instance, had argued over military affairs; Vadier and Robespierre had clashed in the Catherine Théot affair. The Committee of General Security was jealous of the new *bureau de police* established by the Committee of Public Safety because it threatened to encroach on its own powers of political police. Already the important reports on the Hébertists and the Dantonists had been entrusted to Saint-Just instead of to the Committee of General Security, and this committee had not been consulted on the Law of 22 Prairial. It is possible, too, that Robespierre's opponents resented the government's social policies, embodied in the Ventôse decrees, that envisaged the liquidation of suspects' property for the payment of poor relief. But on 4 and 5 Thermidor, Barère and Saint-Just reached a compromise on this issue.

Beyond these personality clashes and power struggles lay a growing suspicion of Robespierre's own dictatorial pretensions and of his religious policy. Robespierre seemed to have strong personal influence over the Jacobin club, the Paris Commune, the Parisian National Guard, and the Revolutionary Tribunal. He seemed to be aspiring to a personally dominant role in Prairial, when he had presided over the Festival of the Supreme Being, an occasion that gave rise to serious rumblings of discontent among Montagnard deputies. Montagnards like Vadier suspected Robespierre of working toward a policy of religious appeasement with Catholicism, which they felt might assist the forces of clerical counterrevolution in the provinces.

Robespierre was therefore overthrown by a disparate group of *conventionnels*, some of whom looked forward to a relaxation of the Terror, while others intended to intensify it.

The temporary unity of the Thermidorians dissipated soon after 9 Thermidor when it became clear that public opinion favored the moderates against the extremists and dechristianizers. Within a few months, the events of 9 Thermidor had led to a dispersal of the authority of the two leading government committees, the release of suspects, the dismantling of economic controls, and the proscription of left-wing Thermidorians like Barère, Billaud-Varenne, Collot d'Herbois, and Vadier. The events of 9 Thermidor were a reaction against political overcentralization and a triumphant reassertion of the role of the National Convention. But the Thermidorians still had to demonstrate that the war could be won and Revolutionary gains consolidated without resorting to the Jacobin solutions of centralized control and political repression.

P. Sainte-Claire Deville, *La Commune de l'an 2: vie et mort d'une assemblée révolutionnaire* (Paris, 1964); M. Lyons, "The 9 Thermidor: Motives and Effects," *Eur. Stud. Rev.* 5 (1975); A. Mathiez, *Autour de Robespierre* (Paris, 1926); *Réimp. de l'Ancien Moniteur*, 32 vols., vol. 21 (Paris, 1863); G. Rudé and A. Soboul, "Le maximum des salaires parisiens et le 9 thermidor,'' *Ann. hist. de la Révo. française* 26 (1954); A. Soboul, *Les sans-culottes parisiens en l'an II: Mouvement populaire et gouvernement révolutionnaire, 2 juin 1793-9 thermidor an II* (Paris, 1958).

M. Lyons

Related entries: BARERE; BARRAS; BATTLE OF FLEURUS; BILLAUD-VARENNE; BOURDON; BUREAU DE POLICE GENERALE; COMMITTEE OF PUBLIC SAFETY; COUTHON; CULT OF THE SUPREME BEING; DE-CHRISTIANIZATION; LAW OF 22 PRAIRIAL; SAINT-JUST; THERMI-DORIAN REACTION; TALLIEN; VADIER; VENTOSE DECREES.

NOOTKA SOUND CONTROVERSY (1789-90), dispute between Great Britain and Spain over the Northwest Territory, leading to the collapse of the Family Compact between France and Spain. The origins of the controversy can be traced to 1789 when the Spanish government, apprehensive of American, British, and Russian encroachments in the Pacific Northwest, dispatched a fleet to establish a garrison at Nootka Sound and secure the coast southward to San Francisco. After seizing three English ships near Vancouver Island, Spain warned the British government not to trespass on Spanish territory. The British contended that they had every right to colonize the coast by virtue of Captain J. Cook's exploration and British settlements. This—the right to establish colonies in the Pacific Northwest and to fish off the coast—became the central issue in the Nootka dispute.

When the owner of the seized ships published an exaggerated account of the seizures, the cry of war ran throughout Great Britain, the cabinet drew up a declaration "demanding an immediate and adequate satisfaction for the outrages," and W. Pitt prepared for war. Meanwhile, Spain attempted to isolate Britain by forming a quintuple alliance with Austria, Russia, Denmark, and France. Spanish efforts for a grand alliance, however, were in vain, not because the continental powers were unsympathetic but because they were so preoccupied with their own aggrandizement that they could not spare any resources for Spain. Only France, Spain's traditional ally through the Family Compact, most recently renewed in 1761, was free from external interests, but France was absorbed in domestic politics as the first anniversary of the Revolution approached.

France played a key role in the Nootka issue because Spain was helpless without French assistance. For this reason Spain and Britain intensified their efforts to win French support. Spain wanted a clear, unequivocal endorsement of the compact, but it felt uneasy with the Revolutionary government. Almost all of France was sympathetic to Spain and hostile to Britain, but French anglophobia was offset by a dislike of a dynastic compact with autocratic Spain and by the conviction that the responsibility for starting and ending wars should reside with the National Assembly, not with the king. In May 1790 the Assembly expressed its sympathy to the Spanish government, mobilized fourteen ships, but referred to its newly established Diplomatic Committee the questions of a national versus a dynastic compact and the king's versus the Assembly's authority in matters of war and peace. Unfortunately for Spain, the Diplomatic Committee could not make its report to the Assembly before August, putting Floridablanca's ministry in a precarious position for the next three months.

Exploiting this dead-center position in Franco-Spanish relations, Pitt sent two unofficial envoys, W. Miles and H. Elliot, to Paris to assure the Assembly that British armaments were not directed against France, that Britain wanted a peaceful settlement, and that Spain was the only counterrevolutionary threat to France. Both envoys were to achieve this by making contacts with French political leaders (Miles with the marquis de Lafayette and Elliot with H.-G. R. Mirabeau). At no time was either to identify himself with the British government, which was officially neutral toward the Revolution, and neither was entrusted with money, as is often alleged, to bribe Mirabeau and other members of the Assembly. Both were Francophiles who served as lobbyists to widen the split between the Bourbon partners during the most critical periods in Anglo-Spanish negotiations.

Pitt succeeded in isolating Spain, which, without French support, had no choice but to succumb to his ultimatums of 5 July and 2 October, which insisted that Spain admit in writing that its claims to the Nootka territory were not founded on treaties, that its seizure of British ships was illegal, and that the British could fish, trade, and settle in the Pacific Northwest. For Britain, the Nootka settlement was its greatest victory between the Peace of Paris (1763) and the Treaty of Vienna (1815); for Spain, it long remained a symbol of appeasement and marked the beginning of the end of its great American empire.

H. V. Evans, "The Nootka Sound Controversy in Anglo-French Diplomacy—1790," *J. of Mod. Hist.* 46 (1974); W. R. Manning, "Nootka Sound Controversy," *Ann. Report of the Am. Hist. Assoc. 1904* (Washington, D. C., 1905); C. de Parrel, "Pitt et l'Espagne," *Rev. d'hist. dipl.* 44 (1950).

H. V. Evans

Related entries: FLORIDABLANCA; MILES; PITT.

NOTABLES, ASSEMBLY OF. See ASSEMBLY OF NOTABLES.

NOYADES DE NANTES (November 1793-May 1794), literally the Nantes drownings. The *noyades* have come to signify the extensive executions conducted in Nantes, largely by local authorities, as part of the Republic's pacification of the Catholic and royalist rebellion in the Vendée. Between November 1793 and the following May, a maximum of 3,500 people died at Nantes of disease, exposure, or some form of execution, including the *noyades*. Exactly how many of these 3,500 were victims of drowning is conjectural, though estimates go as high as 200 to 300. Given the amount of misinformation surrounding the *noyades de Nantes*, the episode should be viewed in the same light as the Parisian September Massacres: institutionalized hysteria that has been factually misrepresented.

The city of Nantes, situated at the mouth of the Loire River at the geographic edge of the rebellious west, served as the center and headquarters for the Republic's campaign of pacification and republicanization of the area. From October

1793, the city also housed facilities where captured Vendéans were detained and tried. As a city of 80,000 people, Nantes and its public services became increasingly overstrained, particularly after General J.-B. Kléber's victory at Savenay on 23 December 1793 over the Catholic and Royal Army commanded by J.-N. de Fleuriot. By the turn of the year, over 6,000 prisoners and suspects were incarcerated at Nantes.

From this point, although the first *noyades* had already taken place in early November, the dramatic influx of prisoners filled the regular jails and such auxiliary places of detention as the Entrepôt beyond capacity. Fear of an epidemic—typhus was present in the jails—and of a mass escape from the prisons led to the policy of mass executions, including the use of firing squads, the guillotine, and increasing the *noyades*, wherein barges packed with prisoners were set adrift in the Loire River where they were sunk by cannon fire.

A major difficulty is the question of responsibility, which historians have laid on J.-B. Carrier, representative on mission to Nantes from October through February. Yet an examination of his correspondence for this period reveals that Carrier was involved primarily with the military aspects of the pacification and that he rarely concerned himself with judicial or police matters. The actual initiation and implementation of republican justice, predating Carrier's arrival in the city, was the work of local radicals, *les Marats*, a group that had seized control of the city government. Carrier knew of the group's activities, but he failed to prevent or limit its actions. Consequently, responsibility for the brutality at Nantes must be shared by Carrier, *les Marats*, and even the National Convention itself, which proved incapable of restricting Nantes' radicals until the summer of 1794, when, with the end of the Terror, the city returned to nearly normal conditions.

Although the events at Nantes have been exaggerated and even distorted and Carrier's name blackened unfairly, the episode represents one of the darker sides of the Revolution, if only because many of those executed were given summary trials. The atrocity is ameliorated slightly by the fact that approximately 3,000 detainees were released by Carrier and his successor after January 1794.

E.-H. Carrier, ed. and trans., *Correspondence of Jean-Baptiste Carrier* (London, 1920); C.-L. Chassin, *La Vendée patriote, 1793-1795* (Paris, 1895); G. Martin, *Carrier et sa mission à Nantes* (Paris, 1934); A. Velasque, "Du nombre des victimes de la terreur à Nantes," *Rev. hist. de la Révo. française* 14 (1922).

E. A. Arnold, Jr.

Related entries: CARRIER; KLEBER; SEPTEMBER 1792 MASSACRES; VENDEE.

O

OBSERVATIONS A MES COMMETTANTS. See *AMI DU PEUPLE, L'*.

OCTOBER DAYS (1789), one of the memorable events of the Revolution, best known for the women's march to Versailles and the transfer of the royal family to Paris. The fifth and sixth of October 1789 saw a regrouping of forces as a result of conditions existing after 14 July: urban hardships and tensions owing in part to Revolutionary disruption of the economy, rural rebelliousness, untested local governments and militias, and at the national level the unsteady exercise of authority as Louis XVI and his ministers contested with the National Assembly over the shaping of France's political institutions.

The crisis was one in which the outcome of a struggle between the crown and the National Assembly was decided by popular intervention. The surface aspect of this struggle concerned three bodies of legislation, the Assembly's decrees of 5-11 August implementing the resolutions of the night session of 4-5 August dealing with feudal remnants in French society and government, the Declaration of the Rights of Man, and the first nineteen articles of a written constitution. Louis XVI kept withholding his acceptance of these acts and stating reservations. At stake was the king's share in constitution making and the passage of ordinary laws. Decisions on these matters were crucial to the relative shares of political power to be held in the future by the aristocracy and the newer elite of wealth and talent. Accordingly, the deputies to the National Assembly were divided in their attitudes toward the king's attempts at leadership. A minority of aristocrats supported the king or wanted him to show greater firmness. The Assembly's majority of patriots was increasingly impatient. Breaking off from the patriots, a minority known as *monarchiens* of Anglophile persuasion, led by J.-J. Mounier, wanted a compromise between the old aristocracy and the new elite, based on an absolute veto for ordinary laws and a bicameral legislature. Another minority consisted of democrats like M. Robespierre.

As tensions heightened during the weeks of delay, the patriots, fearing a resort to force in the interest of a coalition of crown, aristocrats, and *monarchiens*, looked for support to political allies in Paris; the details of their efforts are not known. The *monarchien* leaders accused their rivals of profiting from the intimidation of moderate deputies. Early in September the *monarchiens* tried to influence the king to move the Assembly to a location farther from Paris. Louis XVI refused, but on 14 September he sent for the Flanders Regiment, which, on its arrival, was fêted by the King's Bodyguard at a banquet in the course of which the tricolor was insulted. News of this event reached Paris, where the threshold for social antagonism and resort to force was already low.

On Monday, 5 October, the scattered disorders of previous days merged into two major Parisian demonstrations in which multiple complaints tended to focus on setting things right by going to Versailles. In the morning, several thousand women, accompanied by some men, invaded the Hôtel de Ville but were diverted toward Versailles by S.-M. Maillard, an imposing figure identified with the taking of the Bastille. Too late to witness this event, the marquis de Lafayette and the Paris National Guard took control of the area, which continued to fill up with a dangerous crowd. From late morning Lafayette was faced with the fact that his own troops sympathized with the crowd and were determined to march to Versailles. Lafayette tried for hours to dominate this situation but finally secured permission from the municipal authorities and at about 5 P.M. set out on the twelve-mile march to Versailles with his troops and a considerable civilian mob.

As the two phases of this crisis in Paris were developing, the National Assembly at Versailles was debating the king's resistance to its legislation and arguing about the banquet given by the King's Bodyguard. News of the women's march heightened tension in the Assembly and, in the early afternoon, brought the king back from hunting to attend a council meeting. At about 3:30 the National Assembly ordered Mounier, its president, to convey to the king its demand for unconditional acceptance of its acts; but before Mounier could leave, the women marchers from Paris crowded in. After a disorderly period during which Maillard and others voiced complaints, the Assembly had Mounier escort a women's delegation to the palace, where Louis XVI promised remedies. Maillard and some of the women then left for Paris.

This apparent success did little to quiet the apprehensions of the king and his advisers. Messages of reassurance arrived from Lafayette at about 9 P.M., but news of his approach with thousands of armed men renewed anxiety concerning the general's purposes. At one point the royal family agreed to withdraw to less accessible Rambouillet, but eventually Louis decided to remain and meet with Lafayette. At 10 P.M. he informed Mounier of his unconditional acceptance of the Assembly's decrees and at once sent the news to Lafayette, as did Mounier. "Once again," as Lefebvre wrote in *The Coming of the French Revolution*, "a mass movement had assured the success of a juridical revolution." By a little after midnight, Lafayette's forces and their hangers-on were in Versailles. In a dramatic confrontation with the king, Lafayette pledged his loyalty and that of his troops and explained that it had been impossible to oppose the popular will on the subject of the march. The Paris delegates who were with Lafayette then reported their constituents' wishes, one of which was that the king move to Paris. Louis spoke reassuringly but made no comment about moving.

The next morning, 6 October, the crowd from Paris invaded the palace, killed two of the Bodyguards, and rushed up a staircase toward the queen's apartment. Order was restored by the National Guard, but by the time Lafayette arrived, there was still danger from a mob in the courtyards. In a series of appearances on a balcony by Lafayette and the royal family, the innocence of the Bodyguards was proclaimed and the king agreed to move to Paris. The heterogeneous procession left Versailles at about 1 P.M.

Henceforth the king and his advisers would be hostages to the Parisians whose protests, spontaneous yet mobilized and directed to an extent hard to determine, had tipped the scales in the crisis. The Assembly, arriving in Paris on 19 October, would share this hazardous environment. Lafayette would be the hero of the October Days and would try to mediate between the court and the victorious patriot majority. Necker had been unable to forestall or control the recent events and had lost prestige. H.-G. R. Mirabeau was suspected of having tried to turn the popular unrest to the advantage of the duc d'Orléans. The *monarchiens* were, like the king and the aristocrats, the defeated parties; the effort of Mounier and his associates to balance new social forces with elements of tradition had encouraged the court's resistance to change and accentuated the fears of the patriot majority. King, aristocrats, and *monarchiens* in the future would be counterrevolutionaries but would never work together wholeheartedly. The victory of the patriot majority in October had consolidated the social gains and constitutional steps of August and September, but at the cost of strengthening the precedent of popular intervention. On the Left there were political figures capable of applying this lesson to later manifestations of the people's force, but that road would not be open again until more issues divided the Revolutionaries and further developments in the counterrevolution had taken place.

J. Egret, *Necker, ministre de Louis XVI* (Paris, 1975) and *La Révolution des Notables. Mounier et les Monarchiens, 1789* (Paris, 1950); L. Gottschalk and M. Maddox, *Lafayette in the French Revolution through the October Days* (Chicago, 1969); G. Lefebvre, *The Coming of the French Revolution*, trans. R. R. Palmer (Princeton, 1947) and *La Révolution française* (Paris, 1951).

P. H. Beik

Related entries : *ANGLOMANES*; COUNTERREVOLUTION; FLANDERS REGIMENT; 4 AUGUST 1789; LAFAYETTE; MAILLARD; *MONARCHIENS*; MOUNIER; NECKER; PATRIOT PARTY.

OCTROIS, consumption taxes. Local taxes administered by towns and communities, the *octrois* were levied on beverages, livestock, tallow, wood, construction materials, and even on grain and flour. Collected usually at the town gates, these taxes were the most important source of municipal revenue. The *octrois* of Paris were important enough to be included in the royal lease to the farmers general. In the course of the eighteenth century, the municipalities created special *octrois* to pay for local hospices, to repurchase local offices from the crown, and to furnish gifts to the king in times of national emergency. An increasing portion of the receipts were siphoned off to Paris so that by 1789 the *octrois* produced even more revenue than the *capitation*: 46 million *livres* compared to 41 million from the *capitation*.

As consumption taxes, the *octrois* were very unpopular, especially with wine and wood merchants, and with local tradesmen generally. Town governments were reluctant to raise the *octrois* on wine, which fell heavily on cabaret owners and their clientele among the *menu peuple*. The reforming minister, A.-R.-J. Turgot, attempted to exempt grain and flour from the *octrois* to aid the poor but without success. On the other hand, certain establishments such as the Bastille, the Invalides, and religious communities were exempt from the *octrois*, as were *bourgeois de ville* who carted produce to their town houses from their country estates. As with other direct and indirect taxes, extensive exemptions and the inequity of assessment were as irritating to the average consumer as the weight of the tax. No wonder the new wall around Paris, built by C.-A. de Calonne in the 1780s to enforce collection of the *octrois*, became the object of popular hostility, even of violence—the hated *mur d'octrois*. Yet local consumption taxes, abolished by the Revolution, were gradually revived by the First Empire. Ironically, the communes of the early nineteenth century clung tenaciously to their *octrois* as one of the last resources of local independence against the centralizing State.

J. F. Bosher, *French Finances, 1770-1795: From Business to Bureaucracy* (Cambridge, Mass., 1970); G. Chaussinand-Nogaret, *Les financiers de Languedoc au XVIIIe siècle* (Paris, 1970); M. Marion, *Histoire financière de la France*, 6 vols. (Paris, 1914-26); G. T. Matthews, *The Royal General Farms in Eighteenth Century France* (New York, 1958).

R. Forster

Related entries: CALONNE; *CAPITATION*; FARMERS GENERAL.

OGE, VINCENT (1750?-91), Haitian revolutionary. See TOUSSAINT L'OUVERTURE.

OPERA. See MUSIC.

"ORATEUR DU PEUPLE, L'." See GONCHON

ORDINANCE, SELF-DENYING. See SELF-DENYING ORDINANCE.

ORLEANS, LOUIS-PHILIPPE-JOSEPH, DUC D' (called EGALITE) (1747-93), earlier duc de Montpensier and duc de Chartres, prince of the blood, deputy to the French National Assembly (1789-91) and member of the National Con-

vention (1792-93). Son of Louis-Philippe, duc d'Orléans, and Louise Henriette
riette de Bourbon-Conti, Louis-Philippe-Joseph d'Orléans was born at Saint-
Cloud 13 April 1747. In 1769 he married L.-M. Adélaïde de Bourbon-Penthièvre,
daughter of the grand admiral and heiress to his fortune. This marriage made
him one of the richest men in France and brought about one-twentieth of the
land of the nation under his control. In 1771 Orléans (then the duc de Chartres)
championed the parlements in their struggle with Chancellor R.-N. de Maupeou.
A few years later, as commander of the Blue Squadron under the leadership of
the comte d'Orvilliers, the duke participated in the naval battle of Oressant
(1778) and was commended for his courageous performance under enemy fire.

Orléans' mad pursuit of pleasure, which involved prostitutes and other women,
as well as horseracing and gambling, decreased the impact of his political ideas.
In the years immediately preceding the Revolution, although not completely
consistent in his views, he talked a great deal about changes that would place
limitations on royal power. As chairman of the Third Bureau of the first (1787)
and second (1788) Assembly of Notables, Orléans opposed ministerial projects.
While the various electoral districts were preparing *cahiers* and electing deputies
to the Estates General in the spring of 1789, Orléans approved the printing and
distribution of *Instructions pour les personnes chargées de ma procuration aux
assemblées des bailliages relatives aux états généraux*. One of his secretaries
and agents, P. Choderlos de Laclos, prepared the pamphlet that bears Orléans'
name and summarizes the duke's ideas at this time. In the *Instructions*, Orléans
recommended that property be safeguarded and that no new taxes be levied
without the consent of the Estates General. Individual rights were to be protected,
and taxes were to be paid by all without distinction as to class. He also advocated
ministerial responsibility, the alienation of the royal domain, reform of the civil
and criminal codes, civil divorce, and abolition of the *capitaineries*. He seems
to have been influenced by ideas generated during the American Revolution and
by the liberal philosophy of Madame de Genlis, at one time his mistress and for
many years the tutor of his children.

Orléans was elected a deputy to the Estates General by several electoral
districts, but he chose to represent the nobility of Crespy-en-Valois. When the
Estates General met in May 1789, the duke called for the joint meeting of the
three orders to verify credentials and supported those who advocated vote by
head rather than vote by order. On 25 June Orléans and forty-six other liberal
nobles joined the Third Estate, which had declared itself the National Constituent
Assembly on 17 June.

On 3 July the Assembly elected Orléans president, but he declined the honor.
After J. Necker's dismissal on 11 July, wax busts of the duke and Necker were
carried by the crowds in Paris, and medals with the likeness of Orléans and with
the inscription *père du peuple* were distributed. Royalist supporters of Louis
XVI accused the duke and his agents of fomenting the disturbances associated
with the fall of the Bastille in July and the march of the women on Versailles

in October, in the hope that Orléans would become king. To get him out of France, the duke was sent on a mission to England, and he did not return and take his seat in the National Assembly until July 1790.

In October the National Assembly cleared him of charges that he was involved in the disorders of the summer and fall of 1789, but his role during this period of the Revolution is still steeped in controversy. Orléans repeatedly stated that five bodies stood between him and the throne and rejected completely the idea that the Revolution was an Orleanist conspiracy. Answering questions from members of the Revolutionary Tribunal on the day he was guillotined in November 1793, he denied that he had conspired with H.-G. R. Mirabeau and C. Dumouriez or that he had been involved in any effort to undermine the Revolution or become king. However, Orléans, with a taste for aimless political intrigue, did little or nothing to prevent disturbances on the grounds of his Paris residence (the Palais Royal) or elsewhere.

The bourgeoisie never really liked him, and most members of the nobility hated the duke. He loved and encouraged the cheers of the crowd, and while he and his agents were charged by Louis XVI's friends with encouraging revolt so that Orléans could become king (or regent), there is little evidence that he was that ambitious or had the audacity and ability essential to the success of such a venture. Orléans was irresolute and indecisive in time of crisis; he talked enough to compromise himself but vacillated when events demanded immediate action. His program of limited reform was achieved during the early stages of the Revolution; he was unprepared and frightened when the Revolution became more radical and moved far beyond the modest proposals of the liberal nobles in 1789.

The flight of the comte d'Artois and comte de Provence, the king's brothers, and Louis XVI's attempt to escape from France in June 1791 created a situation that Orléans might have exploited, and earlier Mirabeau seems to have considered him as a possibility to replace Louis XVI as king. But the duke made no real effort to promote himself, and his relationship with Mirabeau and G.-J. Danton is far from clear. Orléans was elected as a deputy to the National Convention from Paris early in September 1792, and officials of the Commune of Paris assigned him the name Citizen Philippe Egalité. He disliked this but was too weak and frightened to object.

The duke, who had been a member of the Jacobin party since 1790, sat on the extreme left in the Convention. Although his sons advised him to abstain, Orléans, under pressure from members of the Convention and uneasy about his own future, voted for the death of Louis XVI. As the Revolution moved to the Left, Orléans' rank and wealth made him an object of suspicion despite his contributions to the Revolution. When the duke's eldest son, Louis-Philippe, deserted from the army in the company of General Dumouriez, all members of the Bourbon family remaining in France were ordered imprisoned. Although Orléans protested that he had immunity as a member of the Convention, he was arrested on 6 April 1793.

He languished in prison for many months, and it was not until the Terror was fully in progress that he was accused by decree of the National Convention on 3 October 1793. Along with forty Girondists he was charged with "conspiring against the unity and indivisibility of the Republic and against the liberty and safety of the French people." On 6 November, after a short trial before the Revolutionary Tribunal, during which he denied all charges, the duke was sentenced to death. At his own request he went to the guillotine at 4:00 P.M. on the same day.

A. Castelot, *Le prince rouge* (Paris, 1950); B. Hyslop, *L'Apanage-Philippe Egalité, duc d'Orléans* (Paris, 1965); Louis-Philippe, *Memoirs, 1773-1793* (New York and London, 1977).

V. W. Beach

Related entries: ARTOIS; ASSEMBLY OF NOTABLES; *CAHIERS DE DOLE-ANCES*; COMMITTEE OF THIRTY; DUMOURIEZ; *EMIGRES*; LOUIS-PHI-LIPPE; MIRABEAU; NECKER; OCTOBER DAYS; PROVENCE; REVOLUTIONARY TRIBUNAL.

P

PACHE, JEAN-NICOLAS (1746-1823), political functionary under the Old Regime and the Revolution, minister of war (October 1792-February 1793), and mayor of Paris (March 1793-April 1794). Pache began his administrative career under the patronage of the maréchal de Castries, whose children he had tutored. He served as first secretary in the naval ministry, then as naval intendant of Toulon and as director of naval provisions. Under J. Necker he acted briefly as financial controller for the Maison du Roi. Pache then chose to retire to Switzerland just before the outbreak of the Revolution in 1789. Following the death of his wife, Pache returned to France in 1792 and was taken up by J.-M. Roland de la Platière, who gave Pache a post in his Ministry of the Interior. Dismissed with the rest of the Girondins in June 1792, Pache returned to power with them after 10 August and replaced J. Servan as minister of war on 18 October.

In the emerging struggle between Girondins and Montagnards, Pache sympathized with the Mountain. As minister of war he clashed with C. Dumouriez over the provisioning of the army; Pache wanted to centralize purchasing, while Dumouriez preferred to deal with private contractors among his associates. Pache drew apart from Roland and developed a reputation for running a *sans-culotte* ministry. When Roland fell in January 1793, the Girondins took revenge by expelling Pache from his post. He was now seriously adopted by the Jacobins and was elected mayor of Paris on 13 February.

As mayor, Pache was caught between the power of the Paris sections and the Convention's distrust of the Paris Commune. Had the Commune held authority sufficient to dominate the sections, its influence might have threatened the Convention, and this dilemma bounded Pache's mayoral career. Pache supported G.-J. Danton's call for a Revolutionary Tribunal in March 1793; at the request of the Luxembourg section, he and the *procureur* P.-G. Chaumette demanded that the Convention impose a Revolutionary tax; he supported partial amnesty for participants in the prison massacres of September 1792; he acted in May to suppress the *muscadins* (young Girondin supporters who were the social predecessors of the *jeunesse dorée* of the Year III). Although the Girondins were later to regard Pache as a principal organizer of the insurrection of 31 May, there is little evidence that he played an instigating role, although he was instrumental in preventing bloodshed. Pache never gained—nor could afford to gain—control over the political life of the sections. Indeed, in late August 1793 his arrest was sought because he had refused the sections' food-supply commissioners entry into the Paris granaries.

While Pache was mayor, Chaumette was *procureur* and J.-R. Hébert was Chaumette's substitute. In consequence, Pache was frequently accused by witnesses during the trials of the Cordeliers in March and April 1794 (Ventôse-Germinal Year II). His name figured frequently in spy reports to the Ministry of the Interior during this period; he was a natural target for informers whose business was slow. M. Robespierre, however, was well disposed toward Pache and had him arrested for safekeeping on 21 Floréal (10 May).

Transferred from prison to prison after Thermidor, Pache was finally brought to trial by his Girondin enemies in Prairial Year III (May 1795), only to be released by the amnesty of 4 Brumaire Year IV (26 October 1795). He published three political pamphlets during the Directory, of which the best known is *Sur les factions et les partis* (1797), his response to the government's efforts to implicate him in the Babeuf conspiracy of 1796. Pache subsequently retired to his Ardennes estate to lead a profoundly apolitical existence until his death in 1823. His unfinished metaphysical treatise, *Introduction à la philosophie*, was published by his son in 1844.

Although Pache was not a careerist, it is unquestionable that much of his activity in the Revolution consisted of keeping pace with his political milieu. He was a good Jacobin but not a creative one, and his responsibility for events in Paris during the Terror was minor. He wrote of himself in 1797 that he had no illusions about his actual influence, but the persecutions he had suffered from all factions proved that it was allegedly great.

L. Pierquin, ed., *Mémoires sur Pache* (Charleville, 1900); A. Sée, *Le procès Pache* (Paris, 1911); I. Woloch, *Jacobin Legacy: The Democratic Movement under the Directory* (Princeton, 1970).

C. Ramsay

Related entries: CHAUMETTE; CONSPIRACY OF EQUALS; HEBERT; *JEUNESSE DOREE*; NECKER; PARIS COMMUNE; ROLAND DE LA PLATIERE, J.-M.; SECTIONS; SERVAN DE GERBEY.

PADUA CIRCULAR. See LEOPOLD II.

PAINE, THOMAS (1737-1809), English political writer and activist in the American and French revolutions. Born on 29 January 1737 in Thetford, England, Paine was the son of Quakers; his father was a corset maker. He attended grammar school until thirteen years of age and then was apprenticed to a tradesman in his father's occupation, and tried various pursuits while continuing to educate himself. Married twice briefly, he lost his first wife within a year (1759) and separated legally from his second wife (1774). Appointed as an excise man, he drafted an appeal for higher wages for his coworkers and was dismissed as a result. After meeting B. Franklin, he sailed for Philadelphia in October 1774 with a letter of introduction from him. Shortly after his arrival, he turned journalist.

On 10 January 1776 he published *Common Sense*, in which he argued for a complete break with England and urged a strong federal union. His reputation was now made. In December 1776, after joining the army, he published the first letter of *The Crisis*. He also served as clerk of the Pennsylvania Assembly and went to France with J. Laurens to seek financial assistance for the American rebels. With the peace, New York State granted him a farm at New Rochelle, and Pennsylvania gave him 500 pounds in cash in recognition of his efforts. Meanwhile, he continued to write on various subjects, promoted his invention of an iron bridge, and returned to Europe in 1787. When the Bastille fell, Paine was in Yorkshire. He left for Paris late in 1789 and for the next three years commuted between the capitals of France and Great Britain.

After the appearance of E. Burke's *Reflections on the Revolution in France* (1 November 1790), Paine wrote the first part of his *Rights of Man* (1791), dedicated to G. Washington, and the following year published the second part, which was inscribed to the marquis de Lafayette. Both documents are eloquent defenses of individual rights. He rejected Burke's premises that posterity is bound forever as a result of a submission made by its ancestors at some previous date, in this case 1688. The eloquent passage in which Burke bemoaned the passing of the age of chivalry Paine repudiated indignantly as "the Quixotic age of chivalric nonsense" and accused Burke of embracing arbitrary power at the expense of the wretched and the weak. In part II, Paine proposed specific remedies for the ills of English society—remedies that have been accepted in all civilized states long since—old age pensions, free, public education, a progressive tax on the wealthy, and the end of primogeniture. The book sold 200,000 copies before Pitt's government suppressed it.

After the fall of the French monarchy, Paine was elected by four departments to represent them in the Convention. Although unable to speak French, he took his place as a deputy from the Pas-de-Calais, having been made an honorary French citizen (August 1792) together with other champions of liberty and equality, among them Washington. His politics were moderate, and he became a Girondist by temperament and association. His republicanism appeared as early as June 1791, after the flight of Louis XVI to Varennes, when Paine joined with the marquis de Cordorcet and N. de Bonneville, one of the founders of the Cercle Social, in a republican club and issued a letter in which he argued that the idea that a republic is suitable only for a small country was monarchist propaganda. The larger the nation, the less possible it was for one man to govern it, he held.

When Louis XVI was about to be tried by the Convention, Paine argued (21 November 1792) that although the king should be judged like other despots of

Europe, he should be exiled to the United States rather than be executed. J.-P. Marat interrupted the reading of Paine's appeal, shouting that Paine's Quaker principles made him incompetent to vote objectively on the question. After some tumult, the reading was allowed to proceed. Paine warned that what appeared today as an act of justice may tomorrow look like an act of vengeance, that he would rather see a thousand errors on the side of mercy rather than one act of severe justice, and that Louis' execution would wound the feelings of Americans. Despite this statement, Paine opposed the appeal to the people promoted by his friends, the Girondists.

Paine served as a member of the Committee on the Constitution along with B. Barère and Condorcet (1793) and helped draft a new version of the Declaration of Rights. Perhaps the most trenchant observation on the course of the French Revolution was made by him in a letter to G.-J. Danton (6 May 1793). He began by admitting that he was disturbed by the jealousies and party strife among the deputies and suggested that France ought not to interfere in the internal affairs of other countries; that the capital should be removed from Paris; and that price fixing, if it were to be resorted to at all, should be done by municipalities rather than from the center. Otherwise the policy will result in "dearness and famine," not "plenty and cheapness," and he cited his own experience in the American Revolution to buttress his argument. Finally, he suggested that there ought to be some regulation of denunciations that now prevailed because this practice led to destruction of all authority and promoted "private malignancy or private ambition." The deputies proscribed by the militant sections (his friends among the Girondists) were all known to him as patriots. Danton was in no position to act on his suggestions.

After the arrest of the Girondin leaders, Paine ceased attending sessions of the Convention, and when the Convention ruled that no foreigner could represent the French people, he lost his immunity and was arrested on 28 December 1793 and imprisoned in the Luxembourg. His detention resulted from an intrigue by G. Morris, American minister to France, who was a royalist sympathizer termed counterrevolutionary by Lafayette in a letter to Washington asking for his recall (15 March 1792). Paine's successful intervention on behalf of American crews held captive by the French aroused the hostility of Morris, who had hoped to aggravate differences between the two countries so as to break the French alliance in favor of an understanding with Britain. As a result Paine spent ten months in prison until rescued, finally, by J. Monroe, who had replaced Morris as minister. Paine never forgave Washington for abandoning him.

While in prison he wrote *The Age of Reason*, a profession of faith of a deist. Although critical of all churches, he professed his belief in God and in the immortality of the soul, principles that had nothing in common with atheism, of which he was accused by various critics. Paine rejected miracles and revelation and the idea that priests could forgive sins. Moreover, he saw the same spirit of religious intolerance that destroyed so many of his friends transferred to politics.

Paine was nursed back to health by Monroe and his wife, then restored to the Convention in July 1795; he remained in France until the Peace of Amiens (1802), before sailing for America. He spent the last seven years of his life near New Rochelle, a victim of poverty, bad health, and social ostracism, dying on 8 June 1809.

M. D. Conway, *The Life of Thomas Paine*, 2 vols. (New York and London, 1893) and *The Writings of Thomas Paine*, 4 vols. (New York, 1902-08); E. Foner, *Tom Paine and Revolutionary America* (New York, 1976); D. F. Hawke, *Paine* (New York, [1974]); T. Paine, *The Age of Reason* (1793 in French, no copy extant; 1795 first English edition; many editions) and *The Rights of Man* (many editions); W. M. van de Weyde, *The Life and Works of Thomas Paine*, 10 vols. (New Rochelle, N.Y., 1925).

M. Slavin

Related entries: BURKE; CERCLE SOCIAL; DANTON; GIRONDISTS; MARAT; MORRIS; VARENNES.

PANCKOUCKE, CHARLES-JOSEPH (1736-98), publisher of periodicals during the Old Regime. See *MONITEUR UNIVERSEL*.

PARIS COMMUNE (1789-95), Revolutionary and radical municipal government of Paris. The word *commune* shares a common root with the English *common*, as in commoner, common people, and commonwealth. In the struggle against feudal exactions imposed on towns by lord and bishop, the commoners often combined for self-defense and mutual aid. When the struggle erupted into open warfare, the people would arm themselves and would form a municipality under arms, the precursor of the future citizens' militia. This fight to free themselves from the feudality lasted for centuries. The medieval historian and theologian abbot Guibert de Nogent recognized the menace to the privileged classes in the organization of a people's commune when he stated in 1115: "Commune is a new and extremely bad name; it releases vassals from their due servitude." Almost seven centuries later, B. Barère shared this sentiment when he confessed in his *Mémoires* that the Paris Commune was "incompatible with public tranquility and with the calm necessary for the work of the Convention."

Undoubtedly there was some truth in these observations. The Commune tended to embody those principles and practices of popular sovereignty that troubled deputies of both the Right and the Left because it defended the needs and aspirations of the common people, at first the middle class and its allies, and later, the *sans-culottes*. More important than the ungentlemanly conduct of its members and spokesmen, the Commune demanded measures like the maximum and the guarantee of provisions, which were at variance with laissez-faire economics, accepted by the Mountain and the Girondins. Thus, on the one hand, it played an important political role by serving as a rallying point and expression of popular sovereignty, and, on the other, it performed those administrative functions that all large cities must engage in, from collecting taxes to dispensing aid for the poor. Furthermore, under the pressure of prolonged political and economic crises, it participated actively in the great *journées* of the Revolution.

The municipal law of 14 December 1789 had established the legality of communes that had risen spontaneously after 14 July. A further law of 21 May 1790, promulgated on 27 June, defined the municipal government of Paris. This institution was composed of 144 delegates, 3 from each of the 48 sections that constituted the new division of the capital, after the liquidation of the 60 districts. The representatives to the Commune were residents of the section that had elected them for a period of two years by the active citizens in their primary assemblies. Until 10 August 1792, voters had to be twenty-one years of age, living from their revenue or their labor. After the fall of the monarchy, delegates were elected by universal male suffrage. Before taking their seats, they had to pass a *scrutin épuratoire*, a close scrutiny, by their fellow representatives. If twenty-five or more sections rejected a delegate, his section was notified to replace him. This was done so that the parent body could establish control over imperfect purges and scrutinies by individual sections.

The affairs of the municipality were divided among five departments: subsistence, police, national estates and finances, public institutions, and public works. The municipal body (*corps municipal*) was composed of 48 officials elected by the sections from among the 144 representatives. Sixteen administrators were elected from this body who formed the *bureau municipal* and who administered the five different departments. They were presided over by the mayor. The 32 officials who were not members of this *bureau* made up the municipal council (*conseil municipal*) of Paris. Finally, the General Council of the Commune (*conseil général de la commune*) was composed of this municipal council plus 96 representatives, notables elected by the sections.

The General Council of the Paris Commune discussed such important matters as the acquisition or alienation of landed property, extraordinary taxes, local expenses, and loans. In addition, it passed various ordinances and decrees. The *corps municipal* concerned itself with lesser matters, such as the management of the Commune's property, budget, public works, roads, the allocation and receipt of direct contributions, and the deposit of funds. The Commune also had the power to limit the price of bread and meat and enjoyed other rights to regulate the local economy. One of its more important prerogatives was the right to call out the armed forces of the city and, in emergencies, to proclaim martial law.

Theoretically Paris as a municipality was under the jurisdiction of Paris as a department and had no legal right to execute laws passed unless approved by the latter. Since the sections elected both groups of officials, however, when the Commune spoke, the department was inclined to agree. Moreover, the mayor, the *procureur*, and his two substitutes were inviolable and thus could hardly be touched by the central authorities. In addition, the municipality was sole mistress of the Parisian Guard and controlled the police administration as well. Finally, since each company of the Garde parisienne elected its own officers, the political opinions of the latter tended to be of the same persuasion as that of the militiamen who had elected them.

From the very beginning, certain differences developed between the Paris Commune and the districts. The latter insisted that their delegates to the General Council were mere proxies or mandatories, sent to the Commune to carry out the will of their constituents and subject to recall by them. This doctrine was embodied in the term *mandat impératif*. The Commune rejected this principle of direct democracy and argued that delegates of the districts were representatives, not mandatories, and once elected, they no longer belonged to individual districts but to the Commune as a whole. Closely linked to this dispute was the question of *censure*—whether individual districts had the right to exercise critical control over their delegates to the Commune. Here again the General Council repudiated the idea of direct democracy as leading to anarchy. Finally, there was a sharp conflict over the question of *permanence*: whether the districts possessed the right to convoke themselves and to remain in session until dissolved by their own act or whether they could meet only when summoned by higher authority. The same division of opinion occurred. These disputes continued even after the districts gave way to the electors.

In times of crisis, the sections possessed one weapon, however, which the Commune was powerless to control. In order to bypass the representatives of the Commune whom they could not recall legally, the sections elected special commissioners whom they often endowed with unlimited powers. The assembly of these extraordinary commissioners would then elect an executive committee charged with the necessary powers to take decisive action. This was done during the insurrection of 10 August 1792, as well as against the Girondins on 31 May-2 June 1793. In each case, however, after removing the General Council from power, the commissioners of the sections immediately reinstated the Commune's officials and delegates in their former functions. This act was more than symbolic, it signified that the commissioners were expressing their confidence in the Paris Commune as the legally installed representative of Paris. Nor was this mere comedy as some historians believe. The confidence in the Commune by the Legislative Assembly and by the Convention, shaken though it might have been, nevertheless, remained intact. This would hardly have been possible had the authority of the Commune been supplanted by extraordinary commissioners sent by the more radical sections.

The social composition of the Commune tended to parallel that of the electorate. When active citizens alone enjoyed the suffrage, representatives to the General Council were largely members of the bourgeoisie or the liberal professions or high officials. The elections of September 1790, for example, returned an overwhelming majority (about 75 percent) of merchants and members of the legal profession. Once universal male suffrage was introduced, however, after the dethronement of Louis XVI, this class structure changed. Of the 206 members of the Commune whose occupation is known, only 26 were linked to the law. Nevertheless, the majority of this *commune provisoire* were small employers, not *sans-culottes*. After July 1793, the *commune définitive* reflected a more democratic trend. The number of merchants declined (from 37 to 21), while the number of artisans and workers almost tripled (from 12 to 32). In short, delegates tended to represent the *petits gens* after the overthrow of the Girondins. After the fall of M. Robespierre, this tendency was reversed.

Within certain historical limits, it is possible to speak of dual power when comparing the real and potential control exercised by the Paris Commune in contrast to that enjoyed by the Legislative Assembly or the Convention. This reference is to the well-known tension that existed between the Petrograd Soviet and the Provisional Government of revolutionary Russia in 1917 after the abdication of Nicholas II. The measures taken by the insurrectionary Commune after the fall of Louis XVI were so far-reaching that for a time it was the real authority in France, as it launched a policy of mass arrests of suspects, dispatched commissioners into the departments, requisitioned food, limited prices of necessities, and assisted the poor. Moreover, it still controlled the armed forces of the interior. After the insurrection of 31 May-2 June 1793 during which it had imposed its will on the Convention (under the direction of the Comité des Neuf, then under the Comité central révolutionnaire of the Evêché Assembly), it gradually surrendered its powers.

The Law of 14 Frimaire Year II (4 December 1793) put an end to its independent role, as national agents of the Revolutionary government were substituted for the *procureurs*. The execution of the Hébertists in March 1794 destroyed the leaders of the Paris Commune and converted it into a tame organ of the central government. With the fall of Robespierre, whatever communal policy still remained was finally suppressed. Under the Constitution of the Year III, its role was limited to purely fiscal and administrative affairs. After that the Paris Commune disappeared as a political expression of any sort.

B. N., Lb[40] 2, *Affiches de la Commune*; B. Barère, *Mémoires*, 4 vols. (Paris, 1842-44); F. Braesch, *La Commune du dix août 1792. Etude sur l'histoire de Paris du 20 juin au 2 décembre 1792* (Paris, 1911); Guibert de Nogent, *Opera omnia*, ed. J.-P. Migne (Petit-Montrouge, 1853); S. Lacroix, ed., *Actes de la Commune de Paris pendant la Révolution*, série I, 7 vols., série II, 8 vols. (Paris, 1894-1900) in *Collections de documents rélatifs à l'histoire de Paris pendant la Révolution française*; P. Sainte-Claire Deville, *La Commune de l'an II* (Paris, 1946); M. Tourneux, ed., *Procès-verbaux de la Commune de Paris (10 août 1792-1er juin 1793)* (Paris, 1894).

M. Slavin

Related entries: ACTIVE CITIZEN; HEBERTISTS; LAW OF THE MAXIMUM; *SANS-CULOTTES*; *SCRUTIN EPURATOIRE*; SOCIAL CONTRACT.

PARLEMENTS, supreme courts of appeal, whose extrajudicial powers made them the main source of institutionalized opposition to the *ancien régime* government. Originally the king had only one sovereign (supreme) court, the Parlement of Paris, but as he gained new provinces, each was endowed with a parlement of its own. The first provincial parlement was that of Languedoc, established at Toulouse in 1437. By 1789 there were thirteen, established (in chronological order) at Paris, Toulouse, Grenoble, Bordeaux, Dijon, Rouen, Aix, Rennes, Pau, Metz, Besançon, Douai, and Nancy.

Although it was possible for their judgments to be overruled by the Privy Council, parlements normally were the final courts of appeal on all nonfiscal civil or criminal cases. They also possessed extensive administrative powers and could issue *arrêts de règlement*, or bylaws binding throughout their jurisdictions, on any matter they deemed important. Above all, they kept registers in which all new laws had to be entered before taking legal effect. Before registration, parlements had the right to send remonstrances to the king pointing out defects in new laws; by thus delaying registration pending the king's reply, they could effectively hold up the operation of government. Louis XIV curtailed these powers by permitting remonstrance only after registration; but in 1715, in return for agreeing to override Louis' will, the parlements had their power of prior remonstrance restored by the regent.

By skillful manipulation of these procedures, they developed into a formidable engine of opposition. By *lettres de jussion*, the king could order registration regardless of remonstrances, but parlements could continue to delay matters by sending *itératives remontrances*. A further ploy was to register laws only with provisoes or reservations, and as a last resort, recalcitrant magistrates could go on strike. Sometimes they even resigned en masse. In reply the king would try to compel obedience by transferring the sittings of a recalcitrant court to some inconvenient small town, a sort of mass exile, and formally he retained the last word in a *lit de justice*, a session in which he or a personal representative came to the court and ordered registration on the spot. In the presence of the source of all justice, the authority of the magistrates was temporarily nullified, and so they were bound to obey. This did not prevent them from declaring *lits de justice* null and illegal in subsequent sessions. By printing and publicly distributing such declarations and copies of their remonstrances, they attempted to enlist public opinion on their side. In this they had considerable success, and the parlements were popularly regarded as champions of public liberties until September 1788. Behind their public posturings, however, they were often far less resolute in opposition than they appeared, being deeply divided on most issues both within and among themselves. Modern scholars are also coming increasingly to emphasize the degree to which collusion and cooperation, whether overt or tacit, was the norm in their relations with the government.

Offices in the parlements were venal, so it was impossible to dismiss a troublesome or incompetent magistrate without paying heavy compensation. In effect this gave the 1,200 magistrates of these courts complete security of tenure. Together they made up the core of the so-called nobility of the robe. By the eighteenth century, only a small minority of them had actually been ennobled by their offices, and the formal exclusion by a number of courts in the latter half of the century of those without a distinguished noble ancestry emphasized their aristocratic quality. Everywhere robe nobles intermarried freely with sword families, and the fusion of the two once-distinct categories seemed complete. This has led some scholars to see in the parlements the spokesmen of noble interests as a whole, to whom all other nobles now looked for a lead. The most recent work, however, emphasizes continuing divisions and jealousies between robe and other nobles in the 1780s. These came to the surface in 1789, when few members of the parlements were elected by their fellow nobles to sit in the Estates General.

The high point of the parlements' opposition to the government came in the 1750s and 1760s when they successfully limited tax increases and thwarted royal efforts to promote rival appellate authorities. They also maneuvered the government into expelling the Jesuits from France. Simultaneously, in the provinces, there were spectacular clashes between sovereign courts and intendants or provincial governors. The most serious of these, between the parlement of Rennes and the duc d'Aiguillon, led in 1770 to a confrontation between the government and the Parlement of Paris. The chancellor, R.-N. de Maupeou, lost control of the situation and in order to retrieve his position undertook a radical remodeling of the sovereign courts. Venal offices and judicial fees were abolished, the jurisdiction of the Paris Parlement was undermined by powerful new *conseils supérieurs*, and half of the magistrates in the country were dismissed and exiled. Outraged at their treatment, certain parlements in their remonstrances launched the call for the convocation of the Estates General to remedy such royal despotism, and there was an explosion of pamphleteering in their favor. Nevertheless, Maupeou soon reduced the remodeled courts to silent impotence, and his system lasted from 1771 until the death of Louis XV in 1774.

Louis XVI, anxious for popularity, dismissed Maupeou and restored the old parlements. Many historians regard this as the fatal mistake of his reign, the abandonment of a chance to bring in reforms without opposition. Others have observed, however, that despite Maupeou's talk of reform, little had been undertaken and that the restored parlements between 1774 and 1787 gave little trouble, being chastened by the Maupeou experience and often bitterly divided between those who had cooperated with him and those whom he had exiled. The Parlement of Paris was particularly supine; its earlier opposition was overridden, and it became vocal again only in opposing C.-A. de Calonne's insistent demand in the mid-1780's for the registration of new loans.

Thirty-eight members of the parlements sat in the Assembly of Notables of 1787, but they did not take a lead. Only when that body was dissolved, having called for the Estates General, did the courts come to the fore by refusing to register reform proposals that excluded the Estates. Even then both sides sought compromise. But after the government's attempt to dictate terms at the royal session of 19 November, six months followed during which the parlements refused to register anything and bombarded the king and public with defiant remonstrances. In May 1788 Keeper of the Seals C.-F. de Lamoignon attempted to break the deadlock by remodeling the courts even more drastically than Maupeou, vesting the power of registration and remonstrance in a single plenary court, and creating powerful new intermediate appeal courts, the *grands bailliages*. This plan was abandoned after the government collapsed three months later, but not before the fate of the parlements had aroused a public outcry and redoubled demands for the prompt convocation of the Estates.

Support for the parlements rapidly collapsed, however, particularly after the Paris Parlement declared, on 25 September, that the Estates General should meet under the "forms of 1614," for these forms were seen to guarantee dominance to the first two orders. Parlements came to be seen as mere mouthpieces and protectors of noble vested interests, and patriots viewed them with growing suspicion. The parlements in turn showed little sympathy for the work of the National Assembly, which in August 1789 abolished venality and judicial fees and committed itself in principle to a total reform of the judiciary. Pending this reform, the parlements were put on perpetual vacation by a decree of 3 November 1789 and were finally abolished by a decree of 6 September 1790. Eventually, perhaps two-thirds of their members emigrated, while around 300 were executed in the Terror. Many, however, resurfaced under Napoleon and played an important part in the judicial reorganization of 1811.

While it is undoubtedly true that the parlements were able to obstruct reforms, the Maupeou episode shows that they were not an insuperable obstacle. Their main Revolutionary significance lay not so much in preventing reform of the old order as in educating public opinion, through their remonstrances, in concepts such as despotism, patriotism, national rights, and fundamental laws. In 1787-88 they gave the agitation for the Estates General a lead and a focus, and after September 1788 their obvious conservatism did much to alert the third estate to the dangers of noble political ambitions.

F. Bluche, *Les Magistrats du Parlement de Paris au XVIIIe siècle (1715-1771)* (Paris, 1960); H. Carré, *La fin des parlements, 1788-90* (Paris, 1912); W. Doyle, *The Parlement of Bordeaux and the End of the Old Regime, 1771-1790* (London and New York, 1974) and "The Parlements of France and the Breakdown of the Ancien Régime, 1771-88," *Fr. Hist. Stud.* 6 (1970); J. Egret, *Louis XV et l'opposition parlementaire, 1715-1774* (Paris, 1970) and *Le parlement de Dauphiné et les affaires publiques dans la deuxième moitié du XVIIIe siècle*, 2 vols. (Grenoble, 1942); M. Gresset, *Gens de justice à Besançon (1674-1789)*, 2 vols. (Paris, 1978); B. F. Stone, "Robe against Sword: The Parlement of Paris and the French Aristocracy, 1774-1789," *Fr. Hist. Stud.* 9 (1975).

W. Doyle

Related entries: ASSEMBLY OF NOTABLES; GRENOBLE; JUSTICE; LAMOIGNON DE BASVILLE.

PARTHENOPEAN REPUBLIC, short-lived (January–May 1799) sister republic of France in the former Kingdom of Naples. After the annihilation of the French fleet at Aboukir on 1 August 1798, the king of Naples, on the advice of England and Austria, attacked the French troops stationed in the new Roman Republic. On 27 November, the Neapolitan army, commanded by the Austrian General K. L. Mack, occupied Rome—except for the castle of Sant' Angelo,

where a small French garrison continued to resist. But the bulk of the French
army, under the orders of General J.-E. Championnet, retired in good order to
the ridges of the Apennines. After receiving reinforcements from the north, the
French took the offensive, reentered Rome 13 December, and soon moved into
Neapolitan territory. The king of Naples and his family abandoned the capital
on 23 December and left for Sicily on the English ships commanded by Lord
Nelson, while the *lazzaroni* (the most miserable element in Naples' population)
rose in insurrection. On 11 January, Mack, incapable of fighting the *lazzaroni*
and the French at the same time, requested and was granted an armistice; the
French army was to occupy the north of the kingdom, except for the city of
Naples.

The French Directory had not anticipated the conquest of the Kingdom of
Naples and had given no instructions to its commissioners or its generals to
cover such an eventuality. In light of the situation, the likelihood of a new
coalition against France being formed, it was prudent not to provoke the states
of the Old Regime by creating new democratic republics in Italy. However,
General Championnet was jealous of the glory acquired by N. Bonaparte in
northern Italy; he desired to imitate, even to equal, him. He opened negotiations
with the Neapolitan Jacobins and claimed that they called on him to repress the
revolt of the *lazzaroni*. Championnet then declared that the king of Naples was
not observing the armistice, that the kingdom's ports remained open to the
English, and that the war indemnity, provided for by the treaty, was not being
paid. In these circumstances he ordered his army to enter Naples, and, despite
the warning of the army commissioner, G.-C. Faipoult, on 26 January 1799 he
proclaimed the Neapolitan Republic (also known as the Parthenopean Republic,
after the Greek name for Naples, Parthenope).

In Paris, the Directory was angered by this initiative; it supported Faipoult,
dismissed Championnet, and replaced him with General J.-E. Macdonald. The
provisional government of the Parthenopean Republic still continued to function.
It sent representatives to Paris to plead its case and elaborated its constitution.
This constitution, promulgated on 23 January 1799, was more original than the
constitutions of the other republics created by France in Italy. It began with a
long statement of the rights and duties of man, of the citizen, and of the people.
It put in the first rank of these rights, equality, then the right to subsistence, and
only afterward, liberty. Citizens who paid taxes would elect a Council and a
Senate; these then appointed five archons who exercised executive power. The
Parthenopean constitution devoted much attention to national education but was
mute on the religious question. In a major innovation, it provided for a tribunal
of five censors, at least fifty years of age, who were charged with judging the
morals of citizens. Those who lived "in a dissolute or voluptuous manner" could
be deprived of their civic rights for up to three years. Another original feature
was the assembly of ephors, one of whom would be elected by each department;
these men formed a kind of court charged with judging the constitutionality of

laws voted during the preceding year; they could also propose revisions of the constitution to the senate.

This constitution was never implemented. While withdrawing to Sicily, King Ferdinand IV had called the inhabitants of the Kingdom of Naples to insurrection. If the *lazzaroni* of the capital, who had accepted the Republic, did not budge, peasants, on the contrary, organized an Army of the Holy Faith at the instigation of Cardinal Ruffo. The republican government was incapable of winning over the peasants, for it did not abolish the feudal regime, which was very harsh in the Kingdom of Naples. In contrast, Cardinal Ruffo rallied them by pointing out that the barons were allies of the French. The Holy Faith forces marched on the capital. Macdonald evacuated Naples on 5 May 1799 in order to avoid having his retreat cut off by Austro-Russian troops, who were advancing through Italy from the north. A small garrison, left in the forts, capitulated on 19 June and was granted repatriation to France, along with the Neapolitan patriots who had joined it. On the advice of Admiral Nelson, however, Queen Marie Caroline had the patriots arrested; 120 of them, including the woman journalist, E. de Fonseca Pimentel, were condemned to death and hanged; more than 1,100 received long prison sentences. Thus ended the Parthenopean Republic after five months' existence.

G. Cingari, *Giacobini e sanfedisti in Calabria nel 1799* (Reggio, 1978); B. Croce, *La rivoluzione napoletana del 1799* (Bari, 1953); J. Godechot, *Les Commissaires aux armées sous le Directoire* (Paris, 1938).

J. Godechot

Related entries: BATTLE OF ABOUKIR; CISALPINE REPUBLIC; CISPA-DANE REPUBLIC; MACDONALD; ROMAN REPUBLIC; SECOND COALITION.

PASSIVE CITIZEN, a citizen who lacked at least one of the qualifications needed to be an active citizen entitled to vote in the first stage of an election in the period 1789-92. In its inclusive sense, the term covers the men over age twenty-five with little or no property and also unknown numbers of vagrants and domestic servants, as well as approximately 8 million women, 11.5 million persons younger than twenty-one years of age, and more than 900,000 men aged twenty-one to twenty-four who were defined as underage in the electoral law of 1789 but not in 1792 and later.

Political debate centered on a narrower meaning of the term. In this, the passive citizen was considered solely as the man qualified to vote in every way except that he did not have enough property to be obliged to pay a direct tax amounting to triple the daily wage for common labor. There may have been approximately 2 million men in this position. The term *passive citizen* ceased to be used after 11 August 1792 when they were granted the right to vote.

L. Henry and Y. Blayo, "La population de la France de 1740 à 1860," *Population* 30 (November 1975); R. R. Palmer, *The Age of the Democratic Revolution*, vol. 1 (Princeton, 1959).

P. Dawson

Related entries: ACTIVE CITIZEN; SIEYES.

PATRIOT PARTY (1789-91), national coalition of officials and politicians committed to moderate social and constitutional reform within the context of a national monarchy. The patriot party is said to have taken its name from those political forces in the parlements who opposed the Maupeou reforms of the early 1770s as ministerial despotism. The broad-based coalition that early appeared in the Estates of Dauphiné in 1788 opposed the imposition of the plenary court and other administrative reforms of C.-F. de Lamoignon without the consultation and approval of a national representative assembly. In appeals such as the *Lettre écrite*, those supporters urged that local privileges be retained only when they did not conflict with national needs.

Although both the proposals of J.-J. Mounier and E.-J. Sieyès opposed Montesquieu's view of the nobility as a separate and distinct political body from the nation, the two caused an early schism in the ranks of the patriot party by their differing views on the nature of the needed reform. Mounier had endorsed the idea of separation of powers; Sieyès maintained that all power should lie with the representatives of the nation. The early high point of the coalition was achieved in August 1789 with the abolition of some noble privileges, and opponents of the patriot party soon became identified under the title aristocrats.

Other members of the coalition included the duc de La Rochefoucauld-Liancourt, the marquis de Lafayette, the marquis de Condorcet, and Bishop Talleyrand of Autun. In the aftermath of the autumn votes on the proposed constitution, the patriot party suffered the defection of the club *monarchique* (*monarchiens*) who claimed that the actions of the Assembly had done the monarchy irreparable harm.

The chief success of patriots was in the formation of the local and regional federations or provincial leagues that swore allegiance to the nation first, then the king, and the new constitution. These assemblies occurred in Valence in November 1789, Pontivy and Dôle in February 1790, Lyon in May, and Strasbourg and Lille in June. Finally the national fête de la fédération was held in Paris on 14 July 1790, the high point of the patriot movement. Following the violence of the Champ de Mars in July 1791, the patriot party began to break down into factions, one of constitutional monarchists and the other of republicans.

A. Cochin, *La campagne electorale de 1789 en Bourgogne* (Paris, 1904); R. Crout, "The Garde Nationale as a Revolutionary Network: Impressions from the *Cocarde Nationale*," in *Pro. of the Cons. on Revo. Eur.* 13 (1984); J. Egret, *La Révolution des Notables: Mounier et les Monarchiens, 1789* (Paris, 1950); L. Gottschalk, *Lafayette in the French Revolution: Through the October Days* (Chicago, 1969).

R. R. Crout

Related entries: *MONARCHIENS*; MOUNIER; SIEYES.

PAUL I, czar of Russia, (1754-1801), whose reign marked the first occasion during the Revolutionary wars when Russia actively fought the French Republic. Paul was the son of Catherine II, his father was either Czar Peter III or one of Catherine's lovers. Fearing that Paul might become the focal point of plots against her, Catherine kept him isolated from public life; Paul, in turn, came to dislike her and her advisers.

Coming to the throne on his mother's death in 1796, Paul brought his own circle of courtiers to power. Rumors soon spread that the czar was mad. The work of his enemies, these stories were exaggerated accounts of the czar's eccentricities; there is no sound evidence of madness. His policies were motivated by a desire to strengthen the Russian government at home and abroad.

In foreign affairs, Paul at first sought to prevent Russian involvement in the wars of the Revolution in order to restore his state's financial position and concentrate on absorbing the new Polish provinces obtained by the partitions of 1792 and 1795. The French Egyptian expedition, however, seemed to pose a threat to Russian interests. Napoleon's seizure of Malta alienated Paul, who was grand master of the Order of the Knights of Malta, and the invasion of Egypt inserted French influence into regions long regarded by Saint Petersburg as being within Russia's areas of interest. The czar therefore decided that he would have to take up arms against France. At the end of 1798, he concluded an alliance with the Ottoman Empire and joined England in the Second Coalition. Paul agreed to send Russian combat units to Italy, Switzerland, and Holland. His objective was the same as England's: the overthrow of the Republic, the reduction of France to the frontiers of 1792, and the restoration of the pre-1789 status quo in Italy.

The campaign of 1799 began with a series of coalition victories, many of them won by Paul's chosen general, A. V. Suvórov. The Austrians, however, soon betrayed the coalition in pursuit of their particular expansionist aims. Vienna intended to seize northern Italy and Belgium, and Austrian forces that were to cooperate with a Russian corps in Switzerland moved into the Rhineland in order to attack Belgium. The Russian army was isolated, and the French crushed it at the Battle of Zurich. The French also inflicted grave losses on Suvórov's force as it tried to advance into Switzerland to assist the corps at Zurich. Shortly after, the British commander of the Anglo-Russian army in Holland capitulated to the French.

Angered by the disloyalty of his allies, Paul left the coalition at the end of 1799. In the following year, he adopted a pro-French policy, forming a League of Armed Neutrality, and even planned an invasion of India. Before either of these schemes had taken effect, Paul was murdered on 23 March 1801. A clique of aristocrats who objected to a number of Paul's domestic policies aligned themselves with Paul's son, Alexander, and killed their ruler.

A. Lobanov-Rostovsky, *Russia and Europe* (New York, 1947); H. Ragsdale, "A Continental System in 1801: Paul I and Bonaparte," *J. of Mod. Hist.* 43 (March 1970); A. Rodger, *The War of the Second Coalition, 1798-1801* (Oxford, 1964).

S. T. Ross

Related entries: BATTLE OF ZURICH; EGYPTIAN EXPEDITION; SECOND COALITION; SUVOROV-RYMNIKSKII.

PEASANTRY, by far the largest element in the population of France at the time of the Revolution, constituting 80 percent or more of the total but exhibiting such enormous variations in wealth, condition, and status that perhaps the only generally applicable definition would be inhabitants of the countryside whose primary or sole occupation was agricultural in nature. Because of the substantial regional differences in climate, soil, topography, property holding, farming techniques, even language, it is impossible to provide a general description of the French peasantry of the eighteenth century that would be valid for the country as a whole. On the other hand, to be completely precise would almost require a village-by-village analysis. Nevertheless, a generally accurate overview of the condition of French peasants can be presented, always bearing in mind the necessary qualifications and reservations.

In almost every rural community there were some well-to-do farmers—called variously *laboureurs, cultivateurs, fermiers, propriétaires*—who owned or rented enough land to support their families, employ labor, and enjoy a comfortable life-style even in difficult times. They also sometimes exercised official duties, such as tax or dues collections, and enjoyed great local influence and power since they hired hands, rented out animals for plowing, and were agricultural entrepreneurs (for example, merchants or millers).

A much more numerous group among the peasantry included tenant farmers and sharecroppers who either owned no land or held an amount insufficient to sustain themselves. While both types of land tenure existed throughout the country, sharecropping was the more common, particularly south of the Loire River and in western France. These peasants, who rented their land for payments in money or kind, were described as *laboureurs* and *fermiers* (the intermixture with the previous group being due to regional and linguistic variations), as well as *ménagers, métayers, closiers, bordagers, haricotiers,* and even *travailleurs*. All of them were essentially dependent on wealthier landowners, particularly in periods of economic crisis. Comparable to these were the wine growers (*vignerons*) and truck farmers (*jardiniers* or *airiers*), who were also dependent farmers but more closely tied to a market economy. During the last decade or so of the Old Regime, the wine growers, both proprietors and renters, had been especially badly hurt by a deteriorating market, a problem that was national in scope because of the extent of this industry.

The lowest echelon of peasant society included very diverse groups. There was a very large proportion of day laborers—*journaliers, manoeuvres* or *manouvriers, brassiers, laboureurs à bras*—whose survival depended on employment by larger farmers, at least on a seasonal basis. In addition, there existed a group of servants who comprised not only domestics but also such employees as shepherds, cowherds, and gamekeepers. Plus, there were ancillary rural occupations, including charcoal makers, fishermen, hunters, and woodsmen. Still in 1789, there remained roughly a million serfs in France, located mostly in eastern (Franche-Comté, Lorraine, Burgundy) and central (Auvergne, Bourbonnais, Nivernais) France and on the estates of the church. While their legal rights were less than those of the poorest peasants, they at least had some claim on the obligations of their lords during times of distress. All but the wealthiest free peasants faced an uncertain economic existence; a poor harvest could send hundreds of thousands of them on the road as migrants, beggars, or brigands, and fear of such a disaster dominated the peasant mentality well into the nineteenth century.

Two additional considerations affected the survival of the French peasantry in the late eighteenth century. First was the traditional right to common land, notably to graze their livestock on community fields or to gather firewood or food (nuts, berries) in village woods. Second, home or cottage industry, especially in textiles, furnished an increasingly essential supplement to the household income of peasants who saw their opportunity to acquire land decline markedly as the number of those dependent on income from agriculture rose significantly. Between 1715 and 1789, the population of France grew from 18 million or 19 million to 26 million or more, and virtually all of this increase came in the countryside. This demographic change intensified the peasants' land hunger, a condition exacerbated in some regions, particularly the northern plains, by an enclosure movement on the part of large landowners.

These developments added to what was already an almost intolerable burden of obligations on peasants. In addition to their tithes, required to support the established church, they had to pay an array of government taxes that included the *taille* on property, the *capitation*, a head tax, the *vingtièmes* on income, plus indirect taxes such as the *aides* on drinks and certain manufactured products, the *traites*, internal customs tolls, and the infamous *gabelle* or salt tax. The fact that indirect taxes were often farmed out to private tax gatherers and that all taxes were levied inequitably increased peasant resentment. Service obligations, such as the *corvée*, a tax in labor, and service in the militia fell on the peasants exclusively. On top of these came feudal dues and obligations. There were the customary rents in money, the *cens*, the *lods et ventes* on any transfer of property by sale or inheritance, and the *champart*, levied as a proportion of the crop, among others. Furthermore, local lords enjoyed special privileges at the expense of the peasantry, including a monopoly of low justice, the seigneurial *corvée*, the *banalités* or monopolies over mills, ovens, and wine presses, as well as exclusive rights to hunting, fishing, and maintaining dovecots. The allegory of the peasant supporting the rest of the population on his back, common at the time of the Revolution, bore a striking resemblance to reality.

While barely tolerable in normal times, the condition of the peasantry deteriorated in times of economic crisis, such as that of the late 1780s. Already pressed by demographic pressures and by the growing seigneurial reaction, which sought to revive and enforce feudal privileges that had fallen into disuse, French peasants had been victims of increasing prices and rents for years, but the unusually poor harvest of 1788 created a crisis. Prices of necessities rose 50 to

100 percent, and foodstuffs, especially the most basic food, cereals, increased most. While large farmers profited from the sale of their crops, the vast majority of the peasants, subsistence farmers, who had little or no surplus to market, were affected like other consumers. Beyond this, because of the paltry harvest, the demand for day labor declined, thus depriving small peasants of an alternative source of revenue. And finally, since food took up an increasing proportion of one's income, the demand for manufactured goods, notably textiles, declined precipitously, thereby all but eliminating the supplementary income derived from home industry. By the spring of 1789, most French peasants were in dire straits.

The one great hope, regardless of how well founded, for most of them lay in the coming meeting of the Estates General, scheduled for the beginning of May 1789. Even before this, from February on, there had been incidents of peasant violence in Dauphiné, Lyonnais, Languedoc, Brittany, and Provence, most of which was directed against feudal obligations and which often included attacks upon châteaux. The largest and most effective expression of peasant discontent, however, did not come until after the fall of the Bastille. Beginning on 20 July and lasting into the first week of August, the Great Fear swept vast areas of France. Rumors of armies of brigands—supported by foreign troops in frontier regions—and of an aristocratic plot led the peasants to arm and organize themselves. When their panic subsided, the peasants moved on to assume local authority and to attack and destroy the remnants of feudalism, usually accomplished by burning the feudal dues records or *terriers*.

Hoping to appease the peasant fury and at the same time protect property rights, leaders of the National Assembly, including liberal nobles, initiated legislation to abolish the more objectionable aspects of feudal rights and obligations on the night of 4 August. Although the renunciation and denunciation of feudal privileges went further than intended during that session and although specific decrees worked out during the following week began by declaring the total destruction of the feudal regime, the reality was less radical. All feudal privileges based on personal obligations were abolished, but those based on property rights had to be compensated for by redemption payments. By and large, peasants ignored the distinction and made their payments only when the authorities possessed adequate armed forces to implement the law—and sometimes not even then.

Local peasant violence occurred sporadically when redemption payments were demanded—for example, in the department of the Cantal in early 1790 and in the Lot in December of the same year—and more general recurrences of widespread fear took place during national crises, such as the attempted flight of Louis XVI in June 1791. The peasant attitude toward redemption was partially vindicated by legislation in June and August 1792, which required the seigneur to furnish the original title (often long lost) to justify repayment for certain dues, such as *lods et ventes* and *champart*. Finally, the National Convention definitively abolished all feudal obligations without indemnity on 17 July 1793.

Meanwhile, great changes had been taking place in the French countryside.

Church property had been nationalized in November 1789 and subsequently put on sale in exchange for *assignats*. Since these properties were sold in large parcels, it is unlikely that any but the wealthiest peasants were able to increase their holdings. In June 1793 two measures did more to improve the lot of the poorer peasantry: property confiscated from the *émigrés* was put on sale in small lots that could be purchased over a ten-year period and the Law of 10 June 1793 provided for the partition of commons among all members of the community. The famous Ventôse decrees (February-March 1794) went even further by ordering the distribution of confiscated property among indigent patriots. While these measures undoubtedly spread property holding more widely, it appears that the primary beneficiaries among the peasantry were the better-off farmers.

Not all peasants reacted to the Revolution in the same way. Major centers of peasant opposition to Revolutionary policies developed, particularly in the west and southeast, where hostility toward the measures of the central government and toward its representatives resulted in violent counterrevolution. In these regions, political, social and economic, as well as religious factors combined to lead to sporadic rebellion throughout the Revolutionary period. Nor were all peasants in a given region united in their response to Revolutionary developments. Small and large peasants disagreed strongly about the partition of commons. In general, the poorer peasants wanted the redistribution by head; those better off advocated that this be done by household and feared the *loi agraire* that their most radical brethren endorsed. Similar divisions developed over the law of the general maximum, which larger proprietors, who produced for the market, opposed.

It was the latter who benefited from the end of price fixing that came with the Thermidorian Reaction, while poorer peasants, like their counterparts in the towns and cities, suffered seriously from food shortages in 1795, a situation exacerbated by the exceptionally harsh winter. Problems involved in the partition of commons (such as costs of implementation, conflicting claims, opposition from certain groups of peasants) frustrated the implementation of this policy, and in 1796 the Directory gave up attempts to divide common lands among members of the community. The same regime also saw its various attempts to establish some new civic religion come to naught in the face of peasant devotion to tradition.

What, then, was the impact of the Revolution on the peasants of France? As with virtually every other element of French society, the peasantry in 1799 displayed characteristics of both change and continuity. Despite some occasional and isolated remnants, the feudal system that had persisted into the eighteenth century had been irrevocably destroyed. In addition, although local studies show the inevitable variations from region to region and although the bourgeosie and wealthy farmers bought most of the newly available *biens nationaux*, there can be little doubt that the total number of peasant proprietors increased significantly. On the other hand, French agriculture continued to be dominated by small farmers employing traditional techniques, who played only a very limited role in the market economy. Indeed, the French Revolution may well have retarded a modernization of agriculture. While not untouched by a decade of revolution, established peasant traditions remained firmly in place well into the next century. In short, the experience of the peasantry paralleled that of most other Frenchmen who lived through this momentous period.

P. Bois, *Les paysans de l'Ouest* (Le Mans, [1960]); J. Dupaquier, *La propriété et l'exploitation foncières à la fin de l'Ancien régime dans le Gâtinais septentrional* (Paris, 1956); G. Lefebvre, *The Great Fear of 1789: Rural Panic in Revolutionary France*, trans. J. White (New York, 1973), *Les paysans du Nord pendant la Révolution française*, 2d ed. (Bari, 1959), and *Questions agraires au temps de la Terreur*, 2d ed. (La Roche-sur-Yon, 1954); P. de Saint-Jacob, *Les paysans de la Bourgogne du Nord au dernier siècle de l'Ancien régime* (Dijon, 1960); A. Soboul, *Problèmes paysans de la Révolution (1789-1848)* (Paris, 1976).

S. F. Scott

Related entries: *BANALITE*; *BIENS NATIONAUX*; *CHAMPART*; *CORVEE*; FARMERS GENERAL; FEUDALISM; *GABELLE*; GREAT FEAR; LAW OF THE MAXIMUM; VENTOSE DECREES; *VINGTIEME*.

PERE DUCHESNE, LE. See HEBERT; HEBERTISTS.

PETION DE VILLENEUVE, JEROME (1756-94), Jacobin, mayor of Paris, federalist. Son of a lawyer and court official, Pétion practiced law until his election to the Estates General, where he gained prominence by fighting for the Declaration of the Rights of Man and for increasing the powers of the National Assembly. As a member of the Constitutional Committee of 1790-91, he advocated abolition of religious orders, establishment of the *assignats*, and complete judicial reform. He also demanded that the legislature receive sole authority to declare war or negotiate peace.

Immensely popular, Pétion shared with M. Robespierre the epithet "Incorruptible." Along with A. Barnave and M.-C. Latour-Maubourg, he brought Louis XVI back from Varennes. Although he fatuously recounted the impression he had made on Madame Elisabeth, he still urged that the king be tried and condemned. Pétion presided over the Jacobin Society in August 1791 and in the same year was elected to the Criminal Tribunal of Paris and to the mayoralty of Paris, the latter of which he won by a vote of 6,798 to 3,924. His opposition to the wearing of the red liberty cap as a superficial symbol won him respect from M. Robespierre and others. Still greater popularity was gained after the department of Paris suspended him from the mayoralty when he failed to prevent a crowd from invading the Tuileries on 20 June 1792. Three weeks later, he received a great ovation at the Champ de Mars in the presence of the king, and in early August he headed a delegation of the Paris sections that demanded that Louis be removed from the throne. A crowd of royalists kept him locked in his lodgings during the events of 10 August. Like most other political leaders, he disliked the September massacres but could do nothing to stop them. Elected to the National Convention from his native Eure-et-Loire, Pétion became president of that body and also presided over the Jacobins from 24 September to 8 October 1792.

Pétion parted company with the Jacobins and opposed Robespierre largely out of personal motives. He defended F.-N.-L. Buzot's attacks on the Paris Commune and declined the mayoralty when reelected in 1792. His attacks on Robespierre and his vote for a suspended death sentence for the king cost him his popular following. The Jacobins attacked him for alleged involvement in C. Dumouriez' defection in the spring of 1793, and he was included in the proscriptions of 31 May-2 June. Pétion fled to Normandy, Brittany, and the Gironde as the federalist revolt collapsed. Discovered while attempting to escape by sea, he hid in the woods with Buzot. The two men apparently shot themselves; their bodies were discovered the next day, half eaten by wolves.

J. Pétion, *Mémoires inédites* (Paris, 1866).

D. Stone

Related entries: BARNAVE; BUZOT; DUMOURIEZ; ELISABETH DE FRANCE; FEDERALISM; LATOUR-MAUBOURG; SYMBOLISM; VARENNES.

PHILIPPE EGALITE. See ORLEANS.

PHYSIOCRATS. See DU PONT DE NEMOURS.

PICHEGRU, JEAN-CHARLES (1761-1804), general and politician. Born at Les Planches-près-Arbois (Jura) in February 1761 to an obscure peasant family, Pichegru was educated in the local collège des Minimes, and his scientific aptitudes won him a place as tutor in mathematics at the future military school of Brienne. There he decided to become a soldier, not a priest, and enlisted in the artillery. He campaigned in America and rose to be a sergeant major by the summer of 1789. His officer potential had already been recognized, and by the summer of 1792 he was a lieutenant. Active in clubs and in support of the Revolution, he resigned his commission to take up the presidency of the Besançon club. He was, however, opposed to the Jacobins. In October 1792 he was elected commander of a battalion of volunteers from the Gard, which passed through Besançon, and served with them in the Rhine Army, rising to captain in March 1793 and general of brigade by late August 1793.

Following a staff appointment, he was made general of division that autumn and was then appointed commander in chief by L. Saint-Just in October. He demonstrated his talent for lightning attacks at the siege of Landau and the recapture of the lines of Wissembourg. This won him the praise of M. Robespierre and the Jacobins, so that the royalists threatened his life. In January 1794 he was transferred to the Army of the North where he repeatedly defeated the duke of York's forces and went on to capture Holland early in 1795. He also put down the riots of Germinal.

By then he was one of the most promising and well-respected generals, but his experiences in the Rhine and Moselle Army in the spring of 1795 made him cool to a government that left both him and his army totally denuded of money and equipment. He also resented the fact that others were promoted over him and his friends. This was noted by royalist agents, who, after watching him from May 1795, made contact at Blotzheim on 16 August 1795. L.-J.-C. Fauche-Borel, impressed by the way he had put down the *sans-culottes*, tried to suborn him by offering money and office. A long series of contacts began, although Pichegru was not trusted by the English and always seems to have been halfhearted in his activities, refusing to commit himself too far. Hence he never pursued the royalists' basic idea of a march on France in conjunction with the forces of the prince de Condé and Austria. His peasant loyalties and *ancien régime* army background may also have made him grateful to the monarchy, and he was certainly attracted by the availability of easy money to support his costly way of life. He was naively attracted too by the apparent weakness of the Republic.

Knowledge of his dealings seems to have encouraged the Austrian army, and this, together with the exhaustion of a smaller French force, meant that no great breakthroughs were made by the French. Pichegru was slow to capture Heidelberg and Mannheim and then withdrew his forces, suffered a crucial defeat outside Mannheim on 24 October 1795, thereby losing many earlier conquests, and signed a truce with the Austrians. The Directory was dissatisfied but dared not dismiss him. Knowing that he was under surveillance, he chose to resign in March 1796. He was offered the Stockholm embassy but preferred to live on his estates, maintaining contact with the royalists, until March 1797.

Then, despite the fact that evidence of his treason had fallen into the hands of J.-V. Moreau and N. Bonaparte, he allowed himself to be elected with English money to the Council of Five Hundred in April 1797. Although regarded as a leader of the opposition, he was again overcautious as president. He grasped the necessity of strengthening the National Guard too late and was taken by surprise by 18 Fructidor. Deported to Guyana, he escaped in June 1798 and with difficulty reached London. In 1799 he advised the allied forces in Holland, but the Austrians would not use him against France. He got in contact with G. Cadoudal and came to Paris only to be betrayed. Arrested on 28 February 1804, he was found strangled in his cell on 5 April, possibly at Bonaparte's behest.

G. Caudrillier, *La trahison de Pichegru* (Paris, 1908); H. Mitchell, *The Underground War against Revolutionary France* (Oxford, 1965); E.-M. Saint Hilaire, *Cadoudal, Moreau et Pichegru* (Paris, 1977).

C. Church

Related entries: CONDE; COUP OF 18 FRUCTIDOR YEAR V; MOREAU.

PILLNITZ, DECLARATION OF. See DECLARATION OF PILLNITZ.

PITT, WILLIAM (THE YOUNGER) (1759-1806), prime minister of Great Britain, 1783-1801, 1804-06. By 1789 Britain's youngest prime minister was already a veteran of parliamentary politics. He had withstood every attack from

Fox's opposition, placed the nation's finances in order, established reciprocal trade agreements with Ireland and France, scored a great diplomatic victory over France in the United Provinces in 1787, formed the Triple Alliance in 1788, endeared himself to the public, and survived the greatest threat to his ministry, the regency bill crisis, during George III's illness in the winter of 1788-89. The regency crisis, however, pointed out how fragile his position was without a healthy king to support him.

Persuaded by A. Smith's doctrines that international peace, free enterprise, and free trade were prerequisites for British prosperity, Pitt was anxious to maintain tranquility in Europe, to preserve the balance of power on the Continent, and to refrain from any interference in French internal affairs during the Revolution. He predicted confidently in February 1792 that expectations for a lengthy peace had never been better. The start of the Revolutionary wars two months later and the invasion of Poland by Russia and Prussia before the end of the year shattered his illusion.

Throughout the early years of the Revolution, Pitt expressed few sentiments or judgments about that event. He was obviously relieved that France's financial collapse and apparent military impotence removed any fears of renewed rivalry. Unlike E. Burke who viewed the Bourbons as essential for France's peace, stability, and welfare, Pitt, the son of the Great Commoner, evinced no feelings of compassion toward that royal family. Even in April 1790 when he noted that the distressing condition of France entitled it to compassion, he was probably following the advice of his ablest diplomat A. Fitzherbert "to drop a word in their favour" at a moment when Britain was exercising every effort to isolate Spain, break the Family Compact, and gain Vancouver during the Nootka Sound controversy. When the crisis was over in October, Pitt revealed his true sentiments: Britain must avoid any appearance of cringing to France at all times, even during France's present moment of weakness. And when H. Elliot, his emissary in Paris, returned to London in November, Pitt rebuked him for eulogizing that "Glorious" Revolution and for condemning Burke's *Reflections* as a "great libel," an opinion not shared by Pitt.

Pitt hoped to avoid the Revolutionary wars and decried Austro-Prussian intervention. As late as 7 November 1792 his foreign minister, W. W. Baron Grenville, was optimistic about keeping free of war, but France's conquest of the Austrian Netherlands that same month made war inevitable. The age-old cornerstone in British foreign policy—keeping France out of the Low Countries—remained the stumbling block for peace. From the fall of the Belgic provinces in November 1792 until the Lille negotiations in 1797, when British power was at its nadir, Pitt's ministry consistently and adamantly rejected any peace proposal that gave Belgium to France. The Scheldt Decree (16 November 1792) and Propaganda Decrees (19 November and 15 December) merely confirmed British suspicions of French intentions in the Low Countries. Unless France withdrew its forces from Belgium, there was no hope for peace in the winter of 1792. After November Pitt's ministry prodded the lethargic Dutch government into preparing for war and it negotiated with Austria, Prussia, Russia, and Sardinia to take concerted action to force France to withdraw its troops and cease fomenting troubles in neighboring countries. The execution of Louis XVI and the subsequent expulsion of F. Chauvelin from London were superficial incidents in the origins of the war.

Pitt's wartime policies were fourfold: to subsidize the armies of England's continental allies, to seize the colonial possessions of France, to support counterrevolutionary movements in France, and to employ Britain's small army in limited operations in friendly areas on the Continent. Except for the seizure of France's and its allies' colonies, Pitt's policies were failures. He admitted that he knew little about military affairs, appointed the wrong persons into key offices, and took advice from a few close but inept friends. Even his most sympathetic biographers agree that he was incompetent as a war minister and denounce his repressive wartime measures. At the time of his death, just a few weeks after Austerlitz, he had nothing to show for the millions of pounds that he had given to three coalitions and to the counterrevolutionary movements. Every British military campaign from the attack on Dunkirk in 1793 to the expedition to Hanover at the time of his death ended in a disaster. Meanwhile Napoleon had pushed the limits of his empire nearly to its zenith.

Not all of this was Pitt's fault. He had pursued essentially the same policies that his father, Lord Chatham, had executed so brilliantly during the Seven Years War. But Pitt the Younger lacked a single, strong ally on the Continent, such as Frederick the Great, to inject vigor into the coalition armies. Catherine the Great, the only powerful monarch of the period, was more interested in carving up Poland and the Ottoman Empire than in fighting a distant war against France, and Austria and Prussia wanted to share the spoils in Poland.

Only on water was Pitt successful. From the early naval victories at Toulon (1793) and Brest (1794) to the great battles of the Nile (1798) and Trafalgar (1805), Britannia ruled the seas. The seizure of French, Dutch, and Spanish islands in the East and West Indies, Ceylon, and Cape Colony was impressive, and yet they counted for little at the negotiations in Paris (1796), Lille (1797), or Amiens (1802). Whenever Britain offered to make full restitution of all French possessions but to retain two or three colonies belonging to France's allies, the Directory consistently rejected the offer, until Napoleon, anxious for peace after 1799, permitted Britain to keep Ceylon and Trinidad by the Treaty of Amiens. Although the settlement at Amiens was W. Addington's, Pitt defended it as honorable.

Clearly Pitt's best years preceded the outbreak of war in 1793. During the first ten years in office, he laid the foundations for making Britain the most powerful nation in the world. His strong points were finance, trade, taxation, and administration. His India Bill (1784) established India's government for seventy years; his Act of Union with Ireland (1800) lasted for over a century, but some of its failings remain today; his innovative income tax still exists and has been copied by most of the world. His omissions were equally significant.

He did nothing to patronize the arts; his suppression of civil liberties cannot be justified; he reneged on his youthful promises to reform Parliament, abolish the slave trade, emancipate the Catholics, and moderate the penal codes, although in fairness to him it must be said that he supported W. Wilberforce's bill to abolish the slave trade and resigned from office when the king opposed his bill to emancipate the Irish Catholics. His diplomatic successes over the French in the United Netherlands in 1787 and the Spaniards at Nootka Sound in 1790 were offset by his failures against the Russians at Ochakov in 1791 and the French throughout the Revolutionary and Napoleonic periods.

In spite of his limitations as a prime minister, the heroic legend of the great "Pilot who weathered the storm" persists. Perhaps it is because his most enduring virtue and strength was the respect he commanded from even his most inveterate enemies for his convictions, patriotism, integrity, and charisma that enabled him to dominate Parliament for more than two decades. The deference with which he was treated at the time of his death made it appear that even in defeat he had won the war, and the people's awe of him after his death made him the very symbol of rugged British determination to destroy Bonapartism.

Chatham Papers, P.R.O. 30/8/101-363, 373; J. Ehrman, *The Younger Pitt: the Years of Acclaim* (London, 1969); J. T. Murley, "The Origins and Outbreak of the Anglo-French War of 1793," (Ph.D. dissertation, Oxford University, 1959); Pretyman MSS, Ipswich and East Suffolk Record Office; J. H. Rose, *Life of William Pitt: Part I, William Pitt and National Revival* and Part II, *William Pitt and the Great War* (London, 1923); Earl Stanhope, *The Life of the Right Honourable William Pitt*, 4 vols. (London, 1861-62).

H. V. Evans

Related entries: ANNEXATION; BATTLE OF JEMAPPES; FIRST COALITION; FOX; GRENVILLE; MILES; NOOTKA SOUND CONTROVERSY; SECOND COALITION.

PIUS VI (1717-99), pope. Giovanni Angelo Braschi was born into a noble but not wealthy family in Cesena in the Romagna. His election to the papacy in 1775 ended a long conclave and came only after his choice had been cleared politically with several Catholic monarchs, who were concerned that he would not attempt to restore the Jesuit order. In his first decade in office, he had to confront several challenges to papal authority, most notably the efforts of the Hapsburg emperor, Joseph II, to bring the ecclesiastical authorities in his lands more directly under the control of the crown.

Pius VI's career before the French Revolution recalled the Renaissance popes in both the best and worst senses. He greatly expanded the papal collections, encouraged excavations of classical antiquities, and welcomed the scholars and artists who came to Rome to rediscover the ancient glories. He began the draining of the insalubrious Pontine marshes, helped to draw up an elaborate plan for the economic development of the countryside around Bologna, and concerned himself with the more efficient governing of the ramshackle Papal States. He also lavished offices and benefices on his relatives.

Until 1789, Pius VI's relations with the French state had been comparatively serene, but the Revolutionaries' religious reforms and his own intransigence were to produce the most serious crisis for the papacy since the fifteenth century.

Always politically cautious, Pius avoided taking a public stand concerning either the nationalization of church property in late 1789 or the Civil Constitution of the Clergy of 12 July 1790, hoping perhaps that the French bishops or the king would prevent their implementation, but Louis was persuaded to sanction them, and in March 1791 C.-M. Talleyrand made possible the new national church's apostolic succession by consecrating the first bishops elected under the new constitution.

Pius had been placed in a very difficult situation. To oppose the National Assembly's religious reforms could lead to a diplomatic rupture with the French state and could endanger his sovereignty over the papal enclave in Provence, but to approve them, especially following decades of similar efforts by various Catholic rulers, would encourage other states to do likewise. The eight months' delay before the pope spoke out, however, placed the French clergy in a tragic dilemma, which many of them saw as forcing them to choose between their country and their church.

When Pius did declare himself, in two briefs published in March and April 1791, his condemnation included not only the Civil Constitution of the Clergy but also the French regime's support for religious toleration, freedom of the press, and human equality, all of which he said were contrary to the principles of the church.

With the outbreak of the war in April 1792, a war that Pius' emissary and adviser, the *émigré* abbé J. S. Maury, represented as a crusade against the godless Revolution, French Catholic clergy and laity who followed the pope in rejecting the constitutional church came to be seen as subversives and traitors and were subjected to ruthless measures, including imprisonment, deportation, and death. Active persecution ceased with the end of the Reign of Terror in August 1794, but relations between the papacy and the French government did not improve, and the schism persisted.

In early 1798, the French engineered the overthrow of papal authority in Rome and the creation of a Roman Republic; the pope's nephew, Duke Braschi, participated in its founding. When Pius refused to leave the city of his own accord, he was placed under house arrest and sent to Siena. While it is true that crowds turned out to see and honor him as he traveled north, it is also true that there was no popular protest against the ending of the pope's temporal rule.

Pius's health had been precarious since 1791, and by 1798 he was an invalid. The French hoped to transfer him to Sardinia, but because of his health, they deferred the move. When in March 1799 the war was resumed, he was moved to Parma and then to Turin. With Austro-Russian invasion imminent, Pius, by now nearly paralyzed, was moved again, over the Alps into France. He died at Valence 29 August 1799, after a reign of twenty-four and a half years, the longest since the supposed twenty-five years of Saint Peter himself.

Although Pius VI was, in O. Chadwick's words (1981), the "least satisfactory" of the eighteenth-century popes, his determined resistance to the French Revolution and the sufferings of his last years served to elevate popular regard for the office, if not for the man, and to help to make possible the revival of Roman Catholicism after 1800.

O. Chadwick, *The Popes and European Revolution* (Oxford, 1981); J. Leflon, *Pie VII*, vol. 1 (Paris, 1958); L. Pastor, *The History of the Popes*, vol. 40 (London, 1953).

C. Garrett

Related entries: AVIGNON; CIVIL CONSTITUTION OF THE CLERGY; JOSEPH II; MAURY; ROMAN REPUBLIC; TALLEYRAND-PERIGORD.

PLAIN, THE (otherwise known as the Marsh or the Belly), the body of deputies during the life of the National Convention (1792-95) who refused to take up a predetermined attitude in political disputes and who during crises such as the trial of Louis XVI or the fall of M. Robespierre held the balance of power. After participating in the trial of the king (January 1793), these deputies played no prominent part in politics until after 9 Thermidor (27 July 1794), when some of them became conspicuous supporters of the Thermidorian Reaction.

L.-M. La Revellière-lépeaux described the prototype Plain deputy as a man who always allowed himself to be carried away by the most intimidating party, without even daring to ask if it was the most legitimate, and the acccusation of time serving, or alternatively fence sitting, has been repeated ever since. It has also been argued that to remain with the Plain was a matter of deliberate choice, and certainly a number of these men showed an independence far removed from mere time serving.

Since the Convention had no formal political organization, any attempt to establish the membership of the Plain must rest on a priori assumptions. To qualify, a deputy should lack clear political commitment but should go more or less with the tide. Down to June 1793, while the Girondin-Montagnard contest was still undecided, one might expect some reluctance to back the Mountain, but from that date, equal reluctance to share in the protest against the exclusion of the Girondins. Those who explicitly aligned themselves with either side do not belong to the Plain. Thus deputies such as P.-J. Cambon and B. Barère, who sat with the Plain when the Convention met but who from early 1793 followed a Montagnard line at points of crisis, must be excluded because they behaved in a way suggesting that their conduct under the Terror was a matter of choice rather than of opportunistic response to pressure. Similarly, it seems logically necessary to rule out any deputy who, being otherwise unknown, voted with the Mountain during the king's trial, refused to support the Gironde in April and May, and then went on to cooperate under the Terror; this too implies a consistent political attitude. (Any sign of wavering, such as a vote for the *appel au peuple* even if followed by steady left-wing voting, places a man with the Plain.) Traditionally, members of the Plain were concerned with distancing themselves from both factions. The number of those who demonstrably did this was considerable, though not as large as has sometimes been supposed; it was about 250 of the Convention's original 749 members.

The problems of adopting this kind of definition are obvious. All depends on the related definitions of *Montagnard* and *Girondin*, since if definitions of the factions are very rigorous, the numbers of the Plain will grow accordingly. Given the character of Convention politics, one must make one's individual judgment. Two points may, however, be made. First, the recent discussions of the factions, while producing various numerical estimates, have consistently tended to reduce the proportions of the Plain to a good deal less than the legendary great majority, a legend dating from a time when avowed Montagnards had also to accept implicit responsibility for a discredited Terror. Second, among the deputies difficult to classify are forty or so who could alternatively be called back-bench Montagnards. To place these men with the Plain would sharpen the Convention's internal divisions; any political group has its less committed as well as its outspoken supporters. P.-A. Merlin de Douai, said by some to be no Montagnard, was a consistent regicide and the *rapporteur* for the Law of Suspects, who gave a Montagnard-type reason for his abstention over J.-P. Marat's impeachment. This consistency of behavior over a period of months does not place him with the Plain. It may be added that were the Plain to be enlarged, as suggested, by the addition of a group of mostly unobtrusive quasi-Montagnards, this would imply a more widespread early acceptance of Montagnard leadership within the Convention than most historians have so far claimed.

In any case, a total of 250 is respectable, especially given the reduced size of the Convention after the removal of the Girondin leaders and their most vocal supporters. It would not be the great majority even if the suggested Montagnard right wing were added to it, but it could have been important in the politics of 1793-94, especially since so many Montagnards were away on mission. How did its members behave?

On the great issues of early 1793, their stance was significant. They showed either strong conservatism, such as would keep them quiet in the months to come, or moderation coupled with reluctance to become openly committed. Those who withdrew under the Terror included only a handful of regicides, and they voted with the Right during April and May, if they voted at all, which many did not; the withdrawal was already foreshadowing itself. The majority of their more active colleagues wanted to see Louis live but were divided over the *appel au peuple* and in April-May found it hard to decide what to do; they disliked Marat and Paris but lacked great enthusiasm for the policies being pushed by the Gironde.

Under the Terror, these attitudes developed in one of three ways. A small minority of deputies from the Plain, about one in seven, were willing to take on the heavy, sometimes dangerous duties of work on mission. About another two in five accepted office on one or another of the Convention's committees or otherwise showed willingness to accept the regime. Finally, not quite half withdrew from active politics for the time being. These last did not necessarily go home or even fail to attend sessions of the Convention; one such deputy refused in 1795 to consider reelection partly on the ground that he had sat for three years without leave of any kind. Leave of absence from the Convention had to be asked for and granted, and the applications from obscure sources appearing in the 1793-94 *procès-verbaux* are a reminder of the existence at that time of men who would do nothing to assist Jacobin government but who remained its silent witnesses until on 9 Thermidor they could (if they chose) make effective use of the rights they had never abandoned.

After Thermidor, many deputies became more politically active than they had been for some time, but only within certain significant limits. Of those who had completely faded out of politics, more than seven in ten now returned, either to committee work or actually to go on mission in the Thermidorian interest; anyone seeking the Convention's true right wing could surely find it here. The rest continued much as before, some now with identifiably Thermidorian sympathies but many others simply doing the tasks that came to hand: perhaps, as La Revellière-lépeaux was to say, being swept along, but also helping the government of the Republic to continue functioning. But the Plain was not equally represented at all levels of responsibility. After Fructidor Year II (August 1794), some of the committees—for example, Transports, postes et messageries and Pétitions, correspondance et dépêches—were virtually taken over by the Plain, or by the Plain plus returning Girondins; but on two key committees, Législation and Salut publique, ex-Montagnards remained important, on Securité générale the decisive swing to the right did not come until the spring of 1795, and on the comité de guerre the ex-Montagnards were consistently much the strongest single element. Before Thermidor, the Plain as a whole had offered little leadership. After Thermidor, it still left much of the running to others, and in crucial matters rarely led the field.

Since these deputies tried to stand aside from the lethal feuds in which their colleagues were embroiled, the few deaths among them during the session were mostly from natural causes, although the exceptions are revealing: C.-L. Antiboul was executed for cowardly conduct when captured by federalists on mission in Marseille, J. Féraud was lynched by the mob within the Convention itself during the Prairial rising—the only *conventionnel* actually to die at his post—and B. Albouys died of poverty, perhaps because of the inflation, before the session ended. After their parliamentary careers were over, in 1795 or 1797 or 1799, about two-thirds of the survivors achieved some temporary or permanent official post, a figure fairly close to that of the Convention as a whole.

The general background and character of the group is of some interest in that the Plain was seen at the time as the refuge for those deputies whose natural place in any parliamentary assembly would be on the back benches. In some ways, there was little to distinguish them from colleagues readier to commit themselves. For example, there are no clear social boundaries between the Plain and the rest of the Convention. Certainly there was no high nobility—the assembly's duke and eight marquises were committed elsewhere—but otherwise the social range was a broad one. Landowners, lawyers, doctors, and clergy were represented, and the range ran down to the fringes of the *sans-culotterie*, where a poor peasant offered cooperation to the Terror and a corset maker recoiled from it. If distinctions can be drawn, they rested partly on age and partly on nuances of geographical and political, rather than social, background. The members of the Plain were on average older than either the Montagnards or the Girondin leadership, and the most conservative among them, those who withdrew from the Terror, were the oldest group in the Convention. They had also a slightly lower than average level of sophistication and experience; there were notably few men from large cities, few representatives from the large number of *conventionnels* who had graduated from the Legislative Assembly, and a solid group of deputies with no political experience at all. The above-average proportion from local government background hardly compensated for this lack of political training at a national level or in a complex social environment. Some of them made it obvious that they felt out of their depth. There could be few better reasons for staying out of the limelight.

Few from the Plain have been much noticed by historians—P.-T. Durand-Maillane (perhaps because of his memoirs), E.-J. Sieyès, J.-B. Mailhe, J.-J. Cambacérès, F.-A. Boissy d'Anglas—and even among these, Boissy is exceptional in having made something of a reputation from his Convention career; true, he made it in 1795. The Plain is often remembered mainly for its alleged cowardice, for the spite of its Thermidorians when their time ultimately came, and for the inertia of its nullities, of whom J. Fabre is only the most extreme example. Yet some of its members should be remembered for other reasons: C.-F.-G. Morisson, that impassioned opponent of the king's trial, who nevertheless worked loyally for the Republic in the Vendée and helped to avert civil war in the Seine-et-Marne; N. Bourgeois, maintaining republican principles in the teeth of the Thermidorian Reaction but writing wryly at the foot of his 1795 financial declaration, "*Rien dans les mains, rien dans les poches, et vive la Republique!*"; T.-F.-A. Jouenne-Longchamp, a regicide supporter of the *appel au peuple*, who was one of the mainstays of the comité de secours, and who, paying in 1816 for his regicide, continued in exile the work for medical education which he had begun in 1793. The positive contribution from the Plain was patchy and unspectacular, but it was not negligible.

A. Kuscinski, *Dictionnaire des conventionnels* (Paris, 1916-20); G. Lefebvre, *Les Thermidoriens* (Paris, 1937); A. Meynier, *La Revellière-Lépeaux* (Paris, 1905); G. Pariset, *La Révolution, 1792-1799* (Paris, 1920); A. Patrick, *The Men of the First French Republic* (Baltimore, 1972); A. Soboul, ed., *Actes du colloque Girondins et Montagnards (1975)* (Paris, 1980).

A. Patrick

Related entries: BOISSY D'ANGLAS; GIRONDINS; LAW OF SUSPECTS; MONTAGNARDS; 9 THERMIDOR YEAR II; SIEYES; THERMIDORIAN REACTION.

POLAND. During the era of the French Revolution, Poland underwent its own revolution, which sometimes reflected French developments. In occupying the attention of Prussia, Austria, and Russia, it thereby protected France against military defeat.

Polish decline, symbolized by the *liberum veto*, was easily observed by patriotic Poles. Reforms enacted by the 1764 Diet, however, touched off dissatisfaction, which, coupled with foreign involvement, led to civil war, the First Partition, and a Russian protectorate in 1772. When Russia went to war with Turkey in 1788, Polish republicans threw off Russian control and ignored King Stanislaw August Poniatowski. A progressive faction emerged, which, allied with Poniatowski, wrote the reformist Constitution of 3 May 1791. A handful of embittered conservatives formed the Targowice Confederation and, with Russian aid, overthrew the new government. Early in 1793, while Russia and Prussia proceeded to partition Poland for a second time, Austria continued to fight against France. Military occupation of Poland coinciding with an economic slump further contributed to Polish anger, and T. Kościuszko returned from exile on 24 March 1794 to begin an insurrection. A few days later, Warsaw's guilds, in cooperation with the army, expelled the Russian garrison, and other rebellions soon broke out, notably in Wilno. For a little over six months, this Kościuszko uprising established Polish independence and occupied Russian and Prussian military attention. Popular participation included a minor September massacre, when a mob in one city seized seven important inmates from prison and hanged them after a brief, tumultuous trial on the market square. Popular support for the insurrection continued until A. V. Suvórov took Warsaw in early November, after which the third partition followed.

Isolated, Poland sought French assistance, without success. As early as February 1789, the Diet had named Count S. Potocki minister plenipotentiary to France, but the French foreign minister, A.-M. Montmorin, wrote to French agents in Warsaw that Poland should continue good relations with Russia. Potocki soon became occupied with other matters and never left Poland. In February 1791, F. Oraczewski replaced Potocki and went to France, while the marquis Descorches de Sainte-Croix became France's minister to Poland with instructions to watch events carefully without interfering. Descorches arrived shortly after the enactment of the 1791 Constitution and became convinced that Polish reformers would make good allies. The French foreign minister C.-A. Delessart saw no advantage to this policy, but his Girondist successors during the spring of 1792 developed far-reaching schemes for an eastern alliance of Poland, Sweden, and Turkey, designed to sustain France against Austria, Prussia, and, if necessary, Russia. No progress occurred, however, before the Targowice Confederation had recalled Oraczewski and expelled Descorches.

The French diplomat went only to Dresden, where he met with Polish *émigré* leaders who hoped to stage an insurrection with French assistance; P. Parandier, French agent in Saxony, participated in the discussions. But a Polish *émigré*, A. Turski, took it on himself to approach the National Convention on 30 December 1792 and beg for help. Kościuszko, renowned hero of the American Revolution and the 1792 Russo-Polish War, who had been granted honorary French citizenship, came as the official representative of the Polish *émigrés* in January 1793. He asked France to assist Poland in raising an insurrection by organizing a Swedish and Turkish alliance against Russia. The *émigrés* promised to establish a republican government in Poland with institutions similar to France's and to cooperate militarily against their common Prussian and Austrian foes. Foreign Minister P.-H. Lebrun dispatched Descorches to Constantinople with formal proposals, but neither Turkey nor Sweden was impressed, particularly as Russian and Prussian troops moved into their partition zones in Poland. Kościuszko finally left Paris in July 1793, unhappy that the fall of the Girondists had ended Lebrun's ambitious schemes.

The Jacobins were less sympathetic to Polish *émigré* hopes, but Poles continued to try to win them over. The *Moniteur* accused the Poles of insufficient revolutionary zeal and opined editorially against helping them, and the federalist and royalist insurrections of late 1793 further distracted the Jacobins from foreign adventures. In hope of reviving contact, a Polish burgher, F. Barss, came to Paris in February 1794 with Parandier. They advised the ministry that a new Polish revolution would break out as a national movement compatible with French ideals and requested financial aid to raise 500,000 insurgents. Their numerous memorials went unanswered by the Jacobin ministry. The outbreak of the promised 1794 uprising, however, met a generally favorable response from the French public, and Barss gained an invitation to meet with the Committee of Public Safety on 13 July 1794. On this date, however, L. Saint-Just informed him that France would send neither money nor men since the Polish revolution was trying to keep Austria neutral and was halfhearted in enacting social reform. Two weeks later, the Robespierrist Committee of Public Safety was overthrown, replaced by the Thermidorians, who were more sympathetic than their predecessors to Poland and thought of reviving the Girondin-inspired eastern alliance when the military situation improved. It was the Directory, however, that Barss persuaded to send Parandier to Poland to check on the insurrection and demonstrate France's goodwill. On 19 November diplomatic support was indeed finally authorized, but without financial aid. These gestures, little enough in terms of Poland's needs, came too late. Poor communications had delayed news of Polish military defeats—Kościuszko's capture and the fall of Warsaw (October and November 1794).

Two Polish *émigré* groups sought French help to restore Poland after the third partition in 1795; both cultivated ties with conspiratorial groups in Poland. The rising star of N. Bonaparte attracted Poles who wished to fight their way to freedom. Six thousand troops under General J. H. Dabrowski participated in the 1797 Italian campaign, although technically only as part of the Lombard army. J. Wybicki wrote *Jeszcze Polska nie zginęła* (''Poland is not lost'') for them; and it became the Polish national anthem. Kościuszko returned from American exile but suspected French motives and rejected any involvement with them.

Resumption of hostilities in 1799 brought the organizations of new legions under Generals J. Zajaczek and K. Kniaziewicz. While the legions eventually fought their way to Poland and Napoleon formed the Grand Duchy of Warsaw, hopes for restoration of an independent Poland were not fully realized.

S. Askenazy, *Napoleon a Polska* (Warsaw, 1918); J. Grossbart, "La politique polonaise de la Révolution française," *Ann. hist. de la Révo. française* 6 (1929); H. Kocój, *Francja a Upadek Polski* (Cracow, 1976); A. Kraushar, *Barss, Palestrant Warszawski; jego misya we Francyi* (Warsaw, 1904); B. Leśnodorski, *Polscy Jakobini* (Warsaw, 1960).

D. Stone

Related entries: COMMITTEE OF PUBLIC SAFETY; KOSCIUSZKO, LEBRUN; LESSART; SUVOROV-RYMNIKSKII; THERMIDORIAN REACTION.

POLICE GENERALE, BUREAU DE. See BUREAU DE POLICE GEN-ERALE.

PRAIRIAL, COUP OF 30. See COUP OF 30 PRAIRIAL.

PRAIRIAL, LAW OF 22. See LAW OF 22 PRAIRIAL.

PRAIRIAL MARTYRS, the seven Montagnard deputies who, in the aftermath of the insurrection of 1-4 Prairial Year III (20-23 May 1795), either committed suicide (P. Rühl, G. Romme, C.-A. Goujon, E.-D.-F. Duquesnoy, P.-A. Soubrany) or were guillotined (J.-M. Duroy and P. Bourbotte). N.-S. Maure, who shot himself on 16 Prairial (4 June) after being denounced in the Convention, is not usually included.

There is no substantial evidence to suggest that any Montagnard deputies had a hand in the Prairial insurrection, which seems to have been planned by old *sans-culottes* militants, in particular by a group of patriots held in the Plessis prison. The arrest of forty-one Montagnards, decreed in the evening of 1 Prairial and during the next twelve days, was deliberately designed by the most reactionary elements in the National Convention to eliminate the leftist opposition. The ferocity with which the Montagnard remnant, as well as the insurrectionists from the sections, was pursued resulted partly from the personal fear engendered by the crowd on 1 Prairial, notably by the murder of the deputy J. Féraud. It was, however, even more the product of the social fear engendered by the appearance of a far more explicit popular democratic program in Prairial than had been the case in Germinal. It seems that although the committees of government had sufficient forces to disperse the crowd in the Convention by the end of the afternoon of 2 Prairial, they deliberately held back to allow leading Montagnards to compromise themselves in the early evening debates under the presidency of T. Vernier, a member of the Committee of Public Safety. Indeed, the selection of the future Prairial martyrs for the severest reprisals (as distinct from other arrested Montagnards or those already in custody after the Germinal uprising) was determined by their statements in the Convention at that time.

These men were all instrumental in getting the Convention to vote a series of measures designed both to meet popular demands and to regain the political initiative from the reactionaries: the baking of a single type of bread, the permanence of the sections, the release of patriots detained since 9 Thermidor and of the deputies arrested after 12 Germinal, the replacement of the Committee of General Security by a temporary Commission of Four (on which Duroy, Bourbotte, P.-L. Prieur de la Marne, and Duquesnoy agreed to serve).

The campaign to destroy the Montagnard spokesmen of 1 Prairial was orchestrated with remarkably vicious vindictiveness by F.-L. Bourdon le l'Oise and J.-B. Clauzel, whose objective was to send them to the military commission established to judge the rebels. The significance of this was that military commissions tried without jury, defense lawyers, or debates, on the simple establishment of identity and of basic facts. For Bourdon, the guilt of his enemies was self-evident and no trial was necessary. This campaign did, however, encounter resistance among some Thermidorian deputies. Although a first attempt to send them to the commission on 5 Germinal was voted, this was rescinded as a dangerous precedent breaking the safeguards of the Law of 8 Brumaire Year III, which provided that no deputy might be sent for trial before the Assembly had heard his defense. However, the news of the Jacobin revolt of Toulon allowed Bourdon and Clauzel to succeed on 8 Prairial. Rühl, Romme, Duroy, Goujon, P.-J. Forestier, A.-L. Albitte the elder, Bourbotte, Duquesnoy, Soubrany, Prieur de la Marne, and J.-P. Peyssard were to be tried by the commission as authors or accomplices of the rebellion of 1 Prairial. Whereas the others had been transported to a château near Morlaix on 2 Prairial, Rühl, Prieur, and Albitte were being held in Paris. The latter two escaped, but Rühl committed suicide. The news of his death brought a stormy debate in the Convention where former Girondists (led by D.-T. Lesage, J.-D. Lanjuinais, and J.-B. Louvet de Couvray, but supported by F.-P. Legendre and even L.-M.-S. Fréron), moved perhaps by the memory of the Girondist C.-E. Valazé's suicide in similar circumstances, sought without success to have the trial removed to the due process of law in a criminal tribunal.

The trial lasted from 24-29 Prairial (12-17 June). It was less summary than might have been expected; the accused were allowed to cite witnesses in their defense (though several deputies failed to appear) and to cross-examine the prosecution witnesses. The indictment concerned only the debates in the Assembly on 1 Prairial and was based on the tendentious and often inaccurate reports of reactionary journalists. Forestier, whose role had been invisible, was acquitted but left in prison in connection with events before 12 Germinal; Peyssard was sentenced to deportation. The remaining six were sentenced to death. On the stairs leading from the court, Goujon stabbed himself through the heart; Romme seized the knife and stabbed himself; Duquesnoy plunged a pair of scissors into his heart; Bourbotte stabbed himself with another knife and passed it to Soubrany; Duroy only had time to wound himself slightly. Goujon, Romme, and Duquesnoy died instantly. Soubrany died on the cart and his body was guillotined. Only Bourbotte and Duroy were executed.

The suicide of the Prairial martyrs, including that of Rühl, had a deeper significance than an escape from the execution. The suicide of Rühl on learning of the decree of 8 Prairial and the correspondence of Goujon and Bourbotte make it clear that these men expected no other issue than death. The suicides of 29 Prairial were premeditated; these men swore to do it when they heard of Rühl's death, but Goujon had already discussed the possibility between 12 Germinal and 1 Prairial, and Bourbotte began making efforts to get a weapon for this purpose as early as 4 Prairial. The weapons, together with opium, were passed to Goujon by his family on 26 Prairial. The suicides were a gesture of defiance against the injustice of their trial and the tyranny into which the Convention had fallen. More than a gesture of defiance, however, it was an act of explicit political morality in the logic of Cicero's neo-Stoic doctrines, echoed by J.-J. Rousseau, and it was modeled on the suicide of Cato the Younger, to whom Bourbotte referred in his notes for his defense. In this perception, the authority of the legislator derived from his own virtue as much as from the sovereignty of the people; his function was the moral education of men by the power of example. The suicide of the Prairial martyrs was an act of virtue, a gesture imbued by its authors with an educative value designed to distinguish the true virtue of men devoted to the public welfare from the passion of self-interest that had reduced the authority of the Assembly to a technicality and its power to the possession of force. It is doubtful whether their message had any practical effect. G. Babeuf coined the phrase of ''martyrs'' for them and considered the Equals as their heirs, but he saw in them a greater understanding of popular aspirations than they in fact possessed.

R. Andrews, ''Le néo-stoicisme et le législateur montagnard,'' in *Gilbert Romme et son Temps* (Paris, 1966); L. Thénard and R. Guyot, *Le conventionnel Goujon* (Paris, 1908); P. F. Tissot, *Souvenirs de la journée du 1 Prairial an III* (Paris, an VIII) and *Histoire complète de la Révolution française*, vol. 5 (Paris, 1834-36); M. de Vissac, *Romme le Montagnard* (Paris, 1883).

C. Lucas

Related entries: BABEUF; BOURDON; COMMITTEE OF GENERAL SECURITY; COMMITTEE OF PUBLIC SAFETY; CONSPIRACY OF EQUALS; ROMME.

PRELIMINARIES OF LEOBEN, an agreement between France and Austria signed on 18 April 1797 (29 Germinal Year V) as the first step in ending the war that began in 1792. Napoleon, having invaded the Po Valley in April 1796 and defeating the Austrian armies sent against him, succeeded in pushing the forces commanded by Archduke Charles north toward Vienna. Worried about his ever-lengthening supply lines, concerned by unrest in occupied Italy, and anxious about the possible victories of rival French generals in Germany, Napoleon wrote to Charles on 31 March to suggest an armistice. At the same time he continued his advance toward the Austrian capital, occupying Leoben on 7 April. Faced with an imminent invasion and losing confidence in its allies, the imperial government agreed to negotiate, and on 13 April it sent a delegation to the French headquarters at the château of Eggenwald near Leoben.

After swift negotiations, the two sides signed the preliminaries of peace, Napoleon for France and General M. Merveldt and the marchese del Gallo for Austria. Under the formal terms of the agreement, Austria agreed to surrender Belgium, as well as recognize the limits of France as decreed by the laws of the Republic, thereby implicitly accepting French annexation of the left bank of the Rhine. Austria was to receive an indemnity (not specified in the public terms) at the signature of the definitive peace. The two sides agreed to save other outstanding issues for a congress (never held) in Switzerland. The secret articles of the agreement, however, provided that Austria would renounce all claims to Lombardy and be compensated for its loss with territory from the Republic of Venice, including Dalmatia and Istria. Napoleon, who signed the preliminaries without direct authorization from the Directory, gained considerable prestige among the French, who wanted peace after long years of war. The final peace terms, which partitioned the Republic of Venice, were eventually signed at Campoformio on 17 October, 1797.

E. Gachot, *La première campagne d'Italie (1795-1798)* (Paris, 1901); R. Guyot, *Le Directoire et la paix de l'Europe* (Paris, 1912).

J. Friguglietti

Related entries: FIRST COALITION; TREATY OF CAMPOFORMIO.

PRIEUR DE LA COTE-D'OR, CLAUDE-ANTOINE (1763-1832), member of the Committee of Public Safety. Prieur, whose name was actually Prieur-Duvernois, was born in the Burgundian town of Auxonne on 22 December 1763. His father held the minor royal post of receiver of finances, and, although the family thus occupied only the lowest rung of the aristocracy of the robe, Claude-Antoine was able to claim noble birth and gain admission to the school of military engineering at Mézières in December 1781.

After graduating from Mézières as a second lieutenant, Prieur served in the royal army. He spent, however, only about a fourth of his time at his military posts and instead conducted experiments under the direction of his friend, the eminent chemist L.-B. Guyton-Morveau. Prieur supported the Revolution from 1789, arguing with his fellow officers in favor of democratic principles and progressive reforms while on duty at Belfort. Elected to the Legislative Assembly from the Côte-d'Or in 1791, he voted consistently with the Left and began the first of his many committee assignments when he was appointed to the Committee on Public Education.

When the monarchy was overthrown on 10 August 1792, Prieur was sent, along with L. Carnot, to inspect the Army of the Rhine and to spread the news of the Revolution. He was on another mission to the camp at Châlons when he learned that his department of the Côte-d'Or had elected him to the National Convention.

During his first year as a deputy, Prieur was away from Paris on mission a good part of the time. In October and November 1792, he spent six weeks on the eastern border with Switzerland, inspecting French defenses. He was in Paris for the king's trial and voted with the majority for the death penalty. His next mission took him to Brittany and Normandy where, from January to May 1793, he spent over a hundred days inspecting and improving coastal defense installations from Lorient to Dunkerque. He was in Normandy on yet another mission when he was arrested on 9 June 1793 at Caen by town officials who then held Prieur and his colleague G. Romme hostage to ensure the safety of Girondin deputies who had fled to Normandy after their expulsion from the Convention. Prieur was released after the federalist forces were defeated at Vernon (13 July 1793).

After his election to the Committee of Public Safety on 14 August 1793, Prieur was again sent on mission. In October he visited the Army of the West and in December the departments of the Nord and the Pas-de-Calais. However, his principal efforts were directed to organizing and vastly improving the production of munitions and arms for the beleaguered Republic. With his friend L. Carnot assuming the direction of overall military strategy, Prieur emerged as the Convention's de facto minister of armaments and materiel. For fourteen months, he worked intensely at an enormous range of activities. He established and improved factories in Paris and throughout France to produce artillery pieces, rifles, side arms, and gunpowder. Enlisting the aid of friends who were both scientists and patriots, he established a military proving ground at Meudon for research and development of new weapons, including balloons, which were constructed there. He directed or influenced virtually every aspect of defense production and organization, including the tanning of leather, the construction of C. Chappe's telegraph, the reorganization of the mining administration, and the establishment of special "Courses on the Revolutionary Production of Weapons and Explosives," to teach workers from all of France how to increase production. In all, Prieur's incessant labors entitle him to a large share of Carnot's fame as the "organizer of victory."

Prieur was not involved in the fall of M. Robespierre, either as a victim or conspirator. On 10 Thermidor, he hailed Robespierre's execution as a blow against tyranny and continued his work on armaments on the Committee of Public Safety until 6 October 1794 when a third of the committee was replaced according to the decree of 24 August. Returning to the Convention, he sat on the Committee of Public Education where he helped to establish the school that was to become the Ecole Polytechnique. He also contributed to the development and implementation of the metric system, a project that had long interested him.

After the Côte-d'Or elected him to the Council of Five Hundred in October 1795, he continued to work on armaments and the new system of measurements. Above all, he became the legislative champion and defender of the Ecole Polytechnique whose establishment and survival owed much to his efforts. Prieur's political career ended 18 May 1798 when he left the Council of Five Hundred.

He then held minor administrative and consultative positions connected with fortifications and the Ecole Polytechnique, but left public service definitively in December 1801 when his request to retire from military duty for reasons of health was granted. He held the rank of *chef de brigade*. Prieur's attempts to make a living as a wallpaper manufacturer in Paris were not at first successful, and he tried repeatedly but futilely to reenter military or bureaucratic service. His request in 1803 to return to active military duty was denied, and he was unable in 1804 to obtain either a position at the Ecole Polytechnique or a Legion of Honor from Napoleon's government. In 1808 he asked Napoleon for a position as an inspector in the new educational system, but without effect.

By April 1811 Prieur was old enough to go into full retirement from the army. He then devoted himself to his then successful manufacturing concern and to scientific work of no significance. His last years were spent in Dijon where he died 11 August 1832.

P. Arbelet, "La jeunesse de Prieur de la Côte-d'Or," *Rev. du d-h. siècle* 5 (1918); A. Birembant, "Prieur de la Côte-d'Or en 1815-1816," *Ann. hist. de la Révo. française* 28 (1956); G. Bouchard, *Prieur de la Côte-d'Or, Un organisateur de la victoire* (Paris, 1946); P. Gaffarel, *Prieur de la Côte-d'Or* (Dijon, 1900); R. R. Palmer, *Twelve Who Ruled: The Year of the Terror in the French Revolution* (Princeton, 1970).

R. Bienvenu

Related entries: CARNOT; CHAPPE; COMMITTEE OF PUBLIC SAFETY; COUNCIL OF FIVE HUNDRED; EDUCATION; FEDERALISM; GIRONDINS; REPRESENTATIVES ON MISSION; ROMME.

PRIEUR "DE LA MARNE," PIERRE-LOUIS (1756-1827), terrorist, member of the Committee of Public Safety. Prieur (called by his contemporaries Prieur de la Marne to distinguish him from his colleague in the Convention, Prieur de la Côte-d'Or) was born 1 August 1756 in Sommesous. His father, L.-J. Prieur, was a local court clerk. After studying law at Reims from 1772 to 1775, the younger Prieur became an *avocat* of the Parlement of Paris and then moved to Châlons-sur-Marne to practice law. A successful and popular lawyer and an early advocate of the Revolution, he was elected on 24 March 1789 a deputy to the Third Estate of the Estates General.

In the Constituent Assembly, he was one of the most active and radical members. An ally of M. Robespierre, he was one of the few who argued for democratic measures. He contributed substantially to many constitutional, administrative, and judicial reforms. He helped establish, and then led, the comité de mendicité through which he aided orphans, reformed prisons, and developed a home for the deaf and dumb. He supported the nationalization of church lands, clerical salaries, harsh measures against the *émigrés*, and an investigation of the king after the abortive flight to Varennes.

On the dissolution of the Assembly in 1791, three localities offered him important public positions. He moved to Châlons-sur-Marne, accepting the post of member of the directory and substitute *procureur-général-syndic* of the department of the Marne. Here he was confronted with the difficult task of organizing a defense against the approaching hosts of Austrians, Prussians, and *émigrés*. He succeeded well in rallying the local population in the crucial weeks before the battle of Valmy in September 1792. When the local assembly met at Reims on 3 September to elect deputies to the National Convention, it chose him to preside over the sessions and then elected him the first deputy by a vote of 386 to 56.

In the Convention he was a spirited orator of the left wing, the Mountain. He engaged in debates with the Girondins, voted for the immediate death of Louis XVI and against all appeals, helped set up the Revolutionary Tribunal, and went on numerous missions to the departments. In September and October 1792, he visited the armies of the east to renew their Revolutionary zeal in the new offensive. In March and April 1793, he traveled to Orléans to investigate agitations and restore order. From April to July he traveled in Normandy, helping to organize and raise finances for a new army. In July and August he worked on reorganizing and reinforcing the armies of the Nord, Ardennes, and Moselle. From October to December he traveled about Brittany raising armies to fight, successfully, against the Vendéan rebels. To deal with the rebels, he set up a special court, which eventually sentenced 2,905 of them to death. On 29 December the Convention directed him to organize Revolutionary governments in the Morbihan and Loire-Inférieure, areas of rebel sympathy. On 8 February 1794 he was sent to Nantes to replace the notorious J.-B. Carrier. In all of these areas, he applied measures of the Terror and established at least a minimum of Revolutionary order, but he did not go to the wild excesses associated with representatives on mission such as Carrier. In May he traveled to Brest to join A.-J. Saint-André in the building of a new fleet.

Prieur, who was hardly ever in Paris, had nothing to do with the factional struggles or the overthrow of Robespierre in 1794. On 31 July his term on the Committee of Public Safety expired, but he was elected again and served from 6 October 1794 to 3 February 1795. He was president of the Convention from 22 October to 5 November 1794. In time, the Thermidorian leaders denounced him and maneuvered his arrest on 20 May 1795. Ordered to prison on 12 June, he escaped through a window of his house and disappeared from the police. All charges against him were dropped in the general amnesty of October 1795.

From 1796 to 1816 he earned a modest living practicing law in Paris. Although he kept in contact with some of the old Jacobins and showed some interest in politics, he was not elected to any office. In 1798 and 1799 he was an administrator of the *hospices-civils* of Paris. On the approach of the Allies in 1814, he joined the National Guard as a sergeant and fought bravely. After the law of 1816 against the regicides, he voluntarily left for Brussels. There he enjoyed the company of other Jacobins in exile and practiced law but declined into poverty. He died in Brussels on 30 May 1827 at the age of seventy-two.

P. Bliard, *Le conventionnel Prieur de la Marne en mission dans l'Ouest* (Paris, 1906); G. Laurent, *Notes et souvenirs inédits de Prieur de la Marne* (Paris, 1912); R. R. Palmer, *Twelve Who Ruled: The Year of the Terror in the French Revolution* (Princeton, 1941).

R. J. Caldwell

Related entries: CARRIER; COMMITTEE OF PUBLIC SAFETY.

PRIMOGENITURE, usually known in French as *le droit d'aînesse* or (less frequently) as *le privilège de la masculinité,* designated in pre-Revolutionary France the feudal laws and practices governing the transferral of noble or seig-neurial lands from one generation of proprietors to the next generation. As a rule, primogeniture applied to the nobility in the various regions of France, although often commoners holding seigneurial properties also found these prop-erties subject to the *droit d'aînesse.*

Primogeniture in the medieval era had reflected the desire of noble families to preserve the integrity of their fiefs and thus maintain long-term familial interests in troubled times. By the eighteenth century, therefore, primogeniture had be-come long recognized in feudal law as a tradition stating that the oldest son in a seigneurial family (the *fils aîné,* hence the term *droit d'aînesse*) was favored over any younger brothers and all sisters in the central matter of the inheritance of the father's (and, where applicable, the mother's) property. The specific provisions of primogeniture, like so much else in French law, varied widely from province to province and from customary law to customary law, but in general the oldest son was likely to inherit the family's château or principal manor house, with the courtyards, moats, gardens, and other enclosures im-mediately depending on it; also the largest portion of the noble or seigneurial lands in the family; and often, as well, such family treasures as portraits, arms, charters and titles, and so on. The younger sons and the daughters of the family received the rest of their parents' inheritance, often, it would seem, in equal shares. If the family possessed fiefs in more than one province or area of cus-tomary law, the oldest son received his predominant share of the family wealth, or *préciput,* in each of these separate holdings. The perplexing variation of provisions of primogeniture from one area to another must be stressed. If, for instance, customary law in Troyes and Auxerre limited somewhat the extent of the eldest son's *droit d'aînesse,* the customs of Anjou, Maine, Bordeaux, and other regions were markedly more favorable in certain respects to the *fils aîné.* The principle of equal inheritances for all offspring generally prevailed in the matter of non-noble lands and other properties held by noble or seigneurial families, although in this area, too, there were local variations.

The legislators of the French Revolution had a variety of reasons for abrogating the laws of primogeniture. For one thing, the *droit d'aînesse* was only one of three major tendencies governing the bequeathing and inheriting of landed prop-erty in late eighteenth-century France, the other two being the regime of cus-tomary law, which in the north favored the parceling out of non-noble patrimonies among all heirs, and the Roman law of the south, which allowed the testator much more discretion in the bequeathing of non-noble lands. The Revolutionaries wished to replace these complicated and confusing practices with a system uniform for all France, furthering national unity and assuring somewhat greater equity among heirs of all classes. Also, to destroy primogeniture would be to strike a political blow—and reinforce other blows—against those feudal aristocrats who in 1789 loomed as the primary enemies of the Revolution. Furthermore, the new regime's correlation of landed wealth and voting rights lent the issue of equity among heirs an altogether unprecedented political significance.

Accordingly, the abolition of primogeniture insofar as it concerned the nobility was implied in the general condemnation of the feudal regime on the famous night of 4 August 1789; it was explicitly and definitively accomplished by the Constituent Assembly in a law of 15 March 1790. Subsequent legislation of 8 April 1791 abolished those practices of primogeniture that in certain provinces had come to affect bequests among commoners. The abrogation of primogeniture was only one of many actions of those years affecting the complex and controversial question of inheritance. Nonetheless, it heralded the transformation of the Old Regime's social elite and foreshadowed the egalitarianism in inheritances that would help ensure the socioeconomic conservatism of the new France.

J. P. Cooper, "Patterns of Inheritance and Settlement by Great Landowners from the Fifteenth to the Eighteenth Centuries," in J. Goody, J. Thirsk, and E. P. Thompson, eds., *Family and Inheritance: Rural Society in Western Europe, 1200-1800* (Cambridge, Eng., 1976); J. Godechot, *Les institutions de la France sous la Révolution et l'Empire*, 2d ed (Paris, 1968); M. Marion, *Dictionnaire des institutions de la France aux XVIIe et XVIIIe siècles* (Paris, 1923); R. Mousnier, *The Institutions of France under the Absolute Monarchy 1598-1789: Society and the State*, trans. Brian Pearce (Chicago, 1979).

B. Stone

Related entries: ARISTOCRATS; FEUDALISM.

PRISONS. In its effort to reform the management of prisons, the Constituent Assembly drew on the scientific and administrative expertise of the monarchy. The Committee on Mendicity sent M.-A. Thouret and the abbé C.-A.-J. Leclerc de Montlinot, experienced royal consultants, to inspect Bicêtre in 1790. In a report to the Royal Society of Medicine in August 1791, F. Doublet, an inspector of prisons and hospitals under J. Colombier in the 1780s, reviewed the current state of the prisons of Paris and urged the need for reform. Problems of management were held to be contingent, however, on issues of legal reform and civil rights.

The Declaration of the Rights of Man in 1789 guaranteed the French citizen, in principle, against arbitrary arrest (articles 7, 8, and 9), and the Constituent Assembly approved a new criminal code, 16 and 25 September 1791, as a final stage in its effort to reconstitute the monarchy. Imprisonment, viewed narrowly as a measure of public safety under the Old Regime, was the form of punishment preferred by the reformers of the Constituent Assembly. L.-M. Lepelletier de

Saint-Fargeau recommended to his fellow deputies the rehabilitative function of prison (each inmate was to be provided work of a suitable nature), leading ideally to a second "civic baptism," a formal reintegration of the wrongdoer into the community.

A decree of 16 September 1791 provided (Title XIV) that municipalities would be responsible for the maintenance of prisons for the penal detention of convicted criminals. Two additional facilities were to be attached to each district tribunal: a house of arrest (*maison d'arrêt*) for those detained by police warrant and a house of justice (*maison de justice*) for those who had been formally indicted and served with an *ordonnance de prise de corps*. A decree on criminal procedure, 29 September, authorized penalties for the crime of false imprisonment, reiterated the distinction between pretrial detention and the penalty of imprisonment, and ordered that prisons and *maisons d'arrêt* and *maisons de justice* be kept secure. The decree added that these houses must "be clean and well-aired, so that the health of persons detained cannot be impaired by their enforced stay therein." An earlier "Decree relating to the organization of a municipal and correctional police," of 19 July 1791, provided that houses of correction would be established for young offenders under twenty-one years of age and for those condemned *par voie de police correctionelle*, including those detained for morals charges, disorderly conduct, gambling, petty larceny, mendicity, and unlawful assembly.

These provisions were greatly modified in practice by the operations of Revolutionary justice, local committees of surveillance, the Jacobin régime, and the Terror. The classic prison literature of the Bastille (Latude and Linguet), Vincennes (H.-G. R. Mirabeau), and Bicêtre (L.-M. Musquinet de la Pagne) gave way to the fulminations and laments of a new breed of martyrs. After Thermidor, presses groaned to requite the demand for titles such as the *Almanach des Prisons ou Anecdotes sur le régime intérieur de la Conciergerie, du Luxembourg, etc., et sur différents prisonniers qui ont habité ces maisons sous la tyrannie de Robespierre, avec les chansons, couplets qui y ont été faits*. This title went to a third Paris edition in the Year III of the Republic.

The oldest prison of Paris was the Conciergerie on the Ile-de-la-Cité. The *concierge du palais de Paris* had once exercised jurisdiction over the palace and its environs, but at the outbreak of the Revolution, he guarded prisoners subject to the criminal jurisdiction of the Parlement of Paris, the great hall of which adjoined the towers of the prison. In thirteen cavelike vaults referred to as *chambres de la paille*, inmates lay two to four per straw-covered bunk, fifteen to thirty per room. Five rooms, known as *chambres de la pistole*, held ten to twelve inmates paying 7 *livres*, 10 *sous* per month to the concierge for rental of furniture. For a *demi-pension* of 22 *livres*, 10 *sous*, three or four persons could share a room. A private room cost 45 *livres* (these rates from 1791). The least fortunate, including those convicted of capital crimes, slept in straw-lined pens no better than pigsties, in underground cells (*cachots*) behind walls ten to twelve feet thick. Air vents were sealed to prevent escape, and doors opened only for passing food and removing pails of refuse. Sick male inmates of the prison were transferred to a tunnel-like infirmary, cold and humid, containing thirty beds; sick women went to a separate room with ten beds.

During the day, prisoners who were not in *cachots* were allowed to circulate in the prison and its exercise yard (*préau*) and to receive visitors. Searches failed to suppress a thriving nocturnal production of counterfeit *assignats*, bills on the *caisse patriotique*, and other notes. Daring escape attempts, frequent at the end of 1791 and in 1792, led at least one editor, A.-J. Gorsas of the *Courier des 83 Départements*, to suppose that powerful outside agents aided the malefactors within. The local police commissioner, J.-F. Lambert, urged the Legislative Assembly to improve security, but a major overhaul of the prison occurred only after the massacres of September 1792. Crowds set free 110 and killed 378 of the 508 inmates being held at the time. The Revolutionary Tribunal, created 10 March 1793, sat in the old Palais de Justice, and the Conciergerie became the most famous "antechamber of the guillotine." J.-S.-Bailly, Marie Antoinette, G.-J. Danton, Madame Roland, J.-R. Hébert, Madame du Barry, and M. Robespierre awaited trial and execution behind walls that once held R.-F. Damiens, F. Ravaillac, and L.-D. Cartouche.

Another ancient prison of Paris was the Châtelet, headquarters of the commissioners of police for the city. Before the Revolution, the Petit Châtelet, once used as a women's prison, and the episcopal prison of Fors-l'évêque had both been demolished. To take their place, a new prison with five sections was established in a former residence, the Hôtel de la Force, in 1782. The sections housed defaulters on payments to wet nurses, civil debtors, detainees by *ordres du roi* or *de police*, convicted female felons, and beggars and vagrants awaiting transfer to royal *dépôts de mendicité*. An adjoining building was acquired in 1782 as a prison for women of ill repute. The Parlement of Paris approved a regulation especially for La Force, and the chief royal inspector of prisons and hospitals, J. Colombier, had his office there. From 1789, the regulation was ignored, and the sections were merged into two classes: the *pistoliers* who paid rent and the *pailleux* who did not. The divided layout of the prison made supervision difficult under the new conditions. Police commissioners of neighboring Paris sections insisted on searching the premises and found ample evidence of counterfeiting. A fire on 20-21 January 1792 severely damaged the prison. An ensuing inquiry and report by the *ingénieur* P. Giraud was relayed from the Department of Police of Paris to the Directory of the Department, to the minister of the interior (J.-M. Roland), to the National Assembly, requesting authority to purchase outright the convent of the Madelonettes (used formerly as a women's refuge and reformatory). With a capacity of 200, the convent offered some relief to the dangerous overcrowding of the prisons of Paris, a topic of insistent public debate throughout 1791-92. Before it was ready for use, the September Massacres occurred, claiming 171 victims at La Force, including the duchesse de Lamballe. The Paris Commune ordered the surviving prisoners for debt transferred to Sainte-

Pélagie, a former convent and women's reformatory (like the Madelonettes), sponsored by Madame de Miramion in the seventeenth century.

The Abbaye, the prison attached to the abbey of Saint-Germain, was used under the Old Regime for disciplining members of the Gardes françaises and for debtors of high social status. On 30 June 1789, crowds forced the release of eleven guardsmen who had been imprisoned there for refusing to fire on the people at Versailles on the night of 22-23 June. The use of the Abbaye as a prison for soldiers continued. Political prisoners and those accused of *lèse-nation* were also kept there; police informers from other prisons were sent there to be safe from reprisals. A standard of provisioning higher than that of other prisons prevailed at the Abbaye, but there was no exercise yard, inmates were kept in their cells, and the buildings themselves were insalubrious. Overcrowding postponed improvements urged by Giraud and others in 1791. Scene of the first of the September 1792 Massacres, the Abbaye was badly damaged. In a separate action, crowds broke into the prison of the Carmes in the rue de Vaugirard (a former convent of the Carmelite order converted into a *maison d'arrêt* in 1792) and killed the bishops and priests held there.

After 10 August 1792, the National Assembly imprisoned the deposed King Louis XVI in the tower remaining of the largely demolished fortifications belonging to the monastery of the Knights Templar (the Commune ruled out using the Luxembourg). J. Michelet calculated the expense for boarding the king and his family at 333 *livres* per day at the Temple. Louis went from the Temple to his execution 21 January 1793. Marie Antoinette was transferred to the Conciergerie on 3 October 1793 for trial. Their daughter, Marie-Thérèse, was allowed to emigrate, and their son, Louis, died in the Temple (the date of his death is still in doubt). The Directory later imprisoned there thirty-three who were arrested after the Camp de Grenelle affair and a number of leading journalists.

The prison of Saint-Lazare owed its name to an ancient leper hospital converted in the seventeenth century to the use of St. Vincent de Paul's *Congrégation de la Mission*. Among their many activities, the Lazarists chastised wayward youths sent to them by virtue of *lettres de cachet* and sheltered the insane. The pillage of 12-13 July 1789 severely damaged the house and its contents. When the Lazarist order was officially dissolved in August 1792, work began on converting the house to a prison. It opened 18 January 1793. The poet A. Chénier and the painter H. Robert were among the first inmates to enjoy its relative comfort. Over 400 prisoners were transferred there by the end of the month, including some 200 formerly held at Bicêtre. Shortly before Thermidor, a commission sent to investigate prison plots designated those inmates who were enemies of the people and had them executed.

The charitable archipelago of the Hôpital Général was still, in 1789, the main agency for that "Great Confinement" of the poor, the insane, the idle, and the wayward depicted by M. Foucault. In April 1790, the vast hospital for men, Bicêtre, included 422 prisoners among its 3,979 inmates. The women's hospital, La Salpêtrière, held 6,704 persons, including some married couples. Under lock and key were some 500 to 600 women of ill repute and 350 insane women. The Constituent Assembly answered petitions from inmates of these houses with a promise to remedy abuses with a new penal code. J.-S. Bailly warned against freeing *mauvais sujets*. A.-L. de Jussieu energetically investigated conditions in Paris hospitals on behalf of the municipal government of Paris, but the reforms his committee proposed in May 1790 remained in limbo; the directory of the department at that juncture took over responsibility for the hospitals of Paris and created its own commission of inquiry in April 1791. The National Assembly received meanwhile the report of F.-A.-F. duc de la Rochefoucauld-Liancourt's Committee of Mendicity, which urged the creation of two new hospitals to care exclusively for the insane who were still confined at Bicêtre, La Salpêtrière, the Petites Maisons, Charenton, and the Hôtel-Dieu. Problems of discipline and security plagued Bicêtre and La Salpêtrière in 1792, and conflicts developed between civil authorities and religious administrators. Inmates bilked outsiders of thousands of *livres* by imaginative *lettres de St. Jean de Jérusalem* purporting to share hidden treasure. The September Massacres left scars of terror on the minds of many surviving inmates. Little changed from 1792 to 1794, although there was some reapportioning of inmates among prisons. A group of suspects transferred from La Force and Madelonettes in the Year II objected to being confused with criminals at Bicêtre and asked to be transferred to the *maison d'arrêt* of Plessis.

From August 1792, the growing number of arrests swelled the prison population. The Law of Suspects of 17 September 1793 precipitated the most dramatic increase. The *Moniteur* reported 1,877 detained in the *maisons d'arrêt* of Paris on 13 September 1793; it reported a total of 7,541 on 28 Germinal Year II (by 26 Ventôse Year III, the total was back to 2,200). Religious houses in use or set aside as *maisons d'arrêt* in 1792 included the Madelonettes and Sainte-Pélagie, Saint-Lazare and its dependency, the seminary of Saint-Firmin, and the former convent of Port-Royal de Paris (renamed Port-Libre). The collèges of Le Plessis and Louis-le-Grand were added later. The detention center at the Mairie was always full. The Bonnet-Rouge section used the Maison des Oiseaux in the rue de Sèvres, a former barracks of the Gardes françaises, and other barracks, convents, and private houses were pressed into service. Most famous of the *maisons d'arrêt* was the Palace of the Luxembourg, vacant after the emigration of the comte de Provence. G.-A. Réal reported to the Thermidorian Convention that the *concierges* of the Luxembourg and the Carmes had gone out of their way to tyrannize inmates and remind them of their likely fate. *Maisons d'arrêt* were improvised throughout France, for example Toulouse made use of the convents of the Visitation and the Carmelites. The comtesse de Bohm (*née* Girardin), arrested at Senlis, was transferred to Chantilly and ultimately to Paris; Le Plessis was the only prison that would agree to take her convoy. A relatively sober observer of detail, she comments on prison inspections by J.-C. Poullain de Grandpré, a former protégé of Roland at the Ministry of the Interior.

The decrees of early 1793 on prisons and houses of correction may have

brought some improvement in prison management, but the Terror imposed unmanageable burdens on the system. The Thermidorians took revenge on their
tormentors, imprisoning many Jacobins (the theme of prison revolts and rumored
plots took on a new political hue). In its first year, the Directory devoted some
8 million to 10 million francs to the prisons of Paris, but the improvements were
modest. P. Pinel was put in charge of La Salpêtrière in 1795, after working for
two years at Bicêtre, where he had observed the methods of J.-B. Pussin, keeper
of the insane. By 1795, Saint-Lazare became a women's prison, receiving prostitutes from La Salpêtrière, Vincennes, and La Force, and employing them in
workshops set up at the recommendation of P. Paganel and the Comité de Secours
Publics. This committee inherited the perennial task of prison reform.

G. Belloni, *Le Comité de Sûreté Générale de la Convention Nationale* (Paris, 1924);
P. Deyon, *Le temps des prisons. Essai sur l'histoire de la délinquance et les origines
du système pénitentiaire* (Paris, 1975); J. B. Duvergier, ed., *Collection complète des
lois, décrets, ordonnances, règlements et avis du Conseil d'Etat* ... , 24 vols. (Paris,
1825-28); M. Lescure, ed., *Mémoires sur les Comités de salut public, de sûreté générale,
et sur les prisons (1793-1794)* (Paris, 1878); M. Perrot, ed., *L'impossible prison* (Paris,
1980); A. Tuetey, ed., *L'assistance publique à Paris pendant la Révolution*, 4 vols.
(Paris, 1895-97), and *Répertoire générale des sources manuscrites de l'histoire de Paris
pendant la Révolution française*, vol. 6 (Paris, 1902); D. B. Weiner, "Health and Mental
Health in the Thought of Philippe Pinel: The Emergence of Psychiatry during the French
Revolution," in *Healing and History: Essays for George Rosen*, ed. Charles E. Rosenberg
(Kent, England, 1979).

T. M. Adams

Related entries: BASTILLE, THE; CHATELET, THE; DECLARATION OF
THE RIGHTS OF MAN AND OF THE CITIZEN; *LETTRE DE CACHET*;
REVOLUTIONARY TRIBUNAL; SEPTEMBER 1792 MASSACRES.

PRIVILEGE DE LA MASCULINITE. See PRIMOGENITURE.

PROPAGANDA. The French Revolution marked a watershed in the development of propaganda, foreshadowing the use of mass communications in modern democratic and totalitarian states. Propaganda is the deliberate manipulation
of people's thoughts through a variety of symbols: words, pictures, domestic
objects, staged events, and the like. It is distinguished from a free exchange of
ideas by its emphasis on one side of a controversial issue and its exclusion of
independent or critical thinking. The propagandist is usually not in the same
group or class as his audience. He is aware that controversial issues are highly
complex, but for his own reasons he wants to squelch real debate and implicitly
insists that only one approach is correct. The propagandist may or may not
respect the intelligence of the receiver; in either case, he tries to appeal to the
irrational side of the receiver's personality. For this reason, the propagandist
must have an objective, yet intimate, understanding of his audience. Therefore
propaganda is most successful in a society in which there is a self-conscious

intelligentsia that is socially distinct from a large group of relatively uninformed people.

The Enlightenment created that kind of self-conscious intelligentsia in eighteenth-century France, but it was not until the Revolution that propaganda emerged as a potent force. The *philosophes*, though they often advocated a particular viewpoint on controversial issues, were not propagandists. Instead, they fostered a spirit of critical and independent thinking among their readers. In fact, one of the major programs of the Enlightenment was precisely to bring free inquiry into social and political matters. Moreover, unlike propagandists, the *philosophes* wrote for members of their own social class; they were the spokesmen for a ruling elite; and although they called for fundamental reforms, they did not address themselves to peasants or artisans. When D. Diderot wrote that the aim of the *philosophes* was to "change men's common way of thinking," he meant the men who counted—that is, the small number of people at the apex of French society who determined the course of public affairs.

The French Revolution transformed intellectual life by establishing the new regime on the theory of national sovereignty. This meant that every working individual was theoretically part of the nation and shared equally in its sovereign authority. In practice this meant that no government could achieve political stability without the approval and loyal support of French peasants and artisans. Thus, if intellectuals wanted to influence the course of public affairs, they now had to go beyond their traditional bourgeois and aristocratic readers and address themselves directly to the people. But that was not easy. Most Frenchmen were virtually illiterate, and few had the critical skills necessary to understand *philosophes* of the high Enlightenment. For that reason many Revolutionaries were anxious to begin a system of national education. But the education process would take decades, and the Revolution needed to be consolidated as soon as possible. Revolutionary intellectuals had to find quick, effective ways to communicate with their semiliterate countrymen.

Propaganda provided the means. It flourished during the French Revolution because pro-Revolutionary intellectuals believed in an ideal of national unity based on popular sovereignty. They believed that converting peasants into loyal citizens was an urgent task on which political stability depended. Critical thinking and balanced presentations could only prolong ignorance of new political values and endanger the Revolution. Therefore when intellectuals addressed the people, their goal was not to educate them to think for themselves but to foster support for the new regime.

French Revolutionary propaganda can be divided into three genres: literary (books, newspapers, almanacs), artistic (paintings, posters, prints, songs, hymns), and theatrical (religious services, state ceremonies, fêtes).

The most important newspaper written explicitly for peasants was the *Feuille villageoise*. Its editors, a small group of Parisian intellectuals, admitted in the 13 December 1792 issue that the paper "is not really a newspaper at all; rather it is a course of popular instruction, where principles take precedence over facts."

The paper's Prospectus had been even more candid about its propagandist character: "We do not want to teach the people to argue over laws, but only to be loyal to them." Each of its weekly issues discussed national affairs in an Aesopian language that reduced important and controversial decisions to popular formulas. Since most peasants could neither afford to buy the paper nor had the skills to read it, the editors urged rural priests to read parts of it to their parishioners after Sunday Mass. It appears that many priests followed this advice, and by 1791 the *Feuille villageoise* had become one of the most popular Revolutionary newspapers in the nation.

A different type of literary propaganda was J.-M. Collot d'Herbois' *Almanach du Père Gérard*, the winner of a contest sponsored by the Paris Jacobins for the best piece of propaganda that could explain the Constitution of 1791 to peasants. The pamphlet described a mythical member of the Constituent Assembly who returns to his rural village, where he is loved by everyone. Through a series of dialogues, this Goodman Gérard advocates the principles of national sovereignty and fraternity by reducing the Constitution to a popular catechism.

Musical propaganda also tried to reinforce Revolutionary ideology. Between 1789 and 1794 over 2,200 political songs were published in France. Songs were sung in various patriotic ceremonies, on national holidays, and in club meetings. The most intense period of song publication came after the declaration of war against Austria in April 1792, when composers wanted to inspire troops going off to battle. The most enduring of these military songs was the "*Marseillaise*," composed by J.-C. Rouget de Lisle for the Army of the Rhine. Its balance of militarism and nationalism set to an easily learned melody and a magnetic rhythm made the song an overnight sensation in France and placed it among the best-known political songs in modern European history.

Thousands of posters, paintings, sculptures, and engravings were disseminated throughout France during the Revolution. Artists, like writers, entered political life with greater ease than members of other groups and wanted their art to be used for the nation's benefit. The most famous Revolutionary artist was J.-L. David, whose *Death of Marat* (1793) became a model of visual propaganda. In this famous painting, David intentionally chose not to depict the dramatic moment when Marat was stabbed by C. Corday, realizing that the presence of a female royalist in the picture at the moment of Marat's death would diminish its heroic quality for the viewer. What kind of hero would allow himself to be stabbed by a woman? Rather, David chose to portray Marat as he had seen him the day before his death: sitting in his bathtub, pen in hand, writing what would be the last issue of his popular newspaper, *L'Ami du peuple*. In this way, David was able to idealize the tragedy of a patriotic journalist dying in the act of serving the people.

David was also instrumental in developing the fête, a highly organized ceremony combining art, music, oratory, drama, and costumes into a powerful patriotic event. Fêtes involved the active participation of common people in ways which other forms of propaganda could not, and for this reason they may have been the most effective approach to propaganda to emerge from the Revolution.

During the early years of the Revolution, public ceremonies had a religious character. Ceremonies inaugurating divisions of the Parisian National Guard during the summer of 1789 featured a mass and a sermon led by a priest. In the most renowned of these, the abbé C. Fauchet tried to convince Frenchmen that the Revolution was in perfect harmony with the Gospel. By 1792, however, the Christian character of these occasions had diminished. Instead of Christ, new patriarchs including B. Franklin, F.-M. Voltaire, and J.-J. Rousseau were venerated by advocates of the young regime. By 1794, with the ascendancy of fêtes, not even the traditional *Te Deum* was sung, and indeed many fêtes carried anti-Christian messages.

One of the most elaborate celebrations was the Fête of 20 Prairial Year II (8 June 1794), under the direction of David, who by then had become pageant-master of the Republic. At dawn, patriotic music was played throughout Paris, calling citizens to gather at the Tuileries garden. M. Robespierre ended a speech by burning figures symbolizing atheism, ambition, egoism, discord, and false simplicity. Then he led a parade from the Tuileries to the Champ de Mars, which included thousands of citizens wearing costumes covered with patriotic symbols and floats featuring special patriotic objects, such as a printing press, a plow, and a tree of liberty. The Champ de Mars had been renamed the Champ de Réunion and an artificial mountain, symbolizing Jacobin strength, had been constructed in the middle of the field. After Robespierre led the crowd to the top of the mountain, all joined in singing the *"Marseillaise."* The fête was climaxed by girls throwing flowers into the air and boys presenting swords to their fathers, reenacting the dramatic scene depicted in David's *Oath of the Horatii*.

The development of Revolutionary propaganda could not have occurred without an organized network of patriots willing to spend time and money to disseminate their message throughout the nation. The hundreds of clubs to which French intellectuals belonged were crucial in providing the necessary manpower and financial support. By the summer of 1791, over 400 provincial towns had clubs affiliated with the Paris Jacobins. These clubs spread literary propaganda among their provincial countrymen and organized special fêtes and other ceremonies.

As the Revolution advanced, the executive branch of the government became increasingly involved with pro-Revolutionary propaganda for two reasons. First, until the spring of 1792, the king's ministers had not been interested in spreading Revolutionary ideology since their own support for the Revolution had been only halfhearted; second, the outbreak of war made propaganda even more urgent. After the king was overthrown in August 1792, the Roland government established the government's first real propaganda center, the Bureau de l'Esprit Public. With a budget of 100,000 *livres*, it subsidized various Girondin projects, including J.-B. Louvet's *Sentinelle* (a journal posted on Parisian streets for *sans-*

culottes), the *Feuille villageoise*, and the influential propaganda of the Imprimerie du Cercle Social.

This trend toward the centralization of propaganda by the national government continued during the Terror. The Committee of Public Safety not only planned lavish fêtes but subsidized newspapers and pamphlets supporting Jacobin policies. The committee also encouraged visual propaganda in a more organized fashion. During the spring of 1794, it sponsored a series of contests for the best paintings, sculptures, and engravings that glorified the nation. By the time of Robespierre's fall, over 400 models, plans, and sketches had been presented to the committee. When prize money was finally awarded in 1795, the total came to 442,000 *livres*.

Few French Revolutionaries expected propaganda to become a permanent feature of the new regime. They hoped that a national system of public education eventually would replace propaganda networks once the war was won and the Revolution consolidated. Today there are many people who view propaganda as a threat to liberty. But French Revolutionaries thought differently. For them, inculcating the French people with Revolutionary political values provided a solution to the difficult problem of how to achieve a democratic revolution in a country where the bulk of the people were uneducated.

L'art de l'estampe et la Révolution française (Paris, 1977); D. L. Dowd, *Pageant-Master of the Republic: J.-L. David and the French Revolution* (Lincoln, Neb., 1948) and "Art as National Propaganda in the French Revolution," *Pub. Opin. Q.* 15 (1951); J. Ellul, *Propaganda*, trans. K. Kellen and J. Lerner (New York, 1965); J. A. Leith, *The Idea of Art as Propaganda in France, 1750-1799: A Study in the History of Ideas* (Toronto, 1965); M. Ozouf, *La fête révolutionnaire, 1789-1799* (Paris, 1976); C. B. Rogers, *The Spirit of Revolution in 1789: A Study of Public Opinion as Revealed in Political Songs and Other Popular Literature at the Beginning of the French Revolution* (Princeton, 1949).

G. Kates

Related entries: ALMANACH DU PERE GERARD, L'; CERCLE SOCIAL; COMMITTEE OF PUBLIC SAFETY; DAVID; *FEUILLE VILLAGEOISE, LA;* "*MARSEILLAISE, LA*"; MUSIC.

PROTESTANTS. See RABAUT SAINT-ETIENNE.

PROVENCE, LOUIS-STANISLAS-XAVIER, COMTE DE (1755-1824), prince of the blood, brother of Louis XVI, self-styled regent of France (1792-95), self-proclaimed king of France (1795-1814), king of France (1814-24). The comte de Provence was born at Versailles on 17 September 1755, the third son and fourth child of the dauphin Louis and Marie-Joséphine of Saxony and the grandson of Louis XV. One year younger than Louis XVI, he received a poor education under the direction of the duc de la Vauguyon. More liberal than his brothers, the count professed admiration for F.-M. Voltaire and the wisdom of the *philosophes*. In 1771 Provence married Marie-Joséphine-Louise de Savoy, eldest daughter of King Victor-Amadeus III of Sardinia. Until a son was born to Marie Antoinette in 1781, Provence was of importance as the heir presumptive to the throne, and he spent one or two days a week at Versailles.

Louix XVI denied Provence's request to sit on the Royal Council. The count kept busy entertaining poets and writers at his establishment in the Luxembourg Palace and in his château at Brunoy. In anonymous political pamphlets and other writings, he criticized Louis XVI's ministers and courted popularity with the crowd by posing as the enemy of abuses and the advocate of reform. Yet there is little to indicate that he understood the magnitude and the seriousness of the problems facing the monarchy. Indolent and vacillating, the count was much influenced by a series of intimates and favorites on whom he relied for advice. The comtesse de Balbi and the comte d'Avaray in turn played significant roles in his entourage during the Revolutionary era.

At the meeting of the first Assembly of Notables in 1787, Provence was chairman of the First Bureau and contributed to C.-A. de Calonne's downfall as controller general. In the summer of 1787 he encouraged the remonstrances of the parlements, denied that the king was infallible, and talked vaguely about a balanced monarchy. At the second Assembly of Notables, which met in 1788, Provence's Second Bureau, the only one of seven committees to do so, voted its approval for double representation of the Third Estate and provided J. Necker, who had succeeded E.-C. Loménie de Brienne as controller general, support for this proposal, which was finally approved by the king. While the comte d'Artois was being hissed and jeered as the leader of the party that seemed to be obstructing every attempt at reform, Provence was being acclaimed by members of the Third Estate and criticized by the court.

After the fall of the Bastille on 14 July, Artois headed for the border and made good his escape from France, but Provence remained in Paris. The count congratulated Necker when he returned to Versailles on 18 July (after his dismissal as controller general on 11 July). On 5-6 October the count remained in his apartment while the mob threatened Louis XVI and Marie Antoinette and forced them to leave Versailles and move to the Tuileries Palace in Paris. In December 1789 Provence offered his services to Louis XVI as lieutenant general of the kingdom. The king seems to have approved his project, but Marie Antoinette intervened and insisted that the nomination be withdrawn. Provence declared his support for the Revolution in guarded and general terms but remained, for the most part, a passive spectator between May 1789 and June 1791. In February 1791 rumors spread in Paris that he was going to flee France, but he told a delegation that called on him at the Luxembourg Palace that he had no intention of emigrating. But in June, at the same time that Louis XVI and Marie Antoinette's escape plans miscarried at Varennes, Provence was making good his escape to Brussels (as the comte de Lille) and soon was severely criticizing Louis XVI for approving Revolutionary programs forced on him by the National Assembly.

From Brussels Provence soon made his way to Coblentz where he joined his brother the comte d'Artois on 7 July 1791. Provence soon presided as regent over a shadow government in which Calonne played the role of first minister and tried to resolve the financial problems of the government, while Monsignor de Conzie, bishop of Arras, assumed the title of chancellor. The comte de Vaudreuil styled himself secretary of war and shared authority with the prince de Condé who was to direct military operations. Provence appointed agents to represent his court at Vienna and Berlin, and emissaries were dispatched to other European capitals in search of loans and military assistance. Provence and Artois sent messages in the name of the king, their brother, from whom they professed to have all the powers.

The declaration of Pillnitz (27 August 1791), in which the Holy Roman Emperor Leopold II and Frederick William II of Prussia stated that the reestablishment of absolute monarchy in France was the concern of the rulers of Europe, indicated that the monarchs were worried but that no immediate action was contemplated. On 10 September 1791, in a protest against acceptance of the Constitution of 1791 by Louis XVI, Provence and Artois proclaimed that they would be the spokesmen for what they described as the captive king. Provence, spurred on by Artois and Calonne, was challenging the National Assembly rudely and provocatively and making the situation of Louis XVI and Marie Antoinette infinitely worse.

On 31 October the Legislative Assembly ordered Provence to return to France by 1 January 1792 or forfeit his rights of succession to the throne. France declared war on Austria and Prussia in April 1792, and an *émigré* army of over 14,000 under the titular leadership of Provence, but actually commanded by the duke of Brunswick, participated in the Allied invasion of France. Attached to the Prussian corps, the army of the princes made no real contribution. At Valmy, on 20 September, the French army muddled through to victory, and the *émigré* army was disbanded soon after. Provence retired to Hamm in Westphalia where he received news of the execution of Louis XVI in January 1793. Provence declared himself for Louis XVI's surviving son (styled Louis XVII by the royalists) and proclaimed Artois lieutenant general of the kingdom. The powers, however, paid little attention to the count's pronouncements, and he drifted to Verona from where it was thought that he could encourage royalist insurgents in southern France. When Louis-Charles died in the Temple on 8 June 1795, Provence proclaimed himself king as Louis XVIII and issued an uncompromising proclamation in which he again declared war on the Revolution.

Established in a modest villa in Verona, Provence (Louis XVIII) and his entourage followed a routine that became the pattern in exile. He met with his "chancellor," held audiences, convened his "council," read books, and played whist. A monthly allowance of 20,000 francs from the king of Spain provided necessary financial support. Frequently in a state of near destitution, it was not until he went to England in 1807 that an annual allowance from the British government (16,000 pounds for himself in 1809) provided an income sufficient to support the prince and his entourage.

In April 1796 the Venetian government capitulated to French demands and expelled Provence from Verona. He soon joined the army of the prince de Condé on the right bank of the Rhine. From his base in England, the comte d'Artois (supported by the English) was trying to provide help for royalist insurgents in the Vendée. The *chouans* were disrupting efforts to implement Revolutionary legislation in the western departments, diverting republican troops from other fronts, and keeping royalist hopes alive. Louis proposed to put pressure on the republicans from the east. But the count soon found himself unwelcome in the Rhineland, and in 1797 he accepted the invitation of the duke of Brunswick to settle in Blankenburg. Elections in France in May of that year were favorable to the royalists, but the coup d'état of 18 Fructidor dashed *émigré* hopes that the monarchy could be reestablished by legal means.

When Provence found it necessary to move again, Czar Paul I permitted him to settle his entourage at Mittau in Courland, where it remained until 1801. It was there that Marie-Thérèse, only daughter and sole surviving child of Louis XVI, married her cousin the duc d'Angoulême (the eldest son of the comte d'Artois). In 1800 the future king asked Bonaparte, now first consul, to restore the Bourbons, but Bonaparte contemptuously refused. Paul expelled the Bourbons from Mittau in 1801, and the next three years were spent in Warsaw. Provence tactfully declined the suggestion of the first consul (1803) that he abdicate in return for an indemnity. In October 1804, Artois and Provence, seeing each other for the first time in a decade, met in Kalmar, Sweden, where they protested Bonaparte's assumption of the title of emperor of the French. Warned not to return to Poland, Provence again settled in Mittau, but the Treaty of Tilsit made it necessary for him to resume his travels. In 1807 he was given permission (reluctantly) to settle in England, first at Gosfield in Essex in 1807 and then at Hartwell, about thirty miles from London, in 1809. In January 1814 Louis announced that he was willing to accept some of the Revolutionary changes, and Napoleon's downfall in 1814 paved the way for the Charter of 1814, which preserved much of the legacy of the Revolution.

The restored Louis XVIII served as king in fact between 1814 and 1824. With his proclamations, manifestos, circular letters, and intrigues, Provence had kept the idea of French monarchy alive during the long years of exile. He was the first of three *émigré* princes (Provence, Artois, Orléans) to serve as king of France during the first half of the nineteenth century.

V. Beach, *Charles X of France: His Life and Times* (Boulder, Colo., 1971); Duc de Castries, *Les hommes de l'émigration, 1789-1814* (Paris, 1979); G. de Diesbach, *Histoire de l'émigration* (Paris, 1975); J. Turquan and J. d'Auriac, *Monsieur Comte de Provence* (Paris, 1928).

V. Beach

Related entries: ARTOIS; ASSEMBLY OF NOTABLES; CALONNE; *CHOUANNERIE*; COBLENTZ, CONDE; COUP OF 18 FRUCTIDOR YEAR V; DECLARATION OF PILLNITZ; *EMIGRES*; LOMENIE DE BRIENNE; LOUIS XVI; NECKER; WICKHAM.

PROVINCES, the oldest political and administrative units into which pre-Revolutionary France was organized. Provinces were not the product of any single administrative act but rather reflected the way in which the kingdom had grown over the centuries. French kings had preferred to maintain the character-istics and, often, particular institutions of newly acquired territories rather than reorganize them. The result was enormous diversity in size, institutions, priv-ileges, and customs. It is not possible to say precisely how many provinces there were, since many incorporated subprovinces which laid claim to an independent status whenever the occasion arose. In 1776, however, the number of provincial governors was fixed at thirty-nine, and since no important province was without one, this is perhaps the most reasonable estimate of their number on the eve of the Revolution.

The provinces ranged from vast regions such as Brittany, Languedoc, or Dauphiné, to tiny enclaves smaller than a modern department, such as Flanders, Sedan, or Foix. In the course of the seventeenth century, most provinces had ceased to be living administrative units. Most everyday administration was car-ried out by the intendants in *généralités*, which most often were not coterminous with old provinces. Nor was there always any close correspondence between provincial boundaries and those of the jurisdictions of the various parlements. Provincial governors retained certain military functions and could exercise enor-mous and often underestimated political influence informally as a result of their exalted social position, but the office was nevertheless largely honorific. Certain provinces enjoyed important privileges, such as the lower indirect tax burdens of peripheral regions or the exemption of Brittany from the *gabelle*, but the only provinces with a strong institutional identity were those that retained represen-tative estates, the *pays d'états*. By the later eighteenth century, the only large provinces to retain estates of any importance were Brittany, Languedoc, Bur-gundy, and Provence, but twelve other smaller territories retained their estates, notably on the northeast frontier and in the Pyrenees. In these areas the estates granted, assessed, and distributed taxation, and the *taille* was levied on a real rather than a personal basis. But even provinces with estates were included in the network of *généralités* and were subject to the authority of intendants. The areas represented by J. Necker's two *administrations provinciales* of 1778-79, or the provincial assemblies generalized in 1787, were not historic provinces, but new administrative units carved out of *généralités*.

Despite the administrative obsolescence of the provinces, they continued to command strong loyalties among their inhabitants, and in the later eighteenth century provincial parlements in those without estates began to call for the resurrection of these defunct bodies as a barrier to ministerial despotism. Min-isterial experiments with new assemblies failed to satisfy these aspirations since assemblies were believed to be more subject to the tutelage of the intendants. These demands reached a climax in the summer of 1788 when the provinces reacted to the attempts of E.-C. de Loménie de Brienne and C.-F. Lamoignon to force their reform program through by taking refuge in their own privileges, customs, and history and demanding estates to protect them. The lead came from Dauphiné, where an assembly of the three orders of the province met at Vizille on 21 July and demanded that the government convoke estates that had last met in 1628. These, it was declared, were the only authentic spokesmen of the Dauphinois nation. These moves found echoes elsewhere, and there was much talk of Breton, or Provençal, or even Artesian nations. On 8 August 1788, in the decree convoking the Estates General for the subsequent year, Loménie de Brienne conceded that meetings of provincial estates—existing, revived, or newly constituted, according to the precedents—would precede the national body. Led by members of the nobility, a wave of discussion swept the country over the forms and procedures that these estates should adopt. In Dauphiné and Franche-Comté, revived estates actually met. In many regions, however, the campaign dissolved into bickering over the areas to be represented, small regions often showing reluctance to be swallowed up and demanding estates of their own. Disagreements also arose about whether, or how, estates were to be elected, whether they were to represent orders and if so in what proportions, and whether they were to vote by head. These matters were important so long as it was assumed that provincial estates were to elect the Estates General, but when it was announced in January 1789 that the electoral units were to be *bailliages* and *sénéchaussées*, interest in provincial estates rapidly lapsed except among certain nobles. With the approach and meeting of the Estates General, provincial particularism largely disappeared until the federalist revolt of 1793. The provincialist agitation during 1788, however, had done much to familiarize the public with the great issues surrounding representative institutions and alert the Third Estate to noble political ambitions.

The *cahiers* of 1789 show that most articulate Frenchmen expected provincial administration in the future to be conducted by estates. The National Assembly, however, while sharing the desire for decentralization that had partly inspired the agitation of 1788, was soon considering far more sweeping proposals for reorganizing provincial government. Late in July 1789, it was proposed to divide the country into seventy uniform areas, and discussions continued from then until the law of 15 February 1790, when eighty-three *départements* were formally established and provinces abolished. This reform was far from arbitrary, however, and the historic geography of provincial France was borne in mind in the creation of the new units. Nor could the abolition of provinces destroy provincial loyalties, customs, and dialects, as the particularist revolts of 1793 demonstrated.

M. Bordes, *L'administration provinciale et municipale en France au XVIIIe siècle* (Paris, 1972); J. Egret, *Les derniers Etats de Dauphiné. Romans (sept. 1788-jan. 1789)* (Grenoble and Paris, 1942); J. Godechot, *Les institutions de la France sous la Révolution et l'Empire*, 2d ed. (Paris, 1968); J. Plantadis, *L'agitation autonomiste de Guienne* (1787-93) (Brive, 1910).

W. Doyle

Related entries: BAILLIAGE; DAUPHINE; FEDERALISM; *GABELLE*; GRENOBLE; INTENDANTS; LOMENIE DE BRIENNE; PARLEMENTS; *TAILLE*.

PROVINCIAL ASSEMBLIES, local consultative and administrative bodies established by the royal government in the last years of the *ancien régime*, which foreshadowed the departmental assemblies established at the beginning of the Revolution. The creation of provincial assemblies signaled a partial shift from centralized administration and opened possibilities for limited public participation in local government. The example of these assemblies stirred aspirations among the French, which drove them to oppose sharply, first the royal government and then the aristocracy, thus contributing significantly to the coming of the Revolution.

A series of municipal assemblies in parishes, districts, and provinces, terminating in a national "municipality," was a reform that the controller general A.-R.-J. Turgot (1774-76) contemplated. Through administrative activities, the public would learn about problems of government; and local residents, gathered in assemblies to assess taxes, would better ensure equitable levies. Landholding taxpayers would be the sole members; income from land would determine eligibility and voting rights; and clergy and nobles would participate with commoners, with no distinctions marking the orders. A memorandum detailing these ideas was written in 1775 by Turgot's assistant, P.-S. Du Pont de Nemours but was never presented to the king before Turgot's dismissal in 1776 and was unknown to the public until 1787. Variations on this theme circulated, especially through the writings of the physiocrats V.-R. marquis de Mirabeau and G.-F. Le Trosne and the former minister M.-R. Voyer de Paulmy d'Argenson, forming a fund of ideas on local participation from which individuals in government and in the public could draw.

The first provincial administrations were introduced in Berry in 1778 and in Upper Guyenne in 1779 by J. Necker, the director general of France. One assembly operated in each province. Members were appointed by the king, they in turn co-opting others; each order was assigned a proportion of the seats, the Third Estate having a number equal to the combined total of the clergy and nobility, and all the deputies voted together, by head. Necker looked to the assemblies to reduce the power of provincial intendants and of parlementary courts, yet he restricted their authority in matters of taxation and public works. Their jurisdiction was further limited by succeeding ministers. Within their limits, the two assemblies initiated partial reforms to make taxes more certain and equitable. Their example encouraged hopes for better government through local participation and prompted demands that provincial assemblies be granted wider powers and that representatives be elected.

A system of assemblies for provinces without provincial institutions was a key reform which the Controller General C.-A. de Calonne proposed to the Assembly of Notables in February 1787. His plan, also drafted by Du Pont de Nemours, resembled Turgot's: a hierarchy of parish, district, and provincial assemblies, membership and voting rights determined exclusively by landownership and income from land (600 *livres* for parish and district assemblies, with those earning less having a collective vote and those earning more casting multiple votes, and 1,000 *livres* in landed income for provincial assemblies), with no distinctions among the orders. Prosperous landowners in the provinces, noble and non-noble, would dominate. The assemblies would assess the new land tax Calonne intended to substitute for the *vingtièmes*, administer public assistance, supervise some public works, and recommend policy, but they would be barred from consent to taxes, raising funds, and initiating or executing policies, since these rights would be retained by the royal intendants in the *généralités* and the Royal Council in Versailles.

The Notables approved the concept of provincial assemblies but criticized their composition and powers, and the changes they proposed drew on examples and opinions of preceding years and set themes for future debate. They insisted on maintaining the distinction of orders, with the clergy and nobility allotted up to one-half the seats in the provincial assemblies, in an effort to use privilege in the form of a quota to ensure political preeminence for the first two orders within the body of wealthy landowners. They also demanded more authority for provincial assemblies over taxes, public works, debt payment, and public assistance, and greater financial autonomy and policy initiative, free from intervention and supervision by the royal intendant. They desired to replace centralized administration through the intendants with self-government by local inhabitants. This call for stronger provincial government was welcome to a public whose aspirations to participate in political affairs had obscured briefly the claim to power of the privileged orders.

The provincial assemblies established in June 1787 differed from the original plan. The orders were reintroduced, a concession to the Notables; the clergy and nobility were given one-half the seats, and the deputies voted by head. Taxes on any income, not just landownership, permitted wider entry, while the greater numbers were countered by two-tiered local assemblies. A parish assembly, open to those who paid 10 *livres* in taxes, was to elect members to a municipal assembly, limited to those who paid 30 *livres* in taxes, which administered the parish and chose deputies for district (or departmental) assemblies. Other changes weakened the appeal of these assemblies. Parish seigneurs alone could represent the nobility in departmental and provincial assemblies, all other nobles voting with and being elected to the Third Estate, thus reducing the proportion of non-nobles and making the assemblies more aristocratic. Deputies of all orders in the first provincial assemblies were appointed, the crown naming one-half and the appointed members co-opting the rest, thus depriving the assemblies of their representative role; and the elections were delayed until 1790. Despite the appointment as principal minister of E.-C. Loménie de Brienne, archbishop of Toulouse, who as a Notable was a leading critic of the fallen minister Calonne, the assemblies gained no additional authority.

In November 1787 the new provincial assemblies met, twenty in all (municipal assemblies in rural parishes also met, but urban governments retained their existing forms). Their major efforts were to limit increases in the land tax that the crown sought, propose reforms of other levies, investigate local conditions, and recommend policies to aid the poor and promote economic development.

Not surprisingly, with little authority, virtually no money, and a working session of one month, their intentions, though valiant, produced few results. Some royal intendants cooperated with the assemblies, but others contested their actions. The public, which placed its hopes in provincial government, gave no allegiance to deputies whom it did not elect.

The provincial assemblies lost favor to a competing model—the provincial estates. Calls for estates signaled efforts to institutionalize, through the distinction of orders, the political preeminence of nobles and clergy in provincial affairs. Provincial estates, as in Brittany and Languedoc, served as examples of institutions exercising greater authority, having the right to levy and control the administration of taxes and public works, and were able to make and carry out policy. Provinces that had estates in the past demanded their reestablishment and rejected provincial assemblies; provinces with no historical precedent also requested estates; and members of provincial assemblies sought to convert their assemblies into estates by enlarging their initiative in policy making and taxation.

The provincial assemblies never met again. Necker, who had established the first assembly in 1778, cancelled all of them in 1788 because of preparations for the Estates General, but he promised provincial estates later.

Provincial assemblies, conceived by royal ministers to nurture the education of the French in government, became schools of political opposition. A public whose aspirations were greater than the limited role assigned to them in provincial assemblies sought insistently to participate in more activities of government. Their experience schooled them first in the general claim to participation and in specific claims for particular groups. Opposition to the crown receded; conflict within the public mounted. Poor peasants excluded from municipal assemblies sought entry. Townsmen, ruled by officials who bought their posts, requested elected city governments. Provincials, wanting to increase the representation of the Third Estate, borrowed from the assemblies and demanded doubling of the Third in existing or reestablished estates. And patriots throughout France, invoking provincial precedent, especially the new estates of Dauphiné, urged doubling and the vote by head in the Estates General. Political schooling in the provinces in 1787 and 1788 made the French familiar with issues and goals, which they transferred to national politics in late 1788 and 1789.

The political culture that earlier bred hopes for greater local self-government persisted. The Constituent Assembly, among whose members a number had served in provincial assemblies, established in December 1789 departmental assemblies (along with district and municipal assemblies), composed of elected representatives exercising wider powers of self-government, which corresponded more closely to the aspirations that gave local force to the Revolution.

F. Mourlot, *La fin de l'Ancien Régime et les débuts de la Révolution dans la généralité de Caen, 1787-1790* (Paris, 1913); R. Reichardt, "Die Revolutionäre Wirking der Reform der Provinzialverwaltung in Frankreich 1787-1791," in E. Hinrichs, E. Schmitt, and R. Vierhaus, eds., *De l'Ancien Régime à la Révolution française, recherches et perspectives* (Göttingen, 1978); P. Renouvin, *Les assemblées provinciales de 1787, origines, développement, résultats* (Paris, 1921).

V. Gruder

Related entries: ASSEMBLY OF NOTABLES; CALONNE; INTENDANTS; LOMENIE DE BRIENNE; NECKER; *VINGTIEME*.

PRUDHOMME, LOUIS-MARIE (1752-1832), bookseller, publicist. Born in Lyon, Prudhomme first entered the book trade there as a clerk. After migrating to Paris, he established his own shop where he stocked supplies as well as books. This store specialized in underground literature, including some political critiques whose vigor led to problems with censorship. Prudhomme did more than sell such writings; he recruited authors to produce saleable works. Such materials multiplied during the pre-Revolutionary crisis, and Prudhomme estimated that he marketed over 1,500 different pamphlets between 1787 and July 1789. So seditious was one booklet that the police suppressed it at a time when they seemed to tolerate most other political writings.

Associated with the boldest thinkers before the seizure of the Bastille, Prudhomme held to such convictions as the Revolution unfolded. In July 1789 he founded the weekly newspaper, *Révolutions de Paris*, which supported radical positions favoring direct democracy and opposed all challenges to this goal. This newspaper also provided interesting critiques and an immense volume of information concerning political activity in Paris. The periodical became enormously popular. Although Prudhomme hired journalists to do the writing, most scholars agree that his guidance determined content and point of view.

By late 1792, Prudhomme and his political allies began increasingly to diverge on the question of political repression. Prudhomme, so rigorous in suppressing royalists, wished to tolerate more dissent among republicans. Perhaps his emphasis on leniency made him appear soft on the Brissotins, and he was briefly arrested after the Montagnard victory. Then doubly convinced about the need for tolerance and somewhat fearful, Prudhomme became more disturbed about the Revolution as the Terror intensified during the summer of 1793. He interrupted publication of the *Révolutions de Paris* in the autumn and ended it in 1794.

After returning to the book business under the Directory, he wrote a critique of the Revolution. Later he found Napoleon too much a continuation of the Revolution and welcomed the Bourbon Restoration. Continuing in publishing until his death, Prudhomme marketed, edited, and wrote many books opposing the very ideas he had promulgated before the Terror.

L. Gallois, *Histoire des journaux*, vol. 2 (Paris, 1846); E. Hatin, *Histoire de la presse*, vol. 6 (Paris, 1861).

J. Censer

Related entries: GIRONDISTS; *REVOLUTIONS DE PARIS*; TERROR, THE.

PUBLIC INSTRUCTION, COMMITTEE OF. See CHENIER, J.-M; ROMME.

PUBLICISTE DE LA REPUBLIQUE FRANCAISE, LE. See *AMI DU PEUPLE, L'*.

PUBLICISTE PARISIEN, LE. See *AMI DU PEUPLE, L'*.

PUISAYE, JOSEPH-GENEVIEVE, COMTE DE (1755-1827), royalist commander in Brittany (1794-98). As a deputy to the Constituent Assembly (1789-91) Puisaye appeared largely in sympathy with the regime until after the September Massacres (1792) and the growing ascendancy in government of the Montagnards. Outlawed after leading the federalist army in Normandy (May-July 1793), he took refuge in Brittany, soon conceiving a plan to transform the sporadic activity of *chouan* bands into an effective antirepublican force, which, supported by the British government, would detonate a general insurrection. Having linked up various groups, he launched in August 1794 the first stage of a large-scale plan and, this having failed, he crossed to London to concert, in what was meant to be a brief visit, a combined operation.

Welcome to a ministry already decided on sending troops and supplies to western France, he was also accepted, reluctantly, by the comte d'Artois and accorded the Brittany command although suspected by the pure royalists of being both a constitutionalist and dangerously subservient to W. Pitt. The failure of the Quiberon expedition (June-July 1795) blasted any hope Puisaye had of winning the Bourbon princes' confidence, and, while in 1796 he tried to recreate a *chouan* confederation and link it with other counterrevolutionary forces in Anjou and the Vendée, certain royalist elements influential in Louis XVIII's court worked to displace him. The republicans' temporary success (spring 1797) in quashing the *chouannerie* forced Puisaye to hide and then to emigrate to England, where his intemperate criticisms facilitated his being removed from his command.

Twenty months after leaving Brittany, Puisaye arrived in York (now Toronto), heading a group intended to found an *émigré* colony. The project faltering, Puisaye withdrew (1799), first to Niagara and then (1802) to England, where he carried on drafting his memoirs, each wordy tome of which (6 vols. in 7, London 1803-08) purported to demonstrate that his opponents' intrigues had been solely responsible for ruining the opportunity he had opened for the Bourbons to achieve their restoration to the throne. One opponent being the king's confidant, Puisaye was finally held in disgrace by the Bourbons and never returned to France. Nearly his own worst enemy, Puisaye had in fact been loyal and brave in serving, nonmyopically, the Bourbon cause in 1794-98, but his memoirs (never completed; they end, in effect, with Quiberon) damaged that cause, so that his subsequent reputation has suffered quite as much from royalist as from republican insinuations and strictures.

M. G. Hutt, *Chouannerie in the 1790's: Puisaye, the Princes and the British Government* (Cambridge, Eng., 1983) and "Note sur les sources de l'histoire de la contre-révolution: Puisaye," *Ann. hist. de la Révo. française* 36 (1964); P. Sainte-Claire Deville, "Etudes sur le comte Joseph de Puisaye: épisodes d'un grand chef royaliste (1792-94)," *Mém. de la Soc. d'Hist. et d' Archéologie de Bret.* 12, 15, 16 (1931-35).

M. G. Hutt

Related entries: ARTOIS; *CHOUANNERIE*; MONTAGNARDS; PITT; QUIBERON; SEPTEMBER 1792 MASSACRES.

Q

QU'EST-CE QUE C'EST LE TIERS ETAT? (1789), influential political pamphlet written by the abbé E.-J. Sieyès. This was one of the most widely acclaimed pamphlets of the French Revolution and would probably rank among the half dozen most important of the modern era. It was published in January 1789 just as the controversy over the composition and organization of the Estates General convoked for the following May was moving toward its climax. It was so popular that two more editions appeared during the spring, the second one in two slightly different versions, and finally in a considerably revised and amplified third edition. During the Revolution, it was translated into German and other European languages. While there is no firm estimate of the number printed that spring, it must have reached the tens of thousands. It seems to have been as popular in the provinces as in Paris.

The abbé Sieyès was a cleric of modest middle-class origin who had achieved moderate success as an ecclesiastical administrator but who was barred by birth from the higher ranks of the clergy. A frequenter of the Paris salons, he seems to have been associated with the group known as the patriots during the pre-Revolutionary ferment. He wrote other pamphlets during this period and later, but none approached the success of *Qu'est-ce que c'est le tiers état?* It brought him immediate popular acclaim and a reputation as a profound political thinker and potential leader. It was unquestionably responsible for his election as a deputy to the Estates General by the Third Estate of a Paris district after he had failed to be elected by his own order.

The issue that Sieyès addressed in his pamphlet was the mode of organization of the Estates General scheduled to meet in the spring of 1789. The Parlement of Paris had declared on 25 September 1788 that the Estates should be organized in the same manner as the last one held in 1614, with the three estates having an equal number of representatives and voting being done separately by order. Spokesmen for the Third Estate immediately attacked the parlement's declaration on the grounds that the parlement's aim was to protect the special rights and privileges of the first two orders and did not take sufficient account of the fact that the Third Estate included over 90 percent of France's 25 million people.

Because there were only a handful of newspapers and they offered almost no political news or comment, the pamphlet provided the only medium for the discussion of political issues. Contrary to the traditional view, the royal edict of 5 July 1788 was not responsible for the flood of pamphlets in the fall of 1788. The number had been rising steadily since the convocation of the first Assembly of Notables in February 1787. It reached about 150 in that year but then rose to about 500 during the parlementary crisis of the summer of 1788. Another 600 were published in the fall of 1788, and the figure rose to 1,500 in the spring of 1789. Most of those written after 25 September 1788 dealt with the issue of the doubling of the Third and the vote by head, and most favored the Third's position. This effort to arouse public support seemed to have gained a partial success when a royal declaration of 27 December approved the doubling of the Third. The issue of the manner of voting was still unresolved when *Qu'est-ce que c'est le tiers état?* appeared in early January.

Sieyès' earlier pamphlets, including one published in October attacking noble privileges, seem to have received slight notice, and his new one offered little that was strikingly original either in its demands or its supporting arguments. Its spectacular success seems to have derived from the simple, direct, and forceful way the arguments were presented and the author's skillful choice of supporting evidence. Although it is true that the main issues (doubling and the vote by head) were relatively simple, the arguments and evidence used by pamphleteers on both sides were often extremely complex. In many cases, they depended for their effectiveness on a fairly sophisticated knowledge of French history as well as of traditional or prescriptive rights and powers. Although hundreds of pamphlets discussed the issues, it was Sieyès' genius to cut through old, obscure historical precedents and reduce the matter to a simple question of numbers. The Third Estate, he argued, constituted nineteen-twentieths of the population of France and did all the essential productive work required to sustain the nation; therefore, it should exercise the political power that until then had been wielded by the nobility. Furthermore, since within the nation all inhabitants are by nature free and equal, no class or group can legitimately claim special rights, privileges, or powers without the approval of the people. Prescriptive rights, whatever their age, cannot stand against the will of the sovereign people. His attack on traditional privileges was devastating in its logic and irony.

These arguments were presented in the first three sections of the pamphlet, each of which was headed by a rhetorical question followed by a one-word answer. "What is the Third Estate?" "Everything." "What has the Third Estate been in the political order up until now?" "Nothing." "What does it want to be?" "Everything." Although other pamphleteers had made similar assertions, what made Sieyès' effective was his linking them symbiotically with the idea that sovereign power in the nation belonged to the people as a whole. While this idea had been discussed in the eighteenth century and was implicit in the theory of enlightened despotism as well as J.-J. Rousseau's ideas about the general will and direct democracy, it was Sieyès' destiny to present these ideas to the general public under the right circumstances at the right time. Shortly after, they found their definitive expression in the Declaration of the Rights of Man and of the Citizen.

The last two-thirds of the pamphlet (again divided into three parts) reviewed the steps taken by the royal government up to the time of writing to organize the procedures to be followed in the Estates General (the principal one was the reconvening of the Assembly of Notables to consider the matter) and indicated what Sieyès thought should have been done differently in the light of the principles enunciated in the first part of the pamphlet. The final and longest part gave specific advice to the Third Estate on the tactics it should employ when the Estates met in order to obtain its ends. He recommended that it should simply ignore the privileged orders' demands for the vote by order and boldly refuse to do anything until the demands of the Third Estate had been met. It added greatly to Sieyès' reputation that these tactics were actually successfully implemented in May and June and that it was on his motion that the Third Estate declared itself to be a National Assembly on 17 June 1789.

The pamphlet is a classic example of effective political propaganda. Its simple, direct message seemed so logical and compelling that those who tried to point out the complexities it overlooked or oversimplified never made much headway. The main argument—that the whole of the people constitute the nation and should be effectively sovereign—has influenced political developments in Europe and the rest of the world since. Its democratic and egalitarian philosophy has provided a base for both liberal and socialistic movements in the nineteenth and twentieth centuries, although one recent Marxist scholar considers Sieyès to have been more of an apologist for an individualistic capitalism than the harbinger of an egalitarian socialist state.

P. Bastid, *Sieyès et sa pensée* (Paris, 1939); M. B. Garrett, *The Estates of 1789* (New York, 1935); E.-J. Sieyès, *Qu'est-ce que c'est le tiers état?*, critical edition with notes by R. Zapperi (Geneva, 1970) and *What Is the Third Estate?* trans. M. Blondel and ed. with historical notes by S. E. Finer; introduction by Peter Campbell (New York, 1964).

R. W. Greenlaw

Related entries: PATRIOT PARTY; PROPAGANDA; "RESULT OF THE COUNCIL"; SIEYES.

QUIBERON, a peninsula on the southwest coast of Brittany where in July 1795 a British-backed *émigré* expedition was routed. The undertaking stemmed essentially from the desire of W. Pitt's government to open another front after that in the Low Countries had collapsed and from the insistence by some of his colleagues on the opportunity afforded by the Vendée and, more recently by the *chouannerie*, to defeat the Republic and effect the restoration of the Bourbons— this being the best way, it was thought in 1794-95, to advance British interests. That policy was naturally concurred in by the comte d'Artois, and it coincided closely with the projects of the comte de Puisaye, who, once ashore, was to command the enterprise. In establishing a beachhead, *émigré* troops were first to detonate an insurrection; 3,000, followed by 4,000, and another 7,000 British troops would then arrive to hold the perimeter of what would serve as a supply base; and the comte d'Artois would arrive to create a unified command over all royalist forces in western France.

The scale of supply was appropriate to that of the undertaking; 100 transports, protected by a dozen warships, disembarked, beginning on 27 June, arms and equipment for some 70,000 men. The number of troops, though, was not. The thousands of *chouans* who assembled were not well suited to the regular operations now required; only 3,000 *émigré* troops had been landed, another 1,200, under C. Virot vicomte de Sombreuil, not having arrived from Germany in time to accompany them. Furthermore the colonel of the former, L. d'Hervilly, behaved insubordinately. This, plus the weakness of Puisaye's tactical concepts and the limited nature of the insurrection farther inland, meant that the landing force plus the *chouans* failed to break out beyond the Auray-Landevant line before L. Hoche's forces checked them. With 10,000 men rapidly pulled to this critical area by 3 July, Hoche then launched a counterattack to drive "the anglo-*émigré chouans*" back into the peninsula of Quiberon. On 16 July, just as Sombreuil's division was arriving, the royalists were mauled in a badly executed effort to break out and five days later were routed when the "blues" skillfully penetrated their ill-manned defenses. Perhaps only some 300 were killed or drowned, about 2,000 getting away to the ships, but some 5,000 *chouans* and over 1,000 *émigré* troops were captured, and, despite claims that a capitulation had been made, 640 of the latter were shot. It was this severe enforcement of the law against armed *émigrés*, and not the clemency shown the *chouans* (108 executed, only about 200 imprisoned), that gripped foreign observers and horrified royalist opinion.

Although the disaster did not put an immediate stop to expedition plans, in the medium term it fostered a policy of subversion in place of armed confrontation, not least because it increased the reluctance of *émigrés* to serve—particularly in Brittany—for in the savage recriminations that followed, especially bitter opinions were expressed about the unreliability of the *chouans* and Puisaye's courage and loyalty. Quiberon also enhanced the reputation of Hoche, who followed up this resounding success by forcing a general, if fragile, pacification of northwestern France in the spring of 1796, and it encouraged London to begin sounding out (December 1795) what chance there was of supporting its interests by negotiating with the Republic—further "proof" of that perfidy which the British had (in the eyes of royalists) demonstrated, yet again, at Quiberon.

M. G. Hutt, "The British Government's Responsibility for the 'Divided Command' of the Expedition to Quiberon, 1795," *Eng. His. Rev.* 76 (1961); C. Robert, *1795: Expédition des émigrés à Quiberon; le comte d'Artois à l'île d' Yeu* (Paris, 1899); D. Sutherland, "'L' expédition de l'île d'Yeu en 1795," *Ann. hist. de la Révo. française*

45 (1973); J. Vidalenc, "L'Affaire de Quiberon," *Actes du 87me Congrès national des sociétés savantes, Poitiers, 1962—Section d'histoire moderne* (Paris, 1963).

M. G. Hutt

Related entries: ARTOIS; *CHOUANNERIE*; HOCHE; PITT; PUISAYE; VENDEE.

R

RABAUT SAINT-ETIENNE, JEAN-PAUL (1743-93), Protestant minister, deputy to the National Assembly and to the National Convention. Rabaut Saint-Etienne, the foremost leader of the Protestants in the French Revolution, was the eldest son of the celebrated pastor of Nîmes, P. Rabaut. Like his father, he became a devoted Calvinist minister and a stalwart defender of Protestantism. He had a distinguished career as a writer, member of the Estates General, and was elected deputy and president in both the National Assembly and the Convention. He was also a noted journalist who helped J. Cérutti found *La feuille villageoise* and collaborated in *La chronique de Paris*.

Rabaut Saint-Etienne had as his main goal to give Protestants full religious and civil freedom. His hope was that the Revolution would bury the anti-Protestant prejudices of the past and break the chains of Protestant oppression. For Rabaut the Revolution was the heir of the Enlightenment. Indeed, he was imbued with the philosophical views of the Enlightenment, specifically those regarding the doctrines of toleration and progress. Man, gifted with reason, can infallibly arrive at a better world, if he will only use his reason. Man can distinguish between good and evil, ignorance and error, since there is no limit to the perfectability of reason. With this legacy from the Enlightenment, Rabaut Saint-Etienne manifested these views in his thoughts and deeds.

He was one of the major formulators of the Edict of Toleration approved with limitations by Louis XVI in November 1787. Although it was a breakthrough in that Protestants were given freedom of conscience, they were not given full religious and civil equality. Rabaut Saint-Etienne desired to obtain freedom of worship for Protestants, the legalization of Protestant schools, the acceptance of Protestants as lawyers, doctors, notaries, and in other professions still closed to them, and the termination of existing laws still in effect against the Protestants.

On the eve of the French Revolution, Rabaut plunged into the political debate regarding the status of the estates in French society with the publication of his *Considérations sur les droits et sur les devoirs du tiers-état* (1788). Basically, he contended that the third estate was the nation whose representation in the forthcoming Estates General should be preponderant. The popularity of his essay and some of his other writings, such as *Le vieux cévenol* (1784) and *A la nation française sur les vices de son gouvernement, sur la nécessité d'établir une constitution* (1788), so enhanced his reputation that he became the principal drafter of the *cahier* representing the Third Estate at Nîmes and was elected a delegate to the Estates General. His demands in the *cahier* were not radical but basically emphasized religious freedom for Protestants and full recognition of their civil rights.

With the formation of the National Assembly, he had the honor of being elected president in March 1790, despite the fact that he was a Protestant minister. In the Assembly he was an impassioned and skilled orator who convinced his colleagues to have freedom of conscience inscribed in the Declaration of the Rights of Man but was unsuccessful in having them guarantee freedom of worship for Protestants. Although Rabaut took no active part in the discussion regarding the Civil Constitution of the Clergy, he agreed with the establishment of a state church compatible with the principles of the Revolution. According to the historian B. Poland in *French Protestantism and the French Revolution* (1957), Rabaut Saint-Etienne wanted to humanize the priests. Celibacy, religious brotherhoods, religious processions, and holidays should be abolished or diminished. Concurrently, the state should take steps to make useful citizens. Marriage and taxation of priests should be encouraged. In brief, Rabaut Saint-Etienne believed in the utility of a simplified religion, stripped of all accessories.

As a member of the committee on the constitution in the National Assembly, he assisted in the writing of the first constitution of the Revolution. He believed the document should be the code of morality for the state. Rabaut desired a monarchy with the suspensive veto and a unicameral legislature. But his position toward the monarchy changed when he was elected deputy to the Convention from the Aube. The hostility of Louis XVI to the constitution and his attempts to align himself with the counterrevolutionaries had a profound impact on Rabaut. Nevertheless, in December 1792 he joined with the Girondins to delay the monarch's trial by denying that the Convention had the right to try the king. When this endeavor failed, Rabaut Saint-Etienne, a former supporter of the king, voted for his exile or imprisonment. The trial of Louis XVI became a major political issue in a struggle for power between the Girondins and the Jacobins.

As the political struggle between the two factions intensified, Rabaut became one of its victims. The Convention established a Committee of Twelve comprised of Girondins, including Rabaut Saint-Etienne, to undermine the increasing power of the Jacobin Paris Commune. It was to no avail. Rabaut and the other Girondins were declared outlaws by the Jacobins in May 1793 and were to be arrested. He escaped, however, and found a haven near Versailles. Subsequently he returned to Paris in October 1793 and was given shelter by a Catholic family originally from Nîmes. He was discovered by the authorities on 5 December 1793, was immediately executed, and was buried in the Madeleine cemetery.

At fifty, the career of the leading spokesman for Protestant liberty during the Revolution had ended.

J. A. Dartigue, *Rabaut de Saint-Etienne à l'Assemblée Constituante de 1789* (Nantes, 1903); A. Dupont, *Rabaut Saint-Etienne, 1743-1793* (Strasbourg, 1946); A. Lods, "Rabaut Saint-Etienne, sa correspondance pendant la Révolution, 1789-1793," *Révo. française* 35 (1898); R. Mirabaud, *Un président de la Constituante et de la Convention: Rabaut Saint-Etienne* (Paris, 1930); C. de Plancy, ed., *Oeuvres de Rabaut Saint-Etienne*, 2 vols. (Paris, 1826).

C. A. Gliozzo

Related entries: CHRONIQUE DE PARIS; CIVIL CONSTITUTION OF THE CLERGY; COMMISSION OF TWELVE; COUNTERREVOLUTION; ENLIGHTENMENT; *FEUILLE VILLAGEOISE, LA; QU'EST-CE QUE C'EST LE TIERS ETAT?* SUSPENSIVE VETO.

REACTION, THERMIDORIAN. See THERMIDORIAN REACTION.

REASON, CULT OF. See CULT OF REASON.

RECAMIER, JEANNE-FRANCOISE-JULIE-ADELAIDE BERNARD, MADAME (called JULIETTE) (1777-1849), hostess of a literary and political salon. Juliette Bernard was the only child of J. Bernard, a royal notary in Lyon, and his wife Julie. Madame Bernard's connections with C.-A. de Calonne led to her husband's appointment to Paris as *receveur des finances* in 1784. Juliette remained in Lyon for several years at the Benedictine convent of La Déserte.

In Paris in 1793, aged fifteen, she married J.-R. Récamier (born in Lyon, 1751), a rich banker and friend of her parents. Whether Récamier was really her father remains controversial; in any event it was a marriage in name only. Her career as a society figure began under the Directory, when her name was linked with those of J. Beauharnais, P. Barras, L. Bonaparte, J. Moreau, Madame Tallien, M. de Montmorency, and C. Jordan. Her friendship with Madame de Staël, which brought her into close contact with the literary world, began in 1798. Her rejection of L. Bonaparte's advances, combined with her friendship with opposition figures, left her in difficulty with the Napoleonic regime. After Napoleon ordered her to leave Paris in 1805, she went into exile in Italy, returning to Paris to reopen her salon after the Restoration.

Duc de Castries, *Madame Récamier* (Paris, 1971); E. Herriot, *Madame Récamier et ses amis* (Paris, 1924); A. Lenormant, ed., *Souvenirs et correspondance tirées des papiers de Madame Récamier* (Paris, 1859).

L. J. Abray

Related entries: CALONNE; DIRECTORY; STAEL-HOLSTEIN.

REFLECTIONS ON THE REVOLUTION IN FRANCE. See BURKE.

REINHARD, MARCEL (1899-1973), historian. Born in Paris to a family of Alsatian origin, Reinhard enlisted in the military after completing secondary schooling in 1917 and was decorated with the *croix de guerre*. After having passed his *agrégation*, he taught successively at the Military School of La Flèche and the *lycées* Carnot and Louis-le-Grand. He successfully defended his doctoral thesis in 1935. Demoted by the Vichy government, he participated in the fighting of 1945 and was made *chevalier* and subsequently officer of the Legion of Honor for his military service.

He showed himself a pioneering historian of the French Revolution, beginning with his dissertation on the department of the Sarthe under the Directory. This thesis was at one and the same time a model of regional and global history in his demonstration of how the Directory actually functioned. His biography of L. Carnot put "the organizer of victory," who, until Reinhard, had been cast as too heroic a figure, into proper balance. He cast new light, too, on the foreign policy of the Convention and the Directory. After becoming interested in G. Babeuf, Reinhard published his correspondence with the Academy of Arras and showed how Babeuf had formed his communist ideas before 1789. In *La chute de la royauté* (1969), he continued earlier work on the events of 10 August 1792 and completed it with numerous unedited documents that provided information on what he considered a second revolution, that of equality. He was also a pioneer in the research that he undertook, beginning in 1946, on eighteenth-century demography. After establishing the history of demographic investigations, he published his first results in 1949 and 1956. In 1965 he presented to the historical congress in Vienna a demographic summary of the world in 1815.

As an organizer, he established centers for the study of historical demography at Caen and later at Paris and was one of the founders of the Société de démographie historique and of the *Annales* of this organization.

As a director of research, he launched numerous young researchers on investigations of various subjects, including religion, the press, and the army during the Revolution. Each of them found in him a warm guide and, with his flawless scholarship, a master of great integrity.

J. Dupaquier, "Avant-propos" to Société de démographie historique, *Hommage à Marcel Reinhard* (Paris, 1973); J. Dupaquier, J. Surratteau, and A. Soboul, "Marcel Reinhard (1899-1973)," *Ann. Hist. de la Révo. française* 46 (1974).

J.-P. Bertaud

Related entries: LEFEBVRE; SOBOUL.

REMONSTRANCES. See PARLEMENTS.

RENAULT, AIMEE-CECILE (1773?-94), failed assassin of M. Robespierre. The daughter of a paper merchant, she lived with her family on the Ile de la Cité in Paris. On 23 May 1794, Renault left home carrying two small knives and a change of linen and went to Robespierre's lodgings. Told that he was not at home, she became angry and declared that as a public official he should be available to those who came to him. When she refused to explain why she wanted to see Robespierre, she was taken to the Committee of General Security. On the way, according to the testimony of the men who arrested her, she said she would shed all her blood to have a king again. In the course of several interrogations, she remained impassive. She offered little further information, but she insisted that the knives had not been intended for the murder of Robespierre. Asked about the change of linen, however, she said she knew she would need it in prison before going to the guillotine.

There is no evidence that Renault was insane, and she was certainly not part of any anti-Revolutionary plot. It is clear, however, that Renault's apparent assassination attempt, which was the second on leaders of the Committee of Public Safety in two days, profoundly affected Robespierre. Less for the sake of his personal safety, perhaps, than for the success of the new moral society he wished to establish, he was more than ever determined to assure its survival by ruthless repression of opposition. Renault was made the central figure in a show trial that produced fifty-four executions. Among the victims were Hébertist conspirators, people formerly in the service of the king, Renault's father and oldest brother, and her aunt, an ex-nun.

E. Lairtullier, *Les femmes célèbres de 1789 à 1795*, 2 vols. (Paris, 1840); A. Tuetey, *Répertoire général*, 11 vols. (Paris, 1914); G. Walter, *Robespierre*, 2 vols. (Paris, 1961).

C. Garrett

Related entries: COMMITTEE OF GENERAL SECURITY; COMMITTEE OF PUBLIC SAFETY; HEBERTISM; ROBESPIERRE, M.

RENTE, an annuity or fixed return on a capital sum, ranging from 5 to 8 percent in the three centuries before the French Revolution. Devised as a way around the church usury laws, the *rente* was legally distinct from interest since the capital was permanently alienated to the borrower in return for an annual payment in perpetuity (*rente perpetuelle*). There was no time limit for the return of the capital; the lender—technically, the purchaser of the *rente*—could not demand his capital back, while the borrower—technically, the seller of the *rente*—could repay the capital at his or her discretion (with some advance notification so that the lender could find an alternative investment outlet). Under the law, a *rente* was bought or sold for a capital sum much in the way a piece of land was bought or sold for a guaranteed rent or income from the land. In fact, before 1600 most *rentes* were guaranteed by a piece of land representing a return on the capital transferred and so specified in the notarized *rente* contract. In the course of the following two centuries, however, *rentes* were increasingly assigned to all of the property (land or not) of the borrower as a guarantee for the *rente*. Thus the *rente* became a lien or mortgage on the entire estate of the individual who sold or constituted the *rente* initially. By the eighteenth century, *rentes* represented almost invariably 5 percent on the capital transferred, a rate of return below the commercial rate.

Rentes were very popular among families with some surplus capital. They were especially appropriate for paying family charges. Instead of transferring large amounts of capital or land, the family head would pay portions and dowries to children and relatives in the form of annual *rentes* until the capital was raised, which in the case of bachelor sons or daughters in holy orders was seldom necessary. Families that needed the capital—those faced with demanding sons-in-law, for example—usually borrowed by means of the constituted *rente* since it represented no immediate threat to family solvency and avoided the sale of land. The family papers of the well-to-do always included files of *rente* contracts, representing a web of mutual obligations and often interfamily aid.

Rentes were more cumbersome for commercial transactions since there was no legal obligation to return the capital as long as the annual *rente* was regularly paid. Most merchants needed to turn their capital over and make fresh investments; reassigning *rente* contracts to third parties was awkward under the best conditions. The bill of exchange (*lettre de change*) was a more flexible instrument of commercial credit, though its enforceability in the courts was less certain and its status less prestigious than the *rente*. The *rente* was considered lineage property (*propres*) and thus fell under special provisions of the inheritance law favoring entail and the preservation of the family fortune. Like the land itself, the *rente* (and the *rentier* who received it) bore high social prestige in a society that regarded trade as degrading and the taking of interest as sinful. In the hierarchy of social values, it was better to be a modest *rentier* than a prosperous merchant or a rich usurer. The preference for *rentes* encouraged incremental saving and risk aversion, though it was a rational response to uncertain commercial conditions and not simply a social bias.

Since the early sixteenth century, the French government used the *rente* to borrow capital from the general public (*rentes sur l'Etat* or *rentes sur l'Hôtel de Ville*). Remember that investment opportunities (beside land and offices) in Old Regime France were limited, especially safe ones. Hence even a government that often delayed or occasionally defaulted on its *rente* payments was still able to attract large amounts of private capital into its coffers. By the eighteenth century, the royal treasury had developed a reputation as a safe placement for private funds. Moreover, compared to land, government *rentes* were easy to manage, subdivide, and transfer; for many urban notables, widows in particular, they were preferable to real estate. The appeal of public *rentes* reached its apex in the years after the Seven Years War (1756-63) when the royal government devised a series of attractive *rente* issues, many in the form of lifetime annuities (*rentes viagères*), which paid as much as 10 and even 12 percent for the lifetime of the purchaser. Benefiting from the imperfect state of the actuary tables, the *rentiers*, usually from healthier levels of French society and often designated as children in the *rente* contracts, recovered their capital many times over in their long lifetimes.

The royal government became increasingly dependent on *rentes* to cover the escalating deficits after the American Revolution (1778-83). By 1789 the service charges on the public debt reached 50 percent of the national budget. When the *rentiers* of the state lost confidence, began to doubt the future solvency of the government, and then refused to lend fresh capital to the treasury, the French government was forced to declare national bankruptcy, leading to the convening of the Estates General.

R. de Roover, *L'évolution de la lettre de change, XIV-XVIIIe siècle*, vol. 4 (Paris, 1953); B. Schnapper, *Les rentes au XVIe siècle* (Paris, 1957); G. V. Taylor, "The Paris Bourse on the Eve of the French Revolution, 1781-1789," *Am. Hist. Rev.* 67 (1962).

R. Forster

Related entry: AIDES.

RENTIER. See *RENTE.*

REPRESENTATIVES ON MISSION, members of the National Convention assigned from 1792 through 1795 to oversee the armed forces, to enforce the law in the departments, to supervise the conscription of men or the drafting of horses for the army, or for other specific purposes that involved enforcing the laws and policies of the national government. The representatives on mission were numerous; from March 1792 to July 1794, as many as 130 deputies might be absent from the Convention on mission at any time. Because they extended the power of the Convention over the armed forces and the localities and suppressed counterrevolutionary movements, it is doubtful that the Revolutionary government could have succeeded or even survived without them.

The Convention dispatched its first deputies on mission on 22 September 1792, two days after its first session, by sending three of its members to Orléans to restore public order there. At the end of the same month, other deputies were dispatched to the *département du Nord* to restore order and replace all military officers and civilian officials who were unworthy of trust. On 9 March 1793 the Convention divided France into forty-one sections, each consisting of two departments, and assigned two representatives on mission to each section. Other missions were established from time to time, including several to the armed forces. One member of the Convention was assigned to form and administer a war technology experiment station in which scientists worked to perfect balloon observation for combat and find new ways of making gunpowder, and he was carried on the lists of the Convention as a representative on mission.

Until the enactment of the Law of 14 Frimaire Year II (4 December 1793), which codified the conduct of the Revolutionary government and all its agencies, a representative on mission had a free hand and virtually absolute authority. As R. R. Palmer says, they could arrest persons, establish Revolutionary courts to try them, and have them executed by guillotine or by other measures. They could suspend the execution of a law. They had the power to issue decrees and proclamations in their own names. They could fix prices, requisition commodities, confiscate private wealth, and levy and collect taxes of their own creation. Some representatives on mission abused these powers, and that is why the Convention enacted the Law of 14 Frimaire. But even when that law was in force, many representatives on mission, having become accustomed earlier to making and following their own decisions, continued to act arbitrarily, without observing the restrictions the law imposed on them.

The representatives on mission took the authority of the Revolutionary government into places where it had previously been seen as remote and even irrelevant and in which the Revolution itself was badly understood. In their correspondence they referred often, with astonishment, to the ignorance of Revolutionary purposes and doctrines that existed in many towns and villages of the departments. One of their major tasks, therefore, was that of Revolutionary evangelism, of teaching Revolutionary principles, and creating local cadres that could not only carry on the functions of government but also spread the Revolutionary gospel. The proliferation of Jacobin clubs in the small towns and villages during the Year II was one aspect of this effort. But if some representatives on mission succeeded in developing support for the Revolution in the departments, others seemed capable only of producing reactions against the Revolution. Generally representatives who educated the people reasonably and without threats or bluster were more successful than those who relied on unnecessarily harsh policies and what may be called verbal terrorism. It should be kept in mind that in effect representatives on mission were nominated by the Committee of Public Safety and confirmed by the Convention. The committee, which from July 1793 was Montagnard, tended to choose members acceptable to the Montagnard faction. Accordingly, the moderates of the Plain rarely went on mission until the Thermidorian Reaction was under way, and the representatives on mission before that time were on the whole remarkable for the aggressiveness, activism, and severity that characterized the Montagnard temperament.

The immediate task of the representatives on mission in the summer of 1793 was to break the federalist revolt, in which the administrations of some forty departments and several cities were implicated. That the representatives on mission succeeded in so doing testifies to the energy and assurance with which they acted. At Lyon and in the southern valley of the Rhône, federalism had to be defeated by military action; elsewhere the effort was made through political action, propaganda, and the broadcast intimidation that the Terror was expected to accomplish. On arriving at a departmental capital in his section, a representative on mission would confer with a few republicans he had been told were sound and loyal and from them would learn the details of the local situation. Next he would convoke the Revolutionary club and conduct a *scrutin épuratoire*, or purgative ballot, in which each member would present himself in his turn to be challenged, criticized, and judged as a supporter of the Revolution, with the representative present. Those who received the affirmative votes of the club maintained their membership and usually remained in whatever offices they held; the others were dropped from the club and from public office. Once the *scrutin épuratoire* was completed, the representative had a detailed knowledge of who on the local scene could be trusted in positions of authority, and he reconstructed the local administrations on that basis. Persons suspected of federalism and other political crimes were imprisoned, and if necessary a Revolutionary court was established to try them. In these and other ways, representatives on mission shattered the federalist movement and proceeded to mobilize resources for war and national defense, an urgent matter in 1793.

Every representative on mission was responsible for his acts and was therefore required to report regularly to the Committee of Public Safety, enclosing with his report copies of the ordinances and proclamations he had issued. If his conduct was unsatisfactory, he could be recalled. Even so, when he returned from mission to Paris, he would face his own *scrutin épuratoire* in the Paris Jacobin club. In general, a representative on mission was expected to fulfill the tasks he had been appointed to accomplish with firmness, efficiency, and severity. To have a record of indulgence or compassion was disadvantageous: one might be accused of protecting conspirators from the punishment they deserved. But it was also dangerous to be found to have acted with too much violence, to have discredited the Revolution with excessive terrorism.

This being true, representatives on mission took pains in their reports to describe their activities in such a way as to avoid suspicions of having been lenient or having been unreasonably brutal. But they could not control all the information about them that reached the Committee of Public Safety, much of it emanating from hostile sources. Persons of their jurisdictions would write to the committee or the Convention complaining of the way they exercised authority and demanding their recall or worse.

In the winter of 1793-94 the committee employed an agent, M.-A. Jullien, to observe the representatives on mission in the west of France. In February 1794 Jullien reported to the committee that the representative J.-B. Carrier, at Nantes, had tolerated the execution without trial of more than 2,000 imprisoned persons, mostly Vendéans, who were drowned in the Loire. In May Jullien was at Bordeaux, where he reported that local terrorists had extorted bribes from suspects about to be brought before the commission militaire, the local Revolutionary court, and that in several cases in which bribes had been paid, the court had assigned punishments short of death. It is possible that the representatives on mission at Bordeaux, J.-L. Tallien and C.-A. Ysabeau, were implicated in that scandal. On being recalled, many representatives asked to be allowed to remain on mission or simply neglected to abandon their duties, either because they feared having to account for their missions or could not bring themselves to abandon the prestige and the power over others that had become central to their lives. The reluctance of representatives on mission to surrender their authority and return to Paris was so much of a problem that on 17 December 1793 the Convention instructed public prosecutors to proceed against and punish all representatives of the people and other governmental agents who continued to exercise authority in the departments or the armed forces after that authority had been revoked.

After the conspiracy of 9 and 10 Thermidor (27 and 28 July 1794) against the Robespierrists, the institution of the representative on mission survived, and in a few weeks new representatives on mission were appointed. They were being appointed, however, to organize the Thermidorian Reaction in the departments. From this point, they were chosen from the Plain or from the seventy-three survivors of the seventy-five deputies who in June 1793 had signed a petition for the release of the Brissotins and, in return, had been imprisoned until August 1794. Some of the Thermidorian deputies were suspected of having become royalists, such as A.-F. Laurence, who harassed republicans at Toulouse and energetically disarmed, imprisoned, and punished the terrorists of the Year II.

Popular traditions in France about the representatives on mission of the Year II are derived mostly from Thermidorian exaggerations and myths that identify all of them as radical terrorists or *buveurs de sang*. A few deserve to be seen in that way. Carrier at Nantes, J. Fouché and J.-M. Collot d'Herbois at Lyon, and G.-F.-J. Le Bon at Arras seem in fact to have had no consciousness of limit in the trials and executions they set in motion in the departments entrusted to them. And yet in contrast to them we have representatives such as G.-A. Couthon, who went to extremes to save as many as possible of the departmental administrators of the Puy-de-Dôme, so that in the end only two of them were judged and put to death. Taken as a whole, the representatives on mission were as diverse as human nature itself. Some were able; others were of low competence. Some were scrupulously honest; others were corrupt. Some succeeded in winning the common people to the cause of the Republic, while others who were maladroit drove them in the opposite direction. They were neither totally evil nor totally benevolent, constructive, and humane. In revolution, as in life, no faction has a monopoly on virtue.

F.-A. Aulard, ed., *Recueil des actes du Comité de Salut Public avec la correspondance officielle des représentants en mission*, 28 vols. (Paris, 1889-1962); P. Gaffarel, *La mission de Maignet en l'an II* (Aix, 1912); C. Lucas, *The Structure of the Terror: The Example of Javogues and the Loire* (Oxford, 1973); R. R. Palmer, *Twelve Who Ruled: The Year of the Terror in the French Revolution* (Princeton, 1971); H. Wallon, *Les représentants du peuple en mission et la justice révolutionnaire dans les départements*, 5 vols. (Paris, 1889-95).

G. V. Taylor

Related entries: COMMITTEE OF PUBLIC SAFETY; JULLIEN; LAW OF 14 FRIMAIRE; 9 THERMIDOR YEAR II; PLAIN, THE; *SCRUTIN EPURATOIRE*; THERMIDORIAN REACTION.

REPUBLIC, BATAVIAN. See BATAVIAN REPUBLIC.

REPUBLIC, CISALPINE. See CISALPINE REPUBLIC.

REPUBLIC, CISPADANE. See CISPADANE REPUBLIC.

REPUBLIC, CISRHENANE. See CISRHENANE REPUBLIC.

REPUBLIC, HELVETIC. See HELVETIC REPUBLIC.

REPUBLIC, LIGURIAN. See LIGURIAN REPUBLIC.

REPUBLIC, PARTHENOPEAN. See PARTHENOPEAN REPUBLIC.

REPUBLIC, ROMAN. See ROMAN REPUBLIC.

REPUBLICAN CALENDAR. See CALENDAR OF THE FRENCH REPUBLIC.

REPUBLIC OF MAYENCE (or MAINZ) (1793). In September 1792 the Army of the Rhine under A.-P. Custine advanced into Germany from Landau, while the minor princes offered little resistance. On 25 September the French took Spire, on 5 October Worms, and on 21 October Mainz, as the elector-archbishop K. F. von Erthal, along with the upper clergy and nobility, fled his capital.

As early as 1790 there had been disturbances among the artisans of this city, and a middle-class opposition to increasingly despotic rule had developed, led by frustrated intellectuals, who were concentrated in *Lesegesellschaften* (reading rooms) sympathetic to the Revolution. It was the latter who founded the Society of the Friends of Liberty and Equality on 23 October. The German refugees, F. C. Cotta and A. J. Dorsch, an enlightened theologian and former professor of philosophy at Mainz, had accompanied Custine's army from Strasbourg and helped to establish this Jacobin club. G. Boehmer (1761-1839), assistant headmaster of the Protestant gymnasium at Worms, hailed Custine at Spire and became his secretary and the director of the *Mainzer Nationalzeitung*. The leaders of the club were A. J. Hofmann (1752-1849), professor of natural law, and the famous author G. Forster (1754-94), who soon became the guiding spirit of the club, which in turn became the center of local politics. Although it was not affiliated with the mother society in Paris, there was correspondence between the two clubs. Other members active in the society were professor of medicine G. C. Wedekind (1761-1831), the theologian F. A. Blau (1754-98), the mathematician M. Metternich (1741-1825), the mathematician and army officer R. Eickemeyer (1753-1825), the theologian F. G. Pape (1766-1816), the police commissioner F. K. Macke (1756-1844), and J. N. Vogt (1756-1836), professor of history who was a follower of Anacharsis Cloots (the "Citizen of the World") and wrote *A History of the Universal Republic*. The club members were predominantly petty bourgeois: intellectuals, students, minor officials, clerks, shopkeepers, and a good number of artisans and craftsmen as well. Peak membership reached 480.

Initially Custine promised not to interfere in local administration or with the political decisions of the people. Representatives of the merchants declared themselves in favor of a somewhat reformed Old Regime, while the *clubbistes* urged the general to appoint a new administration, which he did for the entire region between Landau, Bingen, and Mainz on 19 November. However, the moderate Custine and the new administration under Dorsch were slow in abol-

ishing feudal rights as the National Convention had ordered for all occupied
territories in its decree of 15 December. Both the Jacobins of Mainz and leaflets
that reflected peasant views and grievances raised objections.

After a heated campaign, on 24 February 1793 elections finally took place
for a Rhenish-German National Convention, the first in German history. Few
of the eligible voters participated and fewer proportionally in Mainz than in the
country. The influence of the Catholic church was still strong; and the Revolutionaries were suspected of being Protestants, defrocked clergy, and Freemasons. Furthermore, the economic benefits from the new order had not been
realized. Property confiscated from exiles and *émigrés* was not put on sale
immediately, and other advantages were negated by the heavy contributions
required by the occupiers, who were living off the country. In addition, the
French began to suffer military setbacks. They had lost Frankfurt on 2 December,
and the Prussians and Saxons were threatening to besiege Mainz. On 12 February
Custine ordered every household to set aside food reserves for seven months.
Such an atmosphere was not conducive to accepting the existing situation as
definitive or to countering effectively counterrevolutionary propaganda with convincing arguments for the passive majority, even though the Revolutionary press
tried its best.

The Rhenish-German National Convention, to which half of the deputies were
peasants, opened on 17 March, with Hofmann presiding. The next day it declared
its separation from the Holy Roman Empire and the abolition of the privileges
of the clergy and nobility. Simultaneously, at the initiative of A.-C. Merlin de
Thionville, the Jacobin club of Mainz was purged of its moderate members and
Forster was reelected chairman. Realizing the impossibility of establishing a
republic of Mayence that was capable of sustaining itself, on 21 March the
Convention adopted Forster's motion for a reunion with the French Republic as
the common homeland of liberty, equality, and fraternity. This request was
accepted by the French National Convention unanimously, and at its last session
on 31 March, the Rhenish-German assembly selected Hofmann to be in charge
of effecting this change. (This example of *Anschluss* had been preceded by the
burghers and peasants of Bergzabern and some thirty other communities of the
Palatinate who had revolted against the duke of Deux-Ponts and had opted to
join the French Republic on 14-15 March 1793.)

The siege of Mainz—described by J. W. Goethe in *Die Belagerung von
Mainz*—lasted from 10 April to its capitulation on 23 July 1793. Some of the
Mainz Jacobins like Hofmann, Dorsch, Wedekind, and Eickemeyer escaped the
harsh repression by fleeing to Strasbourg or Paris; others, such as Metternich,
Blau, and Boehmer, who would later play a part in the Cisrhenane movement,
were captured and not released from prison or exchanged until the Treaty of
Basel in 1795. Mainz itself was to remain the last outpost of the Holy Roman
Empire on the left bank of the Rhine until 1798.

F. G. Dreyfus, *Société et mentalité à Mayence dans la seconde moitié du dix-huitième
siècle* (Paris, 1968); F. Dumont, *Die Mainzer Republik, 1792-1793* (Alzey, 1982); A.

Hofmann, *Darstellung de Mainzer Revolution* (Frankfurt/Leipzig, 1793-1794); H. Mathy, *Als Mainz französisch war* (Mainz, 1968); H. Scheel, *Die Mainzer Republik*, vol. 1 (Berlin, 1975); C. Träger, *Mainz Zwischen Rot und Schwarz: Die Mainzer Republik in Schriften, Reden und Briefen* (Berlin, 1963).

W. Markov

Related entries: CLOOTS; CUSTINE; FORSTER; MERLIN DE THION-VILLE; TREATY OF BASEL.

"RESULT OF THE COUNCIL" (27 December 1788), a declaration of the Royal Council on the composition of the Estates General convoked for 1789, which doubled the number of representatives of the Third Estate (commoners) to equal the combined number of deputies of the First and Second Estates (clergy and nobility). J. Necker, minister of finance and architect of the policy, persuaded Louis XVI and the queen, and a majority of the ministers to accept doubling. Anger at the nobility, who had been contesting royal authority since 1787, induced the royal couple to agree. Necker favored doubling to secure financial support for the government. He also argued, in a report published with the "Result of the Council," that the importance the Third Estate had acquired— their greater numbers, wealth, and enlightenment, the heavier tax burden they bore, their knowledge of economic affairs—justified their increased representation, which public opinion also demanded.

The government's decision momentarily ended the controversy raging in the autumn of 1788 over representation in the Estates General. An aristocratic party of *parlementaires*, royal princes, upper clergy, and nobility favored equal representation of the orders to ensure the first two estates, especially the nobility, of maintaining political preeminence. Patriots, or the national party, a coalition of liberal nobles and clergy and bourgeois, supported by individuals and groups in the Third Estate, demanded doubling and vote by head, whose effect would be to strengthen the political role of the Third Estate.

The decision to double the Third brought popular support for the crown, but government silence on voting procedure, whether by order or by head, prompted renewed controversy. Necker, in his report, indicated the orders would deliberate separately, meeting and voting together only by mutual consent. The effect of doubling being in doubt, the contest for political power continued and centered on the mode of voting. Two months of stalemate in the Estates General ended on 27 June 1789, when the king, clergy, and nobles accepted deliberations in common and vote by head, making the Estates General a single National Assembly.

J. Egret, *Necker, ministre de Louis XVI* (Paris, 1975); M. B. Garrett, *The Estates General of 1789; The Problems of Composition and Organization* (New York, 1935); J. Necker, *Résultat du Conseil d'Etat du Roi, tenu à Versailles, le 27 décembre 1788* (Paris, 1788).

V. R. Gruder

Related entries: ASSEMBLY OF NOTABLES; NECKER; PARLEMENTS; *QU'EST-CE QUE C'EST LE TIERS ETAT?*; SIEYES.

REUBELL, JEAN-FRANCOIS (1747-1807), French Revolutionary and director. Reubell was born in Colmar, Alsace, where his father J. Reubell was a royal public notary and a secretary-interpreter of the Conseil souverain, the equivalent of a parlement. Jean-François attended the University of Strasbourg from 1764 to 1766 and received his *diplôme de licencié-ès-lois*. On his return to Colmar, he was appointed a lawyer at the Conseil souverain. Soon Reubell acquired an outstanding reputation as a lawyer. One case that added to his fame was the legal battle between the peasants of the villages of Riquewehr and Horbourg against the duke of Wurtemburg, who attempted to raise the amount of *corvées* of his Alsatian peasants. Reubell defended the peasants and won their case in 1776 and 1785.

In March 1789 Reubell was elected a deputy of the Third Estate to the Estates General from the district of Colmar-Sélestat. In the Estates General he was the first to suggest on 8 May 1789 that the delegates of the Third Estate declare themselves the nation and begin the renovation of the monarchy without the aid of the delegates of the nobility and the clergy.

In the National Constituent Assembly, Reubell distinguished himself as a fairly radical deputy who combated subversive, anti-Revolutionary elements, supported the suppression of the seignorial system, opposed the granting of a suspensive veto to the king, demanded a rigorous enforcement of Revolutionary measures such as the Civil Constitution of the Clergy, advocated a forced loan of 170 million *livres* to solve the financial crisis, and endorsed the annexation of Avignon and the Comtat Venaissin.

He and other Alsatian deputies strenuously opposed the granting of citizenship to Jews because of their constituents' fear of Jewish financial power in their province. On 27 September 1791, the Assembly finally granted citizenship to all Jews but, at Reubell's insistence, also agreed that the district directories of the Upper and Lower Rhine departments issue instructions on the manner of liquidating debts owed by Christians to Jews.

Reubell also advocated citizenship for the so-called free colored in the French colonies and on 13 May 1791 persuaded the Assembly to accept his proposal that guaranteed them the rights of active citizenship. Colonial representatives opposed this decree and succeeded in having it revoked in September 1791.

In June 1791 Reubell refused to join those who called for the abolition of the monarchy. He resigned from the Parisian Jacobin club and joined the more moderate Feuillants.

He was elected *procureur-général-syndic* of the Upper Rhine department on 16 July 1791, a position he assumed the following September. In his new function Reubell vigorously enforced Revolutionary measures, policies that aroused the hatred of many. He advocated a defensive war and a war of liberation against the German princes as early as December 1791 in order to protect his native Alsace.

In September 1792 he was elected deputy to the National Convention where he associated himself with the more moderate elements. On 15 December he,

A.-C. Merlin de Thionville, and N. Hausmann were elected commissioners to the Army of the Rhine. In the city of Mainz and in other German communities, Reubell and his colleagues vigorously enforced Revolutionary measures. In July 1793 Reubell and Merlin, who were in the besieged city of Mainz, negotiated the surrender terms and later successfully defended their actions before the National Convention, where many deputies had been critical of the surrender and even accused the commissioners of having been bribed by the enemy. Another rumor had it that Reubell and Merlin had enriched themselves in Mainz by stealing the silver, gilt, jewelry, and vases of the elector. This charge was not without foundation, and in October 1793 a Revolutionary committee found and confiscated two trunks of silver in Reubell's Parisian residence. Meanwhile, Reubell and Merlin were ordered to accompany the former Mainz garrison to the Vendée, but Reubell was recalled in the fall of 1793. Subsequently, he lived in obscurity until July 1794.

He joined the Thermidorians and, according to his own account, saved the counterrevolution on 27 July when he prevented F. Hanriot, commander of the Paris National Guard, from seizing the guns and men that protected the National Convention. In March 1795 he was elected to the Committee of Public Safety, serving in the diplomatic section. He and E.-J. Sieyès were sent on an important diplomatic mission to the Batavian Republic, where they concluded the Treaty of the Hague in May. In August 1795, Reubell was dispatched on mission to the Army of the Rhine and Moselle and to Basel where he was to assist in the preparation of a campaign across the Rhine river.

After his return to Paris, Reubell was elected a director of the new regime, the Directory. Many contemporaries and historians have treated neither the Directory nor Reubell very kindly. The regime is often depicted as corrupt and inefficient, and Reubell seemed to have personified most, if not all, of the evils of the new government. Furthermore, Reubell is often described as a rude, coarse, harsh, and irascible person. Much of the criticism could be justified. Reubell was irascible and short-tempered, a condition caused in part by his physical ailments. But he was not corrupt, and he had an excellent mind and linguistic skills. Because of the forcefulness of his character and personality, Reubell became the most influential person in the Directory during the first few years.

Reubell's principal interest was foreign affairs. He remained a fervent advocate of the annexation of the Rhineland and Belgium, which had been annexed by the National Convention in October 1795. He wanted to maintain French influence in the Batavian Republic and favored close and friendly ties with Prussia. He disapproved of the Treaty of Campoformio in 1797 because it failed to transfer the entire Rhineland to France and did not provide compensation for Prussia. He strongly supported the Swiss revolution in 1798 which he, N. Bonaparte, and the Swiss revolutionary P. Ochs planned in December 1797. Although French armies were initially welcomed in various Swiss cantons, much of the initial enthusiasm dissipated, especially as a result of French requisitions and meddling in internal affairs. Reubell's brother-in-law, J.-J. Rapinat, became the special butt of popular wrath. Reubell opposed the Egyptian expedition and once even urged General Bonaparte to resign. Furthermore, he came to regret the policy of revolutionizing other nations, except Switzerland, and confessed that repeated victories had puffed pride and perhaps corrupted heads.

Reubell retired from the Directory on 9 May 1799 when he drew the negative lot. He had been elected to the Council of Ancients in April 1799, and he had to defend himself in the months following against many charges, including corruption and treason, during his directorship.

After the coup d'état of 18-19 Brumaire, Reubell withdrew from public life. The first consul, who respected Reubell for his ability, was eager to include him in his government but wanted the latter to ask for a position. Reubell was unwilling to do so, although he faced serious financial difficulty. He retired to Colmar, where he died on 24 November 1807.

He left his widow, M.-A. Mouhat, only 100,000 francs, although she was subsequently granted a pension by Emperor Napoleon. Reubell had two sons, Jean-Jacques, born in 1777, and François-Xavier, born in 1780. The former was a general in Napoleon's army until 1809.

R. Guyot, *Le Directoire et la paix de l'Europe* (Paris, 1912); R. Guyot, ed., *Documents biographiques sur J.-F. Reubell, 1747-1807* (Paris, 1911); G. D. Homan, *Jean-Francois Reubell, French Revolutionary, Patriot, and Director, 1747-1807* (The Hague, 1971).

G. D. Homan

Related entries: ACTIVE CITIZEN; ANNEXATION; AVIGNON; BATAVIAN REPUBLIC; CIVIL CONSTITUTION OF THE CLERGY; COUP OF 18 BRUMAIRE; DIRECTORY; FEUILLANTS; JEWS; MERLIN DE THIONVILLE; REPUBLIC OF MAYENCE; THERMIDORIAN REACTION; TREATY OF CAMPOFORMIO.

REVEILLON RIOT (27-28 April 1789), popular disturbance in Paris on the eve of the meeting of the Estates General. The only certain facts about the so-called Réveillon riot are that the factory and residence of a wealthy Parisian wallpaper manufacturer named Réveillon in the rue de Montreuil were forcibly entered and ransacked by a mob on the night of 28 April 1789. The premises were guarded by troops who fired on the attackers and caused a significant but disputed number of casualties, a fact that suggests that the crowd was in either a very angry or determined state of mind. It is also agreed that none of Réveillon's workers were involved and that he had a reputation of being a good employer who paid higher than usual wages. Virtually all other aspects of the affair are conjectural or controversial.

There is also general agreement that the triggering factor was a rumor, although the accuracy of that rumor is a matter of dispute. According to this rumor, Réveillon, in a meeting of the Third Estate of his district on 23 April 1789, had made some remarks to the effect that he would like to see a return to the old days when wages were 15 *sous* per day rather than the current 20 *sous*. He had reportedly been seconded in this by another manufacturer of the faubourg Saint-

Antoine named Henriot. An official report by the chief of police confirms the fact that by evening, this rumor was causing some grumbling among the workers of the *faubourg*, but nothing further came of it until Monday, 27 April, a workers' day off. Around 3 P.M., some 500 to 600 citizens gathered at the Bastille, burned Réveillon in effigy, and proceeded to parade dummy figures of both manufacturers around the city. By evening the mob was reported to have numbered 3,000 and to have taken up a position in the place de Grève in front of the Hôtel de Ville. Although temporarily persuaded to disperse by three electors of the Third Estate, the crowd formed again near Réveillon's factory. Finding his house well guarded by troops, it turned away to Henriot's house nearby and ransacked it but was then dispersed by troops without any known loss of life.

During the following day, however, despite the fact that it was a workday, apparently successful attempts were made to recruit additional supporters from the shops and workplaces of the *faubourg* and its neighboring districts. By 5 P.M. Tuesday, the assembled mob was evidently larger than that of the previous evening because it swept aside the fifty men guarding Réveillon's establishment and proceeded to vent its feelings by destroying whatever it could, no doubt consuming large quantities of his wine in the process. Additional troops arrived and fired on the crowd; by 8 P.M. matters were under control.

It is difficult to believe that the rumored remarks made by two members of the seemingly popular Third Estate could have provoked such a violent reaction among working people who were not even their employees, even in the highly charged political atmosphere of that moment. It is even more difficult to credit the reports stating that the crowd had shouted *"Vive le tiers état"* and *"Vive M. Necker,"* as well as *"Vive le Roi."* It is this great contrast between seeming cause and effect that has led G. Rudé, who has made the most thorough investigation of this incident as part of his study of the crowd in the French Revolution, to conclude that the real cause of the violent reaction was the shortage and the corresponding sharp and sustained increase in the price of bread that workers had experienced during the winter and spring of 1789. The wage earner, who normally spent about half his income on bread, now found it taking almost three-quarters of his earnings and an employer was now advocating the reduction of his income still further. Seen in this light, the workers' anger becomes more understandable. Although Rudé considers the possibility that the attack might have been stirred up by personal animus against the two businessmen (they vehemently denied ever having made the remarks attributed to them) or by clerical or aristocratic bribes, he concludes that hunger was the main motive behind the disturbances. The only direct evidence that he can cite, however, is the statement of the bookseller diarist, Hardy, that the rioters, after the attack on Réveillon's, did talk of continuing their activity the next day "in order to obtain a decrease in the price of bread," and the fact that the only other establishments that suffered damage were food shops. A contemporary pamphlet also attributed the fracas to hunger.

Conclusions about the number of casualties and the social composition of the crowd seem equally tentative. The official figures were twenty-five killed and twenty-two wounded, but Rudé claims that the authorities underestimated the numbers in order to keep from inflaming the situation. Other contemporary accounts speak of hundreds killed, but such rumors or unverified reports were probably highly inflated. The names and other information given in the official police report of some seventy-one persons killed, wounded, or arrested show that a majority of this sample of the rioters were from the faubourg Saint-Antoine and its immediately adjoining districts. The record also shows that a majority were wage earners (fifty-eight out of seventy-one).

The fact that thirty-two of the thirty-seven arrested (a less random group presumably than those shot) were wage earners provides perhaps the most compelling evidence of Rudé's thesis that the rioters were primarily a working-class group engaged in a typical Old Regime protest against the shortage and high cost of bread, with little or no participation by the bourgeoisie. Thus he distinguished this essentially localized pre-Revolutionary type of riot from the subsequent Revolutionary *journées*, which typically were characterized by the participation of all elements of the Third Estate from all areas of the city.

C. L. Chassin, *Les cahiers et les élections de Paris en 1789*, 4 vols. (Paris, 1888-89); J. Collot, "L'affaire Réveillon," *Rev. des ques. hist.* 121 (1934-35); G. Rudé, *The Crowd in the French Revolution* (New York, 1959).

                                                                                    R. W. Greenlaw

Related entries: FRENCH GUARDS; *JOURNEES*.

REVELLIERE-LEPEAUX, LOUIS-MARIE. See LA REVELLIERE-LEPEAUX.

REVOLTS, MUNICIPAL. See MUNICIPAL REVOLTS.

REVOLUTIONARY ARMIES. See *ARMEES REVOLUTIONNAIRES*.

REVOLUTIONARY GOVERNMENT, THEORY OF. See THEORY OF REVOLUTIONARY GOVERNMENT.

REVOLUTIONARY SYMBOLISM. See SYMBOLISM.

REVOLUTIONARY TRIBUNAL, a special high court established in 1793 to try crimes against the Republic. The destruction of the Old Regime in France after 1789 meant the total reorganization of the established system of justice. Legislation enacted in 1790-91 established a new basis for legal authority and provided for a rationalized, decentralized, and elective system of courts. At the summit was a high court created to judge crimes against the nation. The penal code enacted in September and October 1791 represented a far more humane system of justice than had existed previously.

The reorganized legal system was severely strained following the outbreak of war in 1792, the overthrow of Louis XVI, and the rising wave of counterrevolution within France. Ineffectiveness by the high court in handling cases brought before it led the Legislative Assembly to establish a special tribunal on 17 August 1792 to handle the large number of political suspects, particularly those associated with the fallen monarchy. This new court, from which there was no appeal, functioned slowly and acquitted numerous well-known royalists. Its inadequacies, combined with tensions caused by the Allied invasion, led to a massacre of suspects in Paris prisons in early September, when some 1,100 individuals fell victim to popular vengeance. The court of 17 August was finally abolished in November 1792.

Not until March 1793 was a new court established to take its place. This body, which became famous as the Revolutionary Tribunal, was instituted at a time when Revolutionary France seemed in a desperate situation. Military defeats in the Low Countries, the treason of General C. Dumouriez, the eruption of counterrevolution in the Vendée, and riots in Paris impelled the government to create a court that would judge political crimes. On the proposal of the deputy J.-B. Carrier, the Convention on 9 March 1793 approved the principle of a Revolutionary court. A decree establishing and organizing a special criminal tribunal was approved the following day after hurried discussion. It was to have jurisdiction over "all counterrevolutionary activities, all attacks on liberty, equality, unity, the indivisibility of the Republic, the internal and external security of the state, and all plots tending to reestablish the monarchy or any other authority hostile to liberty, equality, and the sovereignty of the people." Situated at Paris, the tribunal was composed of five judges, a twelve-man jury, and a public prosecutor with two assistants. Its members were to be chosen by the Convention and placed under the supervision of a Commission of Six, all deputies. The tribunal was to follow the general rules of criminal procedure then in effect, but the property of those condemned to death would be confiscated by the state. The power of control by a commission was soon removed, however, before the tribunal began hearing cases early in April.

Its work load was expanded when the Convention ordered lower criminal courts to send before the Revolutionary Tribunal all cases described in the enabling law and when the court was permitted to arrest all those who were denounced to it by public officials and private citizens. Initially the procedure that the tribunal followed was orderly. A suspect would be arrested, interrogated, and then sent to Paris to await trial. There the accused would be given a preliminary hearing, which was conducted by a judge, the public prosecutor, or one of his assistants (the most famous being A.-Q. Fouquier-Tinville). This examination was brief and served primarily to establish the identity of the accused, to obtain a statement from him about the evidence gathered, and to learn whether he had secured legal counsel. The actual trial involved presentation to the jury of an act of accusation and the evidence against the suspect, the summoning of witnesses for the prosecution and the defense (or written depositions from them), the judge's charge to the jury, the deliberation of the jurors, their rendering of a verdict, and the passing of sentence by the presiding judge. Sentences ranged from acquittal to death, deportation, imprisonment, or referral of the case to another court.

Until September 1793 the Revolutionary Tribunal proceeded slowly and deliberately, with only forty-nine death sentences being imposed. (Among them was that of C. Corday, convicted of assassinating J.-P. Marat.) To improve the efficiency of the court, the Convention increased the number of jurors to thirty and divided the tribunal into two sections, which could deliberate separately. Nonetheless, the slowness and leniency of the court angered both Jacobins and *sans-culottes*, who felt that Revolutionary justice was being cheated at a time of great national danger. Pressured by an outburst of popular agitation in the capital, the Convention on 5 September made terror the order of the day and transformed the Revolutionary Tribunal in order to speed up its work. The number of judges was increased to sixteen, that of jurors to sixty, and the staff of the public prosecutor expanded. Four different sections could now function independently. Many more accused now filled the prisons of Paris as a result of the Law of Suspects passed on 17 September, which extended the definition of crimes committed against the Republic. A special prison, the Conciergerie, was put at the disposition of the court.

Under its new president, M.-J.-A. Herman, the Revolutionary Tribunal stepped up its death sentences, with executions rising to a total of 209 between September and December 1793. Among those condemned were the former queen Marie Antoinette, twenty-one leading Girondins, the duc d'Orléans (Philippe Egalité), the ex-mayor of Paris J.-S. Bailly, and the Feuillant A. Barnave. By the spring of 1794 the work load of the tribunal further increased as local Revolutionary courts were closed down in the interests of centralization and as the Allied invasion and civil war intensified. Death sentences numbered 942 between January and the end of May 1794. Notable among the victims were the farmers general (including the chemist A. Lavoisier), Madame Elisabeth, sister of the late Louis XVI, J.-R. Hébert and his followers, and G.-J. Danton and his associates. Increasing use was made of the amalgam, the grouping together of individuals charged with the same crime.

Harsh as the Revolutionary Tribunal had been until now, it was made even more severe by the Law of 22 Prairial Year II (10 June 1794). Enacted after a sharp debate in the Convention, it reorganized the court, allocating the number of judges at twelve and that of jurors at sixty. While continuing to operate in sections, each would be composed of three judges and nine jurors, seven of whom were necessary to reach a verdict. More important, the legislation dispensed with the preliminary questioning of the accused, left the summoning of witnesses to the discretion of the court, which could act on written evidence alone, and effectively denied the accused legal counsel. The list of enemies of the people who might be brought before the Revolutionary Tribunal was greatly expanded to include economic as well as political criminals, specifically those accused of hoarding and dishonest contracting; defeatists who spread unfavorable news about the war effort; and corrupt public officials. The law implicitly included members of the Convention itself, a fact that caused disquiet among the deputies. The severity of the law may be traced to assassination attempts made against J.-M. Collot d'Herbois and M. Robespierre in May and the widespread belief in a vast counterrevolutionary conspiracy.

The Law of 22 Prairial inaugurated the Great Terror, which lasted until late July. The large number of suspects in prison—more than 8,000 in Paris alone—and the simplified legal procedure resulted in a dramatic increase in death sentences passed—more than 1,300 during the summer of 1794. Over 900 were executed in the capital in July. Batches of prisoners, often unknown to each other, were condemned at one time and sent to the guillotine in slow-moving tumbrils through the streets of Paris. Among the victims were a group of Carmelite nuns, the poet A. Chénier, and suspects accused of conspiracy in the prisons.

The fear generated by this acceleration of the Terror combined with military successes on the frontiers that seemed to make it less necessary led to the overthrow of Robespierre on 9 Thermidor (27 July). He, along with other members of the Convention and Paris Commune, were condemned to death by the Revolutionary Tribunal without a formal trial, simply on the basis of the establishment of their identities. They were followed to the scaffold by seventy-one members of the Commune on 29 July and twelve more the next day, all without formal proceedings being held.

On 14 Thermidor (1 August) the Thermidorian Convention repealed the Law of 22 Prairial and nine days later ordered that the legal procedures governing the operation of the Revolutionary Tribunal would be those previously in effect. New members of the now purged court were chosen and the public prosecutor, Fouquier-Tinville, who had become notorious for his severity, was ordered arrested. Because the number of prisoners awaiting trial was rapidly reduced through relaxation of the law, a sharp decline in the work of the Revolutionary Tribunal took place. Only forty-six death sentences were meted out between August and December 1794. Among them was the Jacobin deputy J.-B. Carrier, accused of excesses in repressing the Vendée rebellion.

During the remaining five months of the existence of the court, the case load dropped dramatically. Only seventeen persons were condemned, sixteen of them former members of the tribunal itself, including Herman and Fouquier-Tinville, the latter convicted of judicial murder following a lengthy trial. The group was guillotined on 6 May 1795 to great public rejoicing.

With the Revolutionary Tribunal no longer needed, the Thermidorian Convention formally abolished it by its decree of 31 May. The crimes that had once fallen under its jurisdiction were transferred to the criminal courts of the various departments. During its existence from March 1793 to May 1795, the Tribunal pronounced more than 2,700 death sentences. Of the victims whose occupations can be identified, 20 percent came from the nobility, 9 percent from the clergy, 53 percent from the middle classes, and 18 percent from the lower classes. If harsh in its treatment of suspects, particularly in the summer of 1794, the court served to intimidate enemies of the Republic and thereby assure it of victory in its struggle against enemies at home and abroad.

E. Campardon, *Le Tribunal révolutionnaire de Paris*, 2 vols. (Paris, 1866); J. L. Godfrey, *Revolutionary Justice: A Study of the Organization, Personnel, and Procedure of the Paris Tribunal, 1793-1795* (Chapel Hill, 1951); D. Greer, *The Incidence of the Terror during the French Revolution: A Statistical Study* (Cambridge, Mass., 1935); H. Wallon, *Histoire du Tribunal révolutionnaire de Paris*, 6 vols. (Paris, 1880-82).

J. Friguglietti

Related entries: CARRIER; CORDAY D'ARMANS; FOUQUIER-TINVILLE; LAW OF 22 PRAIRIAL; 9 THERMIDOR YEAR II; SEPTEMBER 1792 MAS-SACRES; TERROR, THE; VENDEE.

REVOLUTIONS DE FRANCE ET DE BRABANT, newspaper written and edited by Camille Desmoulins, 28 November 1789-July 1791, which sprang from his political activities in 1789. That year found him eagerly anticipating the new opportunities that might emerge with the meeting of the Estates General. Frustrated in his law career and committed from school days to republicanism, he was receptive to change. His first real chance to participate in these momentous events occurred in July 1789. Parisians, convinced a plot existed against them, heard on 12 July that the seemingly progressive minister J. Necker had been dismissed. They feared this signaled an attack on them. Desmoulins may have shared this view, but he also felt that the reforms proposed by the nation's representatives would benefit from an insurrection. Haranguing the crowds gathered in the Palais Royal, he and other orators urged listeners to defend themselves with arms. They swarmed out into the streets, gained additional followers, and two days later seized the Bastille. Contemporaries believed this action fixed France on a Revolutionary course. They credited Desmoulins with instigating the uprising and immediately elevated him to fame. He cemented this success by publishing two popular pamphlets. His desire for a more permanent forum led him in November to establish a newspaper, the *Révolutions de France et de Brabant*.

To produce the periodical, Desmoulins contracted with a printer named Garnery who promised him the substantial amount of 1,000 *écus* annually for his efforts. If subscriptions topped 3,000, the salary would quadruple. Together they marketed a weekly of forty-eight pages selling for 6 *livres* 15 *sous* quarterly. On the front of each issue appeared a political cartoon.

Desmoulins' accomplishments as a newspaperman added to his notoriety. Although in theory the periodical was to report events, in actuality it provided a platform for the journalist to advance his goals for the Revolution. He strongly advocated direct democracy, defending and praising those who agreed with him while blasting opponents. He delivered this message in inimitable style, satirical, pungent, and powerful. Scholars generally consider his paper the best written of the period. Parisians too appreciated the journal, evidenced by the substantial circulation. Desmoulins' enemies also paid tribute to his skills in riposte by instituting legal actions and political protests against him. Although ordered to pay 1,200 *livres*, a large settlement, to one plaintiff, Desmoulins generally escaped such complaints unscathed.

Despite successes, Desmoulins decided to quit after six months of publishing his paper. Speculation on his motives includes disagreements with the publisher, exhaustion combined with a lack of resolve, a desire to remain home with his bride, disappointment that no republic seemed to be emerging, and dissatisfaction with his remuneration. Desmoulins' retirement permitted Garnery to recruit J.-L. Carra to continue the journal. But no sooner had Desmoulins relinquished his role on the *Révolutions* than he resumed publication with a new publisher, J.-J. Laffrey. Again Desmoulins' motives remain unclear, although it appears pressure from his political allies and his need for acceptance encouraged his return. His resumption of publication forced out Garnery and Carra after only three issues. With renewed vigor, Desmoulins worked with Laffrey until the seventy-third issue, when he negotiated a new agreement with a printer named Caillard.

Desmoulins continued the popular journal through the eighty-sixth issue, published in July 1791, when the Champ de Mars protest disrupted matters. The journalist had been an avid supporter of this popular antiroyalist rally. When the government smashed this demonstration with a hail of bullets, Desmoulins, fearing further repression, quit his post. Some of those factors that had led to his first resignation may also have reinforced the decision, for when difficulties abated, he did not resume the paper. The journalist intended that his unfilled subscriptions be completed by the *Révolutions de Paris*, but his printer Caillard secured J.-F.-N. Dusaulchoy to write the periodical. The new recruit, a career journalist, was neither as radical nor interesting as Desmoulins, and the journal lasted only eighteen weeks more. A year later, in October 1792, in order to improve his then flagging political fortunes, Desmoulins tried to revive the *Révolutions de France et de Brabant*, but he could not recapture his original verve and gave up after two months.

J. R. Censer, "The Political Engravings of the *Révolutions de France et de Brabant*," *Eighteenth Cent. Life* 5 (1979); L. Gallois, *Histoire des Journaux*, vol. 2 (Paris, 1846); E. Hatin, *Histoire de la presse*, vol. 5; (Paris, 1860); J. Janssens, *Camille Desmoulins, le premier républicain de France* (Paris, 1973).

J. Censer

Related entries: BASTILLE, THE; CARRA; CHAMP DE MARS "MASSA-CRE"; DESMOULINS; NECKER.

REVOLUTIONS DE PARIS, weekly newspaper published by Louis-Marie Prudhomme from 1789 to 1794. First issued on 12 July 1789, *Révolutions de Paris* quickly established itself as one of the most influential journals of the Revolution. C. Desmoulins stated that it attracted 200,000 subscribers, and although such a high figure seems unlikely, it surely indicates a very large circulation. This journal owed its popularity to several factors. Although it generally espoused radical politics, the intelligence of its analyses and the completeness of its reporting could interest more moderate readers. Also well organized, the *Révolutions de Paris* often possessed a print of some current event.

Although Prudhomme (1752-1832), an Old Regime bookseller of antiestablishment materials, founded the journal and probably set its general goals, he did not do the reporting. For this he hired a number of journalists, including E. Loustalot, P.-S. Maréchal, and A. Chaumette, who wrote but did not sign their articles. Prudhomme took responsibility for producing the periodical. Early in the Revolution he purchased his own print shop, where he turned out the weekly. At the beginning he marketed the forty-eight-page paper for 36 *livres* annually.

Révolutions de Paris continued through 225 issues until Prudhomme ended it on 28 February 1794. Problems had begun for Prudhomme in late 1792 when be began to object to Revolutionary violence. Although he had previously joined with radicals to support the repression of royalists, he wanted toleration among republicans. As suspicion focused on him, he was briefly arrested in June 1793. Reinforced in his hostility to the Terror, concerned for his own future, and increasingly alarmed as executions augmented in the summer of 1793, Prudhomme stopped publication from August to October. When he resumed, he chose the strategy of obeisance. Apparently this neither removed his fear of the Terror nor his animosity to it, and he voluntarily ended the journal four months later.

G. Villacèque, "Les Révolutions de Paris" (doctoral dissertation, University of Toulouse, 1961).

J. Censer

Related entries: CHAUMETTE; LOUSTALOT; MARECHAL; PRUDHOMME.

RIGHTS OF MAN AND OF THE CITIZEN, DECLARATION OF THE.
See DECLARATION OF THE RIGHTS OF MAN AND OF THE CITIZEN.

RIVOLI, BATTLE OF. See BATTLE OF RIVOLI.

ROBESPIERRE, AUGUSTIN-BON-JOSEPH DE (called ROBESPIERRE THE YOUNGER) (1763-94), deputy to the Convention, representative on mission. Born at Arras on 21 January 1763, the younger brother of M. Robespierre in his youth followed the same pattern as his elder brother: a scholarship to the collège Louis-le-Grand in Paris, then, on returning to his birthplace of Arras, a position as a barrister that he began to exercise on the eve of the Revolution. The first years of the Revolution saw him participate in local Revolutionary politics as *procureur-syndic* of the city of Arras and subsequently as administrator of the department of the Pas-de-Calais (1790-91).

Thanks to his brother's prestige—doubtlessly—he was elected deputy to the National Convention (in nineteenth place) on 16 September 1792. He sat with the Mountain and took an active role in the struggles and denunciations that led to the fall of the Girondins in the early summer of 1793. Sent on mission to the Army of the Alps, he participated in operations in the region of Nice (September-October) before contributing, along with other representatives (J.-F. Ricord, P. Barras, L.-M.-S. Fréron), to the capture of Toulon (December 1793) where he noticed and appreciated N. Bonaparte. On the way back to Paris, he was active in the Haute-Saône and the Doubs, which provided him the occasion of denouncing dechristianization and what he judged to be local excesses of the Terror.

After his return to Paris, he seems to have had somewhat strained relations with his brother during his last months, probably because of his public expressions of moderation (for example, at the Jacobins on 3 Thermidor). But he clearly showed his solidarity with his brother when in the Convention on 9 Thermidor he asked to share Maximilien's fate. Wounded at the Hôtel de Ville when he attempted to commit suicide, he was carried to the scaffold dying on 10 Thermidor Year II.

On the whole, he needs to be reevaluated by going beyond the deprecatory judgments inspired by hatred and insisting on his mediocrity, as in the distorted view of their sister C. Robespierre in her prying—not to say abusive—memoirs, which were published after the fact and for a long time were almost the sole source of knowledge about the two brothers.

Anonymous, *Les arrêtés de Robespierre jeune et de Ricord dans les Alpes Maritimes* (Besançon, n.d.); H. Fleischmann, *Charlotte Robespierre et ses mémoires* (Paris, 1910); G. Michon, *Correspondance entre Maximilien et Augustin Robespierre*, 2 vols. (Paris, 1926); M. Sicard, *Robespierre jeune dans les Basses-Alpes* (Forcalquier, 1900).

M. Vovelle

Related entries: DECHRISTIANIZATION; GIRONDINS; MOUNTAIN; 9 THERMIDOR YEAR II; ROBESPIERRE, M.

ROBESPIERRE, MAXIMILIEN-FRANCOIS-ISIDORE DE (1758-94), lawyer and political leader who played a prominent role in the French Revolution from 1789 to 1794. A sincere democrat, Robespierre, like J.-J. Rousseau, believed that moral virtues were inseparable from the exercise of sovereignty. During the meeting of the Estates General, he took his place among the extreme elements of the patriots. The people, who appreciated the rigor of his principles, dubbed him the Incorruptible. His enemies attributed to him a dictatorial power that in fact he did not possess, while popular militants reproached him for lacking audacity. In the same way, historians have depicted him as some kind of bloody creature or a timorous bourgeois, according to their own political opinions.

His family, which had settled in Carvin (Pas-de-Calais) around 1650, counted a number of lawyers, including his grand-father and his father, François, who married the daughter of the brewer Carrault. Four months after the marriage, on 6 May 1758, Maximilien was born; then came two sisters, in 1760 Charlotte and in 1761 Henriette, who died young, and his brother Augustin in 1763. Another infant did not survive birth and cost their mother her life. The father left home, traveled abroad, and died in Munich in 1777, leaving the maternal grandparents to raise the orphans. From 1765 Maximilien attended the collège of the Oratorians at Arras and in 1769, thanks to the canon Aymé, obtained a scholarship from the abbey of Saint-Vaast to the collège Louis-le-Grand in Paris. A brilliant student, he obtained the bachelor's degree in 1780 and was admitted to the bar the following year. He then registered as a barrister with the bench in Arras and, along with his sister Charlotte, established himself on rue du Saumon (then called rue des Jésuites). He rapidly made a reputation for himself and was called to sit in the episcopal court whose jurisdiction extended over the provostship (*prévôté*) of the bishopric. He successfully pleaded numerous cases, including the famous lightning rod case, and his work afforded him a certain affluence.

In 1783 Robespierre was admitted to the Academy of Arras, became its chancellor two years later, and subsequently its president. He socialized with local notables and did not live an isolated and quiet life, as was for so long believed. F. Dubois de Fosseux, the perpetual secretary of the academy, depicts him mixing with the young people of the canton and "enlivening their dances by his presence." He participated in the meetings of the academy, and his *Mémoire sur les peines infamantes* was crowned at Metz. He joined the literary society of the Rosati and wrote elegies in the fashion of the period. It is claimed that around this time he became engaged to his cousin A. Desherties. By 1788 his unselfish skill was already well known. A lawyer for the poor, he upset people of privilege, speaking out against royal absolutism and arbitrary justice (*Mémoire pour le sieur Durand*). At the announcement of the Estates General, he launched his appeal *A la nation artésienne sur la nécessité de reformer les Etats d'Artois*. In late March 1789, the inhabitants of Arras chose him as one of their electors, and the Third Estate of the *bailliage* elected him fifth out of eight deputies for Artois. Thus began his political career; he was not yet thirty-one years old.

In Versailles and later in Paris, where he established himself on the rue de Saintonge, Robespierre kept his old habits, his careful dress, and his simple manners. Despite his youth, he very quickly attracted the attention of the National Assembly, which counted so many illustrious names. He spoke for the first time, it appears, on 18 May and intervened more than 500 times in the course of the Constituent's deliberations. In spite of his weak voice and the opposition that he aroused, he was able to get a hearing, and his motions were applauded. As evidence of his growing popularity, the royalist papers relentlessly pursued this "Demosthenes" who believed everything he said, this "monkey of Mirabeau's." He was excluded from committees and from the presidency; only once, on 19 June 1790, was he elected secretary of the Assembly. In April 1790 he was elected president of the Jacobin club, of which he had been a member since its creation. He was appointed judge in the district court of Versailles. He always tried to devote his energies entirely to his mandate as a deputy. His place was at the rostrum where the constitution was being elaborated. Nurtured on ancient history and the writings of the *philosophes*, he applauded the majestic principles of the Declaration of the Rights of Man and demanded that they be observed. He tenaciously fought for universal suffrage, for free access to the National Guard, to public employment, to military ranks, and for the free exercise of the right of petition; he opposed the royal veto, abuses of ministerial power, and religious and racial discrimination; he defended actors, Jews, and black slaves; he supported the unification of Avignon to France (September 1791). On 16 and 18 May 1791, he was responsible for the decision that deputies were ineligible for reelection to the next legislature.

Robespierre's ardent struggle for liberty increased the number of his enemies. After the attempted flight (20-21 June 1791) of the king, whose trial he demanded in vain, the slanders redoubled in their violence. He pressed for a vote on the constitution (8 September 1791) in order to call on "as large a democratic element as possible," by inviting all patriots to unite in his *Adresse aux français* (July 1791). Despite everything, the Jacobins were divided. Robespierre, whose life was threatened, moved his quarters to the home of M. Duplay. He succeeded in preserving the Society of the Friends of the Constitution. At the end of the Constituent's sessions, the people of Paris arranged for him, together with his friend J. Pétion, a genuine triumph, a celebration repeated in Artois in the course of a brief visit there (October 1791), the only respite in his five years of struggling.

Having excluded himself, along with all his colleagues, from the Legislative Assembly, Robespierre did not reduce his political activities. He did give up the lucrative post of public prosecutor in the criminal court of Paris, to which he had been elected on 11 June 1791. Henceforth he reserved his speeches for the Jacobins; up to 10 August 1792 he spoke there some 100 times. There he took his stand against the war that J.-P. Brissot wanted; he denounced the secret plots of the court and of the royalists and their collusion with Austria, the unpreparedness of the army, the possible treason of noble officers, whose discharge he requested yet one more time on 10 February 1792, while he defended the patriot soldiers, such as those of the Châteauvieux Regiment who had been imprisoned after the mutiny at Nancy. In May 1792 he founded a newspaper, *Le défenseur de la constitution*, a new weapon that reinforced his activity. He violently attacked the marquis de Lafayette, whom he suspected of wanting to establish a military dictatorship, and asked for his dismissal, which the Assembly rejected. The reverses suffered by French armies and the threatening invasion rallied the people to him. Although he had defined its objectives, he hesitated to advise insurrection. He told the *fédérés* gathered in Paris, "Fight the common enemy only with the sword of the law." The uprising of 10 August 1792 occurred without him. Like G.-J. Danton and J.-P. Marat, he did not participate in the fighting at the Tuileries. However, that very afternoon his section (Picques) named him to the Insurrectional Commune. He was designated to preside over the extraordinary tribunal of 17 August that had to judge those who had defended the king, while Danton, the minister of justice, named him to the Council of Justice, in vain. As a member of the Parisian electoral assembly, Robespierre followed its operations with care; there he received news of the September

Massacres and took the side of their authors. On 5 September, the capital elected him the first of its deputies to the National Convention.

In the Convention, the Girondins, who controlled the government and the administration, used the tactics of the counterrevolutionaries against Robespierre. From the first sessions they accused him of dictatorial ambitions, but the Assembly did not go along with them. In the king's trial, which opened in November 1792, Robespierre intervened eleven times, demanding death without delay; his speech of 3 December rallied the hesitant. With the help of his new paper, *Lettres à mes commettans*, he kept the provinces informed. The king was executed, but the struggle between Girondins and Montagnards remained indecisive. The popular masses, however, were disturbed by the scarcity of necessities and high prices; and General C. Dumouriez's treason precipitated crisis. A sort of popular front developed between the Parisian *sans-culottes* and the Mountain; the Girondin plan for a departmental guard was rejected. Then, on 26 May 1793, Robespierre invited the people to prepare an insurrection. On 31 May, he supported the decree of indictment against the Girondin chiefs and the accomplices of C. Dumouriez, which was voted in the case of twenty-nine of them on 2 June.

The democratic Constitution of 1793, adopted on 21 June, contained several articles drafted by Robespierre; however, those that limited property rights, that proposed the right of all to work, the establishment of a progressive tax, and of a Society of Nations appeared too audacious. Moreover, the implementation of the constitution, submitted to popular ratification and adopted by an enormous majority, was deferred until the peace.

At this point, the situation of the country seemed desperate. Threatened within by federalism and the Vendée and on the frontiers by the enemy coalition, the Revolution, in order to conquer, mobilized all its resources, human and material. What was needed was *une volunté une*, noted Robespierre in his diary, and such a dictatorial power characterizes the Revolutionary government. On 27 July Robespierre entered the Committee of Public Safety, which had been renewed on 10 July. As president of the Jacobin club since 7 August and then of the Convention since 22 August, he denounced the machinations of the *Enragés* and of J.-R. Hébert who would profit from the shortages to stir the Paris sections to revolt. To realize the *levée en masse*, the democratic dictatorship, total war, Robespierre also demanded the Terror. "It is weakness toward traitors that is destroying us," he declared while affirming the necessity of "a prompt, severe, and inflexible justice," guided by the laws against suspects (*Oeuvres complètes*). Nonetheless, he rejected useless executions and protected the deputies who protested the arrest of the Girondins and Madame Elisabeth, the sister of Louis XVI. The massacres tolerated by representatives on mission disgusted him; he demanded the recall of J.-L. Tallien, J.-B. Carrier, and P. Barras, who he said were dishonoring the Revolution. Public virtue, love of the fatherland, should guide their actions.

After L. Saint-Just and J.-N. Billaud-Varenne, Robespierre devoted his report of 15 Nivôse (25 December) to justifying the collective dictatorship of the Convention, administrative centralization, and the purge of the authorities. He spoke out against the factions that threatened the government. The Hébertists and popular militants would have desired more radical measures, would support dechristianization and the prosecution of those who monopolized provisions. Their excesses made the peasants fear that the decrees of 8 and 13 Ventôse, providing for a distribution of suspects' property among the indigent, would not be able to satisfy their expectations. Returning to the Jacobins after a month of illness, Robespierre denounced the Hébertists, who were executed on 12 Germinal (24 March 1794) together with foreign agents. Those who, like Danton, wanted to put a stop to the Terror and the war, attacked the policy of the Committee of Public Safety more violently. Robespierre, who still had some hesitation, won over the Convention against these so-called Indulgents. The Dantonist leaders and some deputies compromised by the liquidation of the Company of the Indies were guillotined on 16 Germinal (5 April). Public opinion, quite disconcerted, held Robespierre alone responsible for their fall and the ebbing of the Revolution.

A deist in the same way as J.-J. Rousseau, Robespierre condemned the "masquerades" of the Cult of Reason. In his report of 18 Floréal (7 May), he proclaimed the existence of God and the immortality of the soul and strained to rally patriots around a civic religion and the Cult of the Supreme Being. Robespierre's popularity remained great, as the testimonies that poured in to him after the unsuccessful assassination attempt by Admirat (3 Prairial, 22 May) demonstrate. The Jacobins, the Commune, and the National Guard, which F. Hanriot commanded, were devoted to him. The Convention elected him to its presidency on 16 Prairial by a vote of 216 out of 220 votes cast. In this capacity, on 20 Prairial he conducted the celebration of the Supreme Being in the Tuileries gardens. This provided, for his enemies, a new weapon.

After the passage of the Law of 22 Prairial (10 June), which reorganized the Revolutionary Tribunal and which Robespierre had endorsed, the opposition to him grew under the leadership of the representatives on mission whom he had threatened. His influence was challenged in the midst of the Committee of Public Safety, on one side by L. Carnot and on the other by J.-M. Collot d'Herbois and Billaud-Varenne. The Bureau of Police, which he directed along with Saint-Just and G. Couthon, gave umbrage to the Committee of General Security, which tried to set traps, like the Catherine Théot affair, for him. And P.-J. Cambon, who controlled finances, detested him.

His intensive work and his numerous speeches in the Assembly and at the Jacobins—which, since the beginning of the session, numbered around 450—had compromised Robespierre's health; he became irritable and distant. Embittered by the slanders spread about him, he stopped participating in the sessions of the Convention, then the meetings of the committee after 10 Messidor (28 June), and limited himself to denouncing the intrigues of counterrevolutionaries at the Jacobins. The people, who now saw the Republic victorious on the frontiers, tolerated the restrictions and requisitions more and more poorly. From his retreat, Robespierre followed the raging violence of the Terror and the growth of social opposition, stupefied.

Robespierre struggled to regain the support of public opinion and appeared again at the Committee of Public Safety on 5 Thermidor (23 July) and then on 8 Thermidor at the Convention, which he wanted to serve as an arbitrator. His last speech was at first applauded but then created a disturbance as the parliamentary majority turned against him. Despite the success that he had that evening at the Jacobins, the next day his opponents were able to prevent him from speaking before the Convention, which issued an indictment against him, together with his brother and his friends. Doubtlessly, he could have continued the struggle at the Hôtel de Ville where some of the sectional troops, who had been assembled by the Commune, were waiting; but Robespierre, who was not admitted to the Luxembourg prison, hesitated to lead an insurrection. In the confusion, some loyal forces left the Place de Grève. Declared an outlaw, Robespierre seriously wounded himself in the jaw with a pistol, and his supporters fell into disarray. Armed columns of the Convention rounded up the survivors, who were dumbfounded by their quick defeat. In the evening of 10 Thermidor (28 July), the first twenty-two condemned men, after the simple verification of their identity, were executed and buried in the cemetery of the Errancis. In all, 108 persons paid for their attachment to his ideas with their lives.

Robespierre disappeared—he was thirty-six years old. There followed an implacable campaign against his memory; a large part of his papers were destroyed. During the popular movements of the nineteenth century in France and abroad, people rendered homage to him, and his most famous speeches were reprinted. Nevertheless, his social ideal was restricted to reducing the extreme inequality of fortunes, to increasing the number of small property owners, and to ensuring work and education for all. A man devoted to ideas and to government policy, he remained a man of his time. If he was determined to destroy the monarchy, he did not propose any new socioeconomic structure to replace it.

Actes du colloque Robespierre (Paris, 1967); M. Bouloiseau, *Robespierre*, 5th ed. (Paris, 1976); M. Gallo, *L'homme Robespierre* (Paris, 1979); J. Massin, *Robespierre* (Paris, 1956); J. Poperen, *Robespierre. Textes choisis*, 2 vols. (Paris, 1957); M. Robespierre, *Oeuvres complètes de Maximilien Robespierre*, 10 vols. (Paris, 1939-); G. Rudé, *Robespierre* (Englewood Cliffs, N.J., 1967); J. M. Thompson, *Robespierre*, 2 vols. (Oxford, 1939); G. Walter, *Robespierre*, 2 vols. (Paris, 1961).

M. Bouloiseau

Related entries: AVIGNON; BATTLE OF FLEURUS; BILLAUD-VARENNE; BRISSOT DE WARVILLE; CALENDAR OF THE FRENCH REPUBLIC; CAMBON; COLLOT D'HERBOIS; COMMITTEE OF GENERAL SECURITY; COMMITTEE OF PUBLIC SAFETY; DECHRISTIANIZATION; ENLIGHTENMENT; *ENRAGES*; FEDERALISM; GIRONDINS; HEBERT; INDULGENTS; JACOBINISM; LAW OF 22 PRAIRIAL; MIRABEAU; MONTAGNARDS; 9 THERMIDOR YEAR II; PETION DE VILLENEUVE;

SELF-DENYING ORDINANCE; ROBESPIERRE, A.; SAINT-JUST; THE-
ORY OF REVOLUTIONARY GOVERNMENT; VENDEE; VENTOSE
DECREES.

**ROCHAMBEAU, JEAN-BAPTISTE-DONATIEN DE VIMEUR, COMTE
DE** (1725-1807), marshal of France. Rochambeau was born in the town of
Vendôme in 1725. As a sixteen-year-old cornet, he was a part of the army
Marshal Belle-Isle led into Bohemia during the War of the Austrian Succession;
he was present at the siege of Namur in 1746 and was wounded leading his
regiment in a charge at the Battle of Laufeldt the following year. He emerged
from this war a colonel.

Rochambeau served with distinction throughout the Seven Years War, participating in the capture of the fortress of Port Mahon in Minorca and receiving
a severe wound at the Battle of Klosterkamp, where his regiment was instrumental
in gaining a French victory. He subsequently was awarded the rank of *maréchal
de camp*.

After the war, Rochambeau was named inspector general of infantry, in which
capacity he was responsible for the tactical training of the French army. Because
he had carefully digested the lessons learned from the Seven Years War, Rochambeau was generally progressive in his thoughts on tactics, discipline, and
training, which made him an ideal choice to command the French troops sent
to aid General G. Washington's army in the War for American Independence.
A sensitive and sensible man, Rochambeau was well suited for the role of
commanding auxiliary forces in a military coalition, and he deservedly shares
credit for the final victory at Yorktown in 1781.

On his triumphant return to France. Rochambeau was given command of the
northern district, comprising Flanders, Picardy, and Artois. During the last years
of the *ancien régime*, Rochambeau reacted as an enlightened aristocrat to the
growing financial crisis in government, to those of the Second Estate who were
"very interested to perpetuate the abuses," and to the signs of growing discontent.

In July 1789 Rochambeau was reassigned to Alsace, where there was infectious
disorder. Passing through Paris two days before the storming of the Bastille, he
could hear shots and see patrols from the French Guards fraternizing with the
people. Rochambeau's understanding and character were probably as instrumental in maintaining order throughout Alsace as his sparing use of troops.

In 1790 he was assigned to command the *Armée du Nord*, and the following
year Louis XVI named him marshal of France because of his loyalty to the
crown. He enjoyed the dubious distinction of being the last marshal created
during the *ancien régime*. He was even offered the position of minister of war
in 1792, but his health and aversion to politics caused him to decline. His
experience with the *Armée du Nord* was not a happy one. The troops lacked
discipline, many of the officers had emigrated, and the army had become heavily
politicized. When France declared war against the Holy Roman Emperor in April
1792, Rochambeau was under heavy pressure to mount an offensive in the Low

Countries even though he knew that his army was unprepared to take the field. One of his chief subordinates, however, intrigued with General C. Dumouriez, minister for foreign affairs, and Dumouriez ordered an immediate advance to liberate the Belgians from Austrian control. Both the decision and the political interference disgusted Rochambeau, and he subsequently resigned, but not before he was able to avoid a rout of the raw French troops by a timely arrival with three regiments and eight guns at the Battle of Quiveran. In June 1792, Rochambeau retired to his estate near Vendôme.

In August, following the storming of the Tuileries and the fall of the monarchy, Rochambeau's peaceful retirement was disrupted when he was arrested, carried to Paris, and imprisoned because of his aristocratic background. He probably would have been a victim of the guillotine had the Thermidorian Reaction not occurred when it did. After six months' imprisonment, he was released and permitted to return to his estates, where he lived the life of a quiet observer until his death in 1807. A few years before, when he was presented to Napoleon, the emperor had greeted him with the words: "Marshal, behold your pupils." Rochambeau rejoined in kind: "General, the pupils have surpassed their master."

R. Keim, *Rochambeau* (Washington, D.C., 1907); J.-E. Weelen, *Rochambeau, Father and Son; a Life of the Maréchal de Rochambeau. . .and the Journal of the Vicomte de Rochambeau* (New York, 1936), A Whitridge, *Rochambeau* (New York, 1965).

J. Luvaas

Related entries: DUMOURIEZ; GUIBERT; 10 AUGUST 1792; THERMIDORIAN REACTION.

ROEDERER, PIERRE-LOUIS, COMTE (1754-1835), Revolutionary, journalist, administrator. Roederer's father was an assistant prosecutor with the Parlement of Metz, and Pierre-Louis was born in this town in 1754. He began a legal career as a first step in his ambition for a high administrative post and in 1779 bought a seat in the Parlement of Metz. He quickly became a leading figure there and in the Academy of Metz. Roederer was elected to the National Assembly in October 1789 as a replacement (*suppléant*). There he became part of the group of constitutionalists around E.-J. Sieyès and distinguished himself in matters of financial legislation. A member of the Jacobin club, he left it to join the Feuillants in July 1791 but soon returned.

After the dissolution of the Assembly, Roederer was chosen *procureur-général syndic* of the department of Paris in November 1791 by the electors of that department. He supported the institutions of the constitutional monarchy, but his position had little actual power. He was unable to protect the king from the humiliation of 20 June 1792 and the attack on the Tuileries of 10 August. As the crowd approached the palace on 10 August, Roederer led the royal family to the safety of the Legislative Assembly. His role was equivocal, for a determined defense of the palace by the more than 4,000 royalist defenders with the king present might have driven off the attackers.

Criticized by the Paris Commune for his action on 10 August, Roederer went into hiding in Paris but published frequent articles in the daily *Journal de Paris*, where he opposed the king's execution. From February to May 1793, he felt safe enough to appear in public but went underground again with the crisis that led to the fall of the Brissotins or Girondins. Emerging again after Thermidor, he recommenced his journalistic career in the *Journal de Paris*, of which he became part owner in January 1795. He also published the *Journal d'économie publique*. Roederer won election to the Institut National as a member of the Academy of Moral and Political Sciences. His moderate and anti-Robespierrist views almost led to his deportation after the coup of Fructidor, but C.-M. Talleyrand crossed his name off the list, and thereafter Roederer concentrated on literary journalism.

Basically a man of the eighteenth century, he regretted his more Revolutionary stance of the early 1790s and now longed for a more orderly government. He eagerly joined Sieyès and Talleyrand in the movement that led to Brumaire. At first he was a close adviser of N. Bonaparte, who appointed him to the Council of State. Active on this body, he was not enthusiastic about Bonaparte's movement toward an empire and ultimately found himself outside the inner circle. Roederer helped draft the constitution for the Republic of Italy in 1801. Director of public instruction for a few months in 1802, he became a senator in 1803. Also in that year he prepared a draft for the Act of Mediation for Switzerland.

In 1806 Roederer's close friend, King Joseph Bonaparte of Naples, appointed him finance minister there, where he served very effectively until 1808. In 1809 Napoleon named him a count in the imperial nobility. The following year he became minister of the Grand Duchy of Berg. An efficient and reliable administrator, Roederer remained loyal to Napoleon until his exile to Elba and rallied to him during the Hundred Days. Thereafter he retired to his estate in Normandy where he busied himself with historical and literary essays. Louis-Philippe named him a peer of France in 1832. He died in 1835.

O. Connelly, *Napoleon's Satellite Kingdoms* (New York, 1965); K. Margerison, *P.-L. Roederer*, in *Trans. of the Amer. Phil. Soc.* 73 (1983); M. Reinhard, *La Chute de la royaute: 10 août 1792* (Paris, 1969); *Oeuvres du Comte P.-L. Roederer*, 8 vols. (Paris, 1853-59).

J. M. Laux

Related entries: COUP OF 18 BRUMAIRE; COUP OF 18 FRUCTIDOR YEAR V; FEUILLANTS; GIRONDINS; JACOBINS; *JOURNEES*; 10 AUGUST 1792; THERMIDORIAN REACTION; SIEYES.

ROLAND DE LA PLATIERE, JEAN-MARIE (1734-93), civil servant and minister of interior. The youngest of five sons of a Beaujolais family who claimed ancient origins, possessed property, offices, and honors, and cultivated pretensions that accompanied success, Jean-Marie, christened in the parish church at Thizy on 19 February 1734, early showed the obstinance and persistence that were to remain his lifelong and dominant traits. Alone among his brothers, he rejected the priesthood and ran counter to family tradition and pressure in choosing to make his fortune in the world of commerce and industry; when he was eighteen, he commenced an apprenticeship in business. After briefly considering (and abandoning) immigration to the New World, Roland moved to Rouen in 1754, where a kinsman sponsored his entry into the Corps of Inspectors of Manufactures and Commerce. For the next thirty-eight years, he was to serve the inspectorate. His early career was spent in Rouen, but in 1764 he was transferred, briefly, to Languedoc to a more responsible post as under-inspector at Clermont-en-Lodève. In the autumn of 1766, he was appointed inspector at Amiens, a post more commensurate, in his eyes, with his abilities and achievements. It was at Amiens that he firmly established his career and such renown as he was to achieve in pre-Revolutionary France.

As the year passed, Roland came to feel that his career had reached a plateau, if not a dead end. Efforts to improve his position culminated not in a title, for which he sought letters patent, but in being transferred as inspector to Lyon, a post of greater importance and remuneration than Amiens and one that made it possible to return to his native region. Five years after moving to Lyon, the Revolution began; and on 27 September 1791 the Inspectorate of Manufactures was abolished, abruptly ending Roland's career and leaving him feeling frustrated and bitter after nearly four decades of devoted civil service and hard work. Roland had transcended the narrow limits of his job by engaging in many other activities, some directly, some only tangentially related to his work as inspector. Much of his extravocational activity consisted of travel and observation; he toured extensively in France and abroad, in England, the Low Countries, Germany, and Italy. Wherever he went, he carefully observed and collected information relevant to his profession or to satisfy his own persistent curiosity. These trips resulted in a flood of memoranda, technical studies, and occasionally works of greater length and more general nature, such as the six-volume *Lettres écrites de Suisse, d'Italie, de Sicile et de Malte. . .en 1776, 1777, et 1778*. Roland was also an active participant in a number of scientific societies and academies and a contributor to the *Dictionnaire des manufactures, arts, et métiers*. His professional expertise received some recognition, but it was often grudgingly given and seemed not to affect his career in ways that satisfied him. For this lack of suitable reward, Roland, irascible and dogged, must bear some of the blame.

The achievement of his career as inspector that had most impact on his Revolutionary career was his marriage on 4 February 1780 to M.-J. (Manon) Phlipon, a Parisian some twenty years his junior. Theirs was a lengthy and stormy courtship, marked by doubts and a certain amount of self-deception on the part of each, and the marriage was hardly more placid or candid. But Manon did bring to Roland a vitality that he lacked; she provided energy, loyalty, and the practical support that he needed and expected. She was, like her husband, determined and ambitious; she was much quicker than he to see the opportunities that the Revolution offered them. The Revolution had ended Roland's career as an inspector; being willing to take risks and seize the opportunities offered by the Revolution, Madame Roland was able to insinuate her elderly and disappointed husband into a new Revolutionary career, one for which he was temperamentally unfit and one that she was not always able to direct and control satisfactorily.

Soon after the Rolands settled in Lyon, they became friendly with a number of young men who were actively involved in early Revolutionary politics. Undoubtedly the most important of these acquaintances was J.-P. Brissot, to whose journal, the *Patriote français*, both Rolands began to contribute. Roland also became involved in Lyon municipal politics, and this led to his being sent on a mission to Paris to seek nationalization of the Lyonnais debt. The trip to Paris in the winter of 1791 placed the Rolands at the center of Revolutionary activities, a position from which they were henceforth unable to retreat more than briefly. After completing his mission in the summer of 1791, the Rolands returned to Lyon, only to discover that the inspectorate had been abolished and with it his source of livelihood. Urged by Manon, the Rolands returned to Paris in December 1791 to seek a pension in compensation; this time they remained in the capital permanently, and, whatever his own preferences, Roland was to find himself politically active at the Revolutionary vortex. He joined the Jacobin club, and his acquaintance with Brissot and other moderate Jacobins resulted in his nomination, as the most desirable and qualified candidate, for minister of interior in the Girondist ministry that Louis XVI appointed in March 1792.

Roland's rapid rise in national politics came at the crucial moment when France went to war with anti-Revolutionary Europe. The Girondist ministry, an interesting experiment in quasi-parliamentary government, was a failure, coming to grief over the war, which went badly, the king's lack of confidence, and the lack of political expertise exhibited by the ministers and their partisan supporters in the legislature. As the war effort collapsed, so too did the Girondist ministry. Roland took a prominent part in trying to salvage the government from political disaster. It was decided that the court should be presented with an ultimatum in the form of three emergency measures: Louis XVI was required to abolish the King's Guard (provided him by the constitution), to deport nonjuring clergy, and to encamp 20,000 *fédérés* outside the walls of Paris. The king agreed to abolish the Guard, which left him defenseless, but he would not act on the other two measures. The Girondists considered Louis' response insufficient, and the resulting stalemate spurred Roland to respond. His action, direct and peremptory, was to address a letter to Louis demanding that he cease circumventing the will of the majority and accept the decrees that the Girondists believed necessary for the safety of the nation. Louis' answer, the dismissal of Roland and two other Girondist ministers, was not perhaps what Roland had in mind, though he suddenly found himself acclaimed a patriot minister and accorded some of the recognition and popularity that had so long eluded him. The dismissal of the Girondist government was followed by the insurrection of 20 June 1792, which proved a dress rehearsal for the insurrection of 10 August, when the monarchy was toppled. In the provisional government created after the monarchy, Roland found himself again minister of interior, a post he was to hold until 22 January 1793.

These were stormy months of transition from monarchy to republic, of the king's trial and execution, of the struggle between moderate and radical Jacobins, between Girondists and Montagnards, for political dominance. Roland was caught in a maelstrom that increasingly went beyond his control. His helplessness became clear during the September Massacres, that purging of Paris in the face of invasion, of which Roland strongly disapproved but was unable to curb. Increasingly, Girondist political acumen faltered before Robespierrist pressure and attacks, and Roland was frequently the focus of the anti-Girondist campaign. In late 1792, as his political career floundered, so too did his marriage; though Manon remained at his side, she made it clear to him that her affections had been transferred to another (revealed as the young Girondist deputy, F.-N.-L. Buzot, only in 1864). This combination of disappointments resulted in Roland's resignation from the ministry the day after the execution of Louis XVI.

Roland was determined to remove to the family property in Beaujolais but was not allowed to do so. His repeated appeals for permission to leave Paris were denied. As the Robespierrists consolidated their hold in Paris, Roland's papers were seized, threats were made against him, and on 31 May, the first evening of the insurrection that saw the arrest and expulsion of the Girondists from the Convention, Revolutionary commissioners appeared at Roland's home to arrest him. He was not to be found; Madame Roland, who had not fled with him, was imprisoned. The fugitive Roland managed to make his way first to Amiens and finally to Rouen, where old friends hid him. On 10 November 1793, when he learned of Madame Roland's condemnation by the Revolutionary Tribunal, Roland left Rouen, perhaps to return to Paris and speak out against the Robespierrist-dominated Convention and make himself available to the guillotine. He got no further than a neighboring village, where his body was found impaled on his sword cane.

Rigid and austere, with straight white hair and a rather pinched expression, Roland, according to C. Dumouriez, resembled something out of Plutarch. His was not a warm or particularly attractive personality; he was inflexible, righteous, and obstinate. But he was also hard working, had wide-ranging interests, and was not afraid of ideas or innovations. Roland was better suited to the bureaucratic life of an inspector than to the turmoil of Revolutionary politics, yet he received scant recognition and small worldly success as a civil servant of the Old Regime. It is his career as Revolutionary minister for which he is usually remembered, though he was obviously not a man for revolutionary seasons.

    E. Bernardin, *Jean-Marie Roland et le ministère de l'intérieur, 1792-1793* (Paris, 1964); A.-Th. Girardot, *Les ministres de la République française: Roland et Mme Roland* (Paris, 1860); A. Join-Lambert, *Le mariage de Madame Roland: trois années de correspondance amoureuse, 1777-1780* (Paris, 1896); C. A. Le Guin, *Roland de la Platière: A Public Servant in the Eighteenth Century* (Philadelphia, 1966); C. Perroud, "Le premier ministère de Roland," *Révo. française* 42 (1902).

                                                                    C. A. Le Guin

Related entries: BOSC; BRISSOT DE WARVILLE; BUZOT; FEDERALISM; GIRONDINS; JACOBINS; *JOURNEES*; ROLAND DE LA PLATIERE, M.-J; REVOLUTIONARY TRIBUNAL; SEPTEMBER 1792 MASSACRES; 10 AUGUST 1792.

ROLAND DE LA PLATIERE, MARIE-JEANNE "MANON" PHLIPON

(1754-93), writer and political figure. A native Parisian bourgeoise, Manon Phlipon was born near the Seine, the daughter of a master engraver. Much doted on by her parents, she was a pretty and precocious child, attributes that she retained throughout her life. As an only child of a comfortable household, Manon was raised with latitude and every advantage her parents could afford. In childhood she was profoundly impressed by steady and extensive reading and by insensitivities, real or imagined, that she experienced in the society in which she found herself. At nine she discovered Plutarch's *Lives*, and it made an indelible impression on her. Madame Roland later credited Plutarch with making a republican of her; much about the world seemed lacking to her when measured by Plutarchan standards. She discovered and became devoted to J.-J. Rousseau, who like her had read Plutarch at the age of nine and who reinforced that love of freedom and virtue that she had imbibed first in the *Lives*.

Young Manon took traditional religion seriously and at age eleven expressed a desire to embrace the monastic life. Her parents acquiesced to a year's trial, and on 7 May 1765 she entered a convent. While there she met the two Cannet sisters from Amiens, whose friendship was to have an important impact on her future. Her year in the convent convinced Manon that religion was not her vocation, and she decided to return to the world in the spring of 1766, taking up a quiet residence with her grandmother Phlipon on the Ile Saint-Louis. It was during this period, on a visit to a condescending noblewoman who had employed her grandmother, that Manon had one of several youthful encounters that made her critical of and hostile to the society in which she had to live.

Returning to the more exciting life at her paternal home on the Cité, Manon continued her pattern of exhaustive reading, relieved by forays into society. As a result of this regimen, her attitudes became clearly and sharply critical, and she became increasingly aware of her social and intellectual isolation, an awareness heightened by the death of her mother in 1775 and by the pressures of courtship. At the time of her mother's death, Manon was twenty-one and unmarried. Shattered by her loss, Manon assumed the role of mistress of the Phlipon household, a task that proved burdensome because of the disintegration of her father's personal life and the decline of his business. He pestered her with suitors, none of whom she approved and all of whom made her sensitive about being unmarried. Manon's own preference lay with older men, often older than her father; in them she found intellectual and social companionship, uncomplicated by physical attraction. But no suitor fulfilling her image of a husband materialized until 1776, when she made the acquaintance of J.-M. Roland de la Platière, an inspector of commerce and manufactures at Amiens. Roland was introduced to

Manon by her convent schoolmates, H. and S. Cannet. Soon after taking his post at Amiens, Roland had become friendly with the Cannet family, especially with the older sister, Henriette. It was S. Cannet who arranged the first meeting between Roland and Manon, which took place during one of his professional trips to Paris in January 1776.

Manon soon convinced herself that in Roland she had found the man with whom she wished to share her life, a decision perhaps hastened by growing tensions between her and her father. Twenty years Manon's senior, Roland appeared to her more respectable than seductive. She found him serious and enlightened, and he attracted her from first acquaintance, despite his tendency to talk too much about himself. His successful career, his broad interests, his gravity of mind appealed to her. At very least she saw in him an acceptable means of delivering herself from an increasingly unpleasant domestic situation; at most Roland answered her intellectual, if not emotional, needs. As for Roland, Manon soon came to occupy the unfulfilled place in his life.

Their courtship was lengthy, indecisive, and emotionally stormy. There were problems to overcome: M. Phlipon's objections, the attitude of Roland's family, Roland's friendship with H. Cannet. They would have been more easily resolved had Roland and Manon been less obstinate and vain, more certain and candid. They became engaged in April 1779, after which marriage seemed to be deferred constantly. Frustrated by Roland's hesitancy and tergiversation, Manon again took up residence in a convent (November 1779), a feint that finally resulted in her rescue by Roland. They were married on 4 February 1780 and made a trying and tiring wedding trip to meet Roland's family in Beaujolais. After the honeymoon, they returned to Amiens, Roland to his profession, Manon to the routines of homemaker and civil servant's wife and assistant. On 4 October 1781, their only child, Marie-Thérèse-Eudora, was born.

The routine and life-style that the Rolands created in Amiens was to remain relatively consistent until the outbreak of revolution. In her role as mother and housewife, Manon had the faithful and invaluable aid of the loyal M.-M. Fleury, who provided Manon with the same devoted service and support that Manon gave to her husband. As a hostess, she made social life easier for her husband, but more important, she shared his professional and intellectual labors by acting as his secretary and amanuensis. She initially approached this task with humility; ultimately she succeeded in making herself indispensable to Roland, and he became very dependent on her. She progressed from being his copyist to becoming his editor and, in time, virtually his partner. The work she did in the first years of their marriage consisted mostly of professional and technical articles and monographs, which were important to Roland's career but must have seemed increasingly tedious and boring to Manon. Their work also entailed travel to other parts of France and a journey to England (1784), where she felt as intrigued as many other eighteenth-century French travelers, and it led to making the acquaintance of a number of young men, among them L.-A.-G. Bosc and F. Lanthenas, who were to become useful and faithful friends of the Rolands.

The confidence that Madame Roland inspired in her husband was recognized by him toward the end of their residence in Amiens, when he sent her to Paris to seek his letters patent of nobility. Manon shared her husband's belief that his claim to ennoblement was soundly based on his ancestry and, more practically, on the record of his professional and intellectual activities. They believed that such recognition was Roland's due and that it should come before he retired. Madame Roland's pursuit of a title was a splendid example of the charm, intelligence, and persistence with which she undertook any task, but for all her efforts and abilities, she was unable to overcome hostile official attitudes toward her obstinate, arrogant, and badgering husband. The best she could achieve was a transfer from Amiens to Lyon, without title, without promotion, but with an increased income and an opportunity to live inexpensively in his former home. In the spring of 1785, the Rolands established themselves in Lyon, though they spent as much time as possible at the Roland family estate, Le Clos, a place whose beauties and rural pleasures Manon at first greatly admired and enjoyed. Four years remained before the outbreak of revolution suddenly changed the tenor of their lives.

The Revolution proved a godsend to Manon. Her initial fascination with rural life wore thin; her routine as Roland's assistant began to irritate her, all the more so because there seemed no exit from the life she found them living at Le Clos and Lyon. Visits from their friends and the formation of new friendships, such as with J.-P. Brissot and L.-A. Champagneux, seemed only to spotlight the finality of Manon's situation. Her perspective changed with the outbreak of revolution; this exciting event revived her Rousseauist and Plutarchan enthusiasms and opened paths of opportunity she had considered closed to her. She had only to encourage and inspire her husband to Revolutionary zeal, a task made easier by the influence she had accumulated over him for nearly a decade. The Rolands' earliest moves into the arena of Revolutionary activity came when they became Lyonnais correspondents for the *Patriote français* of their friend Brissot and when Roland stood for mayor of Lyon (he was elected only to serve on the General Council of the Lyon Commune, however).

It was in her husband's service to Lyon that Manon found the means of liberation from the confining life in Beaujolais. She accompanied Roland to Paris in February 1791 when he was sent on political mission by the Lyon Commune. During the six months of this mission, Madame Roland established her first political salon, at the Hôtel Britannique in the rue Guénégaud, where they resided. Back in her native city, in the midst of Revolutionary excitement there, Manon was in her element; she added to their circle of friends, especially those who would be valuable to her and her plans for her husband.

The mission to Paris spoiled Manon for a return to the provinces, and she went back to Beaujolais with undisguised impatience and a determination to remove permanently to Paris. Her ambition was to be fulfilled when Roland was deprived of his profession as a result of the abolition of the inspectorate at the end of September 1791. Instead of retiring permanently to Le Clos, as he preferred, they decided to return to Paris in quest of a pension, which Roland felt he deserved for his thirty-eight years as a government servant. The Rolands settled in a flat on the rue de la Harpe near the Sorbonne; Paris was henceforth their home, and Manon was ready to make a triumphal reentry into Revolutionary politics in the capital, her husband being her agent, their friends being their means, her salon being the point of confluence.

Roland's friends brought him into the Jacobin club in January 1792, and shortly after included him in the newly formed ministry. He became minister of interior in the Girondist government that was in power from March to June 1792. The Rolands' political involvement was significantly expanded by his elevation, and Manon's role as a minister's wife and hostess suited her talents. Her salon, transferred to the Hôtel de l'Intérieur, became the social and political hub of the new government. From this vantage point Manon and Jean-Marie reached a pinnacle of her ambition. During this first Roland ministry, Manon's influence was largely indirect, though she is generally credited with having an important part in preparing the letter by which Roland challenged Louis XVI to accept the emergency war measures, sponsored by the Girondists in the Legislative Assembly, and by which the ministry was brought down on 13 June 1792. During Roland's second term as minister of interior (10 August 1792-22 January 1793), Madame Roland's role was more open and direct. She had special interest in and influence over the Bureau d'esprit publique, an official information service funded by a grant of 100,000 *livres* from the Assembly. This bureau proved a potent and dangerous political weapon and became a major focus of the rapidly growing radical opposition to the Rolands and their Girondist associates.

In the autumn of 1792, the Robespierrist campaign against the Rolands became heated; Manon shared the brunt of the attack with her husband. Their enemies insisted that retaining Roland as minister meant keeping Manon in the ministry as well. In response to these attacks, Manon made a dramatic defense of herself and her politics before the bar of the Convention on 7 December 1792, after which she was voted honors of the session. Her success only served to convince her enemies that she was the power behind the Girondist faction.

As the political struggle between Girondists and Montagnards approached its vortex, Manon was caught in another crisis, a personal one. At some point in autumn of 1792, she admitted to herself that she felt romantically attracted to the Girondist deputy from Evreux, F.-N.-L. Buzot. At some point before Roland resigned from the ministry on 22 January 1793, Manon told her husband. She continued to live and work with Roland, but their life together must have been severely strained and unhappy, the misery of their personal relations matched by the uncertainty and growing danger of their political position. They were prohibited from leaving Paris for retirement to Le Clos, despite frequent requests and protests. They were in Paris during the insurrection of 31 May-2 June, which resulted in the arrest of the Girondist leadership. Manon helped to engineer Roland's escape, though she did not leave herself. Commissioners who came to arrest the absent Roland returned to arrest his wife on the night of 31 May. From this time until 8 November, when she was executed, Manon spent her time in prison, principally in the Abbaye, seeking release and writing her memoirs, a remarkable personal account of her life and beliefs.

"Penelope" Roland, as J.-P. Marat labeled her, was destined to perish along with the Girondist leaders with whom she was associated, whom she admired and served. The Girondists' Egeria was beheaded one week after the execution of twenty-one leading Girondists on 31 October 1793. Apocryphal, perhaps, but characteristic and fitting was the remark she is claimed to have addressed to David's statue of Liberty as she approached the guillotine: "Oh Liberty, what crimes are committed in thy name!"

J.-M. Clemenceau-Jacquemaire, *Madame Roland* (Paris, 1926); C.-A. Dauban, *Etude sur Madame Roland et son temps* (Paris, 1864); G. May, *Madame Roland and the Age of Revolution* (New York, 1970); J.-M. Phlipon Roland, *Lettres de Mme Roland*, ed. Cl. Perroud, 4 vols. (Paris, 1900, 1902, 1913, 1915) and *Mémoires de Mme. Roland*, ed. Cl. Perroud, 2 vols. (Paris, 1905); I. M. Tarbell, *Madame Roland, A Biographical Study* (New York, 1905).

C. A. Le Guin

Related entries: BOSC; BRISSOT DE WARVILLE; BUZOT; PRISONS; RO-
LAND DE LA PLATIERE, J.-M.; ROUSSEAU.

ROMAN REPUBLIC (1798–99), French-sponsored revolutionary regime in central Italy. Despite the steadily worsening relations between the French government and the papacy from 1790, France made no overt moves to challenge the pope's remarkably incompetent government until N. Bonaparte's dramatic incursion into the Po Valley in 1796. In June, the French army occupied the papal legations of Bologna and Ferrara, and both cities declared their independence. The Papacy decided now to resist. A ramshackle army was assembled, and priests preached a holy war against the French. In January 1797, Napoleon declared war in order to force the pope's acceptance of the new order in northern Italy. After several military disasters, Pope Pius VI did accept the French Republic and its Italian satellites, but his authority continued to erode as Ancona and several towns in the Marches region along the Adriatic declared their independence as well.

In Rome itself, a city of 165,000 situated in the most desolate part of the peninsula, with no industries save the church and tourism, chaos was general, exacerbated by both the weakness of the government and the subversive activities of radical activists. Most of these so-called Jacobins had come from the north, but they included the distinguished Roman sculptor G. Ceracchi. Several attempts at fomenting a revolution in Rome were failures, but on 28 December 1797 a demonstration in front of the palace in which the French ambassador, J. Bonaparte, was staying led to the probably accidental shooting of French General L. Duphot by papal troops.

The ambassador's initial response was restrained. He filed a diplomatic protest and moved the embassy to Florence. The French government in Paris, meanwhile, launched a well-orchestrated campaign to deflect the attention of Austria and Naples by hinting at possible territorial acquisitions elsewhere. Then, on 11 January 1798, the Directory secretly ordered General A. Berthier, who had replaced N. Bonaparte as commander of the Army of Italy, to march on Rome and to engineer the establishment of a Roman Republic, but without making it appear that the French were behind it. The French arrived in Rome in February, occupied all strategic points, and managed to disarm most of the papal army without firing a shot.

On 15 February, in the cow pasture that had once been the Roman Forum, a small group of Romans promulgated an Act of the Sovereign People, declaring that the pope's civil authority was at an end. A few days later, the aged pope began his northward journey in search of a haven. Pius VI's career had been distinguished by neither piety nor political effectiveness, but his callous treatment by the French now turned him into a martyr.

Four weeks later, the French produced a constitution for the infant regime. The pope's central Italian territories were divided into nine departments, there was to be an elaborate administration, and the spiritual authority of the church was not to be disturbed. One article stated that no law would be valid until it was signed by the French military commander.

In the nine months until the regime collapsed before the invading armies of the Neapolitans, the Roman Republic staggered from crisis to crisis. The economy, never healthy, was close to disaster with the loss of the wealthy northern territories and the huge French exactions. French troops were frequently insubordinate, and there was continuous tension between the generals and the Directory's civilian agents. There were a series of rebellions in the countryside and in the Roman Trastevere section. Despite promises to respect the church, the French and their Roman collaborators became militantly anticlerical. Neither the occupying army nor the new Roman government was remotely interested in dealing with the desperate plight of either the urban poor or the peasants in the countryside.

In November 1798, the English and Austrians encouraged Bourbon King Ferdinand of Naples to move against Rome. The invading army took Rome as easily as the French had done, but General K. L. Mack's army was humiliatingly defeated north of Rome by a much smaller French army. The invasion was followed by a rout of the Neapolitans, and for the time being the Roman Republic was reestablished. The French moved on to conquer Naples and to establish the last and most ephemeral of the Italian republics. By March 1799, with the occupation of Tuscany, nearly the entire peninsula was under French control.

With the victories of A. V. Suvórov's Russian armies in the Po Valley in April, most of the French troops moved north, and the Italian republics quickly collapsed. In much of the territory of the Roman Republic, the French and their Italian allies were confronted with a savage guerrilla war. At the final French withdrawal from the city, however, there was no bloodbath. Rome resumed its traditional apathy toward politics.

Although the Roman Republic was a failure in practical terms, it did promulgate ideas of liberty and equality, however feeble their implementation, and it introduced the issues of lay government and separation of church and state that would be decisive for the nineteenth-century Risorgimento.

A. Cretoni, *Roma giacobina* (Rome, 1971); R. De Felice, *Italia giacobina* (Naples, 1970); R. R. Palmer, *The Age of the Democratic Revolution*, vol. 2 (Princeton, 1964).

C. Garrett

Related entries: BONAPARTE, J.; BONAPARTE, N.; DIRECTORY; PIUS VI; SUVOROV-RYMNIKSKII.

ROMME, CHARLES-GILBERT (1750-95), deputy to the Legislative Assembly and National Convention. Born into a petit bourgeois family of the Puy-de-Dôme and educated by the Oratorians, Romme served as tutor to the son of a Russian aristocrat from 1779 to 1789. When the Estates General convened, he expressed the views of a very moderate reformer. Yet he later supported the more radical measures of the National Assembly and founded two clubs to promote Revolutionary action. The Amis de la Loi, organized in January 1790, sought to foster civic education for French children. Another society, established in June 1790 to commemorate the Tennis Court Oath, first brought Romme into prominence as a political leader.

Elected as a deputy to the Legislative Assembly in 1791, he maintained an independent posture despite friendly personal relations with some of the Girondists. He voted for war in April 1792 and in August approved the suspension of the king, while making it clear that he was in no way affiliated with the extremist Paris Commune. In the National Convention he sat with the Plain, worked for a reconciliation of all republican deputies, but voted with the Mountain for the execution of the king. When the Girondist leaders were arrested, he was on mission in Normandy, where Girondist sympathizers allayed any Montagnard suspicions about his loyalty by holding him hostage for fifty days.

Important as his political activities were, Romme accorded priority to his duties as a member of the Committee of Public Instruction. He admired the plan for public education that the marquis de Condorcet presented to the Legislative Assembly in April 1792 and adopted its basic structure for his own proposals in 1793. He departed from Condorcet mainly in advocating Rousseauist education to shape moral character as well as instruction in academic subjects for elementary students. The same goal of moral regeneration, coupled with his growing anti-Christian sentiments, motivated him in his work on the Revolutionary calendar.

The new calendar and his earlier support for the Cult of Reason seemed to put the deputy from Riom on a collision course with M. Robespierre, who saw both as signs of a dangerous drift toward materialism. Another appointment as deputy on mission from February to October 1794 probably saved him from an open clash with the Incorruptible. The overthrow of Robespierre during his absence clearly caused him no distress. The political reaction that followed was a different matter. Especially disturbing to Romme was legislation lifting all restraints on Catholic priests and abolishing economic controls, which had served to protect the lower classes from inflation and exploitation. Although he was undoubtedly sympathetic to the uprising of 12 Germinal Year III (1 April 1795) and to other antireactionary demonstrations, there is no evidence that he participated in them. It was not until 20 May (1 Prairial) that he declared himself, presenting an impassioned plea in the Convention for a return to the social democracy of 1793. Revolutionary leaders ordered him and a number of like-minded deputies arrested that night, and on 17 June a military tribunal condemned him and the other "martyrs of Prairial" to death. Minutes after he was sentenced, he committed suicide with a hidden dagger.

Romme was representative of political figures throughout the Revolution, but especially in the Plain during the National Convention, who struggled with deeply ambivalent feelings. A man of thought and the written word, he found himself caught up in the Revolutionary maelstrom requiring action and oratory for success. An admirer of many of the policies of the Montagnards, he was hostile to some of them personally and often scorned their tactics. A proponent of a rigorous academic curriculum in public schools, he gave more attention to character building in his public utterances on the subject. A martyr to the cause of the *sans-culottes*, he found them frightening in person and thoroughly distrusted them as potential wielders of political power.

A. Galante-Garrone, *Gilbert Romme, Storia di un rivoluzionario* (Turin, 1959) and in French translation by A. and C. Manceron (Paris, 1971); *Gilbert Romme (1750-1795) et son temps, Actes du Colloque tenu à Riom et Clermont les 10 et 11 juin 1965* (Paris, 1966); M. de Vissac, Un conventionnel du Puy-de-Dôme, Romme le montagnard (Clermont-Ferrand, 1883).

R. Vignery

Related entries: CONDORCET; CULT OF REASON; PARIS COMMUNE; PLAIN, THE; PRAIRIAL MARTYRS; TENNIS COURT OATH.

ROUGET DE LISLE, JEAN-CLAUDE (1760-1836), composer of the music and lyrics of the French national anthem, the "*Marseillaise.*" Rouget de Lisle was born on 10 May 1760 in Lons-le-Saulnier in the modern department of the Jura to parents of the minor provincial nobility. His childhood appears to have been typical for a boy of his social standing, although apparently his mother, who introduced him to music, spoiled him, and this caused problems in his relations with others in later life.

In 1784, after an undistinguished career at the Royal Military School of Mézières, Rouget was commissioned a second lieutenant in the Royal Engineer Corps. Not a particularly conscientious officer, he preferred poetry and music. Consequently his superiors' fitness reports on him were lukewarm. In 1790, after garrison duty in various places in France, he was promoted to captain and sent to the frontier garrison of Strasbourg to join General N. Luckner's *Armée du Rhin*. There he came to know the great French composer I. Pleyel and Baron

Dietrich, the mayor of the city. Both men admired Rouget de Lisle's musical talents and provided him encouragement and aid.

Rouget composed the "*Marseillaise*" on 25-26 April 1792, after the Revolutionary government had declared war on Austria and Prussia. He then rejected the more radical direction of the Revolution, particularly after the events of August 1792, and he deserted the army, going into hiding in the mountains of the Jura. In September 1793, on the personal orders of L. Carnot, who disliked the young officer, he was arrested, tried, and sentenced to death on the charge of royalism. The charge was based on his refusal in September 1792 to swear an oath of loyalty to the new Republic. The end of the Terror and the temporary eclipse of Carnot brought about his release from prison in August 1794. After distinguished military service at Quiberon Bay in July 1795, he resigned from the army.

Rouget de Lisle's subsequent efforts to make a name for himself in the literary and musical circles of Paris ended in failure. In 1798, he was given a minor clerical post in the embassy of the newly established French satellite, the Batavian Republic. However, in 1803 Napoleon abruptly dismissed him, ostensibly because Rouget had demanded the directorship of the Paris opera. He was not to hold regular employment for the remainder of his life, and he occasionally was placed under police surveillance. Rouget de Lisle alienated his younger brother, a general in the army, who objected to Rouget's self-indulgence. Rouget was even forced to sell most of his inheritance in Lons-le-Saulnier.

While living until 27 June 1836, Rouget's last years were difficult. Unsuccessful in his musical endeavors, in 1824 he suffered the loss of a pension granted him by Louis XVIII, and he served a term in debtor's prison. Louis-Philippe granted Rouget de Lisle a pension of 1,500 francs in 1830; this was soon doubled on his being awarded the Legion of Honor in recognition for writing the "*Marseillaise*." This enabled him to spend the last years of his life in relative material comfort.

Although many eminent European musicologists of the 1860s and 1870s denied Rouget's authorship of the original, unsigned version of the "*Marseillaise*," in the 1880s and 1890s his authorship was established definitively. On Bastille Day 1915, in the midst of much military pageantry, his remains were removed from Lons-le-Saulnier to the Invalides.

E. A. Arnold, Jr., "Rouget de Lisle and the 'Marseillaise,' " in *Proc. of the WSFH* (1978); M. de la Fuye and E. Gueret, *Rouget de Lisle inconnu* (Paris, 1934); J. Tiersot, *Rouget de Lisle, son oeuvre, sa vie* (Paris, 1892).

E. Arnold, Jr.

Related entries: CARNOT; DIETRICH; "*MARSEILLAISE, LA*"; MUSIC; QUIBERON.

ROUSSEAU, JEAN-JACQUES (1712-78), *philosophe*, novelist, political and social theorist. Rousseau was born in Geneva, Switzerland, on 28 June 1712. His early years gave no hint of future fame. He was brought up by relatives, his mother having died in childbirth and his watchmaker father having abandoned him. He was apprenticed to an engraver but ran away at the age of sixteen. There followed years of wandering, an intermittent liaison with a Madame de Warens, a temporary conversion to Roman Catholicism, employment as a servant, as a tutor, and secretaryship to the French ambassador at Venice.

Then followed the years in Paris, where he became a member of the encyclopedist group of D. Diderot and the other Paris *philosophes*. Stimulated by his contacts with this group, he had read widely and reflected and had contributed to the *Encyclopédie*. Fame came suddenly with his *Discours sur les sciences et les arts* published in 1750, the award-winning essay in the Academy of Dijon's contest. His reputation was enhanced by a second essay, *Discours sur l'origine et les fondements de l'inégalité parmi les hommes* in 1755. Other writings of this period included a well-received operetta, *Le divin du village*.

Then within a period of three years he published *Julie ou la Nouvelle Héloïse* (1760), a long and immensely popular sentimental novel, set in a rural social utopia; the *Contrat social* (1762), his major contribution to Western political theory; and that same year, his *Emile*, a pioneering, idealistic treatise on education. In each of these, as in his earlier works, he extolled the simple, natural life—not that of the savage, noble or otherwise, contrary to popular misconception then and since. Man is born good, according to Rousseau, but has been corrupted by society. Reason and conscience are part of his nature, and he will be happy if he will reform himself and his society. Rousseau was basically a moralist, and for him the natural man is the rational, ethical person. His seriousness of purpose in all of this perhaps reflects the influence of his Calvinist, Genevan upbringing, but more apparent was his great admiration for Sparta and republican Rome.

Rousseau's fame was now at its height, for two of these three works had brought him an international reputation and the beginnings of a literary cult for their author. The *Nouvelle Héloïse* quickly became a best-seller, and its impact on readers was unprecedented. *Emile*, his idealistic description of a natural education and its exposition of a sentimental deism in the section entitled "Profession de foi d'un vicaire savoyard" had a similar reception, but it also brought condemnation in Paris by both church and state and the threat of arrest.

Rousseau by this time had broken with his encyclopedist associates, Diderot, J. d'Alembert, and F.-M. Voltaire for both personal and ideological reasons, and with the oversophisticated Parisian salon society, which for a variety of reasons he now found quite uncongenial. There followed another period of wandering as Rousseau, now clearly the victim of paranoia exaggerated by actual persecution by his former associates, wandered from place to place in Switzerland, France, and England, finding successive patrons and then quarreling with each of them in turn. In 1770 he returned to Paris where he supported himself as a music copyist until 1778, when he retired to the estate of the marquis de Girardin at Ermenonville. Here he died a few months later that same year. The literary cult of Rousseau as the author of the *Nouvelle Héloïse* and *Emile* flourished during the next decade, with his tomb at Ermenonville the object of pilgrimages by his disciples.

The *Contrat social* had been largely forgotten, for it had been banned in France. It was neither a popular nor a revolutionary work but rather a sophisticated and abstract treatise on political theory. Rousseau was not a radical thinker. In fact, he might better be labeled a cautious conservative, although revolutionary implications could be and still are read into some of his epigrammatic statements. The most quoted of these was the beginning of chapter 1 of the *Contrat social*: "Man is born free but everywhere he is in chains." The paragraph concludes with his insistence that he can justify the legitimacy of this bondage. But generations of readers have recalled only the ringing affirmation of the first sentence. Rousseau never contemplated a revolution for France, and when he was asked to make recommendations for the Polish patriots trying to maintain their country's independence, his *Considérations sur le gouvernement de Pologne* was a decidedly conservative program for minimal change.

In the *Contrat social*, he took the familiar concept in political theory of a social compact or contract and gave it new justification, deriving from it sovereignty of the people and therefore by implication (but only by implication) giving a theoretical justification for democracy, but not a democratic state. As a follower of Montesquieu, he was quite undoctrinaire as to forms of government, and he recognized the validity of a variety of governmental forms, while having as his models an idealized Sparta and his native Geneva, also idealized. Being basically a moralist, he presented the social contract as an agreement that there should always prevail the general will, the enlightened consensus of the group whose members had risen above their individual wills to see and desire what promoted the permanent and best interests of the group. Thus the relationship between the individual and the community, so crucial to liberal thought, posed no problems in this abstract, idealistic work. But Rousseau, while ignoring in his theory the Lockean concept of natural rights and placing no limits on the sovereignty of the people, was no admirer of even enlightened despotism, for kings to him were simply executives, serving at the pleasure of the sovereign people. Nor was he, as has been claimed, a prophet of later authoritarian and totalitarian government.

Such a sophisticated and theoretical work had thus inevitably been largely forgotten, but with the political controversies that began with the calling of the Estates General in 1788 and the beginnings of the Revolution in 1789, the work, logically or not, came into its own. There is no good evidence that Rousseau's abstract and idealistic theories had any real influence on the thinking of those who made the Revolution. Putting into practice his theories, which were premised on the existence of a small, homogeneous community such as Sparta or Geneva, would have been impossible in France. But both supporters and opponents of the course of events began to cite Rousseau in support of their respective and sometimes contradictory positions. The conservative, anti-Revolutionary themes in the *Contrat social* and his other writings were quoted by opponents of the

Revolution in pamphlets and books; the opposing themes of popular sovereignty
and equality were cited by supporters of the Revolution in their speeches and
writings. As the Revolution progressed, the latter group prevailed, and supporters
of the Revolution, and opponents later, came to accept the thesis stated by
J.-S. Mercier in the title of his book, published in 1791, *De J.-J. Rousseau
considéré comme l'un des premiers auteurs de la Révolution*.

By that time a patriotic lay cult of the Revolution had come into existence,
and it was as part of this larger cult that a political cult of Rousseau in turn
appeared, overshadowing the literary cult of the pre-Revolutionary period. It
was clearly a product of the Revolution; Rousseau came to be assigned the role
of the leading prophet of the Revolution, and his *Contrat social* came to be
considered a sacred writing of this new Revolutionary religion. His bust and a
copy of the book were given a place of honor in the National Assembly, and
that body in December 1790 decreed that a statue of Rousseau be erected with
the inscription: *La nation française libre à J.-J. Rousseau*. The *Contrat social*
was now republished in four separate editions in 1790, three more in 1791, and
thirteen more between 1792 and 1795, including editions in pocket Bible format.
Its author was cited and sometimes quoted in the legislative debates and in the
Revolutionary press. An iconography of Rousseau and of the *Contrat social*
came into existence. Books, eulogies, poems, and hymns were written in his
honor. His bust was a standard fixture in patriotic ceremonies.

This political cult was largely an impersonal phenomenon, unlike the pre-
Revolutionary literary cult, but disciples more or less sincere were to be found
in each of the various Revolutionary factions. Several of the Girondin leaders
were followers. Both G.-J. Danton and L. Saint-Just had volumes of Rousseau
in their libraries. G. Babeuf at his trial appealed in his defense to the "immortal
author of the *Contrat social*." But M. Robespierre was the best known and most
earnest of Rousseau's political disciples. He and his young associate, Saint-Just,
envisioned a France as a moral utopia, and in his 5 February 1794 speech on
the principles of political morality that should guide the government of the
Revolution, he spoke of moral reform for France as the goal of the Revolution,
in terms Rousseau would have found familiar. Although there is no evidence
that he, or anyone else, was a rigid follower of Rousseau's ideas, Robespierre
cited Rousseau in support of his program and eulogized him on a number of
occasions in genuinely emotional terms. At the height of his power, he told the
Convention that if Rousseau had witnessed the Revolution of which he was the
precursor, he would have warmly embraced its justice and equality. In this same
speech, he paraphrased the often-quoted phrase from the *Contrat social*: "Man
is born for happiness and freedom and everywhere he is enslaved and unhappy."
His project for a cult of the Supreme Being was an idea advanced by Rousseau
and others. But he was not the originator of the project, and he resolutely rejected
the Rousseauian injunction that atheists should be banished.

It was not, however, until after the overthrow of Robespierre and the beginnings of the Thermidorian Reaction that the honors of the Pantheon, which had

previously been accorded Voltaire and various Revolutionary heroes, were given to Rousseau's remains. This was accomplished on 11 October 1794 in a typical Revolutionary ceremony. Plans for a statue of Rousseau were revived, but it was never erected.

During the more prosaic period of the Directory, the political cult of Rousseau declined and disappeared. At the end of the decade of Revolution, First Consul N. Bonaparte, on the occasion of a visit to Ermenonville, declared that it would have been better for France if Rousseau had never lived. The myth of Rousseau's influence on the Revolution, affirmed by both supporters and opponents of the Revolution—as well as by those who profited greatly from it—persisted. Only in the twentieth century has there come a reassessment.

A. Cobban, *Rousseau and the Modern State* (London, 1964); P. Gay, *The Enlightenment, an Interpretation*, vol. 2 (New York, 1969); J. Guehenno, *Jean-Jacques*, 3 vols. (Paris, 1948-52); J. McDonald, *Rousseau and the French Revolution, 1762-1791* (London, 1965); G. H. McNeil, "The Cult of Rousseau and the French Revolution," *J. of the Hist. of Ideas* 6 (1945); R. D. Masters, *The Political Philosophy of Rousseau* (Princeton, 1968); J.-J. Rousseau, *Oeuvres complètes*, ed. B. Ganebin and M. Raymond, 4 vols. (Paris, 1959); E. H. Wright, *The Meaning of Rousseau* (London, 1929).

G. H. McNeil

Related entries: BABEUF; CULT OF THE SUPREME BEING; *ENCYCLOPEDIE*; MABLY; MONTESQUIEU; ROBESPIERRE, M.

ROUX, JACQUES (1752-94), the most famous and controversial of the *Enragés*, called by A. Mathiez "the true leader of the party" (although, in fact, they never constituted a party). Roux was born on 21 August 1752 at Pranzac-en-Angoumois (now in the department of the Charente) to a well-to-do family of the provincial bourgeoisie. In 1767 his father, a judge, started him on a clerical career. In 1777 Roux became a curate and in 1778 almoner of the collège of Saint-Louis and professor at the seminary of Saint-Pierre in Angoulême. He became involved in an accidental killing in 1779, was placed under arrest for some weeks, and was pardoned by the king in 1780. He left for the diocese of Saintes (1785-86) and served as curate at Cozes in 1787 and at Saint-Thomas de Conac in 1788.

In 1789 he welcomed the Revolution in a sermon entitled "The Triumph of the Brave Parisians over the Enemies of the Public Welfare." Accused of favoring peasant riots in April 1790, he was placed under interdiction by his superiors. He subsequently appeared in Paris where on 16 January 1791 he took the oath to the Civil Constitution of the Clergy at Saint-Sulpice. He joined the Cordeliers club and continued to serve as a curate at Saint-Nicolas-des-Champs in the section of Gravilliers.

In 1792 (probably in May) he sheltered J.-P. Marat, who was in hiding, and joined the popular movement that led to the overthrow of the monarchy on 10 August. He came into his own when the formerly passive citizens entered the sectional assemblies. Known for his patriotism and his charitable work, Roux emerged as the popular leader of Gravilliers and became an elector of the section and a delegate to the General Council of the Commune of Paris. In his discourse of 1 December—*Sur le jugement de Louis-le-dernier avec la poursuite des agioteurs, des accapareurs et des traîtres*—he ably summarized popular grievances. On 21 January 1793, as a representative of the Commune, he accompanied Louis XVI to the scaffold.

He opposed popular violence against shops, but when such riots took place on 25 February, he excused the rioters. For this, the bourgeoisie reproached him for propagating "the pillage of property." In the spring of 1793 he joined the Mountain to bring down the Girondins, and his prominent role during the last days of this struggle (27-31 May) made him well known throughout the capital. The Commune later appointed him to record the history of the revolution of 31 May.

Roux, however, overplayed his position after the Mountain came to power. With the assistance of other *Enragés*, J.-F. Varlet and J.-T.-V. Leclerc, he composed an address to the Convention (25 June 1793), that P.-J.-B. Buchez has labeled the "Manifesto of the Enragés." In it he insisted that the national assemblies had not done nearly enough for the poor. Liberty, he argued, is only an empty phantom when some men can starve others with impunity; equality is equally meaningless when the rich monopolize the right of life and death over their fellow men.

The Montagnard leaders, who feared division in the popular support on which their leadership was based, strongly attacked Roux. Both the Jacobins and the Commune joined in denouncing this "suspect priest"; and under their pressure, the Cordeliers withdrew their support. Nevertheless, Roux' fortunes revived after the assassination of Marat when he borrowed the name of Marat's former publication, *Publiciste de la République française*, for a newspaper of his own (July-November 1793). On 18 August he was elected chairman of the General Assembly of the Gravilliers section, but due to the intervention of the Commune, he was removed and arrested on 22 August, only to be released on bail five days later. During the *journée* of 5 September, at the instigation of the Jacobins, he was again arrested and taken to Saint-Pélagie prison, from where he continued to publish the *Publiciste* and give instructions to his followers. In order to crush this nucleus within the Gravilliers, where he was also backed by the popular society of the section, Roux was shifted to the Bicêtre prison on 27 October, and his followers were rounded up in the next two months. He was summoned before the Correctional Tribunal on 14 January 1794, and this court ordered his transfer to the Revolutionary Tribunal. Roux attempted to commit suicide but recovered in the prison hospital of Bicêtre. Nonetheless, he later succeeded in taking his life on 10 February, and this first left-wing victim of the Terror was buried at Gentilly.

Roux made a distinct impression on his contemporaries. Some depicted him as an anarchist. He was, in fact, neither a communalist nor an atheist. He was, rather, a radical egalitarian with a belief in the people and high esteem for the role of women in revolution. An advocate of direct *sans-culotte* democracy, he was not an original thinker but a passionate front-line fighter who tried, unsuccessfully, to combine popular aspirations into a coherent program. To his credit, he had a deep understanding of the importance of the socioeconomic components of revolution. He was among the first to appreciate the social limitations of Jacobin democracy, which allowed the development of a new class division between rich and poor, rulers and ruled, oppressors and oppressed. He served, perhaps, as the prototype for V. Hugo's character Cimourdain in *Quatre-vingt-treize* and figures in P. Weiss' *Marat*.

W. Markov, *Exkurse zu Jacques Roux* (Berlin, 1970) and *Jacques Roux oder vom Elend der Biographie* (Berlin, 1966); A. Mathiez, *La Vie chère et le mouvement social sous le Terreur*, 2d ed. (Paris, 1927, 1973); R. B. Rose, *The Enragés: Socialists of the French Revolution?* (Melbourne, 1965); Jacques Roux, *Scripta et Acta*, ed. W. Markov (Berlin, 1969).

W. Markov

Related entries: CIVIL CONSTITUTION OF THE CLERGY; CORDELIERS CLUB; *ENRAGES*; LECLERC; MONTAGNARDS; PARIS COMMUNE; PASSIVE CITIZEN; PRISONS; REVOLUTIONARY TRIBUNAL; TERROR, THE.

ROVERE, JOSEPH-STANISLAS-FRANCOIS-XAVIER-ALEXIS (1748-98), marquis de Fontvielle, politician. Rovère was born at Bonnieux in the papal enclave of the Comtat Venaissin. His unsettled early career was scarred by financial difficulties. After squandering his wife's large dowry, he escaped his creditors by moving to Avignon where he purchased a captaincy in the Swiss Guard of the Vice-Legate in 1785. However, he defaulted on payment and had to relinquish the post. He came to prominence in 1791 during the bitter struggles of the Comtat civil war. He commanded volunteers in the patriot Monteux Army against the papal forces at the Battle of Sarrians (19 April 1791) and in the siege of Carpentras (22 April-7 May). Intimately linked with the radical pro-French Avignon party of M.-J. Jourdan (Coupe-Tête), L.-F. Peyre, and N.-J.-B. Lescuyer, he was one of the envoys to Orange for the peace treaty between Avignon and the Comtat in June. In August, he went to Paris with the delegation lobbying for the annexation of the papal enclave. After the annexation, the enclave was organized into two districts (Ouvèze, attached to the Drôme, and Vaucluse, attached to the Bouches-du-Rhône). In the ensuing elections held in July 1792, Rovère became a deputy to the Legislative Assembly for the district of Vaucluse. The immediate disappearance of the Assembly brought him back to Paris as a deputy to the National Convention for the Bouches-du-Rhône.

In the Convention, Rovère quickly achieved some influence through his connections with Girondist leaders, especially those from the Bouches-du-Rhône. In early October 1792 he went on a brief mission to the Yonne with C. Fauchet to supervise grain supplies, and he became a member of the Committee of General Security on 17 October and again on 21 January 1793. However, he was more a man of the Plain than a serious Girondist; he adopted the hard-line position in the trial of the king and, in a mission to restore order at Lyon (February-April 1793), he sought to keep a balance between the factions there. He broke his Girondist connections in mid-May when he quarreled with C.-J.-M. Barbaroux who accused him of illegally obtaining military rank in the Fifteenth Dragoons Regiment. Rovère was indeed fundamentally a corrupt opportunist. In the Year II, he developed relations with the deputies of dubious morality around G.-J. Danton. Rovère was in many senses an archetypal *pourri*. He also typified a certain kind of deputy whose political career was constructed on an elaborate clan of local friends and clients, whose interests and factional struggles he promoted through the power gained from his status as deputy. In this, he resembled M.-G.-A. Vadier or P.-F. Piorry, for example, although neither was corrupt. Indeed, his later manipulations of C.-A. Goupilleau (de Montaigu) during the latter's mission to the south in the Year III in order to pursue partisan revenge resembles Piorry's manipulation of F.-P. Ingrand during Ingrand's Year II mission to the Vienne, in order to further his struggle with the Thibaudeau clan.

These characteristics of Rovère became fully apparent during his mission to the south in the second half of 1793. He was sent with F.-M. Poultier on 24 June to help suppress the southern federalist revolt and to organize the new department of the Vaucluse, composed of the old papal territory. Rovère combined a determined moderation toward federalists with the active pursuit of personal interests. The two aspects were inextricably intertwined. The organization of the new department allowed him to install his clients in the administrations at Avignon. This was another stage in a long local struggle since the civil war, marked for them by both successes (notably the election of his brother, S.-S. Rovère, as bishop of Avignon) and defeats (notably the successive arrests and attempted prosecutions of Jourdan and his friends after the Glacière massacre at Avignon on 16 October 1791 when they murdered sixty antipatriots). The Rovère clan was, however, vulnerable because it was extraordinarily corrupt (Jourdan, for instance, had left 100,000 *livres* of debt behind him in Paris in 1789), murderous (the Glacière affair was only the largest and most notorious example), and tyrannical (in their persistent persecution of opponents in the small towns of the Comtat in 1792-93). They now had a free rein. They established a syndicate to buy national lands at absurd prices through the collusion of friends in the administrations, and Rovère himself profited from this. A protracted struggle opposed them to another Montagnard faction through the autumn and winter of 1793. This faction, in control of the Vaucluse tribunal and the Avignon club, presented themselves as pure Montagnards on a platform denouncing both the moderation and the corruption of Rovère and his friends. Spearheaded by A. Moureau, it sought a government audience through lobbying by southerners on the Revolutionary Tribunal and organized a petitioning campaign by clubs and Revolutionary committees. The campaign long failed to make headway since it was based on the regional assemblies of clubs, which the Committee of Public Safety viewed as a new federalism. Although Rovère was tartly recalled from mission on 5 Frimaire (25 November 1793) after ignoring previous orders to this effect, Poultier was able to get the Convention to decree Moureau's arrest on 12 Frimaire (2 December). However, the scandals implicating the *pourris* and the defeat of the Indulgents undermined Rovère's position, further discredited by his marriage to the ex-comtesse d'Agoult. Simultaneously, the representative on mission, E.-C. Maignet, close to the Robespierrists, began to investigate the Vaucluse. Moureau was released on 26 Germinal (15 April 1794); Jourdan's arrest was decreed on 28 Germinal, and he was sentenced to death at Paris on 8 Prairial (27 May). Under Maignet's patronage, the Moureau faction seized local control.

The months preceding 9 Thermidor were difficult for Rovère. His friends were prosecuted while denunciations and reports poured in from Maignet, the Moureau faction, and the Revolutionary Commission of Orange. It is not surprising, therefore, that he denounced Maignet to the Convention as early as 15 Thermidor (2 August) and had his friend Goupilleau (de Montaigu) sent as replacement. Goupilleau initiated a thorough reaction in the Vaucluse at the expense of the Moureau faction. In the Convention, Rovère emerged as an extreme reactionary among the group around L.-M.-S. Fréron and J.-L. Tallien. He was a member of the Committee of General Security for most of the period of high reaction, from 15 Nivôse to 15 Floréal Year III (4 January-4 May 1795) and again from 15 Prairial to 15 Vendémiaire Year IV (3 June-7 October 1795). It is clear that he worked hard to impose reactionary policies in the committee. Closely associated with the *jeunesse dorée*, he used many of them as a counter-police in Paris. Unlike Fréron and Tallien who became alarmed by the progress of royalism, Rovère went through with the logic of the reaction. Deeply implicated in the preparation of the royalist uprising of 13 Vendémiaire, his arrest was decreed on 24 Vendémiaire (16 October 1795). However, having been elected by the Vaucluse, he took his seat in the Conseil des Anciens. He must be classed as one of the royalist group. In the plotting that preceded the 18 Fructidor coup by the Directory (4 September 1797), he was allotted the role of organizing an antigovernment police, given his experience in the Year III. He was quite justifiably arrested and deported to Guyana where he died.

M. Jouve, ed., *Correspondance intime du conventionnel Rovère avec Goupilleau* (Nîmes, 1908); V. Laval, ed., *Lettres inédites de J.-S. Rovère à son frère* (Paris, 1908); P. Vaillandet, "La mission de Maignet en Vaucluse," *Ann. hist. de la Révo. française* 3 (1926), "Les débuts de la Terreur Blanche en Vaucluse," *Ann. hist. de la Révo. française* 5 (1928), and "Le conventionnel Rovère et les Montagnards du Midi," *Mém. de l'Inst. hist. de Prov.* 8 (1931).

C. Lucas

Related entries: AVIGNON; BARBAROUX; COMMITTEE OF GENERAL SECURITY; COUP OF 18 FRUCTIDOR YEAR V; FEDERALISM; INDULGENTS; *JEUNESSE DOREE*; PLAIN, THE; 13 VENDEMIAIRE YEAR IV; VADIER; WHITE TERROR.

S

SAINT-ANDRE, ANDRE-JEANBON (1749-1813), organizer of the Revolutionary navy, member of the Committee of Public Safety. Jeanbon was born in Montauban on 25 February 1749 to A. and M.-M. Jeanbon. His Calvinist father, owner of a fulling mill, sent him to a Jesuit collège but soon withdrew him. He joined the merchant marine in 1765, made several long voyages, and rose to the rank of captain. In 1771 he entered the Protestant seminary in Lausanne, where he was ordained a Calvinist minister in 1773. He added the Catholic-sounding "Saint-André" to his name to gain protection from religious persecution. He was a pastor at Castres from 1773 to 1782 and then at Montauban in 1788. There he became an early supporter of the Revolution and joined the Jacobins. In November 1791 he was elected to the municipal government.

Elected a deputy of the Lot to the National Convention in September 1792, he joined the Girondins but quickly abandoned them for the Montagnards. Declaring "Royalty itself is a crime," he voted for the immediate death of Louis XVI and against all appeals. On 9 March 1793 he was sent as a representative on mission to the Lot and Dordogne, where he organized military recruitment and enforced strong measures against suspects, émigrés, and refractory priests. Returning to the Convention on 27 May, he supported the arrests of the leading Girondin deputies. After the Montagnards gained dominance, the Convention elected him a member of the Committee of Public Safety (10 July), the most powerful government committee, and president of the Convention (11-25 July). He and P.-L. Prieur de la Marne spent the month of August on mission enlarging, reinforcing, and supplying the armies of the Nord, Ardennes, and Moselle.

Jeanbon's most significant role in the Revolution was to reform the navy. He found a weak and dispirited navy that was no match for the British and left a formidable fleet that could at least challenge the enemy's control of the seas. On 30 September the Committee of Public Safety directed him to go to Brest and take any measures necessary to rebuild the Atlantic fleet. During this mission, he dismissed many officers, filled the ranks with patriots, inspired Revolutionary zeal among the sailors, improved conditions for the sailors, hastened the construction of ships and the manufacture of arms, and secured food and supplies. He proved himself to be one of the most capable administrators of the French Revolution. Because he refused to set up a Revolutionary tribunal in Brest, the committee sent J.-F. Laignelot on mission there.

Jeanbon promptly returned to Paris in a huff, but the committee, planning an invasion of the Channel Islands, ordered him once again (16 February 1794) to Brest with full power to prepare the fleet. On 16 May he sailed with the refurbished fleet to meet and escort a convoy of 116 merchant ships carrying 24 million pounds of flour from America. The British fleet, lying in wait for the convoy, engaged the French flotilla in a grueling battle on 1 June. Although the more experienced British won the battle, they were so disabled that they had to limp back to Plymouth and allow the huge convoy open passage to France.

On 6 July Jeanbon was sent to Toulon to construct a new fleet. Despite the fall of the radical government on 9 Thermidor (27 July), local complaints against him, and challenges to his authority, he contributed a great deal to the building of a powerful Mediterranean fleet before he was recalled to Paris on 29 January 1795.

Along with most of the leading terrorists, he was swept from power in the Thermidorian Reaction. After the popular rising of 1 Prairial Year III (20 May 1795), he was arrested by decree of the Convention for being a terrorist and a Robespierrist. He was released from Quatre-Nations prison by the general amnesty of October 1795.

Unlike many former terrorists, he continued to hold public offices. Aided by C.-M. Talleyrand, he gained appointments as consul to Algiers on 18 November 1795 and to Smyrna on 29 October 1797. When the Porte broke off relations with France, the Turks imprisoned him on 17 November 1798. After three years in jail, he returned to France and secured appointments as *commissaire général* to reorganize the four new departments of the Rhine and as prefect of Mont-Tonnerre (1 December 1801) from Napoleon, the first consul. Serving well as a popular and successful imperial administrator who never abandoned his republican sentiments, he was named to the Legion of Honor and, in 1810, entitled the baron de Saint-André. He died of typhus in Mainz on 10 December 1813, aged sixty-four years.

L. Levy-Schneider, *Le conventionnel Jeanbon Saint-André* (Paris, 1901); M. Nicolas, *Jeanbon Saint-André, sa vie et ses écrits* (Montauban, 1848); R. R. Palmer, *Twelve Who Ruled: The Year of the Terror in the French Revolution* (Princeton, 1941).

R. J. Caldwell

Related entries: COMMITTEE OF PUBLIC SAFETY; GIRONDINS; MONTAGNARDS; 9 THERMIDOR YEAR II; SECOND COALITION; THERMIDORIAN REACTION.

SAINT-DOMINGUE, French colony on the western third of the island of Hispaniola in the West Indies where revolution led to the establishment of the first black-ruled state in the western hemisphere. French planters were long aware of the danger of slave uprisings, especially on Saint-Domingue, where bands of maroons (runaway and rebellious slaves) lived a life of resistance among the rain-filled forests and mountainous retreats. There were many slave uprisings in the eighteenth century, the most violent led by F. Macandal, who from 1751 to 1757 terrorized the island. Nonetheless, seldom has there been a more careless, irresponsible group than the articulate minority of planters who, by imposing their will on the majority of the French residents, contributed to the coming of revolution on Saint-Domingue.

Most planters were wary of the swelling abolition movement, distrustful of the Estates General (and later, of the National Assembly), and suspicious of the aims of the planter minority who sought the transformation of the wealthier planters into a privileged aristocracy that would monopolize the public offices and control Saint-Domingue. The majority preferred a low profile, maintaining the status quo, trusting the French crown to intercede if necessary on their behalf. The vocal minority, however, disregarding the grave threats to life and property until too late, insisted on sending delegates to the initial meeting of the Estates General. They also organized in 1788 a political action committee of wealthy planters living in France and of their merchant allies, popularly known as the Club Massiac (from the marquis de Massiac, a Saint-Marc sugar proprietor in whose town house they met). The Club de Massiac provided the principal opposition to the abolitionist Société des amis des noirs, who sought equality before the law for the mulattoes (*gens de couleur*), consistent with the rights granted them by *Code Noir*, promulgated by Louis XIV in 1685. But the abolitionists not only won this political battle; in February 1794 (15 Pluviôse), after the National Assembly had in 1791 granted equality to free mulattoes, and after the planter minority defied the National Assembly's action, the abolitionists succeeded in having slavery itself abolished.

In 1789 local assemblies at Saint-Domingue, Martinique, and Guadeloupe elected delegates to the Estates General, six of whom were seated after heated debate. This was the first time in European history in which colonial representatives were seated in a metropolitan legislative assembly, and it produced a tremendous reaction at Le Cap, Saint-Domingue, as M.-L.-E. Moreau de Saint-Méry noted. H.-G. R. Mirabeau, in fact, extended the debate to include the very utility of colonies, as well as the immorality of slavery. Thus, by the summer of 1789, the question of enfranchisement and the future of Saint-Domingue became very much a part of the French Revolution. As Moreau pointed out in his *Considérations présentées aux vrais amis du repos et du bonheur de la France, à l'occasion des nouveaux mouvements de quelques soi-disant Amis des Noirs* (Paris, 1791), if the National Assembly legislated on the status of mulattoes, the colonists would believe themselves betrayed, and the mulattoes would take extreme measures. Then, in a domino process, the slaves would rise up. The colonies, he continued, will be a vast shambles. And France? The mulattoes are only pawns in a larger game. For if our slaves once suspect that some power other than their masters controls their fate, if they once see that the mulattoes are successful in invoking this power to gain equality with us, then France must renounce all hope of keeping her colonies.

The rhetoric of freedom, accompanied by a call for abolition, seemed to have inspired considerable fear. Saint-Domingue was in grave peril, a Club Massiac member warned, because the Amis des Noirs were engaged in a writing campaign against the colonists. The note of fear found an echo, as may be seen in an October 1789 dispatch from Saint-Domingue to France that claimed racial violence was imminent. The coming struggle was more complex than that of black and white, however. It was, rather, *grands blancs* and *petits blancs*, royalists and Revolutionaries, mulattoes and blacks, *affranchis* and slaves—all would fight, plunder, and kill in shifting, confused alliances.

The violence itself began in October 1790 when V. Ogé, a young Paris-educated mulatto affiliated with the Amis des Noirs, returned to Saint-Domingue and led an abortive revolt of mulattoes, which was repressed but nonetheless resulted in a wave of support for the mulatto cause. The following August (1791), a slave named Boukman led a terrible slave uprising. Within a few weeks, the entire northern plain was in ruins. Fire was set to cane fields, houses, and sugar mills; whites and blacks were murdered. Roads leading toward Le Cap were choked with refugees, the sky behind them a wall of fire.

This first large-scale revolt in the West Indies could not be suppressed by the few thousand white settlers and the handful of available regular troops without considerable help. The only hope of restoring order lay in the dispatch of troops from France. However, the Jacobins, finding the violence in Saint-Domingue a useful political weapon against their opponents, firmly opposed any such move. Only in September 1792, after the Jacobins had gained control of the Convention, did a French army reach Saint-Domingue. But this was a Revolutionary army, accompanied by three Jacobin commissioners, sent out to enforce the rule of liberty, equality, and fraternity. L.-F. Sonthonax, their leader, a zealous abolitionist, aligned himself with the revolted slaves, who, in June 1793, in part at his instigation, entered and sacked Le Cap. In August he proclaimed a conditional emancipation, subsequently confirmed in 1794 by the Jacobin government of M. Robespierre. Meanwhile, however, the proclamation alienated mulattoes, many of whom were, or had been, slave owners; it affected very little the slaves who—in the north, at least—had made themselves free through their uprising. With the general collapse that followed the destruction of Le Cap, white supremacy was ended, and short of some future significant support from France, was ended forever. But what Saint-Domingue was to be had not yet been decided.

News of these events in Saint-Domingue alarmed the British in Jamaica and the Spanish in Santo Domingo. When England and Spain went to war with France in 1793, both governments sent expeditions to invade Saint-Domingue.

The immediate goal of these invasions was to rescue the white colonists, who had invited intervention, and to suppress the slave rising. But there is little doubt that the British hoped to annex at least part of Saint-Domingue, which, until the outbreak of violence, had been far more profitable than Jamaica. The British, landing at the port of Jérémie in the south, met little resistance at first; in fact, many of the French colonists welcomed them as liberators. In March 1794, they took Port-au-Prince, but a second maroon war in Jamaica in 1795 resulted in a temporary retreat. Although the British would campaign for another four years, an ever-increasing incidence of casualties and of yellow fever led to their ultimate evacuation, which in 1798 F. Maitland negotiated in return for an amnesty and a commercial treaty between F.-D. Toussaint L'Ouverture and England. The Spanish, who also entered the war in 1793, were successful at first. In 1794, however, after Toussaint deserted the Spanish, turned against them, and went over to the French, the Spanish were forced to retreat east into Santo Domingo.

Toussaint soon rose to power following his betrayal of the Spanish; however, it would not be until the affair of 30 Ventôse (20 March 1796) that he would receive recognition commensurate with his real military power. Toussaint had intervened decisively on behalf of E.-M. Laveaux, then commander of the French forces, who was threatened by a mulatto commander. Laveaux was so grateful for Toussaint's intervention that he named him lieutenant governor of Saint-Domingue and promised to do nothing without his advice and counsel. This destroyed French authority on the island. P. de Lacroix, one of Napoleon's generals, later concluded that this event marked the end of white prestige and the beginning of black rule.

After the English and Spanish had been defeated or neutralized, and with the support of General Laveaux, Toussaint turned next on G. Rigaud, perhaps the most feared mulatto leader, who led a sizable force and was virtual ruler in the west. He defeated Rigaud, and, after sacking Les Cayes, the mulatto head-quarters, ordered J.-J. Dessalines, his lieutenant, who later would succeed Toussaint, to pacify the region. Dessalines did, systematically rounding up and murdering an estimated 10,000 men, women, and children.

By 1800, Toussaint was established as the only real power on Saint-Domingue. A year later, he defied the Consulate, invaded Santo Domingo, captured it, and gained virtual control of the entire island. Later that year, a local commission elected Toussaint governor for life, and a new constitution was prepared, which correspondingly reduced Saint-Domingue's ties with France. By now, however, Napoleon, convinced that the Jacobin plan of colonial assimilation was no longer operative, formally abjured the Revolutionary principle in the Constitution of the Year VIII and planned to restore the old system, sugar plantation, slavery, and all, in Saint-Domingue and Guadeloupe. These plans could not be executed while Toussaint ruled Saint-Domingue, but his removal could be achieved only through a military conquest of the island. Toussaint, aware of Napoleon's plans, began to prepare his forces, purchasing large quantities of arms and ammunition from the Americans and British. Meanwhile (1 October 1801) the Peace of

Amiens freed a large number of French regulars for duty in the West Indies, and the British blockade was lifted. Within ten weeks, some 20,000 picked soldiers of the Armies of the Rhine and of Italy were at sea, instructed, as Napoleon told C.-M. Talleyrand, to destroy the government of the blacks in Saint-Domingue and to reestablish the *ancien régime*.

Napoleon put C.-V.-E. Leclerc, his brother-in-law, in command of this large, veteran expeditionary force. The military operation would be divided into three phases: seize the coastal towns and organize for further operations, smash organized resistance, and impose pacification by use of flying columns. Leclerc was also commissioned to restore slavery when he saw fit.

In early December 1801, the army of invasion sailed for Saint-Domingue. When Leclerc landed in February 1802, he had only some 11,000 troops, the rest having been delayed by storms. Toussaint's position was strong. He had an army of around 20,000 regular troops who were well armed and hardened by war. Yet Toussaint decided not to give battle but to retreat and resort to guerrilla warfare and scorched-earth tactics. The French struck quickly. General D.-M.-J. de Rochambeau, with 2,000 troops, was ordered to capture Fort Dauphin, the most eastern point of Saint-Domingue; General J. Boudet with 3,500 men sailed on to seize Port-au-Prince, which isolated the south from the rest of the island. Leclerc with his remaining 5,000 troops made for Le Cap in the north, where he was greeted by mulattoes and many *affranchis*. H. Christophe, in charge of defending the city, decided to set it afire and retreat to the mountains. By 6 February the *plaine du nord* was in French hands.

Within a week, Toussaint's forces were in retreat everywhere, and Leclerc attempted to open negotiations with him. When Toussaint continued to resist, the French general issued a proclamation, putting Toussaint and Christophe beyond the pale of the law and declaring all of their armed adherents guilty of rebellion. Leclerc, having by now received additional reinforcements, moved in a major offensive against Toussaint's defenses in the mountains. Although Toussaint and his men resisted bravely, the end seemed inevitable when some of Toussaint's key supporters, including Dessalines, Christophe, and J. Maurepas, deserted to the French. Finally, early in May, Toussaint entered Le Cap to capitulate. A month later, Toussaint was arrested and sent to France where he was imprisoned. He died a year later.

In the spring of 1802, even as Leclerc began his program of pacification, the yellow fever season began, and the mortality rate of the French was frightful: an estimated thirty men died each day. When news reached Saint-Domingue that summer that the French had restored slavery and the slave trade on Guadeloupe, thousands of blacks, who still had not been disarmed, rose up. When Leclerc himself died of malaria, Napoleon in 1803 decided that he must relinquish his plans for the West Indies. Meanwhile, Leclerc's successor, without the reinforcements he had been promised by Napoleon, evacuated the island and sailed to Jamaica, where he surrendered his starved, ragged, fever-stricken remnant of an army.

Dessalines, who succeeded Toussaint, launched a campaign of extermination against the remaining whites as well as against the white exiles whom he invited to return. In 1804, he proclaimed himself an independent ruler of Haiti. Thus vanished French Saint-Domingue, and the black state of Haiti began its troubled history.

C. L. R. James, *The Black Jacobins*, 2d ed. (New York, 1963); T. O. Ott, *The Haitian Revolution, 1789-1804* (Knoxville, 1973); T. L. Stoddard, *The French Revolution in San Domingo* (Boston, 1914).

L. Apt

Related entries: BRISSOT DE WARVILLE; SOCIETE DES AMIS DES NOIRS; TOUSSAINT-L'OUVERTURE.

SAINT-JUST, LOUIS-ANTOINE-LEON DE (1767-94), deputy to the National Convention, Jacobin. One of the most remarkable figures of the Revolution, Saint-Just became famous for his energy, oratorical ability, military leadership, and political role in the Terror. Born at Decizes (Nièvre), he was the son of a former sergeant of the guard and captain in the artillery who came from peasant stock. His mother was a notary's daughter. His childhood was spent at Nampcel (Oise) and Blérancourt (Aisne), where his father possessed considerable property. When the elder Saint-Just died in 1777, he left his family a considerable inheritance.

Saint-Just was educated at the Oratorian collège of Saint-Nicolas at Soissons, where he studied from 1777 to 1785. An unhappy adolescent love affair led him to leave for Paris, taking family valuables with him. At the demand of his mother, Saint-Just was briefly incarcerated for several months in 1786-87. No doubt it was while confined that he composed his *Organt*, a lengthy, scabrous poem with political overtones, published anonymously in 1789. Chastened by his confinement, Saint-Just entered the service of the public prosecutor of Soissons and later attended courses at the Faculty of Law at Reims. After completing his legal studies, he returned to Blérancourt. There he spent a year of relative idleness, marked only by a trip to Paris in the summer of 1789 where he witnessed the fall of the Bastille.

The outbreak of the Revolution opened a career for the young lawyer, who quickly became involved in local politics. In 1790 he was elected secretary of the town of Blérancourt and wrote an impassioned defense of Soissons as the capital of the newly created department of the Aisne. No doubt because of his military background, Saint-Just was chosen to serve as colonel in the National Guard. In this capacity, he led his unit to Paris to attend the Festival of the Federation in July. That same summer he wrote to M. Robespierre a letter of admiration, calling him the ''deputy of humanity.'' This contact marked the start of a close friendship that lasted until their deaths.

Putting his legal talents to work, Saint-Just gained fame at Blérancourt by his defense of local peasants against a large landowner, a former marquis named Grenet. In 1791 he published a brochure on the spirit of the Revolution and the constitution of France. Writing in the laconic style that became his hallmark, Saint-Just expressed his satisfaction with the work of the Constituent Assembly and the limited monarchy of Louis XVI. He called for the enactment of wise laws that would guarantee equal political and civil rights for everyone and promote virtue. Still an idealist, he disavowed the use of force to compel obedience and believed that institutions would promote human happiness.

Soon afterward came the attempted flight of the king. As a colonel in the National Guard, Saint-Just was called on to escort Louis XVI back to Paris. Eager to play more than a local political role, Saint-Just sought election to the Legislative Assembly in September, but he was denied the chance because he had not yet reached legal age. Consequently, he watched from the sidelines the crisis that developed in 1792: war, invasion, and the overthrow of the king. Although little is known of his attitudes during this time, Saint-Just developed into an ardent republican. He entered national politics in September, when he was elected the fifth of twelve deputies to the Convention from the Aisne department.

At the opening of the Convention, Saint-Just, its youngest member, took his place among the Jacobin democrats and established his reputation as an enthusiastic Revolutionary. In a speech to the Jacobins on 22 October, he attacked the moderate Girondins for their plan to establish a federal guard for the lawmakers. Such a force, he declared, would endanger both deputies and people. Saint-Just gained greater prominence for his speeches made before the Convention during the trial of Louis XVI. He called for the king's judgment and execution, without any resort to popular plebiscite. Louis was guilty of crimes because "it is impossible to reign in innocence."

Saint-Just also touched on other pressing national issues in his addresses. He dealt with the problem of food supply on 29 November, urging the government to relieve the misery of the poor who suffered from rampant inflation. He asked that the property of *émigrés* be sold to pay off the national debt, that the land tax be paid in grain, and that free movement of grain be allowed. His speech on the organization of the Ministry of War (28 January 1793) called for war powers to be vested in the Convention rather than in an individual, and on the reorganization of the army (12 February) he pressed for the speedy amalgamation of regular troops and volunteers into a single force, as well as the election of officers by soldiers.

His grasp of military affairs led his colleagues to dispatch him in March to supervise recruitment for the army in the Aisne and Ardennes departments. Returning to Paris, Saint-Just bitterly denounced P.-P. Beurnonville, the minister of war, for his ineffectiveness in supplying the troops.

Always interested in problems of government, Saint-Just intervened in the debate on the new constitution, presenting his own plan to the Convention on 24 April. He opposed the Girondins' federalism and sought to establish a democratic government that divided power between legislative and executive branches, the former elected directly by the people, the latter chosen by electoral assemblies in the departments.

Saint-Just was rewarded for his efforts by being elected a member of the Committee of Public Safety on 30 May. The elimination of the Girondins from power in the uprising of 2 June further promoted his fortunes. With his colleagues on the committee, he drafted a new democratic constitution for France, which was adopted on 24 June. It was he who on 8 July presented a report on those Girondin deputies who were either in prison or in flight. Saint-Just called on the Convention to punish the fomenters of rebellion but to spare the misguided. His impressive oratory brought his election to the reorganized committee two days later. With his colleagues, Saint-Just now became one of the de facto rulers of France.

During the next year, he became a leading spokesman for the committee, presenting numerous reports to the Convention and serving on several missions to the armies. These oratorical and military efforts won him lasting notoriety. In a speech delivered on 10 October, he described the many dangers that confronted the country and called for a drastic reorganization of the government to overcome them. Saint-Just demanded full civil and military authority for the committee to rule the country and for the suspension of the recently enacted democratic constitution. The Convention responded with a measure that declared the government Revolutionary until the peace and gave the committee control over ministers, generals, and local administrators.

A week later, Saint-Just was assigned the important task of deputy on mission to the Army of the Rhine in Alsace. Along with P. Le Bas, he visited the hard-pressed troops, restored their morale through provisioning of food and supplies, and removed incompetent officers. He also imposed demands for money and supplies on the wealthy of Strasbourg and ousted ineffective local officials. As a result, the army won major victories that drove the Allied forces from Alsace. On his return to Paris, Saint-Just received a second mission, this time to the Army of the North. In January and February 1794, he and Le Bas reorganized the transportation and supply system in preparation for a spring offensive. These successes raised Saint-Just's stock such that he was elected president of the Convention on 19 February.

His oratorical abilities were again put to good use by the Committee of Public Safety during early 1794. On 26 February, he presented a report that justified the Terror, pledged to free innocent political prisoners from detention, but threatened to confiscate the property of those suspected of crimes against the Republic. To implement this proposal, he put forth a plan on 3 March that ordered a census of the poor, an examination of those held in custody, and a scheme to distribute to the poor the property of enemies of the Republic. Although these so-called Ventôse Decrees were never fully carried out, they potentially meant a massive redistribution of property throughout France.

As political divisions over Revolutionary policies widened and the danger of extremists on both Left and Right increased, the Committee of Public Safety moved to eliminate its enemies. On 13 March Saint-Just denounced the foreign factions who aided the enemy by weakening the republican regime from within. The Convention then voted the arrest and trial of such extremists as J.-R. Hébert and F.-N. Vincent, as well as leading foreigners residing in Paris. On 31 March Saint-Just accused G.-J. Danton and his followers of corruption and moderation. They too were tried and executed.

With both Hébertists and Dantonists eliminated, the Committee of Public Safety held the fate of the Revolution in its hands. Thus, the pronouncements that Saint-Just made in its name bore considerable weight. In a report presented to the Convention on 15 April, he declared that the country still faced great dangers and that to overcome them, the police administration should be strengthened. The decree he proposed called for the centralization of justice, with all political prisoners being tried by the Revolutionary Tribunal in Paris. Nobles and foreigners would be expelled from the capital and strategic towns. Local government would be placed under tighter central control. The measure passed, giving the committee enormous power.

Saint-Just turned now to practical action. In late April he and Le Bas were sent on a mission to the armies on the northern frontier, where he remained (with one short visit to Paris) until June. The two deputies strengthened the French positions and prepared for a general assault on the enemy. At his urging, attacks were made against Austrian positions on the Sambre River. Despite repeated setbacks, the French under General J.-C. Pichegru eventually won the day at Fleurus on 26 June, opening Belgium to the republican armies.

His task accomplished, Saint-Just returned to the capital, where he resumed his work on the committee. But the acceleration of the Terror as a result of the Law of 22 Prairial, divisions within the committee, and M. Robespierre's estrangement from it created a new political situation. During July when the internal crisis came to a head, Saint-Just seems to have remained loyal to Robespierre, whose leadership now came under attack. On 26 July Robespierre precipitated a crisis by calling for a new purge of the Convention. This threat to members fearful of punishment for misdeeds led to the overthrow of the Incorruptible and his associates the next day (27 July). Hoping to win over the Convention, Saint-Just began a carefully prepared speech that was soon interrupted and never completed. With four colleagues, he was denounced by the conspirators and arrested. That evening Saint-Just was released from detention and met with his friends at the city hall, where they sought to stir a popular uprising against the Convention. Unsuccessful, they were captured and arrested—Saint-Just submitting stoically—identified before the Revolutionary Tribunal, and guillotined on 28 July.

Saint-Just enjoys the reputation of a dynamic but icy figure. Detractors see him as a sinister terrorist devoted to the ruthless elimination of enemies of the republican regime. Admirers consider him a dedicated Revolutionary devoted to liberty and the welfare of the people. Saint-Just's own political testament, *Fragments on Republican Institutions* (not published until 1800), reveals an idealistic and authoritarian personality, one that combined the rigor of ancient Rome with the faith of the Enlightenment.

G. Bruun, *Saint-Just: Apostle of the Terror* (New York, 1932); E. N. Curtis, *Saint-Just, Colleague of Robespierre* (New York, 1935); P. Derocles (pseud. A. Soboul), *Saint-Just, ses idées politiques et sociales* (Paris, 1937); J. B. Morton, *Saint-Just* (London and New York, 1939); A. Soboul, *Saint-Just: Discours et rapports* (Paris, 1957); C. Vellay, *Oeuvres complètes de Saint-Just*, 2 vols. (Paris, 1907); B. Vienot, "Les origines familiales de Saint-Just," *Ann. hist. de la Révo. française* 54 (1982).

J. Friguglietti

Related entries: BATTLE OF FLEURUS; COMMITTEE OF PUBLIC SAFETY; GIRONDINS; HEBERTISTS; JACOBINS; LAW OF 14 FRIMAIRE; LAW OF 22 PRAIRIAL; PICHEGRU; REPRESENTATIVES ON MISSION; REVOLUTIONARY TRIBUNAL; ROBESPIERRE, M.; TERROR, THE.

SAINT-LAZARE. See PRISONS.

SAINT-PRIEST, FRANCOIS-EMMANUEL GUIGNARD, COMTE DE (1735-1821), diplomat and minister of state. Scion of a distinguished family of Dauphiné, whose father had served as intendant of Languedoc, Saint-Priest was trained for a military career. He was *aide-de-camp* to Marshal de Broglie in the Seven Years War, serving later under Marshal Beauveau in Spain. It was under Beauveau's protection that Saint-Priest entered the diplomatic service, first at Lisbon and then, from 1769 until 1785, at Constantinople, where he replaced C.-G. Vergennes. He was never on good terms with Vergennes, and it was not until the death of the foreign minister in 1787 that Saint-Priest was able to advance in the diplomatic service and finally to become a minister of state. He was sent to the Hague in 1787 where he had the unhappy task of informing the patriot party that France could not send aid to resist British and Prussian intervention on behalf of the stadholder.

At the time of the fall of E.-C. Loménie de Brienne's ministry and the beginning of J. Necker's second ministry at the helm of the royal finances, Saint-Priest was appointed minister without portfolio. He opposed the doubling of the Third Estate in the elections to the Estates General. He sought to have the French government accept the proffered alliance of Catherine II of Russia, believing that this might be useful in containing domestic radicalism. Necker opposed this move, and it was not pursued. During the June crisis of 1789, Saint-Priest supported Necker's position that concessions should be made to the Third Estate. He was dismissed along with Necker on 11 July and returned again after the fall of the Bastille, when he became minister of the interior. In that post, he held important responsibility in the events that followed. Concerned about the steadily dwindling power of the monarchy and the ministry, he sought to persuade the king and royal family to move away from the proximity of the Parisian radical movement. In the October Days he drew up a plan for the king and the royal family to move to the château of Rambouillet and to place troops at the main exits of the city of Paris toward the southwest. Necker opposed this, and the king, after an initial acceptance, also rejected it. After the removal of the royal family to Paris, the ministry lost all power, as Saint-Priest had predicted. He himself became the object of Revolutionary furor and was denounced by H.-G. R. Mirabeau in the National Assembly. He emigrated, going first to England and then to Sweden.

Saint-Priest became a prominent figure in the history of the emigration. He was usually opposed to the policies of the princes, the two brothers of the king, believing they were unrealistic and harmful to the royal cause. But he did think that the Revolution could be suppressed only by outside intervention coming to the aid of domestic opposition. He sought the help of Sweden and Russia to intervene militarily in France. Gustavus III was eager to do so, but Catherine II declined. On the death of Louis XVII in 1795 and the assumption of the crown by Louis XVIII, Saint-Priest finally joined the Bourbon court and became the foremost diplomat of the emigration, finding new asylums for Louis XVIII on his travels. Yet he did not get along well with the Bourbon pretender, feeling that his exaggerated claims to respect by fellow sovereigns did not accord well with his actual diplomatic and political situation. After the establishment of the Consulate, Saint-Priest left the service of Louis XVIII, residing again in Sweden and later in Geneva. He took no active part in the Restoration of 1814 and 1815, although he was nominated to the Chamber of Peers.

Baron de Barante, *Etudes historiques et biographiques* (Paris, 1858); E. M. de Saint-Priest, *Mémoires*, 2 vols. (Paris, 1929).

R. D. Harris

Related entries: *EMIGRES*; LOMENIE DE BRIENNE; NECKER; OCTOBER DAYS; VONCK.

SALTPETRIERE. See PRISONS.

SANS-CULOTTES, a diverse social group comprised of master craftsmen, small shopkeepers, journeymen, and workers in Paris and other cities whose social ideals included economic independence and government regulation and whose political ideals consisted of popular sovereignty and direct democracy. *Sans-culottes*, originally a vulgar expression, was a term of ridicule coined by their enemies to describe the Parisian Revolutionaries, but the latter adopted this description and made it a mark of pride. In fact, they did not wear knee breeches like the aristocrats, but rather trousers held up by suspenders, a short jacket or *carmagnole*, a Phrygian cap (the sign of liberated slaves in antiquity), a tricolor cockade, and wooden shoes. Often, too, the *sans-culotte* carried a sword at his side and pike in his hand, the latter being a sign of popular sovereignty, which, when the need arose, was employed in insurrection, always a sacred right.

It was the pike, a weapon quickly forged and easily handled, that allowed the overthrow of the monarchy on 10 August 1792 and subsequently the establishment of the Republic and the expulsion of the Girondins from the Convention.

It was the pike, in the opinion of the *sans-culottes*, that would bring them victory over the brigands of the Vendée and over the liberticides of Europe. On 21 September 1793 the deputy S.-P. Lejeune noted in a speech to the Convention that this weapon had been too long neglected while aristocrats tried to discredit it; and yet the pike of the *sans-culottes* was worth liberty itself. The pike was called "holy," and all who carried it were referred to indiscriminately as "pikes," "*carmagnoles*," or "*sans-culottes*."

A. Soboul has demonstrated that the *sans-culottes* did not constitute a social class but rather a heterogeneous group that comprised master artisans (some of whom were well-to-do like J.-M. Duplay, Robespierre's landlord), their employees, journeymen who worked side by side with them in their ateliers and shops, and workers in the few factories that existed. What united them was their hatred of aristocracy and their passion for equality. This manifested itself in their social behavior and peculiar language. No more use of "*Monsieur*"; instead, "one is honored by the title of citizen," henceforth used to address and greet people. In December 1792 one patriot observed that the word *vous* was contrary to the principle of equality. It had been used in the past to support principles of feudalism. The word *toi*, he continued, is the true method of address used by free men. *Le Républicain* of 15 Brumaire Year II (5 November 1793) observed, "During the centuries of error from which we are just now emerging there was no true friendship, because friendship is free and friendship uses *toi* as a form of address. A republic is one large society of friends; therefore, it is necessary for people to use *toi*." Thus, *toi* was employed in public life until 1795; it disappeared after the uprising of Prairial Year III (May 1795), when, at the same time, the desire for equality was crushed.

In the Year II this desire had expressed itself in other ways in conversation and correspondence: no more "I have the honor" or "You do me the honor of ...."; no more "I am, sir, your very humble and very obedient servant." The *sans-culotte* did not bow; he kept his head high and his body straight so that former court mistresses and ministers "lowered their eyes" before him. One began and ended letters with: "Your fellow citizen," "Your friend," "Your brother," or "Your comrade" and added "Greetings and Fraternity in Holy Equality." A *sans-culotte* soldier who wrote to a general or a minister ended his letter with, "Your equal in rights." Bowing and scraping existed only in memory. Citizens whom one met had surnames like Liberty, Fraternity, Equality, Terror, the Mountain, Brutus, Marat, or, like G. Babeuf, Gracchus.

Central to the social demands of the *sans-culottes* was cheap bread. If all people did not eat adequately, then equality, and liberty as well, were mere delusions. From demanding the right to existence, the *sans-culottes* soon passed to demanding equality of possessions. The gap between rich and poor, they claimed, should be smaller; let the rich, then, give their superfluous goods to the poor and, if needed, share their possessions with them; or let the state facilitate the acquisition of property by all. Although they wanted to limit the influence of property by regulating the circulation of necessities and by price fixing, the *sans-culottes* were not communists. Their dream was that all should possess as much property as could be worked by a man and his family. The political system, wrote one *sans-culotte*, should assure all the unmolested enjoyment of possessions; but the system should also, in so far as possible, ensure at least a proportional distribution of goods among all citizens.

So that all citizens, while waiting for limitations on property, might have sustenance and thereby their independence, the *sans-culottes* also demanded recognition of the right to work and to public assistance. An address from three united sections of the faubourg Saint-Antoine (on 4 July 1793) stated that since the poor had helped to sustain the Revolution and to frame the Constitution, it was time that they enjoyed their fruits. The address went on to demand the establishment of workshops where the workingman would always find employment and institutions where the elderly, the sick, and the infirm would receive assistance.

In order to establish equality, the right of all to education had to be recognized. On 16 June 1793 an orator from the section Amis de la Patrie denounced the ignorance and fanaticism that was destroying years of struggle and sacrifice while education would dissipate prejudices and make people embrace a revolution whose secure basis was virtue. He demonstrated the need to assure educational opportunity by creating primary schools.

Anticapitalists, sharing the ideal, expressed by J.-J. Rousseau, of the small proprietor free from control by large merchants, the *sans-culottes* went against the current of economic evolution in their own time. They were more innovative in the political domain where their tendency and their practices were those of direct democracy. The people was sovereign. The people made laws or at least sanctioned them by closely supervising the deliberations and decisions of deputies, who were regarded as mere agents. If the latter were unfaithful, they could be recalled by the people. In case of extreme danger, when the tocsin sounded and the drum pounded, the armed people resumed all legislative, executive, and judicial powers; this was the meaning of the massacres of September 1792 and the *journées* of 31 May-2 June 1793 and 4-5 September 1793.

The *sans-culottes* participated in political life by means of assemblies that met within the framework of the sections, popular societies, or clubs. The sections were institutions authorized by public law that exercised administrative functions and that, during elections, united all citizens living in the same neighborhood in a primary assembly. In 1793, under pressure from the *sans-culottes*, these assemblies tended to become permanent. The popular societies were organizations created by private initiative that united citizens who desired to debate the great questions of the day. At the beginning of their existence, they had no official competence. The sections and the popular societies, however, tended, little by little, to resemble each other and sometimes to become indistinguishable from each other. The sessions generally took place at the end of the day, at 6 o'clock in the winter and 7 o'clock in the summer. On the premises, the walls were covered by inscriptions that proclaimed that it was necessary ''To Conquer or Die," to gain "Liberty or Death." Pictures or statues recalled the traits of heroes or martyrs of liberty: L.-M. Le Pelletier, M.-J. Chalier, J.-P. Marat, J. Bara, J.-A. Viala. In the room were benches, chairs, sometimes a stove for cold days, a wooden screen to mark off for the public the space reserved for them, and occasionally a gallery for the wives and daughters of *sans-culottes* who were invited to come to support citizens but almost never to participate actively in their debates or decisions. Behind a long table, on a platform, was a committee on which sat the members elected for a month at a time: the president, vice-president, secretary, and archivist. On the wall above their heads were the Declaration of the Rights of Man and of the Citizen and tricolor flags. The secretary read the minutes of the previous meeting or extracts from the newspapers. People listened to correspondence from patriots in the provinces, and sometimes children were invited to come and read the great texts of the Revolution. Then came the order of the day; all those present were invited to give their opinions on the questions raised. Anyone who asked to speak donned a *bonnet rouge* (red cap), climbed the stairs to a rostrum facing the president, and began his speech. The length of speeches was not limited, but if the president felt that the speaker was monopolizing the rostrum, he could remind him that a laconic style most befitted republicans. When all those who wanted to speak had done so, the president called for the vote. Among brothers, what need was there of a ballot box or secret ballots? Would anyone thus try to hide his opinion? One voted, therefore, by sitting or standing, or by raising one's hand, or sometimes even by applauding. To bring a motion to the Convention, a mere majority was insufficient; unanimity among the voters was required. If this was not obtained, discussion reopened until the opposition was won over.

Some sections were more moderate than others; and real *sans-culottes* would then call on their brothers in neighboring sections to come to their aid. They would come to fraternize and thereby contribute to the elimination of the lukewarm. In the Year II these purges were carried out by the Jacobin allies of the Revolutionary government, which was uneasy about this parallel authority. In the summer of 1793 the government had allowed them to establish themselves and to initiate the Terror. But did not such popular assemblies provide factions with the chance to manipulate crowds, to push them to pressure the Convention and its committees, and to incite them to overthrow the government? Did not the ultra-Revolutionaries, like the *enragés*, act this way? Could one allow public debate over questions essential to the triumph of the Revolution? According to the Jacobins, the war necessitated a policy made by small, secret committees. Under the orders of the Convention, only these committees knew how to motivate and organize citizens and to maintain the unity of the Republic.

In order to prevent the sections from continuing as autonomous agencies, the government forbade the permanence of their meetings. To get around the law, the *sans-culottes* created sectional societies, modeled on the popular societies. After J.-R. Hébert and his friends were guillotined, however, the Montagnards pursued and achieved the dissolution of these societies. Henceforth, the sections and the popular societies became part of the governmental machinery and assumed police and record-keeping functions. In fact, militants had never been more than a minority. Between 1790 and 1792 the proportion of those eligible who attended the general assemblies of the sections varied from 4 to 9 percent. After 1792 participation increased, only to decline anew in the Year II. The importance of the sections and the popular societies as vital centers of political life or as intermediaries in the exercise of governmental power, however, cannot be measured entirely by the number of participants. On the days after their meetings, the militants returned to their workplaces and repeated the discussions of the previous evening; they were told the opinions of their comrades and could, when evening came, repeat them in their neighborhood assemblies.

During the Year II the Jacobins also met in their clubs and tended to form a kind of hegemonic party with which the popular societies were affiliated. According to the historian G. Maintenant, these societies increased from 400 in 1791 to 2,000 in 1794. Thus, across France nearly 100,000 members attended their meetings, at least on occasion. If this network of militants permitted the Jacobins to conduct the war successfully and save the Revolution, it did not provide them with effective aid in Thermidor, and the government of the Mountain fell along with Robespierre. The departure of the staunchest militants for the army, the physical and emotional wear and tear on other *sans-culottes* employed in various tasks in the state apparatus, the disarray in which others were put by the drama of Germinal, then the dissolution of the sectional societies (as L. Saint-Just said, the Revolution was frozen), all explain the partial defection of the *sans-culottes* on 8 and 9 Thermidor. Robespierre's fall is explained further by the contradictions within the *sans-culotte* movement. These included the contradictions between journeymen and small masters, who did not always favor a strict application of the maximum on prices, which sometimes worked against their interests, but who, on the other hand, supported a strict adherence to the maximum on wages. Also there were contradictions between the *sans-culottes* and the Revolutionary bourgeois, who were upset by economic controls and by social measures taken by the Montagnard government.

Nevertheless, 9 Thermidor did not mark the end of the popular movement. The defeat of the *sans-culottes* dates from Germinal and Prairial Year III (April-May 1795)—after the *sans-culottes* uprising that, together with cheap bread, demanded the Constitution of 1793, which recognized the aspirations of direct democracy. Repression fell on the *sans-culotte* militants, and, for a long time, the popular movement was broken.

For how long? While industrialization increased in France during the nineteenth century, with its factories and mass of laborers, the social element represented by the workshop, the small factory, and the small retail outlet persisted in the capital and elsewhere. The small masters and their journeymen, the wage earners of the Old Regime, played an important role in the Commune of Paris of 1871. In this episode was reborn the ideal of the *sans-culottes*, who, in the Year II, had wished to unite "Fatherland and Revolution."

F. Brunel, "Les derniers Montagnards et l'unité révolutionnaire," *Ann. hist. de la Révo. française* 49 (1977); G. Lemarchand, "Jacobinisme et violence révolutionnaire au Havre de 1791 à septembre 1793," *Cahiers Léopold Delisle*, special no. (1966); G. Maintenant, "Le jacobinisme en Haute-Marne: le club de Bourbonne-les-Bains," *Cah. ht.-marnais*, nos. 135, 136 (1978, 1979), "Les Jacobins d' Alençon, 1791—mars 1793," *Bull. de la Soc. hist. de l'Orne* 104 (1976), and "Les Jacobins de la ville de Mayenne (1791-an II): Etude d' histoire politique d'un club 'modéré,' " *Bul. de la Comm. hist. de la Mayenne*, no. 66 (1977); G. Rudé, *The Crowd in the French Revolution* (Oxford, 1959); A. Soboul, *Les Sans-culottes parisiens en l'an II: Mouvement populaire et gouvernement révolutionnaire, 2 juin 1793-9 thermidor an II* (Paris, 1958).

J.-P. Bertaud

Related entries: *ENRAGES*; HEBERT; *JOURNEES REVOLUTIONNAIRES*; LAW OF THE MAXIMUM; MONTAGNARDS; 9 THERMIDOR YEAR II; SECTIONS; SYMBOLISM; 10 AUGUST 1792; TERROR, THE; VENDEE.

SANTERRE, ANTOINE-JOSEPH (1752-1809), commandant of the National Guard of Paris from 11 August 1792 to 19 May 1793, general in command of Parisian volunteers in the Vendée in the summer of 1793. Santerre's father was a Cambrai brewer who had founded an establishment in Paris. A.-J. Santerre inherited the brewery and became a respected figure in the faubourg Saint-Antoine: paternal employer, subscriber to local poor relief through public works, elector of the Third Estate for Paris in 1789. His participation in the attack on the Bastille on 14 July gave him the nickname "general of the faubourg Saint-Antoine"; his prosperity made him a natural spokesman for the artisans and shopkeepers among the victors of the Bastille. By early 1791 he was chief of his National Guard batallion, vice-president of the club Ennemis du despotisme and president of the Quinze-Vingts section.

On 28 February 1791, the people of Vincennes attempted to demolish its château, which had been a prison and was now a fort. The marquis de Lafayette called several National Guard units to the spot but barred Santerre's batallion, which was largely composed of "victors of the Bastille." Santerre's men forced him to lead them to Vincennes, where their role was so ambiguous that an aide-de-camp of Lafayette accused the faubourg Saint-Antoine detachment of preparing to fire on him. Santerre, incensed at both Lafayette and his aide, brought a suit that ended with the court's declaring the case outside its jurisdiction. This incident established Santerre as a bourgeois general in opposition to the leadership of the liberal nobles.

Santerre joined the republican demonstration of 17 July on the Champ de Mars; the demonstrators were attacked by the National Guard and a warrant was sworn out for Santerre's arrest. He fled Paris, to return only after the amnesty that accompanied the ratification of the 1791 Constitution.

In 1792 Santerre's popularity began to extend beyond Paris. A signer of the petition for 10,000 pikes, he participated in the *journées* of 20 June and 10 August and was named commandant of the Paris National Guard after the murder of A.-J.-D. de Mandat. He managed to stay clear of the September Massacres, of which he clearly desired no part. Santerre was now a minor national hero, his face appearing in some decks of patriotic playing cards, a man with a quasi-military reputation for disciplining and leading *sans-culottes*. On 19 May 1793 Santerre accepted the command of a force of Parisian volunteers en route to the Vendée.

The Vendée was disastrous for Santerre's Revolutionary career. His troops were routed at the defense of Saumur on 6 June and again at Coron on 18 September 1793, defeats unfairly blamed on him alone, although the inexperience of his Parisian volunteers was also responsible. The reports of the Interior Ministry's spies in Paris show that Santerre's political capital was depleted; Parisians expected news of his arrest from January 1794 and tended to explain his incompetence as treachery. He was arrested in Rennes on 29 Germinal Year II (18 April 1794) by the Committee of General Security, as an afterthought to the arrest of leaders of the Paris Commune. Santerre was released on 19 Vendémiaire Year III (10 October 1794), well after the fall of M. Robespierre.

Santerre stayed outside Paris during 1795-96, first living with farming relatives in the Seine-et-Marne, then undertaking a textile business in Senlis. His family's assistance, along with shrewd speculation in *biens nationaux* around Beauvais, let him reestablish himself in Paris by 1797. Santerre steered clear of pro-Jacobin circles, though at the coup of 18 Fructidor Year V (4 September 1797) he is reported to have organized a small armed band and offered his support to the insurgent directors. In July 1800, N. Bonaparte (then first consul) recognized Santerre's status as a general, retired him, and gave him a pension. Informers described him in 1803 as a regular in military clubs, complaining of inaction. Further real estate investments in Paris kept Santerre comfortable until his death on 6 February 1809.

Santerre is an example of the Parisian popular leader before the radical *sans-culotte* movement of the Year II. A prosperous commercial figure whose status was tied to the world of work, he could suitably champion the Third Estate in the years 1789-92, when the court and nobles were the Revolution's only declared enemies and popular military prowess was still an unrealized hope. Neither a politician nor a soldier, Santerre's symbolic leadership was swept away by the military and political needs of the Terror.

P. Caron, ed., *Paris pendant la Terreur*, 5 vols. (Paris, 1910-58); M. Carro, *Santerre, général de la République française* (Paris, 1847); M. Dommanget, "Santerre dans l'Oise," *Ann. révo.* 13 (1921).

C. Ramsay

Related entries: BIENS NATIONAUX; COMMITTEE OF GENERAL SECURITY; COUP OF 18 FRUCTIDOR YEAR V; *JOURNEES REVOLUTIONNAIRES;* LAFAYETTE; NATIONAL GUARD; VENDEE.

SCIENCE. During and after the Revolutionary era, French scientists maintained a preeminent place in the European intellectual community despite the disruption of basic research during the Terror, the temporary dissolution of most public scientific institutions, and the executions of A. Lavoisier and other scholars. While the radical governments of 1793-94 employed selected scientists for their technological skills, the moderates after Thermidor created new public educational institutions and learned societies. The ultimate impact of the Revolution was thus to assist the emergence of a professional scientific career and to deepen the generally beneficial, if sometimes constraining, interaction between scientists and government.

The Revolution had varying effects on a wide array of scientific institutions under public sponsorship in the Old Regime. The National Convention in 1794-95 reorganized the elite engineering schools, the Ecole des Ponts et Chaussées (founded 1747), the military Ecole Royale du Génie (1748), and the smaller Ecole des Mines (1783), to give them larger teaching staffs and more socially diverse students. Yet the changes in Revolutionary regimes scarcely affected the public lectureships of the non-degree-granting Collège royal (Collège de France), which, after 1774, had eight scientific chairs out of nineteen. In 1793 the self-imposed reform of the Jardin du Roi (1626), the dramatic change in the Royal Observatory (1667), and the suppression of the Paris Royal Academy of Sciences (1666) demonstrated the severe pressure of the Republic on institutions tainted by corporate privilege and royal patronage.

Some historians have attributed the relative success of the Jardin du Roi, compared to the Academy, to Rousseauist empathy for popular natural history and hostility to mathematical, "aristocratic" Newtonian science. Indeed the Convention debates of 1793 included anti-intellectual outbursts that expressed the sentiments of the alleged, but apocryphal, remark of Lavoisier's judge in 1794: "The Republic needs no *savants*." Many Paris artisans also resented the Academy's traditional consultative role in granting royal privileges and subsidies for inventors. In 1791 artisans petitioned the Assembly against the academicians' domination of the new advisory group, the Bureau de Consultation des Arts et Métiers.

Yet antagonism to the Academy generally did not aim at the scientific enterprise itself, nor did the success of the Jardin reflect scientific rather than political issues. The staff of the Jardin revised their statutes in 1793 to replace the intendant by a director limited to a one-year term and to assure internal equality among all twelve professors. In the Convention in June 1793, J. Lakanal was able to save the "republicanized" Jardin, renamed the Muséum National d'Histoire Naturelle. After the Terror, the museum became a flourishing center of research and teaching in chemistry and the life sciences (for B.-G.-E. Lacepède, J.-B.-P. Lamarck, A.-L. de Jussieu, and later G. Cuvier, among others).

Conversely, the observatory suffered because of the royalist opinions of the director (J.-D. Cassini), who maintained a hierarchy among himself and three unequally salaried assistants. The assistants succeeded in establishing an egalitarian regime in September 1793 and in unceremoniously evicting Cassini. By June 1795, the Convention had established in conjunction with the observatory a new astronomy and navigation school, the Bureau des Longitudes, staffed by eminent scientists such as J.-L. Lagrange. Several in the bureau were also members of the Weights and Measures Commission, which survived the Terror after a purge of suspected moderates. War and domestic insecurity delayed the necessary measurements so that the proclamation of the metric system in French-dominated Europe occurred only in December 1799.

The fatal flaw of the Paris Academy lay in its organization as a privileged royal corporation, with royal approval for elections, royal appointment of officers, twelve honorary members elected for their patronage as prominent nobles or ministers, and a three-step hierarchy among the forty-eight working members (in each of eight sections excluding the permanent secretary). In the political context of abolition of guilds, professional monopolies, and, after 1792, of royal symbols, the Academy was an anachronism. Although academicians proposed statutes in 1790 to eliminate royal influence, internal hierarchy, and honorary members, they insensitively maintained the old rules pending legislative reform. After 10 August 1792, the majority refused to purge émigrés in a vain bid to appear above politics.

Influential journalists and politicians fanned the flames of hostility to elitist academies. Even in 1784 J.-P. Brissot had lamented the injustice of academic commissions that condemned F.-A. Mesmer for charlatanism. J.-P. Marat in 1791 singled out Lavoisier and the marquis de Condorcet in bitter attacks on the Academy, no doubt a reaction to real or imagined slights concerning the reception of his discoveries on light, heat, fire, and electricity. Although Marat was dead and Brissot in prison, in the charged atmosphere of 8 August 1793, the artist J.-L. David swayed the Convention to abolish all academies and to ignore the abbé Grégoire's pleas for the utility of an academy in maintaining scientific projects.

The suppression of the Academy and turbulence of the Terror interrupted basic scientific research. The guillotine claimed six academicians, at least eleven others served prison terms (two of whom died), and fourteen more suspended their scientific work in Paris. Others suffered the tensions of hiding out in the country, possible betrayal by colleagues, loss of property, or imprisonment of relatives. Yet the most notorious executions, of Lavoisier and J.-S. Bailly, and the death of the outlawed fugitive Condorcet were not vendettas against scientists but the settling of political scores. Bailly was vulnerable as mayor of Paris during the Champ de Mars "massacre," Lavoisier as a wealthy tax farmer, and Condorcet as an indiscreet critic of the Constitution of 1793.

Nevertheless, the much-heralded mobilization of savants as personal agents of the Committee of Public Safety did not compensate for the destructive effects of the Terror. The mobilized group (about ten, including L.-B. Guyton-Morveau, A. Fourcroy, C.-L. Berthollet, and J.-A. Chaptal) were less numerous than those with disrupted careers and were a politically acceptable fragment of the Paris scientific community. Their contributions were, of course, genuine: memoirs on weapons manufacture, artillery testing, metal refining, and saltpeter extraction. Some taught crash courses in Paris early in 1794 (the Ecole d'Armes) on munitions manufacture to pupils who diffused the techniques on their return to their departments. In June 1794 at Fleurus, Guyton-Morveau supervised the first balloon-borne artillery spotters; and by August the Convention had realized the plan of C. Chappe to build a Paris-Lille semaphore telegraph to speed dispatches to and from the battlefront.

This approach benefited military technology and inspired a model for remedying shortages of teachers, physicians, and engineers. The planning of new educational institutions began during the Terror, but the Convention acted only after Thermidor. Thus deputies such as Fourcroy and Grégoire could exaggerate Jacobin vandalism.

At J. Lakanal's urging, the Convention created the Ecole Normale in October 1794 for teacher training analogous to the Ecole d'Armes. The distinguished faculty included eight former academicians (Lagrange, P.-S. Laplace, Berthollet, L.-J.-M. Daubenton, R.-J. Haüy, G. Monge, A. Thouin, J. Buache de la Neuville), but the exalted level of the lectures (Laplace's probability theory, Monge's descriptive geometry) to an unprepared audience precluded pedagogical success. Unlamented when it closed in June 1795, the Ecole Normale remained an inspiration for the Imperial *grande école* (1808), where the sciences were an integral component of the curriculum.

To unify civil and military engineering, the Convention founded the much more successful Ecole Centrale des Travaux Publics (September 1794, renamed the Ecole Polytechnique a year later), which also began with a crash course. The regular curriculum, however, was not narrowly vocational but provided a solid education in the physical sciences and mathematics, a prerequisite for admission to the applied engineering schools. The highly competitive entrance examinations and the notable work of the faculty research council during the Directory and early Consulate (including Monge, Lagrange, Fourcroy, Berthollet, and Guyton-Morveau) made the Polytechnique an elite institution, where teaching and research were combined fruitfully. Like the Muséum, the school made several assistantships available as a first apprenticeship for a scientific career and faculty chairs were expanded from fifteen to nineteen by 1813.

While secondary-level scientific education had existed in the philosophy courses of more than twenty of the best *collèges*, the Daunou education law (25 October 1795) specified two courses, natural history and physics-chemistry, in the secularized curriculum of the new central schools. Despite such outstanding individual science teachers in Paris as Cuvier, quantitative study of enrollments shows that more pupils may have studied science in the *collèges* than in the central schools. Lack of laboratory equipment hampered instruction in many departments. Yet the central schools were significant for pioneering efforts in public secondary education, for providing a stage of new secular careers in teaching, and for the *idéologues'* philosophical program.

The culmination of the constructive creations of the Daunou law was the National Institute of Sciences and Arts. While the architects of the law were P.-C.-F. Daunou, F.-A. Boissy d'Anglas, Fourcroy, and Lakanal, the institute represented the fruition of the encyclopedist vision (restated by C.-M. Talleyrand and Condorcet in educational plans of 1791-92) of unifying all knowledge. At the same time, the institute as a new, prestigious research forum atoned for the epoch of vandalism, compensated the cultural elite, and vaunted the civilizing mission and prestige of the Republic.

While the institute reconstructed counterparts of academies, it did not merely resurrect the past. The Second Class of Moral and Political Sciences was a bold venture in extending a scientific approach to human affairs, and it provided a home for *idéologue* philosophy. The sixty-member First Class of Mathematical and Physical Sciences was deliberately republican in its abolition of the honorary category and of internal hierarchy among resident members. It could hardly be a replica of the Academy when one-fourth of working academicians had been lost through death or emigration.

Yet continuity was as evident as the differences in organization. Forty-five of the sixty-eight elected to the First Class in 1795-96 were ex-academicians. By 1815 all but nine surviving academicians (three of whom remained *émigrés*) had been so honored. The academic ceremonies, prize contests, and concern for public utility certainly resembled Old Regime practices, duly adjusted for a Republic. Some interpreters see the Terror as a dramatic break, which increased the scientists' obsession for an ideology of objective, apolitical detachment. They also see the Terror as a precedent for subservience of scientists to an increasingly bureaucratic state. Yet one may argue that the ideal of scientific detachment and the reality of scientists' commitment to utility and dependence on patronage all had characterized the late Old Regime.

Less controversial is the loss of élan in the First Class due to its increasing redundance in the early nineteenth-century world of specialized learned societies, periodicals, and research groups (such as Arcueil). Avant-garde research often appeared elsewhere before the Institute memoirs could be published. The nine-teenth-century Academy of Sciences (renamed in 1816) was also less creative than its predecessor since elections often crowned the careers of aging scholars. Yet its role in peer evaluation, its patronage and incentives through prize contests and grants ensured its continuing significance.

The growth of the state and the specialization of science were long-term trends preceding the Revolution. The new institutions did accelerate professionalization, even though there may not have been more scientific positions in 1799 than in 1789. The Revolution neither created nor destroyed French scientific achievements. It strengthened the fateful entanglement between French science and government. Scientists provided increasingly specialized skills in exchange for career positions, financial stimuli to research, and, in the Empire, for both significant and honorific appointments in the government bureaucracy.

M. Clagett, ed., *Critical Problems in the History of Science* (Madison, 1969); M. Crosland, "The Development of a Professional Career in Science in France," *Minerva* 13 (1975); J. Fayet, *La Révolution française et la science* (Paris, 1960); C. Gillispie, *Science and Polity in France at the End of the Old Regime* (Princeton, 1980); R. Hahn,

The Anatomy of a Scientific Institution: The Paris Academy of Sciences, 1666-1803 (Berkeley, 1971); D. Outram, ''The Ordeal of Vocation: The Paris Academy of Sciences and the Terror, 1793-1795,'' *Isis* (1982).

M. S. Staum

Related entries: CONDORCET; EDUCATION; LAKANAL; LAPLACE; MESMER; MONGE.

SCIENCES AND ARTS, NATIONAL INSTITUTE OF. See SCIENCE.

SCISSION, parliamentary maneuver used by the directors to nullify the elections of the Year VI. See COUP OF 22 FLOREAL YEAR VI.

SCRUTIN EPURATOIRE (1791-94), a process of examination by public presentation at the rostrum of members of a society, of an assembly, or of candidates for political office, which was followed by a vote. This purifying scrutiny was one of the spontaneous innovations most characteristic of Jacobin practice and one of the major weapons of popular democracy during the Year II. Its birth can be dated to the split that occurred in the Jacobin club following the king's flight to Varennes between democrats and moderates who would soon become the Feuillants. In the face of this split and on the initiative of M. Robespierre, the Parisian society reconstituted itself, beginning with an initiation committee composed of six deputies who had remained faithful to the club and six members who were co-opted. From these elements a nucleus of sixty members of the society was created from among those who had recently rejoined the club, after a case-by-case examination. This general purification, designed to regenerate the society, operated on the basis of a series of co-optations that involved the candidate's presenting himself and responding to questions about his Revolutionary record.

From the end of 1791 and especially in 1792-93, this procedure spread, becoming one of the bases of Jacobin political practice. In spreading, it first affected the popular societies, beginning with the Jacobins, who commonly practiced *scrutins épuratoires* in this period, but the Cordeliers and other popular societies were not far behind. In the provinces, whether spontaneously or under pressure from representatives on mission, *scrutins épuratoires* were widely used in 1793-94; the popular society of Cherbourg, for example, underwent five successive purifications.

The practice of *scrutin épuratoire* became general. As early as September 1792, this procedure was demanded within the framework of the elections to the Convention. In Paris some people wanted the deputies chosen by the electors to submit to a *scrutin épuratoire* by the sectional assemblies. The same demand was reiterated in November during the election of the Parisian municipal authorities. In the sectional assemblies, as in the Revolutionary committees, the *scrutin épuratoire* became one of the means of selecting and controlling civil servants and officials. This did not come about without resistance—far from it.

This practice was most widespread at the time of the fall of the Girondins in June 1793, and within the framework of the sectional movement, it culminated in September 1793, at the apogee of the popular movement. It still occupied a prominent place from the winter to the spring of the Year II, during the crisis over dechristianization and during the elimination of the factions between Ventôse and Germinal. But at the same time one can see a distortion of the spirit of the *scrutin épuratoire*, which changed from a means of control from the bottom to a method of sanctioning decisions made at the top. It would be the same when, after Thermidor, the Jacobin club was purged of its terrorist elements.

While it varied considerably according to circumstances, time, and place, the *scrutin épuratoire* exhibited some common traits. Although it was sometimes a regular formality, more often it was motivated by a specific event. It resulted in a drastic reduction in the real strength of societies (for example, from 500 to 110 at Chambéry). Commonly, a purifying nucleus was constituted, which was rounded out by co-optation. The presentation of a member or a candidate was the occasion for a public response to a series of questions about his civism and Revolutionary record. The *scrutin* could open with the postponement of a decision or even exclusion.

In fact, the *scrutin épuratoire*, accused of contributing to the monopolization of power by pressure groups or even of providing the opportunity for personal revenge, could not survive the setback of the *sans-culotte* movement for which it had become a means of action. Robespierre made this unequivocally clear on 26 Ventôse Year II when he attacked the *scrutin épuratoire* on the grounds of the needs of the Revolutionary government, which had no place for dual power—that of the central government and of *sans-culotte* democracy. On this basis, the *scrutin épuratoire*, which had become a method of controlling those whose orthodoxy was faltering, carried with it all the contradictions of Jacobin political practice.

L. de Cardenal, *La Province pendant la Révolution française* (Paris, 1929); G. Martin, *Les Jacobins* (Paris, 1945); A. Soboul, *Les sans-culottes parisiens en l'an II*, 2d ed. (Paris, 1962).

M. Vovelle

Related entries: DECHRISTIANIZATION; FEUILLANTS; GIRONDINS; JACOBINS; ROBESPIERRE, M.

SEANCE ROYALE OF 23 JUNE 1789. See LOUIS XVI.

SECOND COALITION (1798-1801), an alliance organized in response to French foreign policy and violations of the terms of the Treaty of Campoformio. Ultimately, England, Austria, Russia, Naples, Portugal, Turkey, and several minor German states united for various reasons to contain French expansion and redress past grievances. The coalition powers were dissatisfied with many of the provisions of the Treaty of Campoformio (17 October 1797), and they were opposed to French expansion in the Low Countries, Germany, Italy, and Switzerland. The creation of the satellite states—the Batavian Republic in Holland, the Roman Republic in Italy, the Helvetic Republic in Switzerland—the reorganization of the Cisalpine Republic, the annexation of the Rhenish provinces and Piedmont, the destruction of the secular power of the pope, and the continued spread of Revolutionary ideas posed serious threats to the members of the coalition. Similarly, Napoleon's occupation of Malta and Egypt and the expansion of French influence in the Near East, coupled with French efforts to resurrect the old French colonial empire and impose trade restrictions on England, served to solidify Allied resistance against France.

Formation of the coalition was delayed for months because of disagreements between England and Austria and the unsuccessful attempts to include Prussia in the alliance. Austria and Naples formed the basis of a defensive alliance (May 1798), but before the coalition was galvanized, the Neapolitan king, Ferdinand, with the encouragement of Lord H. Nelson, invaded the Papal States and forced the French out of Rome (29 November 1798). The French counterattacked. The Neapolitans were expelled from Rome, and the Kingdom of Naples was quickly conquered by General J. Championnet. The rulers of Naples fled to a British fleet, and the French established the Parthenopean Republic (23 January 1799). Meanwhile England and Russia concluded a treaty to support the alliance against France (29 December 1798). Soon Portugal joined the coalition, followed by the Turkish Porte, incensed by French intervention in the Near East.

The strategy of the Second Coalition called for the reconquest of German and Italian lands, the containment of the French in other areas, and the possible restoration of the Bourbons. A Russian army under Marshal A. Suvórov joined an Austrian army commanded by General M. Melas in northern Italy; together they crushed the French armies between April and August 1799 and drove their defeated forces back into Genoa. With the French ovewhelmed in Italy, the Austrians claimed many of the liberated Italian lands, despite Russian objections. Meanwhile, a second Russian army, commanded by General A. Rimski-Korsakov, marched to Zurich to join an Austrian army under General D. Hötze, in preparation for the invasion of France. Once the victorious Suvórov, advancing through Saint Gothard pass, arrived at Zurich, the invasion would begin, with the army of Archduke Charles, fresh from its victory at Stockach (25 March 1799), covering his flanks. However, Austrian minister F. Thugut decided to transfer Charles's army to the middle Rhine to seize Mannheim, advance in the Rhineland, and protect Austrian interests there.

The French Directory grasped the significance of this movement and reinforced its Army of Helvetia under General A. Masséna at Zurich in order to thwart the anticipated invasion. In a brilliant campaign, Masséna crushed the Austro-Russian army at Zurich and then caught Suvórov in the Linth valley, inflicting appalling losses on the Russian army. As a result, France was spared invasion, and a major split developed between the members of the Second Coalition. Austria had sacrificed the goals of the coalition for its own concerns by transferring Archduke Charles's army to protect its interests and expose the flanks of the Russian army at Zurich.

Simultaneously, Anglo-Russian forces landed in the Low Countries to threaten French control in that area. General G. Brune attacked and defeated the British forces at Bergen, forcing them to sign the Convention of Alkmaar (18 October 1799) for the evacuation of the country, while the abandoned Russians retired to the Channel Islands, captives of the harsh elements. Czar Paul I, incensed by Austria's aggrandizement and what he considered England's abandonment, withdrew from the coalition.

Meanwhile, Napoleon conquered Egypt and invaded Syria, only to be repulsed at Acre (19 March-21 May 1799). On learning of the reverses suffered by the French armies in Germany and Italy, he left Egypt and returned to France in time to take part in the coup of 18 Brumaire (9 November 1799). Instead of marching to relieve the blockaded French troops at Genoa, now under Masséna, he marched across Great Saint Bernard Pass and destroyed the Austrian army at Marengo (14 June 1800), regaining Italy for France. The French army in Germany, under General J.-V. Moreau, forced the Austrian army across southern Germany and overwhelmed it in the decisive Battle of Hohenlinden (3 December 1800). As the French advanced on Vienna, the Austrians sued for peace and signed the Treaty of Lunéville (9 February 1801). As a result, the Second Coalition had ceased to exist. In April, Portugal, still at war with France, was invaded by Franco-Spanish forces in the so-called War of Oranges. After little fighting, Portugal ended the war by the Treaty of Badajoz (6 June 1801), leaving only England and Turkey at war with France. After lengthy negotiations, England came to terms with France in the Treaty of Amiens (27 March 1802), followed soon after by a Franco-Turkish peace treaty (9 October 1802), ending the war in Europe.

The Second Coalition was doomed to failure from its inception because of the many delays in solidifying the alliance, as well as Prussia's refusal to join the Allies. Moreover, Austria's territorial schemes for aggrandizement alienated the other members of the coalition, especially Russia, and England's tendency to pursue its interests without concern for its allies undermined the alliance. Not to be discounted were the abilities of the French commanders and their men in achieving decisive victories over the armies of the Second Coalition at Zurich, Bergen, Marengo, and Hohenlinden.

M. von Angeli, *Erzherzog Carl von Österreich ols Feldherr und Heeresorganisator*, 5 vols. (Vienna, 1896-97); K. von Clausewitz, *Die Feldzüg von 1799 in Italien und der Schweiz*, 5 vols. (Berlin, 1833); H. Huffer, *Der Krieg des Jahres 1799 und die zweit Koalition*, 2 vols. (Gotha, 1904-5); A. B. Rodgers, *The War of the Second Coalition* (Oxford, 1964); S. T. Ross, *Quest for Victory, French Military Strategy, 1792-1799* (New York, 1973).

D. D. Horward

Related entries: EGYPTIAN EXPEDITION; MASSENA; MOREAU; PAUL I; PITT; SUVOROV-RYMNIKSKII; TREATY OF CAMPOFORMIO.

SECTIONS, basic political divisions and centers of Revolutionary activity in Paris, 1790-94. The sections of Paris, like those of all the other major towns of France, played a dual role: first, as geographic and administrative subdivisions of the municipality, and second, as foyers of the Revolution. Like other institutions, they evolved historically with the growth and expansion of the capital itself. Thus, the boundaries of each parish, quarter, or ward tended to differ according to the historical epoch during which they were created. The fifty-two medieval parishes of Paris had never been coterminous with its twenty *quartiers*. The latter gave way to the sixty districts on the eve of the Revolution, within whose limits electoral assemblies gathered to vote for delegates to the Estates General and to draft their *cahiers*. Less than a year after the fall of the Bastille (21 May-20 June 1790), the National Assembly divided the capital into forty-eight sections. The National Convention grouped them into twelve *arrondissements* on 7 Fructidor Year II (24 August 1794) of four sections each, the latter becoming *divisions* under the Directory and after 1812, once again *quartiers*, which disappeared only in 1860.

The division of the capital into forty-eight units developed from the plan of E. Verniquet, an architect whose major objective was the convenience of elections and the efficiency of a section's civil and military service, based on the total number of active citizens. Since the latter constituted 97,631 of the population at the end of 1789, of whom 31,792 lived south of the Seine and 65,839 north of the river, his plan called for fifteen sections in the first area and thirty-three in the second.

Within these limits, the section's political life was embodied in its general assembly. The municipal law of 1790 dealt at some length with the organization of primary assemblies but said little about the regulations and practices of general assemblies. It stipulated the election of a president and secretary but provided for little else. By 1793 the assembly was conducted by a president, assisted by an executive committee (*bureau*) and a secretary-registrar to draft the *procès-verbal*, tellers to count votes, and censors to maintain order. Sessions began by reading the minutes of the previous meeting, followed by decrees of the Convention and ordinances of the Paris Commune. This procedure, together with discussion of the questions of the day, took far longer than had been foreseen, when meetings were legally limited to open at 5 P.M. and close at 10 P.M.

Until the sections gained the right of *permanence* (25 July 1792)—that is, the right to convene themselves by their own authority—the number of sectional meetings were relatively few. The section Postes, whose record is quite complete, met fifty times from 4 December 1790 to 25 July 1792. After this date, meetings became more frequent. More important, perhaps, was the modest number of voters and participants in the primary and general assemblies, not only during the period of the division between active and passive citizens (the *censitaire* epoch) but even after this distinction had disappeared. After the overthrow of the king, for example, when political feeling had reached a high point, the number of voters remained quite modest; no more than one-ninth or one-tenth of the eligible active citizens voted in August 1792. In an effort to encourage participation in the political life of the section, the Convention suppressed *permanence* on 9 September 1793 and limited sessions to two per *décade*, subsidizing the poorer citizens by paying them 40 *sous* for attending sessions of their general assemblies.

These assemblies tended to support the concept and practice of direct democracy, embodied in the term *mandat impératif*, which had long historical roots. Under the Old Regime, a deputy was expected to defend the interests of his own class, not to represent all France. Since each estate knew its own interests, theoretically it could direct the mission of its delegate. This obligation imposed by the electors on their delegates to vote in a predetermined manner on questions considered in advance was expressed in the term *mandat impératif*. Essentially it held that deputies or delegates of the sections were not representatives free to deliberate on the questions before them but were proxies or mandatories who had to carry out the bidding of their constituents. Among their arguments was the well-known axiom of J.-J. Rousseau that the general will could not be represented, that deputies were not representatives but only commissioners of the people.

From the very beginning of the Revolution when the municipal government was taking shape, districts challenged the Commune over the powers of their delegates. J.-S. Bailly admitted that as early as August 1789 "an unceasing war" had begun between him and the representatives of the Commune; while L.-M. Prudhomme, publisher of the popular journal *Les Révolutions de Paris*, argued that the rights of the Commune reside only in the districts. The right of the districts to exercise critical control over their delegates to the Commune and to replace them if they failed to promote the will of the assemblies was expressed in the term *censure*. The sections were to inherit and to champion this concept. Thus, direct democracy in the form of *permanence*, the *mandat impératif*, and *censure* was a widespread feature of the sections' political concept and practice.

When delegates elected to the Commune no longer expressed the changed political beliefs of the sections yet could not be recalled until the date provided for by law, the assemblies resorted to extralegal devices. Meeting in extraordinary session, the body might elect delegates to an illegal gathering, held frequently in the Evêché, the archbishop's palace. A sectional assembly could always circulate a resolution calling on its sister bodies to elect commissioners with limitless powers to deliberate on public affairs and to take whatever steps were necessary to assure the "triumph of the public good." This was the method used to overthrow the Girondins by the insurrection of 31 May-2 June 1793, when the commissioners of the thirty-three sections who made the revolution created their Revolutionary Central Committee, or the Comité de Neuf. In overthrowing the king, representatives of the sections met with those of the Jacobin and Cordeliers clubs and a committee of the *fédérés*, who had arrived some time before to help celebrate the third anniversary of the fall of the Bastille. In both cases the regularly constituted municipal authorities were temporarily suspended until the triumph of the movement was assured. This done, they were allowed to resume their duties until new elections confirmed them or removed them from office. This right of a sacred insurrection was an article of faith widely held by the militants of the sections.

The dramatic days of the Revolution, the *journées*, are perhaps a more accurate gauge of the commitment to the new order of the many thousands of *sectionnaires* than are the elections throughout the period. In revolutionary times, as is well established, action is more important than the counting of votes. The prime movers in these *journées*, from the storming of the Bastille to the attack on the Thermidorian Convention in Prairial Year III, were the districts and sections of the capital. The legal division between active and passive citizens, formalized by the Constitution of 1791, failed to express the political reality of the day. Once the economic and political crisis conjoined with the military disasters of 1792-93 and as the country was proclaimed in danger (11 July 1792), the disenfranchised citizens came storming into the sectional assemblies, thus demonstrating that in time of revolution political activity could not be limited by a legal fiction.

Among the tactics used to win control of the assemblies was the staging of raids by militants of several sections to help their fellow radicals, done under the guise of fraternization. By combining the forces of several sections, militants could impose their will, temporarily, on a vacillating section where a resolution adopted the previous evening would be repudiated the following night, only to be reaffirmed shortly thereafter. Often it was the support or rejection of the Revolutionary assembly in the Evêché that became the point at issue; at other times it was the acceptance or condemnation of a particular resolution that divided an assembly. Sometimes a motion was passed late at night, after the majority had already dispersed or the president of the assembly had officially adjourned the meeting.

Not all manifestations of sectional authority were political in nature. A number of functions remained largely administrative or technical. An example of the latter is the work of the civil committees, established by the municipal law of 21 May-27 June 1790 as organs of surveillance and execution of the ordinances of the Commune. Among other duties they apportioned taxes, affixed and removed seals on papers and effects, took the census, inspected lodging houses, delivered various types of certificates, among which was the important certificate of civism, converted *assignats* into specie, and provided relief for the poor. On 11 August 1792 the civil committees were suppressed by the Commune, and under the decree of 15 August they were henceforth made electable by the general assemblies, thus losing their former independent powers. With the reorganization of Paris by the Law of 7 Fructidor Year II (24 August 1794), they recovered their former importance. On 14 Vendémiaire Year III (5 October 1794), they were charged with delivery of certificates of civism but were finally suppressed on 19 Vendémiaire Year IV (10 October 1795).

Unlike the civil committees, Revolutionary committees were more political in nature. After a number of changes (from *comités permanents* to *comités des recherches*), the Convention established Revolutionary committees on 21 March 1793 for the purpose of watching over foreign residents or enemy aliens. Composed of twelve members and six assistants elected by simple plurality of the voters in each section, committees excluded ecclesiastics, former nobles, seigneurs, or their agents. By a decree of 17 September 1793, they were authorized to issue warrants of arrest and to seal papers of those loosely defined as suspected persons. After the Committee of Public Safety began to appoint them, they lost both their independence and their democratic structure. Unlike the members of civil committees, they tended to be from the lower ranks of the *sans-culottes*.

The large number of poor in the sections, underestimated at 10 percent of the population, led to the establishment of lay committees on poverty, as early as November 1789 (the first being in the district Jacobins-Saint-Dominique). On 21 January 1790 the National Assembly created its Comité de mendicité to supervise relief, now seen as a social duty not haphazard charity. The Paris Commune created its own relief commission on 9 April 1791 and by October denied the right of parish committees to discriminate on the basis of religion in assigning help for the poor, the first step in secularizing poor relief. By December 1792, parish committees were suppressed, and by 19 March 1793 the Convention had adopted a plan of helping the poor. The General Council supplemented the plan of the Convention on 25 July 1793 by providing for the election, by majority vote of the general assemblies, of members of relief committees (Comités de bienfaisance.) These sectional committees were installed on 20-22 September 1793 and usually met with civil committees in providing help to the indigent. The right to equal treatment of the poor with that received "by the rich in their mansions," in the words of section Homme-Armé, was echoed by other sections, many of which sought to give the poor a new sense of dignity.

Important judicial posts in the sections were held by justices of the peace who were endowed with authority to deal with cases of persons or property whose value did not exceed 50 *livres*, without appeal, and in cases of up to 100 *livres* subject to appeal. They were elected by the section's primary assembly for two years and were eligible for unlimited reelection. The municipal law of 21 May 1790 also provided for the creation of police commissioners in each section, elected by simple plurality for a term of two years, with the right to succeed themselves. Given deliberative voice on civil committees, they were endowed with the right to arrest lawbreakers in *flagrante delicto*. The General Council directed them to perform a variety of duties, among which were to watch bill posters, peddlers, and street orators, to interrogate the accused, to affix and remove seals, and to verify the price of bread.

After the abolition of distinctions between active and passive citizens, the General Council authorized each section (13 August 1792) to form military companies. Each company enrolled 126 men and one or several batteries of artillery. Officers and noncommissioned officers were elected by the men; assembled in companies, they also chose their commanding general for three months, subject to reelection for one year. The military committees (Comités militaires or Comités de guerre) created by the sections had become councils of discipline in 1793. They distributed aid to parents and families of volunteers, corresponded with battalions serving at the front, armed and equipped them, and maintained their morale.

In addition to these administrative organs, each section had a political society or two, usually affiliated with the Jacobins or the Cordeliers. Begun as democratic gatherings, which recruited both active and passive citizens and deliberately kept dues low in marked contrast to various bourgois societies, sectional societies were composed of "merchants of fruits and vegetables," and of "carriers of water and other good people," as they were described by contemporary journals. From the very beginning, moderates and patriots differed on their role. The former wanted to limit their activities to educational endeavors, while the latter sought to point them toward political goals. The Convention's decree of 9 September 1793, limiting sectional assemblies to two weekly meetings, encouraged political activists to circumvent this restriction by transferring much sectional business and discussion to these clubs. These societies were suppressed when the Jacobins ruled (15 May 1794) that their members could no longer belong to sectional clubs.

Although the sections made a major contribution to both the political and the administrative life of the capital, their ultimate role was often determined by events outside their confines. Despite this, they promoted the political consciousness of thousands of individuals, a consciousness that gave a self-awareness to countless men and women. Without the sections, the history of the French Revolution probably would have been quite different.

G. Garrigues, *Les districts parisiens pendant le Révolution française* (Paris, n.d.); A. Mathiez, *La vie chère et le mouvement social sous la Terreur* (Paris, 1927); H. Omont, *Catalogue des manuscrits français de la Bibliothèque nationale* (Paris, 1899); A. Soboul, *Les Papiers de sections de Paris (1790-an IV)* (Paris, 1950) and *Les Sans-culottes parisiens en l'an II* (Paris, 1958); K. D. Tønnesson, *La défaite des sans-culottes. Mouvement populaire et réaction bourgeoise en l'an III* (Paris, 1959).

M. Slavin

Related entries: BAILLY; CENTRAL REVOLUTIONARY COMMITTEE; CERTIFICATES OF CIVICISM; COMMITTEE OF PUBLIC SAFETY; GIRONDINS; JACOBINS; *JOURNEES REVOLUTIONNAIRES*; PARIS COMMUNE; *SANS-CULOTTES*.

SEGUR, LOUIS-PHILIPPE, COMTE DE (1753-1830), ambassador and political figure. In 1753 Louis-Philippe, comte de Ségur, was born in Paris into one of France's most distinguished families. A skilled courtier with influence at Louis XVI's court, an army officer of high rank, he was welcomed at the leading Paris salons, where he encountered some of the most brilliant men and ideas of his age—B. Franklin, J.-J. Rousseau, F.-M. Voltaire, and D. Diderot, to name but a few. He became attracted to the cause of the American Revolution and was among the first of the court aristocracy to volunteer in the American war against England; he did not, however, participate in the war until 1782. From 1785 to 1789 he served as ambassador to Russia and effected a Franco-Russian trade agreement favorable to France.

During the early years of the French Revolution, Ségur was a moderate royalist, playing the dangerous role of a negotiator between the court and aristocracy. In April 1791 he was appointed ambassador to the Vatican, in October 1791 he was offered the position of minister of foreign affairs (which he rejected), and in late December 1791 he was sent on a desperate mission to the court of Berlin to try to prevent war between France and Prussia. After the latter mission, he temporarily withdrew from politics, and during the Terror he lived a quiet life in provincial exclusion.

During the period of the Directory, he returned to politics and contributed a lengthy list of articles and poems to periodicals; he wrote the three-volume *Histoire des principaux événements du règne de Fr. Guillaume II, roi de Prusse*, one of the most astute early studies of the era of the French Revolution, and he edited the three-volume *Tableau politique de l'Europe*, a significant document of the eighteenth-century theory of diplomacy. Shortly after the coup of 18 Fructidor (4 September 1797), he became a loyal supporter of N. Bonaparte.

Under the Consulate Ségur was appointed to the Council of State and to the Institut français. As Napoleon's master of ceremonies during the Empire, he staged many spectacles of imperial splendor, including the coronation ceremony, supervised the imperial court, and executed the emperor's plans for celebrating his military victories. In addition, he was appointed to the Senate. In 1814, however, he reluctantly voted to depose Napoleon but hastened to rejoin him during the Hundred Days. After Napoleon abdicated in 1815, the restored Bourbon regime punished Ségur for having flagrantly defected. With his political career presumably ended, he earned his living as a writer, just as he had done before joining the Napoleonic administration.

From 1815 to 1828 he published the fifteen-volume *Histoire universelle*, which was received well by reviewers, including A. Thierry and T. Jefferson, a collection of political and philosophical essays published in three volumes under the title of *Galérie morale et politique*, which went through seven complete editions, the seven-volume *Histoire de France*, which perhaps influenced J. Michelet's celebrated history of France, and three volumes of *Mémoires*, which remain a valuable source for the study of the Old Regime. In addition, he was an articulate and respected member of the liberal minority in the Chamber of Peers. On 27 August 1830, after living to see yet another liberal revolution, Ségur died.

L. Apt, *Louis-Philippe de Ségur: An Intellectual in a Revolutionary Age* (The Hague, 1969); L.-P. de Ségur, *Mémoires: ou souvenirs et anecdotes*, 3 vols. (Paris, 1824-28).

L. Apt

Related entries: ARISTOCRATS; COUP OF 18 FRUCTIDOR.

SELF-DENYING ORDINANCE (16 May 1791), decision by the deputies of the Constituent Assembly that they would not be eligible for election to the next legislature, the Legislative Assembly. On 16 May 1791 M. Robespierre proposed to the Constituent Assembly that the Assembly decree that members of the then present Assembly could not be members of the next legislature. After some debate, the majority of the Assembly approved the decree. The consequent exclusion from the Legislative Assembly of the experienced deputies of the Constituent was, allegedly, a source of weakness in the new body.

This viewpoint probably has little substance, since, while they had not, of course, sat in the Constituent, most deputies to the Legislative Assembly were men of considerable practical experience in various roles in their localities. The constituents did not intend to bar themselves from any public positions. By decreeing on 28 May that all departmental administrators would be reelected after the new legislature was chosen, they opened throughout the country a large number of important positions to which they might aspire. The allegedly detrimental effects of the self-denying ordinance were later cited in support of the two-thirds decree passed near the close of the National Convention in late August 1795.

A.P., vol. 26 (Paris, 1879-1913); J. M. Thompson, *The French Revolution* (New York, 1966).

A. Saricks

Related entry: TWO-THIRDS DECREE.

SENECHAUSSEE. See *BAILLIAGE.*

SEPTEMBER 1792 MASSACRES, violent and murderous attacks on prisoners in Paris by Revolutionaries fearing an allied invasion of Paris combined with a counterrevolutionary inspired insurrection. The immediate background to the September Massacres was a state of mind bent on vengeance for those Revolutionaries who had died during the insurrection of 10 August, three weeks before, a state of mind kept alive by ceremonies honoring the dead, particularly the great ceremony of 26 August directed by the police administrator A.-F. Sergent. Moreover, J.-P. Marat had urged Parisians to go armed to the prisons to kill those Swiss troops there who had fought in defense of the king. A special court had been created, the tribunal of 17 August, to judge counterrevolutionaries, but its justice seemed too slow and too uncertain, disappointing the promises made by the Commune that all the guilty would perish.

Mounting anxiety was also prompted by disquieting reports of the Prussian invasion of France, particularly of the unexpected fall of Longwy on 23 August, encouraging rumors of treason. A call-up of 30,000 additional troops was ordered, as well as domiciliary searches for weapons and suspects.

The Paris prisons were becoming more crowded as a consequence of some 500 arrests since 10 August. People worried about prison conditions: the inadequate supervision, the forging of *assignats* within the prisons, the frequent escapes.

There were stories of plots being hatched within the prisons, particularly at Bicêtre. It was believed that when the enemy reached Paris, counterrevolutionaries would open the doors of these prisons and bring about a massacre of patriots.

There had been present too, a continuing struggle, to determine the outcome of 10 August, between the Girondin rump of the Legislative Assembly and the men of the insurrectional Commune, each party bent on subjecting the other to its own will. Indeed, Marat urged on the Jacobins the need to shed the blood of "the most gangrened members" of the Legislative. The Commune held the upper hand, but on 30 August the Legislative decreed its dismissal and replacement. The Commune threatened reprisals, and two days later, on 2 September, the Legislative revoked its decree, but ill will remained.

On 30 August the Commune requested the police administrator E.-J. Panis to reconstitute the Commune's Committee of Surveillance, responsible for supervising the Paris prisons. He named to the new committee the three other police administrators, Sergent, P.-J. Duplain, and D. Jourdeuil, and six others, including two nonmembers of the Commune who were added belatedly: F.-L.-M. Deforgues, a long-time intimate of G.-J. Danton, and Marat, who had posted placards urging those who were enlisting in the army to first kill the traitors in the Paris prisons before leaving their families for the battlefront. The new committee sat for the first time, at the Mairie, on Sunday 2 September.

Early that morning it was learned at Paris that Verdun was about to fall to the Prussians. The Commune decreed a form of *levée en masse* and sent commissioners into the Paris sections to urge the citizenry to enroll in the army. At noon Danton delivered a remarkable speech to the Legislative that urged attack against the enemies of the fatherland and the need for boldness, ever more boldness.

That afternoon, at about 2 P.M., four carriage loads of prisoners set out from the Mairie for the Abbaye prison. They were insulted along the way and at one point were attacked, their own escort taking part in this attack. Near the Abbaye itself they were again attacked, by a group of some fifty neighborhood patriots, among them a jeweler, a butcher, a café owner, a carpenter, and a couple of National Guards. Someone from the section's Civil Committee (Quatre Nations) asked that they be judged first, but some were killed before they could descend from their carriages. Seventeen of twenty-two prisoners died in this first of the September Massacres. Was it spontaneous? The *fédérés* who escorted the prisoners may have been the same men who had escorted Marat to his duties at the Mairie not long before. We do not know.

The Carmelite prison was the first to be attacked directly, at about 4 P.M. More than 200 imprisoned priests were attacked by an organized band who had come marching toward the prison from the faubourg Saint-Marceau, singing the hymn "*Dies Irae*" as they marched. They killed some of the priests on the spot, without formality; but after a section commissioner intervened, they created a kind of judge who questioned the prisoners one by one before delivering them to the killers, who tossed their bodies into a well.

That same afternoon many of the section assemblies met and undertook initiatives of their own. Section Poissonnière passed a resolution that referred to the evil doers who, when the good citizens had left for the frontiers, might open up the prisons, release the conspirators whose trials had been delayed under various pretexts, and spread desolation and death through Paris. It urged that justice be done immediately to all malefactors or conspirators in the prisons. Poissonnière transmitted this resolution to other sections of Paris. Section Luxembourg, after learning of the massacre at the Carmelites, passed a similar resolution and sent three of its own commissioners to the Commune so as to be sure of acting in a uniform fashion. Other sections acted identically.

The Commune met at about 4 P.M. Informed of the massacres, it decided to effect a separation between those arrested for debt and other prisoners and sent out commissioners to the Abbaye to this end. Someone there objected; if he had to leave for the front he did not want to leave anyone alive in prison who might kill his wife and five children. The commissioners returned to the Commune, where J.-N. Billaud-Varenne proposed that commissioners be sent to the prisons, examine the prison registers, make a selection of prisoners from them, and then turn over to the people all those they thought compromised in the plot of 10 August. The Commune issued a decree to this effect; it then notified the Legislative Assembly of its action.

By early evening the massacres had resumed at the Abbaye, where a special tribunal had been created to judge its prisoners. It was presided over by S. Maillard, who had led the women from Paris to Versailles in October 1789. The courtroom was filled with people, who took part in the judging themselves. National Guards and *fédérés* were on hand. A much larger crowd was waiting outside. The condemned were murdered in the street or in a garden nearby. Among the dead were Swiss troops and royal bodyguards, prominent aristocrats, some judges, justices of the peace who had arrested Revolutionaries, priests in large number, and the former royal minister the comte de Montmorin. Not until 4 September did the killings at the Abbaye cease.

During the first thirty hours of the massacres, no efforts were made by any authority to bring them to an end. On 2 September C. Fauchet told the Assembly about the killing of the priests at the Carmelites, but no one proposed a decree of repression. The deputies confined themselves to sending some of their own members to the prisons, where they were badly received. That evening the Executive Council of ministers met; so did the Paris departmental authorities and Mayor J. Pétion with presidents of the Paris sections. The records are meager; it is not clear from them that the massacres were even discussed. A.-J. Santerre, commander of the National Guard, claimed on 4 September that he had given orders to the Guard, but this claim was denied by the Guard's other leaders, and he clearly made no real effort to get the Guard to act. Apparently no consideration was given to requiring its action against the killings through a declaration of martial law. Would one have dared to propose such action against those who believed they were defending the Revolution by killing counterrevolutionaries, especially in the light of memories of the "massacre" of the Champ de Mars?

The initiatives taken by Poissonnière and the other sections together with the inertia of the authorities explain the extension of the massacres during the evening of 2 September to the Conciergerie; to the Châtelet, where there were many thieves and debtors, who thought at first that they were being rescued and where more than 200 died; and, at midnight, to La Force, where a tribunal was formed in which J.-A. Rossignol took part. Only eight political prisoners died at La Force, one of whom was Madame de Lamballe, the friend of Marie Antoinette. On Monday, 3 September, the killers moved on to Saint-Firmin, where some seventy priests were killed, then to the Bernardins, where seventy-two of seventy-five common prisoners awaiting shipment to the hulks were similarly executed. There were also at least two expeditions to Bicêtre, where it had been rumored that armed prisoners were firing on the people. Here the killers were National Guardsmen who on 4 September carried out the best organized, most systematic, and calmest massacre of all. When they thought their work was done, a prison steward named Boyer called their attention to a group of young prisoners under his care, children in their early teens. They too were killed, as was Boyer. The last prison to be hit on 4 September was the women's prison at La Salpêtrière, where thirty-five women were selected from among those branded on the shoulder; the rest were spared. At La Force the killings continued longest, perhaps as late as 7 September.

There were massacres outside Paris as well: at Meaux, where fourteen were killed after the arrival of gendarmes from Paris urging a purge of the prisons in imitation of Paris; and especially at Versailles, where most of the victims were from a detachment of political prisoners, including the former minister C.-A. Delessart, who had been awaiting trial by the high court at Orléans. Because of the slowness of that court's trial proceedings and the rumored insecurity of the prisons at Orléans, there had been repeated demands from the Paris sections for the transfer of these prisoners to Paris for punishment. On 26 August, after learning that many armed Parisians were setting out for Orléans, the Legislative Assembly authorized a special force of Parisian National Guards to set out for Orléans under the command of the Cordelier, C. Fournier "the American"; but on 2 September the Legislative ordered the escorting force to take their prisoners to a fortress at Saumur, so as to avoid the Paris massacre. Fournier disobeyed or, as he later claimed, was unable to enforce obedience on his troops. The group marched to Versailles instead, and its escort played a large part in the massacre that followed. Forty-five of the fifty-three prisoners from Orléans were killed. The Versailles prison was attacked next, and twenty others died.

At Paris, of a total number of 2,600 prisoners, between 1,100 and 1,400 died, among them 82 Swiss and Royal Guards, 223 priests, and somewhere between 49 and 87 other political prisoners. The great majority of the dead were common criminals. The killers included gendarmes, volunteers to the armies, *fédérés* from the provinces, shopkeepers, and artisans, many of them belonging to the neighborhoods where the massacres occurred. There were also some outsiders, however, who worked together in an organized fashion, moving from one prison to the next. They appear to have been normally decent people but rough and violent in their use of clubs, swords, and pikes against their victims, and there are stories of mutilation and torture that are probably true. They ate and drank while they worked. They expected pay, and they were paid, from Commune funds. They probably believed in the righteousness of what they were doing, in saving the Revolutionary fatherland.

The difficult question is that of assigning responsibility. Were the massacres from below, the spontaneous expression of the rage of ordinary people indignant over the delays of the courts, excited over the recent acquittal of Montmorin, frightened over the peril of royalist plots? So argued J.-L. Tallien, secretary of the Commune, soon after the event, and so argue most historians sympathetic to the Revolution. There was in fact much popular rage during the days that followed the events of 10 August. Marat was not alone in calling for an attack on the prisons before Parisians set out for the frontier.

Or were the massacres arranged, the product of a deliberate effort on the part of certain Revolutionary leaders, through the exercise of terror, to extend their dominion over France, not only against royalists but also against Girondin moderates? This was the position stated by the Girondin J.-D. Lanjuinais in January 1793 when he contended that the massacres were not the effect of popular disturbances but a plot on the part of five or six unnamed tyrants who hired brigands to carry out the massacres. Clearly if some men did plan a massacre, it is unlikely they would have kept minutes of such a meeting or have talked about it afterward. In any case there is no documentary evidence of such arrangements beforehand.

Such indications as there are of premeditation are inconclusive. The Commune had spoken as early as 23 August of separating debtors from political prisoners, but this may reflect its fear of a massacre rather than the desire for one. Toward the end of August, Danton asked the prison concierges for lists of their prisoners and the causes of their arrests; but the Girondins P.-L. Manuel and J.-M. Roland had asked Danton for such lists. Some of the prisoners, such as T.-G. Lally-Tollendal and A. de Beauharnais, were set free on the eve of the massacres, but prisoners could be set free at any time. The fact that the killers were admitted freely into the prisons instead of having to force their way in suggests complicity of the prison authorities, but it may reflect only their desire for self-preservation. The fact that the killers were already organized for the early massacre at the Carmelites does suggest planning, as does the fact that the killers were paid by the Commune, though pay may not have been promised beforehand. More serious still is the fact that the Commune called for the reconstruction of its Committee of Surveillance on 30 August, when the struggle between the Legislative Assembly and the Commune was at its peak, and that Marat, the leading proponent of prison massacres, was appointed to that committee.

Once the killings began, there was a widespread failure on the part of the governing authorities to attempt seriously to bring them to a halt. There was a positive complicity with the massacres on the part of the Commune and its Committee of Surveillance. To promote a separation between debtors and other prisoners and to send out commissioners to ensure this separation, as the Commune did, was to authorize the killing of the latter. The Commune did send its commissioners to the prisons; some of them, such as Rossignol, took part in the judgments that were made; others, such as Billaud-Varenne, encouraged the killers, telling them, "You are immolating your enemies; you are doing your duty."

The direct involvement of the Committee of Surveillance in the establishment of the tribunal at the Abbaye is suggested by a letter published in a Parisian journal in 1796: a letter to Maillard from Panis and Sergent of that committee, and J.-C.-H. Méhée de la Touche, secretary of the Commune, which directed Maillard to judge all the prisoners of the Abbaye without distinction, except for the abbé Lenfant, brother of a committee member, who was to be put in a safe place. P. Caron and G. Lefebvre have, however, seriously challenged the authenticity of this document.

This committee's support of a massacre was made clear in a circular letter, signed by its members, sent out to the eighty-three departments on 3 September. This letter spoke of a frightful plot to kill all French patriots who had forced the Commune of Paris, on 9 August, to recover the power of the people. It spoke of another plot, more recent: the effort made by the Legislative Assembly on 30 August to eliminate and replace the Paris Commune. It then hastened to inform its brothers in all of the departments that some of the conspirators detained in the Paris prisons had been put to death by the people in order to restrain conspirators through terror, and it urged the entire nation to hasten to adopt this necessary means of public safety. This appeal for further massacres was printed on the printing press of Marat. It was sent out under the seal of the minister of justice, Danton. P.-F. Fabre d'Eglantine may have applied the seal, rather than Danton himself, but it is unlikely that Danton had no knowledge of this.

Opposition to a national assembly that had so recently attempted to break the Commune found expression also, on the night of 2 September, at the assembly of the Commune, where Billaud-Varenne and M. Robespierre denounced a plot on the part of J.-P. Brissot and other deputies to place the duke of Brunswick on the French throne. That same night Robespierre's friend, Panis, delivered a warrant for the search of Brissot's lodgings, and the Committee of Surveillance prepared warrants for the arrest of Roland, Brissot, and other Girondin deputies. Nothing incriminating was found at Brissot's. Danton intervened with Marat and persuaded him not to carry out the arrests. Was the intention of Billaud and Robespierre merely to damage the Girondins politically, to prevent their election by Paris to the Convention; or did they seek to make them victims of the massacre itself? We do not know. The Girondins suspected the worst, and this explains in large part the bitterness of their attacks on the Commune and on its former members in the Convention during the months that followed.

S.-A. Berville and F. Barrière, eds., *Mémoires sur les journées de septembre, 1792* (Paris, 1823); B.-J. Buchez and P.-C. Roux, *Histoire parlementaire de la Révolution française*, vols. 17-18 (Paris, 1834-38); P. Caron, *Les massacres de septembre* (Paris, 1935); G. Lefebvre, *La Première Terreur* (Paris, 1952); G. Lenôtre [pseud. L. Gosselin], *Les massacres de septembre* (Paris, 1907); E. Seligman, *La justice en France pendant la Revolution*, vol. 2 (Paris, 1913).

S. Lytle

Related entries: BRISSOT DE WARVILLE; CHAMP DE MARS "MASSA-CRE"; DANTON; FABRE; GIRONDINS; LAW OF SUSPECTS; LESSART; MAILLARD; MARAT; MONTMORIN DE SAINT-HEREM; PRISONS; ROBESPIERRE, M.; SECTIONS; TALLIEN; 10 AUGUST 1792.

SERFDOM, a condition of hereditary personal bondage, which scarcely existed in Old Regime France. *Mainmorte*, a servitude adhering to land, not persons, was the representative form of serfdom in pre-Revolutionary France. A *mainmortable*, one who held land in an area of *mainmorte*, could transmit his land only to his children living with him. He could alienate his land only to another *mainmortable*, unless he obtained prior permission from the lord. If no children were resident with him at the time of the tenant's death, the lord obtained the succession. In most customary law codes, the word *children* had been expanded to include other *mainmortables* living in community with the *mainmorte* tenant. The *mainmortable* was generally subject to heavier seigneurial dues, in particular the seigneurial *taille* and extra *corvées*, than were *censiers* in the same seigneurie. By some customs, the rights of *formariage* were due when the *mainmortable* married outside the seigneurie. A *mainmortable* was free at any time to abandon his tenure; by doing so he was freed from the obligations and condition of *mainmorte*, but he lost his property to the lord.

Mainmorte existed only in limited areas of France, and those areas were perforated with areas liberated from it. The customs of Burgundy, Franche-Comté, Chaumont, Troyes, Vitry, Auvergne, La Marche, Bourbonnais, and Nivernais all retained sections pertaining to *mainmorte*. *Mainmorte* was strongest in Franche-Comté, parts of Burgundy, and the Nivernais. It is estimated that one-third of all Burgundian villages were subject to *mainmorte*. But within these villages many individuals were free from *mainmorte* or had obtained their enfranchisement.

The attack on *mainmorte* was launched well before the Revolution, and the battle was waged on humanitarian and utilitarian grounds. From the humanitarian perspective, *mainmorte* was equated with a personal and barbarous servitude and was condemned as being destructive of human liberty and dignity. This attack on serfdom often took a strong anticlerical bent, in part because ecclesiastical institutions controlled a large share of *mainmortable* land. J.-J. Rousseau's *Discours sur l'origine de l'inégalité* (1755) and F.-M. Voltaire's *mémoires* of the 1770s in favor of the serfs of Mount Jura heralded the appearance of numerous if less illustrious treatises condemning serfdom.

Mainmorte was also attacked from a physiocratic or utilitarian perspective as being harmful to agriculture. The *mainmorte* tenant had little incentive to improve property at risk of it reverting to the lord, and the risks involved and services demanded ensured that *mainmorte* holdings were small and backward. In a 1779 agricultural inquiry, Burgundian curés condemned the harmful effects of *mainmorte*.

Mainmorte found its defenders, however, who argued that it was not a destructive custom but rather one protective of the peasantry and beneficial to both the tenants and the lord. The peasantry had much greater access to the land in areas of *mainmorte* and greater success in retaining their tenures, if only because no bourgeois wished to hold land under such conditions. The labor force proved steadier and the land better worked because one's heritage depended on one's remaining within the seigneurie. The general lot of the peasant was a happier one. Living in a larger household community to avoid the loss of the succession, the peasant shared accordingly in a larger community of resources, and relations with the lord were much more reciprocal and protective in areas of *mainmorte*.

In August 1779 Louis XVI issued an edict, drafted by J. Necker and inspired in part by Voltaire's campaign and by the king of Sardinia's recent abolition of serfdom in Savoy, abolishing *mainmorte* on the royal domains and abolishing in every case the right of pursuit. The king, while regretting that he was unable to decree the entire abolition of *mainmorte* because the state of royal finances would not allow him to reimburse seigneurs for the loss of property such an abolition would entail, urged other lords to follow his example. The edict raised much protest from the parlements in provinces where *mainmorte* was strong. The Parlement of Besançon, for example, registered the edict under duress and not until October 1788. Louis XVI's edict obtained mixed results that have yet to be evaluated. In some cases, it seems that the edict frightened seigneurs into negotiating with their *mainmorte* tenants for fear of an impending abolition of the right. In other cases, the edict seems to have had little effect.

Mainmorte was a profitable right for seigneurs. It provided a cheap, abundant, and available labor force, permitted greater seigneurial exactions, and, if the lord paid close attention to the intricacies and observance of succession rules, it could regularly enrich his coffers. In the case of *formariage*, many lords judged it more profitable not to enforce the right, in the expectation that marriage outside the community would more likely result in the escheat of the succession. Other lords chose to free their *mainmortables* in exchange for a fee, new or additional seigneurial dues, or communal property.

The situation of *mainmorte* in the period preceding the Revolution was mixed. Its physical and intellectual hold had declined since the seventeenth century. Courts took a hard line in cases involving the proof of *mainmorte* and refused to hear cases concerning issues of personal servitude. The condition of the *mainmortable* was increasingly considered a degrading status. The socioeconomic status of *mainmortables* is also difficult to assess, and the arguments of *mainmorte*'s defenders and adversaries are contradictory. *Mainmorte* survived in more backward areas of France, frequently on the poorer lands. Although *mainmorte* added to the burdens of working such land, it cannot be isolated as the cause of agricultural stagnation. An opposite argument suggests that *mainmorte* protected peasant property and that peasants were able to compensate for the heavy exactions by retaining a larger share of the land for themselves than in other areas not subject to *mainmorte*.

The campaign against *mainmorte* reached a crescendo with the Revolution, and several *cahiers* demanded its abolition. The Constituent Assembly's course was much more decisive on this issue than for other seigneurial rights. *Mainmorte personnelle et réelle* was abolished in the legislation of 4-11 August 1789. The decrees of 15-28 March 1790 clarified the abolition and attempted to sort out rights incidental to *mainmorte* that should be redeemed. This legislation in effect made the *mainmortable* a *censier* subject to the customary exactions. As with the abolition of seigneurial rights, *mainmortables* refused to acknowledge the distinction. The Law of 25-28 August 1792 declared *mainmorte*'s full abolition.

D. Ligou, "La seigneurie en Bourgogne," in *L'abolition de la féodalité dans le monde occidental*, vol. 2 (Paris, 1971); J. C. Q. Mackrell, *The Attack on "Feudalism" in Eighteenth-Century France* (London, 1973); "Mainmorte," *Encyclopédie méthodique . . . , Jurisprudence* (Paris, 1782-91); J. Millot, *Le régime féodal en Franche-Comté au XVIIIe siècle* (Besançon, 1937).

M. A. Quinn

Related entries: *CENS*; *CORVEE*; FEUDALISM; 4 AUGUST 1789; NECKER; *TAILLE*.

SERVAN DE GERBEY, JOSEPH (1741-1808), minister of war. A career officer since the 1760s, Servan won notoriety in 1780 with the publication of *Le soldat citoyen*, a long and detailed plan for reforming the army. Its central theme foreshadowed the Revolution by urging universal conscription in a nation that would regard its soldiers as citizens.

Servan became minister of war on 9 May 1792, joining a cabinet already split into two rival factions: one dominated by the minister of foreign affairs, C. Dumouriez, and the other by the minister of the interior, J.-M. Roland de la Platière. Roland wanted to minimize the king's power by having the ministers work directly with the Brissotin leaders of the Legislative Assembly. Dumouriez was more the king's man and distrusted the republican Roland. Dumouriez believed that he could dominate Servan and supported his appointment. When Servan became Roland's strongest supporter, tensions within the cabinet were raised to an unbearable pitch.

The most controversial move of Servan's brief tenure in office was made on 4 June. In a speech to the Legislative Assembly, he proposed the creation of an army of 20,000 men, which would be stationed on the northern outskirts of Paris. This was to be an elite force, composed of five soldiers from each city and town in the nation. Its ostensible purpose was twofold: first, since they represented all parts of the country, the federals would provide a striking patriotic symbol for the national festival set for 14 July; second, they could protect Paris in case of a foreign invasion. But everyone knew of a third purpose, which Servan chose not to discuss: the new troops also could be used to protect the Legislative Assembly from the machinations of the king and his court. Dumouriez was infuriated. In the Executive Council, he claimed that Servan had not informed him or even the king of the new proposal before speaking of it to the Assembly. He believed that such behavior was evidence of a republican attitude festering in the cabinet. At one point the insults between Dumouriez and Servan became so strong that they drew swords on one another in the presence of the king. The Assembly, however, took a different view. With the support of its Military Committee, the Legislative Assembly easily passed Servan's proposal on 6 June. The king refused to sanction the decree; and the affair contributed to the dismissal of Roland, Servan, and E. Clavière (the minister of finance) on 12 June. Dumouriez himself replaced Servan at the Ministry of War and delivered a scathing critique of Servan's administration to the Assembly. The Brissotins immediately retaliated with a well-organized press campaign. In pamphlets such as *Réflections sur le ministère de M. Servan* and *Lettres et pièces intéressantes pour servir à l'histoire du ministère du Roland, Servan, et Clavière*, Servan and his colleagues were made into popular heroes.

Roland, Servan, and Clavière were recalled to their ministries after the insurrection of 10 August. Since June, Servan had been serving in the army as a brigadier general in Soissons, and he was unable to return to Paris before 19 August. On that same day the duke of Brunswick led the Allied forces across the French border, and two days later the fortress of Longwy was taken. The responsibility for stopping the invasion was Servan's; and both the Military Committee and the Executive Council allowed him to direct the war as he saw fit. The generals were less cooperative. After the marquis de Lafayette surrendered himself to the Austrians, Dumouriez became the most important general. Servan put aside his hostile feelings and tried to work with Dumouriez as best he could. But serious differences soon arose. Dumouriez wanted to invade Belgium, where he believed his chances for military success were good. Servan was worried that the Allies would march on Paris and urged the general to draw his troops back to Sedan in order to defend the capital. Dumouriez refused, arguing that the Austrians would never allow troops to go far into France if Belgium were endangered. Servan wondered what good Belgium would be to a France without Paris. So worried was Servan about the situation that he supported Roland's proposal to move the government to safe ground in the Loire region (the plan was killed in Executive Council by G.-J. Danton). It was not until the Allies took Verdun on 2 September that Dumouriez put his full weight behind the defensive campaign. Bad weather slowed the Allied drive and allowed the French time to regroup. The subsequent battle at Valmy on 20 September gave the French a crucial victory. The invasion was stopped, and the French began to win a series of battles during the fall of 1792.

The pace of these events left Servan in a state of physical exhaustion. After little more than a month in office, he asked the Convention to relieve him of his duties. On 4 October he left the ministry and was appointed general of the Army of the Pyrenees. Historians critical of Servan have followed the accusations of some Montagnards in suggesting that Servan allowed a few speculators (notably the abbé d'Espagnac) to make huge sums of money through the sale of munitions. After the fall of the Girondins, Servan was imprisoned and was released only after Thermidor. He was reinstated in the army in 1795 and served in various capacities until his retirement in 1803. He died in 1808.

M. Dommanget, "Les fournisseurs aux armées et Servan," *Ann. hist. de la Révo. française* 2 (1925); H. Libermann, *La défense nationale à la fin de 1792. Servan et Pache (10 août 1792-2 février 1793)* (Paris, 1927); A. Mathiez, "Servan et les premiers marchés d'Espagnac," *Ann. Révo.* 10 (1918).

G. Kates

Related entries: BATTLE OF VALMY; BRUNSWICK; DUMOURIEZ; LAFAYETTE; ROLAND DE LA PLATIERE, J.-M.

SIEYES, EMMANUEL-JOSEPH (1748-1836), abbé, pamphleteer, politician. Sieyès was born in Fréjus, a small coastal town in southeastern France and the seat of an impoverished bishopric. He was the fifth child and third son of H. Sieyès, a minor royal fiscal official and postmaster with some independent means, who with the encouragement of the local bishop seems to have pushed his son toward the church at an early age. After the usual schooling with local clergy, Emmanuel was sent to Paris where he attended the Sorbonne and the celebrated seminary of Saint-Sulpice, obtaining his *licence* in theology in 1774. While there he seems to have read widely and freely in secular as well as sacred writings.

After much effort and many disappointments, he gained an appointment as a canon of the diocese of Tréguier in lower Brittany, and his benefices provided a modest living as well as his title of abbé. While there he sat as representative of his diocese in the Estates of Brittany. In 1780 his bishop was advanced to the more prestigious see of Chartres, taking Sieyès with him and appointing him first *vicaire-général* and later chancellor of the diocese. He gained further political and administrative experience as a representative of his district to the sovereign chamber of the clergy of France and in 1787-88 to the newly established Provincial Estates of Orléans. During these years at Chartres, he seems to have frequented some of the most celebrated salons in Paris, as well as becoming a Mason and participating actively in a number of political discussion and propaganda groups such as the Société des amis des noirs.

His first effort as a political pamphleteer came in response to the royal decree of 5 July 1788 calling for information about past Estates Generals. It dealt with the legislative role of previous assemblies, but by the time it was ready for the printer in October, an Estates General had already been called for May 1789, and the major issue now was the Third's demand for double representation and the vote by head in that body. Accordingly, he withdrew his first effort from the printer and quickly composed and published a powerful attack on the privileges of the first two orders (*Essai sur les privilèges*), but it seems to have attracted little attention. In January 1789, however, he followed it up with his famous *Qu'est-ce que c'est le tiers état?* which immediately became a bestseller. The simplicity of his argument—that no privileges can stand against the rights of the sovereign people—and the force of his rhetoric gave this work such universal and powerful appeal that Sieyès immediately became a celebrity and potential leader of the Third Estate.

While his radical views probably prevented his election to the Estates General as a representative of the clergy, it was unquestionably the widespread appeal of his arguments that led to his selection as deputy by one of the districts of the Third Estate in Paris. Since his famous pamphlet had already recommended a strategy for the Third Estate to follow in its efforts to obtain the vote by head, it is not surprising that he quickly emerged as a leader of that order when the Estates General convened; and it was on his motion that it declared itself to constitute a National Assembly on 17 June 1789. A few days later, he was one of the instigators of the Tennis Court Oath.

As the Assembly assumed its constituent role, he was one of the first elected to the Committee on the Constitution, and therefore he was deeply involved in all of the critical issues taken up by the Assembly over the next two years. He seems to have had most influence on the legislation reorganizing local government and the judiciary. In spite of his emphasis on popular sovereignty, he strongly supported the distinction between active and passive citizenship. His views did not always prevail by any means, and he disapproved of the Assembly's eventual stands on many issues, but especially on the confiscation of church lands, because of his adamant support of property rights. As these disagreements became known, his popularity, and consequently his influence, began to wane. He was a very poor speaker and seemed unable or unwilling to try to appeal to the masses through his writings. He had none of the skills or attributes of the politician. He tended to hold himself aloof from factions and conspicuously disdained any compromise with his principles. As a result, although he was generally respected as an authority on constitutional matters, his political influence seems to have been greatly diminished by the end of the Assembly.

Barred by law from the Legislative Assembly, he remained active in the Paris government and in some of the political clubs. Perhaps because of his personal enmity toward the leaders of the dominant constitutional monarchist faction, the Feuillants, he gained the reputation of being a republican. He seems to have played no significant role in the momentous events of the summer of 1792 but nevertheless emerged in September as a deputy to the Convention. There the pattern of the National Assembly was repeated. He was elected to the original constitutional committee but not the Jacobin-dominated one that replaced it in the summer of 1793. Consistently refusing to align himself with either the Girondists or the Mountain (although he voted for the death of the king), he prided himself on the fact that he survived both the Terror and Thermidor.

Probably his refusal to endorse any consistent line and his lack of any significant political following made him too unimportant to be concerned about. After Thermidor he again became involved in the constitution making that resulted in the Directory, but so many of his proposals were ignored that he had nothing but contempt for the constitution that emerged. His principal objection was that the Convention's reverence for the principle of the separation of powers deprived the new executive Directory of the power it would need to maintain political stability.

In spite of his reservation, however, Sieyès accepted election to the Council of Five Hundred and served until May 1798, when he was appointed ambassador to Prussia. When he returned to Paris in the spring of 1799, he abandoned his customary low profile and accepted election as one of the executive directors. He seems to have believed that this would put him in a position to bring about the changes in the structure of that government that he and several other members of the councils felt were needed if France was to continue to be a great power. He is credited with choosing N. Bonaparte (not his first choice) and master-minding the coup d'état of Brumaire. Although he expected to play a preeminent role in the new government, Napoleon had other ideas. Some of his proposals, however, such as the separation of the debating and voting functions in the legislative bodies and having the voters choose pools of candidates from which legislators and officials would be drawn, were embodied in the constitution, but the final document reflected Napoleon's ideas much more than Sieyès'. He was amply rewarded for his acquiescence by being given the presidency of the new Senate with a handsome salary and perquisites. He became a rich man and in 1808 was made a count in the new imperial nobility. In 1814 and 1815, he weathered the first Restoration, but after the Hundred Days he found it prudent to remove to Brussels where he lived modestly but comfortably until the Revolution of 1830. He then returned to France and died in 1836.

For someone with such a great contemporary reputation as constitution maker and political theorist, it is remarkable that he left no major corpus of political writings. His ideas and theories emerge in his pamphlets, speeches, and reports, and these sufficed in the nineteenth century to make him considered perhaps the foremost spokesman for the liberal state with its two cornerstones of civic equality and popular sovereignty.

P. Bastid, *Sieyès et sa pensée* (Paris, 1939); J. H. Clapham, *The Abbé Sieyès* (London, 1912); E.-J. Sieyès, *Qu'est-ce que c'est le tiers état?* critical edition with notes by Roberto Zapperi (Geneva, 1970); J. L. Talmon, *The Origins of Totalitarian Democracy* (New York, 1960).

R. W. Greenlaw

Related entries: ACTIVE CITIZEN; CONSTITUTION OF 1799; FEUILLANTS; GIRONDINS; MONTAGNARDS; PASSIVE CITIZEN; *QU'EST-CE QUE C'EST LE TIERS ETAT?*; SOCIETE DES AMIS DES NOIRS; 10 AUGUST 1792; TENNIS COURT OATH.

SOBOUL, ALBERT-MARIUS (1914-82), historian and teacher specializing in the French Revolution. Born in Ammi Moussa, Algeria, on 27 April 1914, the son of a peasant settler from the Ardèche, the young Soboul lost his father early in World War I. He and his older sister were raised first by their mother, who died when he was eight, and then by his aunt, the headmistress of a girls' school in Nîmes. After receiving a degree from the lycée of Nimes in 1932, he continued his studies at the lycée Louis-Le-Grand in Paris and then at the Sorbonne.

Soboul received his *diplôme d'études supérieures* in 1936 for a *mémoire* on the political and social ideas of L. Saint-Just, which was published under the pseudonym of Pierre Derocles the next year. In 1938 he passed his *agrégation d'histoire et de géographie*. While a student in Paris, he became associated with a communist student organization and formally joined the Communist party in 1939. Remaining a loyal member throughout his life, Soboul did not always fully agree with its positions. On the eve of World War II, he published his *1789*, a collection of documents from the first year of the Revolution.

Called up for military service in 1939, Soboul served as a private in the artillery. After the fall of France and ensuing armistice, he was demobilized and was assigned to teach at the lycée of Montpellier (1940-42, 1944-47). In July 1942, he was arrested as a result of his participation in a student demonstration and dismissed by the Vichy government. From then until the Liberation, Soboul fought in the Resistance as a soldier in the underground FTP (Franc-Tireurs et Partisans Français). He put his military experience to good use when he published his study of the republican armies, *L'armée nationale sous la Révolution (1789-1794)*, in 1945.

Resuming his interrupted teaching career after the war, Soboul became a teacher, first at the Lycée Marcelin Berthelot in Paris, then at the Lycée Henri IV, where he remained until 1960. He also returned to the study of Saint-Just, publishing his *Republican Institutions* (1948) and an edition of his speeches and reports (1957). Under the direction of G. Lefebvre, who became his mentor and close friend, Soboul turned his attention to the Parisian popular classes. After extensive research, he completed his doctoral dissertation, "Les Sans-culottes parisiens en l'an II," in 1958. (A much-abridged English translation appeared in 1964.) This 1,100-page thesis, which examined the action of the democratic masses of the capital in 1793-94, earned the unanimous praise of the Sorbonne jury.

His success brought Soboul promotion to the post of professor of modern history at the University of Clermont-Ferrand. In 1967, on the retirement of M. Reinhard, Soboul was named professor of the history of the French Revolution at the University of Paris. In addition, Soboul succeeded Lefebvre as head of the Société des Etudes Robespierristes, coeditor of the *Annales historiques de la Révolution française*, and director of the Institut d'Histoire de la Révolution française.

A prolific scholar, Soboul published a long series of important studies: *Die Sansculotten von Paris* (with W. Markov, 1957); *Les Campagnes montpelli-*

eraines à la fin de l'Ancien régime (1958); *Précis d'histoire de la Révolution française* (1962; English translation, 1974); *La Révolution française* (1965; English translation, 1977); *Le procès de Louis XVI* (1966); *Paysans, sans-culottes et jacobins* (1966); *La France à la veille de la Révolution: Economie et société* (1966); *Le Directoire et le Consulat, 1795-1804* (1967); *Les sans-culottes* (1968); *La première République, 1792-1804* (1968); *La civilisation et la Révolution française: La crise de l'Ancien régime* (1970); *Problèmes paysans de la Révolution, 1789-1848* (1976); *Le Siècle des lumières: L'Essor (1715-1750)* (with G. Lemarchand and M. Fogel, 1977); *Comprendre la Révolution* (1981). In addition, he reedited most of Lefebvre's works and published a new, annotated edition of J. Jaurès's *Histoire socialiste de la Révolution française* (1968-73).

Although he denied heatedly that he was a Marxist historian, Soboul placed economic and social forces at the heart of his analysis of the Revolution. His work stressed that the bourgeoisie, having won economic power during the eighteenth century, sought political power as well, seizing it from the ruling aristocracy after 1789. He was especially interested in the conflict that arose between the middle classes and the lower classes, particularly the urban *sans-culottes*, who sought their own egalitarian revolution against the liberal, legal revolution of the moderates. Despite strenuous efforts by popular militants, this revolution from below did not succeed, although some gains were made during the Year II, when popular democracy was at its height. In later years, Soboul devoted more attention to the demands of the peasantry, believing that it carried out an autonomous revolution. Aligned with the classical and scientific school of historiography that extended from A. de Tocqueville through F.-A. Aulard, Jaurès, and A. Mathiez to Lefebvre, Soboul attacked those historians (mostly English and American) who claimed that the Revolution was not fundamentally bourgeois or that it formed part of a larger Atlantic upheaval. He firmly believed that the Revolution destroyed the highly restrictive economic system of the Old Regime, thereby removing the barriers to the development of capitalism and preparing the way for the large industrial and commercial enterprises that characterized the nineteenth century.

Soboul attained international recognition, not only for his numerous publications, but also because of his wide travels abroad. At various times he visited the United States, Canada, Germany, Hungary, Rumania, the Soviet Union, China, Japan, and Australia to attend meetings and deliver papers. His enormous physical energy, vital personality, and effective speaking style all contributed to his worldwide reputation. Soboul died suddenly at his home in Nîmes on 10 September 1982.

Le Monde, 14 September 1982; *London Times*, 17 September 1982; *Great Soviet Encyclopedia*, vol. 24; *Ann. hist. de la Révo. française* 55 (1982).

J. Friguglietti

Related entries: AULARD; JAURES; LEFEBVRE; MATHIEZ; REINHARD; TOCQUEVILLE.

SOCIAL CONTRACT, political philosophy asserting the idea of popular sovereignty, usually identified with J.-J. Rousseau. The idea of a social contract, first conceived as a contract of submission (an agreement between the ruler and the ruled, limiting the exercise of the political authority thereby conferred) but then developed in more radical terms as a contract of association (the prior agreement among men to constitute a political society as a whole, thereby determining its nature and purposes), was by no means novel in the eighteenth century. Invoked in many contexts since the Reformation, it had been elaborated theoretically in the seventeenth century by such thinkers as T. Hobbes and J. Locke, H. Grotius and S. Pufendorf, and became a common idiom in the political discourse of the Enlightenment. However, the idea received its most powerful expression in J.-J. Rousseau's *Du contrat social* (1762). This work, more than any other, laid the theoretical foundations for the Revolutionary conception of national sovereignty.

According to traditional monarchical theory in France, royal authority represented the principle of unity (and the condition of order) in a society defined as a multiplicity of particularistic orders and Estates; the sovereign will inhering in the public person of the monarch was therefore absolute, unitary, inalienable, and indivisible. Rousseau's conception of the social contract transposed these attributes of sovereignty from the monarch to the entire social body, conceived as a union of individual citizens living freely under a common law. To establish the unity of the political body and to create a sovereign power absolute enough to secure the freedom of its individual members one against the other, he argued, it was necessary that the associates give themselves equally and entirely, with all their rights, to the community thereby constituted. But to maintain the individual liberty that was the goal of the association, it was also necessary that the sovereign power inhere inalienably and indivisibly in the citizen body as a whole and that its exercise be the expression of the general will. Defined in terms of the universality of its source and the universality of its object, the general will emanated equally from all and applied equally to all; it therefore expressed the will of the public body for the common good. As a result, it could not be represented by any particular will—hence Rousseau's insistence on the supremacy of the sovereign people over any government (to which executive authority alone could be delegated) and on the impossibility of entrusting legislative authority to a representative assembly. Nor was the preservation of the general will consistent with the existence of any partial associations within the state. In essence, then, the concept of the general will was the abstract antithesis of the monarchical authority and particularistic social order of the *ancien régime*.

The impact of *Du contrat social* on French political discourse has been much debated. While some twelve editions of the work were published in French within the first two years of its appearance in 1762, there were relatively few thereafter until the outbreak of the Revolution. But at least two appeared in the stormy years following the Maupeou coup (1772 and 1775, the latter with an apparently false Philadelphia imprint), and the work was also included in as many as sixteen editions of Rousseau's collected writings published in the pre-Revolutionary period. Traditional assumptions regarding the book's influence that date from the Revolution itself were radically challenged by D. Mornet on the basis of his study of private libraries sold in Paris in the period 1750-80; in 500 sale catalogs, *Du contrat social* was listed only once, as compared with 185 listings for *La nouvelle Heloïse*. Combining this finding with evidence of the paucity of separate editions after 1763, Mornet concluded that *Du contrat social*, the most abstract of Rousseau's writings, went virtually unnoticed in the pre-Revolutionary period. Extending Mornet's argument to the period of the Revolution itself, J. McDonald has claimed that the personal cult of Rousseau exercised a far more powerful influence on the mind of the Revolutionaries than his political theory, of which the Revolutionaries remained largely ignorant.

These conclusions are quite inadequate. Mornet appealed essentially to external evidence for the diffusion of *Du contrat social* itself, without systematically analyzing the political discourse of the pre-Revolutionary period for indications of the direct or indirect impact of its arguments. Yet it is clear that among the many appeals to the principle of the social contract that erupted in the anti-Maupeou propaganda of the 1770s, there were some—most notably the *Catechisme du citoyen* of G.-J. Saige and the *Ami des lois* of M. de Marivaux, pamphlets that were to reappear in the course of the pre-Revolution—that drew specifically on the Rousseauian formulation of the idea. McDonald, in turn, relied heavily on the unsatisfactory procedure of scanning the political literature of the Revolution for explicit appeals to the authority of Rousseau by name; and to the extent that she analyzed political argumentation directly, she tended to look for discrete political positions corresponding to the doctrine of *Du contrat social* as she understood it as a whole. But the abstract and complex character of the argument of this work—and hence its potential for use in a variety of ways and in a variety of particular political situations—suggest that it was more likely to enter into Revolutionary discourse as an underlying problematic or a series of problematics, structuring debate on successive political issues, than as a single doctrine identified with a particular author or party.

Recent research by R. Barny, based on more extensive study of Revolutionary political discourse, confirms that this was indeed the case. The conflict over the forms according to which the Estates General should meet and vote, as over the eventual transformation of that body into a national assembly, was cast in terms of such issues as the ultimate inalienability of popular sovereignty, the universality of the general will and its incompatibility with particularistic corporate interests within the state, and the unity of the nation as a body of citizens living under a common law—all essential themes of *Du contrat social*. In the Constituent Assembly, discussion of the relationship to be established between the legislative and the executive was informed by Rousseau's understanding of the necessary distinction between them, just as the arguments for the royal veto drew force from a distrust of representative government grounded in the principles of *Du contrat social*; at the same time, aristocratic critics of the Revolution were able to invoke Rousseau's critique of representation against the actions and authority of the Assembly itself. During the National Convention, the tension between the practical necessity for representation and the theoretical supremacy of the direct expression of the general will constituted one of the essential conditions of the failure of representative government. Within the Convention, both Girondins (in their demands for a referendum) and Jacobins (in their reliance on direct popular action) sought to appeal beyond the representative assembly to a more immediate expression of popular sovereignty; outside it, the *sans-culottes* combined their claim to constitute the active expression of the general will with a renewed emphasis on the theme of social equality. Similarly, the postulate of unanimity inherent in the concept of the general will offered the ideological underpinning for the Robespierrist dictatorship, just as Rousseau's emphasis on the need for a civil religion became an important feature of the Reign of Virtue through which all hearts would be regenerated. Thus, throughout the Revolutionary period, the problematic of *Du contrat social* structured political discourse, informed perceptions of political realities, and propelled ideological development in complex ways.

R. Barny, "Jean-Jacques Rousseau dans la Révolution française," *Rev. du d-h. siècle* 6 (1974); R. Derathe, *Jean-Jacques Rousseau et la science politique de son temps* (Paris, 1950); D. Echeverria, "The Pre-Revolutionary Influence of Rousseau's *Contrat social*," *J. of the Hist. of Ideas* 33 (1972); J. McDonald, *Rousseau and the French Revolution, 1762-1791* (London, 1965); D. Mornet, "Les enseignements des bibliothèques privées (1750-1780)," *Rev. d'hist. litt. de la France* 17 (1910) and *Les origines intellectuelles de la Révolution française* (Paris, 1933).

K. Baker

Related entries: GIRONDINS; JACOBINS; ROUSSEAU; *SANS-CULOTTES*; THEORY OF REVOLUTIONARY GOVERNMENT.

SOCIETE DE L'HARMONIE UNIVERSELLE. See MESMER.

SOCIETE DES AMIS DES NOIRS, antislavery organization during the early years of the Revolution. On 19 February 1788, a small handful of men gathered in Paris at No. 3 rue Française to organize a philanthropic society that would promote the abolition of Negro slavery and the slave trade. They were led by J.-P. Brissot, a French journalist; E. Clavière, a respected financier and close friend of Brissot; the comte de Mirabeau, the dramatic hero of the Tennis Court Oath; and J.-L. Carra, A.-M. Cerisier, J.-G.-C. Valady and A.-C. B. Duchesnay, associated later with the Girondins. By early 1789, the Société des Amis des Noirs would have 141 well-known members, the most famous of whom were the marquis de Lafayette, the marquis de Condorcet, the duc de Rochefoucauld, E.-C. de Loménie de Brienne, J. Pétion, and the abbé Gregoire.

Brissot, inspired by British and American Quakers, such as T. Clarkson and A. Benezet, who had "stirred the hearts of *philosophes*, journalists and the more enlightened nobility," and taken with the power of the printed word ("Qui a fait la révolution des Etats-Unis?'' he rhetorically asks in his *Mémoires*, ''Les gazettes''), modeled the society on a literary idealization of British and American abolition societies. This is perhaps why recent critics of the French abolition movement argue that the Amis des Noirs, which relied primarily on newspapers, such as *Le patriote français*, the major voice of the society from 1789 to 1793, *L'analyse des papiers anglais*, *Le courrier de Provence*, *Le chronique de Paris*, and *Le journal de Paris*, and on political pamphlets to disseminate its ideas, was elitist, lacked a broad base of support and an effective organization, and was largely ineffective. While some of the historical criticism is just, much of it reflects more that radical age in which the Amis des Noirs was being studied (the 1960s and 1970s) than the era of the French Revolution in which the members of the Amis des Noirs were, with courage and perseverance, the principal advocates of the abolition of slavery.

The Amis des Noirs, for the most part, believed in their humanitarian mission. Brissot, often the target of recent historians, who with disdain call him superficial and an opportunist, more interested in making his fortune in land speculation than in alleviating the lot of black slaves, remained through much of his career a steadfast foe of slavery and an advocate of humanitarian reform. In 1780, his ''De la suppression de la peine de mort,'' influenced by C. B. Beccaria and J. Howard, sought to put an end to capital punishment. In 1781, he published the two-volume *Théorie des lois criminelles*, which proposed reforms of the criminal law code. He further urged legal and political reforms in the ten-volume *Bibliothèque philosophique du législateur, du politique, du jurisconsulte*, published between 1782 and 1785. And in 1786 he published an impassioned defense of the morality and religious and political beliefs of the Quakers and of the rights of blacks and of their ability to live as freemen in *Examen critique des voyages dans l'Amerique septentrionale, de M. le Marquis de Chastellux*. Until he was hunted down and killed by the Jacobins in 1794, he would remain an advocate of the rights of blacks.

Soon after the February 1788 organizational meeting, the leaders of the Amis des Noirs elected a president, Clavière; adopted a lengthy constitution, drafted by Condorcet, which, open to men and women, Frenchmen and foreigners, revealed their faith in the inevitable growth of their movement, even to where it would take on international proportions, and in the seriousness and justness of their mission. (They envisioned an international antislavery society led by W. Wilberforce, J.-P. Brissot, T. Paine and A. Hamilton.) Their goals were disseminated, the issues debated in H.-G. R. Mirabeau's *L'analyse des papiers anglais* with so much zeal that their English supporters became frightened, especially after proslavery forces alleged that the society sought to bring about the immediate abolition of slavery in the English colonies. In July 1789 Clarkson himself came to Paris and insisted on the sharp separation of the French abolition movement from the British, as well as the narrowing of the Amis des Noirs' goal to the abolition of the French slave trade. Meanwhile, in late 1788, Brissot, the nominal leader, had sailed to the United States to study first-hand the problem of slavery in the New World.

In the spring of 1789, on Brissot's return, the Amis des Noirs lobbied the *bailliages*, urging them to instruct their elected deputies to the Estates General to consider ways to abolish the slave trade and slavery itself. Partly as a result of their efforts, 49 of some 600 *cahiers de doléances* called for abolition of the slave trade or for gradual abolition. Although these antislavery *cahiers* represented many parts of France, the Amis des Noirs were unable to create an indomitable upswell of antislavery public opinion. France was more concerned with its pressing political and economic problems than with the problems of slaves in the French West Indies. Moreover, plantation owners from Saint-Domingue, Martinique, and Guadeloupe, supported by merchants and financiers from port cities, such as Bordeaux, Nantes, and Le Havre, lobbied against the Amis des Noirs, using their powerful political influence and scare tactics to protect their investment in the slave system. The abolition of slavery, they warned, would result in economic disaster. Not only that but the slave lobby, which called itself the Club Massiac, accused the Amis des Noirs of conspiring with the English to stir up the blacks to destroy the whites. If the Amis des Noirs should persist in their abolition efforts, they would be attacked with knives, reports warned.

There was little need, we now see, for the Club Massiac to be threatened by the Amis des Noirs. For despite the society's economic and moral arguments for abolition (''Should I be abandoned, should I remain alone, I swear to Heaven ...that I will never abandon the cause of the Blacks,'' Brissot and others pledged), there seemed little reason to believe that its members could persuade the Constituent Assembly to legislate an end to slavery or even of the slave trade. Some members, like Mirabeau, were intimidated by the threats of violence. Others like Brissot often spent more time at Versailles, participating in debates and committees, than in Paris, where they could organize resistance to the Club Massiac. Still other members who held positions with the municipal government of Paris (like J. Pétion) were absorbed in their duties at the Hôtel de Ville, or like Lafayette, were organizing a National Guard.

Even if the Amis des Noirs had not been distracted by their duties, it is doubtful if they could have been more effective than they were. For many months, for instance, the Assembly refused to permit the Amis des Noirs to take the floor to speak against the slave trade. It gave virtual control of the slave issue to the Committee on Colonies, which, dominated by planter interests, recommended that the Assembly agree that the government had no intention of changing even a single aspect of the colonial trade and would outlaw all agitation that threatened property and property holders in the French West Indies. (The government approved this report on 8 March 1790.)

Thereafter, there would be only a single feasible issue, the mulatto question (*gens de couleur*), for the Amis des Noirs. Some wealthy mulattoes were already living in Paris and had organized themselves into a pressure group called the

Colons Américains, headed by V. Ogé and J. Raymond. What is more, it seemed that the Amis des Noirs felt that the mulattoes met every criterion of citizenship under the Declaration of the Rights of Man and of the Citizen, as well as under article 59 of the *Code Noir*. However, the Assembly managed to shroud the legal status of the mulattoes with ambiguity and prevented them from receiving explicit citizenship rights. Thus, it appeared that because of these circumstances, the Amis des Noirs had failed to generate sufficient support to end the slave trade, abolish slavery, or even win acceptance for the mulattoes. But this is a moot point, for while the Assembly was debating such issues, blacks and mulattoes would take matters into their own hands, especially on Saint-Domingue, and, led by F.-D. Toussaint-L'Ouverture, eventually win their independence and freedom after a bloody struggle.

B. D. Davis, *The Problem of Slavery in the Age of Revolution* (Ithaca, N.Y., 1975); G. Debien, *Les colons de Saint-Domingue et la Révolution. Essai sur le Club Massiac, août 1789-août 1792* (Paris, 1953); E. Ellery, *Brissot de Warville: A Study in the History of the French Revolution* (Boston, 1915); D. Resnick, ''The Société des Amis des Noirs and the Abolition of Slavery,'' *Fr. Hist. Stud.* 7 (1972).

L. Apt

Related entries: *BAILLIAGE*; BRISSOT DE WARVILLE; GREGOIRE; MIRABEAU; SAINT-DOMINGUE; TENNIS COURT OATH.

SOCIETE DES CITOYENNES REPUBLICAINES REVOLUTIONNAIRES. See LACOMBE; LEON.

SOCIETY OF 1789, political club of moderate constitutional monarchists, founded in April 1790 to rival the Jacobins and superseded by the Feuillants club in July 1791. The Society of 1789 appeared during the year of the marquis de Lafayette's greatest influence, following the October Days of 1789. Lafayette and some of his political associates—E.-J. Sieyès, J.-S. Bailly, C.-M. Talleyrand, H.-G. R. Mirabeau, and others—decided to form a society that would be smaller and more exclusive than the Jacobin club, where the Lameth brothers and their friends A. Duport and A. Barnave were gaining in influence.

The Fayettists did not break sharply with the Jacobins, but they tried to promote the consolidation of the early gains of the Revolution, safeguard the king's remaining powers, finish writing the constitution with a minimum of radical interference, and have Louis XVI accept it in good faith. They were less conservative than the short-lived Impartials Club, founded late in 1789, which preferred the Anglophile views of the defeated *monarchiens*, and the somewhat similar Friends of the Monarchical Constitution, founded in November 1790, both of which were undeservedly identified by the public with the far right of the political spectrum. The Society of 1789 was more prestigious and lasted longer. It resembled a gentleman's club, with its limited membership, strict entrance requirements, costly dues, and sumptuous quarters in the Palais Royal, with balconies overlooking the park where ordinary citizens gathered. Its members were noble, clerical, and bourgeois deputies, bankers, military men, and intellectuals. The club had its own publication, the *Journal de la Société de 1789*, to which Condorcet contributed.

Infused with rationalism, individualism, and cosmopolitanism, the society's statement of principles denied that the membership was a sect or party and described the organization as a center for the study and promotion of *l'art social*, defined as a body of social scientific knowledge dedicated to the well-being of nations. They proposed to work toward a much-needed integration of political and social theory, economics, philosophy, and the arts, including applied science. Recognizing that this integration could not be achieved optimally without the utmost cooperation, they advocated international division of labor in intellectual matters as well as in commerce. Spreaders of social truths, they would take their first steps by perfecting the French constitution and the well-being of the nation.

There is irony in the appearance of this laudable program in a time of such underlying instability. By the fall of 1790, Lafayette's influence at court, in the National Assembly, and on the public was waning, and his Jacobin rivals, the triumvirate of C. de Lameth, A. Duport, and A. Barnave, were taking the lead in the Assembly. In 1790-91 the Society of 1789 was increasingly under attack by radical journalists (J.-P. Marat, L.-C.-S. Desmoulins). Its posture as consolidator of the gains of 1789 won it no mass support; its efforts at poor relief were interpreted as reactionary aristocratic demagoguery; and its demands for the preservation of military discipline were interpreted as repression.

In the Revolutionary free-for-all of proliferating popular societies in Paris and Jacobin-affiliated clubs throughout France, the Society of 1789, with its vision of a limited monarchy controlled by qualified proprietors, ultimately found itself under siege. Some of its members (Mirabeau, J.-P. Brissot, I.-R.-G. Le Chapelier) returned to the Jacobins. In the Jacobin club itself the once-dominant Triumvirate of Lameth, Duport, and Barnave was increasingly challenged by the more radical democrats led by M. Robespierre and in the spring of 1791 was recognizing that its social and political aims were similar to those of the Fayettists. Well before the king's flight in June 1791 and the Champ de Mars repression in July, the Triumvirate and the Society of 1789 had begun to cooperate in support of the king and of the preservation and conservative reshaping of the constitution. The future of this coalition was assured on 16 July 1791 when the triumvirate led most of the Jacobin deputies out of their club in the hope of destroying it and taking over its affiliates. The result was to be the formation of the Feuillants club, rallying place of Fayettists and Lamethists and their followers in defense of the Constitution of 1791. It would not be long before France would be torn between the Feuillant version of liberty and those of more democratic challengers.

A. Challamel, *Les clubs contre-révolutionnaires. Cercles, comités, sociétés, salons, réunions, cafés, restaurants et librairies* (Paris, 1895); J. Godechot, *Les institutions de la France sous la Révolution et l'Empire* (Paris, 1968); G. Michon, *Essai sur l'histoire du parti feuillant, Adrien Duport. Correspondance inédite de Barnave en 1792* (Paris, 1924).

P. H. Beik

Related entries: BAILLY; CHAMP DE MARS "MASSACRE"; FEUIL-LANTS; JACOBINS; LAFAYETTE; MIRABEAU; *MONARCHIENS*; OCTO-BER DAYS; SIEYES; TALLEYRAND-PERIGORD; TRIUMVIRATE.

SOCIETY OF THE FRIENDS OF THE CONSTITUTION. See JACOBINS.

SOULT, NICOLAS-JEAN DE DIEU (1769-1851), duke of Dalmatia, repub-lican general and imperial marshal. Soult was born on 29 March 1769 at Saint-Amans–La Bastide in the Tarn. His father was a small-town notary. Soult, despite his small size and club foot, joined the army as an enlisted man in 1785. In 1787 he became a corporal and he was promoted to sergeant in 1791. Frustrated by legal restrictions that prevented him from becoming an officer, he decided to return to civilian life, but the Revolution's policy of opening careers to talent regardless of social status convinced him to remain in the army.

The new policy, the emigration of aristocratic officers, and the coming of war in 1792 enabled him to attain rapid promotion. A lieutenant in 1792, Soult soon became a colonel; and in 1794 he served as chief of staff to General F.-J. Lefebvre at the Battle of Fleurus. During the battle, he convinced Lefebvre and F.-S. Marceau to stand fast against the Austrian assaults instead of retreating, thereby contributing significantly to the French victory. He was soon promoted to general of brigade.

He fought hard and effectively during the difficult German campaigns of 1795, 1796, and 1797. By 1799 he was a general of division and as such fought in southern Germany during the opening phases of the War of the Second Coalition. Although forced to retreat, his abilities gained the attention of General A. Mas-séna, who brought him to Switzerland. There, in September 1799, Soult played a major role in the Battle of Zurich. He attacked and defeated Austrian troops protecting the Russian left. Denied reinforcements, the Russians fell victim to Masséna's assault.

In the following year, Soult went with Masséna to Italy and participated in the defense of Genoa, which distracted the Austrians while Napoleon made his thrust across the Alps. Wounded and captured during a sortie, Soult was released after Marengo. He ended the year as governor of Piedmont.

Masséna's praise and his own talents brought Soult to Napoleon's attention, and his rise was swift. By 1804, he was one of the original marshals of the Empire. He later fought with the Grand Army in the central European campaigns of 1805, 1806, and 1807. From 1808 to 1813 he campaigned in Spain, the graveyard of so many French military reputations. He led the pursuit of J.

Moore's army, was driven from Portugal by the duke of Wellington, and fought W. C. Viscount Beresford to a draw at Albuera. Napoleon employed him in Germany in 1813 and then sent him back to Spain in an attempt to hold the Pyrenees. Soult's army was ill trained and contained many conscripts without combat experience. He fought hard but could not stop Wellington, who invaded France in 1814. Still, he did manage to keep the English, Portuguese, and Spanish from cooperating with the Allied forces to the north.

Soult accepted the first Restoration, then supported Napoleon's return from Elba, and after a brief exile following Waterloo, returned to France. After 1830, he served the regime as minister of war and minister of foreign affairs. He even represented France at Queen Victoria's coronation. He retired in 1847 and was created marshal general, a rank held previously by only three men. He died in 1851.

An able leader, Soult like many others, found in the Revolution a path that enabled him to exploit his talents. He learned his trade as a general under the Republic and emerged as one of the Empire's most able military leaders.

K. Blibtreu, *Marshall Soult* (Berlin, 1902); L. Chardigny, *Les maréchaux de Napoléon* (Paris, 1946); R. P. Dunn-Pattison, *Napoleon's Marshals* (London, 1909); N.-J. Soult, *Mémoires du maréchal-général Soult*, 3 vols. (Paris, 1854).

S. Ross

Related entries: BATTLE OF ZURICH; MASSENA; SECOND COALITION.

SPIRIT OF THE LAWS. See *ESPRIT DES LOIS, L'*.

STAEL-HOLSTEIN, ANNE-LOUISE-GERMAINE NECKER, BARONNE DE (MADAME DE STAEL) (1766-1817), novelist, critic, moralist, and miscellaneous writer. Born in Paris on 22 April 1766, Germaine was the daughter of the Swiss financier and millionaire J. Necker, who in 1767 became minister of the Republic of Geneva to Versailles. At a precociously early age, she became familiar with the distinguished group of *philosophes* who frequented her mother's salon. Such interests increased when Louis XVI in 1776 appointed her father, although a Protestant, as director general of finances, a position he resumed in 1788, this time under the title of controller general of finances. In 1786 she married E. Magnus, baron de Staël-Holstein, just named Swedish ambassador to Versailles. Growing up under the spell of pre-Romanticism, she published her *Lettres sur Jean-Jacques Rousseau* in 1788. In her own salon, she quickly demonstrated her brilliant conversational powers and began to take the long procession of lovers who were to come into her life, C.-M. Talleyrand among the first.

When the Estates General opened in May 1789, Necker's inability to have his political and economic views prevail led to his continued frustration until, in September 1790, he resigned and departed for Coppet, his estate outside Geneva, where he would die in 1804. Intensely devoted to her father, Germaine sympathized with the program of moderate constitutional reform prevailing at the outset of the Revolution. Her salon on the rue du Bac became a meeting place for the liberal aristocracy; here she held forth on her ideas: a limited monarchy, a bicameral legislature, representative government based on property, and guarantees of civil liberty for everyone. After the opening of the Legislative Assembly in October 1791, she had some share in the appointment of her lover L. Narbonne, who served briefly as minister of war. When the Convention met a year later, she held no sympathy for the evident radicalism of the Jacobins. She avoided possible danger by going to Coppet late in 1792, subsequently spending several months early in 1793 in England with a circle of royalist *émigrés* at Juniper Hall in Surrey. In this year she published a pamphlet, *Réflexions sur le procès de la Reine*, attacking the treatment of Marie Antoinette. Eventually returning to the Continent, she aided in freeing many French prisoners of aristocratic birth.

Germaine disliked the Thermidorians and in a small pamphlet in 1794, *Réflexions sur la paix*, she urged terminating the European war. She returned to Paris with her new lover, B. Constant, in May 1795, and in her reopened salon made the acquaintance of such new political leaders as P. Barras and J.-L. Tallien. Her *Réflexions sur la paix intérieure* (1795) again urged civil rights for all, with government in the hands of those having the largest stake in the country. She welcomed the Constitution of 1795, saying that it provided a middle path between the absolutists and the anarchists.

After a stay at Coppet, Germaine returned to Paris in 1797, becoming a member of the moderate group known as the Constitutional Circle. When Talleyrand returned from America, she worked furiously—and successfully—to have him appointed minister of foreign affairs, visiting the director Barras at least six times. She developed an admiration for General N. Bonaparte, whom she met on several occasions on his return from Italy in 1797, demonstrating an ardor that he did not reciprocate. Bonaparte variously described her as a veritable pest, an old crow, and a madwoman who should be taken into custody by the police.

Away from Paris for much of the final period of the Directory, Madame de Staël completed a work, *Des circonstances actuelles qui peuvent terminer la Révolution*, unpublished until 1906. It contained her typical constitutional views and declared Bonaparte to be the most extraordinary genius in history. She returned from Coppet to Paris on the evening of 18 Brumaire, approved in general of the coup, and used her influence to have Constant appointed to the new legislative body, the Tribunate. Under the Consulate, she became increasingly at odds with Bonaparte, the situation culminating in October 1803 when, after first being required to live forty leagues away from Paris, she was officially escorted to the frontier. Through her father, she had become a woman of great wealth, and apart from occasional brief visits to France, she lived for the next ten years chiefly in Germany and Switzerland.

Madame de Staël's European reputation was established during this decade, which she described in her *Dix années d'exil*, published posthumously in 1821. Her novels *Delphine* (1803) and *Corinne* (1807) have an assured place in the history of Romantic literature. An earlier work, *De la littérature considérée dans ses rapports avec les institutions sociales* (1800), attempted to show in a wide sweep through the ages how the literature and spirit of a nation are affected by its political institutions. Implied criticisms of Bonaparte may well have marked the beginning of the breach with him. Her most influential work, *De l'Allemagne*, completed in 1813, has been ranked with F.-M. Voltaire's *Lettres sur les Anglais* and A. de Tocqueville's *Democracy in America* in its capacity to analyze the true spirit of a country. Distinguishing between the mentality of the Latin and the Teuton, she made the romanticism of the North, which she was the first to so identify, intelligible to the intellectual world. Despite its merit, the work was condemned by the French government, and the entire printing was confiscated.

In her last year, Madame de Staël completed the manuscript of her *Considérations sur les principaux événemens de la Révolution française*, published posthumously by her son Auguste in 1818. Much earlier in a letter she had described the Revolution as one that centuries had prepared and 29 million people had desired. This provides the theme of her three volumes, which devote over 150 pages to the *ancien régime*. They display a wide knowledge of intellectual and political life and show what abuses the Revolution had destroyed and what institutions it had created. The evaluation of Napoleon is harsh, and in her last chapter she hails the love of liberty inherent in the French people. She died in Paris on 14 July 1817 and was buried at Coppet beneath the tomb of her parents.

B. d'Andlau, *Mme de Staël* (Paris, 1960); C. Blennerhassett, *Madame de Staël*, 3 vols. (London, 1889); C. de Diesbach, *Madame de Staël* (Paris, 1983); J. C. Herold, *Mistress to an Age: A Life of Madame de Staël* (Indianapolis, 1958); F. Kohler, *Madame de Staël et la Suisse: Etude biographique et littéraire* (Lausanne, 1918); D. G. Larg, *Madame de Staël, la vie dans l'oeuvre, 1766-1800* (Paris, 1924), Engl. tr. (London, 1926); A.-L.-G. N. de Staël-Holstein, *Oeuvres complètes*, 17 vols. (Paris, 1820-21).

E. J. Knapton

Related entries: BARRAS; CONSTITUTION OF 1795; COUP OF 18 BRUMAIRE; NARBONNE-LARA; NECKER; TALLIEN; THERMIDORIAN REACTION.

SUBSISTENCE AND PROVISIONS, COMMISSION OF. See LAW OF THE MAXIMUM.

SUN, COMPANIES OF THE. See COMPANIES OF THE SUN.

SUPREME BEING, CULT OF THE. See CULT OF THE SUPREME BEING.

SURVEILLANCE, COMMITTEES OF. See COMMITTEES OF SURVEILLANCE.

SUSPECTS, LAW OF. See LAW OF SUSPECTS.

SUSPENSIVE VETO, constitutional power delegated to Louis XVI by the Constitution of 1791, giving the king authority to withhold his sanction to decrees passed by the legislative body. In such a case, his refusal was suspensive; when two consecutive legislatures immediately following the one that had initially proposed the decree had enacted the same decree in identical terms, the decree was to be considered automatically law.

The question of the royal veto over legislation was a stormy one in the National Assembly, particularly between 27 August and 11 September 1789. Louis XVI had refused to sanction either the 4-11 August decrees abolishing feudalism or the Declaration of the Rights of Man enacted by the Assembly on 26 August. The deputies were confronted with the explosive issue of the monarch's legal authority in the legislative process. On one side stood the advocates of an absolute veto, H.-G. R. Mirabeau and J.-J. Mounier among them, who urged a strong executive on the Constituante, in keeping with the English model. They were opposed by such figures as the marquis de Lafayette, A. Barnave, the abbé Grégoire, and A. Duport, partisans of a suspensive veto, by which they meant that the king could suspend legislative action for a predetermined period. He would have to yield, however, if the deputies persisted in their resolution to have specific legislation enacted. A less numerous group of deputies, including E.-J. Sieyès and M. Robespierre, wanted no veto power at all vested in the monarch, claiming that one man should not have the power to decide the fate of 25 million.

While the debate raged in Versailles over this question, political demonstrations opposed to the granting of a veto to the king were occurring in Paris at clubs and the Palais Royal. Similar disturbances were noted by contemporaries in the provinces as well. In general, Frenchmen feared that the king, armed with any veto power, would halt the Revolution and block constitutional reform. At this stage, with civil insurrection looming, J. Necker, controller general of finances, promised the adherents of the suspensive veto that the king would sign the August decrees provided that the suspensive veto were granted to the monarch. Under this double impetus, the threat of civil disorder and the promise of the king's assent to two vital documents, the partisans of the suspensive veto were successful. On 15 September the monarch was granted this right by a vote of 673 for and 325 opposed. Those deputies urging a strong executive had been defeated along with those opposed to any veto power whatsoever.

Although Necker's promise went unfulfilled until the October Days, when Parisian women marching to Versailles had demonstrated their potential for violence, the Assembly's vote for the suspensive veto seems to have been politically astute at the time; it was the only possible compromise between the two extremes. That feelings remained intemperate over this constitutional right accorded the monarch became eminently clear during the political and ministerial crises preceding the declaration of war in April 1792 and the popular uprising of 10 August. The exercise of the royal suspensive veto in defense of the refractory clergy and the *émigrés*, in addition to the king's refusal to sanction the formation of an armed military camp in Paris for the *fédérés*, led to a monumental political disaster for the monarchy. The constitution itself collapsed with the call for a new National Convention. The suspensive veto passed with it, never really having been given a fair chance to be tested.

F.-A. Aulard, *Les orateurs de la Révolution: l'Assemblée Constituante* (Paris, 1905); J.-S. Bailly, *Mémoires d'un témoin de la Révolution*, 3 vols. (Paris, 1804); E. D. Bradby, *The Life of Barnave*, 2 vols. (Oxford, 1915); M. Deslandres, *Histoire constitutionnelle de la France*, vol. 1 (Paris, 1938); E. Thompson, *Popular Sovereignty and the French Constituent Assembly, 1789-91* (Manchester, 1952).

B. Rothaus

Related entries: BARNAVE; CONSTITUTION OF 1791; DECLARATION OF THE RIGHTS OF MAN AND OF THE CITIZEN; 4 AUGUST 1789; GENERAL WILL; *MONARCHIENS*.

SUVOROV-RYMNIKSKII, ALEKSANDR VASIL'EVICH (1729–1800), Russian field marshal, prince Italiskii. Son of a noble army officer who attained the rank of general, Suvórov was a frail and sickly child who read only of great battles and succeeded in cadet training by force of will. In wars against Turkey and Poland, he won startling victories by his unorthodox tactics of swift frontal attack in concentration and immediate pursuit with the intention of destroying the enemy army. He was a fanatic of the bayonet and contemptuous of the elaborate large-scale patterns of maneuver of his time. His military achievements depended not only on tactical boldness and constant field drill but also on an unusual ability to command loyalty from common soldiers in battle.

Commanding armies of conscripted Russian peasants, Suvórov was able to use religious and national appeals not readily available to the officers of more heterogenous and mercenary armies. Moreover, the method of recruitment and the large population of the Russian Empire ensured an ample supply of new recruits should the assault tactics create large losses. Suvórov insisted on uniforming and training his troops for the conditions of actual combat; his concern for their physical well-being and habit of chatting with the soldiers around the evening campfire made him a legend in his own lifetime among the common people. The causes of his successes in the field were little understood even in his own country, where periodic attempts were made to enforce the preeminence of perfect parade ground display. He wrote a short training manual incorporating his ideas and reflecting his desire that all soldiers understand their role in maneuvers and be capable of initiative (*Nauka pobezhdat'*, *The Science of Winning*); it remained unpublished during his lifetime and largely unheeded long after.

Hampered by plebeian manners and lack of interest in nonmilitary topics, Suvórov was unable to maneuver himself within the political life of the Russian court and the rivalries of competing generals. Slow promotion in midcareer embittered him and fed his growing eccentricity of dress and manner. In later years, foreigners often judged him mad.

Soon after the accession of the universally suspicious Paul I (1796), Suvórov was relieved of command and exiled to his country estate. However, no taint of disloyalty could be found, and as Paul moved closer toward the Second Coalition and renewed warfare, he increasingly sought Suvórov's support and military opinion. Suvórov had concluded some years before that Russia would never eliminate the Turkish and Polish problems until it had dealt with France, supplier of arms and support to both. Now invited to set forth his thoughts on dealing with the Revolutionary menace, he urged predictably that a large coalition army under a single command strike quickly into France at a single point of penetration. Although the Second Coalition opted for multiple and diffuse attacks, nonetheless in February 1799, at Austrian request, Suvórov was appointed to command an Austro-Russian force against France in northern Italy. Suvórov arrived in Verona 14 April, entered Milan late that month, and captured Turin on 26 May, gaining control of all northern Italy in six weeks of rapid movement. He soon discovered, however, that he was unable to control the Austrian generals; he complained that they held back from further advance and thwarted his plan to raise an Italian army among the Piedmontese. After striking victories over the French armies of E.-J. Macdonald at Trebbia River (18-19 June) and B.-C. Joubert at Novi (15 August), Suvórov wished to march against France immediately and elaborated a multiprong plan of attack through and around Genoa. The Allies, however, feared the growth of Russian power in the West, and Francis II ordered Suvórov instead to reinforce a Russian army in Switzerland and free the Austrian forces under Archduke Charles to attack the French. Inadequately supplied with pack animals and guides by the Austrians, Suvórov nonetheless set forth over the Alps in September with a force of 20,000 Russians. Breaking through the French at the Saint Gotthard Pass and Devil's Bridge with great loss of life on both sides (13-14 September), already cold and hungry, the Russian army found itself surrounded by a much larger French force; the Allied armies they were to have joined had been defeated by the French days before. Refusing to consider surrender, Suvórov led his men out of the trap, crossing two high passes to the Rhine River by Glarus in a two-week saga of heroism and endurance in the face of snow, hunger, sickness, avalanche, and enemy fire. Although the horses, mules, and mountain guns had been lost, three-quarters of the men who set forth from Italy reached the Rhine and brought over a thousand French prisoners with them. Suvórov's characteristic tactics of surprise and bold attack, no matter how great the odds, had forced the enemy and brought them through.

The remarkable passage of Suvórov through the Alps, which brought him great fame and admiration in Europe, proved futile. Paul I, increasingly at odds with Austria and England, was already moving toward neutrality. In January 1800 he recalled Suvórov and the Russian armies from Europe. Suvórov, already very sick, had been promised great honors on his return; en route to Russia, however, he offended Paul's high sense of military propriety and was refused all official recognition. He died soon after.

P. Longworth, *The Art of Victory; The Life and Achievements of Generalissimo Suvórov, 1729-1800* (London, 1965); A. F. Petrushevskii, *Generalissimus kniaz' Suvorov*, 3 vols. (St. Petersburg, 1884); *A. V. Suvórov. Dokumenty*, 4 vols. (Moscow, 1949-53).

E. Ambler

Related entries: BATTLE OF ZURICH; FRANCIS II; PAUL I; SECOND COALITION.

SYMBOLISM. At first Revolutionary symbols rose up alongside monarchical and religious ones. As the Revolution became more radical, monarchical and Christian symbols were consciously rejected or transformed to serve the new ideology. For example, the sun, once exploited by Louis XIV, was used to suggest the dawn of a new Revolutionary order, a new beginning for humanity, the enlightenment of the world.

Color has often played a symbolic role in various movements and regimes. Thus, for Christians, white—sometimes replaced by gold or yellow—symbolized light, purity, innocence, joy, and triumph. Red stood for love, fire, fervor, blood, and martyrdom. Blue represented heaven, truth, consistency, and wisdom. Early in the French Revolution, the tricolor—red, white, and blue—came to be used to represent the new order. When the royal family was forced to quit Versailles for Paris, the white of the royal livery was combined with the blue and red of the city of Paris to represent the reunion of the monarch and his people. The tricolor appeared on cockades, ribbons, sashes, crockery, wallpaper, and, above all, flags. It gradually lost all association with the monarchy and became the symbol of the nation.

Another symbol that appeared early was the Phrygian bonnet or liberty cap. It was generally knit of wool and had a high point, which fell over to one side. It was dyed red and usually embellished with a tricolor cockade or rosette. Its origins extended back to the ancient Romans, among whom the bonnet had been worn by emancipated slaves, thus becoming a symbol of liberty. Brutus had placed one between two of the daggers that had killed Caesar. The plebeians had worn it after the death of Nero. In the eighteenth century, it had been used by the followers of J. Wilkes in England, by rebels in the Lowlands, and by American revolutionaries. It appeared on the streets of France in 1789, was popularized by the Jacobins, was forced on the king on 20 June 1792, and then was adopted officially shortly after the overthrow of the monarchy in August 1792. It was worn by members of the Commune of Paris and other municipalities. Gradually it fell into disuse after Thermidor.

The liberty tree, which became one of the principal symbols of Revolutionary aspirations, first appeared in May 1790. It was planted by a curé in a village in the department of the Vienne to mark the installation of the municipal authorities elected under the new constitution. This ceremony was widely publicized in the press and imitated throughout France. The liberty tree was usually decked with tricolor ribbons and cockades and was often capped with a liberty bonnet. This use of a tree for devotional purposes was rooted deep in the past. Ancient peoples had often seen trees as symbols of life-force and dwelling places of the gods. In the Judaic-Christian tradition, there was the tree of the knowledge of good and evil in Eden and the great tree in the center of the heavenly kingdom described in Revelation. In classical antiquity, various trees had been associated with different deities—the laurel with Apollo, the oak with Jupiter, the olive with Minerva, the myrtle with Venus. Altars and votive offerings had been placed before such trees. Something of the sacred tree as a symbol of regeneration had survived in the popular celebrations around the May tree or pole. In France liberty trees proliferated so rapidly that there were about 60,000 by 1792. The National Convention regulated their use by a decree on 3 Pluviôse Year II. Such trees, planted at strategic locations in cities, towns, and villages, served as focal points in Revolutionary ceremonies. Images of liberty trees also served as decoration on posters, crockery, letterheads, and bookbindings. The French army spread the custom as far as Poland. Most of the trees were uprooted during the Restoration.

As the Revolution placed increasing emphasis on equality, the carpenter's level emerged as an important symbol. In the eighteenth century, the level did not use a bubble in a glass tube set in a long block of wood as is familiar today; rather it used a plumb line hanging from the apex of an equilateral triangle. When the weight was at the center of the base, the surface on which the triangle rested was level. The Masons used such a level as a symbol of equality. The shape also gave this symbol divine connotations. Christians had sometimes used an equilateral triangle to denote the Trinity, in which three equal persons constituted a single God. Masons used the same triangle to represent the past, present, and future embodied simultaneously in the Divinity. French Revolutionaries continued to use the equilateral triangle, frequently with a mystical eye in the center and radiating light, as a symbol of the Supreme Being. Since the carpenter's level was the same shape, it too was sometimes portrayed as a sacred object emitting rays in all directions.

As the Revolution entered its most radical phase with the expulsion of the Girondists, the Mountain became a familiar symbol. The radical Jacobins who sat on the high seats to the left of the speaker had become known as the Mountain, a name that evoked deep memories. Mountains, which reach up into the heavens and from their peaks afford a commanding view of the earth below, have played a significant role in various religions. Moses brought down the Ten Commandments from Mount Sinai. Christ preached his Sermon on the Mount. Echoing this memory, some artists showed the Jacobin Constitution of 1793 emerging from a mountain amid thunder and lightning. Others showed the lightning from the peak of the mountain striking down counterrevolutionaries. Symbolic mountains appeared on letterheads, calendars, tobacco pouches, and ladies' fans. In Bordeaux the architect A. Brongniart sketched plans to build an artificial mountain in the nave of the cathedral of Saint-André. In Lille the architect F. Verly presided over the actual construction of such a mountain in the church of Saint-Maurice. Throughout France mountains were erected in open spaces for Revolutionary festivals. In Paris, for the Festival of the Supreme Being, a mountain was erected on the Champ de Mars large enough to accommodate hundreds of officials and a choir of 2,400 on its slopes. During the Thermidorian Reaction, the authorities ordered removal of all such mountains.

Under the Old Regime, fasces, a bundle of staves bound together around an axe, had been used occasionally to represent unity. At the peak of the Revolution, the fasces became the main symbol of the Republic *une et indivisible*. This symbol was derived from classical antiquity where lictors accompanying a Roman magistrate had carried fasces to designate his power. An axe in the center meant that the magistrate could impose a capital sentence to enforce the law. During the French Revolution, some artists made the meaning explicit by showing "False Patriotism" untying the bundle and "True Patriotism" binding it together again. Fasces appeared everywhere, encircling monuments, embellishing civic altars, flanking doorways, decorating triumphal arches, even serving as bedposts capped with liberty bonnets.

Revolutionaries ascribed the success of their movement to force exerted by the people. The most common symbol of popular force was the pike, the inexpensive weapon of the common people, but there were various other signs signifying their power. Cannon and cannon balls frequently decorated posters, calendars, copies of the Rights of Man, textbooks, and other printed works. Another common symbol of popular power was the massive club, often shown resting on broken chains and scepters. During the Terror the architect J.-J. Lequeu proposed an immense gateway for the city of Paris, an "arch of the People," topped by a giant figure of the People dressed in a lion skin, his huge club resting on the shattered symbols of tyranny.

Fraternity, along with Liberty and Equality, was one of the triune ideals of the Revolution. To express this ideal, no single symbol such as the carpenter's level of equality was available; consequently, artists employed various images. France or the Republic was depicted giving similar pikes to two brothers. A cluster of hearts was shown tied together with a cord. A number of eggs was portrayed grouped in the same nest. Hands were depicted clasped in friendship. The fasces, however, provided the main symbol of fraternal union among Frenchmen.

The Revolutionaries adapted the ancient symbols of sun and light to represent the dawn of a new age and the enlightenment of mankind, a natural culmination of what the *philosophes* had called the *siècle des lumières*, which we call the Enlightenment. Frequently the sun was shown rising on the horizon, dispelling the clouds of ignorance, its beams radiating over the globe. One engraving shows the rising sun, bearing what appears to be the face of M. Robespierre, with the slogan "I enlighten the universe." Light was also used apart from the sun to signify enlightenment. Light was shown radiating from the constitution, the Rights of Man, the holy Mountain, or the heads of heroes and martyrs. Like the persons of the Trinity or Christian saints, republican heroes sometimes had halos.

There were various other lesser symbols. The bountifulness promised by the new regime was sometimes suggested by a cornucopia and sheaves of grain, at other times by a female with enormous breasts or frequently with two rows of breasts. The value of agriculture and labor was represented by ploughs, scythes, and spades. One engraving shows a bag of gold counterbalanced on a scale by a scythe and a spade. Often a beehive was used to stand for the community and cooperative endeavor. Thus, at the peak of the Revolution, artists, printers, and decorators had on hand an arsenal, a repertory, a lexicon of signs and symbols to express the promise and nature of the new order.

These symbols always accompanied the allegorical figures that the Revolutionaries used to portray their ideals. Such figures were usually female because in the French language most of the abstract entities, like their Latin progenitors, were feminine—*la France, la République, la Liberté, l'Egalité, la Fraternité, la Nature*, even *la Force*. Only *le Peuple* was masculine. To express the vigor of these ideals, the allegorical females were robust, muscular, and formidable: Liberty generally held a pike capped by a liberty bonnet. Equality carried a carpenter's level, sometimes suspended over a globe. Fraternity grasped fasces and stood alongside a nest full of eggs or a cluster of hearts bound together. Nature with her ample breasts stood by a horn of plenty and sheaves of grain. Force, a veritable virago frequently wearing a lion skin, carried a huge club or a cannon ball. Her male counterpart, the People, was portrayed as a modern Hercules striking down or trampling on the hydra of counterrevolution or the debris of monarchical insignia.

Architects of the period not only could draw on all these symbols and allegorical figures to embellish their projects but by the shape of their monuments could strive to convey the significance of the Revolution. Immense domes, outdoing their classical prototypes, would express the grandeur of the movement. Sometimes they proposed decorating such domes with the outline of the world— with France in the center—on the outside, or the constellation of the stars on the inside, thus linking the Revolution to universal and cosmic forces. Architects also favored massive cubical or round edifices, suggesting the solidness and eternality of the new order. They often planned buildings and altars with identical facades or approaches facing the four corners of the world. Immense triumphal arches, towering columns, and soaring obelisks would signify the accomplishments and thrust of the Revolution. In Lille, Verly proposed a huge temple at the top of an enormous staircase, like a stairway to heaven, and a *théâtre du peuple* with a semicircular facade rising like the sun on the horizon, promising a new beginning for the masses.

Clothing too can serve a symbolic purpose. Under the Old Regime, aristocrats dressed in a fashion intended to distinguish them from the common people. Successful or ambitious bourgeois aped the aristocrats as much as possible. With the advent of the Revolution, patriots took up the liberty cap and tricolor cockade to express the new ideals. At the peak of the Revolution, the clothing of the lower classes became symbolic of the new equality and dignity of the ordinary people. Aristocrats had labeled them *sans-culottes* because they did not wear the breeches and silk hose of the upper classes. Radicals turned this term into a badge of honor. However, the government was not satisfied with such attire and on the eve of Thermidor commissioned the painter J.-L. David to design clothing that would signify the new social order.

For all their potency, symbols have limitations. Some people rejected or ridiculed the new or revised symbols because they stood for ideals that these people loathed. Counterrevolutionaries mocked the liberty bonnet without a head, a reminder of the guillotine. Or they depicted the liberty tree without roots, a sign of the futility of the Revolution. Or they depicted the *sans-culotte* in tricolor attire, with a bloody dagger in his hand or corpses dangling from his pockets. Other Frenchmen turned against the Revolutionary symbols when the ideals that they represented—liberty, equality, fraternity, plentifulness, regeneration—seemed contradicted by terror, strife, and scarcity. Some of the more radical symbols died or were repressed after Thermidor. As we have seen, the expiring Convention ordered all images of Mountains eradicated. Liberty bonnets and carpenter's levels went out of fashion. Later Napoleon restored scepters and introduced the imperial eagle. With the Restoration, many of the old monarchical symbols reappeared. Then through the nineteenth century a drawn-out war of symbols in France accompanied the clash of rival political and social ideals.

M. Agulhon, *Iconographie et histoire des mentalités* (Paris, 1980) and *Marianne into Battle: Republican Imagery and Symbolism in France, 1789-1880* (Cambridge, England, 1981); E. F. Henderson, *Symbol and Satire in the French Revolution* (London, 1912); L. Hunt, "Hercules and the Radical Image of the French Revolution," *Representations* 1 (1983); J. A. Leith, *The Idea of Art as Propaganda in France, 1750-1799* (Toronto, 1965) and *Media and Revolution: Moulding a New Citizenry in France during the Terror* (Toronto, 1968); J. Starobinski, *1789: Les emblemes de la raison* (Paris, 1973).

J. A. Leith

Related entries: CULT OF THE SUPREME BEING; DAVID; DECHRIS-TIANIZATION; ENLIGHTENMENT, THE; FEDERATION; FREEMA-SONRY; PROPAGANDA; *SANS-CULOTTES*; THERMIDORIAN REACTION.

T

TAILLE, basic direct tax under the Old Regime, permanently established in 1439 and abolished by the Law of 17 March 1791. Originally a war tax, in principle the *taille* was payable by all who did not perform military service. Nobles, who were presumed to perform such service, were exempt. So were the clergy, who were forbidden by their calling to fight. Later the privilege of exemption was extended to other categories, such as acquirers of certain offices or burghers of certain important cities. Town dwellers in general always bore a much lighter burden. Accordingly, most of the weight of the *taille* fell on the peasantry.

The *taille* was assessed arbitrarily, according to the government's needs rather than the faculties of the taxpayer. Each year the total sum required was fixed and divided up among the *généralités*. They in turn imposed their own arbitrary assessments on their constituent fiscal districts *(élections)*, and so on down to the village level. Matters were complicated by the fact that the government could, at will, revise or add to each year's total according to its needs. A collector was elected by the assembly of each village community to assess and levy the contribution of each taxpayer. In two-thirds of France, the *taille* was "personal," payable by those of *taillable* status according to the collector's opinion of their faculties. In the *pays d'états*, however, the *taille* was "real," payable on the basis of whether a person's landed property was legally designated noble. Owners of noble land were exempt; owners of non-noble land, whatever their personal status, were required to pay. These and other anomalies have led scholars recently to question the true extent of exemptions. Clearly in the *pays d'états*, many nobles paid the *taille*, and in other areas they often paid indirectly by reducing their tenants' rents to take account of their tax burden. Equally clearly, most wealthy non-nobles managed to escape the burden entirely. Nevertheless, down to 1789, exemption from the *taille* remained the first and most fundamental test of noble status, and it was this rather than the pecuniary advantage that made exemption so constantly sought after.

Ministers and writers on public affairs had exhaustively discussed the inadequacies of the *taille* ever since the seventeenth century. They condemned the injustices of its arbitrary assessment, its slowness of collection, the general avoidance of the thankless office of collector, the tendency of taxpayers to hide their true wealth, the ease with which the really wealthy could secure exemption, and the failure to tap urban wealth effectively. To these long-standing criticisms, the physiocrats of the eighteenth century added the disincentives to agricultural production of a tax that bore no proportion to the wealth on which it was levied. Beginning with the 1740s, attempts were made in certain *généralités* to introduce a *taille tarifée*, to be levied differentially according to the type and quality of a taxpayer's property, an idea first proposed by the abbé Saint-Pierre in 1723. But the drawing up of land registers, an essential prerequisite for any such system, met constant resistance from taxpayers who believed that more accurate assessment must result in a heavier burden, and the *taille tarifée* was never generalized. The only nationwide improvement in the levy of the *taille* came with the royal declaration of 13 February 1780, under which J. Necker effectively discontinued the practice of increasing the total of the tax once it had been fixed for each year by making such alterations subject to registration by the sovereign courts, whose hostility and obstruction could be predicted. As a result, the total of the *taille* ceased to grow between 1781 and the Revolution, and collection was much simplified. The basic unfairness of a tax from which most of the richest and most influential Frenchmen were exempt remained, however, and it lay at the heart of the demand for fiscal equality, one of the most universal aspirations of 1789.

G. Ambrosi, "Aperçus sur la répartition et la perception de la taille au XVIIIᵉ siècle," *Rev. d'hist. mod. et cont.* (1961); E. Behrens, "Nobles, Privileges and Taxes in France at the End of the Ancient Regime," *Econ. Rev.* 2d ser., vol. 3 (1963); G. J. Cavanaugh, "Nobles, Privileges, and Taxes in France: A Revision Reviewed," *Fr. Hist. Stud.* 8 (1974); F. Hincker, *Les Français devant l'impôt sous l'Ancien Régime* (Paris, 1971).

W. Doyle

Related entries: ARISTOCRATS; BOURGEOISIE; FEUDALISM; PEASANTRY.

TAINE, HIPPOLYTE-ADOLPHE (1823-93), historian and literary critic. Of all the accounts of the French Revolution, few have generated as much controversy as that of H. Taine. A major source of argument between F.-A. Aulard and A. Cochin, Taine's work helped to inspire a small school of historians unsympathetic to the French Revolution, including P. Gaxotte, in the early decades of the twentieth century. During the last few decades, however, Taine has on balance been the object more of strong attack than of admiration as both his methods and political ideas have gone increasingly out of fashion.

Son of a lawyer, Taine was educated at the boarding school of Saint-Honoré in Paris and at the Ecole normale. Failing his examination for the *agrégé de philosophie*, Taine taught at *lycées* in Nevers and Poitiers. Rejection of his doctoral thesis on the problem of sensation in 1852 led to the composition of a thesis on La Fontaine, defended successfully in 1853. Living at the margins of the academic establishment and largely dependent on his publications for income, Taine became a phenomenally prolific author, tossing off scores of articles and major books on philosophical, historical, and literary subjects during the 1850s and 1860s. By the 1870s Taine's fortunes began to improve considerably. Already in 1865 a professor of aesthetics at the Ecole des beaux-arts, he was elected in 1880 to the Académie française.

Although Taine was never a dogmatic positivist, he nonetheless did share with the positivists a methodological interest in applying scientific methods to the study of cultures and a political predisposition to seek social progress by perfecting social order. Taine's fear and loathing of the people at large—enhanced by the events of 1848 and the Paris Commune of 1871—is infamous and seriously distorted his account of the French Revolution. But it is necessary to observe that Taine was no uncritical supporter of the party of order—he opposed the rule of Louis Napoleon—and that he made serious efforts to study the plight of the poor, which included personal visits to working-class districts. His works, while consistently and sharply hostile to the political expression of the people, at least did not obscure the wretchedness of their condition.

Taine's principal study of the French Revolution is contained in his final and greatest project, *Les origines de la France contemporaine*, on which he labored for the last twenty years of his life. Volume 1 dealt with the Old Regime; volumes 2, 3, and 4 covered the events of the Revolution down to Napoleon; volumes 5 and 6 treated developments from Napoleon to the end of the nineteenth century. Neither strikingly original in conception nor thorough in its use of sources, Taine's powerful account of the French Revolution derived its effectiveness from the author's ability to recreate scenes and to recapture moods. But in the end, his propensity to dramatize reduced the precision of his social and historical analyses in that it led to the blurring of crucial distinctions between social groups and time periods.

Taine believed the weakening of the Old Regime to be primarily the result of the concentration of power in the hands of the king, whose expanding bureaucratic government made traditional social and political bodies obsolete. But Taine also placed heavy emphasis on the role of the classic spirit. This spirit, Taine maintained, which had been nurtured in the artificial atmospheres of Parisian *salons* and academies, inclined the *philosophes* and Revolutionaries to think that the same abstractions and verbal gymnastics they used to dazzle and to entertain at social gatherings could also be used as the basis for practical political policy. Spread among the social elite, the *philosophes'* notions of liberty, equality, and nature encouraged privileged social groups, who by 1789 had been thoroughly alienated from the state and isolated from each other, to think that a revolution was desirable. Spread among the lower classes, these notions convinced the masses of people—poor, overtaxed, ignorant, burning with hitherto undirected resentment—that a violent redress of their grievances was possible.

For Taine, the collapse of traditional restraints on social action and the consequent unleashing of mass protest, with all its savagery and violence arising out of the bestial natures of the people, constituted the central drama of the Revolution; the Jacobin conquest and the Reign of Terror, which Taine held to be implied in the logic of the Revolution, constituted its central scene. Developments as early as those of 1788-89, described in a section entitled "Spontaneous Anarchy," were explained largely as a product of the popular movement. The course of events after 1789 was accounted for primarily by demonstrating the varying degrees of success that competing factions had in manipulating the crowd—the Girondins failed because they lost control of it, while the Jacobins succeeded because they pandered to it.

Taine seems to have approved of Revolutionary leaders in proportion to their distance from the fundamental Revolutionary ideology. G.-J. Danton, described as a powerful presence but not as a fanatic, received a relatively favorable judgment; J.-P. Marat was presented as a monster and a lunatic, his physical degeneration associated by Taine with his perverted ideas. M. Robespierre, who, for Taine, most perfectly embodied the classic spirit in politics, was presented as a man loath to mingle with the people but willing to harness popular savagery for the more effective realization of his empty political and social vision.

N. Bonaparte could resolve the Revolutionary crises, according to Taine, because he was precisely what most Revolutionary leaders were not: a perfect pragmatist. Yet in the end even Bonaparte could not solve the deepest problems of contemporary France. The Revolutionary heritage, Taine insisted, lived on in the waste of centralized administration and in the chronic instability of democratic rule.

A. Chevrillon, *Taine: Formation de sa pensée* (Paris, 1932); S. J. Kahn, *Science and Aesthetic Judgment: A Study in Taine's Critical Method* (New York, 1953); C. Mongardini, *Storia e sociologia nell'opera di H. Taine* (Milan, 1965).

T. E. Kaiser

Related entries: AULARD; GAXOTTE.

TALLEYRAND-PERIGORD, CHARLES-MAURICE, COMTE DE (later PRINCE DE BENEVENTO) (1754-1838), foreign minister and diplomat. Talleyrand was born at Paris on 2 February 1754, the eldest surviving son of a noble family originating in Périgord. An early injury left him with a permanently deformed foot, which kept him from the military career he normally would have followed. Following an education at the collège de Harcourt and the Seminary of Saint-Sulpice in Paris, he was ordained a priest in December 1779. Through family influence, he became vicar general of the diocese of Reims and agent general of the clergy of France, and he enjoyed the income from several abbeys. He developed in these offices considerable financial and administrative experience. In January 1789 he was made bishop of Autun, a diocese he rarely visited. Talleyrand enjoyed all the worldly pleasures of aristocratic life under the *ancien régime*, frequented the salon of Madame de Genlis, read the works of the *phil-*

osophes, made the acquaintance of F.-M. Voltaire, H.-G. R. Mirabeau, and C.-A. de Calonne among many others, and became a member of the Freemasons.

Talleyrand was chosen a representative of the clergy of Autun to the Estates General. The *cahier*, which he had helped to prepare, called for a constitution providing for an elected legislature, democratic government at the local level, judicial reforms, and the abolition of the most burdensome feudal privileges. When the Estates General was transformed in June 1789 into the National Constituent Assembly, Talleyrand was named to the committee preparing a constitutional draft. He also joined several of the new clubs discussing such matters. Talleyrand supported most of the great changes adopted by the Assembly, including the nationalization of church lands and the Civil Constitution of the Clergy, to which he swore the required civil oath. On 14 July 1790 he celebrated Mass on the Champ de Mars at the great public Festival of Federation. In January 1791 he resigned from his see of Autun and was placed under papal excommunication. His last important work in the Constituent Assembly was the 216-page *Report on Public Instruction*, which envisioned a pyramidical structure rising through local, district, and departmental schools much like that later effected by Napoleon.

Debarred by the self-denying ordinance from sitting in the new Legislative Assembly, Talleyrand was sent on a diplomatic mission to London (January-May 1792), seeking unsuccessfully to ensure English neutrality in the gathering European storm. After the September Massacres of 1792, which threatened all aristocrats, he sought and obtained G.-J. Danton's permission to return to London, this time unofficially. Here he moved in the growing circle of French *émigrés*. Meanwhile, his property in France was confiscated in December 1792 by the Convention, and two years later when he was ordered to leave England by the British government, acting under the Alien Bill, he decided to go to the United States. He stayed here for two years, mainly in Philadelphia, but also traveled to Maine and Ohio. His impressions of the new nation were decidedly mixed, and he deeply resented President G. Washington's refusal to receive him. After long delays, the Directory approved his petition to return.

Talleyrand arrived in Paris in September 1796 to find that in his absence he had been elected to the newly established Institute of Arts and Sciences. He renewed his acquaintance with Madame de Staël, with whom he had corresponded while in America, and partly through her influence with P. Barras, the most powerful of the new directors, was named minister of foreign affairs in July 1797. His general views were that French interests would best be served by peace, by maintaining a balance of power, along with England and Austria, against Russia and Prussia, and doing whatever possible in the field of colonial expansion.

Talleyrand's relations with General N. Bonaparte, who in 1796 and 1797 was winning spectacular victories in Italy, were of profound significance for the future. On assuming office he wrote to Bonaparte, hailing his successes, promising every support, and continued to do so after the signing of the Treaty of

Campoformio (October 1797). In their exchange of letters, ideas on government emerged that were later embodied in the Constitution of 1799, following the coup of Brumaire. Talleyrand, like Bonaparte, had no active share in the coup of Fructidor (September 1797), which removed two directors suspected of royalist leanings. He gave it, however, his blessing as a temporary departure from the constitution.

Talleyrand's share in the so-called XYZ affair suggests his venality. Widespread French and British interference with neutral shipping had made the United States a chief victim. Consequently, the United States sent three agents to France to resolve the problem. Through subordinate French negotiators, it was indicated that there should be a $250,000 bribe for Talleyrand and a complicated loan arrangement of $10 million to France, which it would eventually repay on terms outrageously favorable to itself. Unacceptable to the Americans, the negotiations stood still until in January 1798 the French government decreed that its navy would seize all ships, including American, with English goods on board or that had put up at a British port. When the documents concerning the negotiations were submitted to the American Congress with the letters "XYZ" disguising the names of Talleyrand's agents, the outcry resulted in a state of undeclared war with France. It was not ended until the Convention of Mortefontaine was ratified in July 1801 when Talleyrand was again foreign minister.

Following Bonaparte's return from Italy in December 1797, he met with Talleyrand on several occasions, where the two were mutually impressed. The general now contemplated an expedition to Egypt, and Talleyrand gave his support. He had read a paper to the Institute in July 1797 that stressed French interests in Egypt, and in two reports to the directors (January and February 1798) he recommended military and naval action. Although Talleyrand had promised Bonaparte that he would resign from the Foreign Ministry and undertake a peace mission to Turkey, he shrewdly managed to avoid what would have been a useless undertaking. When, during the summer of 1799, the Directory was threatened by a resurgence of Jacobinism and royalism, Talleyrand resigned (20 July 1799). This was clearly a case of *reculer pour mieux sauter*.

Talleyrand quickly renewed his friendship when Bonaparte returned from Egypt in October 1799. His *Mémoires*, composed much later, are notably brief about his share in the coup of Brumaire. He met secretly on several occasions with the conspiratorial group at Napoleon's house, which was near his own, gave advice, served as a link with E.-J. Sieyès, and on 18 Brumaire was chiefly responsible for obtaining the reluctant P. Barras's resignation from the expiring Directory. His part on the following day at Saint-Cloud is even less important; he sat in his carriage outside the palace, awaiting whatever might be the turn of events. Within a few weeks, he returned under the Provisional Consulate to the Ministry of Foreign Affairs, a position he held until August 1807.

Under the Consulate and Empire, Talleyrand again turned his brilliant abilities to the service of France. Since he favored the religious Concordat of 1801, the ban of excommunication was lifted, so that in 1803 he was able to marry his long-time mistress, Madame Grand, a woman of remarkably easy virtue. He became grand chamberlain of the empire in 1804 and prince of Benevento in 1806; and his portrait has a prominent place in J.-L. David's great painting of the imperial coronation.

At the time of the secularizations of 1803 when German princes dispossessed on the west bank of the Rhine were to be compensated with confiscated church lands within Germany, Talleyrand's house in Paris became the center of these transactions—to his huge financial advantage. In other areas he tried, unsuccessfully, to prevent the rupture of the Peace of Amiens with Britain in 1803. His growing disapproval over Napoleon's ever-enlarging European conquests loosened his ties with the emperor. He resigned from the Ministry of Foreign Affairs after the Peace of Tilsit (August 1807) but retained his other titles. Talleyrand particularly disapproved of Napoleon's Spanish policy, secretly intriguing with J. Fouché against it. The climax was the famous occasion at a diplomatic reception in the Tuileries (January 1809) when Napoleon, recently returned from Spain, publicly denounced Talleyrand in language fit only for the gutter. Henceforth Talleyrand was in the shadows.

Talleyrand had a minor part in arranging for the return of the Bourbons in 1814, and when the Allies entered Paris, Czar Alexander took up residence in Talleyrand's great house on the place de la Concorde. He was briefly a member of the provisional government then established and served as France's chief representative to the Congress of Vienna (1814-15). Here again, since C. von Metternich and the viscount Castlereagh clearly had the upper hand, his description of his role is exaggerated. Such as it was, it ended when Napoleon returned for the Hundred Days.

After Napoleon's defeat, Talleyrand served Louis XVIII in the Second Restoration as foreign minister and president of the council from 15 July to 23 September 1815; he then retired. At the time of the Revolution of 1830, he emerged to support Louis-Philippe and was offered the post of foreign minister. Instead he chose to go to London for four years as ambassador. He had here some share in establishing an independent Belgium (1831). Talleyrand commented that this was the thirteenth government he had served, and in his *Mémoires* he made the famous defense that he had never conspired, save when he had the majority of Frenchmen as his accomplices.

Talleyrand died in Paris on 17 May 1838. When the last rites were administered, he held out both hands for the anointing, whispering, ''Do not forget that I am a bishop.'' This marks the full circle of an extraordinary life in which the talents developed during the *ancien régime* were put to the service of the Revolution, the Empire, and the restored monarchy.

A. Duff Cooper, *Talleyrand* (London, 1932); G. Lacour-Gayet, *Talleyrand, 1754-1838*, 4 vols. (Paris, 1928-34) and *Talleyrand et l'expédition d'Egypte* (Paris, 1917); G. Pallain, *La mission de Talleyrand à Londres en 1792* (Paris, 1889) and *Correspondance diplomatique: Talleyrand sous le Directoire* (Paris, 1891); M. Poniatowski, *Talleyrand et le Directoire, 1796-1800* (Paris, 1982); C.-M. de Talleyrand-Périgord, *Mémoires*, ed.

Duc de Broglie, 5 vols. (Paris, 1967), Engl. tr., 5 vols. (London, 1891-92) and "Rapport sur l'instruction publique" (September 1791) in C. Hippeau, *L'instruction publique en France pendant la Révolution* (Paris, 1881).

E. J. Knapton

Related entries: CIVIL CONSTITUTION OF THE CLERGY; CONSTITUTION OF 1799; COUP OF 18 BRUMAIRE; DANTON; EGYPTIAN EXPEDITION; FOUCHE; SELF-DENYING ORDINANCE; SIEYES; STAEL-HOLSTEIN; XYZ AFFAIR.

TALLIEN, JEAN-LAMBERT (1767-1820), politician. Born in Paris, the son of the comte de Bercy's butler, Tallien was a lawyer's clerk before the Revolution. Secretary to the deputy J.-B. Brostaret in 1789 and subsequently to A. de Lameth, he became a typesetter on the *Moniteur*. In the early years of the Revolution, he gained some reputation in Paris as a minor journalist and club activist. He founded the *société fraternelle* of the faubourg Saint-Antoine for the civic instruction of the illiterate and in 1791 was teaching civic morality in L. Bourdon's school. Tallien was admitted to the Jacobin club in December 1790 and spoke there frequently. Subscriptions from fellow members funded his anti-Feuillant weekly broadsheet, *L'ami des citoyens*, launched in August 1791. By 1792, he clearly identified with the Paris radicals, being particularly close to such radical members of the municipality as J. Pétion and P.-L. Manuel.

Tallien entered the insurrectionary Commune of 10 August 1792 as secretary. This exposed him subsequently to accusations of complicity in the September Massacres. He was one of the *commissaires* who extricated some women and debtors from the prisons of La Force and Sainte-Pélagie on 2 September. He was also one of the delegates who reported to the Legislative Assembly that evening. There is no evidence, however, that he participated in the massacre. Even P.-J. Cambon, attacking him on this issue in early Year III, only alleged complicity "at least by your opinions." Tallien seems to have shared the radical attitude that the innate good sense of the people should not be impugned, that the Revolutionary crisis justified the massacre, and that it was better to draw a veil over it.

Tallien's differences with M. Robespierre, so important later, were already visible. Robespierre's electoral machine prevented Tallien's election to the Convention for Paris; and, indeed, Tallien presented himself to the electors as neither J.-P. Brissot nor Robespierre. He sat in the Convention for the Seine-et-Oise, quickly distinguishing himself by his ardent defense of Paris and attacks on the Girondists. In the trial of the king, he sought to prevent Louis from being allowed defense counsel and voted the hard-line position. Although he became a member of the Committee of General Security on 15 October 1792 and again on 21 January 1793, he appears to have been more voluble than influential at this point.

On 9 March 1793, he was sent with J.-F.-M. Goupilleau (of Fontenay) to organize recruitment in the departments of Indre-et-Loire and Loir-et-Cher. The Vendée rebellion broke out during his mission and soon presented a military threat to the Indre-et-Loire. Tallien seems to have been active and efficient in organizing its defense. Like many other representatives on mission, he was forced to develop proto-Terror methods: he established a central commission and a network of *commissaires*, imposed domiciliary visits, disarmament of suspects, multiple arrests, forced loans on the rich, and coercive measures to ensure food supply. He does not, however, appear to have acted extravagantly.

After returning briefly to Paris in August, he left for the departments of the Gironde, Dordogne, and Lot-et-Garonne on 23 August in order to help repress the federalist revolt at Bordeaux. Tallien's behavior at Bordeaux during the autumn and winter of 1793-94 is the key to his subsequent career. Although in his speeches and correspondence with the central government Tallien possessed the vocabulary of ardent terrorism, he was clearly in practice a moderate man. Certainly, with his colleague C.-A. Ysabeau, he implemented all the standard apparatus of the Terror (establishment of a Revolutionary committee and a Revolutionary commission, purge of officials, arrests of suspects, *armée révolutionnaire*, tax on the rich, enforcement of the maximum, closure of churches, and destruction of feudal emblems). However, reprisals were in fact limited to the most prominent federalists. He countenanced the fining rather than the execution of wealthy suspects; he curbed the institutions of the Terror; he was indulgent to lesser personalities and listened to the relatives of suspects. This attitude is traditionally ascribed to his liaison with T. Cabarrus, a wealthy ex-marquise and daughter of the Spanish court banker. However, even before entering Bordeaux, he distinguished carefully between leading rebels and lesser offenders (his *arrêté* of 17 September in the Lot-et-Garonne).

The Committee of Public Safety criticized Tallien and Ysabeau from the beginning for their moderation. Although Tallien was retained in the general reorganization of representatives on mission in Nivôse, the pressure on him was intensified by denunciations of his lavish life-style with Cabarrus and by allegations of corruption. He finally returned to Paris in mid-Ventôse (early March 1794) to justify himself to the Jacobins and the Convention. However, his liaison with Thérésia, (who was arrested in Paris on 3 Prairial [22 May]) matched Tallien to Robespierre's conception of a conspiracy of corrupt men connected with foreign courts through banking circles. In the Convention on 24 Prairial (12 June), Robespierre, supported by J.-N. Billaud-Varenne, in effect called him a conspirator. The Jacobin club immediately suspended him. Such evident personal risk brought Tallien actively into the plotting before 9 Thermidor, and he played a determining role in that day's debate. He unleashed the attack on the Robespierrists by interrupting L. Saint-Just's speech; he presented what amounted to the formal indictment of Robespierre; he brought the Convention back from side issues to the point of arresting Robespierre.

The Thermidorian Reaction made Tallien a figure of national importance. Indeed, at the end of the Convention, A.-C. Thibaudeau was to impute the primary responsibility for the reaction to him. Tallien rapidly emerged as a leading spokesman for the right-wing Thermidorians. He broke with the victors of 9 Thermidor in early Fructidor (late August), denouncing the Terror as the work of tyranny and campaigning with L.-M.-S. Fréron and L. Lecointre against the continuators of Robespierre. The campaign had no initial success, and he was again expelled from the Jacobins on 17 Fructidor (4 September). However, the pressure of grass-roots reaction in Paris was on Tallien's side, helped by a possibly fake assassination attempt on him on 23 Fructidor. Throughout the autumn and winter of 1794-95, Tallien remained at the center of attacks on the Jacobins, the institutions and personnel of the Terror, and the controlled economy. On 1 Brumaire Year III (22 October 1794), he refounded his newspaper, *L'ami des citoyens*, as an organ of right-wing views under the editorship of J.-C.-H. Méhée de la Touche who had been his aide in the Commune in 1792. Finally, the salon of Cabarrus, whom he married on 6 Nivôse Year III (26 December 1794), became the focus of Thermidorian high society and the political right.

Tallien did not have great political stamina. His influence seems to have waned after mid-winter 1794-95, although he was prominent in the attacks on Montagnard deputies after the Germinal and Prairial days. His right-wing political stance within the Thermidorian movement is not always easy to define, possibly because of the heterogeneous nature of those who surrounded him at his wife's salon. Although he dissociated himself from *L'ami des citoyens* after 13 Frimaire (3 December), it probably reflected his views, until its demise at the end of Pluviôse (mid-February 1795), in its right-wing republicanism, hostility to royalism and criticism of Fréron. His reputation finally collapsed after the *émigré* landing at Quiberon on 9 Messidor (27 June). Sent to organize the defense of the west, Tallien returned to Paris on the day after the final defeat of the enemy and therefore before the executions. Nonetheless, and despite his release of nearly 3,000 women and children before leaving, sensitive royalist and moderate Thermidorian opinion, appalled by the Terror-style repression, heaped opprobrium on him. Tallien moved to the left and, in the aftermath of the royalist insurrection of 13 Vendémiaire Year IV (5 October 1795), urged the arrest of conservative constitutionalists around Thibaudeau. Thibaudeau riposted on 1 Brumaire (23 October) by a violent diatribe on Tallien's ambition, alleging relations with the comte de Provence (now Louis XVIII).

Although Tallien was elected by the Ariège, Lot, and Haut-Rhin departments and sat in the Council of Five Hundred under the Directory, he was discredited. Hated by royalists and former Montagnards alike, unacceptable now to conservative constitutionalists, his reputation damaged beyond repair, he sank into insignificance. His wife left him for P. Barras, with whom he might otherwise have had a natural affinity. Although he was returned for the Landes and the Gard in the Year V, these elections were annulled for irregularities. Crippled by debt, he obtained a position in the Scientific Commission with N. Bonaparte's expeditionary force in Egypt in 1798. He became a member of the Institute of Egypt and editor of its paper, the *Décade égyptienne*. He was also the French *commissaire* to the divan of Cairo. However, he was subsequently expelled from

Egypt by General J.-F. Menou and, having been captured by the English on the return passage, did not regain Paris until 1801. Ill and bankrupt, he obtained the post of consul at Alicante through C.-M. Talleyrand's patronage in 1804 but returned to Paris after nine months. In 1814, Louis XVIII accorded him a pension, ostensibly for his help to detainees in the Year III, although this must inevitably raise the question of his relations with counterrevolution. Having adhered to Napoleon in the Hundred Days, he lost the pension at the Second Restoration. However, he was exempted from exile as a regicide on account of his ill health. He died utterly abandoned in 1820.

H. Lacape, *Notice sur Tallien* (Bordeaux, 1959); P. Leveel, "La mission de Tallien, représentant du peuple en Indre-et-Loire," *Mém. de la Soc. Archéolog. de Tour.* 54 (1958).

C. Lucas

Related entries: CABARRUS, J.-M.-I.-T.; FEUILLANTS; MANUEL; MENOU; 9 THERMIDOR YEAR II; PETION DE VILLENEUVE; QUIBERON; REPRESENTATIVES ON MISSION; THERMIDORIAN REACTION; 13 VENDEMIAIRE YEAR IV; VENDEE; YSABEAU.

TALON, ANTOINE-OMER (1760-1811), civil lieutenant of the Châtelet, deputy to the National Assembly. Born in Paris on 20 January 1760, descendant of a noted family of French magistrates, Talon had a distinguished career at the Paris Châtelet, where, as civil lieutenant, he was involved in the investigation of the October Days and of the Favras case. Resigning from this post on 30 June 1790, Talon, a month later, won a judgment for damages against L.-C.-S. Desmoulins and J.-F.-N. Dusaulchoy who in their respective journals had accused him of venality in office. Talon also served in the National Constituent Assembly as a deputy of the Third Estate from the *bailliage* of Chartres and voted consistently with the Right. His most active role during the Revolution was as a member of the abortive Mirabeau-Montmorin conspiracy to restore royal authority. He was imprisoned briefly for participation in the flight to Varennes.

Talon fled to England in September 1792 and stated that he subsequently became involved in an attempt to rescue the royal family, which failed because of the refusal of foreign powers to pay the bribe demanded by G.-J. Danton. Allowed to return to France in 1801, Talon was exiled to the island of Sainte-Marguérite in 1803 on the charge of being a royalist conspirator. In 1807, Napoleon allowed the family to bring a mentally deranged Talon back to France, where he died at Gretz on 18 August 1811.

A. Mathiez, "Talon et la Police de Bonaparte," *Ann. hist. de la Révo. française* 5 (1928).

D. Epstein

Related entries: CHATELET; DANTON; FAVRAS; MIRABEAU; MONTMORIN DE SAINT-HEREM; OCTOBER DAYS; VARENNES.

TARGET, GUY-JEAN-BAPTISTE (1733-1806), lawyer and jurisconsult. A barrister's son, Target commenced legal studies at an early age, was received as *avocat* before the Parlement of Paris in 1752, and over the next thirty-five years earned a reputation as the foremost legal expert at the Parisian bar. During C.-F. de Lamoignon's ill-fated tenure as keeper of the seals in 1787-88, Target helped coordinate a lawyer's committee charged with revising the kingdom's civil and criminal laws. Target was one of the prime movers in the Revolutionary national patriot party in 1788-89. Elected Third Estate deputy to the Estates General in 1789, he contributed notably to the Constituent Assembly's legal, constitutional, and administrative reforms. With the institution of the new judiciary in Revolutionary France, Target entered the magistracy, becoming judge and then president of one of the capital's civil tribunals. From 1797 until his death, he served as a judge on the Court of Invalidation *(tribunal de cassation)*, charged with reviewing lower courts' case procedures. He also helped prepare the Civil and Criminal Codes under Napoleon. Target's lifelong stature in legal affairs was reflected in his election to the Académie française in 1785 and his later appointment to the Institut national.

J. Hudault, *Guy-Jean-Baptiste Target et la défense du statut personnel à la fin de l'Ancien Régime* (Paris, Thèse Droit, 1970); M. Pignoux, ''Gui-Jean-Baptiste Target, avocat, magistrat (1733-1806),'' *Vie Judic.* 548 (1956); J. Robinet, *Dictionnaire historique et biographique de la Révolution et de l'Empire, 1789-1815* (Paris, 1899).

B. Stone

Related entries: JUSTICE; LAMOIGNON DE BASVILLE; PATRIOT PARTY.

TARLE, EUGENE V. (1874-1955), one of the greatest Russian scholars of French history and member of the Academy of Sciences of the Soviet Union. Tarlé was the most gifted student of I. V. Loutchisky at the University of Kiev and was deeply influenced by him. His master's thesis, ''The Social Ideas of Thomas More and the Economic State of England at the Time'' was considered ''excellent'' by L. Tolstoy who said that he had read it with pleasure and profit. Since he had been involved in revolutionary activity, Tarlé was appointed assistant lecturer at the University of Saint Petersburg only with difficulty.

Influenced by the Russian Revolution of 1905, Tarlé chose for his dissertation topic the role of the working class in the French Revolution. On this subject he had virtually no predecessors. In 1908 he published *Workers in the National Factories in the Era of the Revolution* and in 1909-11 his dissertation, *The Working Class in France in the Era of Revolutions*, in two volumes. He based his work on archival documents, which gave his book major importance. His most remarkable achievement was the discovery of the fact that during the second half of the eighteenth century French industrial activity was, to a great extent, concentrated in the countryside. Part of this work was translated into French as *L'industrie dans les compagnes de la France à la fin de l'ancien régime*. Tarlé, however, had mistakenly interpreted this fact as the victory of small industry over large. Having demonstrated the role of workers in the Revolution and in establishing the maximum, Tarlé accused them of sponsoring a retrograde measure, although he later changed this negative evaluation.

Tarlé's worldwide reputation was based on his research on the economic history of Napoleonic France in archival documents, which he was the first to study and which was published in *The Continental Blockade: Research on the History of the Industry and Foreign Trade of France in the Era of Napoleon* (1913) and *The Economic Life of the Kingdom of Italy under Napoleon* (1915). Both works were translated from Russian into French with the cooperation of A. Mathiez. In the 1920s he collected archival documents concerning the last of the popular movements in Paris in 1795. His book, *Germinal and Prairial* (1937), was a brilliant work that extended the theme of the working class but without his previous errors.

The result of his research on Napoleon, his book *Napoleon*, appeared in 1936. It was translated into several languages and had a substantial impact. The well-known Russian historian D. Petruchevsky wrote to the author, "It is a true masterpiece of historical science and art and I congratulate you with all my heart. This is the general opinion of all who have read your book." Earlier, in 1934, Tarlé had edited C.-M. Talleyrand's memoirs, with a magnificent preface, which he later revised as a book. In 1938 he published *Napoleon's Invasion of Russia*.

On the occasion of the 150th anniversary of the French Revolution, there appeared in the Soviet Union a major collection edited by Tarlé and V. P. Volguin, *The French Bourgeois Revolution of 1789-1794* (Moscow, 1941). Tarlé's two-volume work, *The Crimean War* (Moscow, 1941-43), dealt with later stages of Franco-Russian relations. Tarlé's collected works were published, in twelve volumes, at Moscow during the 1950s (with a preface by A. Jerulsalimsky).

V. Durnovtsev, "Le nouveau de E. Tarlé," *Annuaire français, 1975* (Moscow, 1977); E. Tachapkevitch, *E. Tarlé* (Moscow, 1977).

V. M. Daline

Related entry: LOUTCHISKY.

TEMPLE. See PRISONS.

10 AUGUST 1792, the date that marked the end of the French monarchy after more than thirteen centuries. Although the monarchy would be restored in 1815, this restoration was ephemeral, and France would thereafter become a democratic and republican state. In order to understand the causes of this event, it is necessary to go back to the beginnings of the Revolution.

In 1789 all Frenchmen were monarchists; none of the *cahiers de doléances* presented to the Estates General sought the abolition of royalty. However, the king's conduct during the conflict in the Estates General, which set the Third Estate against the privileged orders, and the subsequent dismissal of the reform minister J. Necker on 11 July 1789, began to create doubts about the possibility of collaboration between Louis XVI and the Revolutionaries. On 20 December 1790, the journalist J.-P. Brissot wrote in the *Patriote français*, "I want my country to become a republic, but I am neither bloodthirsty nor an incendiary; for equally I wish that he who occupies the throne at this happy time not be pressed to relinquish it by either force or violence.'' When Brissot wrote these words, the royal family was becoming increasingly hostile to the Revolution and was considering leaving Paris, where they were semiprisoners, to join either General F.-C.-A. de Bouillé's troops in Lorraine, who seemed to have proved their loyalty by repressing an insurrection the previous August, or even the Austrian troops whom the German Emperor Leopold (Marie Antoinette's brother) had stationed along the Franco-Belgian frontier.

The flight of the royal family took place during the night of 20-21 June 1791. On the morning of 21 June, then, France was without a king. The royal family was arrested at Varennes in the Argonne on the evening of 21 June and brought back to Paris, but the National Constituent Assembly could not restore power to a sovereign who had so openly broken with the Revolution. Would the Assembly, consequently, be able to proclaim the Republic? The Jacobin extreme Left demanded it, but the majority of the deputies were afraid of such a development. The Assembly spread the legend of the kidnapping of the royal family and confined itself to suspending the king until he accepted the constitution, which it was in the process of completing. This stratagem exasperated the opponents of the monarchy, who organized a petition demanding the immediate proclamation of the Republic. The signers of this petition, however, were bloodily dispersed on 17 July on the Champ de Mars by the marquis de Lafayette's National Guards. Nevertheless, the king remained suspended until he took an oath to the new constitution on 14 September. Thus, for nearly three months France had survived without a king, under what was in fact a republic.

The restoration of Louis XVI to the powers accorded him by the new constitution did not end his ambiguous conduct. After the flight to Varennes, a number of nobles, notably the count of Provence, the king's brother, and many military and naval officers had emigrated. The new assembly, the Legislative, demanded that the king enjoin them to return to France; he did so, but reluctantly. He was suspected of playing a double game, of having a secret agreement with the *émigrés* and the foreign powers who welcomed them and let them form counterrevolutionary armies. Distrust of Louis XVI grew even more when, on 20 April 1792, he declared war on Marie Antoinette's nephew, the king of Bohemia and Hungary, Francis of Hapsburg. Did not the royal family desire the quick victory of the enemy armies? These forces would destroy the work of the Revolution and reestablish Louis XVI to absolute power. Suspicions became more explicit when the French armies were defeated in Flanders at the end of April. People were outraged when the king exercised his veto, as the constitution empowered him, on three decrees voted in May and June by the Legislative Assembly to strengthen national defense: the first dissolved the king's Guard, which was suspected of planning a coup against the Assembly; the second ordered the arrest and deportation of refractory priests (those who had refused to take the oath to the constitution) when they were denounced by twenty citizens from the same department; the third established under the walls of Paris a camp of 20,000 *fédérés* (reputed volunteers from the National Guard assembled to celebrate the anniversary of the federation of 1790 but intended above all to defend the capital against internal and foreign enemies). Parisian Revolutionaries, the *sans-culottes*, determined to force the king to sign these decrees by organizing an imposing demonstration before the Tuileries Palace, where he resided. This took place on 20 June 1792. Workers from the faubourgs Saint-Antoine and Saint-Marceau paraded for eight hours both in front of and even within the palace. They forced the king to wear a Phrygian cap and drink wine with them; they cried "Down with the veto"; they demanded the signing of the decrees and the recall of the Jacobin ministers whom the king had dismissed; they reproached the king for deceiving the people (which he indeed had done, as documents later found in the archives proved); but they did not actually assault him. Despite this, the king was unshaken and firmly refused to withdraw his veto. The demonstration had failed, but the general situation continued to worsen. At the end of June, General Lafayette left his army and came to Paris with the intention of carrying out a coup d'état that would reduce the power of the Assembly and of the clubs and would return the king's powers. He failed, above all, because the queen, who despised him, offered no support. On the frontiers, the Austrians, the Prussians, and the army of the *émigrés* slowly increased pressure. Within the country, orders of the day and petitions from administrative assemblies and clubs, and even from individuals, multiplied. Some of these blamed the demonstration of 20 June on the incompetence of J. Pétion, the mayor of Paris, and P.-L. Manuel, the *procureur* of the commune, who had been incapable of preventing it; they were suspended. Others, more numerous, supported the demonstrators and blamed the veto; some even went so far as to demand the dethronement of the king. The Legislative Assembly hesitated between these two currents but eventually was won over toward the second. On 2 July it overturned the royal veto on one of the decrees, authorizing the *fédérés* to come to Paris to participate in the celebration of 14 July. Many of these, notably the *fédérés* of Brest and Marseille, began their march immediately. The latter, all along their route, sang the *chant de guerre* of the Army of the Rhine (composed by J.-C. Rouget de Lisle at Strasbourg on 25 April 1792 and sung at Marseille by an inhabitant of Montpellier on 22 June); this would become the national anthem of France under the title the "*Marseillaise*." On 11 July, with the announcement of an offensive by Prussian troops, the Legislative Assembly declared the fatherland in danger. This proclamation permitted the application of the decrees voted by the Assembly without regard to the royal veto. But already these measures appeared insufficient. On 12 July, *fédérés* from four departments declared to the Assembly that they would not go to the frontier before the king was suspended. The movement in favor of a new revolution gained ground. On 13 July Pétion and Manuel were restored to their functions. The next day, Louis XVI appeared at the celebration of the federation, but the enormous crowd gave him an ovation only when he welcomed Pétion. Many friends of the royal family advised them to flee, which may have been possible, but they preferred to remain in Paris in expectation of victory by the enemies of France, which they hoped was near. Threats against the royal family, however, became more explicit. On 15 July the Assembly ordered five regiments, believed favorable to the king, out of Paris; and the same day, from the rostrum of the Jacobin club, J.-N. Billaud-Varenne demanded the deportation of the king and the meeting of a new assembly, elected by universal (male) suffrage. On 17 July, the *fédérés* demanded that the Assembly suspend the king immediately.

During this time the Austrians were advancing into northern France; they took Orchies on 15 July and Bavai on 18 July. At Paris a central committee of the *fédérés* was formed, and the enlistment of volunteers was organized on public squares. On 28 July, the manifesto of the commander of the allied army, Brunswick, became known in Paris. In April Louis XVI had charged the eminent journalist J. Mallet du Pan with drawing up a manifesto that would be published by the coalition armies when they entered France. But Mallet was relieved of this task by an *émigré*, the marquis de Limon, who composed an outrageous and provocative text: the city of Paris would be given over to military execution and total destruction if the inhabitants did not submit immediately and without condition to their king. Instead of spreading fear, this manifesto increased hatred of the royal family, whose collusion with the enemy now appeared evident. M. Robespierre demanded dethronement and the meeting of a Convention elected by universal suffrage.

At this time (30 July) the Marseillais *fédérés* arrived in Paris. Since the Assembly had decided not to depose the king, the Parisian *sans-culottes* and provincial *fédérés* resolved to act forcefully. An insurrectionary committee, a secret directory of patriots, was created; it remained only to determine the time and the tactics for a violent coup. On 3 August, forty-seven of the forty-eight sectional assemblies of Paris demanded solemnly that the Assembly decree the dethronement of the king. The latter adjourned debate on this question until 9 August; this had the effect of setting the date for the insurrection.

The court prepared by gathering at the Tuileries its last faithful defenders, the Swiss Guards and noble volunteers. On 9 August when the Assembly had still made no decision about the king's dethronement, the insurrectionary committee moved into action. At midnight the tocsin sounded. The National Guardsmen from the faubourgs Saint-Antoine and Saint-Marceau (led by the brewer A.-J. Santerre and the stockbroker C.-A. Alexandre, respectively) and the *fédérés* in Paris began to march along both banks of the Seine toward the Tuileries. An insurrectionary commune was established at the city hall. A.-J.-G. Mandat, a leader of the National Guard who supported the king, was assassinated. Louis XVI, however, believed he could count on some loyal battalions of the National Guard, but when he reviewed them, they cried, "Long live the Nation!" The king and his family then sought refuge within the Legislative Assembly, which sat not far away, in the Manège on the terrace of the Tuileries, without leaving any clear orders for the garrison of the palace.

When the advance elements of the insurgents appeared before the gates of the Tuileries at 9:00 A.M., the Swiss at first appeared ready to fraternize with them but subsequently opened fire. There were numerous casualties. The insurgents fell back. Behind them came the *fédérés* from Brest and Marseille, and this time the Swiss pulled back. Learning that the situation was hopeless, the king ordered the Swiss to lay down their arms and return to their barracks. The insurgents, however, who had lost about 100 dead and 300 wounded, were infuriated. They felt that they had been betrayed and massacred the Swiss, so easily recognized in their red uniforms—600 of a total of 900 perished.

Finally, the Assembly declared not the dethronement but the suspension of Louis XVI and created, to replace him, a provisional executive council whose principal members were the former ministers, J.-M. Roland de la Platière, E. Clavière, and J. Servan, together with G.-J. Danton, the influential orator of the Cordeliers club. The legislature also ordered the royal family interned in the convent of the Feuillants. But the insurrectionary commune, which enjoyed power as a result of its victory and which included among its 288 members such men as Robespierre, P.-G. Chaumette, J.-R. Hébert, and J.-N. Billaud-Varenne, demanded the king, the queen, and their children and imprisoned them in the tower of the Temple. The monarchy in France had ceased to exist.

F. Braesch, *La Commune du 10 août* (Paris, 1911); J. Godechot, *Fragments des mémoires de C.-A. Alexandre sur les journées révolutionnaires de 1791 et 1792* (Paris, 1952) and *Mémoires inédits de E.-L.-H. Dejoly sur la journée du 10 août 1792* (Paris, 1947); A. Mathiez, *Le 10 août 1792* (Paris, 1931); M. Reinhard, *10 août 1792; La Chute de la royauté* (Paris, 1969); A. Soboul, *The French Revolution, 1789-1799: From the Storming of the Bastille to Napoleon* (New York, 1975); M. Vovelle, *La Chute de la Monarchie, 1787-1792* (Paris, 1972).

J. Godechot

Related entries: BILLAUD-VARENNE; BOUILLE; BRUNSWICK MANIFESTO; *CAHIERS DE DOLEANCES*; CHAMP DE MARS "MASSACRE"; FESTIVAL OF FEDERATION; LEOPOLD II; MANUEL; "*MARSEILLAISE, LA*"; PETION DE VILLENEUVE; *SANS-CULOTTES*; SANTERRE; SYMBOLISM; VARENNES.

TENNIS COURT OATH (*serment du jeu de paume*), dramatic event in the early stages of the Revolution, characterized by formal defiance and disobedience of the Third Estate toward the crown. On the morning of 20 June 1789, the deputies of the Third Estate to the Estates General meeting at Versailles found the doors of their assigned meeting hall unexpectedly closed and guarded by soldiers, supposedly to permit workmen time to prepare the room for a special royal session planned for 22 June. The sight of the royal troops, however, persuaded the representatives that Louis XVI had opted for their forcible dissolution rather than face the prospect of union of the first two estates of France with the third in advancing the latter's demands on the government. On the motion of Dr. J.-I. Guillotin, the deputies retired to a nearby tennis court (*jeu* *de paume*), less than two minutes away. There, several deputies led by the abbé E.-J. Sieyès advocated moving to Paris where, they believed, the population would better protect them from royal intrusion. J.-J. Mounier successfully thwarted this proposal by moving instead that the assembly swear an oath not to separate "but to meet in any place that circumstances may dictate, until the constitution of the kingdom shall be laid and established on a firm basis; and that after the swearing of the oath each and every member shall confirm by their signature this unshakeable resolution."

The first to take the oath, J.-S. Bailly, read and administered the oath to the representatives. Only 1 deputy of the 577 present, M. Dauch of Castelnaudry, refused to sign the document, averring that he could do nothing not sanctioned by the king. The dramatic ceremony is historically significant for it marks the assertion of Revolutionary authority by the Third Estate and established a union of all its members to common action, something that did not exist before. Moreover, in asserting their claims on 20 June, the deputies reaffirmed directly their faith in the doctrine of popular sovereignty. The success of the Third Estate's action was seen one week later when Louis XVI ordered the three estates to meet in common for the purpose of writing a constitution for France.

F.-A. Aulard, *Les orateurs de la Constituante*, 2d ed. (Paris, 1906); G. Lefebvre, *The Coming of the French Revolution*, trans. R. R. Palmer (Princeton, N.J., 1976); J. M. Roberts, ed., *French Revolution Documents*, vol. 1 (London, 1966).

B. Rothaus

Related entries: BAILLY; ESTATES GENERAL; MOUNIER; SIEYES.

TERRIER. See PEASANTRY.

TERROR, CONSTITUTION OF THE. See LAW OF 14 FRIMAIRE.

TERROR, THE, a policy and a set of institutions designed to intimidate enemies of the Revolution into obedience by signal, swift, and merciless punishment. By defining the Terror as a reflexive reaction, motivated by fear and vengeance and aimed at those suspected of hostility toward the Revolution, one can trace the Terror's origins to the first acts of Revolutionary street violence in 1789. Such a definition has the advantage of emphasizing the spontaneous and popular nature of much of the impetus behind the Terror, but it also encourages the misleading tendency to confuse the French Revolution's terror with the often random, destabilizing violence directed against established governments by nineteenth- and twentieth-century terrorists. It is more useful to distinguish among the First Terror of 1792, the Terror as an instrument developed by the Revolutionary government from September 1793 to the spring of 1794, and the Great Terror of June and July 1794.

The First Terror began immediately after the fall of the monarchy when the Legislative Assembly authorized the deportation of refractory priests and the arrest of aristocrats, a generic term for persons who might collaborate treasonously with the armies invading France. A large number of arrests took place throughout France, and in Paris, over 3,000 clergy and aristocrats were imprisoned. The legal or governmental terror was accompanied by riots and lynchings of priests and suspected anti-Revolutionaries. The wave of popular violence reached its climax in Paris during the September Massacres (2-6 September 1792) during which almost 1,400 prisoners were butchered. Of these, less than a quarter were political prisoners; the rest were common criminals. By the end of 1792 when French military victories temporarily ended the crisis, most of the political prisoners were released, bringing the First Terror to an end.

The Terror proper began on 5 September 1793 when a mass of *sans-culotte* demonstrators surrounded the National Convention, mingled with the deputies, and demanded more rigorous repression of counterrevolutionaries. The Convention then adopted terror as the order of the day, thereby declaring that punishment and coercion were to be the sole policy of the government toward its enemies. This declaration was the psychological turning point in the evolution of the Terror for it signaled the Convention's determination to employ ruthlessly instruments of repression that had already been created during the spring and summer in response to the insurrection in the Vendée, C. Dumouriez's treason, and the worsening military situation. On 10 March, the Revolutionary Tribunal was established to punish crimes against the Revolution. The Law of 21 March gave legal status to the Revolutionary committees or Committees of Surveillance that had formed spontaneously and ordered that more such committees be founded. These were given the power to arrest suspects. A number of laws defined sedition and provided the death penalty for several kinds of political crimes. The most important in terms of the numbers subsequently killed under its provisions was the Law of 19 March outlawing rebels who, if captured armed, were to be executed by military commissions in the field within twenty-four hours. A decree of 23 April subjected refractory priests to deportation and, if they returned, death. In addition, from March to September a series of laws authorized the establishment of special commissions to mete out punishment on the spot in areas of insurrection and civil war. Eventually over sixty of these were set up, by both the Convention and representatives on mission.

After the galvanic shock of the events of 5 September, this set of ad hoc responses to crisis and popular pressure for punitive action developed rapidly in scope, intensity, and organizational coherence, gradually becoming an instrument of government of dreadful power. The Law of Suspects (17 September 1793) defined crimes against the Revolution so broadly that over a quarter of a million persons were imprisoned before the end of the Terror. The Revolutionary Tribunal, enlarged on 5 September, increased its guilty verdicts dramatically and conducted the show trials of Marie Antoinette and the Brissotins in October. As the Republic began to reconquer rebellious cities like Lyon (9 October 1793), subjugate the Vendée, and repulse the invaders, the number of executions—some legal, others not—rose sharply, reaching a peak in December 1793 and January 1794. At the same time the Revolutionary government, controlled principally by the Committee of Public Safety, increased its grip on the Terror's machinery. The Law of 14 Frimaire (4 December 1793), often called the Constitution of the Terror, subordinated most of the local organs of the Terror, including the representatives on mission, to the Committee of Public Safety. Although it took time for the Revolutionary government to make its authority over the Terror effective, the process continued steadily and was completed after the Committee of Public Safety, led by M. Robespierre, eliminated its opponents to the Left and the Right, the ultra-Revolutionary Hébertists and the moderate Dantonists (March-April 1794). The Law of 16 April ordered that all persons suspected of conspiracy be transferred to Paris to be tried by the Revolutionary Tribunal. And on 8 May 1794 most of the local tribunals and commissions were abolished, thus centralizing Revolutionary justice and punishment in Paris. Finally the representatives on mission, often the most effective but uncontrolled and violent agents of the Terror, began to be recalled to Paris.

These developments significantly increased the government's ability to regulate the Terror, but although the Terror had eliminated all overt resistance to the Revolution within France, it was not relaxed. Instead, it was intensified when Robespierre and G. Couthon pushed through the Law of 22 Prairial (10 June 1794), which began the period of the Great Terror. The decree abolished normal rules of evidence by allowing moral proofs of guilt, deprived accused persons of any defense, and increased enormously the potential body of suspects by redefining crimes against the Revolution in a way that menaced almost everyone. The law began to have the desired effect of (in Couthon's phrase) "exterminating" the enemies of the Republic. More than 1,300 persons were speedily tried and executed in Paris within the space of six weeks. The bloodshed was showing no signs of abatement when the overthrow of Robespierre and his associates on 9 Thermidor (27 July 1794) unexpectedly led to a reaction, which ended both the Great Terror and, by August, the Terror itself.

The conspirators responsible for the fall of Robespierre included some of the bloodiest terrorists, men who had no intention of ending the Terror. The Convention, however, seized the opportunity and began to dismantle the Terror's machinery almost immediately. It reorganized the Committee of Public Safety, reduced its power over the Convention, and then deprived it of the right to arrest suspects. The Law of 22 Prairial was repealed on 1 August 1794 and the Revolutionary committees suppressed on 24 August. Although the Revolutionary Tribunal continued its work (especially against former terrorists), it was reorganized and obliged by law to take the accused's intentions into account. With the release of imprisoned suspects early in August, the Terror came to an end.

Estimates of the number of the Terror's victims vary considerably, but probably around 17,000 persons were condemned and executed according to procedures established by Revolutionary legislation. To this number must be added from 10,000 to 12,000 who were killed without any kind of trial, such as those shot down on the battlefield after surrendering or killed by order of representatives on mission like J.-B. Carrier who drowned about 2,000 persons in the Loire at

Nantes from November 1793 to January 1794. Finally, those who died in disease-ridden, overcrowded prisons also ought to be included among the Terror's victims, bringing the grand total to 35,000 to 40,000.

The interpretation of the Terror hinges on an examination of where, when, and why people were put to death and on who they were. The Terror weighed heavily on certain regions of France and spared others completely. The bloodiest grounds were in the west, scene of the Vendéan rebellion, and in the southeast, which saw the revolts at Lyon, Toulon, and Marseille. These areas account for almost three-fourths of the executions. The figure amounts to 80 percent if the theaters of military operations at the frontiers and the departments in which there were serious uprisings are added. The connection between the impact of the Terror and armed opposition to the Revolution is also evident in both the chronology of executions and the acts for which people were killed. The great majority of official executions took place from December 1793 through January 1794 in the wake of the Republic's triumph over rebellion and insurrection. About two-thirds of the death sentences were meted out to persons because they had taken up arms against the Revolution. Since the majority of the insurgent forces was composed of peasants and artisans, these two groups contributed proportionally; 60 percent of the Terror's victims were peasants and artisans. Another 25 percent of the victims were bourgeois, and 8 percent were of the nobility.

These figures make it possible to dismiss out of hand H. Taine's contention that the Terror was a weapon used by social misfits, ruffians, and crazed, egalitarian fanatics to destroy their social betters. Instead the Terror's social and geographical incidence, the nature of its indictments, and its calendar seem to support up to a point the thesis of circumstance of F.-A. Aulard, who asserted that the Terror was above all a political instrument of national defense, the response of a unified Revolutionary movement to armed invasion, rebellion, and internal subversion. It was aimed at and struck down those it perceived as enemies, whatever their social rank. It waxed in moments of crisis and waned during periods of relative calm.

This essentially political interpretation tends, however, to ignore the social conflicts that divided Revolutionary patriots whose dynamic, in the view of Marxist historians, explains both the origins and development of the Terror. According to A. Mathiez, the Terror in its first phases was forced on a reluctant middle-class Convention by the *sans-culottes* who demanded not only the repression of anti-Revolutionaries but also the ruthless punishment of hoarders and war profiteers, the imposition of price controls, and the provisioning of food for the poor. Eventually the Terror evolved into an instrument of class war and in the late winter of 1794 began a social revolution when Robespierre and L. Saint-Just introduced the Ventôse decrees (26 February -3 March), which pledged the Convention to redistribute the property of suspects to indigent patriots in order to create a new social order. The fall of Robespierre, Mathiez concluded, destroyed this embryonic social revolution.

The social interpretation was developed further but also greatly modified by

Mathiez's successors, G. Lefebvre and A. Soboul, who also insisted on the popular origins of the Terror while denying that a social revolution was ever intended even by Robespierre and Saint-Just. In fact, the economic terror was accepted by the Convention only under the immediate threat of armed violence against itself. It was never vigorously enforced; only 1 percent of the executions were for crimes against economic legislation. And it was abandoned as soon as the *sans-culottes* were destroyed as a political force. The Ventôse decrees, moreover, were primarily a sop to the popular movement and were not, in any case, implemented. In this view, the Terror's history cannot be understood without examining social forces and social conflict, but in both purpose and application it was a political instrument used against counterrevolution.

The political interpretation of the Terror, modified by an examination of the role of the popular Revolutionary movement, thus explains the nature of the Terror in its broad outlines. It does not, however, provide a satisfactory explanation of the Great Terror. Neither the Law of 22 Prairial nor the great increase in executions at Paris can be seen as a rational response to political or military crisis, for these had ended. Instead it seems necessary to point to the psychology of the terrorists, men who had become so accustomed to viewing opposition as a capital crime that they were unwilling to tolerate the reappearance of ordinary, loyal political opposition after the Revolution had subdued its enemies. This determination to kill political opponents was a generally shared predisposition. In the case of highly principled men like Robespierre and Couthon it was joined to the belief that only the virtuous man deserved the protection of the law. The Great Terror was in large part intended to create a just republic by exterminating all who could not meet an ill-defined, virtually religious standard of virtue.

F.-A. Aulard, ed., *Recueil des actes du Comité de salut public* (Paris, 1889-1925); J. L. Godfrey, *Revolutionary Justice: A Study of the Organization, Personnel, and Procedure of the Paris Tribunal, 1793-1795* (Chapel Hill, N.C., 1952); D. Greer, *The Incidence of the Terror during the French Revolution: A Statistical Study* (Cambridge, Mass., 1935); L. Jacob, *Les suspects pendant la Révolution, 1789-1794* (Paris, 1952); A. Mathiez, *La vie chère et le mouvement social sous la Terreur* (Paris, 1927); R. R. Palmer, *Twelve Who Ruled: The Year of the Terror in the French Revolution* (Princeton, N.J., 1970); H. Wallon, *Histoire du tribunal révolutionnaire de Paris avec le journal de ses actes*, 6 vols. (Paris, 1880-82).

R. Bienvenu

Related entries: AULARD; COMMITTEE OF PUBLIC SAFETY; DUMOURIEZ; JACOBINS; LAW OF 14 FRIMAIRE; LAW OF SUSPECTS; LAW OF 22 PRAIRIAL; LEFEBVRE; MATHIEZ; 9 THERMIDOR YEAR II; *NOYADES DE NANTES*; REVOLUTIONARY TRIBUNAL; ROBESPIERRE, M.; *SANS-CULOTTES*; SAINT-JUST; SEPTEMBER 1792 MASSACRES; TAINE; VENDEE; VENTOSE DECREES.

TERROR, WHITE. See WHITE TERROR.

THEATER. The Revolution was a period of frenzied theatrical activity. Thousands of new dramas were produced and hundreds of new theaters founded. Since plays are performed publicly, the theater had to reflect changing public opinion. "The actors became weather-cocks," the actor B. Fleury wrote later in his *Mémoires*. He might have added, so did the playwrights and producers. Consequently, the history of the theater provides invaluable evidence of the course of the Revolution.

The history of the theater also interests historians because many playwrights and leaders wanted to use dramas to arouse Revolutionary zeal and rally the public around the new ideals and institutions. The *philosophes* had taught Frenchmen to believe that the arts should serve a utilitarian purpose by enlightening the public. As the Revolution became more radical, leaders sought increasingly to turn the theater into a school for citizenship. They valued the theater especially because it could reach the masses, many of whom were illiterate.

Even before the Revolution the controversy surrounding P.-A. Caron de Beaumarchais' *Le mariage de Figaro* underscored the political significance of the theater. Because the play bristled with contemporary issues—the powers of the police, freedom of speech, and the privileges of the aristocracy—Louis XVI and his ministers banned it for a long time. When the king finally yielded to public pressure and the play was produced by the Comédie-française in 1784, it ran for seventy-five nights.

In 1789 politicization of the theater was carried further by the controversy over J.-M. Chénier's *Charles IX*, which had been banned because it depicted that monarch largely responsible, by yielding to Machiavellian ministers, for the Saint Bartholomew's Day massacre. In July popular leaders took up the playwright's cause as a case of royal oppression. Popular pressure forced the Comédie-française, the national theater patronized by the king, to produce the play in November when it began a long run. Eventually the king ordered it stopped, but Revolutionaries had discovered the value of the theater as propaganda.

In 1790 public pressure forced revival of *Charles IX*, but it continued to cause controversy. Conservative actors in the Comédie resisted its presentation. Meanwhile, plays praising the constitutional monarch Louis XVI, condemning aristocracy, and lampooning monasticism appeared at various theaters. In July at the time of the great Festival of Federation, there was a spate of patriotic productions, including a reenactment of the storming of the Bastille, but only after H.-G. R. Mirabeau stirred up public opinion did the Comédie consent to revive *Charles IX* for the *fédérés* nine days after the festival. The Comédie was deeply split between conservative "blacks" and more liberal "reds."

Early in 1791 the three state theaters—the Comédie, the Opéra, and the Comédie-italienne—lost their monopoly over serious dramas to a host of new theaters that had sprung up. The post of censor was also abolished. Now that the controls were relaxed, inflammatory plays became more common. Some theaters became like political clubs where patriotic lines set off wild demonstrations. C. de Flins des Oliviers' *Le mari directeur* touched off a series of ribald anticlerical pieces.

Not only did the Comédie lose its monopoly, but half of its troupe, led by the actor F.-J. Talma, quit to join the rival Théâtre-français. The Comédie changed its name to Théâtre de la Nation; nevertheless, radicals still considered it a reactionary stronghold. From the time of the attempted flight of the king from Paris in June 1791 through the following year, the theaters were drawn ever further into political warfare. Different theaters became centers for rival factions and demonstrations frequently interrupted plays. The Théâtre de la Nation attempted to show that it was not an aristocratic nest by producing E.-L. Billardon de Sauvigny's *Washington, ou la liberté du nouveau monde*, but the play was a flop.

The problems of another former national theater, the Opéra, illustrated the political maelstrom in the capital in 1792 as war broke out, the nation was declared in danger, and the monarchy lost support. The Opéra produced *Adrien* by H. Hoffman and E.-N. Méhul. The plot was uncontroversial, but one scene showed a Roman emperor entering in triumph on a chariot drawn by horses that had once belonged to the queen who was now suspected of sympathizing with the enemy. Patriots protested a scene of a triumphant emperor at a moment when the Austrian emperor was invading France. Hoffman, the librettist, refused to change the scene, and the theater withdrew the piece. Hoffman was suspect during the Terror but was saved by friends.

Even after the overthrow of the monarchy on 10 August 1792, the Nation, made up of conservative members of the old Comédie, continued to preach moderation. On the other hand, the Opéra abandoned gallant spectacles for classical works with a Revolutionary significance such as *Miltiade à Marathon*, topical pieces such as *La journée du dix août*, and allegorical pieces such as *La Montagne*. Everywhere audiences demanded rousing plays. The Commune, the municipal government of Paris, dominated by Jacobins, pressured the Opéra and other theatres to offer five free performances of such patriotic plays.

In 1793 the freedom of the theaters was steadily infringed upon. Radicals pressured the Commune to ban such plays as J.-L. Laya's *L'ami des lois*, staged by the Nation, because it portrayed Jacobins as incendiaries. Extremists even attacked J.-B. Radet's and G.-F. Desfontaines' *La chaste Suzanne* because it contained some lines that seemed to criticize *conventionnels* who pressed for execution of the king. Some claimed that Suzanne represented the queen. In August when the Nation presented N.-L. François de Neufchâteau's *Paméla*, with a heroine of noble birth, Jacobins demanded that it be banned. The Committee of Public Safety ordered the theater closed and the author and actors arrested. To play safe other theaters featured Revolutionary plays.

Despite the loss of freedom, interest in the theater was never higher than during the Terror, in Year II. Perhaps as many as 250 new plays appeared, almost half of them political in nature, by almost 140 authors. There were more than forty theaters in the capital, offering about one seat for every ten Parisians.

Many of the political pieces were ephemeral as their names reveal—*comédies patriotiques, divertissements patriotiques, faits historiques, faits patriotiques, impromptus républicains, opéras patriotiques, sans-culottides, tableaux patriotiques*, and *vaudevilles patriotiques*. Often Revolutionary songs were interspersed through such spectacles. Classical plays from the Old Regime were either dropped or expurgated of out-of-date notions. The Committee of Public Safety demanded more patriotic plays.

The Revolutionary government, which steadily expanded its power in the autumn of 1793, developed an ambitious program of propaganda in the following winter and early spring, involving newspapers, pamphlets, paintings, sculptures, caricatures, songs, and festivals. It was an effort to prepare citizens for the inauguration of the new republican constitution, "a vast plan of regeneration," as B. Barère called it. Since theater was considered an important ideological weapon, repertories were examined, some plays were prohibited, and others were revised. Moreover, to preclude criticism, playwrights themselves purged their works of anything offensive to the government.

The Théâtre de la Nation, which had been closed, was reopened as the Théâtre de l'Egalité and ordered to give free performances of patriotic plays several times each month. Provincial theaters were likewise ordered to give free performances every *décade*—the republican ten-day week. At the same time J.-L. David and other artists worked at physically transforming old theaters, removing privileged boxes, designing new curtains, covering the walls with tricolor paint or paper, imposing Revolutionary symbols, and introducing sculptures of republican heroes or martyrs.

Under government pressure, theaters produced three main types of Revolutionary spectacles. They often presented patriotic themes in a classical guise such as M.-J. Martin's *Fabius* presented at the Opéra. Fabius was depicted as a patriot who defeated Hannibal, would-be king of Rome. Second, they offered anticlerical pieces such as A. G. Chiavacchi's *La journée du Vatican*, staged at the Louvois, featuring debauched ecclesiastics. Third, above all they presented topical spectacles such as G. Saint-Armand's *L'ami du peuple*, produced by the Variétés amusantes, glorifying the martyr J.-P. Marat. The government even supplied scarce gunpowder for P.-S. Maréchal's *Dernier jugement des rois* in which the kings of Europe, exiled to an island in the South Pacific, are finally consumed by a volcanic eruption.

This attempt to mobilize theater for propaganda was only partially effective. Some plays favored by the public, such as *Columbine mannequin* by P.-Y. Barré, Radet, and Desfontaines with its comic love plot, were pure escapist entertainment, although they were often combined with patriotic pieces on the same program. In any case the attempt to make the theater part of a concerted propaganda campaign was of short duration. The program was just being fully inaugurated when Robespierre and his colleagues were overthrown and reaction set in. Some theaters that had been glorifying the Jacobin dictatorship produced anti-Jacobin plays such as H. Dorvo's *Le faux député*, A. Charlemagne's *Le souper des Jacobins*, and C.-P. Ducancel's *L'intérieur des comités révolutionnaires*.

Although conditions in the theater became more normal under the Directory, the authorities still censored plays that they thought were controversial or that contained terms from the Old Regime such as *monsieur, château*, or *seigneur*. Controls became especially tight after the coup of 18 Fructidor. Scenes of Catholic worship were especially unacceptable. The theater was not yet free; but before the Directory ended there was one significant accomplishment; the Comédie, torn into rival factions by the same forces that tore France apart, was reunited on the rue de Richelieu. France at last had a national theater again.

With the exception of Chénier's *Charles IX*, the Revolution produced few dramas of literary importance; nevertheless, it represented an important transitional phase in the history of French drama. The Revolution broke many of the restraints of the classical tradition, popularized novel genres, introduced new emotional elements, gave the common people more roles, and broadened the audience, thus preparing the way for the nineteenth century and the advent of Romanticism.

M. Carlson, *The Theatre of the French Revolution* (Ithaca, 1966); P. d'Estrée, *Le théâtre sous la Terreur* (Paris, 1913); J. Herissay, *Le monde des théâtres pendant la Révolution* (Paris, 1922); B. F. Hyslop, "The Theater during a Crisis: The Parisian Theater during the Reign of Terror," *J. of Mod. Hist.*, 17 (1945); H. Welschinger, *Le théâtre de la Révolution* (Paris, 1880).

J. A. Leith

Related entries: BEAUMARCHAIS; CHENIER, J.-M.; MARECHAL; MUSIC; PROPAGANDA.

THEOPHILANTHROPY, a synthetic religion that flourished briefly under the Directory. Although the Revolution had driven the official Catholic church underground, there was always a demand for some sort of religion, whether to provide acceptable ceremonies for marriages and deaths or to provide a basis for republican morality and patriotism, the lack of which frightened many republican intellectuals. Neither the Cult of Reason nor that of the Supreme Being outlasted their political creators, and although the constitutional Catholic church reorganized itself and emerged anew after the separation of church and state on 21 February 1795, this too failed to carry conviction or to surmount changing political circumstances. Many concerned intellectuals, who believed religion and morality to be socially necessary in order to prevent a recurrence of anarchy, drew on eighteenth-century deism to develop new creeds, such as B. Lamothe's Pantheonists and F.-A. Daubermesnil's Culte des Adorateurs. This move was encouraged by competitions run by the Institute of France in 1797-98.

One of these intellectuals was a Parisian bookseller and former Freemason, J.-B. Chemin Dupontès, who in September 1796 published a pamphlet, *Manuel des Théoanthrophiles*, a term later changed to *théophilanthropes*, meaning "lovers of God and man." This described quasi-religious practices already observed in some private homes. The ideas in the pamphlet won the support of a number of leading cultural figures, including V. Haüy, organizer of a school and choir for blind children, and also of the government. Haüy and others organized an administrative committee to run public services, which began in January 1797 in the chapel of Saint-Catherine in Haüy's school, on the corner of the rue des Lombards and rue Saint-Denis.

By May 1797 the movement was noted by the press, and although it was at first refused the use of major churches, by the end of the year it began to expand, producing a yearbook and creating branches throughout the country, mainly due to the effects of Fructidor. It was allocated four churches in the capital, including Saint-Roche, Saint-Sulpice, and finally, in April 1798, Notre Dame, which had earlier been denied. The movement reached its peak in the autumn of 1798 when it had fifteen churches in Paris alone. Outside Paris, it had strength in the department of the Seine and cells in former centers of dechristianization like Dijon, Macon, and Auxerre, although there was little in the west outside of Bordeaux and Poitiers. It also had the interest of leading figures such as H. Bernardin de Saint-Pierre, P. Daunou, P.-S. Dupont de Nemours, S. Mercier, J.-B. Regnault, M.-J. Chenier, T. Paine, and the group connected with the newspaper *La décade*. It was sometimes combined with the Culte décadaire and shared churches with the Constitutional church. All this expansion was due to the patronage of L.-M. La Revellière-lépeaux and P.-J.-M. Sotin de la Coindière, the minister of police from Fructidor Year V to Pluviôse Year VI. La Revellière-lépeaux had a hand in its ideas, although he did not attend its services. The government in general subsidized it indirectly and on a small scale by providing churches and paying for its newspaper, *L'ami des théophilanthropes*, and other publications.

After the coup of 22 Floréal, the government began to withdraw its support since the cult was believed to be too Jacobin in its inclinations. A.-C. Merlin de Thionville and N.-L. François de Neufchâteau, the new directors, then abandoned the deist option in favor of the Culte décadaire, a purely patriotic form of observance aimed at improving public opinion and restraining the Left. Theophilanthropy lingered on, still with some support from La Revellière-lépeaux and still using eighteen churches in 1799, although it had given up Sunday services in favor of the *décadi*. It also tried to reassert itself after 18 Brumaire, only to be banned on 4 October 1801, after which it evaporated save in private uses. These vestiges were still being reported in 1803, and in the Yonne, the movement remained in existence for some time.

At its peak, its organization was of a congregational kind. It consisted of a directing committee at the head of each church, with *lecteurs-surveillants* to run the services. The ritual for these came partly from Chemin and partly from Calvinist models. Its services consisted of readings, drawn from an eclectic range of materials, hymns, either set in plain song or the *chant de départ*, and moralizing addresses, sometimes written by Daunou. Services on occasion shaded off into official activities, such as the public mourning for L.-L. Hoche. Basically the *théophilanthropes* believed in the immortality of the soul and in a God, and although some of their members evolved toward atheism, others claimed to be Christians. Its members viewed it as a minimum religion, or perhaps a set of moral exercises valid for all religions, rather than a new cult in itself. It was not opposed to Christianity, although it had some Calvinist roots and did reject Catholic ritual and dogma. It also rejected the idea of original sin, preferring to see man as motivated by reason and natural law. Although it is doubtful whether theophilanthropy ever enjoyed the influence that some satirists attributed to it, it seems that the latter basically were right and that the idea reflected political circumstances and fears more than a genuine religious movement.

M. Lyons, *France under the Directory* (Cambridge, 1975); A. Mathiez, *Théophilanthropie et le culte décadaire, 1795-1802* (Paris, 1904); J. McManners, *The Church and the French Revolution* (London, 1969); A. Mellon, *L'anti-cléricalisme français* (Paris, 1966); G. Robison, *Revellière-Lépeaux, Citizen-Director (1753-1824)* (New York, 1972).

C. Church

Related entries: CHENIER; COUP OF 18 BRUMAIRE; COUP OF 18 FRUCTIDOR YEAR V; COUP OF 22 FLOREAL YEAR VI; CULT OF REASON; CULT OF THE SUPREME BEING; DECHRISTIANIZATION; DU PONT DE NEMOURS; FRANCOIS DE NEUFCHATEAU; MERLIN DE THIONVILLE; PAINE.

THEORY OF REVOLUTIONARY GOVERNMENT, political ideology that reached its culmination during the Montagnard regime (2 June 1793-28 July 1794). The origins of the theory can be found in the experience and theory of the developing administrative monarchy of the regime which the Revolution endeavored to destroy in its underlying fury. Nevertheless, the theory of Revolutionary government was a philosophical justification of the practices and aspirations of those Revolutionary leaders who eventually expected to bring the Revolution to its ultimate logical conclusion: utopia. The theory began to sprout as soon as the Revolution began, and it was developed by many Revolutionists in varying degrees as the rapidly changing situation led them to glimpse the dawn of a new era. The final phase came during the most radical period of the Revolution. The theory was most thoroughly and logically developed by the one man who then symbolized the nature of the Revolution and who was perceived by much of the knowing world of public opinion within France and outside as its leader: the Incorruptible, M. Robespierre. It was Robespierre who became in effect the leading spokesman, as well as the incarnation, of Revolutionary government.

To understand the theory of Revolutionary government, therefore, it is necessary to concentrate on Robespierre's development as a Revolutionary. Maximilien, advocate and academician in Arras, had been ambivalent toward what was to be called the *ancien régime*. He was dissatisfied but not a revolutionary; the fiscal and political crisis in 1788 and the convocation of the Estates General opened up new vistas for him, as for so many others. He would do his utmost to be elected to the Estates General. The potentialities he had had to become a revolutionary now came into being. He became a vigorous opponent of the local oligarchy, which refused to permit any basic modification of the power structure.

At one of the meetings of the electoral assembly of the Third Estate of Arras, Robespierre brutally castigated the municipal oligarchy of Arras—which included his friend F. Dubois de Fosseux—for oppressing the people. He declared that "the defenders of the people" (such as Robespierre) must not allow personal feelings to interfere with the interests of the people. Thus the interests of society superseded personal loyalties. Intolerance was to reign. A revolutionist had been born.

As Robespierre emphasized in *Les ennemis de la patrie démasqués* (April 1789), the oligarchy of Artois, the forces of evil, had long ago plotted to perpetuate its oppressive regime. A life-and-death struggle between the forces of evil and the forces of good was being waged. "O Citizens, *la patrie est en danger*. Let us fly to its aid. . . . Let us fulfil our duty and let us rely on Heaven itself for the rest of our destiny." Enemies plan to make martyrs out of all the defenders of the people. If they should win, death will be sweet to the martyr. His memory will be dear to all good people. And his soul will enjoy, in the immortal abode of order and justice, the happiness that the tyranny of men has banished from the earth. In this early writing, the future Revolutionary leader revealed not only his religious feelings but also his conception of the fundamental nature of the coming Revolution.

Successfully elected as one of the deputies of the Third Estate of Artois to the Estates General, Robespierre took the new Revolutionary road with verve and without significant hesitation. For him the struggle begun with the oligarchy in Artois was now transformed into a national struggle.

Aligned with the most uncompromising delegates from the opening of the Estates General, he unhesitatingly supported its transformation into the National Assembly and the attack on the Bastille. The day of attack, 14 July, was for him a victory of the Revolution over the plot of despotism and aristocracy to slaughter one-half of the nation in order to oppress the rest. The response of the people of Paris saved the Revolution. The murders of a few officials were unquestioningly approved as just treatment for guilty individuals.

During his service in the Constituent Robespierre developed the germ of an idea of the different nature of the time of revolution and that of a constitutional regime. His expressions of elements of a revolutionary ideology—wherein the end justifies the means—were overshadowed in this period, however, by his vigorous struggle for a liberal constitution, which would be democratic in all its political ramifications. Robespierre became a leader of the radicals, eventually played the major role in saving the Jacobin club, and fought the Feuillants. His uncompromising adherence to democratic principles and his clear-cut incorruptibility were among the factors that made him a charismatic Jacobin leader with national renown by the close of the National Assembly.

During the Legislative Assembly, Robespierre continued to defend his ideals in the Jacobin club in Paris and in his journal *Le défenseur de la constitution*. He fought the Brissotins or Girondins almost single-handedly, striving unsuccessfully to prevent France from being plunged into a war he viewed as a threat to the Revolution. The war came, however, and for a time revolutionized the Revolution. Robespierre's ideas on Revolutionary practices developed further. While he did not participate in the violence associated with the radical transformation of the Revolution in August 1792, he provided guidance and a rationale for the "second Revolution." He was influential in the revolutionary Paris Commune. Dominating the electoral proceedings in Paris, he was the first to be elected from Paris to the National Convention.

In the Convention, Robespierre and his Montagnard colleagues continued the struggle against the Girondins over domestic and foreign issues. The king was found guilty and executed. The ultimate failure of the Girondins to solve the economic and military problems created a loose coalition between the *sans-culottes* and the Montagnard deputies. At the Jacobin club on 26 May 1793, Robespierre for the first time openly called on the people to revolt against the deputies. The expulsion of the Girondin leaders from the Convention (31 May-2 June 1793) opened the way for the more radical Montagnards, including Robespierre, to take over the government.

Threatened in the summer of 1793 by the collapse of the entire Revolutionary effort as a result of the coalition of foreign powers and its invading armies, domestic revolt, economic crisis, and in part by an autonomous *sans-culotte* movement challenging a disorganized central authority, the Convention, under the increasing ascendancy of the Mountain, hastened the reassertion and centralization of governmental authority. Although a rapidly prepared Montagnard liberal democratic constitution was approved in a national referendum, it was suspended, and the power of the central government was increased in stages.

Under the increasingly effective leadership of the new Committee of Public Safety elected by the Convention on 10 July—to which Robespierre was added on 27 July—the challenge to governmental authority was checked. The so-called federalist revolt was ended, the Vendée secured, and nearly all of France cleared of foreign troops by the end of 1793. *Sans-culotterie* was eventually suppressed along with its alleged Hébertist leaders in March 1794. The group of Indulgents, which had appeared in the latter part of 1793 and which wanted to return to normality before the Committee of Public Safety was ready for it, suffered a similar fate soon after. By early April 1794, the new Revolutionary government, as it was now called, seemed to be in full control.

A revolutionary dictatorship, it appeared, had come into being. If all the new institutions and practices became completely effective, the Revolutionary government would become much more absolute than the absolute monarchy of the *ancien régime* ever was. No more were there corps, estates, privileged bodies, or privileges in central or local government. France was now an egalitarian society. Although the Convention was still sovereign in name, it had actually delegated almost all of its authority to its Committee of Public Safety. The committee had jurisdiction over every branch of local government, over the representatives on mission and their virtual rivals and successors, the national agents, over foreign affairs and the conduct of the war, and over the Provisional Executive Council of ministers and its recent replacement, the administrative commissions. The committee also nominated the members of the Committee of General Security, which acted as the chief agent for the enforcement of the Terror (though a police bureau was also organized in the offices of the Great Committee). The centralization of authority was evidenced in the *levée en masse*, the organization of a republican citizen army and the conduct of military affairs, in the use of the Jacobin club organization as a prop of the government, in economic regulation and control, and in the efforts to control and organize the Terror. This in brief was the Revolutionary government.

Professedly the Revolutionary government was provisional. Its continuation and elaboration along with the continued suspension of the Constitution of the Year I required justification. The need to justify the Revolutionary dictatorship became apparent quite early to many Revolutionists. In particular, L. Saint-Just, J.-N. Billaud-Varenne, and primarily Robespierre, leading members of the Committee of Public Safety, in a number of statements, orations, and reports to the Convention and elsewhere completed the development of a theory of Revolutionary government.

Its source is to be found in the theory of the absolute monarchy of the *ancien régime*. The doctrine of public safety dated from Richelieu's period. Domestic or foreign circumstances could justify the temporary suspension of natural laws and the fundamental laws of the kingdom. The theory of the absolute monarchy was most clearly expressed by King Louis XV on 3 March 1766, in the midst of his quarrels with his obstreperous parlements, at the *séance de la flagellation* of the Parlement of Paris. He declared: "The sovereign power resides in my person only...; my courts derive their existence and their authority from me alone;...to me alone belongs legislative power...public order in its entirety emanates from me." Whether the Revolutionaries were acquainted with such expressions of unity and a single will in the state, the statements demonstrate the continuity of French history despite the Revolution and the features it developed that were antithetical to the nature of the regime it had replaced.

On 10 October 1793, L. Saint-Just, reporting for the Committee of Public Safety to the Convention, proposed a law that, besides increasing the committee's powers significantly, proclaimed, "The provisional government of France is revolutionary until the peace." Passed by the Convention, the recently approved constitution was thus formally suspended. The Revolutionary government was now the official political structure of France. In his report, Saint-Just declared that since the sovereign people had manifested its will, anyone who did not actively support this will was outside the sovereign. And anyone outside the sovereign must be governed by the sword. Centralization of authority and a single will went hand in hand. It was also Saint-Just who in March 1794 presented his cold-blooded reports justifying the arrests of the Hébertists and Dantonists in the name of unity of will. Whoever opposed the sovereign—the people—was evil. The factions, representing the foreign enemy, had taken different forms during the Revolution. Again he declared that anyone who was not a loyal supporter of the government was an enemy, and an enemy must be destroyed for the public safety.

J.-N. Billaud-Varenne, added to the committee as a result of the *journées* of 4-5 September, presented to the Convention on 18 November a major report of the committee, which was adopted with modifications on 4 December (14 Frimaire). Demonstrating clearly that he had become a man of government as against anarchy, Billaud-Varenne proposed the rigorous centralization of all Revolutionary activity in the hands of the government. Thereby the enemies of the Revolution could be repressed, and unity of will and order in the Revolutionary government would be created. Under this virtual constitution of the Terror, the Committee of Public Safety, hereafter routinely reelected by the Convention, became the true central authority in government. The national agents were in a way the progenitors of the prefects of Napoleon. The replacement of the ministries on 1 April 1794 by executive commissions was the natural consequence of the decision of the Montagnard leadership to create a single will in France.

Robespierre, who had continued to develop his ideas on Revolutionary government during the increasing foreign and domestic threats to the Revolution since 10 August 1792, consolidated his concepts on Revolutionary government as it reached the pinnacle of its growth. In a series of great addresses to the Convention, in the name of the Committee of Public Safety, the Incorruptible, acting virtually as a premier (though he was not), presented to the Convention, France, and the world *the* theory of Revolutionary government: 17 November and 5 December 1793 on foreign relations, and, especially, 25 December (5 Nivôse, "On the Principles of the Revolutionary Government"), 5 February 1794 (17 Pluviôse, "On the Principles of Political Morality"), and 7 May (18 Floréal, "On the Relations between Religious and Moral Ideas and Republican Principles").

As he had glimpsed in Artois in early 1789, Robespierre now clearly saw two contrary forces contending for the supremacy of the world, the Revolution, the forces of good, versus the counterrevolution, the forces of evil. The latter supported monarchy, aristocracy, tyranny, and the oppression of the people. Although in Robespierre's usage the term *people* had frequently seemed to have a social connotation and include only *sans-culottes*, as opposed to the rich or aristocrats, it was essentially in his mind a moral classification and equated with the true supporters or potential supporters of the Revolution.

The aim of the Revolution, he proclaimed, was to establish and consolidate democratic or republican government (the two terms being used synonymously). While in the weeks immediately following 10 August Robespierre had played a leading role in the direct democratic action of the radicals in Paris, now as a government leader he saw matters in a different light. He declared in his oration of 5 February:

Democracy is not a state in which the people, continually assembled, itself directs all public affairs; still less is it a state in which a hundred thousand fragments of the people, by isolated, hasty and contradictory measures, would decide the destiny of society as a whole....Democracy is a state in which the sovereign people, guided by laws of its own making, performs itself everything it can do well, and through its delegates what it can not accomplish by itself.

In his reports Robespierre contrasted constitutional government with Revolutionary government. The aim of constitutional government was to preserve the Republic. That of Revolutionary government was to bring the war of liberty against its enemies, domestic and foreign, to an end, thereby establishing and consolidating democracy and arriving at the peaceful rule of constitutional laws. While constitutional government was primarily concerned with civil liberty, Revolutionary government must defend public liberty against all factions. Faced with extraordinary and changeable circumstances, Revolutionary government must have more flexible powers than constitutional government in order to defend the public interest or safety.

Since the fundamental principle of the republic or democracy was virtue— public virtue, the love of *la patrie* (including equality), or in other words, the preference of the public interest (or general will) to all private interests—the Convention must direct all of its activities to the maintenance of equality and the development of virtue. The deputies themselves must subordinate their own personal passions to the general passions of the public weal. "Guide the people by the use of reason," Robespierre directed the deputies (5 February).

Robespierre's attitude toward the people had fluctuated from the beginning of the Revolution between adoration and dissatisfaction, depending on whether their views coincided with his interpretation of the general interest. He had learned to employ and consider the Jacobin club in Paris (and its affiliated societies) as a medium to direct the people. He did not always dominate the mother society, but when he did, as in late 1793 and the early part of 1794, he insisted on an *épuration* to rid the club of those who opposed the general will he thought he knew. His ruthlessness surfaced a number of times as he fought the enemies of *la patrie*. The Jacobins were thus expected to become the elite or vanguard to guide the people along the right path to the comprehension and support of the general will.

Revolutionary government owed protection to loyal citizens, "nothing but death to the enemies of the people" (25 December). "If the mainspring of popular government in peacetime is virtue,...during revolution [it] is both virtue and terror—virtue, without which terror is disastrous, and terror, without which virtue is powerless. Terror is nothing more nor less than prompt, severe and inflexible justice." The Revolutionary government was "the despotism of liberty against tyranny" (5 February).

Hitherto it could have been assumed that the emergency Revolutionary dictatorship would end with peace, as the decree of 10 October 1793 had stated. The addresses of Robespierre, however, revealed the more profound objective of bringing the Revolution to its final logical conclusion. On 5 February he urged the Convention to maintain equality and develop virtue. He began by describing the ultimate goal of the Revolution after victory and peace. It was a harmonious society of liberty and equality, where man would have personal as well as public virtue. These would entail such traits as morality, honesty, generosity, pity for the unfortunate, selflessness, contempt for the vices and false values of the monarchy, and love of and service to *la patrie*. (Robespierre had essentially outlined this utopian dream as early as 1784 in his prize essay, *Discours sur les peines infamantes*.) Only democratic government could realize these wonders. On 7 May he proposed and the Convention decreed that "the French people recognizes the existence of the Supreme Being and the immortality of the soul....The worship worthy of the Supreme Being is the observance of the duties of man." All religions, provided they did not disturb the public order, were free to coexist with the civil religion. Although Robespierre was expressing his own religious views in the report, he believed that the tenets of the civil religion provided the necessary impetus to moral action and thus were required for the creation of the new age. Although he included a paean to J.-J. Rousseau in the address, Robespierre, as he had done in the past, was using Rousseau's thought whenever and in whatever way it served his pragmatic purposes. The Festival of the Supreme Being on 8 June (20 Prairial Year II), when Robespierre, then president of the Convention, presided over the ceremonies, was undoubtedly a very satisfying event for him. It also seemed to confirm the belief he had held since the beginning of the Revolution that providence was on the side of that unique historical phenomenon, the Revolution in France.

Robespierre's euphoria was short-lived. The attempted assassination on 22-23 May of Robespierre and J.-M. Collot d'Herbois had reinforced the leaders' fears of an aristocratic or foreign plot. On 10 June 1794 (22 Prairial), G.-A. Couthon, in the name of the Committee of Public Safety, introduced what became the infamous law of that day, which gave the government unlimited control of the Terror and made the application of the Terror completely dependent on the decisions of the Revolutionary dictatorship. Robespierre successfully browbeat the Convention, demanding and obtaining the immediate discussion of the bill. There could be no disagreement, he declared, between men equally in love with *la patrie*. There was the single will. Robespierre seemed to be the final arbiter of the general will. The Great Terror followed. However, dissensions in the Great Committee, between the latter and the Committee of General Security, and the increasing restlessness of fearful deputies weakened the government. Concurrently, the string of military successes of the French armies and, especially, the great victory at Fleurus on 25-26 June seemed to make the need for Terror less necessary. Robespierre, who was now the most prominent member of the Great Committee, became the target of the developing plot. He became more suspicious and isolated. He saw factions again. He absented himself from the Convention and then the Committee of Public Safety, attending and speaking only at the Jacobins. Victory, he told the club on 9 July, would come only when the friends of liberty had conquered the factions. The successes of the French armies were not enough. In his last speech to the Convention on 8 Thermidor (26 July), without giving any names, Robespierre called for punishment of traitors, the purge of the two committees, and the subordination of the lesser committee to the Committee of Public Safety, thereby achieving the unity of the government "under the supreme authority of the National Convention." No end to the dictatorship seemed possible as long as the Incorruptible lived.

Robespierre expressed the inner contradictions of the democratic radicals in the Revolutionary government and of the theory justifying it. There was no way to end the dictatorship and the Terror and still ensure that it would be followed by the democratic utopia. Nevertheless, the theory of a transitional, temporary revolutionary government or dictatorship as a means of establishing a new society was to have a profound effect on the history of modern revolutions.

T. A. Di Padova, "The Views of the Conventionnels Concerning Revolutionary Government, September 20, 1792-July 27, 1794" (Ph.D. dissertation, City University of New York, 1972); J. Flammermont, ed., *Remontrances du parlement de Paris au XVIII*e *siècle*, vol. 2 (Paris, 1898); F. Furet, *Penser la Révolution française* (Paris, 1978); J. Gulaine, *Billaud-Varenne, l'ascète de la Révolution (1756-1819)* (Paris, 1969); *Oeuvres complètes de Maximilien Robespierre* (10 vols., Paris, 1912-1967); R. R. Palmer, *Twelve Who Ruled: The Year of the Terror in the French Revolution* (Princeton, 1941); J. I. Shulim, "The Birth of a Revolutionary: Robespierre in Artois," *Pro. of the Cons. on Revo. Eur.* (1978), "The Birth of Robespierre as a Revolutionary: A Horneyan Psychohistorical Approach," *Am. J. of Psychoanalys.* 37 (1977), "Robespierre and the French Revolution: A Review Article," *Am. Hist. Rev.* 80 (1977), and "The Youthful Robespierre and His Ambivalence toward the Ancien Régime," *Eighteenth Cent. Stud.* 5 (1972); J. L. Talmon, *The Origins of Totalitarian Democracy* (New York, 1960).

J. I. Shulim

Related entries: BATTLE OF FLEURUS; CULT OF THE SUPREME BEING; GENERAL WILL; GIRONDINS; HEBERTISTS; INDULGENTS; JACOBINS; LAW OF 14 FRIMAIRE; MONTAGNARDS; ROBESPIERRE, M.; *SANS-CULOTTES*.

THEOT, CATHERINE (1716-94), religious prophetess. Théot was born in the village of Barenton in Normandy and from earliest childhood had a sense that she was called to fulfill a special religious mission. Having acquired a local reputation for piety, she went to Paris, where she worked as a domestic servant. Inspired in part by the lives of Saints Teresa of Avila and Catherine of Siena, she became more outspoken in her religious convictions. After she began getting up in church to preach against the preachers, she was arrested, together with three followers, and confined in the Salpêtrière, where she remained for three years.

From her release in 1782 until 1793, she lived in the Marais district of Paris, where she once again gathered a circle of followers to hear her millenarian but essentially traditional brand of popular piety. Her activities came to the attention of the Revolutionary government, which began to assemble a dossier on her and interrogated her chief disciple, but the authorities took no further action. The materials collected by the police show that her teachings became more political after the declaration of war in April 1792. The French were God's chosen people, she said, and all nations would submit to them.

In June 1793, Théot moved across the river to the rue Contrescarpe, near the Pantheon. By now her most important disciple was C.-A. Gerle, a former Carthusian prior and a Jacobin member of the National Assembly, who in 1790 had been active in proselytizing for another and very different prophetess, S. Labrousse.

Théot's disciples continued to meet to worship and hear her pronouncements until neighbors complained to authorities about the assemblies. On 17 May 1794, agents of the Committee of General Security attended a meeting, then called in police, who arrested fourteen, including Théot and Gerle. Their official reports show that Théot's sense of her own and France's mission had become more grandiose and more urgent. She called herself the New Eve who pronounced the Word of God. The millennium would begin very soon, and Paris would be its center.

Théot's sect now became obscurely involved in the fall of M. Robespierre. One of Robespierre's enemies on the Committee of General Security, M.-G.-A. Vadier, declared in a speech to the National Convention that the group was part of a great international conspiracy of fanatics and counterrevolutionaries. Then, in the climactic session of 9 Thermidor, Vadier claimed that Théot had singled out Robespierre as divinely called to establish a new cult. Robespierre's other adversaries quickly turned to other, more tangible grievances. Théot died in prison a month later, still serenely convinced of her own divine mission.

While Théot's tangible impact on the French Revolution was surely minimal, she and her followers do show that not only had the traditions of popular piety persisted into the Revolutionary decade, but they had also come to be associated with the new faith of secular revolution.

M. Eude, "Points de vue sur l'affaire Catherine Théot," *Ann. hist. de la Révo. française* 41 (1969); C. Garrett, *Respectable Folly: Millenarians and the French Revolution in France and England* (Baltimore, 1975); A. Mathiez, *Contributions à l'histoire de la Révolution française* (Paris, 1907).

C. Garrett

Related entries: COMMITTEE OF GENERAL SECURITY; 9 THERMIDOR YEAR II; PRISONS; VADIER.

THERMIDORIAN REACTION, the complex of phenomena associated with the dismantling of the political, economic, and religious policies of the Terror, commonly equated with the last fifteen months of the National Convention between 9 Thermidor Year II (27 July 1794) and 4 Brumaire Year IV (26 October 1795). Although dating makes sense generally, it is not wholly accurate. The repressive aspects of the Terror had moderated in many areas before 9 Thermidor, and the national and local political struggles of the Year III continued under the Directory. In economic terms, the maximum was seriously infringed in some areas before 9 Thermidor, while the Year III inflation and collapse of the *assignat* accelerated under the Directory. Finally, the religious revival of the Year III merely foreshadowed an exponential growth in religious dissidence up to the Concordat. The only problem that the reaction resolved was that of the threat posed to property owners by the democratic popular movement. In all other respects, the period reformulated, aggravated, and delegated to the Directory the crucial dilemmas bedeviling the pursuit of a secure, liberal regime of property owners.

9 Thermidor was a palace revolution by Montagnard factions who did not intend to end the Terror; however, it returned political initiative to the Plain and the moderate Montagnards in the Convention who had acquiesced in the Terror only as a function of a national emergency now relieved by military success. They took quickly the initial steps to dismantle the Terror apparatus. The power and coherence of the committees of government were destroyed by the monthly renewal by a quarter of their membership and by their restructuring into sixteen equal committees (11 Thermidor and 7 Fructidor, 29 July and 24 August); the Revolutionary Tribunal was emasculated by the abolition of the Law of 22 Prairial and by an obligation to acquit an accused whose intentions had been pure, however reprehensible his acts (14 and 23 Thermidor, 1 and 10 August); Revolutionary committees were limited to one per district (7 Fructidor); the Parisian sections were confined to one meeting per *décade*; and the 40 *sols* attendance indemnity for the poor was abolished on 4 Fructidor (21 August).

In Fructidor, moderate opinion in the Assembly was still unwilling to follow the Right (led by such turncoat Montagnards as J.-L. Tallien, L.-M.-S. Fréron and L. Lecointre) in its attacks on surviving Montagnard leaders. The Assembly slid into developing reaction from late Brumaire under the combined pressure of four factors: militant grass-roots reaction in Paris, an increasing perception (nurtured by a growing, virulent, Thermidorian press) of horrors committed during the Terror, changes in the Convention's membership, and mounting social fear engendered by popular disturbance. The swelling flood of released suspects (over 3,500 in Paris between mid-Thermidor and mid-Vendémiaire) contributed to growing demands for retribution against Jacobins and fueled a reactionary offensive. Moderates reconquered all but the most radical Paris sections during the autumn and early winter 1794. Simultaneously, groups of reactionary youths (the *jeunesse dorée*) undertook the harassment of Jacobin personalities, institutions, and symbols. These militants were used by the parliamentary Right (especially Fréron) to bring pressure on the Convention. The first major success was the closing of the Jacobin club on 22 Brumaire (12 November) after troubles caused by the youths. At the same time, the Right's anti-Jacobin campaign was given credibility by the trial of ninety-four suspects from Nantes at the Revolutionary Tribunal on 22-29 Fructidor (8-15 September). This demonstrated not the culpability of the accused but the horrors committed by terrorist officials under the representative on mission J.-B. Carrier. The Convention instituted a commission of inquiry whose report on Carrier coincided with the decision to close the Jacobins and resulted in Carrier's trial and execution (3 and 26 Frimaire, 23 November and 16 December). The Carrier affair confirmed the notion of the criminality of the agents of the Terror and legitimized their purge in the Convention and locally.

The repudiation of Jacobinism implicit in the closure of the Jacobin club and the Carrier affair led inevitably to the repudiation of the 31 May 1793 insurrection, which, by purging the Convention of the Girondists, had opened the way to the Montagnard dictatorship. This was expressed in the reintegration of those deputies excluded and arrested in 1793 for protesting this event (18 Frimaire, 8 December) and eventually in the reinstatement of the surviving Girondist leaders themselves (18 Ventôse, 8 March 1795). The reappearance of the excluded deputies helped to shift attitudes in the Convention further, while the extraparliamentary agitation of the reactionary youth put renewed pressure on it. The long struggle of the Montagnard remnant inside the Convention during the winter of 1794-95 was defeated when the Assembly took its second major slide into reaction in Pluviôse-Ventôse, symbolically with the removal of J.-P. Marat from the Pantheon (20 Pluviôse, 8 February), more practically by decreeing the enforced residence of all officials revoked since 10 Thermidor in the commune where they had held office (5 Ventôse, 23 February), and decreeing the arrest of J.-N. Billaud-Varenne, J.-M. Collot d'Herbois, B. Barère, and M.-G.-A. Vadier, the most prominent Montagnards who survived 9 Thermidor (12 Ventôse).

The most powerful stimulus to reaction both inside and outside the Convention was the fear of popular insurrection. Apart from the habitual social fears of property owners, this regenerated the precise fear of a Jacobin revival based on a popular democratic alliance. The unbridled development of anti-Jacobinism coincided with the growing intensity of popular discontent. The root of discontent lay in the Convention's reaction against the controlled economy of the Year II. The key to the Thermidorians' economic attitudes is simple: they believed implicitly in the virtues of private enterprise and the free play of market forces. Although proceeding from the property owners' view of liberty as the free disposition of self and of one's property, there is no reason to doubt that they sincerely believed that the free play of offer and demand would cope better with shortages than a directed economy. They proceeded rapidly to abolish most state enterprises in war materials and, more important though less speedily, to abolish the maximum (4 Nivôse, 24 December). Even under the pressure of subsequent economic and political events, they never retreated from this reassertion of an unregulated market. The consequences were catastrophic. By Germinal Year III, food prices had risen by 819 percent compared to 1790; worse was to come. At the same time, the value of paper money plummeted. By Thermidor Year III, it was worth 3 percent of its metallic equivalent. Peasants refused to supply markets and would accept only coin; hoarders and speculators ran riot. Landowners and peasants with a surplus profited, as did middlemen; purchasers of national lands liquidated their debt to the state in paper money at absurd real values. Nonetheless, not all the middle class benefited. For those deriving their income from *rentes* or leases or salaries, the catastrophe was devastating. For the rural and urban poor, it was even more so, particularly in the context of the exceptionally hard winter. It brought endless queues, riots, and mounting suicide rates.

In Paris, the conjunction of a crisis economy with reactionary harassment produced insurrection. On 12 Germinal (1 April) and again on 1 Prairial (20 May), crowds invaded the Convention, demanding food and a democratic political program. More politically articulate, more sustained, and more dangerous, the Prairial uprising lasted four days and was ended by the armed occupation of the radical faubourg Saint-Antoine. The insurrections marked the final victory of anti-Jacobin vengeance, typified by a summary deportation decree against Billaud, Collot, Barère, and Vadier (12 Germinal), the purge of fifty-five members of the Convention, the trial and death of some Montagnards (24-29 Prairial, 12-17 June), and the decree for a general disarmament of terrorists throughout the Republic (21 Germinal, 10 April).

In the provinces, the incidence of the reaction varied. The progressive release of suspects, the mounting crisis, and the eviction of Jacobin officials occurred everywhere. However, although the laws of 5 Ventôse and 21 Germinal were widely applied, thus placing Jacobins at the mercy of their enemies, the degree of anti-Jacobin persecution varied considerably. In many areas, the reaction meant the transfer of local power to the victims of the Terror, especially federalists. The continued proximity of war zones prevented the frontier departments and the region of *chouannerie* from suffering an intensive reaction after their Year II experience. Apart from the administrative purge and public disabilities of Year II personalities, the reaction took two forms. First, some Jacobin officials were tried in criminal courts for abuses of power or arbitrary acts; more were sued in civil courts for damages or restitution of goods in respect of acts of authority that had been legitimized at the time by government directives. Second and predominantly in the southeast, a system of vengeance through physical assault, street harassment, and murder developed in the late winter and spring 1795. Although the transfer of power was operated swiftly and brutally in a few places (for example, at Marseille and in the Vaucluse in Vendémiaire), the campaign gathered force and violence only from about Pluviôse and culminated in an outburst of prison massacres and manhunts which, though under way as early as Pluviôse, became most widespread between Floréal and Messidor. A combination of factors produced this: the increasingly vengeful character of those being placed in administrations, the return of hardened *émigrés*, the release of the most dangerous detainees at the end of the phase of releases, the fear engendered by the Germinal and Prairial *journées* and by a similar Jacobin rising at Toulon at the beginning of Prairial, and, finally, the supervisory legislation that pinned Jacobins down in hostile environments. This violence is often called the White Terror (though the term is better reserved for similar violence in 1815) and was principally the work of young men (deserters and returned *émigrés*). Often organized into paramilitary groups (obscurely termed Compagnies de Jésus), they became increasingly overtly royalist, as did their Parisian counterparts in the *jeunesse dorée*.

Royalism, indeed, replaced Jacobinism as the dominant problem of the reaction in the summer 1795. Its apparent strength derived from two forces (royalism and the church) whose combination was to arouse fears among property owners by its echo of the pre-Terror menace to the Revolution. The revival of militant royalism was revealed by the attitudes of revenge expressed by activists and by the return of those who had emigrated by conviction rather than by fear. It culminated in the Quiberon landing (9 Messidor, 27 June), insurrectionary plots in the southeast, Massif Central, and Franche Comté, massive electoral intimidation in the southeast in Vendémiaire Year IV, and the royalist insurrection in Paris on 13 Vendémiaire (5 October). At the same time, the Convention's retreat from the Terror's religious policies promoted a resurgence of the refractory church. Although it maintained the Terror's stance on organized religion well into the winter 1794-95, the Convention finally attempted to resolve the religious problem by the Boissy d'Anglas Law (3 Ventôse, 21 February), separating church and state and allowing private worship in reopened churches under priests who agreed formally to observe the Republic's laws. In practice, the constitutional church (damaged beyond repair) did not reassert itself. Profiting from the complacence of conservative local officials, refractory priests came out of hiding or returned from abroad; some occupied reopened churches, and many more extended the clandestine cult. The refractory church could be seen only as an ally, if not an agent, of counterrevolution. Better established in the countryside than in the towns at this point, it articulated widespread peasant grievances against the Revolution and appeared to underwrite the growing anarchy, massive rural resistance to conscription, and royalism of the summer 1795.

The comprehensive defeat of the popular movement and of Jacobinism in Prairial allowed the Convention and its committees to react in turn against the threat from the Right. They moved against royalist extremists in Paris and initiated a policy of releasing detained Jacobins. This reversal reached its apogee with the decision to protect the Republic and the regicide Convention against a royalist electoral victory by the Two-thirds Law (5 Fructidor, 22 August), which imposed the retention of this proportion of Convention deputies in the first assemblies of the Directory. The reversal was confirmed after the Vendémiaire rising by the general amnesty for Revolutionary acts (4 Brumaire, 25 October), essentially aimed at the victims of the reaction. Although there was some relaxation of anti-Jacobinism in the provinces, extreme reactionary groups often remained in control into the Directory.

The Two-thirds law crystallized much middle-class discontent with the discredited Convention. However, the extent to which the mass of Thermidorian opinion was royalist is debatable. Thermidorian circles were heterogeneous and often had conflicting objectives. The foundation of Thermidorianism was the desire to produce a stable, orderly, property-dominated society, erected on the unfettered disposition of oneself and of one's property, in which the victories of 1789 over privilege and despotism were protected by state apparatus firmly in the hands of property owners. This was enshrined in the Constitution of the Year III, voted 5 Fructidor (22 August 1795). Unanimous in its revulsion from the Terror and in the need to repress the social threat of popular democracy, the passage from the politics of middle-class liberties to the politics of vengeance left Thermidorian opinion confused. It could find no coherent principle with which to stem the march of reaction that brought counterrevolution in its wake. Conservatism was always prone to moderate royalism inasmuch as the monarchy could represent an orderly, secure society, yet the line was untenable between moderate royalism and the counterrevolutionary, *ancien régime* royalism of emigration, especially when the death of Louis XVII on 20 Prairial (8 June 1795) gave the crown to the *émigré* comte de Provence. Anti-Jacobin revenge opened the door to anti-Revolutionary revenge. The property owners were caught between two threats to their supremacy and opinion divided and fluctuated over which was the greater.

The moderate Thermidorians' search for a middle way consensus settlement was reflected in a series of proposed or attempted amnesties, in the attempted pacification of the Vendéan and *chouan* areas by negotiation (Frimaire-Pluviôse), in the abolition of emigration laws with respect to cultivators and workers (22 Nivôse, 11 January), and in the Boissy d'Anglas Law. Yet by dismantling the machinery of repression and defeating the popular movement, they deprived themselves of the means to combat counterrevolution, to maintain public order, and to limit the ravages of economic liberalism. Their attempts to transfer responsibility for the Terror onto a few specified individuals deemed guilty of crimes (whether deputies or local terrorists) were vain. They were but symbols of a system legislated by the mass of the Convention and applied by a multitude of officials. In condemning the Terror, moderate Thermidorians could not sustain any distinction among its victims between the innocent or misguided and the real enemies of the Revolution. One could not release some of those detained under the Law of Suspects and not others; one could not relax emigration laws for the ambiguously designated cultivators and not expect determined royalists to return under this pretext. There was no orderly retreat possible from the Terror.

F.-A. Aulard, *Paris pendant la Réaction thermidorienne et sous le Directoire* (Paris, 1898-1902); R. Cobb, *The Police and the People* (Oxford, 1970); R. Fuoc, *La réaction thermidorienne à Lyon* (Lyon, 1957); F. Gendron, *La jeunesse dorée* (Quebec, 1979); G. Lefebvre, *Les Thermidoriens* (Paris, 1937); A. Mathiez, *La réaction thermidorienne* (Paris, 1929); K. D. Tønnesson, *La défaite des sans-culottes* (Oslo, Paris, 1959).

C. Lucas

Related entries: CARRIER; *CHOUANNERIE;* COMPANIES OF JESUS; CONSTITUTION OF 1795; *JEUNESSE DOREE*; LAW OF THE MAXIMUM; LAW OF 22 PRAIRIAL; 9 THERMIDOR YEAR II; REVOLUTIONARY TRIBUNAL; TALLIEN; TERROR, THE.

THERMIDOR YEAR II, 9TH OF.   See 9 THERMIDOR YEAR II.

13 VENDEMIAIRE YEAR IV, unsuccessful right-wing insurrection (5 October 1795) that ended counterrevolutionary hopes of preventing the former members of the Convention from keeping control of the Directorial regime about to be installed and thereby ensured the continuation of the policies laid down by the Thermidorians. The movement that led to the Vendémiaire insurrection grew out of a reaction against the Convention's decrees of 5 and 13 Fructidor Year III, which required voters to choose two-thirds of the deputies to the new legislative councils, set up by the Constitution of 1795, from among the members of the expiring Convention. The Convention, which had just approved the socially conservative Directorial constitution with strong support from the moderate Right, justified this measure on the grounds that the National Assembly's self-denying ordinance in 1791 had undermined the first Revolutionary constitution, and it passed the Fructidor decrees almost unanimously. Many of the Thermidorian Convention's political allies on the Right had supported the new constitution in hope of taking control of the government through elections. The Fructidor decrees frustrated this plan, but they also provided an unexpected opportunity to accuse the Convention of violating the principle of popular sovereignty on which its legitimacy was based.

The Paris section assemblies, dominated by conservative forces since the purge of *sans-culotte* terrorists after the *journée* of 1 Prairial Year III, provided a base for organized resistance to the Convention. The most active sections were the bourgeois strongholds in the western part of Paris, especially the Lepelletier section around the Bourse, and the politically volatile central sections formerly dominated by the Cordeliers club, but the movement eventually won support from all but one of the forty-eight sections. The movement's leaders, who were not united in outlook, were little-known figures, most of whom had been active in political agitation since Thermidor. A number had been in the right-wing *jeunesse dorée*, and many of them also wrote for such popular counterrevolutionary newspapers as the *Gazette française* and the *Messager du soir*. The official agents of the Pretender did not help organize the movement, which took them by surprise, and distrusted its leaders as constitutional monarchists.

The Paris sections and the right-wing press urged voters to reject the Fructidor decrees, which had been submitted to a plebiscite along with the new constitution, and tried to gain support for the Lepelletier section's *acte de garantie*, a resolution committing the sections to come to each other's aid in case of an attack by the central government. The newspapers tried to spread the movement outside of Paris. Well informed about the sections' campaign through the press and its police agents, the Convention nonetheless did little to control it. On 1 Vendémiaire Year IV, it announced the voters' acceptance of the decrees, a result achieved largely by discarding the Paris sections' votes against them on the grounds that they had reported unanimous ballots without specifying the number of voters. The sections responded two days later with a protest accusing the

Convention of planning to use force to implement its unconstitutional measures. In fact, the Convention had only 4,000 troops at hand and was ill prepared for a coup. For ten days, a war of words continued, as the more hot-headed section agitators tried to win support for a movement against the Convention while moderate deputies tried to find a compromise to defuse the situation.

News of the repression of an anti-Convention movement in Dreux on 11 Vendémiaire Year IV provided the final spark for the insurrection, but when only fifteen sections sent delegates to a city-wide assembly at the Odéon theater that day, it became clear that many of them would not support an active attack on the Convention. The assembly broke up without calling for an insurrection, and the initiative passed to the individual sections, some of which proclaimed themselves in revolt the next day. The Convention, meanwhile, voted on 11 Vendémiaire to ban any unauthorized assembly of section delegates and appointed a five-man commission led by P. Barras to organize its defense. The commission ordered the arming of 1,500 *sans-culotte* activists imprisoned since Prairial, a measure that further alarmed moderates in the sections. Among the republican generals who volunteered to help in the defense was N. Bonaparte, although contrary to his and Barras' later claims, he was neither commander nor official second in command during the fighting.

On the evening of 12 Vendémiaire, the Convention sent its military commander, General J.-F. Menou, and his troops to the insurrectionary stronghold in the Lepelletier section with orders to disperse the rebellious National Guards. Menou, a moderate, settled for an unfulfilled promise that the section forces would disperse peacefully and returned to the Tuileries.

The Convention dismissed Menou, but it was too late to forestall the sections' attack. The rebellious sections' National Guards converged on the Tuileries during the day of 13 Vendémiaire; they numbered 25,000 against the 6,000 defenders, but many of the rebels were unprepared for a real battle. It is not clear which side started firing around 4:30 P.M., but the Convention's defenders, armed with cannon, successfully beat off the uncoordinated attacks, first from the rue Saint-Honoré and then from the Left Bank, and the last section strongholds were occupied by the following morning. Despite later legend, Bonaparte did not easily disperse the attackers with a "whiff of grapeshot." The total number of casualties was never officially reported but probably amounted to several hundred on both sides. Outside of Paris, no uprisings occurred.

The Convention exploited its victory with moderation. On 15 Vendémiaire, three military courts were set up to try the rebels, but the city barriers had been left open and most of the section leaders escaped. The courts passed numerous death sentences in absentia but carried out only two executions. The right-wing newspapers, temporarily suppressed after the rising, soon reappeared, and the four Convention deputies ordered arrested for supporting the movement, J.-S.-F. Rovère, J.-B.-M. Saladin, F. Aubry, and J.-B.-C. Lomont, were all allowed eventually to take their seats in the new legislative councils. The Paris section assemblies were abolished and their National Guard units dissolved.

The Convention's moderate response to the Vendémiaire movement contrasted sharply with its repression of the *sans-culotte* insurrections of Germinal and Prairial. It reflected a desire to avoid alienating the bourgeois voters who were supposed to provide the new regime's social base. But the defeat of the Vendémiaire movement did have important consequences. It was the last Parisian street insurrection until July 1830 and thus marked the end of direct popular involvement in the Revolution. The Convention's successful use of the army to put down a citizen's movement was the first intervention of the military in a domestic political dispute since 1789 and cemented the alliance between the troops and the republican politicians in the face of civilian disenchantment with the regime. Finally, Bonaparte's role in defending the Convention brought him to prominence. He was subsequently appointed to command the Army of the Interior and then, in early 1796, the Army of Italy.

W. R. Fryer, *Republic or Restoration in France? 1794-1797* (Manchester, 1965); C. Lacretelle, *Dix années d'épreuves pendant la Révolution* (Paris, 1842); H. Mitchell, *The Underground War against Revolutionary France* (Oxford, 1965); J. Popkin, *The Right-Wing Press in France, 1792-1800* (Chapel Hill, 1980); H. Zivy, *Le 13 vendémiaire IV* (Paris, 1898).

J. Popkin

Related entries: BARRAS; CONSTITUTION OF 1795; *JEUNESSE DOREE*; MENOU; SECTIONS; SELF-DENYING ORDINANCE; TWO-THIRDS DECREE.

THIRTY, COMMITTEE OF. See COMMITTEE OF THIRTY.

THIRY, PAUL-HENRI, BARON D'HOLBACH (1723-89), contributor to and supporter of Diderot's *Encyclopedia*; materialist and atheist. See ATHEISM.

THURIOT DE LA ROSIERE, JACQUES-ALEXIS (1753-1829), lawyer and Revolutionary. Advocate at Reims during the *ancien régime*'s last years, Thuriot commenced his Revolutionary career as an elector of the Parisian municipality in 1789. The following year he became a judge on the new tribunal of the Sézanne district. Thuriot was later elected by his department (the Marne) to the Legislative Assembly. As one of that body's most radical members, he championed harsh measures against *émigrés* and nonjuring clergy, urged prosecution of the war against counterrevolutionary Europe, and justified the Parisian insurrection of 10 August 1792 that toppled the monarchy. Elected by his department to the National Convention, Thuriot became associated in that assemblage with G.-J. Danton and the Mountain. He voted for Louis XVI's execution, denounced General C. Dumouriez and his Girondist allies, served as president of the Convention and (from April to September 1793) as a member of the Dantonist Committee of Public Safety, and embraced the dechristianization campaign. Although his ties with Danton's faction cost him political influence during the Terror, he helped engineer M. Robespierre's downfall in Thermidor (1794).

Thuriot had a vicissitudinous political and judicial career under the Thermidorian Convention, Directory, and Napoleon. Forced out of France at Louis XVIII's accession, Thuriot lived in Liège (Belgium) until his death.

G. de Froidcourt, "Les conventionnels régicides réfugiés à Liège sous la Restauration: Thuriot de la Rosière et ses amis," *Bull. de la Soc. roy. de Vieux Liège* 5 (1956); J. Robinet, *Dictionnaire historique et biographique de la Révolution et de l'Empire 1789-1815* (Paris, 1899).

B. Stone

Related entries: DANTON; DECHRISTIANIZATION; DUMOURIEZ; GI-RONDINS; MONTAGNARDS.

TITHE, fraction of harvests, generally less than one-tenth, paid to the church for the support of the clergy, the maintenance of divine worship, and the relief of the poor. Obligatory since Carolingian times, the tithe was collected in kind, before any other levies and from all producers (including nobles, Protestants, and the poor), on grain, wine, and livestock, as well as on other products (exempt were woods, mines, meadows, hunting, fishing, enclosed plots) and at rates that varied considerably according to local custom. In most parishes, the revenues were assigned not to the priests but to bishops, canons, religious orders, and even laymen (so-called enfeoffed tithes), who commonly farmed out the collection of the tithe and neglected the services it was intended to fund.

The complicated codes and administrative abuses resulted in widespread resistance and litigation in the last decades of the *ancien régime*. The clergy claimed that the prerogative of collecting the tithe derived from divine right and protested the extension of secular jurisdiction in such matters. The parlements frequently ruled against the clergy in cases brought by rural communities, while the crown made efforts to exempt newly cultivated lands from the levy in order to encourage agricultural productivity. The royal Commission on the Administration of Agriculture, which numbered C.-G. Vergennes, A. Lavoisier, and P.-S. Dupont de Nemours among its members, recommended major overhauling of the tithe on the eve of the Revolution.

The *cahiers de doléances* abounded in complaints about the burden and inequity of the tithe. Some demanded its suppression, but most called for reversion of the revenues to the parish clergy. In abolishing feudalism on the night of 4 August 1789, the National Assembly envisioned redemption of the tithe. After the debates of the following week, which included noteworthy statements by both E.-J. Sieyès and H.-G. R. Mirabeau on the question of property rights involved, the Assembly suppressed the tithe on 11 August but sanctioned its continued collection pending other provision for the support of the clergy (enfeoffed tithes, along with certain seigneurial rights, were not abolished outright until 1793). Parish priests naturally favored the reforms, but other ecclesiastical representatives carried on opposition into the spring of 1790. In April the Assembly adopted the report of its Committee on the Tithe appointed to implement the August decree. It declared the tithe abolished as of 1 January 1791 and settled the issue of clerical salaries several months later in the Civil Constitution of the Clergy.

P. Gagnol, *La dîme ecclésiastique en France* (Paris, 1911); H. Marion, *La dîme ecclésiastique en France et sa suppression au XVIIIe siècle: étude d'histoire du droit* (Bordeaux, 1912); J. Rives, *Dîme et société dans l'archevêché d'Auch au XVIIIe siècle* (Paris, 1976).

J. Merrick

Related entries: CIVIL CONSTITUTION OF THE CLERGY; 4 AUGUST 1789.

TOCQUEVILLE, ALEXIS DE (1805-59), historian and political theorist. One of France's greatest social critics, Tocqueville wrote what is arguably the most penetrating analysis of the background to the French Revolution produced in the nineteenth century: *L'Ancien Régime et la Révolution française*. Son of Count Hervé de Tocqueville, a prefect of Versailles under the Bourbon Restoration and himself a historian of eighteenth-century France, Alexis de Tocqueville received a legal education and became a judge in 1827. Although he was originally a supporter of the Bourbon regime, Tocqueville agreed to swear a loyalty oath to Louis-Philippe after the July Revolution in the belief that the new monarchy was the only practical alternative to a republic or outright anarchy.

In 1831 Tocqueville received along with his friend, G. de Beaumont, a government commission to study prison management in the United States, where he lived for two years. His observations on the development of democratic institutions in the United States provided the material for the first of his two major works, *La démocratie en Amérique* (volume 1 published in 1835, volume 2 in 1840), which was an instant success and remains a classic account of the paradoxes and implications of democratic society.

His publication in 1836 of an article on the social and political conditions in France before and after the French Revolution demonstrated a growing concern for the history of his own country. In 1839 Tocqueville was elected to the Chamber of Deputies and, two years later, to the Académie française, where his inaugural address paid particular attention to N. Bonaparte. The Revolution of 1848 and its aftermath proved decisive in his political and intellectual career. Nearly killed during the street fighting of the June days, Tocqueville retained some democratic sentiments and disapproved of Louis-Napoleon's election to the presidency late in 1848. Nevertheless, he accepted the portfolio of foreign affairs in the O. Barrot ministry, only to be dismissed with the Barrot government five months after taking office. Disappointed, Tocqueville bemoaned the popular caesarism he perceived sweeping over the Second Republic and supported a parliamentary protest against Napoleon's coup in December 1851. Political disappointments combined with increasing illness to sap his strength. Tocqueville retired gradually from public life, and devoted the major part of his energies to historical research on the French Revolution in an attempt to solve the political mystery behind France's apparent incapacity to reconcile freedom and order.

Although Tocqueville's interest in the French Revolution was of long standing by the time that he began to conceive of a major work on the French Revolution (1850-51), it took several years before he could settle on a general outline and plan of research. Originally envisioned as a study of the first empire, the work gradually grew in scope following completion of two chapters on the rise of Bonaparte. By 1853 Tocqueville's scholarly attention was increasingly drawn to the background of the French Revolution; what was initially supposed to be two chapters on the Old Regime eventually became an entire volume, indeed, the only completed volume of what was projected to be a multivolumed history of the whole Revolution. Moving from the Bibliothèque nationale to the provincial archives, Tocqueville made especially intensive use of those of Indre-et-Loire in Tours, where he received indispensable assistance from the archivist C. de Grandmaison. Tocqueville also consulted German archives in Bonn, the British Museum, and the Archives nationales, and he interviewed survivors of the Revolutionary era. In 1856 Tocqueville published the first volume of his study, *L'Ancien Régime et la Révolution française*; he subsequently set to work on a second volume, of which he completed only sketches by his death in 1859.

The single published volume of Tocqueville's study is an extraordinarily subtle work with many levels. The author stated from the outset that his purpose was not to write a history of the French Revolution in the traditional sense of an *histoire événementielle* but rather an explanation of how France, in attempting to break with the despotic practices of the Old Regime, was led in the end to accept even more despotic government. Tocqueville put forward this explanation in three parts, each of which had themes of its own but at the same time foreshadowed or recapitulated themes of the other parts. The result was a sinuous line of argument not easily followed.

Part 1 set up the problem of the French Revolution in its historical context. Tocqueville argued that the Revolution, though antireligious in sentiment, was a conflict not primarily over religion but over society and the state. The goal of the Revolutionaries, he contended, was the end of the feudal system in France—the abolition of hereditary inequalities.

In part 2 Tocqueville attempted to explain the decline of feudal institutions through an examination of the monarchy. Here his central point was that the Revolution, far from changing the direction of history, maintained it; in centralizing national power at the expense of traditional and local institutions, the Revolutionaries achieved what the monarchy had been trying to achieve all along. The gradual decline of local and aristocratic corporate bodies, Tocqueville argued, rendered the entire social structure obsolete. Whereas the English nobility had modernized itself and continued to perform important functions within society, the French nobility, shorn of any real political role, fought merely to retain social privileges, whose justification became thinner and thinner. With the nobility, like the other social classes, denied any real access to political power, there developed a cultural homogenization process, which made the possession of privilege seem unrelated to the exercise of political responsibilities and thereby made it all the more resented. The stage was set for a major social struggle.

In part 3, Tocqueville discussed the movements for reform, which, he believed, contributed to the Revolutionary crisis. The monarchy, according to Tocqueville, by initiating political and economic reforms increased popular irritation with remaining abuses to such an extent that reform could not possibly keep pace with the soaring expectations of the people. The *philosophes*, Tocqueville argued, facilitated the outbreak of revolution by indoctrinating the nation in abstract principles of politics derived from little practical experience; their work weakened the power of traditional institutions to restrain social action, thereby increasing the possibility of revolution. But just because the *philosophes*, like the nation generally, had had no experience with governance, their ideology did not, once the Revolution began, promote the institutionalization of freedom that it seemed to promise. Knowing no administration other than that of an authoritarian monarchy, the French Revolutionaries once in power wound up recreating the same kind of bureaucracy they had originally wanted to abolish, and in the process they abandoned the cause of freedom. The failure of the Revolution to establish liberal institutions, in sum, did not, according to Tocqueville, derive from its being blown off course. The failure was already implicit in the structure of the state and society under the Old Regime, a structure that, despite the genuine desire of the Revolutionaries for liberty and innovation, was to reestablish itself basically unchanged under *le drapeau tricolore*. It was the painful lesson of Tocqueville's work that after three revolutions France had still not outlived its pre-Revolutionary past.

E. T. Gargan, *De Tocqueville* (London, 1965); R. Herr, *Tocqueville and the Old Regime* (Princeton, 1962); G. Lefebvre, "A propos de Tocqueville," *Ann. hist. de la Révo. francaise* 28 (1955); J. Lively, *The Social and Political Thought of Alexis de Tocqueville* (Oxford, 1962); M. Zetterbaum, *Tocqueville and the Problem of Democracy* (Stanford, 1967).

T. E. Kaiser

Related entries: AULARD; JAURES; MATHIEZ.

TONE, THEOBALD WOLFE (1763-98), Irish revolutionary. Born in Dublin on 20 June 1763 to an Anglo-Irish Protestant family, Tone was educated at Trinity College, Dublin, and the Middle Temple, London. He was called to the Irish bar in 1789 but was bored by the legal profession and soon turned to politics. Spurred by the democratic principles of the French Revolution, he devoted himself to winning parliamentary reform and civil rights for Catholics. The Society of United Irishmen, which he founded in 1791, aimed at substituting an Irish identity for denominational labels. Tone's activities as secretary of the Catholic Committee were instrumental in gaining the Catholic Relief Act of 1793, but its limited scope and the impossibility of making headway against a reactionary parliament disgusted him with constitutional methods. Convinced that the British connection was the source of political evil, he and his more militant colleagues espoused separatist revolution. Tone made contact with French agents in 1794, urging an invasion of Ireland, but their negotiations were discovered by the authorities. Tone was allowed to avoid arrest by going to America.

Tone spent the latter half of 1795 in the United States, settling his family in Philadelphia and obtaining letters of introduction from French diplomats. By February 1796 he was in Paris, where he won over the foreign minister, C. Delacroix, to the cause of Irish revolution. General L. Hoche was assigned to command an invasion of Ireland, with Tone as adjutant general on his staff. A force of some 15,000 men and more than 40 ships sailed from Brest in December 1796, but half of the fleet was scattered by storms before reaching the Irish coast. Tone, in sight of his homeland, was overruled by the senior officer present, who refused to disembark the remaining troops. A new expedition was planned for 1797 but also came to nothing due to the destruction of the Batavian fleet and the death of Hoche.

Despite Tone's urging to await French support, the forces of rebellion in Ireland could no longer be restrained, and insurrection broke out in May 1798. It was not until late summer that several small French expeditions could be sent to different parts of Ireland, and they were too little and too late to prevent the defeat of the rebellion. Tone's contingent was intercepted by a British squadron on 12 October, and after a fierce naval battle, the leader was captured. Still in his French uniform, Tone was tried by court-martial in his native city and found guilty of treason. Denied a soldier's death before a firing squad, he escaped the ignominy of the gallows by slashing his throat in his cell. After lingering for a week, he died on 19 November 1798.

Tone's grave, in the family plot at Bodenstown, County Kildare, is the site of an annual pilgrimage by those who revere him as the father of the revolutionary nationalism that gave modern Ireland its independence after more than a century of struggle.

F. MacDermot, *Theobald Wolfe Tone*, rev. ed. (Tralee, 1963); R. B. O'Brien, ed., *The Autobiography of Theobald Wolfe Tone*, 2 vols. (London, 1893).

W. D. Griffin

Related entries: HOCHE; IRELAND.

TOULON, a city of more than 20,000 inhabitants, which was the headquarters of the French Mediterranean fleet in 1789. The Revolution commenced here, as at nearby Marseille, with a popular riot on 23 March 1789. Local authorities were constrained to lower bread prices and permit the formation of a citizen guard. In August a permanent council of forty-eight members was created, which administered the city until a new municipal government was installed on 28 February 1790. The following September, the National Assembly designated Toulon to be the capital of the Var department and the chief place of a district.

Tension between aristocratic naval officers and citizens ran high in 1789-90. A riot of 1 December 1789, culminated in the arrest of the fleet commander, C.-H. d'Albert de Rions. Serious disturbances also flared up in May 1790 when the next commandant, J.-B. de Glandeves, sought to lay off workers at the naval arsenal. The years 1791-92 were marred by factional strife between blocs of Jacobins and royalists. The former, whose meeting place was the club Saint-Jean, dominated the municipal government and a part of the National Guard. The latter, who gathered at the club Saint-Pierre, enjoyed the support of district and departmental administrators and the naval general staff. In the summer of 1792 the scales tilted in favor of the Jacobins. Between 28 and 30 July and on 10 September, mobs massacred seventeen people, including four departmental administrators and the commandant, J. Flotte d'Argenson.

Jacobin rule, which became increasingly arbitrary in 1793, was brought to an end on 12 July by a rebellion in the eight sections (city wards). Sectionalism (or federalism) at Toulon was inspired by analogous movements at Marseille, Aix, and Draguignan. The *sectionnaires* closed the club Saint-Jean, hanged twenty-four Jacobins, arrested two representatives from the National Convention, and eventually proclaimed their allegiance to Louis XVII. Threatened by republican armies approaching from the west and northeast, the rebels also surrendered the city to the English on 27-28 August, 1793.

A three-month siege followed. N. Bonaparte, then twenty-four years old, commanded the artillery of republican forces and helped to plan a decisive assault on the heights of Le Caire (14 December). The English, who had been joined by contingents of Spanish, Neapolitans, and Piedmontese, found their position untenable and decided to evacuate (19 December). Those compromised in the rebellion and French royalists who had taken refuge in Toulon were panic stricken and attempted to escape by sea; 7,000 to 14,000 made good their exodus, but scores were trampled to death or drowned when overloaded boats capsized.

A reign of terror began after the entry of republican troops. Toulon's name was changed to Port-la-Montagne. Eight hundred federalists who had stayed behind were shot without trial (20-23 December). A Revolutionary commission pronounced more than 300 death sentences (3 January-17 April, 1794). And additional federalists were sent to Grasse or Marseille for trial.

After the fall of M. Robespierre (July 1794), the moderate representatives on mission, P.-J.-B. Auguis, J.-J. Serres, P. Cadroy, J. Espert, and J.-C.-L. Mariette, freed political prisoners, suppressed the surveillance committee, and removed Jacobin judges and administrators from office. The return of *émigrés* and Jacobin fears of a counterterror led to bloody confrontations in 1795. In May, arsenal workers seized arms from military storehouses and forcibly released Jacobins being held prisoner. Order was restored by the representative on mission, A.-M. Chiappe, and a military court sentenced fifty-two Jacobins to death.

The government of the Directory never received the loyalty of the city's right-wing and left-wing extremists. Napoleon represented order, and the bulk of the population welcomed his accession to power in 1799.

P. Cottin, *Toulon et les Anglais en 1793* (Paris, 1898); D.-M.-J. Henry, *Histoire de Toulon depuis 1789 jusqu'au Consulat* (Toulon, 1855); E. Poupé, *Le département du Var, 1790-an VIII* (Cannes, 1933).

M. J. Kennedy

Related entries: FEDERALISM; LOUIS XVII; MARSEILLE.

TOULOUSE, the major city in southwestern France and one of the few French cities dominated by Jacobins during the Directory regime. With a population of just over 50,000, the capital of Languedoc was a classic Old Regime city; the parlement and the church dominated a very traditional local elite. The city was administered by eight *capitouls*, whose offices conferred noble status. Noble estates of the region produced grain for much of the Midi, and aristocratic social and political life in town completely overshadowed a relatively feeble bourgeoisie. Commercial and manufacturing interests were minor compared to their counterparts in Bordeaux, Nantes, Marseille, or even nearby Montpellier. In the 1760s, moreover, the notorious Calas affair had made Toulouse a byword for superstition, fanaticism, and barbarity.

Despite this traditionalism, or perhaps because of it, Toulouse did not experience violent change in the first years of the Revolution. The local parlement's resistance to the new regime was easily broken, and the nonjurors among the clergy were replaced. Moderate businessmen and lawyers gained control of the new Revolutionary administration, and they presided over the comparatively peaceful dismantling of the Old Regime. In 1793 many officials of Toulouse declared sympathy with the growing federalist movement, but they stopped short of open adherence. With the help of visiting representatives on mission, local Jacobins purged the city and sectional administrations; six federalist leaders were executed. The quick collapse of federalism spared Toulouse the violent repression experienced in cities such as Lyon and Marseille.

The Terror too was comparatively mild in Toulouse, and the course of repression was more influenced by the military situation on the Spanish front than by events in Paris. A local *armée révolutionnaire* was organized in Toulouse, but its effects were felt in the surrounding countryside rather than in the city itself. In all, about thirty suspects were sent to the guillotine by the Revolutionary Tribunal of the Haute-Garonne, and fifty-four leading *parlementaires* were executed in Paris. The reaction following the Terror was similarly restrained; many terrorists were arrested, but broken windows and fisticuffs rather than lynchings and gang murders characterized the White Terror in Toulouse.

Under the Directory regime, Toulousain politics continued to go against the national grain. While the other major southern cities had been torn by bloody struggles between Jacobins and federalists or royalists, Toulouse had remained relatively calm. Then when most of the big cities settled into indifference or royalist intrigue, Toulouse became a stronghold of Jacobinism. Between 1795 and 1799 a coalition of merchants, shopkeepers, and artisans ruled the city, and many of them had been members of the Jacobin club. When royalists won the national elections of 1797, Jacobins in Toulouse maintained their control and did well even in the departmental elections. In August 1799 the Jacobins organized the defeat of a royalist force of 16,000 men who had marched on the city. With the help of National Guardsmen from neighboring departments, they pushed the royalists back to the Spanish frontier. Royalism did not become an important force again until 1815. In another twist of curious Toulousain fate, the city then became a center of ultraroyalism for many years.

L. Berlanstein, *The Barristers of Toulouse in the Eighteenth Century (1740-1793)* (Baltimore, 1975); R. Forster, *The Nobility of Toulouse in the Eighteenth Century: A Social and Economic Study* (Baltimore, 1960); M. Lyons, *Revolution in Toulouse: An Essay on Provincial Terrorism* (Berne, 1978); M. Taillefer, "La Franc-maçonnerie toulousaine et la Révolution francaise," *Ann. hist. de la Révo. française* 52 (1980).

L. A. Hunt

Related entries: ARMEES REVOLUTIONNAIRES; FEDERALISM; WHITE TERROR.

TOURCOING, BATTLE OF. See BATTLE OF TOURCOING.

TOUSSAINT-L'OUVERTURE, FRANCOIS-DOMINIQUE (1743-1803), revolutionary in Saint-Domingue. Toussaint was born on the Bréda plantation, not more than half an hour's ride from the flourishing port city of Cap Français (now Cap-Haïtien), capital of the French colony of Saint-Domingue (now Haiti), probably in May 1743. For almost fifty years he would be called Toussaint Bréda, before assuming the surname of L'Ouverture, perhaps as a symbol of his efforts to be the "opener" (*l'ouverture*) of the door to freedom for his fellow slaves. The Bréda estate, where he spent his early years, was owned by the comte de Noé, reputed to treat his slaves with relative compassion and kindness.

Toussaint, the son of Gaou Guinou, an educated slave who had converted to Christianity, acquired a profound commitment to Catholicism, an opposition to voodoo, and some knowledge of French, though he wrote and spoke it with difficulty, preferring to use the Creole patois and African tribal language. Known to his childhood friends as *fatras-baton* ("skinny stick") because he was so thin, he later filled out, and by the time he was a teenager had the reputation of being powerful, athletic, and intelligent. Winning the favor of the plantation manager, Bayou de Libertas, who promoted Toussaint to the position of coachman, he worked his way up in time to steward, a position of great dignity and honor for a slave, which gave him considerable prestige. In 1777 he was legally freed and permitted to marry Suzanne, who bore him two sons, Isaac and Placide.

During the early months of the French Revolution, Toussaint revealed little interest in the debate about slavery. This perhaps leads one to question the popular legend that as a young man Toussaint read the abbé Raynal's *Histoire philosophique des deux Indes* and believed himself destined to lead the black slaves to freedom. He did not support V. Ogé, a mulatto member of the Amis des Noirs, who in March 1790 was tortured to death when he attempted to stir up an uprising of free blacks. Toussaint also remained uncommitted during the early days of the August 1791 slave revolt in the north province, led by Boukman, a black slave from Jamaica. Later, however, he joined the black forces, though in a limited role, caring for the wounded. It did not take Toussaint long to realize that there was an opportunity to replace the black leaders, who were inept, and to collect an army of his own, which he trained for guerrilla warfare and led in raids along the northern plain.

When, in 1793, the French Republic and Spain went to war, Toussaint and other black leaders joined the Spanish of Santo Domingo, the eastern two-thirds of Hispaniola. Commissioned as a general, knighted in the Order of Isabella, Toussaint demonstrated creative military skills, attracted a force of some 4,000 irregular troops, including two future monarchs of Haiti, J.-J. Dessalines and H. Christophe. Toussaint won several battles in the north, which, combined with some successes in the south of the *gens de couleur*, led by A. Rigaud, and the British occupation of the coasts, brought the French close to surrender. But in May 1794, alarmed by the progress of the British, who Toussaint believed had entered the war in part to restore slavery, and moved as well by personal ambition, he deserted with his troops from the Spanish army, murdered the Spanish officers who opposed his defection, and offered his services to the shattered and discredited army of republican France. The French National Convention, he noted after he had switched sides, had on 4 February 1794 freed all slaves, while Britain and Spain had refused. His switch was decisive, and the Spanish armies soon were driven across the border into Santo Domingo. A year later, on 22 July 1795, Spain signed the Treaty of Basel with France, agreeing not only to withdraw from the War of the First Coalition but to cede Santo Domingo to France, which, however, made no effort at occupation. England, meanwhile, confronted with a slave rebellion of its own in Jamaica, began to find that the invasion of Saint-Domingue was not cost-effective, though it vainly continued to struggle for two more years, withdrawing finally in 1798, when T. Maitland, the English commanding officer, agreed to withdraw his depleted forces in return for an amnesty for his partisans and a commercial treaty.

By 1798, the fame of Toussaint was widespread in the West Indies. Idolized by blacks, respected by whites, he worked hard to reduce racial tensions. Blacks, he felt, had to learn from whites and mulattoes. *Emigré* planters he encouraged to return—in defiance of French Revolutionary legislation—and the economy, disrupted by revolution and war, was restored and stabilized; former slaves were forced to return to work on the plantations, including several owned by Toussaint and other revolutionary leaders, though the whip was abolished.

Toussaint's efforts at gaining political power, however, were tragic. He worked well with E. Laveaux, the governor of Saint-Domingue at the time of the defeat of the Spanish. But he eased out Laveaux in 1796. He had more difficulty working with L.-F. Sonthonax, the French commissioner appointed by the Terror government, who wished to renew racial tensions, urging blacks to rise again and exterminate whites. Sonthonax was dangerous for he rivaled Toussaint for popular support. Blacks regarded him as their white emancipator and friend, *notre ami Sonthonax*. But Toussaint, threatening the capital city with his loyal troops, maneuvered him out in 1797. The Directory sent a replacement, G. Hédouville, who arrived in Le Cap in May 1798. Hédouville attempted to pit Rigaud, a mulatto leader who all but ruled a semi-independent state in the south and west and was himself a fierce fighter, against Toussaint. However, Toussaint turned on Rigaud, defeated him, and sacked his headquarters at Les Cayes. There followed a systematic roundup, torture, and murder of some 10,000 mulattoes, men, women, and children that was directed by Toussaint and his agent, Dessalines. The purge was so brutal that reconciliation with the mulattoes was impossible. As if to complete the tragedy, torrential rain fell through much of the autumn of 1800, breaking the irrigation dams of the Artibonite and Cul-de-Sac, weakened by ten years of neglect. Much of the prosperity of the west and south depended on these irrigation works, which were never repaired, leaving the area eroded wilderness. Meanwhile, Hédouville fled and was replaced by P. Roume, who deferred to Toussaint. Hence, by 1800 Toussaint was politically supreme within the colony, having been able to secure either the compliance or the removal of all officials sent to Saint-Domingue from France. But his real power was military and personal.

With Saint-Domingue in his control, Toussaint turned to Santo Domingo, where slavery persisted, as it did on the British West Indies islands. In January 1801, ignoring the orders of N. Bonaparte, who by now had become first consul, Toussaint overran Santo Domingo. In command of the entire island, he drew up a constitution that made him governor-general for life with near absolute powers, including the right to name his successor. Catholicism was made the state religion, and many Revolutionary principles received at least perfunctory notice. Some clauses had a distinct modern ring, such as the one in which Saint-Domingue was held to be "une seule colonie qui fait partie de l'Empire français, mais qui est soumise à des lois particulières," which sounds much like C. de Gaulle's plans for Algeria prior to his need to acknowledge its independence. There was no provision for a French official, however, as Toussaint insisted that he was French and loyal to Bonaparte.

But there was not enough room in the French Empire for two such powerful men as Napoleon and Toussaint. That political fact combined with Napoleon's irritation at the "pretensions of gilded Africans," which perhaps betrayed Napoleon's antiblack prejudices, his political plans for alliance with Spain, threatened by Toussaint's invasion of Santo Domingo, his feeling that Toussaint was an obstacle to the restoration of Saint-Domingue as a profitable colony, and his intent to restore slavery in Saint-Domingue and Guadeloupe led Bonaparte to plan the military reconquest of the island.

In January 1802, a French invasion force under General C.-V.-E. Leclerc began a systematic campaign to remove Toussaint from power. Many of Toussaint's supporters—Dessalines, Christophe, J. Maurepas, and others—entered French service, bringing their bands of followers. Toussaint was taken by deception and shipped to France, where he was confined at Fort de Joux in the French Alps. It was there that he died on 7 April 1803.

S. Alexis, *Toussaint Louverture, libérateur d'Haiti* (Paris, 1949); C. L. R. James, *The Black Jacobins: Toussaint L'Ouverture and the San Domingo Revolution*, 2d ed. (New York, 1963); R. Korngold, *Citizen Toussaint* (New York, 1965).

                                                                                                                                L. Apt

Related entries: SAINT-DOMINGUE; SOCIETE DES AMIS DES NOIRS; TREATY OF BASEL.

TRACY-DESTUTT, ANTOINE-LOUIS-CLAUDE, COMTE DE (1754-1836), politician and philosopher. Although largely forgotten today outside a limited circle of specialists, Tracy-Destutt (or Destutt de Tracy) was in his own day internationally renowned as a *philosophe* and in particular as having coined the term *ideology* (*idéologie*) and as having founded the school of ideologists during the 1790s.

During a lifetime spanning an epoch of political and social upheaval, Tracy-Destutt combined a career of public service with a career of letters. Born into the high nobility, he served as a prominent spokesman of his class in the Estates General and Constituent Assembly, served in the army under the marquis de Lafayette in 1792, was incarcerated during the Terror, and was released after Thermidor (1794). Early in 1796 he was elected as *philosophe* to the prestigious Institut national. At the time of N. Bonaparte's 1799 coup d'état, Tracy-Destutt was involved in the Directory's attempt to establish a national system of public education. Tracy-Destutt abetted the opposition to Napoleon as senator under the Consulate and Empire and proposed the emperor's deposition in 1814. Later, he figured in the liberal opposition to Louis XVIII and Charles X, visited the barricades of the revolutionaries of 1830, and lived long enough into the new Orléanist regime to become disillusioned by its factionalism and narrow political base.

Tracy-Destutt, however, found his true vocation in philosophy rather than in politics. As early as 1792, he began to read deeply in the epistemological and scientific works of the Enlightenment. Like E.-B. Condillac, J.-O. de La Mettrie, C.-A. Helvétius, and the other *philosophes* in the Lockean tradition, Tracy-Destutt became convinced that man's certain knowledge was limited to what he learned (or thought he could learn) from his physical environment through his senses. For Tracy-Destutt, as for most other *philosophes*, this meant that man, in attempting to secure a sure foundation for the moral and political sciences and indeed for all knowledge and activities must throw off the prejudices bequeathed by the metaphysics or false sciences of the past and accept as truth only that which was empirically demonstrable. Tracy-Destutt became obsessed with the need for a science of ideas, a science of environmental factors and of human perceptions of, and reactions to, such factors. He envisioned such a new science as being both an analytical method and a body of derived and reasonably certain knowledge; moreover, he insisted from the beginning that this derivative knowledge be used in the political and social realms to better human life. Soon after Tracy-Destutt was elected to the Section of the Analysis of Sensations and Ideas in the Class of Moral and Political Sciences at the Institut national in 1796, he began using the term *idéologie* (from the Greek for "science of ideas" or "study of perception") to designate his new science. Ideology was to be objective as well as rigorously analytical—objective, that is, in the sense that as the first of all sciences, it would reflect none of its exponents' and practitioners' values and personal interests but would exist purely as a method for gaining knowledge to be used on man's behalf.

Tracy-Destutt, however, was destined to be frustrated in his quest. He lacked the originality of other French philosophers. His ideas languished in the nineteenth century as fundamental thought moved in new directions and achieved new perspectives. Perhaps more important, politicians and thinkers alike came to regard *idéologie* as something very different from what Tracy-Destutt had originally intended. Napoleon and some later statesmen regarded ideology as the subversive speculation of republican politicians rather than as an objective science; philosophers found in ideology some very subjective elements such as its reductionist tendencies, its claim to infallibility, and its messianic message. It only remained for K. Marx to endow the term with what is still its commonly accepted meaning by characterizing ideology as a reflection of historical and socioeconomic processes rather than as an objective science or purely intellectual phenomenon. Nonetheless, however much Tracy-Destutt's reputation may have waned and whatever the transformation of the term he coined, he remains significant in the long history of human endeavor to understand the origins and processes of human thought and behavior.

E. Kennedy, *A Philosophe in the Age of Revolution: Destutt de Tracy and the Origins of "Ideology"* (Philadelphia, 1978); M. Lowery, "Sensationalism in Revolutionary France: The Epistemology of Destutt de Tracy" (Ph.D. dissertation, Duke University 1977); F. Rastier, *Idéologie et théorie des signes: Analyse structurale des éléments d'idéologie d'Antoine-Louis-Claude Destutt de Tracy* (The Hague, 1972).

B. Stone

Related entry: EDUCATION.

TREATY OF BASEL (5 April 1795), first treaty between the Republic and a monarchy, by which Prussia left the First Coalition. During the first years of the Revolutionary wars, Prussia was at best a halfhearted member of the anti-French First Coalition. Berlin agreed to fight only after attaining promises of subsidies and territorial aggrandizement at Polish expense. Moreover, many in Berlin were as hostile to the traditional Hapsburg enemy as they were to Revolutionary France.

After the Valmy campaign, Prussia threatened to leave the war unless Austria allowed it immediate compensation in Poland. The Second Partition of Poland excluded Austria and poisoned relations between Berlin and Vienna. Angered by Prussia's duplicity, Austria began negotiations with Russia for a third partition that would exclude Prussia. Berlin soon became anxious to free its hands in the west in order to concentrate attention and battalions on the Polish question. Moreover, by late 1794 it was obvious that the coalition would not defeat the Republic; in fact, the French had overrun Belgium and most of the Rhineland and were poised to invade Holland.

The French were, however, intent on splitting the coalition by concluding a separate peace with one of its members. They also wanted diplomatic recognition and acceptance of some, if not all, of their conquests. Therefore, France and Prussia opened negotiations at Basel in the winter of 1794 and concluded a treaty in April 1795. By terms of the treaty, France agreed to withdraw its armies from the right bank of the Rhine. France would hold the Rhineland until the conclusion of a general peace, and Prussia agreed to support French claims to the region in return for compensation elsewhere in Germany. Prussia was to remain neutral in the war between France and the coalition. German states north of the Main River were also to adopt a neutral stance, and Prussia was to guarantee their neutrality.

France had thus divided the First Coalition and gained recognition from a great power. Prussia gained a dominant position in northern Germany and was able to attain a portion of Poland in the Third Partition. For the next decade, Prussia enjoyed the advantages of a neutral in the midst of a war-torn continent.

S. S. Biro, *The German Policy of Revolutionary France*, 2 vols. (Cambridge, Mass., 1957); R. H. Lord, *The Second Partition of Poland* (Cambridge, Mass., 1915).

S. T. Ross

Related entries: BATTLE OF VALMY; POLAND.

TREATY OF CAMPOFORMIO (27 October 1797), peace treaty between France and Austria. After the fall of Mantua in early 1797, Napoleon received reinforcements from France and launched an attack against the Austrian crown lands. By the end of March, he had reached Klagenfurt against weakening enemy resistance, and the Austrians sought an armistice. Napoleon was far from his bases, and the satellite governments he had created in Italy were far from secure. He therefore agreed to a suspension of hostilities on 31 March 1797.

On 18 April he signed a preliminary peace with the Hapsburgs at Leoben. The peace was in fact very different from the one desired by the Directory. Paris wanted to secure Belgium and the Rhineland and was willing to trade gains in Italy to secure that end. Napoleon, however, had committed himself to the Italian republicans and was willing to exchange German for Italian conquests. By the terms of the Leoben treaty, Austria ceded Belgium to France and recognized the French regimes in Italy. In return, Napoleon offered the Austrians compensation at Venetian expense, and he occupied Venice in order to facilitate the trade. The treaty was silent concerning the future of the Rhineland. The Directory was unhappy with the treaty but, plagued by a rising tide of royalist sentiment that fed on French war weariness, the government decided that Napoleon's peace was better than no peace at all.

After Leoben, Bonaparte continued to reorganize Italy. He transformed Genoa into a republic and merged two regimes in central Italy into the Cisalpine Republic. He also concluded a final peace with Austria, the Treaty of Campoformio, in October. Austria recognized the Cisalpine Republic and the French annexation of Belgium. Austria also promised to support French claims to the Rhineland at a future conference (in fact never held) that would conclude a peace between France and the Empire. In return, Venice was divided among Austria, the Cisalpine Republic, and France. Austria gained the lion's share, taking the city itself, Dalmatia, Istria, and most of the mainland. The Cisalpine Republic gained a strip of the Venetian mainland, and France received the Ionian Islands. Austria was also promised compensation in Germany for any land relinquished in the Rhineland.

The Directory, having just survived a royalist bid for power with the help of troops from Bonaparte's army, again accepted their general's treaty. The treaty brought momentary peace between France and Austria but was in fact little more than an armed truce. Austria had no intention of accepting all of the French gains and awaited a favorable opportunity to renew hostilities.

G. Ferrero, *The Gamble: Bonaparte in Italy, 1796-1797* (London, 1961); A. Fugier, *La Révolution française et l'Empire napoléonien* (Paris, 1954); A. Heriot, *The French in Italy, 1796-1799* (London, 1957).

S. T. Ross

Related entries: BELGIUM; CISALPINE REPUBLIC; DIRECTORY; PRE-LIMINARIES OF LEOBEN.

TREATY OF THE HAGUE. See BATAVIAN REPUBLIC.

TREILHARD, JEAN-BAPTISTE (1742-1810), lawyer, deputy to the Constituent Assembly, National Convention, and Council of Five Hundred. Treilhard was born in Brives in 1742. He early made a reputation for himself as a lawyer by his pleadings against the Noailles family. On 15 May 1789 he was elected as a deputy from Paris to the Estates General. Named as a member of the Ecclesiastical Committee of the Constituante, Treilhard was involved in, and supported the enactment of, the Civil Constitution of the Clergy. He claimed that clergy could own property only with the state's approval and the state had the right to withdraw its sanction whenever it wished. Treilhard's successful motion of 13 February 1790 withdrew official recognition of existing clerical vows and allowed the clergy to abandon the church without recrimination. His decree differentiated between educational and charitable institutions, which were supposed to continue their functions, and the mendicant orders, which were to be abolished. It also prohibited the taking of religious vows in the future. He served as the president of the Constituent Assembly from 17 July to 31 July 1790.

On 19 June 1791 Treilhard helped enact a law that created an office of public prosecutors to enforce legal proceedings against nonjuring clergy who were still performing priestly duties. He also helped to organize the admission of Voltaire to the Panthéon during the early summer of 1791. Ineligible to serve in the Legislative Assembly, he was elected in September 1792 to the Convention from the department of the Seine-et-Oise; and he served as the president of the Convention from 27 December 1792 to 9 January 1793. Although he voted for Louis XVI's death, he favored a reprieve. On 6 April 1793 he was elected to the Committee of Public Safety by 160 votes but left the committee shortly before its great reconstruction in July. He proved himself an ineffectual antifederalist commissioner in the southwest, where he was sent on mission by the Committee of Public Safety. His criticism of the Paris Commune and the Jacobins forced him to act discreetly during the Terror. After the Convention's close, he was elected to the Council of Five Hundred and served as its president from December 1795 to January 1796, when he supported the provision of the law that revived earlier legislation sanctioning deportation and death for nonjuring priests. The same legislation also excluded close relatives of the *émigrés* from serving in any public capacity.

He was named by the Directory as minister plenipotentiary to Naples and in 1798 represented France at the Congress of Rastadt. On 9 March 1798 the German Diet accepted provisionally the claims of Treilhard that France should occupy the entire left bank of the Rhine, including Cologne. Little more than two months later he replaced N.-L. François de Neufchâteau as a director. On 16 June 1799 he resigned from this position because of a constitutional decree that forbid any member of the legislature from serving either as a director or as a minister. He was replaced by L.-J. Gohier.

Named a count of the Empire Treilhard enjoyed a well-rewarded career of public service under Napoleon. He died in 1810, a counselor of state.

M. Lyons, *France under the Directory* (London, 1975); J. McManners, *The French Revolution and the Church* (London, 1969); A. Patrick, *The Men of the First French Republic* (Baltimore, 1972); M. J. Sydenham, *The First French Republic, 1792-1804* (London, 1974).

N. Chaudhuri

Related entries: CIVIL CONSTITUTION OF THE CLERGY; COMMITTEE OF PUBLIC SAFETY; FRANCOIS DE NEUFCHATEAU.

TRIBUNAL, REVOLUTIONARY. See REVOLUTIONARY TRIBUNAL.

TRIUMVIRATE (1789-92), A. Barnave, A. Duport, and A. de Lameth, three Revolutionary leaders who led the attack on the monarchy until 1791 when they became its staunch defenders. The middle-class lawyer Barnave, the aristocratic jurist Duport, and the royal army officer Lameth formed close personal and political ties early in the National Assembly despite differences in their social backgrounds. As members of the Jacobin Society, they supported wide-ranging changes in the social and political structure of France between 1789 and 1791. Above all, they dedicated themselves in that early period to the destruction of the power of the royal court, which they saw as the greatest obstacle to the achievement of liberty. That goal brought them into conflict with the royalists and moderate Anglophiles, including J.-J. Mounier, Barnave's former confederate during the revolt in Dauphiné in 1788. Their relationships with H.-G. R. Mirabeau, who was working to maintain a reasonably strong monarchy, were never cordial, though he and Barnave displayed a certain mutual respect. Lameth had participated in the American Revolution with the marquis de Lafayette, but the efforts of these two men to join forces politically on several occasions after 1789 had no lasting success.

Fellow deputies often said of the Triumvirate that Duport was the thinker, Barnave the orator, and Lameth the man of action. As spokesman for the group, Barnave introduced into the National Assembly dozens of legislative proposals designed to wipe away the old political, social, and religious order and to replace it with a new one. Duport, for example, was instrumental in formulating the new judicial organization. Barnave, a Protestant, showed special interest in breaking the power of the Catholic clergy and the crown. The zealousness with which they pursued their Revolutionary goals won them reputations among their less radical colleagues as irresponsible extremists.

After several years of Revolutionary activism, the Triumvirs did an apparent about-face in the last months of the National Assembly. Instead of continuing their attacks on the monarchy, they began warmly to defend it. In fact, they even tried to restore some of the royal powers they had earlier struggled so hard to eliminate. According to legend, that political conversion resulted from Barnave's accompanying the royal family back to Paris after its unsuccessful attempt to flee from the country in June 1791. Supposedly the handsome young bachelor was smitten by the beautiful Marie Antoinette and became a champion of the monarchy because of his love for her. The real motivations were probably less romantic and more complicated. Ambition and vanity undoubtedly were factors. So, too, was the death of Mirabeau, who had been an obstacle to any close understanding between the Triumvirate and the court. Most important, Barnave and his associates came to realize that the executive authority they had deemed so powerful was actually in danger of collapsing completely, and for them, despite their reputations as fanatics, to curb royal power had never meant to destroy the monarchy itself. They also recognized the threat to themselves and to traditional French institutions posed by more radical leaders like J.-P. Brissot and M. Robespierre. During the Legislative Assembly, Barnave, Duport, and Lameth continued their efforts on behalf of the monarchy as founders and leaders of the Feuillant Society. However, for several reasons they proved less effective as supporters of the king than they had as his antagonists. Because of the Self-Denying Ordinance, they were ineligible to serve in the Legislative Assembly and had to lobby for their cause on the outside. Their newly assumed moderate posture and intimate relations with the court cost them the support of the Parisian crowds. And their enemies on the Left lost no opportunity to accuse them of betraying the Revolution, while stalwart royalists continued to treat them with hostility.

In January 1792 Barnave returned to his home in Grenoble, thus ending the collective work of the Triumvirate. The Revolutionary government ordered him arrested in late 1792 when his secret communications with the court came to light, and the Revolutionary Tribunal sentenced him to death fifteen months later. Duport remained in Paris as a criminal prosecutor until 10 August 1792, when he fled to avoid trial as a royalist. He returned to France briefly after 9 Thermidor, then took up residence in Switzerland, where he died in 1798. Lameth resumed his military career, spent three years as a prisoner of the Austrians and another several years in exile before returning to France in 1799. He died in 1829 after serving in a number of administrative and political positions under Napoleon and the restored Bourbons.

Although many of their contemporaries and some historians have charged them with inconsistency and with conduct that was exclusively self-serving, the Triumvirs were dedicated to France's interests as they saw them. Their failure stemmed not from changing their objectives but from remaining staunchly loyal to those objectives under rapidly changing conditions. By the spring of 1791 they realized that the Revolution was going far beyond what they had hoped for in the way of political, social, and religious change. They also discovered they were powerless to calm the winds of change they had done so much to unleash.

E. D. Bradby, *The Life of Barnave*, 2 vols. (Oxford, 1915); J.-J. Chevallier, *Barnave, ou les deux faces de la Révolution, 1761-1793* (Paris, 1936); A. de Lameth, *Histoire de l'Assemblée Constituante, 1789-1790*, 2 vols. (Paris, 1828); G. Michon, *Essai sur l'histoire du parti Feuillant: Adrien Duport* (Paris, 1924); J. Mills Whitham, *A Biographical History of the French Revolution* (Freeport, N.Y., 1968).

R. Vignery

Related entries: ANGLOMANES; BARNAVE; DU PORT; FEUILLANTS; LAMETH, A.-T.-V.; MIRABEAU; MOUNIER; SELF-DENYING ORDINANCE.

TRONCHET, FRANCOIS-DENIS (1726-1806), lawyer, jurisconsult, deputy to the Constituent Assembly and the Council of Elders. Inscribed on the list of lawyers in 1745, Tronchet was elected *bâtonnier* of the Paris order of lawyers in 1789 and selected to represent the third estate in the Estates General from Paris. There his first act was to urge the transformation of the Estates into a national assembly, which earned him the title from H.-G. R. Mirabeau of Nestor of the Aristocracy. Although his influence on the floor of the Assembly was minimal, he played a significant role on the judicial committee. There he authored reports on seigneurial *rentes*, the abolition of the *dîme*, and the jury system. In the reform of the judicial system, he was a tenacious defender of the jury system.

After the adjournment of the Constituent, Tronchet became a judge of the high court, and he was one of three commissioners ordered to receive declarations from the royal family following the king's return from Varennes. He also served as one of Louis' lawyers in the subsequent trial. Tronchet stayed in hiding during the Terror. Under the Directory he reopened his legal practice, and he served as a deputy of the Seine-et-Oise to the Council of Ancients from 1795 to 1799. There he was influential in drafting legislation on legal matters, such as reports on the punishment of criminal intent and on bastardy. Under the consulate he became president of the Cour de Cassation and presided over the commission that formulated the Code Napoleon.

F. Tronchet, *Observations...concernant les pères, mères, ascendans & parens d'émigrés, ainsi que les droits de successibilité de la république* (Paris, 1799), and *Opinion...sur le jugement par jury* (Paris, 1790).

R. R. Crout

Related entries: JUSTICE; LOUIS XVI; *RENTE*; TERROR, THE; TITHE.

TWELVE, COMMISSION OF. See COMMISSION OF TWELVE.

22 PRAIRIAL, LAW OF. See LAW OF 22 PRAIRIAL.

TWO-THIRDS LAW, decreed by the National Convention at the end of the Year III, to preserve two-thirds of the retiring *conventionnels* in office, within the new Corps Législatif. This law was embodied in two decrees of 5 and 13 Fructidor Year III initiated by the deputy P. Baudin. The decrees stipulated that in the new Corps Législatif, two-thirds of deputies must be chosen from among the ranks of *conventionnels*, excluding about sixty-seven Montagnards declared ineligible in the anti-Jacobin measures following the Parisian insurrections of Germinal and Prairial Year III. This attempt by the Convention to perpetuate its membership in power was presented by its supporters as a means of stabilizing and terminating the Revolution and avoiding the alleged error of the Constituent Assembly, which had disqualified its members from reelection to the Legislative. But the law's enemies regarded it as a violation of the principle of popular sovereignty.

The Constitution of the Year III was submitted for ratification to the primary electoral assemblies; and L.-M. La Revellière-lépeaux invited the electorate to pronounce on the decrees of 5 and 13 Fructidor at the same time. Although the constitution was overwhelmingly supported, not all voters expressed a view on the Two-thirds Law. The official figures were 205,498 in favor of the law and 108,754 rejecting it (although these figures do not include those primary assemblies that expressed a unanimous opinion without specifying the number of votes).

Nineteen departments rejected the decrees. A strongly hostile reaction to them was recorded in parts of the center (Allier, Nièvre) and the Massif Central (Ardèche, Lozère), as well as in the Seine valley and Parisian basin (Eure, Eure-et-Loir, Loiret, Seine-et-Oise, Seine-et-Marne, Oise, Aisne). Above all, the decrees were rejected by forty-seven of the forty-eight Paris sections; only the section Quinze-vingts approved them. The government, fearing disorder in the sections, had introduced troops into Paris, and this, together with the Two-thirds Law, helped to provoke the royalist insurrection of 13 Vendémiaire Year IV in the Paris sections.

The Two-thirds Law was an attempt to counter a growing royalist menace against the Republic; the incoming third included at least 117 deputies whom J. Suratteau classifies as royalists or counterrevolutionaries. The Two-thirds Law, however, deprived the elections of the Year IV of much of their real significance and prefigured the electoral manipulations carried out in future years by the Directory. It was perhaps a directorial coup d'état before the Directory had even assumed office.

G. Lefebvre, *Les Thermidoriens* (Paris, 1937); G. Rudé, "Les sans-culottes parisiens et les journées de vendémiaire an IV," *Ann. hist. de la Révo. française* 31 (1959); J. Suratteau, "Les élections de l'an IV," *Ann. hist. de la Révo. française* 23 (1951) and 24 (1952).

M. Lyons

Related entries: SELF-DENYING ORDINANCE; 13 VENDEMIAIRE YEAR IV.

U

UPRISING OF 12 GERMINAL (1 April 1795), the first of the two Parisian insurrections of the Year III. The technical cause of popular distress in the spring of 1795 was the removal of price controls with the abolition of the maximum (24 Nivôse, 13 January 1795). This was compounded by the disappearance of the coercive apparatus of the Terror, which rendered illusory any government attempt to maintain regular food supply from rural areas.

Paris enjoyed a privileged status after the abolition of the maximum since, unlike elsewhere, an official subsidized distribution of bread (at 3 *sols* per pound) and meat (at 21 *sols* per pound) was continued. Holders of bread cards were normally entitled to one and a half pounds per head daily for manual workers and one pound for others. A free market was permitted in addition to the subsidized market. However, incoming supply rapidly contracted, leaving massive shortages while, after an initial surge following the abolition of the maximum, prices on the free market continued to rise steeply. During Nivôse and Pluviôse, the subsidized distribution of bread was maintained only at the cost of running down reserve grain stocks. In Ventôse, these were exhausted and the subsidized distributions frequently fell to eight ounces or less, with significant numbers of people receiving nothing. Supply from outside the city failed to arrive in any quantity. By the beginning of Germinal, the twenty-five districts designated to supply the capital had defaulted on 700,000 quintals of grain. At the same time, the free market prices rose relentlessly, bread reaching 25 *sols* just before the Germinal rising and 65 *sols* just after it. Price levels placed the free market out of reach of the mass of the population, among whom real wages were probably back to the crisis levels of 1789. Popular misery was aggravated by an exceptionally hard winter and by the scarcity and exorbitant price of wood and of other foods not subject to subsidy.

The political crisis of the spring of 1795 occurred at two levels. In the Convention, although matters remained confused and the committees of government hesitant, the reinstatement of the proscribed Girondists on 18 Ventôse (8 March) both testified to and stimulated the reactionary temper of the majority. This was expressed in early Germinal in a struggle over the four Montagnard leaders (J.-N. Billaud-Varenne, J.-M. Collot d'Herbois, B. Barère, and M.-G.-A. Vadier) whose arrest had been voted on 12 Ventôse (2 March). More important, Pluviôse and Ventôse saw struggles in the sections as moderates attempted to control those of the center and east of the city that had been the heartland of the popular movement. This was accompanied by the continuing piecemeal arrest of Jacobin sectional personnel. At the same time, the intensifying harassment by the *jeunesse dorée* (militant reactionary youth) of Jacobin personalities and gatherings intensified into a crisis during the last *décade* of Pluviôse (8-18 February) with their attacks on the busts of J.-P. Marat, counterdemonstrations in the faubourg Saint-Antoine, and the closure of the sectional clubs in the faubourgs Saint-Antoine and Saint-Marceau. There is little doubt that the attack on Marat's memory, whose symbolic importance was central to *sans-culotte* perceptions, reactivated popular militants who had been disoriented after 9 Thermidor.

Popular agitation became menacing during the third *décade* of Ventôse (10-20 March) with the deepening supply crisis. Long, overnight breadlines, often resulting in the distribution of merely a few ounces of bread, brought partial riots (especially by women) and delegations to the Convention in late Ventôse and during the first *décade* of Germinal (21-30 March). At the same time, there appeared a sketchy revival of classic *sans-culotte* attitudes and techniques. On the one hand, there was an attempt to revive the sectional movement during the days preceding 12 Germinal, not merely by sectional delegations to the Convention but also by the holding of unofficial assemblies in traditionally radical sections, notably Quinze-vingts, Gravilliers, and Droits de l'Homme. On the other hand, a political program began to emerge in placards and speeches calling for the application of the Constitution of 1793, the release of arrested patriots, and the restoration of a municipality with elected and accountable officials. By early Germinal, an explosion was visibly imminent. The government attempted to combat this in two ways. First, it sought, without success, to defuse the food problem by raising a forced loan of two-thirds of available grain in the supplying departments (4 Germinal, 24 March) and by stipulating the delivery of bread by household in order to end breadlines (8 Germinal, 28 March). Second, it equipped itself for repression by the Sieyès Law of 1 Germinal (21 March), which established punishments for disturbances and attacks on the Convention, by arming reliable citizens (2 Germinal), and finally, on the evening of 11 Germinal, by summoning the reactionary *jeunesse dorée* to the defense of the Assembly.

Nonetheless, the uprising took the government by surprise, despite an abortive attempt by women from the Gravilliers section to invade the Assembly on 7 Germinal and despite the collapse of food distribution from 9 Germinal. The movement began in the Cité section, but by 11 A.M., large crowds (estimated by one source at about 10,000) drawn from the central sections, from the eastern and northern faubourgs, and from the Invalides section were milling around the Convention. At about 2 P.M. brushing aside the *jeunesse dorée*, they swept into the hall. They remained there for about four hours, for the most part in total confusion, calling for bread. Sufficient order was eventually established to enable the spokesman for the Cité section, a militant named Van Heck, to make a speech calling for the application of the Constitution of 1793, the end of food shortages, the release of imprisoned patriots, and the dispersal of the *jeunesse dorée*. Later, delegations from Fidélité, Fraternité, Bonnet-de-la-Liberté, Bonne-Nouvelle, and Thermes sections presented petitions about the food supply. Van Heck had ended his speech with a scarcely veiled appeal to the remnants of the Montagnard deputies (the "Crête") to take control. Although many right-wing deputies apparently left the Assembly when the crowd entered, the Crête made no effort to profit from the situation and consistently urged the crowd to leave. Meanwhile, the Committee of General Security and the Military Committee were mobilizing the National Guard of the bourgeois quarters of the west, while a number of deputies tried to calm disturbances elsewhere in the city (F. Auguis was beaten up by a crowd and J.-A. Pénières was shot at). By about 6 P.M. these forces reached the Convention and the crowd dispersed, although it is not clear whether it was forcibly ejected from the hall. In the evening, the Convention placed Paris in a state of siege under the command of General J.-C. Pichegru with P. Barras and A.-C. Merlin de Thionville as his assistants. The troubles continued in a more fragmentary fashion on 13 Germinal. The day was marked above all by some attempts to consolidate the movement through illegal sectional assemblies under former Year II militants, notably in the Bon-Conseil and Panthéon sections and in the faubourg Saint-Antoine sections of Quinze-vingts and Montreuil, all four traditional radical centers. Only the Quinze-vingts movement was serious and it evaporated under the threat of Pichegru's forces.

Popular discontent focused on the Convention for a number of specific reasons beyond the traditional protest reflexes. It was seen as the only power capable of ensuring the food supply and therefore responsible for the penury. The chaos in the distribution inside the city, which meant an uneven supply to different quarters, was imputed to the government. Moreover, the Convention had actively drawn the attention of popular anger to itself. It had promised that 9 Thermidor and the abolition of the maximum would result in better conditions; it had closed the troublesome state arms workshops in Pluviôse, apparently aggravating unemployment; it had doubled its own salary to 44 *livres* per day (23 Nivôse, 12 January); it had ordered workers in lodging houses to buy only on the free market; it had voted a clause in the Sieyès Law allowing it to move to Châlons in case of trouble, thus recalling the plan of the Girondists in 1793; it had appeared to favor (even though it did not vote) A.-C. Merlin de Thionville's proposal to hand over authority to a new Assembly (8 Germinal), thus seeming to abandon the food crisis that it was its duty to resolve.

The Germinal uprising was not, however, a predominantly popular political movement comparable to those of 31 May 1793 and 5 September 1793. Although there were attempts at a sectional movement, the uprising was not organized or coordinated by sections. The initiatives of the Cité section came nearest to this, but the petitions presented by other sections on 12 Germinal had been arranged two days earlier and coincided with the uprising without being fully part of it. Although there were echoes of classic *sans-culotte* attitudes in the growing talk of hoarding and speculation, in the expressed hatred of the rich and merchants, and in the demands put forward by placards and some delegations, none of this amounted to much of a program. Van Heck's speech was but a feeble ghost of the full tide of *sans-culottisme* in 1793, and his appeal to the Crête was pathetic testimony to the militants' inability to formulate and achieve a program of independent action. Certainly, inasmuch as some leading areas of the rising had a low percentage of indigent population (Cité section, for example, only had 6.7 percent in Germinal compared with 36.1 percent in Quinze-vingts), one must see other forces than hunger as playing a role. Nonetheless, the uprising was more characteristically a confused mass demonstration of unarmed, hungry people with little program beyond a cry for bread. It continued and amplified fifteen days of small food riots and coincided with a seasonal shortage that produced major disturbances in other areas (at Rouen and Amiens, for example). Among the crowd, the call for the Constitution of 1793 was less prominent than it would be in the Prairial days. The failure of the uprising can be imputed less to the Montagnards' unwillingness to seize the opportunity than to this lack of clear objective, coupled with the absence of any real popular control of areas of Paris, where the sectional movement failed to establish itself while the crowd was occupying the Convention.

The uprising resolved nothing in the relations between the government and the Parisian masses. Unlike after the Prairial days, the pattern of crisis and disturbance continued unchecked. In political terms, however, it resulted in the consolidation of the reactionary movement. On the evening of 12 Germinal, the deportation of J.-N. Billaud-Varenne, J.-M. Collot d'Herbois, B. Barère, and M.-G.-A. Vadier to Guyana was decreed without further ado. At the same time and during the next few days, prominent members of the Crête were arrested: P. Choudieu, P.-J.-M. Chasles, A. Foussedoire, L. Bourdon, P.-C. de Ruamps, P.-J. Duhem, J.-B-A. Amar, P.-J. Cambon, C. Hentz, L. Lecointre, F.-O. Granet, E.-C. Maignet, R. Levasseur de la Sarthe, and N. Crassous. On 21 Germinal (10 April) the Convention decreed the disarmament of all terrorists throughout the Republic and, on 22 Germinal, the abrogation of the outlawry proclaimed against those who had participated in the federalist revolts of 1793. The way was now open both to the violence of the counter-Terror and to the final abandonment of the ideals of the earlier Convention by the formulation of a new constitution.

R. Cobb, ''Les journées de germinal an III dans la zone de ravitaillement de Paris,'' *Ann. de Norm.* (October-December 1955); R. Cobb and G. Rudé, ''Le dernier mouvement populaire de la Révolution à Paris,'' *Rev. hist.* 214 (1955); E. B. de Salverte, *Journées des 12 et 13 germinal* (Paris, an III); E. Tarlé, *Germinal et Prairial* (Moscow, 1959); K. D. Tønnesson, *La Défaite des sans-culottes* (Oslo and Paris, 1959).

C. Lucas

Related entries: CONSTITUTION OF 1793; *DECADE*; FEDERALISM; *JEU-NESSE DOREE*; LAW OF THE MAXIMUM; 9 THERMIDOR YEAR II; PICHEGRU; SECTIONS.

V

VADIER, MARC-GUILLAUME-ALEXIS (1736-1828), deputy, president of the Committee of General Security. Born in Pamiers (Ariège) in 1736, Vadier was the son of a *receveur des dîmes*. Educated at the Jesuit collège in Pamiers and then at the collège de l'Esquile in Toulouse, he joined the Piedmont regiment in 1753 and was promoted to lieutenant in 1755. He fought in the Battle of Rossbach in 1757 and then resigned his commission. He married in 1762 and was to have four sons. He became the leading landowner in his village of Montaut, near Pamiers, and in 1770 purchased the office of *conseiller* at the *présidial* court of Pamiers.

Vadier was elected to the Estates General in 1789, as representative of the Third Estate of the *sénéchaussée* of Pamiers. He signed the Tennis Court Oath and on 4 August 1789 supported the surrender of the privileges of the Comté de Foix. He defended the passive citizens of Pamiers against attempts to partition a plot of common land, known as La Boulbonne. Here, Vadier came into conflict with his local rivals, the Darmaing family, and in this conflict he represented the interests of Pamiers against those of the *chef-lieu*, Foix.

During the period of the Legislative Assembly, Vadier became president of the district court of Mirepoix (Ariège). After the flight to Varennes in 1791, Vadier, in a rare public speech, called for the suspension of the king, but finding this view too advanced for his audience, he withdrew the suggestion, and J.-P. Marat accused him of moral cowardice for doing so. In 1792, he denounced the royalist activities of the Darmaing family and was elected deputy for the Ariège to the National Convention. Vadier voted for the death of Louis XVI without reprieve and aligned himself with M. Robespierre in opposing a national referendum on the fate of the king. He vigorously opposed the federalist revolt in Toulouse. He was a member of the Jacobin club of Paris, the Convention's Comité de Secours Publics; and in September 1793 he entered the Committee of General Security. In Pluviôse Year II, he was elected the committee's president, probably because he was the oldest member, after the resignation of A. Boucher Saint-Sauveur and in the absence of P.-J. Rühl.

With the aid of his network of supporters in the Ariège and Haute-Garonne, led by his eldest son (known as Carpe-Vadier), Vadier secured the arrest of the Darmaing brothers and other suspects from the Ariège, including the so-called *chapeaux noirs* of Montaut. He wrote privately to the public prosecutor, A.-Q. Fouquier-Tinville, recommending the death sentence for several of those local enemies, and this he obtained. Within the Committee of General Security, however, his chief responsibility was for political police in the Paris area.

Vadier became a bitter and ironic antagonist of both G.-J. Danton, whom he described as a stuffed turbot, and of Robespierre, whose sententiousness Vadier detested. He had frequent consultations with Fouquier-Tinville during the trial of G.-J. Danton and even visited the jury while it was deliberating to argue successfully for a conviction.

Vadier employed P.-A. Taschereau de Fargues to spy on Robespierre, but he became a double agent. Like other members of the Committee of General Security, Vadier was perhaps jealous of the increasing powers over political police exercised by the Committee of Public Safety. In addition he resented Robespierre's pontifical role in the Cult of the Supreme Being, which Vadier may have interpreted as the beginning of a fatal policy of appeasement toward Catholicism. On 27 Prairial Year II Vadier presented his report on the C. Théot affair. Théot, an eccentric visionary, had allegedly declared Robespierre the new messiah. Although Robespierre prevented the case from going before the Revolutionary Tribunal, Vadier used the affair to heap ridicule on the clerical counterrevolution and also to undermine Robespierre's credibility. Some of the acrimony in Vadier's rhetoric may be explained by the bitterness caused by the deaths in the Year II of his wife, mother, and two of his sons. Vadier promoted the Law of 21 Messidor Year II, which allowed for the release of suspect artisans and agricultural workers at harvest time. When, however, he actively supported the overthrow of Robespierre on 9-10 Thermidor, he probably did not anticipate the relaxation of the Terror.

He continued to mix in Jacobin circles, and to defend the Revolutionary government in the Jacobin club and in the Convention, where he dramatically appeared with a pistol at his head in response to L. Lecointre's accusations. But in Ventôse Year III, J.-B.-M. Saladin's report on the ex-Montagnards accused Vadier of exerting illegal pressure on the Revolutionary Tribunal, and Vadier went into hiding.

He was granted amnesty in Brumaire Year IV but exiled from Paris in Floréal. He walked to Toulouse, where he was arrested in Prairial Year IV as an accomplice in the Babeuf conspiracy. Vadier, in typical fashion, denounced the Babeuf conspiracy as a foreign plot and used the Vendôme trial to make another strong public defense of the Terror. He was acquitted but detained by virtue of a deportation order of the Year III, never carried out. He was imprisoned in Cherbourg, where he met F. Buonarroti, but was released in the Year VII.

He emerged from private life in the Hundred Days to approve Napoleon's *Acte Additionnel*, and in 1815 he was arrested in Toulouse as a Bonapartist *fédéré*. The Bourbons exiled him as a regicide, and he settled in Brussels, where he renewed his acquaintance with Buonarroti, whose Robespierrist and Rousseauist sympathies Vadier challenged. He died in Brussels in 1828.

Described by his biographer as the Gascon Voltaire for his acerbic tongue, Vadier was of an older generation than idealistic Rousseauists like Robespierre, who could not equal Vadier's boast of "*soixante ans de vertus.*" Vadier used his enormous police powers to eliminate personal enemies, and he thus acquired a reputation as a bloodthirsty monster. Buonarroti described his political creed as simply a hatred of nobles and priests; if so, Vadier remained consistent in his political outlook throughout and beyond the Revolutionary era.

A.N., AD XVIIIa. 66 Vadier: speeches and reports and F7 .4445₃₇, d. 2 Dossier Vadier; M. Eude, "Les députés méridionaux membres des comités gouvernement en 1793-1794," *Actes de 96ᵉ Congrès national des sociétés savantes, Toulouse, 1971, section d'histoire moderne et contemporaine* (Paris, 1976); M. A. Lyons, "M.-G.-A. Vadier (1736-1828): The Formation of the Jacobin Mentality," *Fr. Hist. Stud.* 10 (1977); A. Tournier, *Vadier, président du Comité de Sûreté Générale sous la Terreur* (Paris, n.d.).

M. Lyons

Related entries: BUONARROTI; COMMITTEE OF GENERAL SECURITY; COMMITTEE OF PUBLIC SAFETY; CONSPIRACY OF EQUALS; CULT OF THE SUPREME BEING; DANTON; FOUQUIER-TINVILLE; ROBESPIERRE, M.; TENNIS COURT OATH; THEOT.

VAINQUEURS DE LA BASTILLE. See BASTILLE.

VALMY. See BATTLE OF VALMY.

VANDALISM. See GREGOIRE.

VAN DER NOOT, HENDRIK (1750-1826), Belgian revolutionary. See VONCK.

VARENNES, place of arrest of the French royal family during their attempted escape from Paris in June 1791. The incident came to be known as the flight to Varennes, and it was used by the Revolutionaries as evidence of treasonous activity by the king.

After the summer of 1789, the idea of removing the king and his family from Revolutionary Paris and appealing to the supposedly loyal provinces or to foreign powers to restore his authority was frequently raised in royalist circles. In mid-1790 H.-G. R. Mirabeau secretly urged Louis XVI and Marie Antoinette to withdraw to Normandy and appeal to the nation, promising reform and a constitution. The king shrank from fomenting civil war, and Mirabeau died in April 1791.

By the fall of 1790, however, Louis was greatly aroused over the National Assembly's treatment of the clergy. He now received a new proposal from the *émigré* baron de Breteuil in Switzerland for the royal family to take refuge near France's eastern frontier under the protection of General F.-C.-A. de Bouillé and to appeal to the European monarchs for money and troops. This course was strongly favored by Marie Antoinette.

Montmédy, near the Luxembourg border, was selected as the royal redoubt, and secret negotiations with foreign powers, particularly Austria, were carried out, partly by Breteuil in Switzerland and partly by Marie Antoinette herself, through the comte de Mercy-Argenteau in Brussels. While the evidence is scanty, it seems clear that the queen and her confidants counted on foreign support to restore royal absolutism. By June 1791, there seemed some prospect of aid from Spain, Sardinia, and the Swiss, provided Austria also participated, but Emperor Leopold II, then at war with Turkey, temporized until the last minute before promising support. By then, Louis XVI had overcome his last hesitations when a crowd prevented him from attending Easter services conducted by a nonjuring priest at Saint-Cloud. Marie Antoinette was determined to proceed as planned to force Leopold II's hand, if need be.

In Paris, the Swedish count A. von Fersen prepared for the actual escape of the royal family and a few trusted retainers. A large coach or *berline* was constructed for two Russian ladies, Mesdames Stegelmann and von Korff, who also took out passports for travel to Germany. Considerable funds and the queen's jewelry were secretly sent abroad.

After various delays, the royal party managed to slip out of the Tuileries palace by an unguarded door close to midnight on 20 June 1791 and were driven out of Paris by Fersen, disguised as a coachman, to where the *berline* awaited them. They traveled as ''Madame von Korff,'' her children, and servants, on Madame von Korff's passport.

From the beginning, however, there were delays, and the cumbrous *berline* moved slowly. Bouillé posted army detachments in advance along the intended route as far west as Sainte-Menehould, but as time passed, they attracted so much unwelcome attention that they withdrew from their advance posts. Near Châlons the royal couple was recognized. When they reached Sainte-Menehould, from which Bouillé's detachment had already withdrawn, the local postmaster, J.-B. Drouet, by now forewarned, rode on ahead to Varennes to alert the local authorities, who arrested the royal party on its arrival that night, before Bouillé's small detachment there could reassemble from its quarters. The rapid mobilization of the National Guard throughout the region quickly ended any possibility of further military intervention. The following day, the *berline* and its occupants, accompanied by National Guard units, began the return to Paris, where they arrived on 24 June.

The flight to Varennes destroyed the fiction, at home and abroad, that the king and the nation could work together in good faith. Louis XVI had, moreover, left behind him a manifesto stating his irreconcilable grievances against the

Revolution. Already, on 21 June the National Assembly had suspended his powers. Although he was reinstated on 14 September on his acceptance of the new constitution, true confidence could not be restored. It was Varennes that made republicanism a force to be reckoned with in France, as shown by the serious rioting at the Champ de Mars in July. It also compelled the monarchical powers of Europe to recognize the de facto captivity of the French royal family and to officially condemn the Revolution, a reaction that further strengthened republicanism in France. The monarchy could not long survive the coming of the War of the First Coalition in April 1792; it collapsed with the storming of the Tuileries on 10 August 1792.

C. Aimond, *L'enigme de Varennes* (Paris, 1936); H. A. Barton, *Count Hans Axel von Fersen* (Boston, 1975); V. Fournel, *L'événement de Varennes* (Paris, 1890); G. Lenotre [pseud. A. Gosselin], *Le drame de Varennes* (Paris, 1908).

H. A. Barton

Related entries: BOUILLE; CHAMP DE MARS "MASSACRE"; DROUET; *EMIGRES*; FERSEN; FIRST COALITION; MERCY-ARGENTEAU.

VARLET, JEAN-FRANCOIS (1764-1832), orator, pamphleteer, and political activist. Historians place Varlet with J. Roux, T. Leclerc, and the two republican feminists, C. Lacombe and P. Léon, in a loosely defined group termed the *Enragés*. Although they constituted no distinct political tendency in opposition to the many militants in sectional assemblies or popular societies, they tended to be more consistent in defense of the *sans-culottes* and the working poor. Shortages and inflation coupled with the steady decline of the *assignat* encouraged them to champion the maximum, call for drastic penalties against profiteers, and to urge the acceptance of *assignats* as fiat money. Suspicious of representative government and confident in the basic goodness of the common people, the *Enragés* advocated direct democracy. No other Revolutionist defended this practice more consistently than did Varlet.

Born into a family of some means, Varlet was able to attend the collège d'Harcourt where his professors predicted that he would become either a saint or a devil. The young *Enragé* assured his readers, however, that virtue had won out in the end. When the Revolution broke out, he welcomed it enthusiastically, composed patriotic songs, addressed crowds in the Palais Royal, and bore petitions in defense of popular causes. He was present at Versailles when the Declaration of the Rights of Man was adopted, and he helped to prepare the Champ de Mars for the Festival of the Federation in the summer of 1790. After Varennes, Varlet became widely known for his sharp attacks against the king launched in harangues from a portable podium in the Terrasse-des-Feuillants of the Tuileries gardens. The "massacre" on the Champ de Mars intensified his hatred of the marquis de Lafayette, whom he accused of being a traitor.

On 24 May 1793 he was arrested together with J.-R. Hébert by the Girondin Commission des douze, only to be liberated in triumph three days later and sent as its delegate by his section, Droits-de-l'Homme, to the Evêché Assembly to prepare the insurrection of 31 May-2 June 1793. Elected provisional president of the Comité de neuf, Varlet gave the signal to sound the general alarm and signed the order suspending the powers of the municipal authorities.

Although no theoretician in the formal sense, Varlet tended to develop his ideas systematically in a number of publications. Among his more important writings is an essay written in 1792, *Plan d'une nouvelle organisation de la société de la constitution suivi de la réligion du Philosophe dédié aux indigens* (Paris, 1793), in which he criticized the Jacobin club for its undemocratic procedure. His objections were based on his personal experience of being prevented from expressing his views on a number of occasions and being expelled from the Jacobins for manifesting "an excess of *civisme*." In another brochure, *Projet d'un mandat spécial et impératif, aux mandataires du peuple à la Convention Nationale* (Paris, 1792), he appealed to the deputies to recognize the principle of popular sovereignty and to become what originally they were meant to be: mandatories of the people's will. In one of his more important pamphlets, *Declaration solennelle des droits de l'homme dans l'état social* (Paris, 1793), Varlet posed the question of what it was that made for conditions of inequality and replied that it was the possession or lack of property. Property was a social category, he argued, placed under the protection of the public and hence subject to its regulation. Moreover, the propertyless possessed the inherent right to defend themselves against "the oppression of the rich," he wrote. Society had the right, he concluded, to dissolve "the enormous disproportion of wealth."

On 17 September 1793 Varlet made a provocative and ill-timed speech in the Convention, in which he rejected the 40 *sous* subsidy voted by the deputies for poor *sans-culottes* who had spent three days under arms in the late rebellion against the Girondists. His remarks provoked sharp replies by various deputies, including M. Robespierre. He was arrested the following day and not freed until 8 Brumaire (29 October 1793), after numerous protests had been launched by his friends in the section and in the Paris Commune. After Robespierre's fall, Varlet was arrested again on 19 Fructidor Year II (5 September 1794). Once again he published an important pamphlet, *L'explosion*, in which he denounced "the revolutionary dictatorship, decreed in the name of public safety" and embraced the principles of moderation. Varlet was released shortly after the royalist coup of Vendémiaire, became a Bonapartist, and ended his days in Nantes where he welcomed the overthrow of Charles X in the Revolution of 1830.

A. Mathiez, *La vie chère et le mouvement social sous la Terreur* (Paris, 1927); R. B. Rose, *The Enragés: Socialists of the French Revolution?* (London and New York, 1965); J. M. Zacher, *The Revolutionary Movement of the Enragés* (in Russian) (Moscow, 1961).

M. Slavin

Related entries: CHAMP DE MARS "MASSACRE"; *ENRAGES*; FESTIVAL OF FEDERATION; GIRONDINS; LACOMBE; LECLERC; LEON; ROUX.

VENDEE, department created in 1790 but familiarly used to describe the insurrection in the *Vendée militaire*, an area south of the Loire and northwest of

the line Saumur-Bressuire-Fontenay, where revolt occurred when local authorities in March 1793, sought to raise their quota of troops in accordance with the
central government's orders to levy 300,000 men.

La Grande Guerre, stage 1. Towns in and west of the *bocage* (hilly and
wooded areas around Cholet) were overrun as insurrection swept the area, bands
coalescing into columns under leaders, a council being established to govern the
zone and coordinate three armies, in the *marais* (flat and marshy areas), the
center, and the *bocage*. When operational these bands consisted of men permanently mobilized (approximately 12,000), in addition to even more lightly
armed reserves brought into action by captains of parishes; the *Grande Armée*
of the *bocage* could consist in this manner of some 30,000 men, twice the size
of the other two combined. Failing to capture Nantes (29 June 1793) and to
retain Saumur and Angers, the Vendéans ceased to expand their perimeter, and
cooperation between the armies diminished still further.

La Grande Guerre, stage 2. The counterassault was conducted ruthlessly, the
Republic already being in danger from foreign invasion and federalist revolts.
While the *marais* held out, led by F.-A. Charette de la Contrie, the other armies
were able to escape only by retreating across the Loire (18-19 October), some
30,000 combatants with as many refugees fleeing the punitive terror now unleashed in the Vendée.

It has recently become clear that this was a popular and not merely sectional
insurrection. Priests and royalist noblemen might lead Vendéans into battle, but
no more than in the case of the *chouannerie* did they engineer the rising. In the
poor and rather remote areas of the *marais* and *bocage*, the Revolution seemed
to have benefited only limited sections of the population, sections whose relative
emancipation from traditional values and established elites was consecrated by
local government reorganization (1790) and whose unpopularity was vastly increased by their interference in parish affairs when trying to implement the Civil
Constitution of the Clergy. Interconnecting with a severe recession in the textile
industry—whose putting-out entrepreneurs were town inhabitants and whose
weavers lived in the *bocage*—that interference aggravated an increasingly bitter
polarization. Soon the royalists were an oppressed minority in, for example, the
Val Saumurois, whereas just to the west the Mauges came to be solidly antipatriot
as parish companies swept aside the National Guards and, for a time, held troops
at bay in a rising, the conduct of which was unprecedented in Europe. Fought
cruelly, this punitive civil war was of immediate consequence for an already
endangered Republic, swallowing troops needed on the frontiers. It also had
long-term consequences for the political stance in the nineteenth century of a
(by then) devotedly clerico-royalist zone in which the words *republic* and *monarchy* were each stained, for a bitterly partisan population, by the blood of
martyrs.

La Grande Guerre, stage 3. While the *brigands* and their accomplices were
hunted, imprisoned, drowned, or shot in a purge conducted by the ''blues,'' the
Grande Armée marching into Normandy still offered a serious threat to the

Republic, if only because it afforded its British enemies an ally and perhaps a bridgehead on French soil. At the Channel coast, that army failed, however, to capture a harbor (13-14 November) and fell back, vainly assaulting Angers (3 December), as a British landing force appeared off the target port, Granville, on the Cherbourg peninsula. The Vendéans never again posed such an actual threat after 1793, but despite the Terror in the *Vendée militaire* and the smashing of the Grande Armée at Le Mans and Savenay (12 and 23 December), violence and resistance continued, nurtured by the new hatreds as well as old conflicts, the latter barely touched by the less terroristic and slightly conciliatory stance adopted by the government after the anti-Robespierrist coup of 9-10 Thermidor (27-28 July 1794).

La Petite Guerre, 1794-early 1795. The activity of the remaining Vendéan forces in the *marais* and the eastern *bocage* was now sporadic and unconcerted, their leaders increasingly estranged, and their ill-armed, part-time guerrilla followers incapable of other than local actions. These persisted, however, until an amnesty was offered (December), plus certain concessions (including the free practice of religion and exemption from conscription). When Charette made peace at La Jaunaye (February 1795) J.-N. Stofflet anathematized him, but when his own base area was overrun, he also concluded an ill-kept peace (Saint-Florent, 2 May).

The Third Insurrection, 1795-early 1796. During this period, republican strength was increased by reinforcements and by the establishment of a unified command under L. Hoche, whereas the Vendéans' chances of achieving those same advantages were blasted at Quiberon (July 1795) and blocked in the autumn, for the British followed up a delivery of arms to Charette (11-12 August) by taking (30 September-mid-December 1795) the Ile d'Yeu; republican forces, though, prevented the Vendéans from getting through to the coast, which in turn meant the comte d'Artois did not cross from the island to take command of isolated and dwindling forces to which a cowed population gave diminishing support. With Stofflet killed (24 February) and Charette executed (29 March 1796), open insurgence was quelled. An attempt was made to pacify the area by disarming the inhabitants of the *Vendée militaire* (of whom at least some 15 percent died in the various insurrections) and by restoring civil government to the area (March 1796); but discontent persisted and showed—as did, repeatedly, British ships—though even when the coup of Fructidor Year V was followed by anti-clerical measures, full-scale rebellion did not ensue. The peace was extremely fragile, however, the more so whenever troops were withdrawn because of alarms on the frontiers. Incidents were frequent, *chefs* being able easily to raise raiding bands in the Mauges (summer 1799), despite Republican countermeasures and despite the tactical disapproval of those appointed by the Bourbon princes to be the Vendée's commanders. These latter, C.-M.-A. Baumont d'Autichamp, A. de Grignon, P.-J.-B. Constant Suzannet, renounced, when north of the Loire insurrection again exploded, the submission they had made to the Republic, calling *rassemblements*, which totaled perhaps 8,000 men before one column was dispersed in battle near Bressuire (November 1799) and others split into semiformed *attroupements* in the *marais* and the *bocage*. Raids and reprisals diminished only with the signature by the *chefs* of another armistice (December) and were only suppressed (not eradicated) when the newly installed Consulate (1799) reestablished a sternly repressive military government in the area, made peace with England, encouraged the *ralliement* of *émigrés*, and signed the Concordat. Even if the mass rising of 1793 was never repeated, religion (and revenge) were still exploitable by the Republic's, and the Empire's, enemies abroad. So in 1813 the Vendée could be stirred yet again by conscription, royalist leadership, and news of Louis XVIII's being proclaimed at Bordeaux (12 March); and what tiny chance there might have been of reconciliation in this ravaged area was finally destroyed by the opportunities offered for purges during the collapse of the Empire and again in the Hundred Days, when the British once more sent in supplies and the Vendéans kept some 20,000 troops away from the eastern front, and again (though the White Terror was less savage in the Vendée than in Provence) during the Restoration, when devotion (as powerful propaganda represented it) to altar and throne became, with valor (or cruelty) and fidelity (or backwardness) connotations attached to the word *Vendéan*.

C.-L. Chassin, *Etudes documentaires sur la Vendée et la Chouannerie*, 11 vols. (Paris, 1892-1900); L. Dubreuil, *Histoire des insurrections de l'Ouest*, 2 vols. (Paris, 1929-30); M. Faucheux, *L'insurrection vendéenne de 1793: Aspects économiques et sociaux* (Paris, 1954); J. Godechot, *The Counter-Revolution: Doctrine and Action, 1789-1804*, trans. S. Attanasio (Princeton, N.J., 1971); T. Le Goff and D. Sutherland, "The Social Origins of Counterrevolution in Western France," *Past and Present*, no. 99 (1983); M. Lidove, *Les Vendéens de '93* (Paris, 1971); H. Mitchell, "The Vendée and Counter Revolution: A Review Essay," *Fr. Hist. Stud.* 5 (1968); C. Petitfrère, "Les causes de la Vendée et de la Chouannerie: Essai d'historiographie," *Ann. de Bret.* 84 (1977) and *La Vendée et les Vendéens* (Paris, 1981); C. Tilly, *The Vendée*, 2d. ed. (New York, 1967).

M. G. Hutt

Related entries: ARTOIS; CHARETTE DE LA CONTRIE; *CHOUANNERIE*; CIVIL CONSTITUTION OF THE CLERGY; FEDERALISM; *LEVEE EN MASSE*; QUIBERON.

VENDEE MILITAIRE. See VENDEE.

VENDEMIAIRE YEAR IV, 13TH OF. See 13 VENDEMIAIRE YEAR IV.

VENTOSE DECREES (26 February and 3 March 1794), political and social legislation that provided for the sequestration of the property of enemies of the Revolution and its distribution to indigent patriots, proposed by L. Saint-Just, passed by the Convention, but never implemented. These decrees constitute a combination of measures whose political direction and ideological and social dimensions are so closely correlated that it is impossible to identify the dominant factor. On the political level, it was a matter of the Revolutionary authorities' consolidating the support of the *sans-culottes* and the *menu peuple* for the Jacobin dictatorship; here the circumstantial and tactical element is dominant. On the social level, in contrast, it was a matter of taking bold measures to make a commitment to a combined strategy for the transformation of society—a limited transformation, to be sure, but a genuine and significant one nonetheless.

With the first successes achieved by the Revolutionary government at the end of the autumn of 1793 and with the regularization of the operation of the state by the decree of 14 Frimaire Year II (4 December 1793), many bourgeois, capitalists, manufacturers, *gens à talent*, and men of property looked to a liberal relaxation of the policies of the Terror and of economic regulation. They supported the press campaign of the Indulgents, encouraged by C. Desmoulins in the *Vieux Cordelier* and inspired by G.-J. Danton and his friends. On the other hand, the problems of provisioning the workers, artisans, small shopkeepers, and poor peasants were being aggravated by winter. The black market was a scandal, as waiting lines multiplied and there were shortages in Paris, in other big cities, and in the countryside where large farms predominated. The Cordeliers club, most of the Paris sections, J.-R. Hébert's *Père Duchesne*, P.-G. Chaumette's friends in the Commune of Paris, and the unassigned personnel of the Revolutionary army served as spokesmen for popular anger. Committed patriots opposed the new moderates. In any event, in the countryside class relations were in a state of flux; the abolition of the remnants of feudalism by the decree of 17 July 1793 had favored landowners, large and small, and the big agricultural operators; but neither the laborers nor the tenants benefited from this since there had been no agrarian reform. The sale of *biens nationaux* and even the Law of 23 June 1793, authorizing the division of commons, had favored the rich or those who were landowners already and did little for others. Yet clearly it was on this mass of poor peasants, artisans, and workers that fell the task of defending the fatherland, supporting the war in the Vendée, the mobilization, and the strain of producing and transporting goods. At the same time, restrictions and shortages weighed on them. In the Committee of Public Safety J.-M. Collot d'Herbois and J.-N. Billaud-Varenne, who constituted the militant Left, served as representatives of the aspirations of the poor by demanding social measures and intensification of the Terror.

The Revolutionary government was conscious of the risk of breaking up the Revolutionary unity that had organized around it since the summer; it decided to preserve this unity at any cost. To have the support of the *sans-culottes*, it was necessary to strike against the Indulgents, but to maintain the interests and the confidence of manufacturers, property owners, *exploitants*, and merchants, so indispensable to the war effort, it was necessary to disassociate itself from the political leaders and cadres of the sections who had the *sans-culottes'* confidence because they expressed their social and moral ideal. The Ventôse decrees bore the mark of these contradictions in their very formulation and stipulations; they translated into words the game of complex and subtle compromises that the reality of the Jacobin movement inspired. The men who directed the Committee of Public Safety were themselves torn between conflicting necessities. Saint-

Just, who reported the two decrees, used all of his political talent attempting to overcome these basic contradictions by a concrete, political approach and by seeking a compromise in advance.

The Indulgent campaign had been sufficiently effective to impose on the Committees of Public Safety and of General Security the obligation of examining the cases of detained suspects in order to free those whose incarceration was improper. Saint-Just was charged with making a report that he presented to the Convention on 8 Ventôse. He was skillful enough to exploit the impact of the Indulgents' campaign and to use it to satisfy one of the principal demands of the *sans-culottes*, the sequestering of the property of suspects and of enemies of the Revolution. However, it was necessary to go further in the direction of social security (in the phrase of E. Labrousse), the foundation on which the Robespierrists hoped to consolidate the Republic. Already, on 12 Pluviôse and 3 Ventôse (1 and 21 February 1794), the Convention had voted 10 million francs for the assistance of the poor and had introduced the new general maximum. But to respond a little better to the demand for equality of possessions while at the same time taking advantage of what had been gained on 8 Ventôse, Saint-Just proposed in his own report of 13 Ventôse, that the property sequestered from enemies of the Revolution be distributed to "indigent patriots" (article 1). The decrees in Ventôse, thus, appear to be a single measure in two steps, with the distribution, clearly a social policy, following from the sequestration that was legitimized by political considerations. On the issue of sequestration, however, the Convention was going beyond a simple policy based on circumstances: counterrevolutionaries were denied the right to keep any part of the national patrimony. As for the distribution, the decree of 13 Ventôse was going further again than the recent measure on the division of commons: the principle of gratuity was established and the right of the poor ("all unfortunates" in article 2) was limited only by the requirement of patriotism. This was, in fact, to introduce the Revolutionary criterion of ideological conformity into a system of social welfare.

Six popular commissions had the task of sorting suspects into three categories: those who were to be freed, deported, or sent back to the Revolutionary Tribunal. The property of the last two categories was subject to sequestration. For its distribution, the communes were charged with drawing up a list of parties entitled to it. The Committee of General Security was charged with drawing up a model formula to be proposed to each committee of surveillance in order to establish a list of enemies of the Revolution. The Committee of Public Safety was charged with assembling and classifying all records, while relying on the representatives on mission to expedite the process.

The application of the Ventôse decrees ran into insurmountable obstacles. When the sequestered goods were not land but rather buildings or other property, would the beneficiaries be indemnified with the income from their sale? This would contradict the very spirit of legislation that aimed at assuring the economic independence of the beneficiaries. On the other hand, who were indigents? Those who did not pay taxes? In fact, many poor peasants paid some tax while at the same time they lived on the margin of indigence. Moreover, from place to place the criteria varied as much for the definition of suspect as for that of indigent, and of patriot to boot. Finally, Saint-Just dreamed of founding an egalitarian social republic on the emergence of a class of free landowners who owed everything to Revolution. But the Ventôse decrees, whose wording was ambiguous, were inadequate for this and the Robespierrists were not strong enough to go any further, even if they intended to do so. Finally, the bourgeois majority in the Convention was opposed, preferring to establish public charity rather than ensure the economic independence of the poor by measures that would diminish the security of the *assignats*, which were based on land. Also, the Convention preferred to allocate 500,000 francs to eliminate begging and to undertake the preparation of the important law on assistance of 22 Floréal Year II, while lumping the application of these decrees all together.

In other words, the application of the Ventôse decrees was neatly thwarted, sabotaged at the commune and district level, and perverted by administrators. This issue became a subject of discord even among the members of the Committee of Public Safety after the elimination of the factions, which had no more given them the means of resolving the problem of supplies than of obtaining the support of the *sans-culottes*. As A. Mathiez recognized, Saint-Just's plan heralded a republic that would go beyond the established order—"The unfortunate are the powers of the earth." "Happiness is a new idea in Europe"—but in practice the decrees did not go as far as the *sans-culottes* wished and were not sufficiently precise or effective to receive serious application from the beginning.

In the end, the decrees exercised an impact limited to the immediate political situation, but they preserved a very strong dose of Revolutionary propaganda and egalitarian ideology.

A. Mathiez, *La Révolution française* (Paris, 1960) and *Girondins et Montagnards* (Paris, 1930); A. Ollivier, *Saint-Just et la force des choses* (Paris, 1954); R. Schnerb, "L'application des decrets de ventôse dans le district de Thiers (Puy-de-Dôme)," *Ann. hist. de la Révo. française* 6 (1929), and "Les lois de ventôse et leur application dans le département du Puy-de-Dôme," *Ann. hist. de la Révo. française* 11 (1934); A. Soboul, *Saint-Just, discours et rapports*, 2d ed. (Paris, 1957).

C. Mazauric

Related entries: ARMEES REVOLUTIONNAIRES; BIENS NATIONAUX; CHAUMETTE; CORDELIERS CLUB; COMMITTEE OF GENERAL SECURITY; COMMITTEE OF PUBLIC SAFETY; DESMOULINS; HEBERT; INDULGENTS; SAINT-JUST; *VIEUX CORDELIER*.

VERGNIAUD, PIERRE-VICTURNIEN (1753-93), deputy of Bordeaux (Gironde) to the Legislative Assembly and the Convention and leader of the Girondins. Vergniaud attained eminent positions during periods of Girondin ascendancy. He was successively vice-president (31 August 1791) and president (31 October 1791) of the Legislative Assembly and was elected to this latter position again during the Revolution of 10 August 1792, at which juncture he declared the destitution of Louis XVI. He served as spokesman for the Committee of Twenty-one, which attempted to assume the functions of government between the fall of the monarchy and the first meeting of the Convention, and as one of four deputies named secretaries of the Convention after its inception. He was a member of the constitutional committee named on 10 October 1792 and later presided over the trial of, and pronounced sentence on, Louis XVI (January 1793). His last official function was as a member of the Commission of Twelve through which, in May 1793, the Girondin deputies sought to control the activities of the Paris Commune.

In spite of the respect shown him by his fellow Girondins, he was less decisive than J.-P. Brissot in determining the policies of the loosely bound group and distinguished himself mainly by the eloquence that he had developed earlier in his career as a lawyer and poetaster. He made a number of impressive and often influential speeches, among which contemporaries particularly noted his indictment of the *émigrés* (25 October 1791), his attack on Louis XVI's foreign minister, C.-A. Valdec de Lessart (13 March 1792), his philippic of suppositions against Louis XVI (3 July 1792), and his demand for an armed force to protect the Convention against the Paris crowd (20 May 1793). He is also credited with the celebrated aphorism that the Revolution, like Saturn, devours its own children.

Vergniaud espoused most of the causes and policies with which the Girondins are identified. Under the Legislative Assembly he was an outspoken advocate of war and played a conspicuous role in the campaign to intimidate and co-opt Louis XVI. During the National Convention he championed the departments against Paris and opposed measures sponsored by the Mountain for controlling prices and suspending juridical guarantees. He was a vociferous critic of J.-P. Marat and M. Robespierre's major forensic adversary during the months preceding his fall. But in his personal relations, he stood apart from many prominent liberal republicans and diverged from them on important substantive issues. During the trial of Louis XVI, though he advocated submitting the king's fate to the electorate and indirectly disavowed the prime movers of the revolution of 10 August, he voted for death without possibility of reprieve. At the height of the Girondin-Montagnard struggle in the spring of 1793, he sought to conciliate the warring factions and disassociated himself from the efforts of J.-B. Boyer-Fonfrède and A. Gensonné to expel the more extreme Montagnards from the Convention. Madame Roland, and others in her circle, suspected him of inconstancy and opportunism; and L. Saint-Just excluded him from the first category of guilty Girondins. But in a pamphlet issued from prison after the purge of 2 June 1793, Vergniaud unequivocally proclaimed his hostility to the victorious Montagnards; and the day following his trial (30 October 1793), he shared the fate of other proscribed Girondin deputies on the guillotine.

C. G. Bowers, *Pierre Vergniaud: Voice of the French Revolution* (New York, 1950); E. Lintilhac, *Vergniaud: le Drame des Girondins* (Paris, 1920); A. Mathiez, *Girondins et Montagnards* (Paris, 1930).

M. R. Cox

Related entries: BRISSOT DE WARVILLE; COMMISSION OF TWELVE; GENSONNE; GIRONDINS; LAW OF THE MAXIMUM; ROLAND DE LA PLATIERE, M.-J.; 10 AUGUST 1792.

VETO, SUSPENSIVE. See SUSPENSIVE VETO.

VICTOR AMADEUS III (1773-96), king of Sardinia-Piedmont. Unlike his predecessors, Victor Amadeus III failed to strengthen his kingdom. The traditional policy of the House of Savoy had been to enhance its authority by reducing the influence of the church and aristocracy and abolishing serfdom. In foreign affairs, the Savoyard dukes traditionally balanced themselves between the French and Austrians and exacted territorial compensation from whichever power was seeking Piedmont-Sardinia as an ally. Although Victor Amadeus did enlarge his army, he also dismissed his reforming ministers and restored clerical influence. After 1789 he became hostile to the Revolution. In 1790 he ordered Masonic societies to cease meeting and in 1791 allowed Turin to become a center for French counterrevolutionary *émigrés*.

In 1792 he rejected French offers of an alliance, thus failing to apply the traditional policy of balancing between France and Austria, and at the end of the year, the French overran Nice and Savoy. He joined the war against France but gained little by joining the Austrians save for the loan of a small contingent of Hapsburg troops.

Subsequent fighting along the line of the Alps remained indecisive for several years. In 1796, however, N. Bonaparte launched his first Italian campaign and forced Sardinia out of the war. Victor Amadeus' successors remained neutral until 1799 when they began to prepare for new hostilities against France. The French struck first and annexed Piedmont, which remained under French control until 1814.

J. Colin, *Etudes sur la campagne de 1796-97 en Italie* (Paris, 1898); C. Tivaroni, *Storia Critica del risorgimento italiano, 1735-1870*, 2 vols. (Turin, 1888-97).

S. T. Ross

Related entries: *EMIGRES*; FIRST COALITION; SECOND COALITION.

VIEUX CORDELIER, newspaper written and edited by Camille Desmoulins, 1793-94. On 5 December 1793 Desmoulins (1760-94) released his first issue of the *Vieux Cordelier*. This issue and the following one, published on 10 December, criticized the Hébertists, advocates of stringent measures including economic egalitarianism and Revolutionary violence. Since the Hébertists had leveled carping critiques at the government, M. Robespierre and the majority of the Committee of Public Safety made no objection to the first editions of the *Vieux Cordelier*. In fact, Robespierre even admitted reading the proofs of the second issue. Furthermore, as part of a plan to evaluate members, the Jacobin club on 14 December certified Desmoulins's Revolutionary purity. But the publication of the third issue of the *Vieux Cordelier* changed the views of the Jacobins and the Committee of Public Safety. This edition, published on 15 December, and the subsequent one released five days later, attacked the Terror and proposed clemency. To a government relying heavily on Revolutionary justice, Desmoulins' demands appeared treasonous. To be sure, his assaults were indirect but their subtlety did not obscure their force for contemporaries.

A lack of documentary evidence has forced historians to conjecture about Desmoulins' motives for the attack on the Hébertists and the far more dangerous assault on the Terror. His biographers especially have stressed personal reasons. They note that although Desmoulins played a very active role in the early Revolution and had been particularly effective as a journalist, his election to the Convention in 1792 signaled his eclipse. The stuttering Desmoulins found the legislative forum ill suited to him and appeared there rarely. Instead, always tempted by epicurean pleasures, he enjoyed the company of his beautiful wife, Lucile, and the gambling tables. Pleasures and relaxation made Desmoulins regret the executions of the Brissotins and become hostile to the Terror. In addition, these biographers posit, the rise in late 1793 of the Hébertists with their emphases on equality and Revolutionary allegiance challenged Desmoulins. His life-style and absence from the Convention raised their suspicions. One of the Hébertists, P.-S. Deschamps, attacked Desmoulins from the floor of the Convention on 1 December 1793. Consequently, some historians interpret Desmoulins' journalistic venture as an attempt to fend off the Hébertists and to try to modify the Terror that then troubled him.

Other investigators have taken a different perspective on Desmoulins' decision to publish the *Vieux Cordelier* and have focused on his alliance with G.-J. Danton. Among such scholars is A. Mathiez, who believed the strictures of the *Vieux Cordelier* against the Terror were simply a means to protect the Dantonists from punishment for financial peculation. He insisted, furthermore, that the attack on the Hébertists was only a feint to distract the Committee of Public Safety. The journalist always planned to criticize the Terror, but emerging evidence about the Dantonists' guilt hastened the attack. Historians more sympathetic to the Dantonists have envisioned Desmoulins' newspaper as an expression of that faction's humane wish to modify Hébertist austerity and to end the Terror.

Finally, some researchers have concentrated more on daily circumstances than on prior planning, either by Desmoulins or the Dantonists, to explain the escalating vituperation, first against the Hébertists, then against the Terror. But whatever the motivations, the *Vieux Cordelier*'s charges against the Terror set off a hail of criticism against its author. Conservative circles' praise of the periodical only exacerbated the Revolutionaries' hostility. The publicist, probably fearful and somewhat intimidated, countered with a defense that was a partial retraction in his fifth edition, published on 5 January 1794. But it proved to be too little, for on 5 and 7 January, the Convention and the Jacobins decided to scrutinize his actions. Because of Desmoulins' prior contributions to the Revolution and his agreeable personality, many inclined toward separating the man from his writing. Robespierre, who knew Desmoulins from *collège*, urged that course. But impulsively returning to the offensive once again, Desmoulins insisted during the debate that his objections must be answered. The response undid the efforts of those who were trying to defend Desmoulins the man rather than his periodical, and responsibility fell on Desmoulins. Wavering, he produced another defense as the sixth issue of the *Vieux Cordelier* (dated 25 January 1794 but not published until February), but it was ignored. He had irrevocably associated himself with a policy critical of the Terror.

Whether Desmoulins deliberately acted in concert with the Dantonists or not, they too were advocating a lessening of repression. Thus, Desmoulins' opposition to the Terror linked him to the Dantonists. Their fate became his, and his problems increased theirs as well. When the Committee of Public Safety decided to eliminate all opposing factions, they naturally included Desmoulins. At his arrest, investigators discovered drafts of a seventh issue of the *Vieux Cordelier* and other fragments that indicated renewed aggressiveness, for in these pages he leveled charges against the political leadership. On 13 April 1794, the authorities sent Desmoulins to the guillotine.

C. Desmoulins, *Le Vieux Cordelier*, ed. H. Calvet and A. Mathiez (Paris, 1936); L. Gallois, *Histoire des journaux*, vol. 2 (Paris, 1846); E. Hatin, *Histoire de la presse*, vol. 5 (Paris, 1860).

J. R. Censer

Related entries: COMMITTEE OF PUBLIC SAFETY; DANTON; DESMOULINS; GIRONDINS; HEBERTISTS; INDULGENTS; ROBESPIERRE, M.

VIGEE-LEBRUN, MARIE-LOUISE-ELISABETH (1755-1842), most celebrated French woman artist of the eighteenth century. Born in Paris on 16 April 1755, Elisabeth Vigée-Lebrun shares with A. Kauffmann the reputation of being the most renowned woman artist in their time. Her father, L. Vigée, a professor at the Académie de Saint-Luc and a pastel portraitist, placed his precocious child in a convent, where she revealed her passion for painting at an early age. Encouraged by her father and his closest friends, G.-F. Doyen and C.-J. Vernet, she continued her art lessons with P. Davesne and G. Briard. Denied formal instruction in the academies because of her sex, she copied the masters, notably Rubens, Rembrandt, Van Dyck, and Raphael, in the galleries of Paris. When her father died prematurely when she was thirteen, she supported her mother and younger brother by selling copies of paintings in the Louvre.

It was not until she was admitted to the Académie de Saint-Luc in 1774 that she received the credentials to qualify as a legitimate artist. The following year she presented portraits of cardinal de Fleury and J. de La Bruyère to the Académie Royale and received, in return, its highest compliments. In 1776 she married J.-B.-P. Lebrun, an important art dealer but an incorrigible gambler and spendthrift who squandered her money. In that same year she painted the king's brother, the future Louis XVIII, and three years later the queen. During the next decade, she executed nearly forty, mostly life-size, portraits of Marie Antoinette, painted every member of the royal family except the comte d'Artois, and became the fashion of the *haute société*. Largely through the efforts of the queen, she was admitted to the Académie Royale in 1783. Her reputation catapulted and her salon attracted such notables as the minister C.-A. de Calonne, the duc d'Orléans, the duchesses de Chartres and de Polignac, the marquis de Choiseul, the comte de Vaudreuil, the comtesses de Brionne and de Sabran, the vicomte de Ségur, and Madame du Barry. A list of her clientele reads like a directory of the *ancien régime*. She became equally famous for her musical *soirées*, which attracted the finest artists, actors, and savants of Paris. "In those days," she lamented in her memoirs, "women reigned; the Revolution dethroned them."

More aristocratic in outlook and manners than the aristocrats themselves, she soon became the target of the Revolutionaries. After numerous threats on her life, she disguised herself as a working woman and escaped from Paris on the same October evening in 1789 that Louis XVI and the royal family were escorted from Versailles to the Tuileries. For the next three years, she traveled throughout Italy, joining the art academies of Rome, Parma, and Bologna. Wherever she went, her reputation preceded her, and she became the darling of the courts. She spent two years with the Hapsburgs in Vienna (1793-95) and six years with the Romanovs in Saint Petersburg (1796-1801), where she was admitted to the Imperial Academy. In the meantime, her husband, who remained in Paris, and her fellow artists signed petitions to remove her name from the list of *émigrés*, making it possible for her to return to Paris in 1801. Still suspected of loyalty to the Bourbons, Vigée-Lebrun journeyed to England for three years and later to Switzerland. When she finally returned to France, she bought a country retreat in Louveciennes where she continued to paint and send her works to the Salon until 1824. In the 1830s she published her *Souvenirs*, depicting her aristocratic friends as gracefully in words as she had painted their portraits in oils.

In her *Souvenirs* she lists 662 portraits, 15 subject paintings, and 200 landscapes. There may have been more portraits, but virtually all of her landscapes have disappeared. Her fame rests on her portraits, especially of women, whom she presented as youthful, charming, and gracious figures. In a period when prettiness was in vogue, she adhered to her dictum that women must be flattered and excelled in capturing the color and charm, simplicity and sweetness of her feminine subjects. Her settings, too, reflect the gentility, affability, and urbanity of aristocratic society. Louis XVI's comment, "I know nothing about painting, but you make me like it," speaks for many admirers of France's most successful female artist of the century if not of all time.

L. Hautecoeur, *Madame Vigée-Lebrun* (Paris, 1917); W. H. Helm, *Vigée-Lebrun, Her Life, Works, and Friendships* (London, 1916); P. de Nolhac, *Madame Vigée-Lebrun: Painter of Marie Antoinette* (Paris, 1912); M.L.E. Vigée-Lebrun, *Souvenirs de Mme. Vigée-Lebrun*, 2 vols. (Paris, 1835-37).

H. V. Evans

Related entry: DAVID.

VINCENNES. See PRISONS.

VINGTIEME, widely resented tax on income during the Old Regime. The *vingtième* was a royal tax of one-twentieth of the income introduced in France in 1749 after long and bitter opposition from both the Parlement of Paris and the Church. It was the added expense and burden of debt occasioned by the War of the Austrian Succession (1740-48) that led the finance minister, L.-C. de Machault d'Arnouville, to try to reintroduce a percentage tax on income like the royal *dîme* of Louis XIV. It was to be paid by all recipients of income from both real and movable property. His attempt to include church property failed, but the levy of a *vingtième* on most forms of lay property was finally reluctantly registered by the Parlement of Paris.

Besides the fact that it was to fall on the property of the nobility as well as the Third Estate, the *vingtième* was also unique in that it was intended to reach new categories of income, such as minor offices, and income producing intangibles as well as commerce and industry. In this it failed since typically less than 5 percent of the revenue of the tax ever came from movable property.

The original hope of the government was that as a percentage tax, the revenue from it would increase along with the wealth of the country, but, as the price of registration, the Parlement of Paris amended its terms so that the amount collected by the government in any year could not exceed the amount collected in the initial year (57 million *livres*). When a second *vingtième* was added in 1756, everyone paid just twice their original assessment plus a small surtax. In 1760 and again in 1782, a third *vingtième* was added to help meet the additional expenses of war. The government had been requiring parishes in the *pays d'élections* to establish accurate property registers so the assessments would be more accurate, but in late 1782 the Parlement of Paris demanded that the process be stopped as the price of its registering the third *vingtième*. The practice of allowing *abonnements* (lump sum payments by various corporate entities such as certain of the *pays d'états*, as well as some towns and cities and other corporate groups) certainly also reduced the government's yield and probably tended to favor the rich and the powerful.

M. Marion, the authority on Old Regime taxation, states that the tax was systematically evaded by the privileged and in practice became merely a supplement to the *taille*. A contemporary scholar, C. B. A. Behrens, points out that many members of the Third Estate were exempted from the *taille* or found other ways of evading the tax burden. Certainly they benefited equally from *abonnements*. It is her conclusion that the nobility did feel the burden of the *vingtième* and probably paid more in direct taxes than their English counterparts (gentry).

C. B. A. Behrens, "Nobles, Privileges and Taxes in France at the End of the Ancien Regime," *Econ. Hist. Rev.*, 2d ser., vol. 15 (1962-63); M. Marion, *Dictionnaire des institutions de la France aux XVIIe et XVIIIe siècles* (Paris, 1923) and *Histoire financière de la France depuis 1715*, 3 vols. (Paris, 1914-28).

R. W. Greenlaw

Related entry: *TAILLE*.

VIRIEU, FRANCOIS-HENRI, COMTE DE (1754-93), deputy to the National Assembly. Virieu was an army colonel from a distinguished noble family of Dauphiné, a Freemason, interested in public affairs, who saw merit in E.-C. de Loménie de Brienne's provincial assemblies but resisted the judicial reform of Loménie and C.-F. Lamoignon in 1788. After carrying to Versailles a petition from the nobility demanding recall of the parlement and revival of the Dauphiné Estates, he became a noble deputy to the Estates General and gradually moved into an alliance with his friend J.-J. Mounier in support of the *monarchien* program for representative government along English lines.

Virieu was cautious about preserving royal prerogatives and the property rights and political influence of the aristocracy. He joined the National Assembly on 25 June, supported the *monarchien* strategy on 4 August 1789, and was an aggressive partisan of the two chambers and absolute veto defeated in September and made hopeless in October. Unlike Mounier, Virieu remained in the National Assembly after the October Days and was active until after the king's flight in June 1791. He was living in Lyon in 1793 when the city rebelled against the Convention. During the siege, he became one of the royalist commanders. He was killed in October when the city fell.

J. Egret, *La Pré-Révolution française (1787-1788)* (Paris, 1962) and *La Révolution des Notables. Mounier et les Monarchiens. 1789* (Paris, 1950); J. Michaud and L. G. Michaud, eds., *Biographie universelle, ancienne et moderne*, vol. 43 (Paris, 1866).

P. H. Beik

Related entries: LYON; *MONARCHIENS*; MOUNIER; OCTOBER DAYS.

VIZILLE. See DAUPHINE.

VOLTAIRE, FRANCOIS-MARIE AROUET DE (1694-1778), *philosophe*. Although he later claimed to be the bastard son of an obscure nobleman, François-Marie Arouet was born into a middle-class Parisian family on 21 November 1694. Educated at the illustrious Jesuit collège Louis-le-Grand, where he excelled as a student, he soon gained a reputation as a rising young poet and became associated with the licentious Parisian society of the Temple. At the age of twenty-four, he assumed the pen name Voltaire and established himself as France's leading playwright with the production of his tragedy *Oedipe*. By 1726 he had outdistanced most of his rivals as a man of letters, had set out on the road to riches through investment and speculation, and had managed twice to get himself imprisoned in the Bastille for personal and literary indiscretions. Released from his second confinement when he agreed to go into exile in England, he spent three years observing the land of Newton and Locke firsthand and viewing his homeland from a new perspective. The result was his first major reformist publication, *The Philosophical Letters on the English*, published in France in 1734.

During the ten years after publication of the *Philosophical Letters*, Voltaire lived with his brilliant mistress, Madame du Châtelet, at Cirey, her estate in

Champagne. There he composed a popularization of Newtonian physics, began to write the *Age of Louis XIV*, and sketched out a plan for the *Histoire des moeurs*. After three turbulent years as court historiographer at Versailles, he returned to Cirey, but he resumed his travels a few years later when Madame du Châtelet died giving birth to another lover's baby. The years 1750 to 1753 found Voltaire again playing the courtier, this time at the palace of Frederick II, with whom he had previously carried on an extensive correspondence. Although the Berlin period was productive in historical studies and a variety of short works, it was marred by professional and personal quarrels, including a nasty lawsuit over a questionable joint venture with a Jewish businessman in currency speculation. For two years following his departure from Berlin, he moved from place to place; in 1755 Voltaire took up residence at an estate near Geneva, which he named Les Délices. In that delightful setting he wrote *Candide* and a number of other works yet still found time to carry on a bitter verbal battle with the Calvinist authorities of Geneva. The fighting ended only when the famous but combative *philosophe* decided to depart in 1760.

The last eighteen years of his life Voltaire spent as the lord of Ferney, an estate on the border of Switzerland and France, where the *philosophe* who now called himself the comte de Tournay set up housekeeping with his niece and lover, Madame Denis. Despite his age and chronic bad health, he continued to write prolifically. At the same time, as lord of the manor, he made Ferney a laboratory for testing the social, religious, and economic reforms he advocated. It was also during this time that he launched the practical part of his crusade for religious toleration by denouncing the official persecution of J. Calas, the chevalier de la Barre, and the Sirven family. By 1778 he had become the undisputed intellectual sovereign of Europe. In recognition of his international stature the French government allowed him to visit Paris, whose inhabitants showered him with expressions of love and admiration. Overtaxed by the exciting homecoming, his frail body gave way, and he died on 30 May.

At his death, Voltaire left a substantial financial fortune. His literary legacy was equally immense and incredibly varied. His total output, including correspondence, numbered over 23,000 separate pieces of writing. In form they range from histories, tragedies, and epic poems to philosophical tales, short poems, and letters. In content they are nothing less than encyclopedic. The vast volume and scope of the legacy is relatively easy to determine; not so its impact on events since Voltaire's death in 1778. One reason is that so many different, sometimes conflicting, causes have claimed Voltaire as patron saint during the past two centuries. That practice had its origin in the French Revolution.

Historians have debated Voltaire's contribution to the coming of the Revolution in 1789, but they have generally agreed that the Revolutionaries themselves regarded him as one of their precursors. His name appeared frequently in the Revolutionary debates, published pamphlets, and newspapers. His collected works went through three editions in the first three years of the Revolution. The Theater of the Nation revived his tragedy *Brutus*; other theaters staged plays about his life; painters and sculptors portrayed him in popular works of art; Revolutionary songwriters praised him in their lyrics; and in July 1791 the National Assembly organized a magnificent procession to transfer his remains from the abbey of Scellières in Champagne to the Panthéon in Paris. That ceremony, by glorifying one of the best-known enemies of the church, marked a symbolic turning point in the religious policies of the Revolution

With a few exceptions, especially among clergymen, literate Frenchmen of the Revolutionary decade seem to have shared their leaders' admiration for the most famous of the *philosophes*. However, they saw him in very different ways. Supporters of the king took the position that Voltaire never wavered from his basic attachment to the monarchy, despite his reformist activities. Early Revolutionary moderates thought of him as the champion of the natural rights of man, constitutionalism, and political participation restricted to the propertied classes. As the Revolution moved to the left, so too did the image of Voltaire. It came not only to be associated with republicanism but with Jacobin radicalism, with Montagnard martyrs such as J.-P. Marat and L.-M. Lepelletier, and with the militant *sans-culottes*. Thus from a self styled nobleman who favored reforms from above, Voltaire was transformed into a symbol of democracy and even terrorism. Like the Revolution itself, the image of Voltaire has remained, and undoubtedly will remain in the future, a point of profound scholarly and popular disagreement.

T. Besterman, *Voltaire*, 3d ed. (Oxford, 1976); G. Lanson, *Voltaire*, trans. Robert A. Wagoner (New York, 1966); J. A. Leith, "Les trois apothéoses de Voltaire," *Ann. hist. de la Révo. française* 51 (1979); K. N. McKee, "Voltaire's *Brutus* during the French Revolution," *Mod. Lang. Notes* 56 (1941); R. Waldinger, *Voltaire and Reform in the Light of the Revolution* (Geneva, 1959).

R. Vignery

Related entries: *ENCYCLOPEDIE*; ENLIGHTENMENT; JACOBINS; MONTAGNARDS; *SANS-CULOTTES*.

VOLUNTEERS, NATIONAL. See NATIONAL VOLUNTEERS.

VONCK, JEAN-FRANCOIS (1743-92), lawyer and Belgian revolutionary. Son of a successful farming family from Baerdegem, near Alost, Vonck studied humanities at the Jesuit collège in Brussels and law at the University of Louvain. His brilliance soon made him a leader among Brussels' lawyers. A reader of the *philosophes*, he was offended by violations of Belgian rights by Joseph II, the Holy Roman Emperor and ruler of the Austrian Netherlands. In 1787, Vonck collaborated with H. van der Noot in organizing resistance to the Austrians.

While van der Noot sought foreign support, Vonck believed Belgians should free themselves. Through a secret Brussels society, Pro Aris et Focis, he enlisted volunteers and, for commander of the patriotic army, J. van der Mersch. Financial and moral support was supplied by clergy anxious to reverse Joseph II's reforms affecting the church. Flushed from Brussels by the Austrians in October 1789, Vonck's forces joined with those of van der Noot at Breda in Dutch Brabant.

Successful invasion of Belgium and defeat of the Austrians in November was followed by a falling out between the Vonckists, or progressives, and van der Noot's statists, or conservatives. In a pamphlet, *Considérations impartials sur le position actuel du Brabant*, published in June 1790, Vonck advocated constitutional reform. Lesser nobles and lower clergy should be added to the first two estates. The Third Estate was to be doubled in size and include educated and financially successful bourgeois and representatives of small towns and small landowners, as well as the present city burgomasters and trades corporation leaders. Full democracy was not envisioned; the vote would be granted only to men who could meet a significant property requirement. Vonck further challenged the right of the Provincial Estates to combine in their hands both the legislative and executive powers. A liberal reformer, Vonck believed the time of popular sovereignty had arrived. Van der Noot and the Estates of Brabant held, however, that sovereignty rested with the Provincial Estates, and the privileged classes were not interested in expanding the franchise.

Although Vonck's contacts with France were limited, involving some correspondence with H.-G. R. Mirabeau and others, and though he himself was not anticlerical, he lost the support of many nationalists and clergy. His followers were attacked by peasants, under clerical leadership, as symbols of the Enlightenment and French influence. The admiration of left-wing Vonckists for the French National Assembly, which was now planning serious anticlerical measures, further stimulated conservative suspicions. For its part, the upper bourgeoisie had prospered under the Austrians and saw little reason to flock to the progressive cause.

A sensitive and reflective bachelor plagued by ill health, Vonck could not match van der Noot's bombast and popularity. Vonck's position in the crucial province of Brabant was weak; his strength lay in Flanders and with the Flemish-speaking populace, among some army officers, and with a few nobles. Van der Noot was supported by the French-speaking aristocracy, the leading clergy, the Brabant peasantry, and the Provincial Estates. Strengthened by rural terror, in May 1790 the statists proscribed Vonckists from Brabant, banned Vonck's club, the Société patriotique and its blue colors, and attempted to arrest the signers of Vonck's 15 March petition for modernization of the *Joyeuse-Entrée*. Vonck fled to Lille. Shortly before his death there in 1792, he published a tract, written before May 1791, entitled *Onzeidige Aenmerkingen*; in it he further detailed his spirit of individualism and what H. Pirenne has termed his "liberal opportunism" and his hope for an "elective aristocracy."

Briefly the leader of the Brabant revolution and the initiator of armed revolt, Vonck shifted his primary concern over a period of months from nationalism to democratic reform; in exile Vonck's followers would support importation of foreign revolution to their homeland. Early writers often were critical of Vonck as they set van der Noot's nationalism against the French influence allegedly represented by Vonck. Since 1918, historians have vindicated the progressive cause.

H. Pirenne, *Histoire de Belgique*, 7 vols. (Brussels, 1909-32); S. Tassier, *Les démocrates belges de 1789. Etude sur le Vonckisme et la Révolution brabançonne* (Brussels, 1930).

J. E. Helmreich

Related entries: BELGIUM; JOSEPH II.

W

WATTIGNIES, BATTLE OF. See BATTLE OF WATTIGNIES.

WEISHAUPT, ADAM (1748-1830). See ILLUMINATI.

WESTERMANN, FRANCOIS-JOSEPH (1751-94), soldier, Revolutionary militant, general. Born at Molsheim (Alsace) in 1751, he became a hussar at fifteen in the Esterhazy regiment and by 1773 was a noncommissioned officer with the Royal Dragoons. He later served as an equerry in the stables of the comte d'Artois (1787). A year later he became *échevin* at Strasbourg, then a secretary in the Revolutionary municipality of Haguenau (1789), where he accused his predecessors of mishandling funds. Accused of insurrectionary activity in 1790 and pursued by P.-F. Dietrich, mayor of Strasbourg, he sought refuge in Paris, where he was protected by the Cordeliers (J.-P. Marat, P.-F. Fabre d'Eglantine, and the lawyer C.-R. Buirette de Verrières).

On the eve of 10 August 1792 he was a member of the directory of the *fédérés*, and in the insurrection he played a leading role as commander of the *fédérés* from Brest, fighting in the vanguard as if he were hungry for death. He was sent by G.-J. Danton to C. Dumouriez, to participate in the negotiations with the duke of Brunswick that ultimately led to the Prussian retreat from France, as well as to serve as an aide to Dumouriez. Appointed colonel, commanding the *Légion du Nord*, he served at Jemappes.

A member of Dumouriez' general staff, he supported Dumouriez in his struggle against the minister of war, J.-N. Pache, for control over supplies needed by Dumouriez' forces in Belgium. He was denounced by the Lombards section of Paris for slandering their volunteers when he accused them of flight. Their commander was the Robespierrist L.-J.-B. Lavalette. He was attacked also by Marat. Taking part next in Dumouriez' invasion of Holland (February 1793), he was successful at Gertruydenberg and Breda but was stopped at Aix-la-Chapelle and escorted back across the French border by Austrian forces. On

Dumouriez' defection, Westermann was arrested and investigated by a Convention commission headed by A. Lecointre of Versailles. He conceded an Austrian effort to bribe him into betrayal but was cleared of all charges (April-May 1793). Dispatched next to the Vendée, where he fought in turn under Generals A.-L. Biron, F. Chalbos, and F.-S. D. Marceau (May-December 1793), he was successful at Moulin aux Chevres, had mixed results at Châtillon, was defeated at La Flèche, and was victorious in the savage battle at Le Mans and at Savaney. He was praised, as always, for his personal courage. He was also accused of brutality and pillage, mistreating his own soldiers, insubordination toward visiting civilian agents, and needless burning of enemy châteaux. He was nicknamed the butcher of the Vendée. In July 1793 he was brought before the Convention on a variety of charges; he was court-martialed and then acquitted.

Accused some months later by M. Robespierre and L. Saint-Just of leaving his army without permission, he was defended by the deputy J.-B. Carrier and General Marceau. He was removed from command but cleared by the Convention in January 1794.

His own unmanageability had contributed to his repeated difficulties with Paris, but the principal cause was political: his own associations with the aristocratic Biron and with the Dantonist deputies on mission (such as P.-N. Philippeaux) during a period when Hébertists like Generals J.-A. Rossignol and C.-P. Ronsin were in the ascendancy in the Vendée because they had the support of the by now Robespierre-dominated Committee of Public Safety.

In the trials of Germinal, Westermann was a witness (against Ronsin and the Hébertists) and a last-minute defendant himself when the earlier charges of traitorous connections with Dumouriez were revived against him. It is unlikely that the government believed these charges, but it feared in Westermann a friend of Danton who was a man of action and who, if left free, could give Danton military support. There is a strong tradition, in fact, that Westermann had urged on Danton such a course of action prior to the trial. They died on the scaffold together.

A. P. Herlaut, *Le général rouge. Ronsin* (Paris, 1956); A. Mathiez, "Westermann et la cour à la veille du 10 août," *Ann. révo.* 9 (1917); J. Robinet, *La procès des dantonistes* (Paris, 1879).

S. Lytle

Related entries: BATTLE OF JEMAPPES; COMMITTEE OF PUBLIC SAFETY; CORDELIERS CLUB; DANTON; DIETRICH; DUMOURIEZ; HEBERTISTS; INDULGENTS; MARAT; ROBESPIERRE, M.; VENDEE.

WHITE TERROR, the series of murders and violent reprisals carried out in response to the Jacobin Red Terror of the Year II. There was more than one White Terror; the first was a wave of anti-Terrorist violence in the year following 9 Thermidor. Although this first White Terror, described here, was concentrated in the Year III, counterterrorist acts continued throughout the Directory and into the period of the Consulate. The second White Terror was perpetrated against ex-Jacobins and Bonapartists in the months following the defeat of Napoleon at Waterloo in 1815.

Violent reprisals against the Jacobin terrorists were made possible by the release of suspects just before and, especially, after the overthrow of M. Robespierre. The reprisals were further encouraged by the return to France, during the Thermidorian and Directory periods, of many *émigrés* with royalist sympathies. News of the last *sans-culotte* risings in Paris in Germinal and Prairial Year III provoked the counterterrorists, as did the local rising of Jacobins in Toulon in Prairial Year III. The ex-Jacobins were especially vulnerable targets for the murder gangs after the laws, such as that of 21 Germinal, that confined them to their place of residence for purposes of surveillance and then disarmed them after the Parisian revolts. These measures clearly identified the ex-Jacobins for anyone planning violence against them, and identification was made even easier for White Terrorists by the publication of blacklists of the so-called *buveurs de sang* by newspapers such as the *Anti-Terroriste* of Toulouse.

The economic context of the White Terror was also important, for the White Terrorist murders of the Year III occurred against a background of severe hardship, the end of price control, astronomically high inflation of the Revolutionary paper currency, and the disastrous winter of the famine year of 1795.

The worst excesses of the White Terrorist murder gangs were committed in the Rhône Valley and Provence, but their activities covered the southeast of France from the Swiss frontier to the Mediterranean, and White Terrorist incidents were also reported in the southwest (for example, in the Ariège and the Bordelais). The White Terrorists acted in a spirit of ferocity, with a taste for bravura and the uncompromising hatred of the vendetta, which were peculiar to the Midi.

Lyon, in particular, was the scene of brutal and brazen acts of White Terrorist vengeance. Lyon was the main center of royalist intrigue in France, attracting many returning *émigrés* over the Swiss border. The town was still partly in ruins after the siege and destruction of 1793, and its debris and underground passages provided ideal protections for assassins. In any case, the Lyonnais authorities were notoriously reluctant to convict White Terrorist assassins. In addition, the city's rivers provided a convenient dumping ground for corpses.

In the judicial records of the Bouches-du-Rhône department, R. Cobb found evidence of 846 murders committed in the southeast between the Years III and VII. The deputy G.-G.-A. de Bouvier, however, claimed that 1,500 had been murdered in the Vaucluse alone over a similar period, and Cobb estimates that overall the White Terror accounted for 2,000 popular militants in the Midi.

The prison massacres of Floréal-Prairial Year III alone claimed several hundred victims. On the evening of 15 Floréal Year III, a violent crowd invaded the Lyon prisons of Roanne, the Recluses, and Saint-Joseph, massacring between 100 and 120 victims, many of them former Jacobins. Neither the district nor the departmental authorities intervened, and not a shot was fired at the rioters. Sixty were killed in the prison massacre at Aix-en-Provence on 21 Floréal; and about another hundred fell victim to the White Terrorists who broke into the Fort Saint-Jean in Marseille in Prairial. Other prison massacres were reported in Tarascon, Lons-le-Saulnier, and Montbrison.

The White Terrorist murder gangs benefited from the hesitancy and perhaps the connivance of public authorities and the forces of order. In Lyon, it was safer to allow the prison massacres to proceed rather than to fire on a large, violent crowd when police forces were inadequate to contain such a riot. Police escorts taking ex-Jacobins for questioning were overpowered with suspicious ease. At Nîmes, four prisoners being transferred to another jail were murdered in Ventôse Year III, although they were escorted by 300 soldiers. *Juges de paix* often failed to notify higher authorities that crimes had been committed. In Lyon, individual murders were commonly carried out in daylight. A typical case was the assassination in Lyon of J. Fernex, ex-member of the *Commission révolutionnaire de Lyon*, in Pluviôse Year III. A murder gang seized the victim from an armed escort of fifty who were accompanying him to prison. Fernex was thrown into the River Rhône. No legal proceedings were ever taken against his murderers.

The White Terror was not so violent everywhere. In Toulouse, for instance, it was chiefly limited to beatings, verbal threats, and attacks on the property of ex-Jacobins. Where the Red Terror had been mild, the White Terror was correspondingly restrained; where the Terror had been accompanied by severe repression, as in Lyon, then the White Terror took a heavy toll.

The victims of the White Terror were carefully chosen. They included purchasers of *biens nationaux*, tax collectors, and married priests. They might include anyone who had played a prominent political role in the Year II: members of the local Revolutionary committee, the Revolutionary tribunal, or the *armée révolutionnaire*. In the Lozère, they included many wealthy Protestant farmers, who had bought church property. The victims would include denunciators of the Year II if the White Terrorists could persuade the authorities to divulge their names. Other targets for bloody vengeance were prominent orators of the Jacobin clubs and Jacobin mayors, like J.-J. Groussac of Toulouse, murdered on the Bordeaux road in the Year VI. At least ten *commissaires du Directoire* were also assassinated.

The chief motivation for the White Terror was not the restoration of the monarchy but simply vengeance, usually of a private kind, against the Jacobins. Murders were not spontaneous; they were carried out by groups, who picked their victims, chose their time (often a Sunday evening in summer), and premeditated their attack. Republicans claimed that the White Terrorist murder gangs were organized by the counterrevolutionary secret societies, known as the Compagnie de Jésus and the Compagnie du Soleil, but the existence of these secret organizations has not been decisively proved.

The murders were carried out with internecine cruelty. Victims and murderers were often well known to each other. Sometimes entire families were butchered, and in some cases the corpses were mutilated or dismembered. The weapons (the shotgun at close range, the axe, the pitchfork, or the scythe), like the cruelty of the White Terror, reflected traditional patterns of rural crime.

The murderers probably included some of the royalist thugs of the *jeunesse dorée*, but the gangs of assassins were also recruited from the criminal classes—poachers, smugglers, and horse thieves, not to mention deserters. The desire for vengeance was fueled by local rivalries, like that which festered in Toulouse between the ex-parlementary quarter of Saint-Barthélémy and the popular quarter of Saint-Cyprien on the other side of the River Garonne. Lower-class royalism, however, drew its main strength from traditional artisan trades, especially those who had been dependent on the *ancien régime* for economic security. In Toulouse, for example, it was the disbanding of the parlement and the aristocratic emigration that deprived many artisans of a clientele and strengthened nostalgia for the *ancien régime*.

The White Terror was not confined to the Year III or even to the Directory, itself a period of sporadic brigandage. The vendettas pursued in the Year III were not over and the memories of 1793 were not dead in 1815 when a new upsurge of White Terrorist violence engulfed the south. The continuity of the White Terror is best illustrated in the Gard department, which was unique in the sense that one-third of its population was Protestant. Here religious conflict dated at least from the War of the Camisards, and it was renewed in 1790 when about 300 Catholics were killed in Nîmes. This was the main reference point for the White Terror in the Gard, both in the 1790s and again in 1815. White Terrorism in Nîmes was organized by J.-M. de Froment, a tithe collector, who was responsible for arming the Catholic and royalist *cebets* ("onion eaters"). Through Froment, the White Terror in the Gard was linked to *émigré* circles in Turin. In the Gard religious divisions often coincided with social differences, the Protestant silk manufacturers were opposed by their mainly Catholic employees. Elsewhere the White Terror had an antipopular character, but in Nîmes, it was directed against Protestant property owners. In the Gard then, the White Terrors in 1795 and 1815 cannot be understood without reference to atavistic hatreds that had surfaced most recently in 1790.

The White Terror could therefore be exploited by *émigrés* and the aristocratic counterrevolution. For the most part, however, the White Terrorist murder gangs of the Midi were intent merely on settling old scores and paying off informers and terrorists, to satisfy personal honor and desire for vengeance. Their main achievement was to remove from circulation a large number of popular militants who were already cornered and frightened. The *sans-culotte* movement in Paris was suffering the defeats of Germinal and Prairial Year III; the White Terrorists in the southeast made sure that the defeat of local militants was sealed in blood.

R. C. Cobb, *The Police and the People: French Popular Protest, 1789-1820* (Oxford, 1970) and *Reactions to the French Revolution* (London, 1972); R. Fuoc, *La Réaction thermidorienne à Lyon, 1795* (Lyon, 1957); J. Godechot, *La Contre-Révolution, 1789-1804* (Paris, 1961); G. Lewis, *The Second Vendée: The Continuity of Counter-Revolution in the Department of the Gard, 1789-1815* (Oxford, 1979).

M. Lyons

Related entries: *ARMEES REVOLUTIONNAIRES*; COMPANIES OF JESUS; COMPANIES OF THE SUN; COUNTERREVOLUTION; *EMIGRES*; *JEUNESSE DOREE*; LYON; MARSEILLE; 9 THERMIDOR YEAR II; *SANS-CULOTTES*; TERROR, THE; THERMIDORIAN REACTION; TOULOUSE.

WICKHAM, WILLIAM (1761-1840), British intelligence agent in Switzerland, 1794-1800. After Thermidor, J. Mallet du Pan, the celebrated Swiss publicist, dispatched several memoirs to the British Foreign Office, urging it to send an agent to Switzerland to discuss the possibilities of restoring the Bourbons as constitutional monarchs in France. The British government quickly accepted the invitation and on 15 October 1794 sent Wickham, a fairly insignificant official in the Home Department, to Berne. Having received his degree in law at the University of Geneva, having married into the distinguished Swiss Bertrand family, and having worked with *émigrés* in the Home Department, Wickham was well suited for the confidential mission. Moreover, his intimate friendship with Lord Grenville, the foreign secretary, and his previous experience on secret missions added to his qualifications as a foreign emissary.

Wickham was instructed to maintain good relations with the cantons, to gather intelligence, to recruit men for the British army, to encourage insurrections in the Midi, Lyon, and the Vendée, to serve as W. Pitt's paymaster on the Continent, and, most important, to unite the royalists (supporters of the comte de Provence) and the constitutionalists (defenders of the 1791 Constitution) in their counterrevolutionary crusade. Erroneously believing in 1795 that France would soon collapse because of allied military forces converging on Paris, Wickham spent 94,028 pounds on counterrevolutionary movements (L-J. Condé, J.-P. Imbert-Colomès, the comte de Précy, F.-A. Charette de la Contrie) and bribes (J.-C. Pichegru) to expedite the final disintegration. Wickham, much too optimistic and too misinformed of the political situation in France, failed dismally in that year.

During the next two years, he changed his tactics from subsidizing internal revolts in France to supporting the political campaigns of constitutional monarchists in the elections of 1797. He now believed that the constitutionalists, not the royalists, represented the vast majority of counterrevolutionists and that they feared a royalist restoration without the safeguards of the 1791 Constitution. By providing financial assistance to rightist candidates and journalists, Wickham and his advisers, notably A. de Bellevue, helped a majority of constitutional monarchists and conservatives win in the elections of 1797. Divisions and distrusts between royalists and constitutionalists, however, robbed them of their victory, and the coup d'état of 18 Fructidor ended the last significant attempt of the counterrevolution to restore constitutional monarchy in France. The Directory demanded that Wickham, now recognized as the leading British agent on the Continent, be expelled from Switzerland. In January 1798 he returned to England and was appointed undersecretary of state for the Home Department.

The formation of the Second Coalition in 1798-99 provided Wickham with another opportunity to return to the Continent. By late summer in 1799, the Austrians and Russians had cleared most of Italy and Switzerland of French troops. The overall Allied plan called for an Austro-Russian invasion of Franche-Comté, as well as the completion of the Swiss campaign, an Anglo-Russian invasion of Holland, and financial assistance to the royalists in the Vendée. The objectives of Wickham's second mission were integrated with these military operations: to consult with Austrian and Russian representatives in Switzerland, to assist the Midi uprising, and to explore the possibility of insurrections in eastern and southern France. For support, Grenville provided Wickham with 500,000 pounds.

Wickham left England in June 1799, but it became apparent before the end of the year that his mission was doomed. Austro-Russian jealousies coupled to indecision within Pitt's ministry eliminated any possibility of coordinated action. Consequently, Switzerland fell to the French by October 1799, and by the following spring Napoleon as first consul crushed the Austrians at Marengo. These defeats terminated Wickham's mission, and he returned to London to resume his work in the Home Department. With Bonaparte in command of the Continent, there was even less chance of succeeding in any future counterrevolutionary activities in France.

The remainder of Wickham's career was as brief and obscure as it had been before his missions to Switzerland. His reputation as a secret agent denied him any important diplomatic post abroad during the Napoleonic period. In 1802 he was appointed chief secretary for Ireland; he entered Parliament for Heytesbury but resigned almost immediately in 1804, served on the Treasury Board under Grenville, 1806-7, and retired to the country in 1807.

H. Mitchell, *The Underground War Against Revolutionary France* (Oxford, 1965); W. Wickham, ''Communications from Switzerland,'' P.R.O., F.O. 74/4-31; W. Wickham, ed., *The Correspondence of the Right Honorable William Wickham*, 2 vols. (London, 1870).

H. V. Evans

Related entries: CHARETTE DE LA CONTRIE; CONDE; COUP OF 18 FRUCTIDOR YEAR V; GRENVILLE; PICHEGRU; PROVENCE; SECOND COALITION; SUVOROV-RYMNIKSKII.

WILLIAM V (1747-1806), prince of Orange-Nassau, hereditary stadholder (1766-95) of the Republic of the Seven United Provinces. William was born in 1747, the son of William IV, prince of Orange-Nassau and hereditary stadholder (1747-51). He assumed his responsibilities in 1766 after he came of age. William was weak-willed and failed to provide leadership during a time of crises in the Dutch Republic when the so-called patriots demanded political and other reforms. His position further deteriorated during the disastrous Fourth English War (1780-84).

He left the Hague in 1785 and went to Nimwegen, making no effort to regain his position. Patriots' insults to his more assertive spouse (Wilhelmina, 1751-

1820), sister of the Prussian king Frederick William II, brought Prussian intervention in 1787 and the defeat of William's opponents, many of whom fled to France. Prussian intervention was a serious blow to French foreign policy, which had sought to make the Dutch Republic a sphere of influence after the Treaty of Paris (1783).

In February 1793 the French National Convention declared war on Britain and the stadholder. French armies invaded Dutch territory in 1794-95 and William fled to England. He died in exile in Brunswick in 1806. His son would become King William I of the United Netherlands (1813-40).

P. Geyl, *De Patriottenbeweging, 1780-1787* (Amsterdam, 1947); T. Jorissen, "Willem V," *Historische bladen*, vol. 2 (Haarlem, 1895).

G. D. Homan

Related entries: FREDERICK WILLIAM II; MONTMORIN; VONCK.

WIMPFFEN, LOUIS-FELIX, BARON DE (1744-1814), federalist general. Wimpffen served with distinction during the War of American Independence at the sieges of Mahon and Gibraltar before he retired to Normandy in 1788 with the rank of field marshal. The following year, he was elected from Caen to the Estates General and played a prominent role there, along with other veterans of the American war. He edited the address of the nobles joining the Third Estate. A constitutional monarchist, he was active in the military committees of the Assembly and, following the outbreak of war in 1792, reentered active service as commander of the fortress of Thionville, which he successfully defended against Prussian attack. Despite this, the popular society of Thionville denounced him to the National Convention for corresponding secretly with *émigré* nobles.

As commander of the Army of the Côtes de Cherbourg, Wimpffen joined the federalist revolt in 1793. The Central Assembly of Resistance at Caen appointed him commander of its federalist army, but he failed to act decisively. He took up headquarters in Caen after a month's delay, recruited hesitantly, and made no effort to rally defeated troops after Brécourt. Throughout the period, he maintained secret contacts with London, although they do not appear to have influenced his actions. After the failure of the federalist revolt, Wimpffen took refuge on his estates, where he successfully waited out the Terror. The Directory commissioned him a general of division without duties. He later became a baron of the Empire and served as mayor of Bayeux and inspector-general of the Haras.

P. Heckmann, *Félix de Wimpffen et le siège de Thionville en 1792* (Paris, 1926); R. Postel, *Une rectification du fédéralisme en Normandie. Félix de Wimpffen et les Girondins réfugiés* (Caen, 1867).

D. Stone

Related entries: CAEN; FEDERALISM.

X

XYZ AFFAIR (1797-98), Franco-American diplomatic crisis that led to the undeclared naval war of 1798-1800. The XYZ affair and the ensuing undeclared naval war were much more important to the new, weak American Republic than they were to France. Nevertheless, the American imbroglio did play some role in French domestic politics and naval activities during the last three years of the eighteenth century.

The consummation of an Anglo-American agreement (Jay Treaty) in 1794 set in motion a chain of events that resulted in the undeclared naval war of 1798-1800 and the abrogation of the Franco-American Alliance of 1778, the United States' sole alliance until 1942. By decreasing Anglo-American tensions through acceptance of British interpretations of neutrality law, the Federalist administrations (1793-1801) placed themselves in the anti-French camp, at least insofar as Paris was concerned. Having implicitly renounced the principle of "free ships make free goods," the United States opened the way for the seizure of its vessels trading with England. Between July 1796 and June 1797, the French were alleged to have seized more than 300 American ships. Further exacerbating relations, they refused to receive C. C. Pinckney, the minister selected to replace J. Monroe, and even ordered him out of the country. The French expected that their putative friends in the Republican faction in the United States would gain control of the government because of the failures of Federalist foreign policy. Throughout this period, Paris was ill served by agents in America—J. Fauchet, J.-P. Létombe, and P.-A. Adet—who consistently overestimated the power of the pro-French bloc and misunderstood American nationalism.

As Federalists and Republicans clashed over foreign policy, so too did French factions. Indeed, stiff criticism of the Directory's anti-American measures by a majority of the membership of the Council of Five Hundred contributed to conditions that led to the coup d'état of 18 Fructidor. For his part, C.-M. Talleyrand, who became minister of foreign relations in July 1797, hoped for a reduction in Franco-American tensions but was wary of crossing powerful anti-American members of the Directory.

J. Adams, the American president who took office in March 1797, was not well disposed to the Revolution or to France. Nevertheless, he did want to head off war and settle amicably the differences that had split apart the two old allies. To that end, he dispatched J. Marshall and E. Gerry to France to join Pinckney in a new overture to the Directory. Arriving in the early fall of 1797, the three envoys met unofficially with Talleyrand on 8 October.

Talleyrand refused to initiate formal negotiations at that time. Instead, the foreign minister dispatched several emissaries who presented preconditions that had to be accepted before serious discussions could commence. J.-C. Hottinguer, L. Hauteval, P.-A. Caron de Beaumarchais, a Monsieur Bellamy, and a Madame de Villette were among the agents who demanded from the American commissioners a *douceur* of 1.2 million *livres* and a commitment to purchase a depreciated Dutch bond issue worth 32 million *florins*. Although Talleyrand had earmarked some of the *douceur* for himself, he apparently planned to use a good portion of it to buy the support of directors antagonistic to his moderate American policies. Through his intermediaries, he also demanded an apology from President Adams, who had made uncomplimentary statements about France in May of 1797 during the special session of Congress called because of the crisis.

The demand for a *douceur* did not surprise the Americans. They were prepared to pay Talleyrand for his services after an agreement had been signed, although not as extravagantly as originally demanded; however, not having been authorized to accept a loan, they balked at considering it without instructions from Philadelphia. And they would not agree to an apology for Adams' statements. In response to the French gambit, Pinckney exclaimed, "It is no; no; not a sixpence." This rejection, soon transformed into the more dramatic but inaccurate "Millions for defense, but not one cent for tribute," became the American rallying cry during the undeclared war.

After weeks of fruitless unofficial negotiations, Marshall sent Talleyrand a formal memorial on 27 January 1798, in which he laid out a tough line on the loan and maritime rights. On 2 March, the three Americans finally saw Talleyrand again, but the discussions foundered on the loan precondition. Two weeks later, the French government responded formally to the Marshall memorial in an equally tough note directed to what it perceived to be pro-French interests in the United States.

Informal discussions continued for a few more weeks with no movement on either side. Marshall and Pinckney, two Federalists, maintained a stiffer front than did Gerry, a Republican. The last, who stopped speaking to the other two in April, was willing at least to consider the loan proposition. Pinckney and Marshall left Paris empty-handed in April. Gerry stayed on until July, engaging in desultory negotiations with Talleyrand and his aides.

In the meantime, dispatches from Marshall and Pinckney that had arrived in the United States had been published by Adams. In discussing the bribe and loan negotiations, the president decorously did not refer to Talleyrand's agents by name but labeled them X (Hottinguer), Y (Bellamy), and Z (Hauteval). He did not mention W (Beaumarchais) and thus, the WXYZ affair became the XYZ affair. So outraged was most of the population with the reports of bribery and blackmail that even Republicans supported the naval retaliatory measures proposed by Adams to combat French spoliations.

When the story of the XYZ bribe scheme was revealed in Paris, Talleyrand published an anonymous defense in the *Moniteur* in which he claimed that Hauteval, who was his agent, had done nothing wrong. As for Bellamy and Hottinguer, he refused responsibility for their activities, dismissing them as rank intriguers operating for speculators who owned the depreciated Dutch bonds. Although many in Paris were skeptical of Talleyrand's explanations, the resourceful minister was able to ride out the storm.

Having misread the American people, Talleyrand was genuinely surprised by the onset of naval war that France could ill afford in 1798. Almost as soon as American and French vessels began shooting at one another, he tried to reopen negotiations to head off full-scale war. Here he was aided by a courageous Adams, who, opposing the many hawks in his own party, pulled back from the brink to accept the Convention of 1800 (Treaty of Mortefontaine). The XYZ affair was soon forgotten by the French but remains today one of the glorious legends of the early history of the United States.

U. Bonnel, *La France, les Etats-Unis et la guerre de course, 1797-1815* (Paris, 1961); A. H. Bowman, *The Struggle for Neutrality: Franco-American Diplomacy during the Federalist Era* (Knoxville, Tenn., 1974); A. DeConde, *The Quasi-War: The Politics and Diplomacy of the Undeclared War with France, 1797-1801* (New York, 1966); R. Guyot, *Le Directoire et la paix de l'Europe, 1795-1799* (Paris, 1911); E. W. Lyon, ''The Directory and the United States,'' *Am. Hist. Rev.* 43 (1938); W. Stinchcombe, *The XYZ Affair* (Westport, Conn., 1981).

M. Small

Related entries: BEAUMARCHAIS; JAY TREATY; TALLEYRAND.

Y

YOUNG, ARTHUR (1741-1820), English writer and traveler, whose account of his travels in France in 1787, 1788, and 1789 remains one of the most important sources for the state of the country on the eve of the Revolution. Despite repeated failures as a practical farmer on his ancestral property in Suffolk and elsewhere, Young was a passionate believer in new agricultural techniques and experiments. By the 1770s he was well known as a commentator on agricultural and economic matters. His *Tour in Ireland* of 1780 foreshadowed in its approach and organization his later work on France.

In 1784 he was visited by the two sons of the duc de Liancourt and their Polish tutor, who were touring England. In April 1787 Young was invited to join the Liancourt family on an expedition to the Pyrenean spas, and he set off for France in May, returning in November. Between July and October 1788 he made a second French tour, alone; and between June 1789 and January 1790 he made a third, which included a three-month expedition into Italy. On these travels, which between them took most of the important regions of France, he kept a journal, which he published along with a set of general reflections and observations in 1792 under the title *Travels, during the Years 1787, 1788 and 1789. Undertaken More Particularly with a View to Ascertaining the Cultivation, Wealth, Resources, and National Prosperity of the Kingdom of France*. It was an instant success and was translated into French in 1793 with the official approval of the Convention, which distributed 20,000 free copies. Historians have turned to it ever since for its vivid and carefully observed impressions of agriculture, industry, politics, and manners at the close of the Old Regime and in the early months of the Revolution.

Young was a man of powerful prejudices, and his *Travels* must be read with these in mind. He made no allowance for the difficulty of introducing English agricultural methods into France and by the 1780s was an unrepentant believer in the benefits of free trade. His speculations on the reasons for some of the things he saw, such as the emptiness of the roads or the apparent poverty of peasant dwellings, are sometimes misleading and shortsighted. But he was a meticulous observer, recorded everything he saw in great detail, and wrote vividly. The general picture he gives of an agriculture far behind that of England has never been seriously challenged, even if many of the precise statistics collected in the second part of the *Travels* need to be used with caution. The tour of 1789-90, in addition to economic information and observation, also records the difficulties of traveling through a country in the first stages of revolution. Young was in Paris and Versailles for most of June 1789, personally witnessing some of the crucial events and meeting those involved. He then passed through eastern provinces, disturbed by peasant unrest and by uncertain news penetrating from Paris, encountering constant suspicion as he went.

He left France persuaded that the manifold abuses of the old order had justified the Revolution, despite a number of reservations about its precise ways of proceeding. Within months of the publication of the *Travels*, however, he became convinced that matters had gone beyond control and that property was threatened by the events following the fall of the monarchy. He began to denounce the Revolution and all its works and in February 1793 published *The Example of France a Warning to Britain*. It passed through four English, two French, one German, and one Italian editions within two years and was all the more influential in arousing conservative hostility to the Revolution in that its author had previously been sympathetic to French events and aspirations.

J. G. Gazley, *The Life of Arthur Young* (Philadelphia, 1973); J. Kaplow, ed., *Arthur Young, Travels in France during the Years 1787, 1788 and 1789* (Garden City, N.Y., 1969); C. Maxwell, ed., Arthur Young, *Travels, during the Years 1787, 1788 and 1789* (Cambridge, England, 1929) and *The English Traveller in France, 1689-1815* (London, 1932).

W. Doyle

Related entries: DU PONT DE NEMOURS; PEASANTRY.

YSABEAU, CLAUDE-ALEXANDRE (1754-1831), cleric, Jacobin. After serving as *préfet des études* at the Ecole militaire of Vendôme, Ysabeau became préfet at the collège of Tours in 1789. His reputation as an educator helped him to become a municipal officer in Tours (1790) and later the constitutional curé of the Church of Saint-Martin in that city. In 1792 he abandoned the church and was married. He was elected as a deputy to the Convention (1792) from the department of the Indre-et-Loire and voted for Louis XVI's death. His administrative interests were extended now to the military sphere. With Generals J. Servan and J.-F.-C. Dugommier, during the latter half of 1793, he organized the Army of the Pyrénées-Orientales.

Following the expulsion of the Girondins from the Convention (May-June 1793), the federalist revolt had spread to Bordeaux. Anti-Jacobin demonstrations by the Société populaire de la jeunesse Bordelaise had become quite intense. By August 1793 Bordeaux was filled with refractory priests, *émigrés*, and aristocrats, whose presence created a tense situation. Their threats against the Jacobins were encouraged by the presence in their midst of J. Pétion, M.-E. Guadet, and other Girondin sympathizers. The Convention dispatched Ysabeau and J.-L. Tallien to the city as deputies on mission; they entered the city of Bordeaux on 19 August 1793.

On their entrance, they were stoned and insulted by a band of youths. Ysabeau and his associate were forced to take refuge at La Réole, a Jacobin stronghold. The *sans-culottes*, however, encouraged by the presence of Ysabeau and Tallien, overthrew the Girondin municipal government on 18 September, and the road was open to the Jacobin repression.

Ysabeau and Tallien now established a *commission militaire*, which, in a period of nine months, tried over 800 rebels and put nearly 300 of them to death. The *commission* claimed to have aided, moreover, in the repression of a huge mercantile plot, which by hoarding and refusing to continue business intended to starve the population. The unraveling of this alleged conspiracy led to the arrest of approximately eighty businessmen.

The *commission* had no jurisdiction over the release of the imprisoned suspects; the power of release lay with the deputies in their respective departments. Ysabeau and Tallien established a committee to review the appeals of the suspects. The result was that the businessmen were assessed heavy fines and then released from prison, a decision that led the local vigilance committee to complain to the departmental Executive Council.

The council denounced Ysabeau and Tallien for their luxurious style of living and their immorality. In retaliation, Ysabeau denounced his accusers as British agents. On 31 January 1794, to silence his opponents further, Ysabeau ordered the arrest of members of the Bordeaux vigilance committee for their arbitrariness. This act displeased the Executive Council, which requested his recall as deputy on mission in April 1794.

On 2 March 1795 he became a member of the Committee of General Security but a month later, because of a decree of 11 Thermidor, was forced to resign from that committee. Over a year later (26 October 1796) he reemerged in public office as a member of the Council of Ancients; he later became an inspector of postal services under the imperial administration.

A. Patrick, *The Men of the First French Republic* (Baltimore, 1972); J. B. Sirich, *The Revolutionary Committees in the Departments of France, 1793-1794* (Cambridge, Mass., 1943); J. M. Thompson, *The French Revolution* (New York, 1943).

N. Chaudhuri

Related entries: CABARRUS, J.; *EMIGRES*; FEDERALISM; GUADET; PE-
TION DE VILLENEUVE; TALLIEN; TERROR, THE.

Z

ZURICH, BATTLE OF. See BATTLE OF ZURICH.

Chronology: Principal Events of the French Revolution

PRE-REVOLUTION (1787-May 1789)

1787

22 February-25 May	First Assembly of Notables; C.-A. de Calonne resigns and E.-C. de Loménie de Brienne succeeds him as controller general of finances.

1788

8 August	Louis XVI consents to the calling of the Estates General.
25 August	J. Necker assumes post of controller general of finances, replacing Loménie de Brienne.
23 and 25 September	Paris Parlement decrees that proposed Estates General will follow precedents and procedures of Estates General of 1614.
6 November-12 December	Second Assembly of Notables fails.
27 December	Louis XVI agrees to the doubling of the Third Estate so that its membership is equal to the combined total of the first two estates.

1789

January	E.-J. Sieyès publishes *What Is the Third Estate?*
February	Elections to the Estates General begin.
27-28 April	Réveillon riots.

NATIONAL CONSTITUENT ASSEMBLY (5 May 1789-30 September 1791)

5 May	Opening session of Estates General.

17 June	Third Estate declares itself the National Assembly.
20 June	Oath of the Tennis Court.
23 June	*Séance royale*, where Louis XVI presents reform program to plenary session of three estates; the Third rejects it.
27 June	Louis orders First and Second Estates to join with the Third as the National Assembly.
11 July	Dismissal of the Necker ministry.
14 July	Taking of the Bastille.
16 July	Necker recalled.
July-August	Peasant revolution, the Great Fear.
4-11 August	Abolition of feudal rights and privileges decreed by the National Assembly.
26 August	Promulgation of the Declaration of the Rights of Man and of the Citizen.
5-6 October	March of the Parisians on Versailles; establishment of the royal family in the Tuileries.
19 October	National Assembly meets in Paris.
2 November	Assembly decrees nationalization of ecclesiastical property.
19 December	Assembly authorizes issuing of *assignats*.

1790

19 June	Abolition of titles of hereditary nobility.
12 July	Assembly enacts the Civil Constitution of the Clergy.
14 July	*Fête de la Fédération*.
27 November	Clerical oath to the nation declared.

1791

10 March	Pius VI condemns the Civil Constitution and the Declaration of the Rights of Man.
16 May	Self-denying ordinance.
20-25 June	Louis XVI and his family attempt flight but are captured at Varennes and returned to Paris.
17 July	Champ de Mars "massacre."
27 August	Declaration of Pillnitz.
14 September	Louis XVI takes oath to the new constitution.
30 September	Final session of National Assembly.

LEGISLATIVE ASSEMBLY (1 October 1791-19 September 1792)

1 October	First session of Legislative Assembly.

1792

20 April	France declares war on Austria; Prussia joins with Austria; beginning of the War of the First Coalition, 1792-1797.
25 April	*"La Marseillaise"* written.
20 June	Parisian crowd invades the Tuileries.
28 July	Brunswick Manifesto (of 25 July) reaches Paris.
10 August	"Second" French Revolution as Tuileries is again invaded. Louis XVI suspended and soon imprisoned.
11 August	Call for convening of a National Convention.
19 August	Defection of the marquis de Lafayette.
2-6 September	Massacres of prisoners in Paris and the provinces.
20 September	Prussians defeated by French at Valmy.

NATIONAL CONVENTION (20 September 1792-26 October 1795)

20 September	First session of Convention.
21 and 22 September	Monarchy abolished and Republic established.
6 November	Battle of Jemappes won by French.
19 November	First propaganda decree offering fraternal aid to subject peoples.
15 December	Second propaganda decree on treatment of occupied territories.
26 December	Trial of Louis XVI begins in Convention.

1793

14-17 January	Louis XVI found guilty and condemned to death.
21 January	Louis XVI (Capet) executed.
1 February	France declares war on England and Holland.
24 February	Levy of 300,000 men for armies of the Republic.
7 March	Convention declares war on Spain.
10-16 March	Revolt in the Vendée begins.
18 March	French lose at Neerwinden; C. Dumouriez deserts to Austrians on 5 April.
6 April	First Committee of Public Safety established by Convention.
4 May	First Law of the Maximum, on grain.
31 May-2 June	Montagnards seize power; Girondins placed under arrest; beginning of the federalist revolt.
24 June	Constitution of 1793 accepted but never put into effect.
13 July	C. Corday assassinates J.-P. Marat.
23 August	General mobilization is ordered, the great *levée en masse*.
27 August	Toulon surrenders to British.
5 September	Terror becomes officially the order of the day.

22 September (1 Vendémiaire Year II)	Republican calendar begins (not voted until October). YEAR II OF THE REPUBLIC
29 September (8 Vendémiaire)	Law of the General Maximum.
9 October (18 Vendémiaire)	Lyon regained for the Republic.
16 October (25 Vendémiaire)	Marie Antoinette executed; French victory of Wattignies.
31 October (10 Brumaire)	Brissotins executed.
10 November (20 Brumaire)	Height of dechristianization; establishment of the Cult of Reason.
22 November (2 Frimaire)	Closing of all Catholic churches in Paris.
4 December	Law of 14 Frimaire.
19 and 23 December (29 Frimaire and 3 Nivôse	British evacuate Toulon; organized resistance to the Republic collapses in the Vendée (Battle of Savenay on 23 December).

1794

26 February-3 March (8-13 Ventôse)	Ventôse Decrees authorize seizure of property of suspects.
24 March (4 Germinal)	Hébertists executed.
5 April (16 Germinal)	Dantonists executed.
8 June (20 Prairial)	Festival of the Supreme Being.
10 June (22 Prairial)	Law of 22 Prairial increases powers of Revolutionary Tribunal; beginning of Great Terror.
26 June (8 Messidor)	French victory at Fleurus.
26 July (8 Thermidor)	M. Robespierre's last speech to Convention.
27-28 July (9-10 Thermidor)	Robespierre and Robespierrists proscribed and executed by Convention.
22 September (1 Vendémiaire)	YEAR III OF THE REPUBLIC
12 November (22 Brumaire)	Jacobin club closed.

24 December (4 Nivôse)	Law of Maximum repealed.

1795

17 February (29 Pluviôse)	Armistice in the Vendée.
21 February (3 Ventôse)	Separation of church and state decreed by Convention.
1-2 April (12-13 Germinal)	Food insurrections in Paris.
5 April (16 Germinal)	Treaty of Basel, ending war with Prussia.
16 May (27 Floréal)	Franco-Dutch alliance, Treaty of the Hague (Holland now the Batavian Republic).
20-23 May (1-4 Prairial)	Insurrection in Paris.
21 July (3 Thermidor)	*Emigré* forces defeated at Quiberon Bay.
22 July (4 Thermidor)	Peace treaty signed with Spain.
22 August (5 Fructidor)	New constitution established with five-man executive, the Directory, and bicameral legislature.
23 September (1 Vendémiaire)	YEAR IV OF THE REPUBLIC Constitution of the Directory proclaimed.
1 October (9 Vendémiaire)	Belgium annexed.
5 October (13 Vendémiaire)	Royalist insurrection in Paris repressed by troops led by Napoleon.
26 October (4 Brumaire)	Last session of the National Convention.

DIRECTORY (26 October 1795-10 November 1799)

1796

19 February (30 Pluviôse)	*Assignats* abolished.
18 March (28 Ventôse)	*Mandats territoriaux* introduced.
27 March (7 Germinal)	Napoleon takes command of Army of Italy.
10 May (21 Floréal)	Arrest of the Babouvists and destruction of the Conspiracy of Equals; French are victorious at Lodi.

22 September (1 Vendémiaire)	YEAR V OF THE REPUBLIC
16 October (25 Vendémiaire)	Cispadane Republic proclaimed at Bologna.
15-17 November (25-27 Brumaire)	French are victorious at Arcola.
15 December (25 Frimaire)	Expedition leaves France for Ireland.

1797

14 January (25 Nivôse)	French are victorious at Rivoli.
4 February (16 Pluviôse)	Paper money, having proved valueless, replaced by metallic currency.
18 April (29 Germinal)	Preliminaries of Leoben with Austria.
27 May (8 Prairial)	F.-N. Babeuf is executed.
4 September (18 Fructidor)	Coup of Fructidor against royalists.
22 September (1 Vendémiaire)	YEAR VI OF THE REPUBLIC
30 September (9 Vendémiaire)	Two-thirds of the public debt repudiated by Directory.
17 October (26 Vendémiaire)	Treaty of Campoformio with Austria.

1798

1798-1801	War of the Second Coalition (Russia, Great Britain, Austria, Turkey, and Naples against France).
15 February (27 Pluviôse)	Proclamation of the Roman Republic.
11 May (22 Floréal)	Jacobins purged from legislative body after election.
19 May (30 Floréal)	Egyptian expedition leaves Toulon.
1 July (13 Messidor)	Napoleon lands army in Egypt.
21 July (3 Thermidor)	Napoleon victorious at Battle of the Pyramids.
1 August (14 Thermidor)	French fleet defeated by Admiral Nelson at Aboukir Bay.
5 September (19 Fructidor)	Jourdan conscription law.

22 September (1 Vendémiaire)	YEAR VII OF THE REPUBLIC

1799

26 January (7 Pluviôse)	Proclamation of the Parthenopean Republic.
16 May (27 Floréal)	Sieyès enters Directory.
4 June (16 Prairial)	First Battle of Zurich.
17 June (29 Prairial)	L.-J. Gohier enters Directory.
18 June (30 Prairial)	Coup of Prairial; P.-A. Merlin de Douai and L.-M. La Revellière-lépeaux resign from Directory as legislature forces them out; replaced by P.-R. Ducos and J.-F. Moulin.
12 July (24 Messidor)	Law of Hostages enacted.
25 July (7 Thermidor)	French victorious at Aboukir.
5 August (18 Thermidor)	Royalist insurrection in the southwest begins.
23 August (6 Fructidor)	Napoleon leaves his troops in Egypt.
23 September (1 Vendémiaire)	YEAR VIII OF THE REPUBLIC
9 October (17 Vendémiaire)	Napoleon lands at Fréjus.
14 October (21 Vendémiaire)	Napoleon arrives in Paris.
9-10 November (18-19 Brumaire)	Coup d'état; Sieyès, Ducos, and Barras resign.
11 November (20 Brumaire)	Formation of provisional Consulate.
15 December (24 Brumaire)	Publication of new Constitution of the Year VIII.

Index

Abbaye (prison), 93, 179, 782; Drouet in, 327; Kellermann imprisoned in, 527; madame Roland incarcerated in, 845; and Maillard, 619; and Marat, 13, 632; mob kills Montmorin there, 681; release of French Guards from, 438; and September 1792 massacres, 892, 893. *See also* Prisons

Abbeville, 379

Abolition movement: and planters on Saint-Domingue, 861

Abonnements: and vingtieme, 3, 1012. *See also* Vingtieme

Aboukir, Battle of. *See* Battle of Aboukir

Aboukir Bay, 80–81, 749

Académie de Saint-Luc: and Vigée-Lebrun, 1010

Académie des Belles-Lettres: Bailly appointed to, 54

Académie des Sciences. *See* Academy of Sciences

Académie française: Bailly's election to, 53; and Bernis, 91; and Condorcet, 229; François de Neufchâteau as member, 413; Gaxotte in, 425; and Mably, 615; and Maury, 645; Montesquieu admitted to, 675; Taine elected to, 927; Target elected to, 936; de Tocqueville elected to, 970

Académie royale de musique (Opéra): and pre-Revolutionary music, 695, 698

Académie royale: and Vigée-Lebrun, 1010

Academy of Arras, 47; Carnot as member, 154; M. Robespierre as member and chancellor of, 830

Academy of Bordeaux: Montesquieu a member of, 675

Academy of Dijon: and Rousseau, 850

Academy of Metz: and Roederer, 836

Academy of Painting and Sculpture: and David, 292, 293, 295

Academy of Sciences, 145; Bailly admitted to, 53; Bosc as member, 111; and Condorcet, 229, 230; and Lamarck, 541; and Laplace, 546; and Lavoisier, 557; and Legendre, 581; Marat denied admission to, 631; and Monge, 665; replaces National Institute of Sciences and Arts, 880

Acre, siege of, 81, 349; and Egyptian expedition, 884; and Kléber, 529

Actes des Apôtres, 3–4

Action française: and Gaxotte, 425

Active citizen, 4–5, 427, 634; compared with passive citizen, 751; in Constitution of 1791, 237, 706; in Constitution of 1795, 243; and election of judges, 522–523; and Legislative Assembly, 582; rejected by Marat, 13; and sections, 885, 887, 888; Sieyès distinguishes from passive citizen, 902

Antonelle, P.-A.: and Conspiracy of Equals, 234; and Jullien, M.A., 520; and Maréchal, 635

Antraigues, comte d', 260

Antwerp: captured by Miranda, 662; defense of in 1814, 156; and Fouché, 404; Malouet's service at, 627; and Moulin, 685

Anvers, 89

Apennines, 750

Appenzell, 462

Architects: and symbolism, 923

Archives nationales: and de Tocqueville, 971; organized under National Convention, 715

Arcola, Battle of. *See* Battle of Arcola

Arcueil, 880

Ardèche (department), 52, 492, 904; and Boissy d'Anglas, 101; and counterrevolution, 219, 268; and Two-thirds law, 986

Ardennes (department): and Great Fear, 443; Pache retires to, 740; and Saint-Just, 866

Argenson, M.-R. Voyer de Paulmy d', 357, 794

Argenson, V. d': and Buonarroti, 130

Argonne: and Murat, 691

Argonne Forest: and Battle of Valmy, 82

Ariège (department): and Lakanal, 537; and Tallien, 934; and Vadier, 995, 996; and White Terror, 1021

Aristocrats, *22–25*; and Assembly of Notables, 33–35; attitude toward bourgeoisie, 118, 119; and *Esprit des lois*, 366; and Great Fear, 441–442, 444; and Hébertists, 460; and Jacobins, 488; in Legislative Assembly, 582; in Marseille, 638; and Montesquieu, 676; Mounier's views on, 686–687; opponents of Patriot party identified as, 752; and primogeniture, 778; and provincial assemblies, 794; and hatred of *sans-culottes* for, 871; and the *taille*, 925; and theater, 947

Arlandes, marquis d', 678

Arles, 639

Arleux, 653

Armée d'Italie. *See* Army of Italy

Armée de la Moselle. *See* Army of the Moselle

Armée de Sambre-et-Meuse. *See* Army of the Sambre and Meuse

Armée des Ardennes. *See* Army of the Ardennes

Armée des Côtes de la Rochelle: and Biron, 101; and Kléber, 528

Armée du Nord. *See* Army of the North

Armée du Rhin. *See* Army of the Rhine

Armées révolutionnaires, *25–28*, 180; Cobb's work on, 200; and Danton, 288; and *enragés*, 365; establishment of, 566; and Hébertists, 460, 461; and Hérault de Séchelles, 464; and Law of 14 Frimaire, 559–561; and National Convention, 713; Tallien establishes in Bordeaux, 933; and Toulouse, 975; and White Terror, 1022

Armoire de fer, *28–29*, 309; and incriminating evidence against Duquesnoy, 341; and Louis XVI, 601

Armonville, J.-B. d', 503, 711

Army of Condé: and Bouillé, 114

Army of England: Moulin given command of, 685

Army of Helvetia: and Battle of Zurich, 83; and Masséna, 642; and Ney, 722; and Second Coalition, 883

Army of Italy, 155, 510; and Battle of Arcola, 75; and Battle of Lodi, 78; and Battle of Rivoli, 79–80; and Biron, 101; and Bonaparte, N., 106, 968; and Genoa, 590; and Hoche, 465; and Joubert, 512; and Jourdan, 513; and Kellermann, 527, 528; and Lyon, 614; and Macdonald, 617; and Masséna, 641, 642; Moreau named general of infantry of, 682; sent to Saint-Domingue, 864

Army of Mayence (Mainz), 512, 642

Army of Naples: Macdonald in command of, 617; and Masséna, 642

Army of Portugal, 722

Army of Spain, 722

Army of the Alps: and Grenoble, 448; and Kellermann, 527, 528; and Le-

of General Defense, 208–209; and Committee of General Security, 210–212; and Committee of Public Safety, 213–216; and committees of surveillance, 219–221; and Companies of Jesus, 224; and Comtat Venaissin, 45; Condorcet in, 232; and Constitution of 1793, 238–242; and Constitution of 1795, 242; and Cordeliers club, 251; Couthon deputy to, 272–274; and Cult of the Supreme Being, 278–280; Danton as deputy to, 283, 286–289; and David, 294–295; and dechristianization, 297; departmental officials in, 307; and Desfieux, 309; and Desmoulins, 312, 1009; Drouet as deputy to, 326–327; and Dubois-Crancé, 328; and Ducos, 328; and Dumouriez, 79, 333; and education, 345; and *émigrés*, 352; engineering schools reorganized under, 877; and *enragés*, 362–365; and Fabre d'Eglantine, 371; and federalism, 261, 375–377; and feudalism, 389, 409; and Forster, 402; and Fouché, 403; and Fouquier-Tinville, 405–407; and François de Neufchâteau, 412; Fréron in, 420; and Garat, 424; and Gard, 51–52; and Gensonné, 430; and Gironde, 432; and Girondins, 433, 434–435; and Gonchon, 438; and Grégoire, 446; and Grenoble, 448; and Guadet, 450; and Hébert, 458, 459; and Hérault de Séchelles, 464; and Indulgents, 471, 474–476; Isnard deputy to, 483; and Jacobins, 486, 491; and *jeunesse dorée*, 503, 504; and Julien, J., 519; and Kléber, 528; and Lacombe, 534; and Lakanal, 537; and La Revellière-lépeaux, 548; and Lasource, 551–553; and Lavoisier, 558; and Law of 14 Frimaire, 559–562; and Law of Suspects, 565–566; and Law of the Maximum, 568–569; and Law of 22 Prairial, 569–572, 825; and Le Bas, 572, 573; and Le Bon, 573–575; and Lebrun, 576; and Legendre, 581; and Lepelletier, 587; and liberty trees, 921; and Lindet, J.-B.-R., 592–593; and

Lindet, R.-T., 594; and Louis XVI, 600–602, 782; and Louis XVII, 603; and Louis-Philippe, 605; and Louvet, 608; and Lyon, 613, 614; and Mably, 617; and Maillard, 619; and Malesherbes, 621; and Manuel, 628, 630; and Marat, 630, 632–633; and Marie Antoinette, 636–637; and Marseille, 639–640; Mathiez on, 645; Merlin de Thionville president of, 654; and Momoro, 663; and Montagnards, 669–673; and Montesquiou-Fézénsac, 677; and *muscadins*, 694; and Museum of Natural History, 541; and Narbonne, 704; and national volunteers, 719; and natural frontiers, 323, 324; and Nice, 724; and 9 Thermidor, 725, 726; and nonjuring clergy, 39, 275; and *Noyades de Nantes*, 730; and Orléans, duc d', 734, 736, 737; and Paine, 741, 743; and Paris Commune, 739, 745, 746; and Paris Conservatory of Music, 698; Pétion elected member of, 758; and Plain, 765, 766, 767; and Polish affairs, 769–770; and Prairial martyrs, 771, 772, 773; and Prieur de la Côte-d'Or, 774, 775; and Prieur "de la Marne," 777; and Quiberon, 260; and Rabaut Saint-Etienne, 805; Reinhard on, 808; and representatives on mission, 811, 812, 813; and Republic of Mainz, 816; and Reubell, 818–819; and Revolutionary Tribunal, 823, 824; Rhineland policy of, 189; and Robespierre, A., 828, 829; and Robespierre, M., 832, 833, 834; and Roland de la Platière, 840; and Roland, madame, 844; and Romme, 847, 848; and Rousseau, 852; and Rovère, 855; and Saint-André, 859; and Saint-Domingue, 862; and Saint-Just, 866, 867; and Science, 877; and *scrutin épuratoire*, 881; sectional assemblies and, 873; and separation of church and state, 192; and September 1792 massacres, 896; and Servan, 901; and Sieyès, 902, 903; and slavery, 977; and social contract, 908; and Talleyrand, 929; and Tallien,

About the Editors

SAMUEL F. SCOTT is Professor of History at Wayne State University. He is the author of *The Response of the Royal Army to the French Revolution* and has contributed articles to *Military Affairs, American Historical Review, Journal of Modern History,* and the *Annales historiques de la Révolution française.*

BARRY ROTHAUS is Professor of History at the University of Northern Colorado. He has contributed articles to *Proceedings of the Western Society for French History* and reviews to *Historical Abstracts.*